THE DESSERT BIBLE

THE DESSERT BIBLE

CHRISTOPHER KIMBALL

LITTLE, BROWN AND COMPANY

New York   Boston   London

Little, Brown and Company
Hachette Book Group
1290 Avenue of the Americas, New York, NY 10104
littlebrown.com

Originally published in hardcover by Little, Brown and Company, October 2000
First Little, Brown paperback edition, May 2015

Little, Brown and Company is a division of Hachette Book Group, Inc.
The Little, Brown name and logo are trademarks of Hachette Book Group, Inc.

The publisher is not responsible for websites (or their content) that are not owned by the publisher.

The Hachette Speakers Bureau provides a wide range of authors for speaking events.
To find out more, go to hachettespeakersbureau.com or call (866) 376-6591.

Designed by Oksana Kushnir

Library of Congress Cataloging-in-Publication Data

Kimball, Christopher.
The dessert bible/Christopher Kimball.
p.   cm.
Includes index.
ISBN 978-0-316-49698-8 (hc) / 978-0-316-33919-3 (pb)
1. Desserts.   I. Title.

TX773.K24   2000
641.8'6—dc21   00-028229

10 9 8 7 6 5 4 3 2 1

RRD-W

Printed in the United States of America

For Adrienne

A bowl of custard, a forkful of cake, a slice of pie — they quiet the children, make the angels sing, and set the stars on their heavenly rounds.

— C.K.

CONTENTS

15. Custards 322

The perfect crème caramel or crème brûlée is a matter of getting the details just right: the ratio of milk to cream, the oven temperature, the proper use of eggs, et cetera. This same attention to details is also important when making chocolate pots de crème, crème anglaise, pastry cream, panna cotta, and zabaglione.

16. Frozen Desserts 347

Few home cooks make ice cream, sorbet, sherbet, ices, gelato, granita, or frozen yogurt — but they should. They are simple and are vastly better than store-bought. Try a cantaloupe sherbet, a coffee gelato, or a lemon Italian ice.

17. Restaurant Desserts at Home 367

Most restaurant desserts cannot be made at home, but here are those popular menu items that do work for home cooks, including roasted apple bread pudding, souffléd lemon custard, lemon curd cheesecake, and more.

ACKNOWLEDGMENTS

Collaboration is the essence of *The Dessert Bible,* as it was for my first two cookbooks, *The Cook's Bible* and *The Yellow Farmhouse Cookbook*. The same holds true at *Cook's Illustrated* magazine, where my role as editor would hardly be recognizable by an editor from any other publication. Discussion and disagreement are the order of the day, and even the most junior editor is expected to contribute.

My wife, Adrienne, has always been my best editor and most perceptive critic and has also tested many of the recipes for midweek dinner, judging their success or failure not only on clarity of instruction but also on the response of our four children, Whitney, Caroline, Charlie, and Emily. Jeanne Maguire, my long-term test cook, has contributed an enormous amount to this book, as she did to *Yellow Farmhouse*. She is a terrific cook, has a great palate, and has limitless energy for pursuing even the most outrageous notion. Also of great help in writing this book was Erica Foss, a professional chef now turned geologist and mapmaker, whose love of detailed research added immeasurably to my understanding of cooking. I also owe a great debt to Nancy Kohl, who worked with me on a number of chapters, including the one on restaurant desserts.

My long-term editor at Little, Brown, Jennifer Josephy, is also to be recognized for her advice and support, as are my agent, Angela Miller, and copyeditor, Peggy Leith Anderson. I have learned most from my colleagues at *Cook's Illustrated,* John Willoughby, Jack Bishop, Kay Rentschler, and Pam Anderson chief among them. I am deeply indebted to the many talented bakers who have gone before me, especially Rose Beranbaum, Nick Malgieri, Flo Braker, Maida Heatter, Carole Walter, Susan Purdy, Nancy Silverton, and Emily Luchetti. A word of thanks also goes to Mark Bittman for his advice and support as well as to Shirley Corriher for her assistance in explaining the science of cooking. I would also like to thank the many restaurants that shared recipes with me: Tra Vigne, Fog City Diner, Pinot's, Aqua, Hamersley's Bistro, Gotham Bar and Grill, and the Claremont Café. Finally, a great big thank you to Marion Cunningham for her limitless enthusiasm for American cooking, which makes even a bad day in the kitchen worthwhile.

INTRODUCTION

One might well ask why any cook would have sufficient nerve to publish a cookbook with *Bible* in the title. Implicit in this nomenclature is the thought that *The Dessert Bible* has both all the answers and all the recipes. Well, let me confess here and now that this book is neither all-knowing nor encyclopedic. What you will find in these pages, however, is exhaustive reporting about my investigations into what makes desserts work, what makes them fail, and why. I hope to be excused from the lack of plenitude by appealing to the experience of home cooks who realize that a cookbook is rarely measured by volume of recipes — quality is best judged by how well the recipes work and how suitable they are for home cooking.

As founder and editor of *Cook's Illustrated* magazine, I have discovered that most of us don't fully understand the whys of cooking. Why does one recipe call for baking soda and another for baking powder? Why does the temperature of butter matter when creaming it? Why is unsweetened chocolate sometimes called for instead of semisweet? And many home cooks are stymied by certain basic techniques. All of us, for example, have trouble making, rolling out, and prebaking pie dough. (Once you read the chapter on pies, you should be able to make really good, foolproof pie pastry.) We are hesitant about whipping and folding egg whites. We find that some cakes rise well, others don't, and still others end up with a domed top. Baking seems mysterious, unpredictable, and often sensitive to small variations in both ingredients and techniques. *The Dessert Bible* has been researched and written to answer a wide range of fundamental questions as well as to provide clear explanations of cooking techniques and a storehouse of truly dependable recipes.

A word about the recipes themselves. For the most part, these are not whimsical creations, the sort of offerings one expects from a fancy restaurant with a pastry chef who majored in art history. (I did major in art history, but I do my best to keep my creative impulses in check in the kitchen.) These are recipes with which you are already familiar. My role is to test every possible approach to these workhorse desserts to find the best, most foolproof method of making them. You may not always agree with my choices, but at the very least this process is helpful in understanding what makes a recipe work. In addition, I can usually ferret out those versions of, say, chilled lemon soufflé, that are too complicated, too fussy, too foamy, too dense, or too rubbery in texture. I can also spend weeks testing puff pastry recipes — so you don't have to — only to discover that none of them is worth doing at home. (Puff pastry is difficult, temperamental, and takes a whole day to make.) You will also get helpful equipment reviews and ingredient taste tests, the sort of material that is hard to come by on one's own.

One final note about my "scientific" approach to recipe development. I believe that good cooking, like playing the piano, must be built on both experience and knowledge. Composers must learn music theory as cooks must understand cooking science. To para-phrase Amelia Simmons, author of America's first cookbook, *American Cookery*, published in 1796, do not confuse my detailed approach to cooking with an "obstinate perseverance in trifles." Rather, I am interested in uncovering rules and maxims that will stand the test of time. If this requires detailed testing, so be it. The other approach, feckless improvisation, is less demanding and more fun, but it is ulti-mately disappointing, as one ends up playing the same song over and over. The good news is that these two approaches merge over time. If *The Dessert Bible* provides you with a solid knowledge of dessert making, you will gain the confidence to think for yourself in the kitchen, balancing a healthy mistrust of recipes (even mine) with enough common sense to rely on your own experience.

Boston, October 2000

THE DESSERT BIBLE

TIPS, TECHNIQUES, AND SHORTCUTS

Many cookbooks hide all the really useful information in an introductory chapter, the one nobody ever reads. For example, an author tells you on page six that he sifts and then spoons his flour into a measuring cup instead of using the dip-and-sweep method, the method used by most home cooks. The result? You end up with 20 percent more flour than called for in the recipe and the cake is heavy and dense. However, from the author's point of view, there is much generic cooking information, the sort of thing that applies to a variety of chapters and recipes, and one doesn't wish to repeat it. So I have yielded to this unfortunate but necessary cookbook convention in the hope that at least a few of my readers will take the time to skim through it. Indulge this earnest cookbook author, take a seat, and give this chapter at least a quick once-over while you are waiting for the oven to preheat. Your kind attention will be most appreciated. (By the way, I measure my flour by dipping and sweeping, so don't sift it first with my recipes unless otherwise instructed!)

KEEPING A CLEAN COUNTER

One of the problems with baking is that it produces all sorts of batter-dripping spoons and spatulas, sticky measuring cups, frothy beaters, and the like. You are often working quickly when baking in order to get a batter into the oven without delay, which means that the counter ends up covered with a sticky mess. The solution is to cut a large piece of waxed or parchment paper before starting on a recipe and laying it on the counter. Simply place all your utensils on the sheet as you work and throw it out when you are done. The counter will remain clean.

NEVER TRUST BAKING TIMES

Baking times are, at best, approximate. All ovens bake differently, some because they are not properly calibrated and some because they are made differently. Since no two ovens are identical, the baking time in a recipe should be viewed as a rough guide, not a precise measurement. Here is what you should do. First, after placing the pan in the oven, set the timer for halfway through the printed baking time. At the halfway point, turn the baking pan around in the oven for even browning. Now set the timer for half of the remaining baking time and then start checking the oven every few minutes after that. I frequently find that baking times are off by as much as 35 percent, even when recipes are properly tested. If you find that your oven is running hot and the top of your cake, for example, is browning too fast, try placing a cookie sheet on a rack just above it. This will reduce the effect of radiant heat on the cake's surface.

HOW TO CALIBRATE AN OVEN

One of the biggest problems for home cooks is that their oven may be improperly calibrated, running 25 to 50 degrees hotter or colder than the setting. I recently had this problem with a new oven and even went to the expense of purchasing three different oven thermometers, placing all of them at once in the oven to gauge the temperature. They consistently showed that the oven was running 25 to 40 degrees cool. I soon found out, however, when a serviceman came to call, that all of them were inaccurate when matched against his expensive measuring device, which showed a markedly smaller margin of error.

He then offered some advice, which I found both amusing and of some value. Purchase two cans of biscuits sold in cardboard cylinders in the refrigerator section of your supermarket. Bake the first batch following the package directions exactly. Since this recipe has been tested a thousand times, the timing will be perfect if your oven is properly calibrated. If the biscuits are not perfectly done, turn the heat setting up or down, give the oven time to adjust, and then bake the second batch. You should now have a roughly accurate reading of how far off your oven is. That being said, this is not a precise method, since recommended baking times are often given in ranges. (You want to

shoot for the middle of the range. If the recipe calls for 10 to 12 minutes, aim for 11 minutes.)

Your gas or electric company should be able to calibrate your oven, although you will be charged for the service call. If you want to purchase an oven thermometer, here is some good advice from a friend of mine, Joe Speiser, who owns a cookware shop in Manchester, Vermont. First, he recommends that you buy a dial thermometer — not a mercury thermometer — since they are easier to read. (By the time you read a mercury thermometer, the oven temperature has dropped significantly.) They cost under $10, and two of the better models are made by Polder and CDN. To choose a thermometer for purchase, Joe suggests, decide which model you want and then look at three or four units on the store shelf to compare the temperature readings. Eliminate any that have readings significantly higher or lower than the others and buy the one with a reading closest to the average. This increases your odds of getting a well-calibrated unit.

DOES OVEN PERFORMANCE CHANGE THE LONGER THE OVEN IS ON?

Many bakers have told me that an oven that has been on for a few hours will bake differently from one that has just been preheated. Since the oven was set to the same temperature, I used to discount those results. But the more I thought about it the more it bothered me, so I decided to do some tests to find out if an oven that has just been preheated to 350 degrees bakes at the same rate as an oven that has been on all day.

I tried two recipes — sugar cookies and biscuits — and noted the baking times and also their appearance to see if they in fact baked differently depending on how long the oven had been on. I also baked squares of parchment for 10 minutes at 2-hour intervals to see if the later squares would brown more quickly than earlier squares. (An old trick to determine an oven's temperature is to bake a piece of parchment paper to see how quickly it turns brown.) Last, I checked to see if an oven thermometer would remain at a constant temperature after several hours of heating.

The results were either comforting or disappointing, depending on one's perspective. The cookies showed no difference at all, both times baking up perfectly after 9½ minutes. The biscuits did show a slight difference; those baked in an oven that had been on for 8 hours cooked in 10½ minutes, and those placed in an oven that had recently come up to temperature baked in 11 minutes. As for the parchment paper squares, there were no discernible differences. Finally, I also used an oven thermometer throughout the tests, and it remained constant. So I concluded that at least for this oven, baking times can shift a bit, but only by 5 percent or so at most.

DOES THE NUMBER OF BAKING SHEETS IN AN OVEN MATTER?

I often find myself having to use more than one baking sheet at a time, and I have found that putting both sheets in the oven at the same time seems to lead to uneven cooking. I was interested in testing whether this is really true and whether the position of the rack makes a difference.

My oven has four rack levels, from the lowest, which I will call A, to the highest, which I will call D. My first test involved baking two sheets of cookies, one sheet on the lowest rack (A) and one on the next highest (B). The cookies on rack B were fine, but those on the lowest rack, A, had problems. The bottoms overcooked and the cookies in the middle of the pan cooked much more slowly, requiring another 5 minutes or so in the oven. So I learned that the bottom rack does tend to overcook the bottoms of baked goods (this might be a plus for a pie, when you want a very crisp bottom crust), and that when one sheet is above another, the food in the center of the lower sheet will cook more slowly than the items around the perimeter.

(My theory is that the top sheet blocks the radiant heat.) I also tried baking a single sheet of cookies on the top rack of the oven, and the color of the cookies was irregular, plus the pan required frequent rotation for even cooking.

I next tried baking the cookies on the middle two racks (B and C). The cookies on the upper rack browned too quickly (before they were cooked through), and those on the lower rack cooked unevenly, the same problem I had with the first test. I did find that I could overcome this problem to an extent by switching the pans' positions halfway through the baking time and also turning the baking sheets around, front to back, at the same time. Still, the cooking time had to be extended by 2 minutes or so, since the cookies were not constantly exposed to the full heat of the oven. In addition, the cookies were still not evenly baked.

I then tried baking two sheets side by side on the middle rack and found that the bottoms of the cookies turned out darker than I would like. My guess is that this method prevents the natural circulation of hot air so the heat concentrates in the lower half of the oven, beneath the sheets.

So the short answer is yes. For best results, put only one cookie sheet in the oven at a time.

THE SCIENCE OF CREAMING

Creaming butter and sugar (beating them together until they are very light) is the basis for thousands of cake and cookie recipes. Beating incorporates a great deal of air into the structure, lightening the texture of the cake. When it is done incorrectly, the results can be disastrous, resulting in a dense, heavy dessert. For most home cooks, the directive "Cream the butter and sugar" is vague at best, giving no indication of its crucial role in producing the perfect texture.

The major factor in creaming butter and sugar is the temperature of the butter. When butter is too cold, it does not whip up properly, and when it is too soft, the results are even worse, since it cannot retain air. I decided to determine the best butter temperature by beating together ½ cup each of butter and sugar, starting with the butter at 42 degrees, 50 degrees, 60 degrees, 66 degrees, 75 degrees, 80 degrees, and melted. Butter at both 42 and 50 degrees took a long time to cream, and the total volume of the mixture was only 1 cup. At 60 degrees, the volume was better — 1¼ cups. At 66 degrees (around the ideal temperature), the butter and sugar whipped up to 1½ cups. At 75 degrees, however, the volume diminished to 1¼ cups, and at 80 degrees, the volume was back to 1 cup. Melted butter was a disaster, yielding only ⅔ cup. I did find that butter that is a bit too cold is vastly preferable to butter that is too warm; a longer beating time helps to warm cold butter and to incorporate more air. (If your butter is too cold, beat it without the sugar for 2 minutes. Scrape down the bowl frequently.)

How does one determine when the butter is at the proper temperature? Of course, an instant-read thermometer will do the trick in a few seconds, but if you don't have one there are other indicators. First, butter at 65 to 67 degrees is easy to spread, although it still has some resistance. (Butter at 60 degrees is hard to spread; butter at 75 degrees is very easy to spread.) Second, you can make an indentation in the stick of butter with your finger

but the butter is still firm. Third, you should be able to bend the stick of butter with your hands but it should still feel firm. Finally, the butter should have a shiny surface but not appear greasy.

Now that I had found the ideal butter temperature, I wondered about the best technique for warming the butter from its starting point, a 40-degree refrigerator. Simply removing the stick of butter and letting it sit at room temperature takes about 2 hours, depending on the ambient temperature. (Cutting the butter into small pieces and placing them into the mixing bowl will reduce the warming time by about half.) I also tried putting butter into an oven with a pilot light, placing it on a warm stovetop, and using a water bath, none of which worked well. One cook told me that she finds the microwave the perfect tool. She places the stick of butter (still wrapped) in a small microwave oven and zaps it three times on full power for 30 seconds each, giving the butter a 10-second rest between cycles and turning it each time so a different side is facing up. I tried this and the butter melted after just 15 seconds! The problem is that different microwave ovens perform differently and not all butter is starting out at the same temperature. I finally settled on a simpler method, which is to cut the cold butter into small pieces, place it in the bowl of an electric mixer, and beat it on high speed for 2

BUTTER FOR CREAMING must be at 65 to 67 degrees for best results.

TO WARM COLD, CREAMED BUTTER, wrap a kitchen towel soaked in hot water around the mixing bowl.

CASE 1: HOW LONG DOES IT TAKE BUTTER TO REACH THE PROPER TEMPERATURE FOR CREAMING?

The single most common problem home bakers have is when they try to cream butter. They simply take the butter straight from the refrigerator and then throw it into the electric mixer, ignoring the admonition about the need to use butter that is malleable but still firm. Other cooks use room temperature butter, which is much too soft. I took one stick of butter straight from the refrigerator and one from the freezer, unwrapped them, and let them sit in an 82-degree kitchen to see how long they would take to reach 65 degrees (the proper temperature for creaming is 65 to 67 degrees).

Elapsed Time	From the Refrigerator	From the Freezer
00 hours	40°: cold to touch, frosty looking	12°: hard and cold
45 minutes	52°: cold but not frosty	28°: cold to touch
1½ hours	60°: cool to touch, finger meets resistance	50°: cool to touch
2 hours	65°: bends easily	60°: cold but finger leaves mark
2½ hours		63°: a little resistant
2¾ hours		65°: bends easily

So it took about 2 hours for the refrigerated stick of butter to come up to temperature and about 2 hours and 45 minutes for the frozen stick. Keep this in mind when you are making recipes that require creaming the butter. It takes some advance planning to make sure that the butter is at the proper temperature.

minutes before proceeding with the recipe. It is not ideal, but it will work in a pinch.

The next question I wanted to answer was what if one starts creaming butter and sugar and the mixture does not whip up light and fluffy (because the butter was too cold)? I tried five methods: heating the mixture in an oven with a pilot light, briefly heating the bottom of the bowl over a low flame, wrapping a kitchen towel soaked in warm water around the bowl while whipping, stopping to immerse the bowl briefly in warm water, and letting the bowl with the butter-sugar mixture sit at room temperature (the butter and sugar are whipped once the

correct temperature is reached). The only two methods that worked well were the warm towel and letting the mixture sit at room temperature, the towel method being the quickest remedy but the latter method being foolproof and simple if one has the time. The other methods often resulted in uneven warming and melted butter.

WHAT DO I DO IF MY EGGS ARE NOT ROOM TEMPERATURE?

The simplest solution is to put whole eggs (in their shell) in a small bowl of hot tap water for 2 minutes. This will gently bring them up to temperature. I found that during this 2-minute period they went from refrigerator temperature (about 40 degrees) to 76 degrees.

A REVOLUTIONARY WAY OF FOLDING FLOUR INTO BATTERS

I am often given to hyperbole, but you are about to discover, as I did, a totally new and vastly superior way of folding flour into delicate cake batters. This is a problem with recipes such as genoise, which call for flour to be incorporated into a very light batter. It takes forever to fold it in, the batter getting thinner by the second. Special tools have been invented to help solve this problem, and cookbooks go on and on about the proper folding methods. (One such tool is a long-handled round spoon with holes in it. The batter is supposed to flow through the holes, which is helpful in incorporating the flour. I have tried it with only modest success.)

My discovery came about in an effort to pin down the best method for folding. I used my

recipe for genoise, a cake that is particularly sensitive to one's skill in folding. I started by simply stirring the flour into the batter, and the resulting cake was a bit short with a small crumb. I then tried folding from the middle of the batter out, and the cake rose a bit better, with some tunneling (holes running through

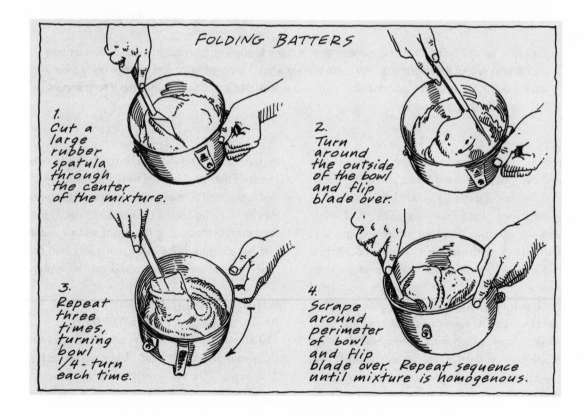

the baked cake). When I folded from the outside in, the rise was the same, but there seemed to be somewhat larger holes, albeit evenly spaced. I tested using a wooden spoon, a baker's spatula (a plastic kidney-shaped scoop used for folding), and a handled spatula, and the handled spatula was the winner. So for most folding tasks, I favor the long-handled rubber spatula, folding from the inside out. (See illustrations.)

I then tried something completely silly. I simply added the dry ingredients to the batter (in the bowl of a KitchenAid standing mixer with the whisk attachment) and let the machine do the stirring on the lowest speed for 10 seconds. (One has to finish off this process by hand with a few strokes.) This was a huge success! The height was better than with any other method, the crumb was fine, and the air bubbles in the baked cake were small and uniform. By con-

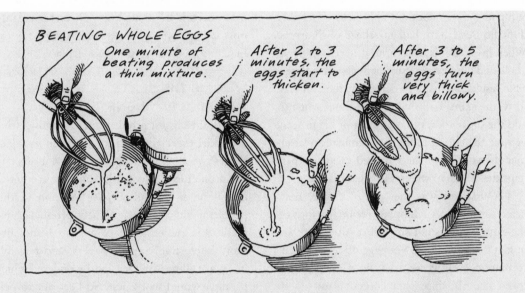

BEATING WHOLE EGGS

One minute of beating produces a thin mixture.

After 2 to 3 minutes, the eggs start to thicken.

After 3 to 5 minutes, the eggs turn very thick and billowy.

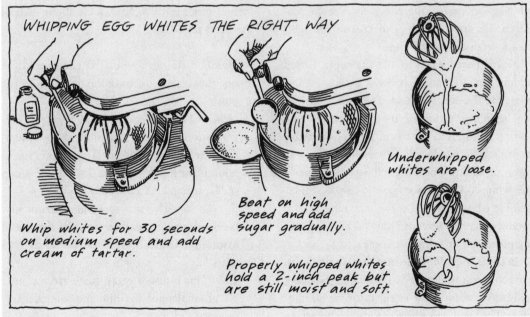

WHIPPING EGG WHITES THE RIGHT WAY

Whip whites for 30 seconds on medium speed and add cream of tartar.

Beat on high speed and add sugar gradually.

Properly whipped whites hold a 2-inch peak but are still moist and soft.

Underwhipped whites are loose.

trast, the other methods resulted in larger holes and uneven tunneling. Why does this method work? It takes far less time, it does a superior job of mixing, and the batter does not become overworked. Hurray for electric mixers! (Note: I only use this method when a recipe calls for folding flour into beaten whole eggs. When folding a batter into beaten whites, I simply use the hand method, which works just fine.)

THE BEST WAY TO WHIP CREAM

Whipping cream does not appear to be terribly difficult, but I have had my share of disasters. When the cream is too warm, it never whips up at all, and I once tried using light cream with terrible results. In trying to determine the best way to whip cream, I also wondered about when to add the sugar — at the beginning of the process or near the end? I thought this might affect either the volume of the whipped cream or perhaps the degree to which the sugar dissolved.

The first test was the type of cream. Both heavy cream and whipping cream performed the same. (This is not surprising, since they are in fact the same thing. See page 49 for more information.) However, the light cream performed poorly, since its fat content is too low to whip up properly. One cup heavy cream produced 2½ cups of whipped cream; the light cream produced only 2 cups.

Next I tested when to add the sugar. I tried adding it straightaway, halfway through whipping, and then near the end. The sugar added at the beginning produced the best result; there was no grittiness to the cream. Adding the sugar in the middle produced a somewhat gritty texture, and adding it near the end was a disaster — the whipped cream was grainy. (Since regular granulated sugar added at the beginning did not produce a grainy texture, I saw no point in testing powdered or extra-fine sugar.)

In terms of chilling the bowl and ingredients, I found it best to place bowl, whisk (or beaters), and heavy cream in the refrigerator for 30 minutes. (The bowl and whisk can also be put in the freezer.) The cream whipped up very quickly, in only 1 minute and 4 seconds. Using a room-temperature bowl and refrigerated heavy cream took somewhat longer (2 minutes, 30 seconds), but the results were about the same. So chilling the bowl does speed up the whipping process, but the outcome is comparable.

Finally, being a slave to the past, I wondered if hand whisking the cream would do as good a job as an electric mixer. The answer was no. It took 4 minutes by hand and only 2 minutes by machine, and the 1 cup heavy cream turned into only 2 cups whipped, versus 2½ cups for the machine method. So use the machine.

WHAT IS THE BEST WAY TO MAKE A BAKING PAN NONSTICK?

One of the biggest problems in baking is getting a cookie, especially a sticky one such as a lace cookie, off a baking sheet or a cake out of a pan all in one piece. Most of us blithely use butter and flour as our all-purpose solution to this problem, but a variety of new products have made this choice more complicated and also more interesting. Sprays, papers, and reusable liners are all possibilities, but I wondered which product would work best. So I set out to perform a series of tests. First, a bit about each of the items tested.

- Unsalted Butter: The classic choice and the one that carries the most flavor. $2 to $3 per pound.
- Crisco: This is hydrogenated vegetable oil, which remains in a solid state at room temperature. It is available in large metal cans (3 pounds for $3.49) or in packs of three 1-cup sticks, which cost about $2.
- Baker's Joy: This is a spray made from soybean oil, propellant, soy lecithin, flour, and assorted chemicals. A 5-ounce spray can costs $2.
- Pam: This is also a spray, made from canola oil, grain alcohol, lecithin, and propellant. A 6-ounce can costs $2.

- Waxed Paper: Although I knew that many bakers use waxed paper for lining cake pans, I wondered how it would perform on a cookie sheet.
- Parchment Paper: You can purchase parchment paper in rounds for cake pans, in sheets, or in rolls. It is a silicon-coated paper made specifically for baking. A 33-foot roll costs about $7.
- Super Parchment: These reusable, light brown, stick-resistant sheets measure 13 x 17 inches and can be cut to fit cake pans or sheet pans. One set of sheets costs $8.50.
- Teflon Bakeware Liners: These are black, nonstick, reusable liners that are available in 9-inch rounds (two for $7) and are also sold in sheets. They can be cut to fit pans if desired.
- Silpat: This is the heaviest of the reusable liners and is made from a silicon-covered fiber. The manufacturer recommends that it not be cut to fit a pan. A full sheet of Silpat measures 11⅞ x 16½ inches and costs $29.99. (It can often be found discounted to $22 to $25.) A half sheet sells for $12.50.

I tried three recipes: butter cookies, lace cookies, and then a sponge cake. The cookies were baked on cookie sheets, and I tested each item based on the final shape of the cookies, what the bottoms looked like after baking, and how easy it was to take the cookies off the sheet. I also noted any difficulties with cleanup. For the cake, I was particularly interested in how well the bottom baked (was it too dark or too light?), and I judged the degree of difficulty in removing the cake from the pan.

I started with unsalted butter, which has an advantage in the taste department, since it imparts flavor to the bottoms of cookies. But beware: butter is useless when baking something really sticky such as lace cookies, and for cakes the pan also needs to be floured. Also, cleaning up a cookie sheet that has been buttered is difficult at best, requiring plenty of elbow grease. Crisco performs in much the same manner as butter but has none of the flavor. Baker's Joy should be renamed Baker's Bane, since it sprays in clumps (it contains flour, which does not spray evenly) and has a noticeable and unpleasant chemical flavor. It also did not do a good job with the lace cookies. Pam performs about the same as Baker's Joy and also has a mildly unpleasant aftertaste. However, it does spray on evenly. Waxed paper was a disaster. Wax melts when exposed to high heat, resulting in cookies that were bonded tightly to the paper. It was even difficult to remove the cake from the waxed paper. (I doubt that this application is recommended by the manufacturer.) Parchment paper was a clear all-around winner. Even the lace cookies did not stick to the paper (although the lace cookies baked on Silpat were superior), and cleanup was a cinch, since the cookies and cake never actually touched the pan. Super parchment also works nicely, but it is reusable and therefore needs to be cleaned after each use. I find it easier simply to discard regular parchment paper rather than having to clean, dry, and store super parchment. The Teflon product is very dark, which made it difficult to tell when the lace cookies were done. (Dark cookies against a dark paper makes it difficult to tell when the edges are browning, a reliable sign that cookies are properly baked.) I also felt that the bottom of the cake became too brown. However, nothing stuck to it. As with super parchment, cleanup is required. Finally, I tried Silpat, which works in a wide range of temperatures — up to 800 degrees. The good news is that nothing sticks to this stuff. The bad news is that, according to the manufacturer, you are not supposed to cut the sheets, so it cannot be adapted to a variety of pan sizes. (It is a very thick rubberlike mat and therefore is only good for baking cookies. You would never, for example, pour a batter over it in a cake pan.) However, Silpat was the clear winner for cookie sheets, since the bottoms of the cookies came out perfectly and the light color makes it easy to tell when the cookies are done.

So, what to buy? The reusable liners (Silpat was best) are more troublesome to use, but they are good for extremely sticky baked goods such as lace cookies. Keep in mind, however, that these liners need to be washed and dried after using. Also, some of them are not supposed to be cut (if you wish to follow the manufacturer's advice), which makes them unsuitable for anything other than cookie sheets. The sprays are universally awful, since they impart an unwelcome aftertaste. Butter or butter and flour for cake pans works well enough and does add a nice touch of flavor, but don't use Crisco, since it performs about the same as butter but has no flavor. However, butter will produce a cookie sheet that is very hard to clean. The overall winner was regular parchment paper, since it is cheap, there is no cleanup, and it can be cut to fit any size pan. You can also slide off a sheet of baked cookies and slide on a new sheet with fresh dough and pop the pan right back in the oven. This makes baking large batches quick and easy.

WHAT IS THE EASIEST METHOD OF CUTTING PARCHMENT ROUNDS FOR CAKE PANS?

Of course, the easiest method for lining a cake pan is to use precut rounds, which are available at many cookware stores. But few home bakers have these available, especially those who make only the occasional cake. So the question is, given a roll of parchment paper, how does one easily and accurately measure and cut a round of parchment to fit the inside of the pan?

I started by pulling out a length of parchment paper and laying it on my counter (it was still connected to the roll). I then placed a cake pan at one end, up toward one corner. I traced the outline of the pan onto the parchment using a pencil. Next, I moved the cake pan down toward the roll but also toward the other side of the paper and traced it again. (I am assuming one needs two rounds of parchment for a two-layer cake. This method also uses the least amount of paper.) I then made a diagonal cut between the two circles and then cut the paper

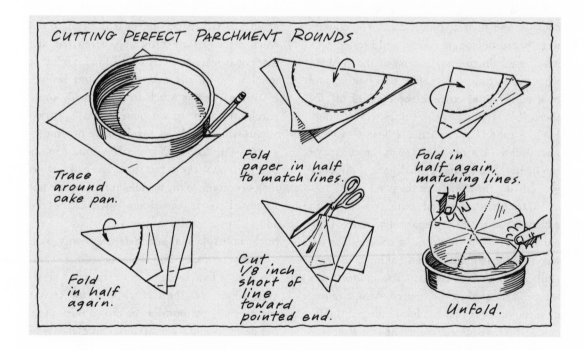

CUTTING PERFECT PARCHMENT ROUNDS

Trace around cake pan.

Fold paper in half to match lines.

Fold in half again, matching lines.

Fold in half again.

Cut 1/8 inch short of line toward pointed end.

Unfold.

from the roll just beyond the second circle. Now I had two pieces of parchment paper, each with a tracing of the cake pan on it. Now the question was how to cut out the rounds.

I started by folding the first circle in half and then cutting, but I found that the paper slipped as I was cutting. Next, I tried folding the circle into quarters, but I still found it difficult to keep the paper from slipping. When I folded the circle into eighths, I hit pay dirt. The paper did not slip, and the circle came out perfectly. I went on to try folding the circle into sixteenths but found that when I unfolded it, each of the creases ended in a small point. Just to make sure that I had not overlooked a better method, I did not trace the outlines of the pan onto the paper but instead simply folded a square of paper into eighths and placed the point above the center of the pan. I then cut a rounded edge at the point where the paper met the edge of the cake pan. The problem with this method is that it is hard to estimate the center of the pan with any accuracy, and the curved edge is hard to cut perfectly, so the circle is irregular when unfolded. Finally, I tried simply cutting around the circle without folding and found that this method produced a ragged, uneven round.

So the best method is to trace the cake pan onto parchment paper, fold the circle into eighths, and cut just inside the traced line. (You need to cut just inside the line to allow for the thickness of the side of the cake pan.)

WHAT IS THE BEST METHOD OF MEASURING FLOUR?

Real bakers always measure their flour by weight; some are even persnickety enough to weigh their baking powder, which I find beyond the pale. (Who in their right mind is going to weigh a half teaspoon of baking powder?) The reality of home cooking, however, dictates that very few of us are going to weigh our flour, even though that is, in fact, the most precise method of measurement. (Besides which, most recipes do not list flour by weight.) The question then becomes, does it make any difference how it is measured? The short answer is an unqualified yes, keeping in mind that what is truly important is that one measure the flour in the same manner as the person who wrote and tested the recipe.

There are three basic methods of measuring flour other than by weight. The first is the classic dip-and-sweep method, which means that

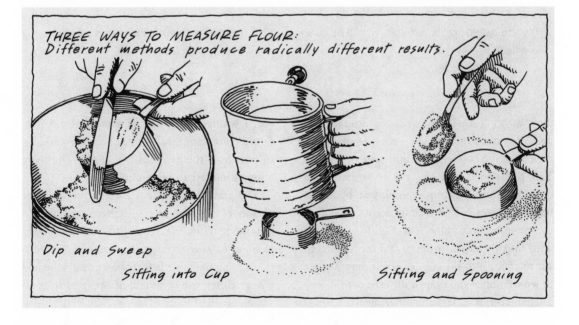

THREE WAYS TO MEASURE FLOUR: Different methods produce radically different results.

Dip and Sweep

Sifting into Cup

Sifting and Spooning

CASE 2: SIFTING, SPOONING, AND SWEEPING

Eight methods of measuring flour were compared to see if they delivered the same weight of flour and to determine which method was easiest.

Method	Weight per Cup	Comments
Sift and then spoon into measuring cup	3.2 ounces	Time-consuming; yields a small weight of flour per cup
Sift and then dip and sweep	3.4 ounces	Need to sift a lot of flour to make this work
Sift directly into measuring cup	3.1 ounces	Must sift lots of flour; yields the smallest weight
Sift and then pour into cup	3.15 ounces	Neat, but yields small weight of flour per cup
Spoon from bag; unsifted	3.8 ounces	Large variations in weight when tested many times
Dip and sweep from bag; unsifted	4.3 ounces	Consistent method, but the most weight
Spoon from a canister; unsifted	3.65 ounces	Less weight than the dip-and-sweep method
Dip and sweep from a canister; unsifted	3.85 ounces	Lighter flour weight than when measured directly from bag of flour

the measuring cup is dipped down into the flour until it is overflowing. The excess is swept off the top of the cup with the dull edge of a knife. This is the method I use and is probably the most common technique employed by home bakers. However, I have come across two other common methods. One is to lightly spoon the flour into the measuring cup, and the other is to sift the flour into the cup (or sift it onto a piece of waxed paper and pour it into the cup). I conducted a series of tests, comparing the various methods and weighing the flour after measur-

ing. I wanted to see if the same method produced consistent results time after time and also to note how the methods compared. The chart above summarizes my findings.

The good news is that each technique gave reasonably consistent results from one time to the next. However, the differences between techniques were striking. The first conclusion is that sifting the flour before measuring will yield a huge difference in weight as opposed to measuring unsifted flour. (There is a 26 percent difference between dipping and sweeping sifted flour and dipping and sweeping directly from a bag.) Therefore, if a recipe calls for sifted flour as a measurement, you had better sift it. Note that there is a difference in meaning between "2 cups flour, sifted" and "2 cups sifted flour." The former suggests that one should measure the flour and then sift it; the latter suggests the reverse. *In this book, I never sift before measuring and always use the dip-and-sweep method.*

Second, there was a sizable difference between dip-and-sweep and either spooning the flour or sifting directly into the measuring cup. (For example, the dip-and-sweep method produced 13 percent more weight of unsifted flour than the spooning method.) So follow the recipe directions carefully. I also suggest that you check the front matter of a cookbook. Cookbook writers don't tell you how to measure flour in each recipe, but they will usually give you this information in the introductory chapters. Unless instructed otherwise, I use the dip-and-sweep method with unsifted flour.

SIFTING FLOUR ONTO WAXED PAPER

Most recipes that call for sifting dry ingredients tell you to sift them into a bowl. I find it easier and less work to sift onto a piece of waxed or parchment paper. It is easier to transfer the flour to a mixing bowl (just pick up the sides of the paper), and you have one less bowl to clean up.

WHAT IS THE BEST METHOD FOR MELTING CHOCOLATE?

Most cookbooks suggest that chocolate be melted in a double boiler, an out-of-date and unwieldy approach. Most home cooks nowadays do not have a double boiler; but they do have a microwave oven, which offers a quicker and simpler solution. To be fair, though, I tested the microwave not only against the double boiler but also against oven heating and direct melting in a regular saucepan on the stovetop. I used 4 ounces of chocolate for all of my tests.

First, the loser. If you have a very heavy-bottomed small saucepan, this method does work in a pinch. Place the chocolate in the pan over low heat and stir constantly until the chocolate is about half-melted. (This will take anywhere from 1 to 3 minutes.) Now take it off the heat and let it sit until completely melted, stirring once or twice. This method will not work if you do not have a very heavy saucepan, as it is easy to burn the chocolate.

Second, I tried the double-boiler method — chopped chocolate is heated in the top of a double boiler or in a bowl placed over simmering water — and it took about 9 minutes with frequent stirring. This was too much time and effort. The oven method worked okay with a 250-degree oven, the chocolate having been placed in a heavy saucepan, but it was difficult to regulate the temperature of the chocolate, since it had to be taken out of the oven periodically to be checked.

Microwaving turned out to be the ideal method. I tried three different power levels — 100 percent, 50 percent, and 25 percent — and I also tried melting the chocolate with and without stirring. I found that without stirring, on either 100 percent or 50 percent power, it was difficult to judge when the chocolate was ready. The 25 percent power method worked fine but took almost 10 minutes. It turned out that 50 percent power with occasional stirring was the best method, since one can judge the exact moment when the chocolate is done. Of course, different ovens and different amounts and shapes of chocolate will produce different cooking times.

So here is the best method: Place the chocolate (it does not have to be chopped) into a microwave-safe bowl and cook at 50 percent power for 1 minute. Stir and cook for an additional minute, still at 50 percent. If the chocolate is not quite ready, continue cooking for 30-second intervals, stirring each time. Note that chocolate often appears solid when heated in a microwave — it retains its shape — until it is stirred. So visual clues are not very helpful.

2

KITCHEN EQUIPMENT BUYER'S GUIDE

A good kitchen detective is always suspicious of claims made by cookware manufacturers. The design of a standing mixer may be exemplary but its performance lousy. A food processor may be expensive but may not perform as well as less expensive models. An all-in-one kitchen appliance may claim to accomplish many tasks but may do none of them particularly well. Clues to the performance of a piece of cookware may not be had from either the design or the price. The only recourse is to try out as many models as possible in the test kitchen and put them through their paces.

And for those of you not inclined to take cookware selection seriously, remember that the wrong mixer will not be able to handle cookie dough, the wrong baking sheet will overcook the bottoms of your chocolate chip cookies, and the wrong food processor won't be able to chop chocolate. Any workman knows that the right tools make all the difference. This is especially true for home cooks, who may be less experienced than a restaurant chef. The right tool can measurably improve the kitchen skills of a beginner cook who is not sufficiently experienced to make up for mediocre performance.

As for shopping, I always find a fair amount of variation in prices from store to store. Generally speaking, the lowest prices are often found at big chain retailers who, contrary to what one might expect, often do carry top-quality kitchen equipment. If you are having trouble finding a source for equipment, I suggest that you refer to my publication *Cook's Illustrated*. We include a resources section at the back of each issue with information on locating a variety of equipment, including 800 numbers that can be used to find a local retailer. (Or contact us at **www.cooksillustrated.com**.) For the sake of convenience, you can also shop by mail. At the end of this chapter is a list of my favorite mail-order catalogs with short descriptions and their phone numbers and Web sites where appropriate.

One last thought. When I, or any other cookbook author, provide times or settings for equipment (e.g., beat 3 minutes on high speed), please take these only as rough guidelines. A hand-held mixer is quite different from a

KitchenAid standing mixer, which is quite different once again from an inexpensive mass-market model such as Sunbeam. It may be 3 minutes or 2 or 4. Rely on the description of the food being processed instead. If it says to whip egg whites until they can hold a 2-inch peak, that's the key piece of information. The same holds true for baking times, which in my opinion are virtually worthless given the huge variation in ovens. Your oven may run 50 degrees hotter or colder than mine. You may have had it preheated all morning while you baked something else, while I may have just turned mine on and brought it up to temperature. Use your head, and don't use published baking times as anything more than rough guidelines.

STANDING MIXERS

A standing electric mixer is perhaps the most expensive and important small appliance one can purchase, and the price ranges from about $100 to $400. A good one can handle almost twice the flour of a lesser model and is also significantly better at dealing with a stiff cookie or bread dough. The question is, which one to buy.

To make that determination, I decided to perform five different tests on each of five different machines. I whipped 1 cup heavy cream, beat 3 egg whites, made a cake batter, creamed butter and sugar to make cookie dough, and then made a simple bread recipe to see how each machine would stand up to some heavy lifting. I took careful notes on the volume and consistency of the whipped cream and egg whites, how well they beat eggs and creamed butter, the difficulty of adding dry ingredients (some machines gave us a minifacial when flour was added), how stable each machine was during the tests, and how well the motors stood up to the tougher cookie and bread doughs.

I selected five machines that ran the gamut from the expensive KitchenAid, at almost $400, to an inexpensive Krups, at just over $100. (I discovered that model numbers change rapidly and, even though these models were checked recently, you may find that newer models are already appearing on store shelves.) Here is a rundown and description of the various models I tested:

- KitchenAid K5SS ($370; 10 speeds): This is the larger of the two KitchenAid mixers, with a 5-quart-capacity bowl and many available attachments. The mixer is engaged by raising and lowering the bowl, not by raising the head of the mixer with the beaters, a design difference that sets it apart from all other tested models. The beaters move in an elliptical path in a stationary bowl. I have found that this method incorporates ingredients nicely, although adding dry ingredients such as flour can lead to an instant facial unless the speed is turned to low or the mixer turned off entirely. (A splashguard is available as an accessory.) The mixer comes with a flat paddle, a whisk, and a dough hook. In my tests, I found that this mixer should not be used with more than 9 cups of flour.
- KitchenAid K45SS ($270; 10 speeds): This is the little sister to the above mixer, with a capacity of 4½ quarts. It is unlike the larger model in that its top portion, along with beaters, tilts upward for adding ingredients or removing the bowl. This mixer comes with the same attachments and also offers a wide range of accessories, although these are somewhat more limited than those for the bigger model. It uses the same motion to move the beaters around the bowl and worked best with no more than 7 cups of flour.
- Krups Power Mix Pro Metal 610 ($100; 3 speeds): This mixer is very lightweight compared with the KitchenAid models and is also the only model that comes with a plastic bowl. It also includes two beaters and a dough attachment. It uses a rotating bowl as well as moving beaters to incorporate ingredients — the only mixer to use both methods. This mixer did not perform well with

anything more than 5 cups of flour. (This model has been replaced by model 613, which costs $150. I did not test the newer version. It comes with a metal bowl instead of plastic.)

- Hamilton Beach 60690 ($130; 12 speeds): This is a medium-weight mixer with a tilting top, two beaters, and a dough hook attachment. It has a revolving bowl with stationary beaters, which requires scraping down the sides of the bowl quite often. This mixer can handle no more than 6 cups of flour.

- Sunbeam Mixmaster 2359 ($160; 12 speeds): This is another medium-weight mixer with a tilting top, two beaters, and a dough hook. It also has a revolving bowl and stationary beaters, requiring multiple stops to scrape the sides of the bowl. For its weight this mixer was quite unstable. Anything over 5 cups of flour made it dance across the counter. Sunbeam also makes a combination standing/hand mixer, model number 2372, which costs only $39. It was so flimsy and unstable that I did not include it in any of the following tests. (This model has now been discontinued and replaced by model 2366.)

Each of the models above was tested using the following criteria:

Whipped Cream: Bowls and beaters were placed in the freezer for 10 minutes. One cup of heavy cream was whipped on low speed for 20 seconds and then on high speed until whipped. I checked consistency and volume of each.

Egg Whites: Three egg whites at room temperature were beaten for 30 seconds at low speed and then on high speed until whipped. Both consistency and volume were rated.

Cake Batter: Egg yolks and sugar were beaten, then dry and wet ingredients (mostly flour and milk) were added in stages. The color and volume of the egg foam was considered, along with the ease of adding dry ingredients

(some models blew the flour back in my face) and the overall smoothness of the batter.

Cookie Dough: This test involved creaming butter with sugar, then adding eggs and dry ingredients. I was looking for a fluffy butter-sugar mixture along with well-mixed dough. I also noted if the mixer was stable during the process.

Bread Dough: I used a simple dough recipe (water, flour, yeast, and salt), and the machines were rated on how well they handled the sticky dough as well as on whether they produced a smooth, elastic dough.

Case 3 summarizes the findings.

FOOD PROCESSORS

Back in the seventies, when the Cuisinart food processor was first introduced, I viewed it as an expensive piece of kitchen gadgetry superfluous to the needs of a good cook. After all, a sharp chef's knife wielded with proper authority should make quick work of most any task involving slicing and dicing. Since that time, however, I have been converted to the use of a food processor for making pie and biscuit dough as well as for kneading bread dough, which can be accomplished in less than 1 minute. It is also handy for grating or slicing a large volume of cheese or vegetables. The question is, is a $250 model really necessary, or can I make do with the cheap, $50 alternative?

I assembled a fair sampling of contestants, ranging from expensive models with an 11-cup bowl to cheaper models that can handle only 7 cups. I performed five types of tests on these machines. For the basic tasks of chopping, mincing, and grinding, I processed an onion, parsley, and then breadcrumbs. Next, I sliced both a zucchini and a carrot, looking for thin, even slices. I grated a carrot and then a block of mozzarella. For pureeing, I tried a simple vegetable soup and then kept adding hot chicken stock to see how much volume each machine could hold before leaking, a serious problem

CASE 3: RATING STANDING MIXERS

Five models were rated on how well each of them whipped cream, beat egg whites, produced a cake batter and cookie dough, and kneaded bread.

Model	Whipping Cream	Egg Whites	Cake Batter	Cookie Dough	Bread Dough
KitchenAid K5SS	Excellent	Excellent	Very good	Excellent	Excellent
KitchenAid K45SS	Excellent	Excellent	Very good	Excellent	Excellent
Krups Power Mix Pro 610	Fair	Very good	Fair	Fair	Fair
Hamilton Beach 60690	Good	Good	Fair	Fair	Poor
Sunbeam 2359	Good	Fair	Poor	Poor	Poor

WHAT TO BUY: KitchenAid wins hands down. Both models made great fluffy whipped cream and egg whites, and smooth cake batter; stiff doughs were created with little effort. There was a bit of flying flour when adding dry ingredients, but this can be mitigated by turning the machine down to a lower setting. The larger model has 25 extra watts of power and more capacity. I find the smaller model to be a bit easier to use, since the head pivots up and away from the bowl, which makes access easier. In general, the other, less expensive models were relatively unstable when working with cookie or bread dough, to the point that they were almost unsafe.

when processing hot liquids. I also pureed a batch of cooked beans and measured the consistency of the texture. Finally, I made a simple American pie dough. Here are descriptions of the models I tested.

- KitchenAid Ultra Power KFP 600 ($249; 11-cup bowl; 12 pounds): This is a heavy-duty machine with a minibowl for small jobs. It has easy-to-use buttons and an easy-to-clean base, since the buttons are completely sealed underneath a clear layer of plastic.

- Cuisinart Pro Custom 11 DLC-8S ($350; 11-cup bowl; 11 pounds): This is also a heavy-duty machine. The controls are very easy to use and the base easy to clean.
- DeLonghi Ultimate FP30 ($270; 11-cup bowl; 7 pounds): This is an odd-looking food processor. The bowl sits at an angle on the base. It has four speeds and a curved blade.
- Krups Master Pro Deluxe ($150; 7-cup bowl; 7 pounds): A lightweight, but easy to use and clean.

IS THE $400 MAGIC MILL MIXER WORTH THE MONEY?

Serious home cooks in the market for a standing mixer do have one other alternative to standard models. It is the Magic Mill mixer, a $400 investment that has been recommended to me by many *Cook's Illustrated* readers. I bought one to find out just how good it really was.

The first thing that became clear was that this machine is radically different in all respects from standard mixers. The metal bowl, which is huge, spins on a stand. A spring-loaded arm extends out over the bowl, and a roller hanging down from it turns against the side of the bowl as it spins. The batter is pressed between this roller and the bowl, which is how the mixing process works. In addition, a stiff rubber spatula positioned against the side of the bowl (this is truly a great idea) scrapes the batter off the bowl as it spins. The machine also comes with a dough hook, which remains stationary as the bowl rotates, and a plastic bowl with a set of small beaters, which are used for whipping cream or beating egg whites. It should also be noted that this is one gorgeous piece of kitchen equipment. It is huge, heavy, and worthy of being included in the permanent collection of the Museum of Modern Art.

That being said, I do not recommend that most home cooks purchase one. This is only for folks who engage in serious baking, needing to work with more than 6 cups of flour at a time, about the limit for the smaller KitchenAid. Whipping 2 or 3 egg whites, for example, is a task much better performed with an electric hand-held mixer. And 3 or 4 cups of flour get completely lost in the gargantuan metal bowl, a bit like seeing only six wildebeests on the Serengeti. However, if you make a lot of bread or are inclined to large quantities, this is the machine for you. No dough is too stiff, no quantity is too large.

- Hamilton Beach Chef Prep 70700 ($50; 7-cup bowl; 5 pounds): This inexpensive and small-capacity food processor makes a mess and also leaks a fair amount.

THE MAGIC MILL mixer is terrific for kneading and for large quantities.

Chopping, Mincing, and Grinding

For the chopping, mincing, and grinding tests, I chopped an onion (quartered), minced parsley (1 cup of leaves), then processed breadcrumbs (2 slices of day-old bread, torn into chunks). The KitchenAid did an adequate job on the onion and parsley, chopping them into small and then smaller pieces (by pulsing) without producing a puree, but the pieces were not all of equal size. However, the breadcrumbs were no challenge for this machine. The Cuisinart did a slightly better job on the onion and parsley than the KitchenAid, although the breadcrumbs turned out uneven. The DeLonghi is the only one that takes practice to use, having four different speeds. Even when the correct speed was used (the manual tells you which speed to use for which operation), the onion became mushy while chunks of unchopped onion were left above the blade. It did a nice job, however, with the parsley (so long as you want it finely chopped), and the breadcrumbs came out fine. The Krups fared well with the onion and parsley, but the breadcrumbs were just okay. The Hamilton Beach was a dud. The onion came out uneven and mushy, the parsley was not adequately chopped, and the breadcrumbs were a disaster.

Slicing

Next, to test each machine's ability to produce even, thin slices, I processed zucchini and carrots. The KitchenAid was terrific at slicing, as was the Cuisinart. The DeLonghi fared reasonably well, although the feed tube for this machine is not quite as large and the slices were not quite as even as with the first two machines. The Krups turned out uneven slices of both vegetables. The Hamilton Beach struggled with the carrot, which seemed to slip in the feed tube, and had trouble even with the zucchini: slices were too thick and also varied in thickness from slice to slice. No thanks.

Grating

I grated a carrot and then a block of mozzarella with each machine. The KitchenAid handled the carrot easily, but the cheese had to be trimmed to fit the feed tube and there were a couple of tablespoons of mashed cheese in the lid after shredding. The shreds were uniform, however. The Cuisinart outperformed the KitchenAid, with the least amount of leftovers in the lid after completion. The DeLonghi did a fine job with the carrot, but there was a great deal of mashed cheese left in the lid after grating the mozzarella. The Krups did an inconsistent job, and the Hamilton Beach once again fell short: its feed tube is small, the lid became mucked up with cheese, and the shreds were inconsistent.

Pureeing

Although I do not consider a food processor the ideal machine for pureeing liquids (I prefer to use a blender), I still wanted to know which of these machines would puree hot foods without leaking. I tried pureeing cooked beans with a small amount of liquid to see which machines could produce a smooth-textured puree. Then I cut up a carrot, an onion, and a stalk of celery,

sautéed them until soft, and pureed them with 2 cups of chicken stock. Then I added hot stock in 1-cup increments until each machine started to leak.

The KitchenAid did an outstanding job: the beans were very smooth and creamy, the vegetable-stock mixture was also homogenous, and the workbowl held up to 6½ cups without leaking. The Cuisinart was fine with the bean puree and the vegetable-stock mixture, but it began leaking at a disappointing 4 cups. The DeLonghi handled the beans nicely, but the vegetable puree was uneven and the machine started to leak at 5 cups. The Krups did a good job all around but started leaking at 4 cups. The Hamilton Beach did a fine job with the beans but the stock mixture started leaking out at 4 cups and the vegetable puree was not as smooth as with the other models.

Making Pastry Dough

In my opinion, making pastry dough is the highest and best use for a food processor. Flour, salt, and sugar are added to the bowl of a food processor and then cold butter is pulsed into the mixture, followed by cold Crisco. For purposes of this test, cold water was then added and the machine pulsed until the dough came together into a cohesive mass. (Normally I add the water only after the dough has been removed from the machine, to avoid overprocessing, but I thought this would make a good test of how well the machines worked the dough.)

Both the KitchenAid and the Cuisinart were winners. In just a few pulses, the fat was cut into very small, even pieces and evenly distributed throughout, and the dough came together quickly and evenly after the water was added. The DeLonghi could not cut the fat into uniform pieces and therefore some of the butter pieces were too large; the Krups produced adequate dough with a bit of extra processing; and the Hamilton Beach did only a fair job, turning out somewhat gummy dough.

CASE 4: RATING FOOD PROCESSORS

Five different food processors were compared using a battery of tests, including chopping, mincing, grinding, slicing, grating, pureeing, and making pastry dough.

Model	Price	Comments
KitchenAid Ultra Power KFP 600	$249	Easy to clean, heavy, quiet, and well made. Holds 6½ cups of hot liquid without leaking, and great with pastry dough.
Cuisinart Pro Custom 11 DLC-8S	$350	Slightly outperformed the KitchenAid in the onion and cheese grating, but holds less hot liquid without leaking and was less successful with bread-crumbs. Still a top contender.
Delonghi Ultimate FP30	$270	This machine was a great disappointment, considering the price. It did a poor job with the onion and the cheese, although it performed adequately with the grated carrot, breadcrumbs, and slicing tasks. Forget the Delonghi and buy the KitchenAid or the Cuisinart.
Krups Master Pro Deluxe	$150	Good for chopping, but lousy at slicing and grating. It started to leak with 4 cups of hot liquid. For an extra $100, buy the KitchenAid.
Hamilton Beach Chef Prep 70700	$50	This machine is a dud, even at the low price of $50.

WHAT TO BUY: The KitchenAid and the Cuisinart are both worth buying; forget the rest of the machines. The Cuisinart does have a wider range of models.

ELECTRIC HAND-HELD MIXERS

Many cookbook authors assume that readers have $250 standing mixers for making cookie dough or whipping egg whites. Although I do have one and use it frequently, this is not a common kitchen appliance among country cooks. For this reason, I have tested electric hand-held mixers to see which models are worth the money. I tested whipping egg whites, whipping cream, and making cookie dough, and I also checked out how difficult it was to clean. The difference in performance was substantial. Some mixers have slow speed settings that are much too fast; I ended up with a face full of flour. Others just don't have enough horsepower to blend cookie dough. Some models were neat, while others threw gobs of dough and whipping cream around the room, splatter-

CASE 5: RATING ELECTRIC HAND-HELD MIXERS

I tested whipping egg whites and heavy cream and made batches of cookie dough. All hand-held mixers are not equal in the ease-of-cleaning department. Some are inexplicably designed with openings and grooves that attract batter like flies to sugar. Others are well sealed to make cleanup a breeze. Items are listed in order of price.

Model	Price	Speeds	Egg Whites	Whipping Cream	Cookie Dough	Cleaning
KitchenAid KHM9PHW	$89	9	Excellent	Excellent	Excellent	Excellent
KitchenAid KHM&TWH	$79	7	Excellent	Excellent	Excellent	Excellent
KitchenAid KHM5TB	$65	5	Excellent	Excellent	Excellent	Excellent
Cuisinart HTM-5	$56	5	Good	Good	Good/fair	Excellent
Sunbeam Mixmaster 2485	$38	6	Good	Good	Fair	Fair
Braun M810	$30	3	Fair	Good	Fair	Good
Hamilton Beach	$25	5	Fair	Good	Fair	Fair

WHAT TO BUY: The 5-speed KitchenAid KHM5TB is the best buy at a reasonable $65. Don't bother with any of the less expensive models; they just won't perform up to speed. The KitchenAid also has a nice range of speeds. The 7- and 9-speed models have a slow setting of just 350 rpm's and a high setting of 1300 rpm's. They also have enough horsepower to work a thick cookie dough, the acid test for any hand-held mixer.

ing everything within three feet. I also looked for mixers without grooves or openings in the housing that make cleanup more difficult. I did find that manufacturers such as Braun also offer lower-priced mixers that are essentially the same machine as the more expensive models but without all of the extra attachments. As with most appliances, I find attachments to be not worth the money. They usually get left in the back of a drawer and forgotten. Case 5 shows how several brands of mixers performed in my tests.

CASE 6: RATING ROUND CAKE PANS

Four different types of cake pans were tested with sponge cake and chocolate cake recipes. Sponge cakes were baked for 16 minutes and the chocolate cakes were baked for 26 minutes. All pans were buttered and lined with parchment — if you do this, cakes will come out of any kind of pan.

Type of Pan	Sponge Cake	Chocolate Cake
Standard heavyweight aluminum	Best height and color. Texture was open and airy with a moist crumb. Top slightly domed.	Best height with excellent texture. Sides and bottom were just browned. Top was domed.
Cushioned aluminum	Bottom and sides of this cake had no color. Good crumb, moist, and the top was flat.	Slightly lower than the above cake. Sides and bottom of cake had no color. Top was flat.
Light gray nonstick	Bottom and sides were dark brown, but the cake was the shortest of the lot. The texture was compact and less desirable.	The shortest cake by a half inch. Very compact texture; not light and airy.
Black-finish nonstick	Similar to the light gray pan, but the sides and bottom were slightly darker.	Average height with a domed top. Sides and bottom darker than with the aluminum pan but lighter than with the light gray. Compact texture.

WHAT TO BUY: Standard heavyweight aluminum pans bake the best cakes: high with a nice light, moist texture. Forget the other models. Note, however, that the cushioned aluminum pan did produce a flat top, although the texture was not as good as with the regular aluminum pans.

ROUND CAKE PANS

I tested four different categories of round cake pans: light gray nonstick, black-finish nonstick, aluminum, and a cushion aluminum model. (The last type uses two layers of metal with air sandwiched between them.) It was interesting to note that all of the nonstick models I tested came with directions indicating that the pans must be greased and floured before baking. As a result, these pans don't save any preparation time. I find that for cake pans, the basic categories of pans are more important than the brands. The pans I tested are as follows:

- Village Baker Professional Weight ($9): This is a standard heavyweight aluminum cake pan. It has a nice shape with very straight sides and a fairly sharp 90-degree joint between bottom and sides.
- Wearever CushionAire Insulated ($11): This is a 9-inch aluminum cake pan with a cushion of air around the sides and bottom of the

pan. This pan has more of a rounded joint at the bottom.

- Baker's Secret Nonstick ($4): This model has a light gray nonstick coating over an aluminum pan. It has slightly sloped sides with a rounded angle at the bottom to give it the least attractive shape of all. This is the lightest-weight pan I tested.
- Calphalon Nonstick Professional Bakeware ($20): This pan has a black nonstick coating over an aluminum pan. It has a nice straight side and a fairly sharp 90-degree joint at the bottom.

I was looking for a pan that browned the sides and bottom both evenly and nicely without burning. Cakes should also be easy to remove from the pan without excessive sticking. I also wondered if the texture of the cakes would vary based on the pan (it did), and if some cakes would have domed tops and others flat (they did). Two cakes were baked in each pan: a sponge cake and a chocolate cake. The results are summarized in Case 6.

BAKING PANS

I have always wondered if it mattered whether a baking pan (a basic square or rectangular pan

CAKE PANS come in many different heights. Two inches is best.

used for brownies, one-layer cakes, et cetera) was made of glass, a dark nonstick metal, a gray nonstick metal, or just plain heavyweight aluminum. In order to resolve this issue once and for all, I purchased one of each model and did three sets of tests. I baked a brownie, a lemon bar, and then a pudding cake. Here are the results.

The Brownie Test

I used the recipe on page 107 and baked it in all three pans. I wanted to find out how well the brownies released from the pan, what the corners looked like after baking, and whether there was a difference in texture or color.

Even when the glass pan was buttered, the brownies stuck a bit. They were the lightest brown of all the brownies I baked, and the round corners made ugly end pieces. Plain aluminum was a better choice: the brownies had a nice medium color, neither too dark nor too light, and they were moist and chewy. They could not be turned out of the pan in one piece but if cut in the pan they were easily removed. The black nonstick pan was great for a quick and easy release — the brownies almost flew out of this piece of bakeware. The bad news is that they were slightly darker and shorter than those baked in a simple aluminum pan, although they were still moist. Gray nonstick bakeware was a surprise, since the brownies actually turned out darker than those baked in the dark nonstick pan. The pan I bought had very rounded corners, which turned out unattractive end pieces.

The Lemon Bar Test

Lemon bars are made with a shortbread crust and a lemon curd filling. The key here was how well the crust baked, since I lined the pan with parchment paper to make it easy to remove the bars after cooking. I checked each recipe after 20 minutes of baking time.

Baked in glass bakeware, the crust was very light brown on the bottom and light brown on

CASE 7: RATING BAKING PANS

Four different models of baking pans (simple square and rectangular pans used for brownies and the like) were tested with three different recipes: brownies, lemon bars, and pudding cake.

Type of Pan	Comments
Glass	Although glass is an excellent heat conductor, my tests showed that it did not brown well. The rounded corners make unattractive end pieces. Not recommended.
Aluminum	This is the best choice overall, producing nicely browned baked goods. Choose heavy, professional-quality pans for the most even cooking, although the cheaper, thinner pans work well.
Black-finish nonstick	The advantage is that baked goods really don't stick in these pans. The bad news is that they can brown a bit too rapidly and slicing baked goods in the pan will eventually damage the finish.
Light gray nonstick	This pan seemed to bake even faster than the darker models. Same pros and cons as the above pan.

WHAT TO BUY: Aluminum is the top choice. It is inexpensive, durable, and bakes evenly.

the top. The sides were barely colored, although the crust was cooked through. The rounded corners made it difficult to line the pan with parchment paper. Aluminum was once again a winner, with even cooking and a crust that turned out a perfect golden brown. The squared corners made the pan easy to line with parchment. Black nonstick cooked unevenly; the top of the crust was golden brown and the bottom was darker brown. The gray nonstick pan turned out the darkest results. The top was dark golden and the bottom was even darker.

The Pudding Cake Test

Pudding cake is a simple cake that separates during baking into a layer of pudding on the bottom and a layer of cake on the top. I was testing for even cooking and the degree of difficulty I had in removing the cake from the pan. In the glass pan, the cake took an extra 5 minutes to bake. The top cracked, and the cake stuck to the sides, although slices could be removed with a spatula. A skin formed on the bottom of the cake. When baked in aluminum, the cake was an even golden brown on top and pulled away from the sides during baking. The cake did stick just a bit, but slices could be removed with a spatula. The black nonstick pan turned out a cake that was an even golden brown; the sides of the cake pulled away from the pan, and the cake slices released very easily. The gray nonstick pan produced a golden brown top, sides that pulled away, and slices that were easily removed.

PIE PLATES

To determine the best pie plate, I baked my pie pastry recipe blind in four different types of pans: tinned steel, aluminum, pottery, and glass. Although all four types of pans worked well — that is, the crust came out nicely browned — I did find that glass tends to work best, since it conducts heat so well. The metal pans are fine, although somewhat slower to brown, and the pottery models provide the least even crust of all. Glass plates have another advantage: one can see the color of the crust as it cooks. A 9-inch Pyrex (glass) pie plate costs only $3; metal plates run $4 to $5 for a set of two. You should also look at the rim of the plate. It should be wide enough to support a fluted edge. Some porcelain pie plates in particular have narrow rims. I also prefer pie plates with two small tabs, or "ears," on the side of the rim. This makes it easier to pick them up and move them.

BAKING SHEETS

A home cook can spend from $3.99 to a whopping $23.99 to purchase a simple baking sheet. Does the color of the surface, the thickness of the gauge, or the type of finish (nonstick or not) really matter? To answer this question, I baked chocolate chip cookies on eight different baking sheets to see what would happen. I lightly greased them first with nonstick Pam cooking spray, and each cookie was made from 2 tablespoons of dough. The only consistent result was that the darker-

PIE PLATES with wide rims are best for single-crust pies.

colored sheets seemed to set up the dough quickly, producing a higher cookie and one that was more browned than the flatter cookies produced by lighter-colored sheets. The big surprise, however, was that price did not seem to be a determining factor. The thin aluminum Kaiser sheet ($6.99) did about as well as the $24 Calphalon model. As far as nonstick goes, I prefer to use parchment paper on my baking sheets, since a freshly baked batch of cookies can simply be whisked off the hot pan and a new batch of dough whisked on and into the oven. (See page 10 for more about making a baking pan nonstick.)

ROLLING PINS

As usual, I have strong opinions about rolling pins, but also as usual, it does depend on the cook. I find thinner, straight or tapered pins to be best, since I get a good feel for the dough. The maple pins with ball bearings attached to the handles are fine, and many people prefer them because they give the cook added leverage. These pins are heavier, which can be important for a short cook who is not towering over his or her kitchen counter and is thus less able to apply a bit of upper body weight to the job. I don't think that marble, nonstick, or ice-filled pins are worth the money. Rolling pins that adjust to produce different thicknesses of dough do work but are large and unwieldy to use. (By turning the adjusters next to the handles, you can set the pin itself to any one of six or so different heights from the work surface.) Two words of advice. Make sure that you have a large enough work area to accommodate the length of your rolling pin. You need a surprising amount of room free from cookie jars, utensil holders, drainboards, and the like to work with even an average-sized pin. Second, pins that have not been treated with a wood sealer should not be washed with water. The surface of the wood can become tacky over time, sticking to the dough. Just scrape off any remaining dough and flour with a dough scraper and wipe clean with a damp sponge.

CASE 8: RATING BAKING SHEETS

Chocolate chip cookies, each cookie using 2 tablespoons of dough, were baked on eight different makes of baking sheets, each of which had been sprayed with Pam. Items are listed in order of price.

Brand	Price	Type	Cookie Size	Cookie Color
Calphalon	$23.99	Heavy-duty aluminum, nonstick	3 inches	Golden
Revere Ware	$16.99	Stainless steel	2½ inches	Very light
Kaiser	$11.99	Thin aluminum, gray nonstick finish	2½ inches	Very dark
Wearever CushionAire	$9.99	Aluminum with air cushion sandwiched inside	3 inches	Golden
Chicago Metallic	$8.99	Aluminum with Silverstone finish	2½ inches	Dark
Ecko	$7.99	Aluminum with shiny gray nonstick finish	2½ inches	Dark
Kaiser	$6.99	Thin aluminum sheet	Just under 3 inches	Golden
Roshko	$3.99	Aluminum with black nonstick finish	2½ inches	Dark

WHAT TO BUY: The Calphalon overall did produce the best cookie, but not that much better than either the CushionAire or the plain aluminum Kaiser, the latter being only $6.99, which is therefore the best buy. If you use parchment paper on your baking sheets, a nonstick surface is not necessary. It was interesting to note that Kaiser's nonstick baking sheet was the worst of the bunch yet its simple thin aluminum model did fine.

WOODEN SPOONS

There are three types of wooden spoons: beechwood are the cheapest, costing from $1 to $5; next are olivewood, priced between $5 and $10; and the most expensive are boxwood, which run $10 to $15. The more expensive spoons are less likely to absorb flavors, but I buy the inexpensive models, using at least two medium spoons, one for savory and one for sweet foods. (This avoids the problem of making a custard with a garlic-infused wooden spoon.) I also suggest purchasing two very large spoons for working with large amounts of batters or dough.

RUBBER SPATULAS

Every kitchen needs to have two of these: one medium and one extra-large. They are essential for folding together ingredients, mixing pie dough, blending batters, and the like. I also suggest purchasing one heat-resistant spatula, which can be used with a hot pan. A wooden spoon has a much smaller head and the oval shape is not well suited for the classic French folding motion, which homogenizes ingredients quickly without overworking batters.

DOUGH SCRAPERS

These are rectangular metal blades with either metal, wood, or plastic handles and are used to move dough, scrape up debris from a counter, move chopped vegetables, and so on. They have a million uses around the kitchen and are well worth the modest $8 price tag. You can also buy scrapers consisting of a flexible plastic blade (these run under $2); they are excellent for any task for which a bit of flexibility is important, such as cleaning a rolling pin or scraping out a bowl. Some are kidney shaped, which

THE DOUGH SCRAPER, also called a bench knife, is indispensable when rolling out dough.

makes them perfectly contoured to the inside of any round pan or bowl.

MIXING BOWLS

You have four choices here: earthenware, stainless steel, tempered glass, and plastic. Although I am partial to my huge ochre-colored earthenware mixing bowls, they are not recommended if you are using a hand-held electric mixer, since they will take a beating over time. Earthenware is also more expensive. For a lot less money, you can purchase a five-piece set of stainless steel bowls from Creative Home for just $15.99 (1½-quart to 8-quart capacity), while Pyrex offers 2-, 3-, and 4-quart bowls from $2.99, $3.99, and $4.99, respectively. A set of eleven glass mixing bowls runs just $30 from Williams-Sonoma. White plastic bowls are also available, and many models come with a gasket around the bottom of the bowl to prevent slippage on the work surface. A set of 3 (1½-quart to 5-quart size) is $20.

You also need to think about sizes. I love huge bowls for mixing. You have more room to work, less flour ends up on the counter and floor, and mixing is a lot easier. So go out and buy at least one huge bowl, one that holds at least 6 quarts. You also want bowls that are stable, with a bottom wide enough to handle the weight and height of the bowl.

MEASURING CUPS AND SPOONS

Stay clear of plastic measuring cups and spoons. The handles break off, they crack, and the ring that holds the spoons together inevitably disappears, leaving the lesser sizes to fend for themselves, obscured by the hundred other things you stuff into your catchall drawer. I also have found that there are two types of metal measuring spoons. One is cheap and uses thin-gauge metal (they cost around $3 per set). These are terrific for seeding cucumbers and peppers, and even for peeling kiwis! (For that last trick, see *The Cook's Bible*.) The metal is so thin that the edges are somewhat sharp, a big plus when scooping out foods. The more expensive stainless measuring spoons (around $10) are recommended for actual measuring, since they will never get dented. The set I have also has very deep bowls, which makes measuring more precise. The shallow-bowl models are less accurate, since the difference between filling a wide bowl almost to the top and actually filling it all the way can be substantial. That is one reason I also like very narrow glass measuring cups over the wider models. They are more accurate. You should also own a 4-cup Pyrex measuring cup and an 8-cup model as well.

ICE CREAM SCOOPS

Ice cream scoops — also sold as "portion scoops" in some cookware catalogs — come in a wide array of sizes and can be used for measuring batter or dough for muffins and cookies. The scoops are graded by number, each number indicating a different size. I didn't know what these numbers meant, so I did some research and learned that dividing the scoop number into the number 32 will tell you how many ounces the scoop holds. For example, a number 8 scoop holds 4 ounces (32 ÷ 8 = 4). That being said, all

SCOOPS come in many different sizes and can be used for measuring cookie dough.

you really need to know is that a number 24 scoop holds 1.3 ounces, or a generous 2 tablespoons, the proper amount for a large cookie, and a number 40 scoop holds 0.8 ounce, or about 1¼ tablespoons, just enough dough for a regular cookie. For muffins, I use a regular-size ice cream scoop. It is the best method for measuring and transferring batter to muffin tins.

CAKE TESTERS

In my experience, cake testers are pretty much worthless, especially the metal ones. (Very little sticks to metal, even a wet, partially cooked batter.) If you are going to use a cake tester, a toothpick, a thin wooden skewer, or a straw from a broom is your best choice. (Use the end of the straw closest to the broom handle. It is clean and intact, unlike the end used for sweeping.) However, a good home cook will press down on the top of a cake to see if it is firm and then watch to see if it springs back when released. (It should.) You can also do this with the flat side of a fork to avoid burning your fingers. Another, sometimes false, clue is whether or not the cake is pulling away from the sides of the pan. This can be a good indication but is not always reliable; the cake sometimes pulls back after it is removed from the oven, even though it may not be done.

WHISKS

Whisks should be stainless steel with a smooth, rounded handle, which is sealed to prevent moisture from penetrating. (Wire handles are fine for small whisks, but a good sturdy wooden or metal handle is best for serious whisking.) Prices range from $5 to $12 for 6-inch to 12-inch models. If most of your mixing and beating is to be done with an electric mixer, you will only need a small to medium-size whisk for blending dry ingredients or whisking a few eggs together or making a salad dressing. However, if you intend to do serious whipping by hand, a larger balloon whisk is advisable. I also find that a flat whisk is excellent for whisking in saucepans when it is important to make good contact with the bottom and sides of the pot. The traditional whisk shape is poorly suited for this application.

POLDER COOKING TIMER/THERMOMETER

This is my favorite kitchen tool, something no home cook should be without. It is a timer as well as a thermometer that monitors the internal temperature of food via a long probe wired to the gauge. Not only will it measure a roast while it cooks (the wire is long enough to run out of the oven to the gauge), but it also accepts a preset temperature — the beeper will go off, say, when the chicken reaches 160 degrees. The display is large and easy to read from a few feet away.

DIRECT MAIL AND ONLINE RESOURCES FOR BAKERS

Here are some of my favorite mail-order sources for equipment.

Amazon.com

The giant of online booksellers recently opened a kitchen store with 6,000 items and "one-click" shopping. (Please note that my magazine,

INSTANT-READ THERMOMETERS are essential for baking.

Cook's Illustrated, does provide editorial material to this site, and therefore I am not entirely unbiased about shopping at Amazon.) They do not have the widest selection of cookware in the business, but I like to read comments from other customers, and the service is outstanding. **www.amazon.com**

Chef's Catalog

This excellent resource is one of the heavyweights in the mail-order cookware business and is owned by Neiman Marcus. They have a well-designed site with plenty of product depth. This is cookware for serious home cooks, and they offer plenty of commercial-quality brands as well as free shipping for orders over $60. **www.chefscatalog.com**

Cooking.com

I can find almost anything at this site, from odd-size cake pans to cardboard rounds for cake decorating. This is perhaps the most reliable cookware site in terms of selection. **www. cooking.com**

A Cook's Wares

A good all-round site for cookware which can be reached at **www.cookswares.com**. They carry many of the top name brands, such as Cuisinart and KitchenAid, and carry a vast assortment of the basics, such as forty different types and sizes of springform pans.

Culinary Replacement Parts

Go to **www.culinaryparts.com** for replacement parts for many kitchen appliances, including Braun, Cuisinart, KitchenAid, Krups, Oster, and BonJour. Just type in your model to search their database.

King Arthur Flour Company

This is perhaps my all-time favorite mail-order company, with knowledgeable and helpful employees. They sell flour as well as baking pans, tools, mixes, appliances, sugar, chocolate, decorating supplies, and equipment. Their plastic flour buckets are incredibly useful since they hold large amounts and provide easy access to the contents. I found the front page of the online catalog a bit slow to load, but this is one company that always leaves you with a smile. **www.kingarthurflour.com**

Professional Cutlery Direct

This is one of my favorite cookware companies, specializing in not just knives but professional high-end cookware and small appliances as well. Order online at **www.cutlery.com**. These folks know their stuff.

Sur La Table

This is another well-respected mail-order supplier of cookware. It sells cookware, foods, electric appliances, linens, tabletop items, and so on. **www.surlatable.com**

Tavolo.com

This is another all-purpose cookware site with a good selection of merchandise. **www.tavolo.com**

Williams-Sonoma

Williams-Sonoma, the largest culinary retailer in the country, can be contacted at **www.williamssonoma.com**. They have gift items, foods, tableware, cookware, and gadgets. This is a good one-stop Web site for home cooks, with a design reminiscent of *Martha Stewart Living*. They do not carry a wide selection of brands but usually offer the highest quality available.

3

INGREDIENT TASTE TESTS AND RATINGS

Cookbook authors and professional chefs tend to use high-quality ingredients when developing and testing recipes, and the home cook is often left trying to make substitutions with less expensive supermarket brands. In addition, even when a specific brand is specified, many home cooks blithely substitute one ingredient or brand for another. This chapter is an exploration of some of the more important dessert-making ingredients — flour, butter, baking soda, extracts, chocolate, frozen puff pastry, jams, and so forth — to determine whether brands matter and, if they do, which brands are worth seeking out. There is no question that there are omissions — to cover all relevant ingredients would take an entire book in itself — but I have attempted to touch on most of the key items used in the recipes in this book.

FLOURS

Does the type of flour (cake, bleached, unbleached, high-protein all-purpose, et cetera) really make a difference in baking? Must one use a different flour for each application? For instance, does a cookie require a different flour than a cake? Or can you purchase one brand or type of flour and make it work for most any application? Exactly what is the difference when baking with a soft flour such as cake flour versus a high-protein all-purpose flour? And what about bleached flour? Is there any reason to buy it?

First, a word or two about protein content. Flour is usually made by grinding kernels of wheat. (A wheat berry contains three elements: the outer bran layer, the germ, and then the heart of the berry, the endosperm. In traditional whole wheat flour the whole berry is ground, whereas all-purpose white flour uses just the endosperm, and the bran and germ are removed.) Not all wheat is the same. Some wheat has very hard kernels, which results in hard flour. Other wheat has softer kernels, which produce softer flour. (You can actually test a kernel of wheat by trying to cut into it with a fingernail. Soft wheat kernels can be cut in half in this manner, whereas a kernel of hard wheat is difficult to cut.) Generally speaking, hard kernels produce a high-protein flour and soft kernels produce a lower-protein flour.

Why is protein content important? Simply

stated, high-protein flours provide more structure to batters and doughs, making them more elastic and able to trap gases as they expand. This, for example, is good for yeast breads, since it makes the dough rise. A cake or pastry flour, which has low protein content (protein content ranges from about 8 percent for cake flour to 14 percent or so for bread flour), tends to make a more delicate, finely textured product.

I started by checking the inventory in my kitchen and found cake flour and King Arthur all-purpose flour. I also keep bread flour and a variety of specialty flours, such as whole wheat, rye, even buckwheat. But I wanted to focus this test on flours found in most supermarkets, so I purchased the following brands: Swan's Down cake flour (bleached, 8 percent protein); Pillsbury all-purpose flour (bleached, 10.5 percent protein); King Arthur all-purpose flour (unbleached, 11.7 percent protein); King Arthur Special for Machines bread flour (unbleached, 12.7 percent protein); King Arthur Sir Lancelot high-gluten flour (unbleached, 14 percent protein). To examine the properties of each, I made both a sponge cake and a sugar cookie with each flour and compared taste, texture, and baking properties. (For a more thorough discussion of flours, see *Cook's Illustrated*, May/June 1999.)

The Sponge Cake Tests

Sponge cake (for the recipe, see page 151) is an excellent test of flour. Unlike a biscuit or a pie pastry, it is a delicate cake indeed, and I suspected that small differences in protein content and milling might show up clearly in the final product. I was not disappointed.

- Swan's Down Cake Flour: This cake was very tender, moist, and crumbly. It did fall a bit in the center, but the texture and taste were both delicate and appealing. This flour produced the loosest batter. The higher the protein content of flour, the more water it can absorb. You can try this at home by mixing ½ cup of high-protein flour such as King Arthur (you can also use bread flour) with 6 tablespoons water and then do the same with cake flour. The high-protein flour will produce a thick mixture, while the cake flour dough will be much looser.

- Pillsbury All-Purpose: This cake was a bit springier than the cake made with Swan's Down, had more bite, and was not as crumbly. I did detect a slight chemical taste, although I did not detect any off flavors with the cake flour, which is also bleached. The structure was more stable than the cake with Swan's Down — the center did not fall — and the batter was slightly thicker. I would not describe the cake as tough, but it was not quite as tender as a sponge cake ought to be.

- King Arthur All-Purpose: This cake was similar to the Pillsbury cake but maybe a touch chewier. There were no off flavors. This flour would be my first choice, since the cake flour did not provide sufficient structure for the cake and the Pillsbury flour, which was bleached, had off flavors.

- King Arthur Special for Machines: The cake was actually gummy in texture, with a wet, coarse crumb. Instead of a fallen center, as with the Swan's Down, this cake had a domed shape. Overall, I found the cake too chewy and too tough.

- King Arthur Sir Lancelot: This very high protein flour (made especially for use in yeasted breads) produced a tough, chewy cake. The batter was stiff, and the top was dome shaped. Forget it!

So I would pick the King Arthur all-purpose flour for this cake, since it provided more structure than the cake flour and had no off flavors as with the Pillsbury bleached flour.

The Sugar Cookie Tests

Unlike a cake, which requires a certain amount of structure to rise and set properly, simple sugar cookies have much less structure and tenderness is more of an issue. I thought that a lower-protein flour might do well for this test.

- Swan's Down Cake Flour: These cookies were very crumbly and fell apart in my mouth. The taste was pleasant, but they were too delicate.
- Pillsbury All-Purpose: These cookies were much better in texture. They had just enough crunch and were slightly soft on the inside. Again, the taste was a bit odd but not unpleasant.
- King Arthur All-Purpose: These cookies were my favorite. The texture and chew of the cookie was very similar to the Pillsbury batch, but I preferred the flavor.
- King Arthur Special for Machines: These cookies were on the crispy, crunchy side, with a harder consistency. They needed to be chewed more than the above, but the taste was good.
- King Arthur Sir Lancelot: This batch was the toughest and chewiest. The taste was good, but the texture was unwelcome.

So once again I preferred the King Arthur all-purpose flour. What conclusions can we come to from these two sets of tests? First of all, if I were going to use just one brand, I would choose King Arthur as a good all-purpose "house" flour. The flavor is good, and it has enough protein to provide structure when needed, as with a sponge cake. But a cake flour is an important pantry staple as well. This low-protein flour will produce more tender muffins or cakes than all-purpose, and this is often desirable. (In the two tests above, a higher-protein flour was best, but in other tests I have found cake flour to be preferable to all-purpose.) Finally, I would avoid purchasing a bleached flour, because it has a slightly odd aftertaste and because there is no compelling reason to keep it on hand — a good unbleached all-purpose flour and a cake flour can handle just about any situation other than bread-baking.

Here are a few observations I have made about flours and baking which might help you in your kitchen.

- If a cake falls in the center when baked, next time use a flour with more protein content.
- If a cake has a high dome in the middle, next time try a flour with lower protein, such as cake flour. (Doming is caused by other factors as well, such as the choice of cake pan, the choice of oven rack, the recipe itself, and the oven temperature. However, the choice of flour is also a factor.)
- If a cookie is tough, try a lower-protein flour. If it is too crumbly, use a higher-protein flour.

HOW MUCH DOES THE CONDITION OF YOUR FLOUR MATTER?

First, what do I mean by "condition"? The same type of flour from the same manufacturer can vary tremendously in cooking attributes over time. Flour that is very dried out and old will require a great deal more liquid than a fresh bag. I discovered just how important this is when I was developing a recipe for cream biscuits, which are made with 2 cups of flour and 1¼ to 1½ cups of heavy cream. Some flour required slightly less than 1¼ cups cream, while other batches needed over 1½ cups; that is a 33 percent difference!

So how do you use this information, since it is impossible for home cooks to accurately measure the moisture content and condition of their flour? Well, the simple rule is to keep flour in an airtight container; but more important, never bake with flour that has been sitting around a long time. A bag of flour that has been open to the air for a couple of months, especially in a dry environment, will produce results quite different from those of a fresh bag.

ARE FLAVORED OILS BETTER THAN EXTRACTS?

I have noted over years of baking that all flavoring extracts are not created equal. In addition, I have found that oils seem to carry a much more intense flavor than extracts. I have also noted that when extracts or oils are used in baked goods, the quality of the flavoring is often masked by other ingredients and by the baking process itself. So the question is, when a recipe calls for a lemon, orange, or vanilla flavoring, which product works best? I decided to make pound cake, buttercream, and, in the case of vanilla extracts, ice cream in order to test the flavor of each brand.

Lemon Flavorings

For the lemon tests, I made pound cake and buttercream with each of four different flavorings and also with lemon zest instead of oils.

- Boyajian Pure Lemon Oil (Natural oil pressed from fresh lemons): Using only 1 teaspoon of the oil, the cake had a true lemon flavor without any mysterious chemical taste. The hands-down favorite.
- Spicery Shoppe Natural Lemon Flavor (soybean oil, oil of lemon, natural flavorings, alpha tocopherol): For this cake I needed to use 2 teaspoons of flavoring. The cake did have a pleasant lemon flavor, but it did not have the fresh lemony taste of the cake made with lemon oil. This product does not have the punch of the lemon oil but still makes a decent cake.
- Scott's Pure Lemon Extract (oil of lemon, water, and alcohol): This also needed 2 teaspoons to get any kind of a lemon flavor, and the alcohol was quite noticeable. This extract was not in the same league as the brands above and is not recommended.
- Durkee Imitation Lemon Extract (alcohol [82 percent], water, oil of lemon, artificial flavor, and artificial color): For this cake I also used 2 teaspoons of extract, but as with the above cake it had an alcohol/chemical taste. To make matters worse, it only had a hint of lemon flavor. I would not even consider using this product again.

With buttercream, the results were even more exaggerated. The Boyajian lemon oil was outstanding, the Spicery Shoppe lemon flavor was okay, and the other two were unacceptable, with a pronounced alcohol flavor.

When I tried lemon zest in both the pound cake and the buttercream, I found it was a reasonable alternative but not nearly as good as the pure oils.

Orange Flavorings

I repeated this series of tests using four orange flavorings as well as zest with exactly the same results. The only difference was that I used Wagner's Pure Orange Extract (oil of orange, alcohol, propylene glycol) instead of Scott's, since that was the brand available locally. Again, pure orange oil was the clear winner.

At first I thought that the Boyajian oils were a bit pricey, at $11 for the lemon and $7 for the orange, but the bottles are 5 ounces instead of the usual 1- or 2-ounce bottles which run $2 to $5. In addition, you only use half as much oil as you do extract, so the natural oils are actually quite economical. Like extracts, they have a long shelf life and can be stored in a cupboard.

Vanilla Flavorings

To test the quality of each vanilla, I made both pound cake and vanilla ice cream. With the ice cream, I also tested using real vanilla beans just for the sake of comparison. Here are the contestants and the results:

- Nielsen-Massey Madagascar Bourbon Pure Vanilla Extract (water, alcohol [35 percent], sugar, and vanilla bean extractives): The pound cake had a fairly rich, pleasant vanilla taste; I did not taste an alcohol flavor. The ice cream had a rich, pleasant vanilla taste but without the intensity of the vanilla bean. Still, I would use it again.
- Spice Islands Pure Vanilla Extract (Bourbon vanilla bean extractives in water and alcohol

[35 percent]): Both the cake and ice cream had a nice vanilla flavor, although slightly different from the Nielsen-Massey extract. Recommended.

- Durkee Pure Vanilla Extract (vanilla bean extractives in water, alcohol [35 percent], and corn syrup): While the cake did not pack the vanilla punch of the cakes above, it was still a pleasant vanilla flavor with a sweet aftertaste. However, the ice cream lacked the intensity of vanilla that was present with the first two extracts. If you're on vacation and this is the only vanilla at the all-purpose grocery/live bait store, it will suffice.
- McCormick Imitation Vanilla Extract (water, alcohol [15 percent], vanillin and other artificial flavorings, and citric acid): This cake had the least vanilla flavor and a sweet, slightly chemical aftertaste. The ice cream had only a mild vanilla flavor and a slight chemical flavor. Forget it!
- The Vanilla Bean (purchased from Nielsen-Massey): The vanilla flavor was rich and intense. No comparison with the extracts. If you can find this brand of vanilla bean, buy it; the beans are soft and plump, unlike many of the dry, leathery beans sold in supermarkets.

In the lemon and orange tests, then, the natural oils were far and away the winners, but the vanilla tasting was a bit more complicated, except to say that the vanilla bean was the hands-down winner. Nielsen-Massey and Spice Islands vanilla extract seemed to do better than the Durkee and McCormick products. It was clear that the quality of a vanilla extract matters more in desserts — such as ice cream — that are not baked and in which the vanilla is a more commanding presence. Other tests performed in the test kitchens of *Cook's Illustrated* have shown that even an imitation vanilla used in a simple cookie is often hard to distinguish from pure vanilla products, since there are so many other competing flavors.

WHAT IS THE DIFFERENCE BETWEEN BAKING POWDER AND BAKING SODA?

Baking powder is nothing more than a mixture of baking soda (about one-quarter to one-third of the total makeup), an acid, and a starch, usually double-dried cornstarch. The acid produces carbon dioxide when it comes into contact with the baking soda in the presence of a liquid, and the starch is a stabilizer. Many cooks believe that since only one-third of baking powder is baking soda — the actual leavening agent — then full-strength baking soda must be more powerful. Although it seems logical, this is incorrect. Baking soda is only fully effective if there is an acid component in the batter for it to react with. In an alkaline (low-acid) batter, a teaspoon of baking powder will be a more effective leavener, since the powder contains both the baking soda and the leavening acid necessary to produce a more complete chemical reaction. This is the reason recipes that contain acidic ingredients such as buttermilk usually call just for baking soda. That being said, even in the absence of an acid, baking soda will decompose during baking and throw off some carbon dioxide gas, but experts claim that the amounts will be relatively small. I decided to test this proposition.

I chose a simple sugar cookie for my experiment, in which I hoped to determine whether the choice and amount of leavener made a difference in the height and structure of the cookie. The recipe included flour, salt, butter, sugar, egg, vanilla, and orange zest. I made several batches, the first with no leavener whatsoever. As expected, there was no rise and the dough did not spread at all during baking. Then I tried 1 teaspoon of baking powder and ¼ teaspoon of baking soda to 1 cup of flour (these were my control amounts), and the cookies rose well and had a speckled color. When I tried doubling the leavening, however, the cookies did not rise at all but took on a nice golden brown color. When I reduced the leavener amounts by half from the original (I used ½ teaspoon baking powder and ⅛ teaspoon baking soda), the cookies rose pretty well, but not quite as high as with the control amounts. These tests confirmed what I already knew, which is that too much leavener can actually reduce the rise in baking; an excess of carbon dioxide is created, eventually causing the structure to collapse. Using too little leavener, of course, means that too little carbon dioxide is produced, creating an insufficient rise.

Next, I wanted to test baking powder versus baking soda. I tried using just baking soda and achieved the highest cookies yet. Doubling the amount of soda actually reduced the rise a bit; and halving the amount of soda actually increased the rise somewhat, but the cookies were pale white instead of golden brown. When I tried using just baking powder, the cookies had about 40 percent less rise than with the soda. Doubling the amount of powder helped a little bit but still fell short of the baking soda cookies, and halving the amount of powder had little effect at all.

I found these results very surprising, since the cookie dough was not particularly acidic, meaning that the baking soda would not have much to react with. To follow up on this test, I then tried two additional tests. First, I baked two versions of a yellow cake: one used 1 teaspoon baking powder and one used just ½ teaspoon baking soda. The baking powder cake was fine, but the baking soda cake did not rise as well, was dark, dense, and rubbery, and had a terrible, soapy aftertaste. My conclusion was that the recipe had insufficient acid for the baking soda. This created both an insufficient leavening effect and an excess of soda, which resulted in the soapy taste. I then tried a similar experiment with oatmeal cookies, making one batch with baking powder and a second batch with half as much baking soda. The results were identical as with the yellow cake: the soda cookies did not rise well, were darker in color, and had a soapy aftertaste.

So what did I learn? First, baking powder is better for batters or doughs that have little acidity. Since baking powder contains acids and baking soda does not, this makes sense. Second, an excess of baking soda will result in a soapy aftertaste, a poor rise, and a darker product. The objective of any recipe using chemical leaveners is to balance the reaction so that all of the baking soda will be used up. The telltale metallic or soapy flavor is a sign that there was either insufficient acid or too much soda. I also learned that baking soda adds color to baked goods, a fact known well by commercial bakers, who often increase the level of baking soda to color cookies. Finally, I was surprised by the cookie test in which the soda actually outperformed the baking powder. However, I explain that result by saying that there is little leavening required in a sugar cookie (as opposed to a cake), and baking soda will release some carbon dioxide gas in the presence of water and heat even with a low-acidity dough. (All doughs contain some acidity, since flour itself is not entirely alkaline.) Put another way, the difference in performance between baking powder and baking soda is more obvious in a cake or thick, high-rise cookie than in a simple sugar cookie.

In order to test my last theory about baking soda producing gas even without much acid, I placed baking soda in a glass of water. Not much happened. But when I heated the water, carbon dioxide gas was released (bubbles were formed). My conclusion, therefore, is that baking soda in combination with liquid and heat does indeed produce carbon dioxide gas even without the presence of acid.

The next issue was whether double-acting baking powders are better than the single-acting variety. Most baking powders are double-acting, which means that two different chemical leavening acids are used in the mixture: one works at room temperature and the other works best at oven temperatures. The theory is that in a cake, for example, it is important to have an early release of carbon dioxide during the batter preparation so that small bubbles are created to form the nuclei of the cell structure. These cells expand during baking due to additional carbon dioxide produced by the action of the second leavening acid, and the dough firms up into the final cake structure. In a stiff cookie batter, however, especially one that has a good deal of structure from butter and eggs, the double-acting issue is less critical. I went back to the kitchen to test one double-acting and two single-acting baking powders to see if this made any noticeable difference. The brands I chose were:

- Davis Baking Powder (cornstarch, sodium bicarbonate, calcium phosphate, and sodium aluminum sulphate): A double-acting baking powder.
- Rumford Baking Powder (calcium acid phosphate, bicarbonate of soda, and cornstarch): This baking powder is not double-acting, since it has only one acid ingredient, calcium acid phosphate.
- Featherweight Baking Powder (monocalcium phosphate, potato starch, and potassium bicarbonate): Again, this baking powder is not double-acting, since it contains only one type of acid, monocalcium phosphate.

I tested each of them in a baking powder biscuit and in a sponge cake recipe. To my great surprise, there was absolutely no difference between them. So my tests proved that all the fuss about double-acting baking powder is nonsense, at least for the two items I test-baked. In addition, for those of us worried about aluminum as an ingredient, I also found that the nonaluminum products (the Rumford and Featherweight) worked just fine. It seems that baking powder is rather simple stuff and brands don't matter a whit.

The question still remained, however, why I noticed no difference between single- and double-acting baking powder. I made some

phone calls to find out. One theory is that double-acting baking powders were developed for situations in which the batter sat around for a while before being baked. This might be true, for example, in a commercial operation. A double-acting leavener would not produce all of its carbon dioxide gas right away and therefore would be able to provide leavening power even after sitting around before baking. To further explain the nature of double-acting baking powder, I recently visited a Web site that detailed an interesting experiment in which baking powder gave off no gas when placed in room temperature water. (The water was cloudy, with much of the baking powder still not dissolved.) When the water was heated, however, carbon dioxide gas was produced. The scientist concluded that the reason baking powder releases most of its carbon dioxide gas when heated is that heat is required to properly dissolve the powder into the liquid in the batter. This would indicate that double-acting baking powders do not, in fact, throw off much carbon dioxide gas at room temperature as I had supposed and therefore act much like single-acting leaveners.

BAKING CHOCOLATE

Selecting a brand of chocolate is endlessly debated among bakers, and not all of us agree since, much like wine, chocolate is very complex and what appeals to one cook may not be suitable to another. I remember tasting chocolates in a seminar given by Alice Medrich, a noted authority on the topic. I found that although I often disagreed with her specific recommendations, I did learn a great deal and agreed with her more generic observations about different types of chocolate. *Cook's Illustrated* has also done many tastings, and the results from these sessions have not always yielded results similar to those of comparable events held by other organizations. In particular, a tasting of unsweetened baking chocolates at *Cook's* resulted in a poor showing for Callebaut, a brand that is universally liked by professional bakers, including me.

First, it is important to understand a bit about the different types of chocolate. You can purchase unsweetened chocolate, bittersweet chocolate, semisweet chocolate, cocoa powder, and chocolate chips. The question is, how do they differ from one another? *Unsweetened chocolate,* often called baking chocolate or chocolate liquor, is made from roasted cocoa beans and contains about 50 percent solids from the beans and 50 percent cocoa butter. *Bittersweet chocolate* (sometimes sold as "dark" chocolate) and *semisweet chocolate* are made from unsweetened chocolate that is ground with sugar and then further refined. Since bittersweet and semisweet chocolates are about 50 percent sugar (bittersweet is 46 percent sugar by weight; semisweet is 57 percent sugar), this means they have less chocolate flavor than unsweetened chocolate, which has no added sugar. However, the flavor is less bitter and more complex, features that are appreciated by many bakers. *Chocolate chips* are made from chocolate (different companies use different types of chocolates) with relatively little cocoa butter, about 30 percent or even less. This is because the chips will not hold their shape with more fat. This lower percentage of cocoa butter makes for a less buttery, grainier texture and flavor. *Cocoa powder* is made from unsweetened chocolate. Much of the fat is removed by pressing, leaving behind the solids. These leftover solids are then fluffed up and packaged. Dutch-process cocoa is less acidic than regular cocoa; many people, myself included, feel this produces a stronger, more interesting chocolate flavor. Other factors that influence the quality of one brand of chocolate over another are the additives. Most processed dark chocolates include vanilla, lecithin (which makes chocolate smoother when poured), and other flavorings, including soy. In addition, some manufacturers roast their beans less, on the theory that when the chocolate is baked by consumers the chocolate will be undergoing additional processing.

As for chocolate tastings, I have noted that preferences often differ depending on whether the chocolates are eaten raw or in baked goods. In brownies, for example, a subtle, sophisticated chocolate often loses its edge to a supermarket brand such as Nestlé or even Baker's. Baking diminishes chocolate flavor and therefore softens unpleasant taste attributes that can be more easily detected when the chocolate is consumed as is. I have also found that many of us who grew up with Baker's chocolate tend to have fond taste memories that, when put to the test in a blind tasting, turn out to be misguided at best. (Many of us have fond memories of cakes made from boxed mixes, but if you tasted them against a homemade cake, you would find them to be rubbery, with a pronounced chemical flavor.) In a brownie tasting some years ago, I rated Baker's highly in a brownie because it had a big, bold, recognizable flavor. Although more expensive chocolates had more complex flavors, their advantages were less obvious in this sort of recipe.

I made a decision to taste semisweet and bittersweet chocolates because I could taste them out of hand as well as in baked goods, and also because I could find a broader selection of these chocolates in local stores. I taste-tested each brand raw, in a chocolate frosting, and then in a fallen chocolate cake. (The frosting recipe is on page 186, and the cake recipe is on page 160.) My tasting notes are in the Case 9 chart.

As for the results, I once again found that when chocolate is baked, the off flavors tend to become muted to the point that even Baker's makes a decent cake. I also found that Hershey's is by far the worst choice of the supermarket brands. As for the premium chocolates, Ghirardelli is not a bad choice at all, and it isn't too expensive. If you can get it, purchase Callebaut, since it was the hands-down winner in all categories. It is available in 11-pound bars if you take your baking seriously.

I also thought that it would be worthwhile to test unsweetened baking chocolates, so I

CASE 9: THE GREAT CHOCOLATE TASTE-OFF

Which brands measure up when tasted raw, in a chocolate frosting, and in a warm chocolate cake?

Brand	Raw	Chocolate Frosting	Chocolate Cake
Baker's semisweet	Waxy, grainy, real off flavor	Same as raw	Off flavors gone, but only modest chocolate flavor
Baker's bittersweet	Same as above; not worth eating	Same as raw	Same as above; cake better than I had expected
Hershey's semisweet	Too sweet and gritty; better than Baker's	Same as raw	Worst of the tasting; off flavors and too sweet
Ghirardelli semisweet	Good chocolate flavor; smooth	Same as raw	Good chocolate flavor; not too sweet; would recommend
Ghirardelli bittersweet	Less sweet than the above and more chocolaty	Same as raw	Same as above
Valrhona bittersweet	Funky; bitter; strong flavor	Same as raw	Bitter, intense flavor; not for me
Callebaut bittersweet	Smooth; big chocolate flavor; clear winner	Same as raw	Complex, rounded flavor; once again the clear winner
Scharffen Berger	Intense chocolate flavor; overpowering; not subtle	Same as raw	Intense but one-dimensional; no complex flavor notes

rounded up the three I could find most readily: Baker's, Hershey's, and Ghirardelli. For this test I made the Chewy, Fudgy Brownies on page 107 and found, not to my surprise, that Baker's and Hershey's did not fare nearly as well as Ghirardelli. The Baker's chocolate clearly out-performed the Hershey's brand, the flavor improving when baked, whereas the Hershey's only deteriorated when subjected to heat. In a pinch, Baker's will do, but Ghirardelli was the hands-down winner.

Finally, I wondered about chocolate chips

CASE 10: GOODBYE, MR. CAROB CHIPS!

A tasting of nine different brands of chocolate and ersatz chocolate chips reveals which are worth buying and which are virtually inedible.

Brand	Comments
Hershey's	Too sweet; candy bar flavor; not enough chocolate flavor
365	Sweet, but not enough chocolate flavor
Ghirardelli	Pretty good; slightly sour, off flavor
Chatfield Carob (contains carob and barley malt; no white sugar)	Truly awful flavor; gritty, powdery
Tropical Source (contains tofu)	Intense chocolate flavor; some tasters thought it was a little bitter
Guittard	Good chocolate flavor; buttery
Sunspire (grain sweetened; no white sugar)	Truly awful taste; waxy; tastes like chocolate-covered cherries
Nestlé	A bit too sweet; pretty good flavor
Baker's	Very sweet; chalky

WHAT TO BUY: The Tropical Source and Ghirardelli chocolates were well liked, as was Guittard. As for supermarket chocolate chips, the tasters preferred Hershey's and Nestlé over Baker's. The 365 brand of chips did surprisingly well, better than any of the supermarket varieties. Avoid the Chatfield and Sunspire brands at all costs.

since, as I stated above, they are usually made with a lower percentage of cocoa butter in order to retain the classic chip shape. This produces a lower-quality chocolate that tends to be grittier and less rich. Unfortunately, Valrhona and Callebaut do not make chips, but I was able to find several other brands to put to the test.

The chart above shows how each fared when tasted as is. I also tried baking the supermarket brands of chocolate chips into chocolate chip cookies and found that Nestlé was the winner over Baker's and Hershey's. The chips were a bit too sweet but very smooth, with decent chocolate flavor.

CASE 11: THE COCOA WARS

In a blind tasting of chocolate cakes and hot cocoa, which brand of cocoa really delivers rich chocolate flavor?

Brand	Appearance and Aroma	Cake	Cocoa
Nestlé	Light brown with soft lumps; barely any chocolate aroma	Cake had the least amount of chocolate flavor	Barely any chocolate flavor; least favorite
Hershey's	Light brown with soft lumps; slight chocolate aroma with a bit of a tang	The cake was better than Nestlé, but still not a huge chocolate flavor	Decent chocolate flavor at the beginning; falls apart as it hits the back of your mouth
Droste	Rich cocoa brown with very few lumps; moderate amount of chocolate aroma; no tang	Cake had a nice rich chocolate flavor; substantially better than brands above	Very nice rich chocolate flavor; the lower acidity makes for a really full chocolate taste
Pernigotti	Very dark reddish brown; lots of lumps; very rich chocolate aroma	Cake was the darkest of all; also had the most chocolate flavor	The best of the bunch; dark rich color and deep chocolaty flavor.

COCOA

Cocoa is an important baking ingredient, and it conveys the deep, rich flavor of chocolate almost better than baking chocolate. I often use it in conjunction with baking chocolate for cookies or cakes. The question is, which cocoa is best? I knew from experience that Dutch-process cocoa is better than regular cocoa. In blind taste tests I have found that Dutch-process provides a significant flavor boost, but I wanted to repeat those tests for this book to make sure that I was right. "Dutch process" involves treating the powder with an alkaline solution to reduce acidity, which makes for a richer, darker chocolate.

To find the best brand, I baked a chocolate cake from *The Yellow Farmhouse Cookbook* and prepared a simple recipe for hot cocoa (1 cup 2 percent milk, 2 tablespoons Dutch-process cocoa, and 1 heaping tablespoon sugar). The contestants were Nestlé, Hershey's, Droste, and Pernigotti. They were all made with 100 percent cocoa except the Pernigotti (packaged under the Williams-Sonoma label), which was 99.9 percent cocoa and 0.1 percent vanilla. The Droste and the Pernigotti were the only Dutch-process cocoas in the test.

As "The Cocoa Wars" shows, the Dutch-process cocoas were clearly superior. Nestlé and Hershey's made unremarkable cake and cocoa, whereas the Droste, which is widely available, was quite good and the Pernigotti was outstanding. I did wonder if substituting a Dutch-process cocoa for regular cocoa might cause a problem in baking. In side-by-side tests I found that Dutch-process and natural cocoas didn't dramatically affect results, with one exception. A cake made with Scharffen Berger natural cocoa didn't rise properly.

BUTTER: DOES THE BRAND MATTER?

Butter is one ingredient that most home cooks think little about yet use almost every time they walk into the kitchen. I have used unsalted Land O'Lakes for more than twenty years and until recently had never thought to actually compare it with other brands. I bought every unsalted butter I could find at local stores, including Keller's, Keller's European Style (this is also sold as Plugra butter), Eshiré (a French butter that is lightly salted), Land O'Lakes, Kate's Homemade (sold at a local natural foods store), and Breakstone. Although Keller's European Style tasted better when eaten as is, I could not tell the difference between butters when using them in baking. Just be sure not to use a salted butter, since almost all recipes, including those in this book, are tested using unsalted butter.

WHY DO RECIPES CALL FOR UNSALTED BUTTER?

Different brands use different levels of salt in their salted butters, so if you cook with salted butter, you never know exactly how much salt you are adding to your recipe along with the butter. It is much more precise for a recipe to call for unsalted butter and salt separately in specific amounts.

IS FROZEN PUFF PASTRY WORTH BUYING?

Very few home bakers make puff pastry from scratch, since one can purchase it frozen in supermarkets. The question is, how does it stack up to the real thing in terms of both taste and texture?

The only brand that I could find in my su-permarket was Pepperidge Farm, so I used that for comparison. The first thing one notices is the lengthy ingredients list, which includes unbleached enriched wheat flour (flour, malted barley flour, niacin, reduced iron, thiamin mononitrate [vitamin B1], riboflavin [vitamin B2], folic acid), partially hydrogenated vegetable shortening (soybean and cottonseed oils colored with beta carotene), water, salt, high fructose corn syrup, distilled monoglycerides (from hydrogenated soybean oil), and soy lecithin. It puffed up nicely when baked on a cookie sheet, when used in a tart, and when making palm leaves. The commercial product was tender, the layers pulled apart easily, and it was very flaky. The problem was flavor. Pepperidge Farm puff pastry contains no butter, which means it has no flavor, a crucial part of the puff pastry experience. So although it looks good and is flaky, it has no taste. The next step was to investigate whether any sane cook would want to make it from scratch at home.

There are two basic methods. The traditional method is to whip butter with a small amount of flour and shape it into a square, at which point it is chilled. Next, a relatively lean dough is prepared and also chilled. The cold square of butter is placed onto the larger piece of chilled dough, the dough is folded up and over the butter, and then this package is rolled and folded about eight separate times with long periods of chilling in between every two folds. This creates literally hundreds of layers of dough and butter and, if done properly, results in the ethereal pastry that all of us have had at least once at a good restaurant. The second method is a "mock" puff pastry — Julia Child herself uses this recipe in *Baking with Julia* — in which butter is worked into flour but still left in lima bean–size pieces. This does eliminate the need to create a separate brick of butter but still requires the same number of folds. I did not find it substantially easier than the classic method.

So what's the problem? First, these recipes take a huge amount of work (from start to finish, including baking time, you can figure on 8 hours or so). My other complaint is that the butter and dough have to be at just the right temperature to make the recipes work. If the butter is too soft, the resulting pastry will be sodden and dense; if too cold, the dough will be hard to roll out. The chances of an inexperienced baker's turning out a good puff pastry on the first shot are low.

I also find that there are plenty of very good substitutes for puff pastry. If you want to make a tart, use either American pie dough or brioche dough. If you want to make a cookie, there are plenty to choose from that are at least as good as bow ties, twisted straws, and palm leaves (traditional shapes for puff pastry) and take just minutes to make. You can also use puff pastry to make a turnover, but here too American pie pastry works well and takes much less time to make. Of course, there are unique desserts for which puff pastry is essential — mille feuille, napoleons, et cetera — but these are best prepared by professional pastry chefs, not home cooks.

If you do want to try your hand at puff pastry, the best recipe I have found is in a wonderful dessert book by Emily Luchetti, *Four-Star Desserts*. The dough has enough fat to make it workable, and the directions are clear and easy to follow.

SPICES

My first experience with taste-testing different brands of spices occurred in the test kitchens of *Cook's Illustrated* when we rated ground cinnamon. It turned out that there were vast differences among the brands, some tasting earthy, some spicy, some flowery, and some just plain bland. We also discovered that almost all "cinnamon" sold in this country is not really cinnamon at all; it's made from the cassia tree. Real cinnamon is much more expensive and has quite a different flavor altogether. Among supermarket brands, the best choice was McCormick, but Penzeys, a mail-order spice company (see page 52), had a clearly superior product. (For more information on cinnamon, see the November/December 1998 issue of *Cook's Illustrated*.)

Having already covered cinnamon, I decided to investigate nutmeg and cloves. For the nutmeg test, I purchased the grocery store brands of both whole and ground nutmeg, along with gourmet brands like Penzeys. To test cloves, I purchased ground cloves. I was surprised at how expensive some of the grocery store brands were. For example, McCormick ground cloves cost $5.99 for just 0.9 ounce. I also purchased Frontier brand bulk spices, which are available at many natural food stores where bulk spices are sold. The bulk spices are the most affordable, since one is not paying for packaging.

Nutmeg

The recipes I used to test nutmeg for perfume and intensity of flavor were the American Baked Custard on page 341 and the Buttermilk Doughnuts from *The Yellow Farmhouse Cookbook*. The results are shown in the chart below. If nutmeg is a predominant flavor in a recipe — such as a custard, with only simple flavors and textures — starting with whole nutmeg and grinding it yourself is slightly better than using the commercially ground variety. That being said, if you did not have the benefit of a side-by-side comparison, you would be quite satisfied with the ground. In the case of custard, I can highly recommend all the brands with the exception of McCormick and Durkee, which were both good but not quite in the same league as the others. When it came to the doughnuts, however, the brand made little if any difference. There were too many other competing textures and flavors to sort out fine distinctions among brands of nutmeg.

Still not completely satisfied, I decided to try an even more complex recipe, to see if one could tell the difference between Spice Islands whole nutmeg and ground nutmegs from Morton & Bassett and Durkee. I baked batches of

CASE 12: THE STATE OF NUTMEG

Is there a difference among different brands of nutmeg? (Whole nutmegs were grated before using.)

Brand	Appearance and Aroma	Custard	Doughnuts
Penzeys whole nutmeg	Walnut-looking exterior, about the size of a red seedless grape; intense nutmeg perfume when ground	Intense nutmeg flavor and perfume	Nice nutmeg flavor; doughnuts were wonderful
Spice Islands whole nutmeg	Slightly smaller and darker than the above; same appearance and aroma as Penzeys when ground	Nice nutmeg flavor and perfume	Nice nutmeg flavor; doughnuts were great
Penzeys ground nutmeg	Uniform reddish-brown color; fairly strong aroma	Good nutmeg flavor; not quite as intense as with whole nutmeg	Nice nutmeg flavor; maybe not as intense as with whole nutmeg
Frontier ground nutmeg	Same as above	Same as above	Same as above
Spice Islands ground nutmeg	Same as above	Same as above	Same as above
Morton & Bassett ground nutmeg	Same as above	Same as above	Same as above
Durkee ground nutmeg	Lighter color and more finely ground than the others; slight soapy aroma	A touch of the soapy flavor, but not bad	Doughnuts were good
McCormick ground nutmeg	Lighter color; slightly lumpy; slight soapy aroma	Same as above	Same as above

hermit bars (I added nutmeg to the recipe on page 116), and, in a blind tasting, nobody could tell them apart. So my advice is to start with whole nutmeg, if possible, when making a dish in which the flavor will be easily noticed. For baked goods that are full of competing flavors, a simple ground nutmeg is just fine and a lot easier to use. I did note that nutmeg sold in plastic containers had a somewhat soapy flavor and aroma, which I attribute, with no specific knowledge if this is true, to the plastic. From now on, I will never purchase nutmeg in plastic, preferring glass jars instead.

Cloves

To test cloves, I made a recipe for clove cookies and also the Hermit Bars from page 116. I tested only commercially ground cloves, since whole cloves are rarely used in dessert recipes other than as a subtle flavoring for sugar syrups and the like. I tested ground cloves from Penzeys, Morton & Bassett, Spice Islands, Frontier, McCormick, and Durkee. They were all the same except for the Durkee, which I thought had a slightly sour flavor. As with the ground nutmeg, Durkee's ground cloves are sold in a plastic container. In any case, I would avoid Durkee, but any of the other brands seemed fine.

FROZEN FRUIT

In Vermont, where I grew up, one simply didn't use frozen fruit. Buckles, grunts, cobblers, and fruit pies were made when the fruit was ready for picking, not in the dead of winter. For the most part, I still follow this rule, since I not only enjoy eating with the seasons but I find, as one might expect, that the ripe blueberries in July make a far better pie than frozen fruit in March (when I might be more inclined to make a custard pie anyway).

In any case, until I began work on this book, I had never tested the quality of frozen fruit and how it would perform in various desserts. This was less a matter of comparing one brand to the next, since most supermarkets do not have a wide selection, than it was an attempt to discover which frozen fruits worked best in which types of desserts. I did find that frozen fruit needs to be individually flash frozen and not in a brick. This means that the bag of frozen fruit ought to feel like loose berries and not a solid mass. You should also look for fruit that contains no additional ingredients. I have discov-

ered that berries frozen with other ingredients tend to turn into a syrupy mess when thawed. Big Valley was the only company at my local grocery stores with a variety of individually frozen fruit, but I did find a local brand of frozen Maine blueberries as well. I tested four frozen fruits:

- Big Valley Raspberries: These berries were slightly bruised and clumped together but not horribly so. The color was bright and beautiful, but the berries were very tart. When only slightly defrosted, they became quite watery and soft.
- Big Valley Strawberries: These berries were quite large and in great shape. They were a little bit on the tart side, compared with ripe strawberries purchased at the same grocery store. The color was beautiful, but when defrosted they were a soggy mess.
- Big Valley Blueberries: Large, plump, and dark purple, these berries were also in great shape. The taste was sweeter than the other fruits. Once again they were useless when defrosted.
- Wyman's Wild Blueberries from Maine: I'm sure this is a local product, and they were fabulous. With intense blueberry flavor, these were tiny Maine blueberries, ripe, sweet, and delicious! And they held up fine when defrosted.

With this rather discouraging start, I set out to make fruit pies, cobblers, buckles, muffins, and sauces. The pies and cobblers were mushy and watery and not worth the effort. Pies should be reserved for fruit in season. It's cheap and abundant and makes a much better pie. On the other hand, the buckles (yellow cake baked with lots of fruit) were very good. My only complaint was that the raspberries were too tart, but the texture and quality of the cake was good. This is certainly a good way to use frozen fruit in a dessert. The muffins were also quite good. Again the raspberries were tart, but per-

CASE 13: WHICH JAMS ARE BEST?

Three commercial brands plus homemade jam were tasted out of the jar to determine if price really makes a difference when purchasing jams.

Brand	Raspberry	Strawberry	Apricot
Smucker's ($2 to $4)	Shiny, dark, and sweet, with good berry flavor	Dark red and shiny, with a slightly cooked aftertaste	Bright orange color, but little fruit flavor
Bonne Maman ($3 to $5)	Shiny, dark, very sweet, with a slightly cooked flavor	Sweet, not a lot of fruit flavor	Dark apricot color, sweet, but little fruit flavor
Wilkin & Sons ($6 to $8)	Reddish brown, very sweet, and less fruit flavor than other brands	Brownish-red color, very sweet, decent berry flavor	Sweet, with a cooked, not fresh, apricot flavor
Homemade	Strong berry flavor, not too sweet	Big, bright strawberry flavor	Strong apricot flavor, not too sweet

haps this could be remedied by tossing them with sugar or by increasing the sugar in the batter itself. In sauces, the frozen fruit worked just fine, producing a good-tasting, brightly colored sauce.

So frozen fruit is not bad if used either in a puree or in recipes such as buckles or muffin batters, where they are not relied on to provide structure. Forget pies and cobblers, which depend heavily on the flavor and texture of the fruit.

JAMS AND PRESERVES

Jams and preserves are often used in baking, and I was curious about whether the inexpensive supermarket products were as good as the pricey imports. Perhaps there was little difference in taste, the extra money simply going for the nicer packaging and the foreign brand name. The types of jam most often found in cooking are raspberry, apricot, and strawberry. Given the huge number of brands available, I decided to limit my investigation to just three different manufacturers, each of whom produced all three flavors. I also threw in my own homemade jams (see *The Yellow Farmhouse Cookbook* for recipes) as a test to see how they would stack up. The brands I used were an inexpensive grocery store brand (Smucker's; $2 to $4 per 12 ounces), a more upscale imported grocery store variety (Bonne Maman; $3 to $5 for 13 ounces), and an imported specialty store brand (Wilkin & Sons; $6 to $8 per 12 ounces). (There are many other brands; these are simply a few of the jams most often available in the Boston area.)

First, I tasted them out of the jar. I learned two things from this tasting. One, price is not necessarily indicative of quality. For example, the Wilkin & Sons brand had less raspberry flavor than Smucker's. The other conclusion, which was not a surprise, was that homemade jam is much better. Why is that? Well, when I make jam I cook it in small batches and then simply refrigerate or freeze it rather than using the water-bath canning process. Commercial producers use more heat to process the fruit so that it will be safe when stored for months or years. This diminishes the fresh taste of the fruit. In addition, they tend to use more sugar — both to increase shelf life and to limit the growth of bacteria — which usually overpowers the taste of the fruit.

That being said, I was curious whether one could taste the same differences when using these jams in baking. (The flavors and textures of the other ingredients might make it more difficult to distinguish one brand from another.) For my first test, I made the Raspberry Rectangles recipe on page 117. As I suspected, the brands were indistinguishable, and therefore Smucker's is fine. I wouldn't even use my own homemade jam for this recipe. A Linzer torte, which calls for a great deal of raspberry jam, was the second test, and the results were the same — Smucker's was more than satisfactory.

With the strawberry jam, I made thumbprint cookies and found that I actually preferred Smucker's to both the other two brands and my own homemade jam, which leaked off the cookies and onto the baking sheet. The apricot jam was used as a glaze for a coffee cake and for a fruit tart. The jam was simmered with a bit of extra sugar on the stove and then strained and brushed onto the baked goods. It turned out that glazes are as much about appearance as flavor, so once again Smucker's was the winner.

So for any situation in which jam is to be baked or used as a glaze, I would simply opt for Smucker's. In situations in which the jam is used fresh from the jar — simply spread on a scone, for instance, or as a cake filling — homemade is clearly superior.

HEAVY CREAM

From experiences with French and Italian recipes in the American home kitchen, I know that the ultrapasteurized cream in our supermarkets is quite a different product from its European counterpart. Fredy Girardet, one of the world's greatest chefs, prepares a Tarte Vaudoise, which is nothing more than a pastry shell covered with a thin layer of cream, sugar, and cinnamon, which are swirled together with the fingers and then baked. I have tried to make this recipe for years with supermarket heavy cream, with little success. The cream never sets up properly. In Girardet's restaurant in Switzerland, however, the cream thickens almost like a custard.

But there is no point whining about the shortfalls of American heavy cream. The real issue is the relative merits of what we can buy here. To determine this, I tested two common supermarket creams, a heavy cream and a whipping cream, both produced by Hood. These are ultrapasteurized products. I then tried a premium heavy cream that was neither homogenized nor ultrapasteurized, from Brookside Farms. I was also interested in discovering the difference between heavy cream and whipping cream, which, it turns out, is nil. The terms are interchangeable, describing cream with a fat content between 36 and 40 percent. The term "ultrapasteurized" means that the cream has been heated to 300 degrees to kill off as many of the bacteria as possible in order to increase shelf life. Somewhat ominously, the Hood cream also stated: "At Hood, we heat our creams to a higher temperature to eliminate virtually all of the bacteria naturally found in cream. This means that cream stays fresh longer without adding preservatives." Yeah, but how does it taste? Here are the contestants:

• Hood Heavy Cream: Cream, mono- and diglycerides (made with vegetable oil, which helps put air into the cream as it is whipping), and calcium carrageenan (which helps hold the whipped cream peaks).

CASE 14: THE GREAT WHIPPED CREAM COMPETITION

How do ultrapasteurized creams perform against nonhomogenized farm creams?

Cream	Whipping Time	Volume	Taste	After 2 Hours	After 4 Hours	After 6 Hours	Next Day
Hood heavy cream (ultra-pasteurized)	90 seconds	1¾ cup	Creamy; airy; good	Same as freshly whipped	Still holding	Bottom of bowl slightly watery	Top intact; bottom quite watery
Hood whipping cream (ultra-pasteurized)	75 seconds	1¾ cup	Same as above	Same as above	Same as above	Same as above	Same as above
Brookside Farms heavy cream (nonhomog-enized)	90 seconds	1⅔ cup	Not quite as airy, but creamier and richer feel and taste	Same as above	Same as above	Same as above	Same as above

- Hood All-Purpose Whipping Cream: Cream, mono- and diglycerides, calcium carrageenan, and polysorbate 80 (made from corn oil: helps create stiff peaks through better emulsification).
- Brookside Farms Premium Heavy Cream: Cream.

To test each cream, I tasted a bit straight from the carton or bottle and then made the American Baked Custard on page 341 and a simple whipped cream. The Brookside Farms cream was tangier and slightly richer than the Hood creams when tasted as is, but when all three were used for the custard, the results were similar; the Brookside product was tangier and creamier, perhaps a bit too rich for this recipe.

The big test, however, was how each of them would perform when whipped. Using chilled bowls and beaters, I whipped 1 cup cream with 1 tablespoon sugar and took note of the time it took to get a 2-inch peak and the resulting volume. I then refrigerated the whipped cream and checked at 2-hour intervals to see if the cream broke down. Finally, I let all of them sit in the refrigerator overnight and checked them in the morning.

The tests showed that there was very little difference in holding power among the three products. I did notice, however, that the Brookside Farms whipped cream had more flavor and a creamier consistency, not quite as airy as the ultrapasteurized creams. However, when the cream is used as an ingredient in a custard, for example, the flavor difference subsides, leaving one only with a richer product, resulting in a heavier mouth feel, which is not always welcome. Since most recipes are tested with ordinary supermarket creams, using a premium product may, ironically, lead to a less desirable end result.

WHAT IS THE DIFFERENCE BETWEEN COCONUT MILK, COCONUT CREAM, AND CREAM OF COCONUT?

First of all, coconut milk is not the thin liquid found inside the coconut itself, which is called coconut water. *Coconut milk* is made by steeping equal parts shredded coconut meat and either warm milk or water. The meat is pressed or mashed to release as much liquid as possible, the mixture is strained, and the result is coconut milk. *Coconut cream* can be made using the same method, but the ratio of meat to liquid is higher, about 4 to 1. (The cream that rises to the top of coconut milk after it sits awhile is also referred to as coconut cream.) Finally, *cream of coconut,* not to be confused with coconut cream, is a sweetened product (the first ingredient listed on the can label is usually sugar) that also contains thickeners and emulsifiers. Cream of coconut and coconut cream are not interchangeable in recipes, since the former is heavily sweetened and the latter is not.

In order to find out firsthand how coconut milk, coconut cream, and cream of coconut compared, I made homemade coconut milk and cream and compared them to commercial products. For the first test batch, I made coconut milk with water. (One cup fresh coconut meat was ground in a food processor with 1 cup warm water. The mixture steeped for 1 hour and then was strained.) Next, I made a batch with milk, using the same proportions and same method. The coconut cream was made using the same method but with 2 cups fresh coconut meat to ½ cup water. I then did a blind taste test against canned cream of coconut and canned coconut milk.

Both the canned coconut milk and the homemade coconut milk were very thin and had only a modest amount of coconut flavor, although the coconut milk made with milk rather than water was superior and enjoyed by many of the tasters. The homemade coconut cream was quite good — thicker, creamier, and somewhat more flavorful than the coconut milk. The canned coconut cream was also very good, not too sweet and much thinner than cream of coconut. The canned cream of coconut was very sweet and syrupy, really inedible right out of the can, with sugar being the predominant flavor. However, I found that it can be used in baking with good results.

In supermarkets, you can find coconut milk, coconut cream, and cream of coconut. My recipe for coconut macaroons calls for cream of coconut, the sweetened product, which is widely available and often sold under the Coco López label. I have also tasted and used Thai Kitchen Pure Coconut Milk and have found that it is much thicker than other brands of coconut milk, really qualifying more as coconut cream than coconut milk. I tried the coconut macaroon recipe in this book with coconut milk and found that since it is unsweetened, it radically changes the nature of the cookie, making it drier, less sweet, and less chewy.

WHAT IS THE DIFFERENCE BETWEEN DESICCATED COCONUT AND SWEETENED, FLAKED COCONUT?

Desiccated coconut, usually sold in natural food stores, is simply dried coconut meat. The sweetened, flaked coconut found in supermarkets is dried and flaked and then rehydrated and sweetened. Although I like the texture of desiccated coconut in baking, the supermarket coconut is actually more flavorful, since it is both moister and sweeter. The desiccated coconut works well for decorating a cake and can also be combined with sweetened, flaked coconut in baking to achieve both good flavor and good texture.

DIRECT MAIL AND ONLINE SOURCES FOR INGREDIENTS

Here are some of my favorite places to purchase ingredients for baking.

American Spoon Foods

This company was started by Justin Rashid and has been on the American culinary scene for almost twenty years. It offers many gift items plus sauces, jams, preserves, dried cherries, fruit butters, salad dressings, et cetera. **www. spoon.com**

Cane Syrup and Molasses

One of the quirkiest Web sites around is Steen's, makers of Steen's cane syrup, which was founded in 1910 by "Grandpa" Steen. The syrup is the South's equivalent of maple syrup and comes in bright yellow cans. I drizzle it on homemade biscuits on Saturday mornings, but you can also use it in baking. Steen's also sells molasses, corn and cane syrup blends, and cane vinegar. **www.steensyrup.com**

Flavored Oils

When I taste-tested extracts versus oils in baking, the Boyajian lemon and orange oils won hands down over extracts. It's like the difference between Baker's chocolate and Callebaut — there is no comparison. Boyajian also makes a variety of other flavored oils including garlic-flavored olive oil, basil oil, rosemary oil, and, spicy sesame oil, as well as flavored vinegars. **www.famousfoods.com/boyajianoil.htm**

Penzeys Spices

These folks are incomparable when it comes to herbs and spices. They sell in small as well as larger quantities and also sell empty jars and labels. Their vanilla extract and double vanilla extract are excellent, as is their choice of basic spices such as cinnamon. They also market barbecue rubs and spices in gift packs. Penzeys spices often win tastings conducted by *Cook's Illustrated* magazine. **www.penzeys.com**

Scharffen Berger Chocolate

This is perhaps the richest, darkest, most intense chocolate I have ever tasted. It may not be as complex and fruity as some brands but if you like a serious burst of chocolate flavor, this is the brand for you. Scharffen Berger sells regular baking chocolates as well as gift bars and cocoa. **www.scharffen-berger.com/index.htm**

4

DROP AND SHAPED COOKIES

If you have ever had a greasy, too-sweet chocolate chip cookie or a peanut butter cookie that was so dry and salty that a large glass of milk was the only remedy, you have experienced what all bakers know to be true — cookie recipes are very difficult to create, since even the tiniest variations seem to make huge differences in the taste and texture of the final product. In essence, drop and shaped cookies (as opposed to rolled cookies) are miniature cakes, with all of the attendant chemistry. In fact, in older cookbooks these sorts of cookies were often included in the cake chapter and listed under the heading "Small Cakes."

Balancing the leavener — baking powder or soda — with the acidity of the batter is crucial, as is adjusting the fat-to-flour ratio to get just the right texture. At the same time, the cook has to keep in mind the level of sugar or other sweeteners, which also affects texture. The size of the cookies matters too — a large cookie bakes up quite differently from a small one. Developing a great cookie recipe is akin to juggling chain saws; you have a lot of variables in the air, and any one of them is potentially destructive.

As difficult as developing a cookie recipe is, simply making and baking them also has its share of difficulties. Here are a few tips that I find helpful when I bake cookies at home:

- Use either parchment paper or Silpat (see page 11 for more information) for baking. This simplifies cleanup and makes large batches of cookies easy to handle. The dough is placed on sheets of parchment, which are then simply slid onto the baking sheet. (I use only one baking sheet at a time in the oven and find that preparing multiple sheets of parchment with dough — slide the baked cookies off the pan and the unbaked dough on — speeds up the process.)
- Baking more than one sheet of cookies at the same time is, in general, a bad idea. See page 5 for more information.
- Most home cooks are afraid of making large cookies. Follow the recipe directions carefully, making sure to form the dough exactly as described. Large cookies tend to have more contrast between the exterior and interior, which makes them more interesting.

CASE 15: JUST A SPOONFUL OF SUGAR

How different ingredients and techniques can affect baking results when making cookies.

Ingredient/Technique	Effect
Sugar	Sugar increases moisture retention and promotes browning; granulated sugar makes sturdier, less crumbly cookies than confectioners' sugar
Baking powder and baking soda	Too much leavener makes a cookie puffy or actually deflate; larger amounts of soda create more browning
Eggs	Whole eggs or egg yolks create structure
Flour	Cake flour produces more tender, crumbly cookies; all-purpose yields a more resilient cookie
Corn syrup	Increases moisture; cookies will be less brittle
Cornstarch	Makes a more tender cookie when added to flour
Size	Larger cookies will be moister inside and crispier outside; small cookies tend to be more uniform in texture
Chilling dough before baking	Cookies bake up thicker; batter spreads more slowly in hot oven

LARGE DROP COOKIES should be the size of a golf ball for best results.

- Baking times listed in recipes should be considered as general guides only, not precise measurements. All ovens are different, and most are not properly calibrated. Check the cookies halfway through the baking time and keep on checking until they are done.
- Baking sheets must be rotated 180 degrees halfway through baking for even cooking. The rear portion of an oven almost always bakes faster than the front.
- *Most cookies should be taken out of the oven long before they "set." The dough will appear very soft. As they cool, they will*

harden. Overbaking is perhaps the single biggest mistake that home cooks make. The result? They end up with dry, hard cookies.

- Chocolate is also best underbaked, since cooking reduces its flavor. Always err on the side of too little oven time when making chocolate cookies.

- Chilling dough before baking often makes the cookies thicker when cooked, since the dough doesn't immediately melt into a puddle.

- If a recipe calls for creaming butter (beating it until light and fluffy), follow the directions carefully. Don't simply melt the butter and be done with it.

- Make sure that your ingredients are the right temperature before starting. Often eggs must be at room temperature and butter must be cool, not cold and not room temperature.

- Finally, try to use the best possible ingredients. This is most important when choosing oils and extracts (see pages 35–37).

⋮

REFRIGERATOR COOKIES

THERE ARE HUNDREDS OF RECIPES for refrigerator, or icebox, cookies, which are a basic sugar cookie. The notion is simple. The dough is rolled into a log in waxed paper or plastic wrap and refrigerated before it is cut into rounds and then baked into cookies. Of all of the variables, the one that varies the most from recipe to recipe is the sugar, different cooks calling for all granulated sugar or differing combinations of granulated, confectioners', and/or brown sugar. As I experimented with icebox cookie recipes, I found that confectioners' sugar produces a very crumbly dough, somewhat like shortbread, which was not the texture I was looking for, since they were a bit too delicate. I preferred light brown sugar mixed with regular white granulated sugar, which boosts the flavor and produces a nice crisp cookie with a hint of chew in the center.

I was testing a recipe that called for 1½ cups

flour. My next decision was how much butter to use, and I found 10 tablespoons preferable to the more common 12 tablespoons called for in many other recipes, since the cookies had a bit more crunch but were still not dry. (Lower amounts of butter produced hard cookies.) I also tested using a whole egg versus just the yolk or just the white, and the whole egg was the winner, but only by a nose — the taste was slightly richer. Now I had an excellent refrigerator cookie that was crisp, showed off a bit of chew (especially when freshly baked), and had the rich flavors of butter and brown sugar, unusual for such a small thin cookie.

•••

Master Recipe for Refrigerator Cookies

A great benefit of this recipe is that the dough can be made well ahead of time and left in the refrigerator for up to 3 days and in the freezer for one month.

MAKES ABOUT 40 COOKIES

1½ cups all-purpose flour
½ teaspoon salt
10 tablespoons (1¼ sticks) unsalted butter, softened but still firm
⅓ cup granulated sugar
⅔ cup packed light brown sugar
1 large egg, at room temperature
1 teaspoon vanilla extract

1. Sift the flour and salt onto a piece of waxed paper. Set aside. In a large bowl, beat the butter and sugars with an electric mixer on medium speed for 2 minutes, scraping the bowl down frequently. Add the egg and beat until incorporated, 20 to 30 seconds. Add the vanilla and beat another 10 to 20 seconds, or until incorporated. Scrape the sides of the bowl as necessary. Add the flour mixture to the bowl and mix on low speed for about 1 minute, or until fully incorporated.

2. Divide the dough in half and, working with half at a time, shape each piece into a log about 2 inches thick and about 6 inches long. Wrap each log in plastic, waxed paper, or parchment and refrigerate for at least 2 hours, or until firm. The dough can be made up to 3 days ahead or frozen for about one month. (If freezing, wrap in plastic and then foil or a heavy freezer bag. Thaw in the refrigerator for about 30 minutes, or until soft enough to slice, before baking.)

3. Adjust the oven rack to the middle position and heat the oven to 325 degrees. Line a cookie sheet with parchment paper. Remove one of the logs from the refrigerator, unwrap, and slice with a sharp knife at ¼-inch intervals. Place slices on the cookie sheet 1 inch apart.

4. Bake 13 to 14 minutes, rotating the sheet halfway through the baking time. Check the cookies every couple of minutes after that. Their edges will be lightly browned when they are done. Cool on the sheet for 2 minutes, then use a cookie spatula to transfer to a wire rack to cool completely.

WHAT CAN GO WRONG? The butter and sugar must be creamed properly until the mixture is very light and fluffy. Since this dough is not rolled out, it is relatively easy to make.

CHOCOLATE VARIATION

Follow the above recipe, replacing ¼ cup of the flour with ¼ cup cocoa powder. Add 2 ounces melted and cooled semisweet chocolate to the batter along with the vanilla. Note that this dough is very sticky and takes a bit of work to form into a log.

SPIRAL VARIATION

Make one-half recipe of the master recipe and one-half recipe of the Chocolate Variation above (or make a full recipe of each and work with half of each dough at a time). Press each dough into a 4-inch disk, wrap in plastic, and

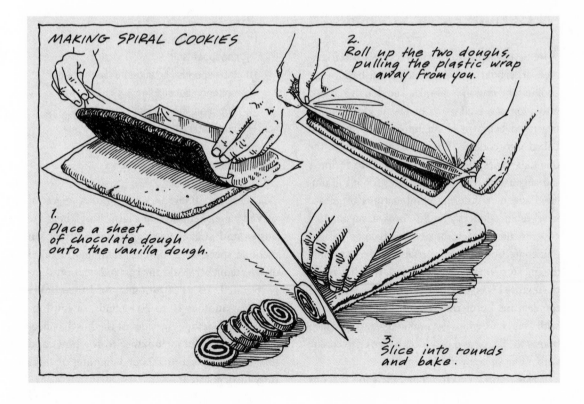

MAKING SPIRAL COOKIES

1. Place a sheet of chocolate dough onto the vanilla dough.

2. Roll up the two doughs, pulling the plastic wrap away from you.

3. Slice into rounds and bake.

chill for 15 or 20 minutes. Roll each disk between 2 pieces of plastic wrap to a rectangle
about 14 x 11 inches. Place the plastic-covered
rectangles onto a cookie sheet and chill for 30
minutes. Place the light dough onto a work surface and remove the top layer of plastic wrap.
Remove a layer of plastic wrap from the chocolate dough. Place the unwrapped surface of the
chocolate dough on top of the vanilla dough,
using the corners of the remaining plastic wrap
to center it as best you can. Next, remove the
top layer of plastic wrap. With the long edge of
the stacked dough in front of you, start to roll
the two doughs together as tightly as possible,
peeling away the bottom layer of plastic wrap
as you go. If at any time during this procedure
the dough seems too soft, stop and refrigerate
for another 30 minutes. When you have formed
your log, wrap in plastic or parchment and refrigerate for 2 hours, or until firm. Proceed with
step 3 of the main recipe.

PINWHEEL VARIATION

Make one recipe of Refrigerator Cookies and
one recipe of the Chocolate Variation. Instead
of dividing each dough in half, divide it into
quarters. Form each quarter into a 1-inch-thick
log. If the dough seems too soft to work with,
refrigerate for about 30 minutes. Lay a piece of
plastic wrap or parchment paper onto a work
surface. Place one light log and one dark log
next to each other on the paper, about 2 inches
from the end. Next, place one dark log on top
of the light log and one light log on top of the
dark log. Roll the logs together into one fat log
(about 2 inches thick). Do the same with the
four remaining logs. Proceed with step 3 of the
main recipe.

SPICE VARIATION

Sift ½ teaspoon cinnamon and ⅛ teaspoon cloves
along with the flour and salt. Replace the ⅔ cup
light brown sugar with ⅔ cup dark brown sugar.
Add ⅔ cup sliced almonds to the mixing bowl
along with the dry ingredients.

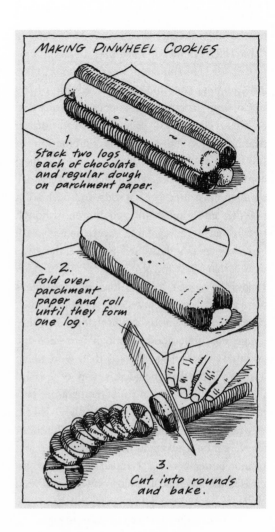

MAKING PINWHEEL COOKIES

1. Stack two logs each of chocolate and regular dough on parchment paper.

2. Fold over parchment paper and roll until they form one log.

3. Cut into rounds and bake.

GINGER VARIATION

Omit the vanilla. Sift ½ teaspoon ground ginger
along with the flour and salt. Add ¼ cup finely
minced crystallized ginger to the mixing bowl
along with the dry ingredients.

PEANUT BUTTER COOKIES

MANY PEOPLE DO NOT ENJOY peanut butter
cookies because they are dry, crumbly, too salty,
and lacking in true peanut flavor. I started out
by trying a number of recipes, including our
own recipe at *Cook's Illustrated* plus recipes

from cookbooks including *Death by Chocolate* (Marcel Desaulniers), *Pillsbury: Best Cookies Cookbook, The Fannie Farmer Cookbook* (Marion Cunningham), and the 1997 edition of *Joy of Cooking* (Irma S. Rombauer et al.). Only two of the recipes used peanuts in addition to peanut butter; most used a combination of brown sugar and white sugar (one recipe used confectioners' sugar, which made a very dry cookie); most used baking soda and no baking powder; and almost all used butter, although one recipe used vegetable shortening instead.

I decided that I wanted a cookie that was thicker than most and also moister in the middle. I liked the *Cook's* recipe a lot, but the cookies were a bit flat for my taste, since I prefer thicker, chewier cookies. I also thought that the Pillsbury recipe was quite good, although it needed the addition of ground peanuts. I then worked up a new recipe that included a cup of ground peanuts, a half pound of room temperature butter, and light brown sugar instead of white sugar. The results were good but not perfect. The cookies were a bit greasy and flat, the bane of many peanut butter cookies. I added more flour, increased the amount of baking powder, and then chilled the dough for 3 hours before using to give it more body. A final refinement was an extra egg for a bit more body and moisture. Finally, a puffier cookie that wasn't at all dry.

Next, I wanted to investigate peanuts and peanut butters. The problem with both ingredients is that major manufacturers put in all sorts of unwanted ingredients that disguise the flavor of pure peanuts. For example, Planters dry-roasted peanuts include peanuts, salt, sugar, cornstarch, monosodium glutamate, gelatin, corn syrup solids, paprika and other spices, dried yeast, onion and garlic powders, hydrolyzed soy protein, and natural flavor. And I thought they were just dry-roasted peanuts! I found the same problem with commercial peanut butters. Skippy contains roasted peanuts, sugar, partially hydrogenated vegetable oils (rapeseed, cottonseed, and soybean), and salt;

the Jif brand also includes molasses and diglycerides. Of course, the natural food store has plenty of peanut butters that include nothing more than peanuts: no salt, no vegetable oils, no diglycerides. It was not surprising, therefore, that cookies made with the natural products won hands down. The pure flavor of the peanuts really came through. I also noted in this tasting that, among supermarket brands, Jif did have a more pronounced peanut flavor than Skippy.

• • •

Moist, Thick Peanut Butter Cookies

Unlike any other peanut butter cookie you have ever had, these are thick and moist in the middle without being greasy. They also have a strong peanut flavor, something often missing from this sort of cookie. The salt level in this recipe is gauged for salted peanut butter and salted peanuts. (See "What Can Go Wrong?" below.)

MAKES ABOUT 3 DOZEN COOKIES

- 2½ cups all-purpose flour
- ½ teaspoon baking soda
- 1 teaspoon baking powder
- ¼ teaspoon salt
- ½ pound (2 sticks) unsalted butter, softened but still firm
- 2 cups packed light brown sugar
- 1 cup extra-crunchy peanut butter (see "What Can Go Wrong?" below)
- 3 large eggs
- 2 teaspoons vanilla extract
- 1 cup roasted salted peanuts, ground to resemble breadcrumbs

1. Whisk flour, baking soda, baking powder, and salt in a medium bowl. Set aside. Either by hand or with an electric mixer, beat butter until smooth and creamy. Add sugar, beat until light and fluffy, about 3 minutes with an electric mixer, stopping to scrape down the bowl as necessary. (This is an important step. Make sure

that the sugar-butter mixture is very fluffy and light.) Beat in the peanut butter until fully incorporated, then the eggs one at a time, then the vanilla. Gently stir dry ingredients into peanut butter mixture. Add the ground peanuts and stir gently until just incorporated.

2. Cover dough with plastic wrap and chill until firm, at least 3 hours to overnight. (In a pinch, you can go ahead and bake them without chilling. The chilling will make thicker cookies, since the cold dough will not spread as much during baking.)

3. Adjust the oven rack to the low center position. Heat oven to 350 degrees. Line a large cookie sheet with parchment paper.

4. Working with a generous 2 tablespoons each time, roll dough into 2-inch balls. The dough can also be scooped with a number 24 ice cream scoop, which yields exactly the right amount and makes this task painless. Place balls on the parchment-lined cookie sheet, leaving 2½ inches between them.

5. Barely press each dough ball twice with the tines of a dinner fork to form a crisscross design, dipping the fork into cold water in between presses. Try to flatten the cookies as little as possible. (This step is optional.)

6. Bake until the cookies are puffed and slightly brown along edges and the bottoms are golden brown, 12 to 13 minutes, turning baking sheet in oven halfway through baking. Cool until set, about 4 minutes, and then transfer to a wire rack to cool completely.

7. Repeat steps 4 through 6 with a new sheet of parchment paper until all the dough is baked.

WHAT CAN GO WRONG? The big problem with peanut butter cookies is salt level. It is best to use a peanut butter with little or no added salt, in which case you may want to try increasing the amount of salt in the recipe to a full teaspoon. On the other hand, if you use a supermarket peanut butter that is particularly salty, the ¼ teaspoon salt called for in the recipe should be about right. If the cookies are still salty, use no

added salt the next time you make them, relying on the peanut butter to provide the salt.

▪ ▪ ▪

Oatmeal Chocolate Chip Cookies

The original version of this recipe was forwarded to me by my sister, Kate, who found it on the Internet. It is the famous "Neiman Marcus" cookie recipe. The story, now thought to be entirely apocryphal, is that a customer was charged $250 for it, not $2.50 as she had assumed when requesting it, and was so furious that she published it on the Internet as a form of revenge. I have made many revisions, including eliminating the baking soda entirely (using only baking powder), increasing the salt level, changing the oven temperature, decreasing the amount of both sugars as well as the oats, and rewriting the directions. The original was good, but a bit dry and too sweet. Do not be put off by the use of oatmeal. This is an outstanding chocolate chip cookie — chewy, rich, and thick (since they do not spread much during baking).

MAKES 30 TO 36 LARGE COOKIES

1½	cups rolled oats
½	pound (2 sticks) unsalted butter, softened but still firm
¾	cup granulated sugar
¾	cup packed brown sugar
2	large eggs, at room temperature
1	teaspoon vanilla extract
2	cups all-purpose flour
1	teaspoon baking powder
¾	teaspoon salt
12	ounces chocolate chips
4	ounces grated semisweet chocolate (see step 3)
1½	cups chopped pecans or walnuts

1. Adjust oven rack to the middle position and heat oven to 350 degrees. Place oats in a blender or food processor and blend until very fine. Set aside.

2. With an electric mixer, beat the butter and both sugars in a large bowl until light, about 3 minutes. Add the eggs one at a time and beat 20 seconds after each addition. Add the vanilla and beat for 15 seconds to blend.

3. Whisk together the flour, processed oats, baking powder, and salt. With a large rubber spatula or wooden spoon, blend the dry ingredients into the butter mixture. (This will be difficult since the batter is very stiff.) Add the chocolate chips, grated chocolate, and nuts. (The easiest method of "grating" chocolate is to chop it in a heavy-duty food processor, such as the KitchenAid or Cuisinart models, fitted with the metal blade.)

4. Form dough into balls about 2 inches in diameter and place on a baking sheet covered with parchment paper. (The parchment is optional.) Bake 14 to 15 minutes, or until the bottoms are lightly browned. The cookies should still feel a bit soft at this point. (They will not spread very much and will look undercooked. *Do not overcook or they will become hard and dry when they cool.*) They will harden as they cool. Remove from oven and let cookies cool for 2 minutes on the baking sheet before removing to cooling racks. Repeat with a new sheet of parchment paper until all the dough is baked. Cool cookies at least 30 minutes before serving.

WHAT CAN GO WRONG? As with many cookies, overbaking will make these dry. These cookies, however, tend to keep their shape in the oven as they cook, so it is difficult to tell when they are done. The best method is to check the bottoms, which should be lightly browned.

❖

THE SEARCH FOR THE ULTIMATE CHOCOLATE COOKIE

OBSESSIONS OFTEN BEGIN with chance encounters, a wry, fetching smile glanced out of the corner of the eye, or perhaps one's first taste of a homegrown tomato. One of my greatest obsessions has been the first transcendent bite of the perfect chocolate cookie, still warm from the oven. My fantasy was that this ultimate cookie would be dense with the rich, buttery flavor of bittersweet chocolate. It would be crispy along the edges, but the first bite would reveal a center of hot fudge sauce, moist, the texture of chocolate bread pudding, with a deep, complex chocolate flavor — the sort of confection that creates intense focus while it is consumed, overloading the other senses to the point of dysfunction.

The problem was that I had, for years, been trying to perfect this cookie. I created large, dense cookies, the equivalent of round, baked fudge. These were rich and decadent, but the chocolate flavor was overwhelming and the texture was, well, on the dry side. I had experimented with thin, crisp cookies (nice but not intense), chewy cookies (good but not showstoppers), and cakelike chocolate cookies, which tended to be dry and uninspired. Our test kitchen also made a half-dozen recipes from various cookbooks and discovered a world of difference in texture, flavor, and appearance, from soft mocha-colored disks to thick mounds of pure fudge. This panoply of outcomes gave me pause, since the ingredient lists seemed to have more in common than the cookies themselves. Figuring out what makes a chocolate cookie tick was going to require weeks of testing and a great deal of detective work.

My first step was to strip the recipes down to their basics to understand the fundamentals. A chocolate cookie is a mixture of melted chocolate, sugar, eggs, butter, flour, baking soda or powder, and salt. Vanilla, coffee, and nuts are extras. There are two schools of thought: one calls for creaming the butter and sugar, and the other suggests beating the eggs until they are thick and lemon-colored and melting the butter along with the chocolate. For the first test batch, we melted the butter and the eggs were whipped. We found the results to be good, but the cookies were a bit cakey and loose without any chew to them. When we started creaming the butter, we noticed an immediate improvement. The cookies had more body and seemed a bit moister as well. So creaming was in and melting was out.

The next issue was one of proportions, that is, the ratio of flour to butter to eggs to sugar to chocolate. This was going to be crucial to the thickness of the cookie, the amount of moisture, the texture, and the degree to which the taste of chocolate dominated. Looking over the recipes we had tested, I felt like the British trying to crack the German secret code in World War II, given the number of permutations. In order to organize the facts, I proceeded as if I were a cryptographer, making a chart of the various ratios of eggs, sugar, chocolate, and butter to flour with related comments on the taste, texture, and shape of each cookie tested. I quickly noted that the ratios of eggs and butter to flour were less important than the ratios of sugar and chocolate to flour. The driest cookie used less than ½ cup sugar per cup of flour; the richest, wettest cookie used 3 cups. After many tests designed to balance sweetness and moisture, I settled on 1 cup sugar to ¾ cup flour. The biggest issue, however, was the amount of chocolate. The cookie with the faintest chocolate flavor and relatively firm, dry texture used only 2 ounces of chocolate per cup of flour, whereas other recipes used up to a pound of chocolate with only ½ cup flour. More tests ended up suggesting using 8 ounces of chocolate per ¾ cup flour. Finally, I had a cookie that had good chocolate flavor and was moist, not dry. However, it still needed better flavor and texture, so I moved on to other ingredients.

The cookie started with all white granulated sugar and then was tested with a mixture of brown sugar and granulated, which seemed to improve the flavor and added just a bit of moisture to the cookie. I also tried corn syrup, which had little effect. A small amount of vanilla extract and instant coffee powder rounded out the flavors. Throughout the testing, I had been using all-purpose flour, but I also tried cake flour, which produced a cookie that was a bit too delicate. To create an even thicker, more stable cookie, I tried replacing some of the butter with vegetable shortening (Crisco), but this created an unattractive greasy-looking cookie, with a pale white sheen. I thought that the choice of leavener might be important, so I tested baking powder against baking soda and found that the cookies were slightly thicker with the powder. To create an even thicker cookie, I tried refrigerating the dough before baking. This worked well, producing a dome-shaped cookie rather than a flat disk. Finally, when I had reached our fortieth test, I decided to revisit the amount of flour in the recipe, increasing it to a full cup (from ¾ cup), and this worked like a charm, adding some chew as well as height.

The cookie was thick and very good but not the sort of thing that would reduce the average adult to tears of joy. The flavor was a bit dull and the texture was moist but unremarkable. To solve this problem, I wondered if the type of chocolate mattered, that is, whether unsweetened was just as good as semisweet or bittersweet. The unsweetened chocolate, an ingredient often called for in chocolate cookie recipes, added a bit of intensity to the flavor but also an aggressive bitter note, even when the sugar level was adjusted. I then tested semisweet chocolate and preferred it for its smooth, rich flavor — due, I guessed, to the additional cocoa butter and other flavorings not found in unsweetened chocolate. Still searching for a truly decadent chocolate experience, I decided to add chocolate chips to the batter, hoping that they would melt during baking, creating a texture much like hot fudge sauce drizzled over warm chocolate cake. This is exactly what happened. This more liquid texture also seemed to boost the chocolate flavor, since the warm, melted chocolate stimulated the taste buds better than firmer, chewier cookies. However, there were drawbacks to this approach. The choco-

Five major brands were tested head-to-head: Nestlé, Baker's, Ghirardelli, Scharffen Berger, and Callebaut. The Baker's turned out a gritty cookie, which received low marks; the Nestlé cookie had an off, somewhat fruity taste; the Ghirardelli produced a muted but pure chocolate flavor that was quite pleasant; the flavor of the Scharffen Berger cookie was the most intense of the lot but not fruity or complex; and the Callebaut cookie was the favorite, with big chocolate flavor that was clean, well rounded, and full of punch. As for the chips, I conducted a tasting (see page 42) which revealed that Tropical Source, Ghirardelli, and Guittard are the best. If you can only get supermarket chocolate chips, Nestlé is preferred.

late flavor was overwhelming, almost too much of a good thing, and the texture suffered as well, losing a bit of its chew. (I finally decided to offer the chips as a variation on the master recipe.) Still searching for a rich chocolate cookie with the right texture, I wondered if a bit of cocoa powder might add depth of flavor. A quarter cup of cocoa was substituted for the same amount of flour, and the chocolate flavor was both smoother and deeper. (I also tried a batch of cookies made with only cocoa powder, no chocolate, and these were disappointing, with only a faint chocolate flavor.) Finally, I had brought my fantasy to life, a double chocolate cookie that was rich, thick, soft, crispy, and with an intense chocolaty center that could drive anyone to distraction.

■ ■ ■

Double Chocolate Cookies

These cookies contain both semisweet chocolate and cocoa powder; hence they are double chocolate cookies. If you add chips as well (see variation below), they turn into triple chocolate cookies! Be absolutely sure to underbake these cookies. *They should still be very soft and wet when taken out of the oven. They will set as they cool. Although 10 minutes is the proper baking time in my oven, all ovens are different, so I suggest baking a couple of cookies as a test, letting them cool, and then judging the texture. Note that if you make smaller or larger cookies, this will dramatically affect the baking time.*

MAKES ABOUT 20 COOKIES

8   ounces semisweet chocolate, coarsely chopped
1   cup all-purpose flour
¼   cup Dutch-process cocoa powder
1   teaspoon baking powder
½   teaspoon salt
5   tablespoons unsalted butter, softened but still firm
¾   cup packed light brown sugar
¼   cup granulated sugar
2   large eggs
1   teaspoon vanilla extract
1   teaspoon instant espresso powder

1. Melt chocolate either in a saucepan in a 250-degree oven for 15 minutes or in a glass bowl in a microwave oven at 50 percent power for 3 minutes, stirring after 2 minutes. If you like, chocolate can also be melted in the top of a double boiler. Set aside. Sift together the flour, cocoa, baking powder, and salt onto a piece of waxed paper. Set aside. Heat oven to 350 degrees.

2. In a large bowl, cream the butter with an electric mixer on high speed for 4 to 5 minutes, or until very pale and fluffy. Add the sugars and beat an additional 2 to 3 minutes, or until light and fluffy. Scrape down the sides of the bowl. Lightly whisk an egg with a fork and then add to the creamed butter, beating 30 seconds. Repeat with second egg. Add vanilla and espresso powder and beat to incorporate for about 20 seconds. Add the melted chocolate and beat another 30 seconds. Scrape down the sides of the bowl. Add the dry ingredients and beat on the lowest speed until well mixed.

3. Using a small ice cream scoop or a large soup spoon, make balls of dough about 1¾ inches in diameter (the size of a golf ball; smaller or larger cookies will dramatically impact the baking time). Place them on a parchment-lined cookie sheet. Bake about 10 minutes, rotating the cookie sheet halfway through cooking. *The cookies should be very soft and appear undercooked when they are removed from the oven.* Do not let the cookies become too browned on the bottom. Remove to a cooling rack to set and cool. Repeat with a new sheet of parchment paper until all the dough is baked.

WHAT CAN GO WRONG? Most folks make these cookies too small, which means that they bake faster and tend to be less moist on the inside. I suggest using balls of dough the size of a golf ball. You will be tempted to make them much smaller, which makes an inferior cookie. Also, chocolate cookies are much better slightly underbaked. They will appear soft and almost raw when you take them out of the oven. They will firm up considerably as they cool. Also note that the less you bake chocolate, the more flavor it has.

Triple Chocolate Variation

Add 6 ounces of semisweet chocolate chips to the batter after the dry ingredients have been incorporated.

▪ ▪ ▪

Thick, Dense Chocolate Cookies

I have searched for years for the best recipe for a thick, dense chocolate cookie. (The recipe above is for a lighter, more refined chocolate cookie.) I like a heavy-duty chocolate cookie to be lightly crisp on the outside and chewy on the inside. The texture should be somewhere in between cakey and fudgy, moist but not wet, rich but not candylike.

Using the recipe I developed above for Double Chocolate Cookies, I played with the amount of flour and reduced it by over 50 percent in relation to the chocolate. This made the cookie denser and more chocolaty. (Chocolate cookies with a higher proportion of flour to chocolate tend to be lighter and cakier.) I also included chocolate chips in this recipe, which adds more chocolate punch. As with most cookies, I found that letting the dough cool in the refrigerator for 2 hours helped the cookies keep their shape when baked, without melting and spreading. These cookies do not hold well and should be eaten within 48 hours.

MAKES 18 COOKIES ABOUT 4 INCHES IN DIAMETER

1	pound semisweet chocolate, coarsely chopped
10	tablespoons (1¼ sticks) unsalted butter
6	large eggs
2	cups granulated sugar
¾	cup all-purpose flour
1	teaspoon baking powder
12	ounces chopped walnuts or pecans
12	ounces chocolate chips

1. Melt chocolate and butter in a saucepan until smooth, or place saucepan in a 250-degree oven for about 15 minutes. Set aside. In a large bowl, whip eggs and sugar until thick and pale yellow, about 5 minutes on high speed. Using a rubber spatula, combine melted chocolate with egg mixture until well blended. In a separate bowl, whisk together the flour and baking powder and then fold into chocolate mixture until fully incorporated. Add nuts and chocolate chips and blend.

2. Chill dough for 2 hours. Heat oven to 350 degrees. Cover a baking sheet with parchment paper. Place mounds of dough 3 inches apart using an ice cream scoop. (The balls of dough should be very large — about 2 inches in diameter. Smaller cookies will bake more quickly than indicated below.) Bake for 18 minutes, rotating the baking sheet halfway through baking. Remove parchment paper with cookies and cool on a wire rack. Repeat with a new

sheet of parchment paper until all the dough is baked.

WHAT CAN GO WRONG? It is crucial to chill this dough before baking and to use very large balls of dough for the cookies. Warm dough will spread quickly in the oven, and smaller cookies will quickly overcook.

▪▪▪

Snipdoodles

According to James Beard, snickerdoodles were called by many different names, depending on the region of the country where the recipe was found. Along the Hudson River Valley they were called schnecken doodles, yet snipdoodles or snickerdoodles were also common names. I am partial to the name snipdoodles as well as to this recipe. I add a bit of nutmeg to the batter, which adds a gentle perfume to what is a very simple cookie. I tested them with Crisco instead of milk, and the cookies were flatter, more spread out, and a bit crispier. I prefer a more delicate, softer snipdoodle and therefore used the milk. The texture of these cookies is heavenly, light but with a nice chew. They bake up nice and thick, almost like a macaroon.

MAKES 20 TO 24 COOKIES

8	tablespoons (1 stick) unsalted butter, softened but still firm
1½	cups plus 3 tablespoons granulated sugar
2	large eggs
1	teaspoon vanilla extract
¼	cup milk
3	cups all-purpose flour
¾	teaspoon baking soda
1	teaspoon cream of tartar
½	teaspoon salt
½	teaspoon nutmeg
1	tablespoon cinnamon

1. Beat the butter and 1½ cups of the sugar in the bowl of an electric mixer or with a wooden spoon until creamy and smooth, about 3 minutes. Add the eggs and vanilla and beat until fully incorporated. Add the milk and stir to incorporate. In a separate bowl, whisk together the next 5 ingredients (flour through nutmeg) and then stir into the butter-sugar mixture. Chill dough for 2 hours. Heat oven to 350 degrees. Line a cookie sheet with parchment paper.

2. Shape dough into large, walnut-size balls, about 1¼ inches in diameter. Mix together the remaining 3 tablespoons sugar and cinnamon in a small bowl. Dip tops of dough balls in sugar-cinnamon mixture. Place balls 3 inches apart on lined baking sheet. Bake for about 12 minutes, rotating the baking sheet after 6 minutes. Cookies will appear undercooked when removed from the oven; the centers will still be very moist and light. Remove cookies to a rack; as they cool, they will firm up. Repeat with a new sheet of parchment paper until all the dough is baked.

WHAT CAN GO WRONG? This is an easy cookie to make, but just be sure not to overbake. They should appear undercooked when removed from the oven.

▾▾▾

THE BEST OATMEAL COOKIE

THE SEARCH FOR THE PERFECT OATMEAL cookie turned out to be akin to finding the Holy Grail. I started with a master recipe that was very heavy on shortening (1 cup butter to 3½ cups flour and oats) and set out to try a few variations. My objective was to create a thick oatmeal cookie with lots of chew and also lots of flavor. I tested refrigerating the dough, a technique that works well with chocolate cookies, to no effect. Adding an extra egg white just made the cookie stickier. Melting the butter instead of creaming it made the cookie thinner and a little greasier. I did find, however, that reducing the baking soda actually resulted in a

CASE 16: OATMEAL COOKIES

What is the best method for making a chewy, moist oatmeal cookie?

Test	Result
Refrigerate dough for 2 hours	Little effect on final cookie
Add 1 egg white	Stickier cookie
Melt butter, don't cream it	Thinner, greasier cookie
Reduce baking soda to ½ teaspoon	Thicker cookie
Add 1 egg yolk	Stickier cookie
Reduce white sugar to ¾ cup	Not quite as sweet; otherwise the same
Reduce butter to 12 tablespoons	Less greasy
Use ¼ cup molasses and reduce sugar slightly	Bitter, unpleasant flavor

thicker cookie, a surprising result. I also tried molasses, which was bitter, as well as adding an extra egg yolk, reducing the sugar, and reducing the butter, all to little effect.

None of the variations I tried did the trick, except the reduction in baking soda, which produced a thicker cookie. (See discussion of baking powder and baking soda on page 37.) However, I still had a relatively thin, very flavorful cookie, not the thick, chewy confection that I had set out to discover. I put aside the master recipe and went through my 1914 edition of Fannie Farmer's *Boston Cooking School Cookbook*. That recipe used a much lower proportion of shortening. The good news was that the cookie finally had some height; the bad news was that it had no taste and was very dry. In desperation, I followed the recipe on the Quaker Oats container, and this worked fairly well, although the flavor was unremarkable.

I finally decided to compromise. I used my master recipe and reduced the baking soda to ½ teaspoon, but I increased the oats to 2¼ cups in a nod to the Quaker Oats version (the latter uses 3 cups, which I felt was too much). I was getting close. The cookie was chewy and flavorful and not as greasy as my original version. Based on a suggestion from one of the *Cook's Illustrated* editors, I also tried mixing the dough with a wooden spoon, not with an electric mixer. This made a slight difference, the cookie had a bit more body and texture. Finally, I reversed the quantities of white and brown sugar, using more of the former than the latter. This worked well; I found that the larger amount of brown sugar had overpowered the flavor of the oats.

•••

Master Recipe for Thick, Chewy Oatmeal Cookies

The most common mistake made when baking these cookies is to take them out of the oven too late, after they look properly baked. Chewy, moist cookies are best removed when they appear undercooked. They will set up as they cool. Also, be sure not to use quick-cooking oats. You want regular rolled oats, which provide better texture.

MAKES ABOUT 24 LARGE COOKIES

½   pound (2 sticks) unsalted butter, softened but still firm

1   cup granulated sugar

½   cup packed light brown sugar

2   large eggs

1   teaspoon vanilla extract

2¼   cups rolled (*not* quick-cooking) oats

1¼   cups all-purpose flour

½   teaspoon baking soda

¼   teaspoon salt

½   teaspoon cinnamon

¼   teaspoon allspice

¼   teaspoon ground cloves

1   cup raisins

1. Heat oven to 350 degrees. Line a cookie sheet with parchment paper.

2. In a large bowl, beat the butter and sugars by hand with a wooden spoon until pale yellow and very light. Add the eggs and vanilla and beat until fluffy. Add oats and mix to combine.

3. In a separate bowl, whisk together the remaining ingredients except the raisins and fold them into the oatmeal mixture using a large rubber spatula or wooden spoon. Stir in raisins.

4. Place dough in heaping tablespoons on parchment paper and bake about 15 minutes, or until edges are brown. Rotate the pan halfway through the baking time for even browning. The cookies will still feel slightly undercooked and soft when removed from the oven. Slip parchment paper off of baking sheet and place on a cooling rack. Repeat with a new sheet of parchment until all the dough is baked.

WHAT CAN GO WRONG? I have watched professional culinary students overbake these cookies, and I have even done it myself on more than one occasion. These cookies will be very pale and look underbaked when they are ready. You almost have to force yourself, against your better judgment, to take them out of the oven when they still look raw and very puffy. If you don't act decisively, the cookies will harden and dry out as they cool. You want soft, chewy cookies.

DATE VARIATION

Substitute 1½ cups chopped dates for the raisins.

GINGER VARIATION

Omit raisins and add ¾ teaspoon ground ginger.

NUT VARIATION

Omit raisins, increase flour to 1⅓ cups, and add ¼ cup ground almonds and 1 cup walnut pieces along with the oats. (Almonds can be ground in a food processor or blender.)

ORANGE AND ALMOND VARIATION

Omit raisins and add 2 tablespoons minced orange zest and 1 cup toasted chopped almonds along with oats. (Toast the almonds in a 350-degree oven for 5 minutes.)

THE PROBLEM WITH CHOCOLATE CHIP COOKIES

*C*OOK'S *ILLUSTRATED* ONCE RECEIVED an article on how to make the best chocolate chip cookie. The author had written a compelling and detailed account of how she had perfected a master recipe after working through forty variations. We baked a batch and found that they were good but not great. Two hours after baking, they became crispy, losing the chewiness that I think is essential to a great chocolate chip cookie. The manuscript was sent back, and two months and another ten variations later, we had her new recipe, which was very good, a real gourmet store cookie. But I still wasn't completely satisfied, although I was somewhat daunted by the difficulties involved. It was clear that developing a chocolate chip cookie is hard work, a little like doing a watercolor in the dark. You never know how it is going to turn out.

I started with a few obvious tests. Refrigerating the dough, a trick I use for chocolate cookies, didn't affect the texture much. I varied the eggs, using 2 whole eggs instead of 1 egg plus 1 yolk. The batter was thin and spread quickly when baked, and the interior was still cakelike, a big problem with the master recipe. However, I then tried using 1 whole egg plus 1 egg white, and this made a much better cookie with more chew. I also tried using 2 whole eggs and 1 white, and the batter was much too thin.

Although I had found that mixing oatmeal cookie dough by hand made some difference, I was surprised to find that an electric mixer will turn chocolate chip cookie dough to soup. This dough must be mixed with a wooden spoon. I also decided to cream the butter instead of melting it, and this was a big improvement. The cookies were much chewier. I was surprised by the results when I substituted ¼ cup Crisco for the same amount of butter. This made a puffier, chewier cookie than the all-butter version. There was still plenty of butter in the recipe, so there was no lack of flavor. Reducing the baking soda to ¼ teaspoon also helped thicken the cookie; I had found this to be true when testing oatmeal cookies as well. I tested reducing the flour to 2 cups (a reduction of 2 tablespoons), and the cookies were too thin. When I tried bread flour, it produced a very stiff cookie.

Just as a benchmark, I made the standard Toll House recipe (the recipe printed on the back of the Nestlé chocolate chip bag) and was quite disappointed. After cooling, these were very crispy cookies, very much like a Pepperidge Farm product. I then tried baking them for a shorter time at 375 degrees — the recipe calls for a 325-degree oven temperature — and this was better. Although they were too soft, the difference in texture was remarkable. I decided to go back and bake my current recipe, which used 1 whole egg plus 1 egg white, Crisco and butter, hand mixing, and a reduced amount of baking soda, at an oven temperature of 375 degrees. There was a big improvement in texture.

I still wasn't totally satisfied, however. I wanted more structure to the cookie, more contrast between a crisp exterior and a chewy interior. I called Shirley Corriher, the *Cook's Illustrated* consulting scientist, and she let me in on one of the secrets of cookie making. She pointed out that if I wanted a thicker cookie, the cookie dough needed to set quickly in the oven. For that to happen, she said, it needed more acidity. Shirley listed a few items that are acidic, including cake flour and brown sugar, and also pointed out that using baking powder instead of baking soda would increase the acidity. I made this substitution and found that the cookie set more quickly, giving me the shape I was after. I also tested freezing the dough for 10 minutes before baking, and this made very little difference at all. Finally, a great chocolate chip cookie with a chewy, moist interior.

▪ ▪ ▪

The Best Chocolate Chip Cookie

MAKES ABOUT 20 LARGE COOKIES

¼	cup Crisco
8	tablespoons (1 stick) unsalted butter, softened but still firm
1	cup packed light brown sugar
½	cup granulated sugar
1	large egg
1	large egg white
2	teaspoons vanilla extract

2 cups plus 2 tablespoons all-purpose flour
¼ teaspoon baking powder
⅛ teaspoon salt
10 ounces chocolate chips (chunks are preferred over chips)

1. Heat oven to 375 degrees. Beat the Crisco and butter in a medium bowl with a wooden spoon until pretty smooth but with a few harder pieces (about 1 minute). Add the sugars and stir until well blended. Add the egg, egg white, and vanilla and beat until smooth. In a separate bowl, whisk together the flour, baking powder, and salt. Add to the batter and mix together until smooth. Add the chips and fold in.

2. Line a large cookie sheet with parchment paper. For large cookies, place heaping tablespoons of dough on the paper with 1½ inches between the outer edges of the balls of dough. Shape the dough quickly with your hand so that each spoonful is compact and not too spread out.

3. Bake for about 12 minutes, or until tops are lightly browned. Rotate pan front to back halfway through baking; do not overcook.

4. Slide parchment paper onto wire racks to cool. Repeat as needed with fresh sheets of parchment paper.

WHAT CAN GO WRONG? The dough is easy to make, but overbaking will turn these cookies into hard little nuggets. I prefer larger cookies, since the exterior is crispy and the interior remains moist and chewy.

Nut Variation

Add 1½ cups of roughly chopped toasted pecans or walnuts to the batter along with the chips.

Coconut Macaroons

Coconut macaroons are a bit like broughams. In the age of horse-pulled transport, a brougham was a light closed carriage with seating for either two or four. When Detroit automakers got hold of this term, realizing that nobody had a clue what a real brougham was, they turned this elegant nineteenth-century conveyance into a description for a rather pedestrian two-door sedan. Macaroons have undergone a similar transformation from their origin a thousand years ago as baked almond paste to quite elegant cone-shaped coconut macaroons, which were popular in the nineteenth century, to their current state as lackluster mounds of beaten egg whites and coconut or, at their worst, nothing more than a baked mixture of condensed milk and sweetened coconut. Further research shows that recipes for coconut macaroons might include a wide range of ingredients, including corn syrup, extracts (such as vanilla, almond, or coconut), salt, flour, sugar, sweetened condensed milk, and even an egg or two in extreme variations.

My initial testing included five recipes, ranging from dense, wet cookies to light, if not dry, mounds of coconut. In the former category were recipes that used unbeaten egg whites mixed with sweetened coconut and sugar; one of them, a Brazilian macaroon, even included eggs and produced a gooey, cavity-inducing cookie with a strong caramel flavor but nary a hint of coconut. The light, airy cookie used beaten egg whites, which resulted in a meringue-style cookie, light and delicate but totally lacking in coconut flavor or chew. (One cookbook author claims that macaroons were based on meringues, so whipping the whites may have some historical precedent.) The test winners were simple enough — unbeaten egg whites mixed with sugar, unsweetened coconut, salt, and vanilla. It seemed that unsweetened coconut, rather than sweetened, resulted in a less sticky, more appealing texture. Still, I had not achieved my goal of the perfect coconut macaroon. I felt that the test winners lacked coconut flavor and were a bit on the dry side, not sufficiently chewy or moist. I set out to find a happy medium between our test recipes.

My testing showed that the type of coconut, sweetened versus unsweetened, had a major effect on texture. But cookies made with just one type were either too sticky or too dry, so I tested a combination of sweetened and unsweetened. This worked well, giving the cookie a somewhat more luxurious texture without being wet or heavy. I also found, to my surprise, that sweetened coconut had more flavor than dried, so the coconut flavor was turned up a notch. Another key issue was the ratio of coconut to unbeaten egg whites. Testing showed that a recipe using 3½ cups coconut to only 1 egg white was dense and heavy; 3 cups coconut to 3 egg whites seemed a better ratio. To add still a bit more moisture to the cookies, I tried using corn syrup instead of sugar as a sweetener and found that the cookies were slightly moister, held together a bit better, and were pleasantly chewy. Melted butter was tried but discarded, since it masked the flavor of the coconut, as did sweetened condensed milk. Flour — I tried both cake flour and all-purpose — was helpful in eliminating the stickiness of cookies made entirely with sweetened coconut, but the combination of sweetened and unsweetened solved this problem without resorting to other ingredients.

I still felt that the cookies were a bit light in coconut flavor, so I tried adding cream of coconut and hit the jackpot. The coconut flavor was superior to that of any other cookie made to date. Finally, a coconut macaroon with real coconut flavor. (Since cream of coconut is sweetened, I did have to decrease the amount of corn syrup.)

Putting it all together is easy, another benefit of not beating the egg whites. The liquid ingredients are whisked together, the dry ingredients are mixed, and then the two are combined. I found it best to refrigerate this dough for 15 minutes to make it easier to work with, but in a pinch you can skip this step. (Cold dough makes thicker cookies.) In an effort to produce a nicely browned, crisp exterior, I experimented with oven temperatures and finally settled on

WERE MACAROONS INVENTED YESTERDAY?

In a word, no. Almond-flavored macaroons have been around for the better part of a thousand years, being, in essence, baked marzipan. One dessert expert and historian, Stephen Schmidt, claims that the term *macaroon* comes from the Italian *macaroni*, the almond paste looking much like a pasta dough as it was extruded through a pastry tube. (Other sources claim that the macaroon is related to the meringue cookie, since both are based on egg whites.) The coconut version came to life much later, perhaps in the late eighteenth or early nineteenth century, probably as an English or perhaps American invention. The coconut was treated much like the almonds, ground with sugar and then combined with egg whites. Whereas almond macaroons were formed into balls, coconut macaroons were shaped into cones. In the nineteenth century, these cookies were made with less sugar and therefore were a bit chewier and drier than the very sweet, almost gooey-textured cookies that we know today.

375 degrees; 400 tended to overcook the bottoms and lower temperatures never produced the sort of browning I was hoping for.

Triple Coconut Macaroons

Cream of coconut, available canned, is a sweetened coconut product commonly used in piña colada cocktails. Note that this is entirely different from coconut cream or coconut milk, both of which are unsweetened. Be sure to mix the can's contents thoroughly before using, since the mixture separates upon standing. Look for unsweetened desiccated coconut in natural food stores or in Asian markets. I am partial to huge, two-fisted cookies, so I call for ¼ cup of batter for each cookie. This also produces a nice contrast between a crispy exterior and a moist interior. However, if you prefer a daintier confection, use just 2 tablespoons and reduce baking time to 16 to 18 minutes. I also found that these cookies are great when the bottom is dipped in chocolate (see variation below). Since the cookie is not overly sweet, the chocolate is a nice complement, not a case of coals to Newcastle. It is best to grease the parchment paper for baking — the cookies are easier to remove.

MAKES 18 COOKIES

- 1 cup cream of coconut
- 2 tablespoons light corn syrup
- 4 large egg whites
- 2 teaspoons vanilla extract
- ½ teaspoon salt
- 3 cups unsweetened desiccated coconut (about 8½ ounces)
- 3 cups sweetened flaked coconut (about 8½ ounces)

1. Adjust an oven rack to upper-middle position and heat oven to 375 degrees. Line 2 cookie sheets with parchment paper and lightly spray parchment with nonstick vegetable cooking spray. (If you don't have any spray, it's okay. The cookies will simply be a bit harder to remove from the paper.)

2. In a small bowl, whisk together cream of coconut, corn syrup, egg whites, vanilla, and salt to combine.

3. In a large bowl, combine unsweetened and sweetened coconuts; toss together with your hands, breaking up any clumps between fingertips. Pour liquid ingredients into dried coconut and mix with rubber spatula until evenly moistened. (If desired, press plastic wrap directly on surface of dough at this point and refrigerate 30 minutes; mixture will be slightly firmer and easier to work with.)

4. Scoop 9 cookies onto the first cookie sheet with a 1¾-inch-diameter ice cream scoop, mounded with ¼ cup dough. (Alternatively, roll ¼ cup dough between palms of hands into golf ball–size balls.) Form cookies into loose haystacks with fingertips or gently flatten with

palm of hand into 2¼-inch rounds, moistening hands with water as necessary to prevent sticking. Bake until light golden brown, about 20 minutes, turning cookie sheet from front to back halfway through baking. Repeat with second sheet.

5. Cool cookies on cookie sheets 2 minutes; remove to wire rack with metal spatula and let cool completely.

WHAT CAN GO WRONG? This is a very simple recipe, since the ingredients are easily combined and then baked. If you mistake coconut cream (unsweetened) for cream of coconut (sweetened), you will dramatically affect the outcome, producing less sweet and less moist cookies. See page 51 for more information.

CHOCOLATE-DIPPED VARIATION
Follow recipe for Triple Coconut Macaroons. Cool baked macaroons to room temperature, about 30 minutes. Line cookie sheet with parchment paper. Melt 8 ounces chopped semisweet chocolate in a small heatproof bowl set over a pan of almost-simmering water, stirring once or twice, until smooth; remove from heat. (To melt chocolate in microwave, heat at 50 percent power for 2 minutes; stir and continue heating at 50 percent 1 minute longer. If chocolate is not yet entirely melted, heat an additional 30 seconds at 50 percent power.) Dip bottom ¾ inch of cookies in chocolate and place on parchment-lined cookie sheet. Refrigerate until chocolate sets, about 30 minutes.

CHOCOLATE MACAROON VARIATION
I tried using unsweetened chocolate to make these macaroons, but the cookies, believe it or not, were not sweet enough. I settled on semisweet chocolate. I started with 4 ounces, decided that the cookies needed a bit more chocolate, and therefore increased the quantity to 6 ounces. I also tried the recipe with 8 ounces of chocolate, and it was too chocolaty.

Melt 6 ounces of semisweet chocolate and

CASE 17: GOING NUTS FOR MACAROONS

Four almond macaroon recipes were baked and compared to find the best combination of ingredients.

Ingredient/ Comments	Recipe A	Recipe B	Recipe C	Recipe D
Almonds	18 tablespoons	13 tablespoons	15 tablespoons	28 tablespoons
Sugar	3 tablespoons brown 2⅓ cups confectioners'	1¾ cup confectioners' ½ cup granulated	18 tablespoons confectioners'	1 cup granulated
Eggs	4 whites	3 whites	1 white	3 tablespoons white
Vanilla extract	1 teaspoon	1 teaspoon	1 teaspoon	None
Other	⅛ teaspoon cream of tartar	2 tablespoons water	1 tablespoon jam	1 teaspoon almond extract
Comments	Sweet, flat, and sticky	Complicated recipe; sweet and gummy	Good, but lacked almond flavor	Very good; low baking temperature solved gumminess

fold into batter with the liquid ingredients at the end of step 3. Bake for 20 to 22 minutes (rotating the sheet halfway through), or until you can just see a bit of color on the tops of the cookies. The bottoms will be slightly browned. Note that it will be very difficult, since these are chocolate cookies, to see when they are taking on color. They should, however, still appear moist and undercooked when done. It is better to slightly undercook these cookies than overcook them, since chocolate macaroons are crunchier and denser than the master recipe (the chocolate hardens as it cools).

ALMOND MACAROONS

I WAS SEARCHING FOR an almond macaroon with a crisp outside, soft, moist center, and nice almond flavor. In addition, I wanted a recipe that was both relatively foolproof and easy to make. The problem was that under the banner of "almond macaroons" there are many different styles of cookies, so I had to do a lot of testing to get a sense of the possibilities.

The first thing I noticed was that there were

two basic approaches: one set of cookies used ground almonds and the other used almond paste. I tried the latter approach first, making recipes from the new *Joy of Cooking, The Fannie Farmer Cookbook,* and *How to Bake,* by Nick Malgieri. I found all of these cookies were gooey on the inside and much too sweet, the sort of macaroon one might find at a suburban mall. In addition, they lacked true almond flavor and a crisp exterior.

I then tested four recipes that used ground almonds instead of almond paste. These tests uncovered many useful techniques. First, granulated sugar was the winner over confectioners', since the flavor and texture were better. Second, a low oven temperature — 300 degrees — was better than higher oven temperatures. One recipe actually called for baking the cookies at a whopping 450 degrees, which gave one little margin for error. I also found that two of the recipes I tested were achingly sweet, using, in one case, over 2 cups of sugar, whereas my favorite recipe, recipe D in the chart, used a mere 1 cup. Too many egg whites also made the cookies gummy, a texture I was not fond of. Other recipes were unnecessarily complicated, calling, for example, for a sugar syrup, which is time-consuming and unnecessary. I also discounted recipes that called for beating the whites, since this made more of a meringue than a macaroon; instead I simply added them to the dough mixture.

So I put together a working recipe that included 1¾ cups almonds, 1 cup sugar, and 1 large egg white. Just to validate my suspicions about the test recipes, I tested confectioners' sugar head-to-head with granulated, and the latter produced a crispier and better-tasting cookie. Whipping the egg white resulted in a dry, airy cookie. I tested both vanilla and almond extract, and the latter won hands down. (One French recipe called for bitter apricot kernels, but these are impossible to find.) Salt, a necessary ingredient in all of baking, did not work here. I could taste a mere ¼ teaspoon, and the flavor was unwelcome.

One cookbook author suggested letting the piped cookies sit for 2 hours before baking, in an effort to make them hold their shape better in the oven. This turned out to work, but I regard this step as optional, since it markedly complicates the recipe. I had already determined in other testing that a lower baking temperature was best for crisp cookies, drying out the center to a nice moist but not gooey consistency. However, since this was a different breed of cookie, I tested again — at 300, 325, and 350 degrees. The lowest temperature was best, producing a moist interior with a nice light color as well.

⋯

Crisp, Chewy Almond Macaroons

Ground almonds rather than almond paste make the best almond macaroon, with real almond flavor and a chewy, not gooey, consistency. The egg whites should not be beaten, the sugar level should be modest, and the oven temperature should be relatively low.

MAKES ABOUT 24 COOKIES

1¾ cups blanched slivered or chopped almonds
1¼ cups granulated sugar
3 large egg whites, at room temperature
1 teaspoon pure almond extract
Sparkling sugar or confectioners' sugar for the
    tops of the cookies

1. Line two cookie sheets with parchment paper.

2. In the bowl of a food processor, place the almonds and the sugar and process (using the metal blade) until the almonds are a fine powder, almost 1 minute. Add the egg whites and almond extract and process until most of the mixture forms a clump and starts rotating around the bowl, 10 to 15 seconds. The batter will be thick and very sticky.

3. Using a pastry bag and a large plain tip,

pipe round knobs about 1¼ inches wide onto the cookie sheets, leaving about 1½ inches between cookies. You can also make somewhat larger cookies (about 2 inches in diameter) using a number 24 ice cream scoop (dip it in water every third cookie so the batter does not stick), but a pastry bag is easier. Moisten your fingertips with water and pat down any peaks on the cookies. Sprinkle with sparkling sugar or sift confectioners' sugar over the tops of the cookies. Let sit for 1 hour but no more than 2. (The waiting period is optional, but the cookies will hold their shape better and not crack as much if they sit before baking.)

4. At least 20 minutes prior to baking, adjust a rack to the center position and heat the oven to 300 degrees. Bake the cookies, one sheet at a time, for about 20 minutes, reversing the cookie sheet front to back halfway through. The cookies will be lightly browned and dry-looking. They will be firm to the touch. Let cool on the pan for 5 minutes and then remove the sheet of parchment to a rack and cool completely. Cookies may then be stored in an airtight container.

WHAT CAN GO WRONG? This batter is extremely sticky, so if you use your hands to shape the cookies, you will need to moisten your fingertips. The size of the cookie will affect cooking times, so watch for light browning and a dry-looking exterior as your guide to when they are done.

MOLASSES SPICE COOKIES

I GREW UP WITH molasses cookies that were as large as a boy's fist, with floured bottoms and a rich, chewy center a ten-year-old could get lost in. Although the local baker in our town in Vermont passed away a few years back, I was determined to find a method for preparing these rich, perfect rounds of baked dough at home for my kids. I started with a recipe given to me by Rose-

marie Brophy, whose son makes her molasses cookies for a Boston restaurant. After one bite, I knew that they were much like the cookies I had enjoyed in the old farmhouse. To get them just right, however, I performed a series of tests, beginning with how to deal with the butter and sugar. Creaming them (beating them together until they are light and fluffy) produced a lighter-textured cookie than using melted butter. Another trick I use for making thick, chewy cookies, chilling the dough before baking, worked here as well. The cold dough doesn't spread out as readily, resulting in a thicker cookie. The proper amount of sugar was also crucial. Too little and the cookies tend to be hard and dry. I tried different quantities and settled on 1 cup of sugar to ¼ cup of molasses. I tested using baking soda and baking powder in different quantities. When I used a full 2 teaspoons of soda, the cookies browned too quickly and spread out flat on the baking sheet. I discovered that this excessive amount of baking soda causes too much of a chemical reaction (the soda reacts with the acid in the molasses, producing carbon dioxide bubbles which produce lift). This causes the delicate cookie structure to rupture, resulting in fallen cookies. I ended up using 1 teaspoon of baking powder, which produced just the right amount of lift and a nice, thick cookie. The most important factor, however, was the size of the cookie. Roll the dough into large, 1¼-inch-diameter balls. This ensures that the inside of the cookies will remain moist when the outside becomes properly cooked.

...

Molasses Spice Cookies

Be sure to make the cookies large enough. Cookies that are too small will cook through, resulting in a drier, tougher confection.

MAKES 20 TO 24 COOKIES

12 tablespoons (1½ sticks) unsalted butter, softened but still firm

1 cup granulated sugar
1 large egg
¼ cup molasses
2¼ cups all-purpose flour
1 teaspoon baking powder
¼ teaspoon salt
½ teaspoon ground cloves
1 teaspoon cinnamon
1 teaspoon ground ginger
Granulated sugar for dipping

1. Beat the butter and sugar in the bowl of an electric mixer or with a wooden spoon until creamy and smooth, about 3 minutes. Add the egg and molasses and beat until fully incorporated. In a separate bowl, whisk together the remaining ingredients (except the sugar for dipping) and then stir into the butter-sugar mixture. Cover bowl with plastic wrap and chill dough for 2 hours. Heat oven to 350 degrees. Line two cookie sheets with parchment paper.

2. Shape dough into large, walnut-size balls. Dip tops in sugar. Place 3 inches apart on lined baking sheets. Bake, one sheet at a time, for about 12 minutes, rotating the pan front to back halfway through. (Refrigerate the second sheet while the first one is baking.) Cookies will appear undercooked when removed from the oven; the centers will still be very moist and light. Remove cookies, still on parchment, to a rack; as they cool, the cookies will harden.

WHAT CAN GO WRONG? This is an easy recipe. Be sure to remove these cookies from the oven when they still look underbaked.

GINGERSNAPS

TWO COMMON SHORTCOMINGS in gingersnaps are, first, that they have no snap and, second, that the mix of spices can be overpowering to the point that the flavor is muddy and dull. I wanted a truly snappy gingersnap, and clean flavors so that I could actually taste each individual spice.

I made several batches from various cookbooks, including *Maida Heatter's Book of Great Cookies; Stars Desserts,* by Emily Luchetti; *Rosie's All-Butter Fresh Cream Sugar-Packed Baking Book,* by Judy Rosenberg; *Classic Home Desserts,* by Richard Sax; and an old recipe from the *Boston Globe* for Alice Read's Molasses Sugar Cookies. (Case 18 shows how the ingredient lists compared.)

Some of these recipes had decent texture — the ratio of 2½ cups flour to 1½ sticks butter with 1 whole egg seemed about right — but many of the cookies had too many spices. In addition, the type and amount of sugar seemed problematic, vinegar was a really bad idea, and the use of shortening instead of butter was similarly questionable. These cookies need the pure taste of butter. Based on these observations, I devised a working recipe using ¾ cup granulated sugar, ¾ cup brown sugar, 2½ cups flour, 1½ sticks butter, 1 egg, ¼ cup molasses, 2 teaspoons baking soda, and spices.

My first set of tests involved the sugar. My working recipe yielded a cookie that was a bit sweet, so I reduced the granulated sugar to ½ cup and preferred the resulting cookie. Then I tried cutting back on the dark brown sugar, to ½ cup, but the cookie was not sweet enough and also lacked flavor. I felt that the cookie needed a full ¼ cup of molasses (but no more), so my final sugar formula was left as ½ cup granulated and ¾ cup dark brown.

The ratio of 2½ cups flour to 1½ sticks butter with 1 egg worked well. The dough was easy to work with, and the cookies were snappy with a nice butter flavor that married well with the molasses. However, I did want to try using less baking soda and even try substituting baking powder. First I reduced the soda to 1 teaspoon, and the cookies had a nice texture, a little less compact but still snappy. Then I took the soda down to ½ teaspoon and still had a great cookie. The cookies were again a tiny bit lighter

CASE 18: CAN ANYONE PUT BACK THE SNAP IN GINGERSNAP?

Looking for the secret to a snappy gingersnap.

Ingredient	Recipe A	Recipe B	Recipe C	Recipe D	Recipe E
Flour	2 cups plus 2 tablespoons	2¼ cups	2½ cups	3¼ cups	2 cups
Baking soda	2 teaspoons	2 teaspoons	2 teaspoons	1½ teaspoons	2 teaspoons
Salt	½ teaspoon	½ teaspoon	½ teaspoon	None	1 teaspoon
Ginger	2 teaspoons	2 teaspoons	5 teaspoons	2 tablespoons	1 teaspoon
Cloves	½ teaspoon	None	None	¼ teaspoon	None
Cinnamon	1 teaspoon	1 teaspoon	2 teaspoons	½ teaspoon	1 teaspoon
Allspice	¼ teaspoon	½ teaspoon	None	None	None
Pepper	¼ teaspoon	¼ teaspoon	None	None	None
Butter	1½ sticks	2 sticks	1½ sticks	1½ sticks	¾ cup shortening
Sugar	1 cup dark brown	1 cup granulated, ½ cup light brown	1 cup dark brown	2 cups granulated	1 cup granulated
Molasses	¼ cup	⅓ cup	¼ cup	½ cup	¼ cup
Eggs	1	1	1	2	1
Other				2 teaspoons vinegar	

and higher but still snappy. Next I tried using baking powder instead and got a soft, "no-snap" gingersnap. Finally, I tried a combination of baking powder and baking soda, and the result was, once again, a soft cookie. So a mere ½ teaspoon of baking soda was the winner.

For spices, I was looking for a delicate balance of ginger, cinnamon, and molasses, while avoiding some of the spicier additions such as ground black pepper, since a truly spicy cookie would not fare well with kids. I tried several combinations, including nutmeg and cloves, but settled on a simple combination of ginger, cinnamon, and allspice. The allspice adds a mild peppery flavor, and the cookies seemed flat-tasting without the cinnamon. Two teaspoons of ginger was just the right amount for a nice zing without being overpowering.

In terms of oven temperature, I tried both 325 and 350 degrees and found the cookies to be crispier and lighter at 350 degrees. The 325-degree cookies were just a touch moist.

▪▪▪

Snappy Gingersnaps

To my surprise, baking powder makes a soft cookie, whereas baking soda makes a snappier product. In this recipe, I have toned down the spices so that they are more delicately balanced than in recipes that use truckloads of the stuff. The low oven temperature also contributes to a snappy texture.

MAKES ABOUT 24 COOKIES

12	tablespoons (1½ sticks) unsalted butter, softened but still firm
½	cup granulated sugar
¾	cup packed dark brown sugar
1	large egg
¼	cup molasses
2½	cups all-purpose flour
½	teaspoon baking soda
½	teaspoon salt
2	teaspoons ground ginger
½	teaspoon allspice
½	teaspoon cinnamon

Granulated sugar for dipping cookie dough

1. Beat the butter and sugars in the bowl of an electric mixer or with a wooden spoon until creamy and smooth, about 3 minutes. Add the egg and molasses and beat until fully incorporated. In a separate bowl, whisk together the remaining ingredients (except the sugar for dipping) and then stir into the butter-sugar mixture. Cover bowl with plastic wrap and chill dough for 2 hours. Heat oven to 350 degrees. Line two cookie sheets with parchment paper.

2. Shape dough into large, walnut-size balls and dip tops in granulated sugar. Place 3 inches apart on lined baking sheets. Bake, one sheet at a time, for about 12 minutes, turning pan front to back halfway through. (Refrigerate second sheet while the first is baking.) Cookies will appear undercooked when removed from the oven; the centers will still be very moist and light. Remove cookies, still on parchment, to a wire rack; as they cool, the cookies will harden. Store in an airtight container.

WHAT CAN GO WRONG? This is another easy recipe, and overbaking is the only major problem. Be sure to chill the dough properly before baking to produce thick cookies.

▾▾▾

MADELEINES

MADELEINES ARE SHELL-SHAPED sponge-cake cookies that should be eaten soon after baking. As Bruce Healy, author of *The French Cookie Book,* says, "Don't even think about trying to keep them overnight." I did, in fact, test this theory and found it to be true. They quickly dry out or become sticky when left to sit. The solution, therefore, is simply to place the batter in the refrigerator for up to a few hours (cover the bowl with plastic wrap) and then bake the cookies when you need them. I found that this chilling period also gives more rise to the cookies; they develop a pronounced hump in the middle during baking.

Another problem with madeleines is one of preparation. That is, soft butter must be beaten and then folded into a relatively light batter. This is quite difficult to do and often results in small pieces of butter floating around intact and unincorporated in the batter. I decided, therefore, to simply melt the butter and stir it into the batter, which worked just fine. I found no deterioration in texture. I also noted that many recipes call for a 450-degree oven, which I feel is too hot. The cookies puff up dramatically and often come out hunchback, displaying a curiously misshapen form. A more moderate 350-degree oven works best, producing pleasing, evenly shaped cookies more like Venus than Quasimodo.

···

Madeleines

MAKES 24 COOKIES

Butter and flour for preparing pans

1	cup plus 1 tablespoon cake flour
½	teaspoon baking powder
¼	teaspoon salt
¾	cup granulated sugar
3	large eggs, at room temperature
1	large egg yolk, at room temperature
1½	teaspoons vanilla extract
½	teaspoon lemon oil
10	tablespoons (1¼ sticks) unsalted butter, melted and cooled

1. Adjust a rack to the lower third of your oven. Butter and flour well two madeleine pans and heat the oven to 350 degrees. Sift the flour, baking powder, and salt onto a piece of waxed paper. Set aside.

2. In a medium bowl, beat the sugar, eggs, and yolk on medium-high speed with an electric mixer until pale yellow and thick, about 3 minutes. Add the vanilla and lemon oil and mix for an additional 20 seconds. Fold the sifted dry ingredients into the egg mixture with a rubber spatula. When almost incorporated, add the butter and continue to fold until the batter is completely mixed.

3. Using a number 40 ice cream scoop or a spoon, fill each shell with 1½ tablespoons batter, or about three-quarters full. Bake for 12 to 15 minutes, or until the cookies are lightly browned around the edges and light golden on top. (Madeleine pans are smaller than baking sheets, so put both pans in the oven, on the same rack. Turn the pans front to back after 6 or 7 minutes.) Unmold and let cool shell side down. Best served soon. Do not hold overnight.

WHAT CAN GO WRONG? The most common problem with these cookies is that they tend to puff up in the center, producing a pronounced bulge. I found that a more moderate oven temperature tends to avoid this. If your cookies develop a hump, try reducing the oven temperature 25 degrees for the next batch.

MAKING MERINGUE COOKIES

THE PROBLEM WITH most meringue recipes is that they are too bloody sweet. I remember taking my kids to Paris, where they encountered huge meringue orbs in Easter yellow and bright pink. One bite, however, was enough to convince even a ten-year-old that these cookies were beyond the pale of edibility. They were achingly sweet and also curiously flavorless.

The basic method for making meringues is simple enough. Egg whites are beaten with cream of tartar and sugar and flavorings are added; the batter is then formed into shapes, baked in a low oven, and allowed to dry in the oven with the heat turned off. Reviewing a few recipes, I noted that the basic ratio of egg whites to sugar was on the order of ¼ cup sugar per white. I immediately scaled down that ratio by half and had much better results. I continued testing nonetheless, ending up with slightly under 2 tablespoons of sugar per egg white. Finally, I had produced a meringue cookie I would actually want to eat.

Next, I discovered that most recipes produced a pitiful number of cookies, since they used only a few egg whites. If you are going to go to the trouble of making meringues, you might as well do a large batch, so I upped the number of egg whites to an even dozen. One recipe I found suggested using a mixture of granulated and confectioners' sugar; this was superior to granulated alone, since it yielded a finer texture and a more durable cookie. I also tried making a sugar syrup and then beating this into the egg whites (this is an Italian meringue). This cooks the whites somewhat, and the results were disappointing, since the outside was done long before the inside was dry (the recipe was also more difficult). Although cream of tartar is almost always called for in meringue recipes, I did test it, and I found that both the color and texture were slightly improved with the cream of tartar, although this would not be noticeable except in a side-by-side taste test. Vanilla is a nice addition, but too much can overpower the delicate meringue.

As for oven temperatures, 250 degrees was as good as 225 degrees and took less time; higher oven temperatures overcooked the exterior before fully drying out the interior.

• • •

Meringue Cookies

The conventional wisdom about meringues is true: they will not dry properly on a hot, humid day. Only make this recipe during cooler, dry weather.

MAKES ABOUT 18 COOKIES

12   large egg whites
⅛   teaspoon cream of tartar
½   cup granulated sugar
½   teaspoon vanilla extract
½   cup toasted chopped hazelnuts, almonds, or pecans (optional)
½   cup confectioners' sugar
½   cup semisweet chocolate chips (optional) (I like the tiny chips best)

1. Heat the oven to 250 degrees and adjust a rack to the center position. Line a cookie sheet with parchment.

2. In a large bowl, beat the egg whites with an electric mixer until frothy. Add the cream of tartar and beat until soft peaks form. Gradually add the granulated sugar and beat until the meringue is shiny and smooth and will hold a 2-inch peak. Beat in the vanilla.

3. If using the optional nuts, grind them with the confectioners' sugar in the bowl of a food processor until they are very finely chopped. Fold them along with the optional chocolate chips into the meringue. If not using the nuts, sift the confectioners' sugar over the meringue and fold until incorporated (see illustrations, page 8).

4. Using a spatula or large spoon, drop blobs of meringue onto the cookie sheet, about 3 tablespoons each. The funky shapes are part of the fun of this recipe. (If you prefer more professional-looking meringues, pipe out the cookies using a plastic storage bag with one corner cut off.) Bake for 1 hour 30 minutes, turning the pan front to back halfway through. The meringues should be very lightly colored, stiff, and dry. Turn off the oven, leaving door closed, and let the meringues cool completely in the oven — about 4 hours. If you can, it is even better to let the cookies sit in the oven overnight, to make sure that they dry out completely. Store in an airtight container.

WHAT CAN GO WRONG? Meringues should only be baked on cool, dry days; hot, humid weather makes it impossible for them to dry properly. I have also found that even small differences in oven temperature can quickly lead to overbrowning of the meringues, so you should watch them very carefully as they bake.

• • •

Cat's Tongues

These thin, dumbbell-shaped cookies are a French classic. I tested using whole eggs versus egg whites and found that the former produced a slightly richer-tasting cookie, which I pre-

ferred. In terms of sugar, some recipes use gran-ulated and others use confectioners'. I prefer the former, since the cookies turn out crisper. Curiously, an electric mixer is not recom-mended here, since the resulting batter is too loose. It is best to use either a wooden spoon or a whisk. I also found that it was best to chill the batter, since it made the cookies easier to pipe through a pastry bag. This batter can also be baked off in simple rounds instead of the classic cat tongue shape.

MAKES ABOUT 60 COOKIES

8   tablespoons (1 stick) unsalted butter, softened but still firm
½   cup granulated sugar
1   large egg, at room temperature
1   teaspoon vanilla extract
¾   cup all-purpose flour
Pinch of salt

1. Adjust an oven rack to the center position and heat oven to 400 degrees. In a medium bowl, using a wooden spoon (not an electric mixer), cream the butter until it is white and smooth and very soft. Add the sugar and stir to combine. Switch to a whisk and add the egg, mixing about 20 seconds, or until fully com-bined. Whisk in the vanilla.

2. Sift the flour and salt over the mixture and stir with the wooden spoon to fully combine. Place batter in the refrigerator to chill for 20 to 30 minutes.

3. Line a cookie sheet with parchment paper and prepare a pastry bag with a small plain tip (about ⁵⁄₁₆ inch, or Ateco #3). Fill the pastry bag with the batter and pipe cookies into a dumb-bell shape. Each cookie should be about 2½ inches long, and they should be about 2 inches apart.

4. Bake 5 to 6 minutes, or until the edges are browned and the centers are still pale. Remove from oven and cool on a rack. Repeat as neces-sary until all the batter is baked. Store cooled cookies in an airtight container.

WHAT CAN GO WRONG? These are not the easi-est cookies, since it is important NOT to use an electric mixer, which produces a very loose bat-ter. A wooden spoon is the best implement. Also, you may not have the right size tip to make these shapes (smaller sizes just won't work very well — I know, I've tried them). You could improvise by using a plastic freezer bag with one corner cut off. You will find it difficult to get the perfect dumbbell shape. Of course, you can simply pipe out the dough into a simple tongue shape if you like.

BISCOTTI

THESE ITALIAN CLASSICS have been American-ized to such an extent that it is hard to remem-ber what the original recipe was like. Classic biscotti contain a low proportion of fat to flour, which results in a very hard, tooth-breaking cookie that must be dunked in either coffee or sweet wine before eating. I find this sort of bis-cotti not very practical for an American cook, since we are much more likely to want to eat biscotti as we would any other cookie — with-out dunking first. At the other extreme, how-ever, are cakey biscotti that are too tender and sandy, almost like a shortbread. These Ameri-can misfits are a different recipe altogether, one that has none of the charm of real biscotti. So I set out to find a good compromise, a cookie that could be eaten on its own without dunking, yet one that still had some real snap to it.

The first issue was the ratio of eggs to flour. Some recipes use only 1 egg or egg yolk per cup of flour, others use close to 2. I liked the lower proportion better, since too many eggs made the biscotti too soft and crumbly. Butter is another common biscotti ingredient. Most recipes I have seen use roughly 2 tablespoons of butter per cup of flour; I found that this was a good proportion. Some recipes also call for creaming the butter and sugar together, but I found that melted butter worked just fine and was easier. I decided that I liked the nuts in small pieces, while most recipes call for them whole. I think any size is acceptable — I just don't like biting into a whole almond. Finally, I decided to use a slightly higher proportion of sugar to flour than is the case with many traditional Italian recipes; this helps to tenderize the dough.

• • •

Master Recipe for Biscotti

Biscotti will hold well in an airtight container, since they are relatively low in fat. This recipe makes small cookies in comparison with the gargantuan Paul Bunyan–style biscotti one usually sees today.

MAKES ABOUT 3 DOZEN COOKIES

2   cups all-purpose flour
¾   cup granulated sugar
1   teaspoon baking powder
¼   teaspoon salt
¾   cup almonds (slivered, sliced, or whole)
2   large eggs, at room temperature
4   tablespoons melted butter
2   teaspoons anise extract or pure anise
     flavoring OR 1 teaspoon vanilla extract

1. Adjust a rack to the center position and heat the oven to 350 degrees. Line a cookie sheet with parchment paper. Place the flour, sugar, baking powder, salt, and nuts in a large bowl and stir to combine. In a small bowl, combine the eggs, butter, and anise or vanilla and whisk to fully combine. Make a well in the center of the dry ingredients and pour in the egg mixture. Using a rubber spatula, mix to combine until a rough dough forms.

2. Turn out the dough onto a work surface and knead a couple of times, or until the dough comes together, adding extra flour sparingly and only if necessary to avoid sticking. Start to form the dough into a big, fat cigar and cut it in half. Form each half into a cigar shape or log

about 1 inch thick, 2 inches wide, and about 12 inches long. Place logs onto the cookie sheet and press lightly with your fingers to slightly flatten.

3. Bake for 25 minutes, rotating the pan halfway through. The bars (cigars) will be firm to the touch and just slightly browned. Remove from the oven and lower the temperature to 300 degrees. Let the bars cool on the cookie sheet for 15 minutes.

4. Remove bars to a cutting board using two spatulas. Using a serrated knife, cut the bars diagonally into slices about ½ inch thick to form the biscotti. Lay them back on the cookie sheet with either cut side down and place back in the oven for 15 minutes. Turn each cookie to expose the other cut side and place back in the oven for another 15 minutes. The cookies will take on the slightest bit of color and feel firm and dry. Let cool on a wire rack to room temperature. Store in an airtight container.

WHAT CAN GO WRONG? Shaping the lengths of dough into logs is not hard but is something new for most home bakers. The dough starts off as a long cylinder when it is placed on the baking sheet. Then it must be slightly flattened on top so that it has only a modest arc. The dough should be neither flat nor totally round on top when you are done.

FIG AND ORANGE VARIATION

Omit the anise in the master recipe. Reduce the sugar to ½ cup. Soak ¾ cup diced dried figs in 2 tablespoons orange liqueur for 30 minutes or so. Add the figs to the dry ingredients and the liqueur to the wet. Also add the finely chopped zest of 1 large orange to the dry ingredients. Add ¼ cup honey and 1 teaspoon vanilla to the wet.

CHOCOLATE-COFFEE VARIATION

Omit the anise and almonds in the master recipe. Add ¾ cup chocolate chips, ¾ cup roughly chopped hazelnuts, ½ teaspoon cinnamon, and ¼ teaspoon ground cloves to the dry

CASE 19: CORNMEAL COOKIES LIGHT

Baking powder makes a lighter cookie.

Ingredient	Recipe A	Recipe B	Recipe C	Recipe D	Recipe E
Butter	16 table-spoons	12 table-spoons	3½ table-spoons	11 table-spoons	12 table-spoons
Sugar	1 cup gran-ulated	¾ cup gran-ulated	½ cup confec-tioners'	9½ table-spoons granulated	¾ cup gran-ulated
Eggs	1 + 1 yolk	1	2 yolks	2	2
Flour	1½ cups	15 table-spoons	10 table-spoons	1½ cups	1¾ cups
Cornmeal	1 cup	⅔ cup	½ cup	1 cup + 3 tablespoons	12 table-spoons
Salt	½ teaspoon	Pinch	None	¾ teaspoon	Pinch
Other	2 teaspoon vanilla	Zest of 1 lemon	Zest of 1 lemon	2 teaspoons baking powder, ¾ cup rum-soaked raisins	

ingredients. Add 1 tablespoon instant espresso powder dissolved in 2 tablespoons hot water to the wet ingredients.

CHOCOLATE VARIATION

Omit the almonds in the master recipe and use vanilla extract instead of the anise. Substitute ¼ cup cocoa powder for ¼ cup of the flour in the original recipe. Stir ¾ cup semisweet chocolate chips into the dry ingredients.

REDISCOVERING CORNMEAL COOKIES

THERE ARE TWO Italian cookies — zaletti and crumiri — that qualify as cornmeal cookies, and the French also have a recipe similar to the zaletti. Unfortunately, cornmeal cookies are often very heavy, rustic cookies, and I was looking for something lighter and more buttery. I started my research by baking cookies from the new *Joy of Cooking, Classic Home Desserts, The French Cookie Book,* and two recipes from *The Italian Baker,* by Carol Field. (See Case 19 for a side-by-side comparison of ingredients.) The only recipe that proved worth making again was recipe D, since it contained baking powder. All the others, since they did not contain any leavener, were heavy and hard. Using that recipe as a starting point, I went back into the kitchen.

My first idea was to use polenta (a coarsely ground cornmeal) instead of the regular finely ground variety. (All of the recipes I had tested up to this point used finely ground cornmeal.) The corn flavor was much better, and the extra crunch in the texture was a bonus. Since I liked the addition of baking powder, I tested quantity and settled on 2 teaspoons: less powder and the cookies were too heavy, and when I increased the amount, the cookies exploded in the center, resulting in a somewhat heavier texture. (Too much leavener can make a cookie rise too much, which results in a fallen cookie, since the dough cannot support the vigorous rise.) Salt was adjusted to ½ teaspoon, and the amount of sugar was decreased to ½ cup (8 tablespoons).

I tried to increase the amount of butter in the dough, but I found that this was impossible — the dough became greasy and difficult to handle. Next, although the consistency of the dough was nice and the cookies baked off to a light texture, I wanted to test whether more egg yolk and less white could result in a richer color and better flavor. Using 1 whole egg and 2 yolks did not significantly change the taste or texture (I had been using 2 whole eggs up to this point), and when I tested using all yolks, the cookies were too yellow and the flavor was unappealing. Last, I wanted to test the vanilla, raisins, and lemon flavors. While I did not care for vanilla in this cookie, I liked both the raisins and lemon zest (but not when used together). Therefore, the basic recipe below uses just the lemon zest, and I have added a variation that omits the lemon and incorporates rum-soaked raisins.

...

Cornmeal Cookies

This is a lighter, more refined version of two Italian cookies — zaletti and crumiri — that tend to be heavy, rustic offerings, usually made without any baking powder or soda. Note that this recipe calls for a coarsely ground cornmeal (often referred to as polenta). Using a finely ground cornmeal will dramatically affect the recipe and is not recommended. These cookies are also good made with raisins (soaked in rum for an even better flavor) instead of lemon zest (see variation below). Many traditional recipes call for shaping the dough into a log and then cutting off individual cookies. I find it much easier to use a small ice cream scoop or large spoon to shape individual cookies.

MAKES ABOUT 4 DOZEN COOKIES

1½   cups all-purpose flour
1   cup polenta or coarsely ground cornmeal
2   teaspoons baking powder
½   teaspoon salt
11   tablespoons unsalted butter, softened but still firm
½   cup granulated sugar
2   large eggs, at room temperature
Zest of 1 medium lemon, finely chopped

1. Adjust a rack to the center position and heat the oven to 375 degrees. Line a cookie sheet with parchment paper. Sift the flour, polenta, baking powder, and salt onto a piece of waxed paper and set aside.

2. Place the butter and sugar in a large mixing bowl and with an electric mixer on medium-high speed beat for 3 minutes. The mixture will be light-colored and fluffy. Add the eggs one at a time and beat for about 30 seconds each, or until incorporated. Add the flour mixture and lemon zest to the butter mixture and mix on low speed until the dough is fully incorporated, about 2 minutes. The dough will hold its shape but be fairly pliable. It should not feel sticky.

3. Using a number 40 scoop or a large spoon, place 2-tablespoon mounds of dough onto the cookie sheet about 1 inch apart.

4. Bake for about 15 minutes, turning the cookie sheet front to back halfway through the baking time. The cookies will look puffy and very slightly browned when they are done.

5. Cool 10 minutes and then remove from the sheet and cool on a rack to room temperature. Repeat as needed with fresh sheets of parchment until all the dough is baked. Store cooled cookies in an airtight container.

WHAT CAN GO WRONG? This is an easy dough to make. Just don't overbake these cookies. These cookies are best made with a coarsely ground cornmeal. If you use a regular supermarket brand, they will lack crunch and flavor.

RUM-SOAKED RAISIN VARIATION

Omit lemon zest from recipe. Soak ⅔ cup raisins in 3 tablespoons rum for at least 30 minutes. Drain them, toss with the flour in step 2, and then add the flour and raisins, as indicated in the recipe, to the butter mixture.

LADYFINGERS

THE FIRST QUESTION I asked myself about these cookies was whether they are really worth making at home. Well, the answer is yes and no. The batter is relatively straightforward: flour, whipped egg whites, and yolks beaten with sugar are all mixed together and then piped into finger lengths. They bake up quickly and taste great. The big problem is having the correct size pastry tube, which must have a large, ¾-inch-wide opening. Smaller tubes will yield funny-looking fingers, hardly befitting a lady. An easy solution is to make your pastry tube with a plastic freezer bag, cutting off one corner of it to the right size. You will not need a tip. These cookies are substantially better than the store-

bought version, and if I were making a dessert that called for ladyfingers, such as tiramisù, a charlotte, or a trifle, I would probably go to the trouble. Of course, they can be served with a simple fruit dessert such as poached pears.

Most recipes for ladyfingers are quite similar; the testing was simply a matter of adjusting the proportions of ingredients to get a light, spongy, but still moist cookie. I started testing with a recipe that called for 4 eggs, 1 cup flour, and ½ cup sugar. This recipe produced cookies that were tough and dry, so I cut the flour to ¾ cup and they were greatly improved. I tried increasing the sugar to ⅔ cup, but the cookies were too sweet, so the original ½ cup was best. Although all ladyfinger recipes call for separating the eggs, I did try one version in which I simply beat the whole eggs, but the cookies were much too dense.

During my research I also found two unusual ingredients: potato flour, which yielded a slightly off flavor, and orange flower water, which was also odd. Stick to the basics.

▪ ▪ ▪

Ladyfingers
(Sponge-Cake Cookies)

If the ladyfingers are to be used to line a bowl in another recipe, the batter can be piped in a continuous series of closely spaced S shapes. Then the whole cookie sheet's worth of ladyfingers can be moved in one piece or cut into large pieces and moved. This is easier than placing one ladyfinger at a time into the bowl.

MAKES ABOUT 4 DOZEN COOKIES

¾ cup all-purpose flour

⅛ teaspoon salt

4 large eggs, separated, at room temperature

⅛ teaspoon cream of tartar

½ cup granulated sugar

1 teaspoon vanilla extract

Confectioners' sugar for sifting (optional)

1. Adjust a rack to the middle position and heat the oven to 400 degrees. Line a cookie sheet with parchment paper. Sift together the flour and salt onto a piece of waxed paper and set aside.

2. In the bowl of an electric mixer, beat the whites on high speed until foamy. Add the cream of tartar and beat until soft peaks form. Gradually beat in ¼ cup of the sugar and beat until the whites will hold a 2-inch peak. Remove whites to a large bowl. In the same bowl used for beating the whites (the bowl does not need to be cleaned), beat the yolks and the remaining ¼ cup sugar on high speed until very light-colored and thickened, about 5 minutes. Add the vanilla and beat another 30 seconds.

3. Fold one-quarter of the yolk mixture into the whites and when almost incorporated fold the rest of the yolk mixture into the whites. Fold the flour into the mixture. Prepare a pastry bag with a fairly large plain tip (about ¾ inch) or place the batter in a large plastic freezer bag and cut off one corner so that the hole is ¾ inch in diameter. Pipe the ladyfingers onto the prepared sheet in strips about 5 inches long and about 1 inch apart. Sift confectioners' sugar over the top of the cookies if you like.

4. Bake about 10 minutes, rotating the sheet front to back halfway through the baking time. When done, the ladyfingers should be golden brown. Remove the ladyfingers, still on the parchment, to a wire rack.

5. Pipe remaining batter onto a fresh sheet of parchment, slide onto cookie sheet, and bake. When all the cookies are baked and cooled, remove them from the parchment with a spatula and store in an airtight container.

WHAT CAN GO WRONG? The key here is having the right size pastry tube, or simply make your own piping tube by cutting off the corner of a plastic storage bag. Cookies made using smaller tube sizes will not be wide enough.

TUILES

A TUILE IS A THIN, very buttery cookie made with almonds which is cooled over a rolling pin or bottle to resemble a curved roof tile (*tuile* is French for "tile"). Tuiles can be shaped, however, in any manner of ways, including into baskets (the hot, still-pliable cookie is draped over a muffin cup or similar mold to cool), which are then filled with ice cream, mousse, Bavarian cream, fresh fruit, pastry cream, et cetera.

Although these thin, shaped, buttery cookies are common in restaurants, they are not as common in cookbooks, a fact I discovered when I went to research the recipe. But this is a good recipe for home cooks: the batter is easy to make, it can be used for special occasions when presentation is important, and a high degree of skill is not necessary. The batter is a mixture of butter (melted or soft), flour (cake or all-purpose), sugar, eggs (whites only or whole), almonds (chopped, ground, or whole), salt, and flavorings. I tested two recipes, one from *Joy of Cooking* and one from *The French Cookie Book,* and discovered that I preferred the nuts in the batter rather than sprinkled on top, that the butter content had to be adjusted to provide flavor without being overpowering, and that whole eggs provided a richer flavor than did egg whites alone. One recipe did not use salt, which turned out to be a mistake, since the flavor was lackluster.

At this point, creating my own recipe was easily accomplished by combining the sugar and nuts in a bowl, stirring in the eggs and vanilla, sifting the flour over this mixture, stirring, and then adding the melted butter. Nothing could be simpler. The problem came in removing the cookies from the baking sheet. They stuck to everything! (On page 11 I discuss the use of Silpat, a reusable cookie sheet liner. This is the only surface to which the tuiles did not stick.) I found that one solution was to use

CASE 20: RULES FOR TUILES

Which ingredients produce a crisp, flavorful tuile cookie and an easy-to-work dough?

Test	Comments
Cake flour instead of all-purpose	Cookies were too delicate
Softened butter, not melted	Butter hard to incorporate fully
Just egg yolks	Cookies too "eggy"
Just egg whites	Not rich enough
1 whole egg plus 1 white	Good flavor; crisp but not brittle cookies
Less flour	Hard to work with the batter
More flour	Bland flavor
Less sugar	Not crisp or sweet enough
Butter variations	2 tablespoons provided good flavor and also a crisp cookie; more butter made cookies too soft
400-degree oven	Cookies burned too easily; not crisp
350-degree oven	Crisper cookies; easier to control baking

parchment paper, but it needed to be lightly buttered. The other problem was timing. The hot cookies need to be draped over wine bottles or rolling pins, so be sure to have enough of them ready. The cookies will cool and stiffen quickly, and that is no time to be searching frantically for one more wine bottle.

I then went back to my recipe and tried to vary the ingredients (Case 20 shows the results). After a great many kitchen tests, I settled on all-purpose flour, a modest amount of butter, enough sugar to crisp up the cookies, 1 whole egg plus 1 white for flavor and texture, and melted butter over softened butter. I was also surprised that the lower oven temperature actually produced a crisper cookie than the 400-degree oven. I finally had what I considered to be the best and easiest-to-make tuile recipe.

▪ ▪ ▪

Tuiles (Shaped Almond Cookies)

If you have Silpat or another reusable, nonstick cookie sheet liner, this is a good time to use it.

The batter is actually easy to prepare. The only trick is shaping the cookies once they come out of the oven and before they start to cool and stiffen. To create cookie cups that can be filled with ice cream or fruit, fit large, hot cookies over an inverted muffin tin and let them cool into minibaskets.

MAKES ABOUT 30 COOKIES

- ½ cup granulated sugar
- 1 cup sliced almonds
- ¼ teaspoon salt
- 1 large egg plus 1 egg white, at room temperature, slightly beaten
- ½ teaspoon vanilla extract
- ¼ cup all-purpose flour
- 2 tablespoons unsalted butter, melted and cooled

1. Adjust a rack to the center position and heat oven to 350 degrees. Line two cookie sheets with Silpat (see page 11), or use parchment paper and apply a light coating of butter to the paper. Have on hand rolling pins or wine bottles to accommodate the cookies as they come out of the oven.

2. In a medium bowl, combine the sugar, almonds, and salt. Stir in the egg until combined. Add the vanilla and stir to combine. Sift the flour over the mixture and stir to combine. Stir in the melted butter. Make sure the almonds are evenly distributed throughout the batter.

3. Working with one prepared cookie sheet at a time, spoon out tablespoons of batter in staggered rows, keeping the cookies at least 2 inches apart. With a fork flatten and shape the blobs into 2½-inch rounds. Bake until the cookies are browned around the edges but still light in the center, 6 to 8 minutes. Start checking the cookies after 4 minutes and do not overbake or they will be impossible to shape later.

4. Let the cookies cool for no more than 30 seconds. With a spatula, place them onto the rolling pins or wine bottles to form their signature arch. Let cool completely on these forms.

(If you like, you can serve them flat, in which case simply remove to a wire rack to cool.)

5. Repeat steps 3 and 4 until all the batter is used. Stir the batter in between batches to make sure it is totally incorporated. After cookies are completely cooled, store in an airtight container.

WHAT CAN GO WRONG? If these cookies are overcooked, they will firm up in just a few seconds after coming out of the oven and will be impossible to shape. The edges of the cookies should just turn a little brown when they are done.

Hazelnut Variation

Substitute an equal amount of chopped hazelnuts for the sliced almonds.

Cookie Basket Variation

Increase the batter per cookie to 1½ tablespoons (a number 40 ice cream scoop works well). Flatten and spread the batter until it is 3½ inches in diameter. (Bake 4 cookies at a time.) Bake for 7 to 9 minutes. After the cookies have cooled for 1 minute, lift onto an inverted standard-size muffin tin. Shape the cookies around the muffin cups to form baskets. Let cool completely. Lift off and store carefully in an airtight container. Makes about 20 baskets.

Pecan Lace Cookies

THESE COOKIES ARE A CROSS between candy and cookie — intensely sweet, thin, and relatively hard, since they have little flour in them. Having made a half-dozen recipes from a variety of cookbooks, including the new *Joy of Cooking, Classic Home Desserts, The Fannie Farmer Cookbook, How to Bake,* and *Maida Heatter's Brand-New Book of Great Cookies,* I knew that pecan lace cookies had their problems. They were often too sweet and sticky and,

CASE 21: KEEPING THE CRISP IN PECAN LACE COOKIES

Which ingredients make a crispy, not greasy, pecan lace cookie?

Ingredient	Comments
Sugar	Dark brown sugar boosts flavor
Corn syrup	Cookies were less brittle, easier to work with
Flour	Used minimum amount for a crispy cookie
Butter	Just enough for flavor; too much butter makes a greasy cookie
Milk or cream	Cream wins testing for texture and flavor
Oats	Good for texture; makes them more of a cookie than a candy

even worse, they often turned out greasy. At the other end of the spectrum were pecan lace cookies that were too tender and thick, not a real lace cookie at all. I wanted a thin, crispy lace cookie that was neither sticky nor greasy.

What is a lace cookie made from? The basic ingredients are sugar (granulated, light brown, or dark brown), flour, pecans, vanilla, and but-

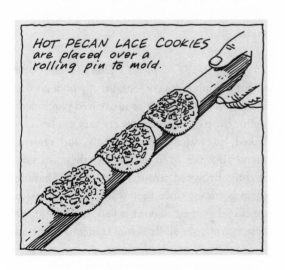

HOT PECAN LACE COOKIES are placed over a rolling pin to mold.

ter. Ingredients that showed up in only some of the recipes were corn syrup, milk or cream, salt, oats, and eggs. The basic method is to cook the sugar, butter, and corn syrup in a saucepan. Off the heat, the rest of the ingredients are stirred in to make a batter and then the cookies are baked in the oven. I quickly found that stirring the flour in before adding the nuts and oats made it easier to tell when the batter was smooth (otherwise it was hard to tell a flour lump from a nut!). Additional testing allowed me to make a number of other observations, summarized in Case 21.

I also tried using eggs, an ingredient in a few of the recipes I tried, and did not like the texture, since the cookies were not crispy enough. I also omitted baking powder and soda for the same reason. Now I had a good working recipe, using dark brown sugar, corn syrup, heavy cream, salt, flour, butter, vanilla, and pecans. I tested oven temperatures of 350 and 375 degrees and preferred the more moderate temperature, since it provided more control over timing; at the higher temperature the cookies had to be watched very carefully to avoid burning.

Like tuiles, pecan lace cookies are often molded after they come out of the oven. (They can also be served flat if you like.) A common shape is the "cigarette," which is made by wrapping the warm cookie around a dowel or the handle of a wooden spoon. It is best to cool the cookies for 1 minute before molding them. I also found that if you intend to serve them flat, it is best to trim off the thin, lacy outer edges. To do this, I use a large round cookie cutter and, as soon as the cookie sheet is removed from the oven, I place the cutter around each cookie and twirl it to trim off the ragged edges. This not only makes a nicer shaped cookie, it makes the edges more durable. Unlike the tuiles, this cookie does not have a major sticking problem: ungreased parchment paper worked just fine. Some bakers coat these cookies with a thin layer of chocolate or dip one end of the cigarette-shaped cookies into chocolate. I find these variations to be too much work for the home cook and therefore have not included them.

●●●

Pecan Lace Cookies

The objective with this recipe was to produce a cookie that was neither a candy, nor greasy, nor a real cookie. Pecan lace cookies should be thin, lacy, and not hard but not cakey either. The secret is corn syrup and just the right amount of butter and flour. These cookies can be shaped (let cool for 1 minute before shaping) by draping the hot cookies over rolling pins or wine bottles, or, for a cigarette shape, wrapping them around a thin dowel or the handle of a wooden spoon.

MAKES 36 TO 48 COOKIES, DEPENDING ON SIZE

¾   cup packed dark brown sugar
½   cup light corn syrup
8   tablespoons (1 stick) unsalted butter
1   teaspoon vanilla extract

1   tablespoon heavy cream
¼   teaspoon salt
6   tablespoons all-purpose flour
½   cup chopped pecans
¾   cup quick-cooking oats

1. Adjust an oven rack to the center position and heat oven to 350 degrees. Line a cookie sheet with parchment paper or Silpat (see page 11).

2. In a medium saucepan, bring the sugar, corn syrup, and butter to a simmer and cook for 6 minutes, stirring frequently. Watch carefully, as the pot can boil over easily. Remove from the heat and stir in the vanilla, cream, salt, and flour. Whisk, do not stir, until smooth to incorporate lumps of flour. Add the pecans and oats and stir to combine.

3. Drop rounded teaspoonfuls of batter in staggered rows onto the baking sheet, leaving 3 inches between cookies. (This small amount of batter will spread a lot.) Bake until the cookies are thin, lacy, have almost stopped bubbling, and are slightly browned, 5 to 7 minutes. Rotate pan front to back after 3 minutes and keep a close watch as the cookies are baking to avoid overcooking.

4. Let cool on sheets for a minute and then shape or transfer to a cooling rack. If shaped cookies are desired, see the headnote. Repeat steps 3 and 4 until all the batter is used, stirring it thoroughly between batches. After cookies are completely cooled, store in an airtight container.

WHAT CAN GO WRONG? Don't even think about baking these cookies directly on a cookie sheet. Use either Silpat or ungreased parchment to line the pan. The cookies are very easily overbaked, so watch them carefully and remove them from the oven as soon as they are very slightly browned around the edges. Shaping them is tricky, since they will cool and harden quickly. I suggest making a very small batch at first to test your skills before trying to shape an entire recipe's worth of cookies.

Pecan Lace Baskets

Follow the recipe above but use a scant tablespoon of batter (about 2½ teaspoons) per cookie. Flatten and spread the batter until it is 3½ inches in diameter. (Bake 4 cookies at a time.) Bake for about 8 minutes. After the cookies have cooled for 1 minute, lift onto an inverted standard-size muffin tin. Shape the cookies around the muffin cups to form baskets. Let cool completely. Lift off and store carefully in an airtight container. Makes about 20 baskets.

5

·ᵥ·

ROLLED COOKIES

Rolled cookies are based on a simple sugar or butter cookie dough that is chilled, rolled out, and then cut into shapes. The cookies can be filled, fruits or nuts can be added to the dough, different spices or flavorings can be used, or the dough can be rolled into a log and then sliced into individual rounds for baking as "refrigerator" cookies. The problem with rolled cookies is the basic dough. If it has too much sugar or eggs, it can become sticky and hard to roll out. Cake flour or cornstarch can lead to a very fragile, crumbly cookie, as will confectioners' instead of granulated sugar. Some rolled cookie doughs are too sweet, others are too rich, and some are too lean, baking up tough. So for such a simple notion, a basic rolled cookie dough, there is actually a great deal to test to devise simple, easy-to-work-with doughs that also taste good.

Before making the recipes in this chapter, you might want to read my testing of nonstick baking surfaces (see page 10) and quickly review the rest of the chapter on techniques. For rolled cookies, unlike drop cookies, the temperature of the dough is critical. If it becomes too soft, it will be hard to roll out. Simply put it back in the refrigerator to firm up. Please note that since cookies bake quickly and since all ovens are not the same, the baking times given below are approximate. Always check cookies halfway through the specified baking time and then keep a close watch on them until they are ready. Turning the cookie sheet from front to back halfway through is also important, since most ovens do not bake evenly. Finally, I recommend that you not use more than one cookie sheet at a time in the oven, since I find that this practice leads to uneven baking results. (For other cookie-baking tips, see page 53.)

·ᵥ·

SUGAR COOKIES

THERE ARE HUNDREDS of recipes for sugar cookies, which start with a simple rolled dough that is cut into shapes and then baked. These are relatively thin cookies and should be crisp, not puffy, and, at their best, have a nice, simple vanilla-and-butter flavor without any off notes. Through detailed investigation, I discovered that a basic sugar cookie contains a simple combination of flour, sugar, baking powder, salt, butter, egg, vanilla, and sometimes a bit of milk, baking soda, sour cream, or cream cheese. To get a handle on what I liked, I tested many recipes, starting with four different sugar cookie recipes from the *Joy of Cooking*, by Irma S. Rombauer, along with recipes from Marion Cunningham's *Fannie Farmer Cookbook*, *Cook's Illustrated* magazine, and *Maida Heatter's Book of Great Cookies*. The winner was the recipe from *Cook's Illustrated*, which called for 2 cups flour, 1 teaspoon baking powder, ½ teaspoon salt, 2 sticks butter, 1 cup sugar, 1 large egg, and 2 teaspoons vanilla extract.

I then started analyzing the ratio of butter to flour, which is crucial to the structure and flavor of the cookie. The recipes I compared ran from ½ stick butter per cup of flour to a little more than 1 stick; I decided to go with 1 stick, 8 tablespoons of butter, per cup of flour. Almost all of the recipes used 1 egg, but the amount of flour ranged from 2 cups to 4. I decided on the middle ground, using 3 cups of flour with 1 whole egg. Sugar ran from a ¼ cup to ½ cup per cup of flour; once again I used a moderate amount, settling on ⅓ cup sugar per cup of flour. I did go with a higher amount of vanilla, using 2 teaspoons with 3 cups of flour. Based on this analysis, I put together a preliminary recipe as follows: 3 cups flour, ½ teaspoon salt, 1 teaspoon baking powder, 3 sticks butter, 1 cup granulated sugar, 1 egg, and 2 teaspoons vanilla.

I baked a batch and found that there was a bit too much leavener, since the cookies became a bit too puffy. I also found the dough to be slightly sticky when rolling and therefore decided to cut back on the amount of butter. The vanilla flavor was fine, as was the sugar level. So I designed a new recipe, reducing the baking powder to ½ teaspoon and the butter to 2½ sticks from 3. I also put in a bit of nutmeg for added flavor.

The results were excellent, but I also wanted to test the oven temperature. Most recipes use either 350 or 375 degrees, but I also tried 400 degrees. I liked 375 degrees best; the higher temperature browned the edges too quickly and the lower temperature produced cookies that did not set up quite quickly enough. Finally, I had developed a simple, flavorful sugar cookie that rolled out easily, was crispy not puffy, and set up nicely in the oven.

▪ ▪ ▪

Master Recipe for Sugar Cookies

This is a simple recipe, but the ratio of ingredients is important. Too much butter yields a sticky, hard-to-roll dough, and too much baking powder makes the cookies too puffy. These are very simple cookies, and I prefer them jazzed up with either a strong flavoring such as a citrus oil or with some sort of glaze or topping. Otherwise, they are on the dull side. See variations below.

MAKES 50 TO 60 TWO-INCH COOKIES

- 3 cups all-purpose flour
- ½ teaspoon salt
- ½ teaspoon baking powder
- ½ teaspoon nutmeg
- 20 tablespoons (2½ sticks) unsalted butter, softened but still firm
- 1 cup granulated sugar
- 1 large egg
- 2 teaspoons vanilla extract

Granulated sugar for sprinkling tops of cookies

1. In a medium bowl, whisk together the flour, salt, baking powder, and nutmeg. In a large bowl, using an electric mixer, cream the butter and sugar for 2 minutes at medium speed. Scrape down the sides of the bowl. Add the egg and vanilla and beat until combined, about 30 seconds. Add the dry ingredients and beat until combined, about 30 seconds more, or until the dough just starts to come together. Press the dough together with your hands to form a ball and then divide in half, shaping each

piece into a 6-inch disk. Wrap in plastic and re-frigerate until firm, about 2 hours. (This dough can be made up to 2 days ahead of time or even frozen. If refrigerated for an extended period, let it sit on the counter, wrapped in the plastic, for about 10 minutes before proceeding. If frozen, let thaw in the refrigerator and then sit on the counter for about 10 minutes.) The dough should be firm but not hard for the best results.

2. Adjust a rack to the middle position and heat the oven to 375 degrees. Line two cookie sheets with parchment. Working on a lightly floured surface, roll half of the dough to about ¼-inch thickness. (Keep the other half cool during this period.) Cut to desired shapes and, us-ing a spatula, place cookies 1 inch apart on one of the cookie sheets. Sprinkle with granulated sugar and bake until golden on the edges and very lightly browned on top, about 8 minutes. Turn the sheet front to back halfway through the baking time. When cookies are done, cool on the sheet for about 5 minutes and then trans-fer to a cooling rack using a spatula.

3. Gather the scraps of dough and reroll, cut, and bake as above. (If the dough becomes too soft, refrigerate for 15 minutes before rolling.) Continue in this way until all the dough is used. Store cooled cookies in an airtight container.

WHAT CAN GO WRONG? The trick with any sort of rolled cookie is to chill the dough to the cor-rect temperature. If too soft, it will be sticky and hard to roll out. If too firm, it will also be difficult to roll. Since all refrigerators are not the same, the suggested 2-hour chilling period is only approximate. If your dough is sticky, just put it back in the refrigerator (or try the freezer for a shorter period) until it firms up.

DROP COOKIE VARIATION

These cookies can also be dropped from an ice cream scoop without chilling the dough. They can then be pressed (to about ⅜-inch thickness) with the flat bottom of a glass (dip the glass in sugar between cookies) and baked.

LEMON OR ORANGE VARIATION

Replace vanilla with 1 teaspoon orange or lemon oil. (Oils are vastly preferable to extracts.)

CHOCOLATE-DIPPED VARIATION

Place two large cooling racks over parchment paper or jelly roll pans. Melt 12 ounces bitter-sweet or semisweet chocolate and dip half of each cookie into the chocolate, placing them on the racks to cool.

JAM SANDWICH VARIATION

Follow the master recipe, rolling out the dough to ⅛-inch thick. Cut dough with a round cookie cut-ter and place half of the circles onto parchment-lined cookie sheets. Spread a thin layer of jam (apricot and raspberry are good choices) over these circles. Using a smaller-diameter cookie cut-ter, cut a hole from the center of the remaining rounds of dough and place the resulting "dough-nuts" on top of the jam-covered circles. Bake 10 to 12 minutes, or until done. Roll out the dough scraps to make more cookies. You can also bake the cookies first and then add the jam (see page 100); in this case, bake about 8 minutes.

ALMOND VARIATION

Substitute 1 teaspoon almond extract for the vanilla. Add 1 cup toasted, slivered almonds to the dough mixture before the last 5 seconds of mixing.

BUTTER COOKIES

SUGAR COOKIES and butter cookies are quite similar, the latter having a higher percentage of butter and eggs. A butter cookie should be more cakey than crisp, moist, and rich with a strong butter flavor.

I started with the master sugar cookie recipe and increased the butter to 1 stick per cup of flour. I then played with the eggs and found that

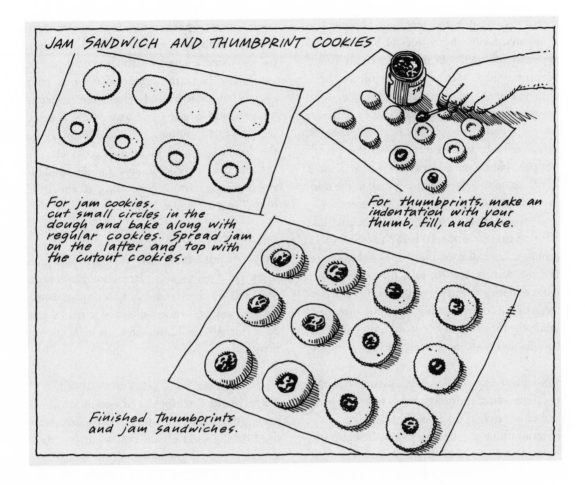

JAM SANDWICH AND THUMBPRINT COOKIES

For jam cookies, cut small circles in the dough and bake along with regular cookies. Spread jam on the latter and top with the cutout cookies.

For thumbprints, make an indentation with your thumb, fill, and bake.

Finished Thumbprints and jam sandwiches.

I preferred yolks to whole eggs for a more tender, richer texture. I settled on 2 yolks for 2 cups of flour. Unlike with the sugar cookie, I found that the butter needs to be whipped for quite a long time; otherwise the batter becomes too stiff when chilled. I also found that a lower oven temperature was necessary to allow the cookies to cook through without becoming too dark on the bottom.

• • •

Master Recipe for Butter Cookies

This recipe can also be made with all-purpose flour, although cake flour is preferred.

MAKES 40 DROP OR THUMBPRINT COOKIES OR
65 REFRIGERATOR COOKIES. YIELDS OF ROLLED

AND JAM COOKIE VARIATIONS WILL VARY
DEPENDING ON SIZE OF COOKIES.

- 2   cups plus 2 tablespoons cake flour
- ½   teaspoon salt
- ½   pound (2 sticks) unsalted butter, softened but still firm
- ¾   cup granulated sugar
- 2   large egg yolks
- 1   teaspoon vanilla extract

1. Sift together the flour and salt onto a sheet of waxed paper. Set aside.

2. Place butter in a large bowl and beat with an electric mixer on high speed for about 5 minutes, or until pale yellow and fluffy. (Be sure to beat butter for the full 5 minutes.) Add the sugar and beat on medium-high speed until

mixture is very pale and very light, another 2 to 3 minutes. Scrape down sides of bowl and add the yolks and vanilla. Beat for 30 seconds, or until incorporated. Add the flour mixture and beat, slowly at first, for about 20 seconds, or until mixture forms a rough dough. Shape the dough into a round (if making refrigerator cookies, dough must be shaped into logs at this point), wrap in plastic, and refrigerate for at least 2 hours, or up to 3 days. Adjust a rack to the middle position and heat oven to 350 degrees.

3. Shape cookies (see variations below) and bake on parchment-lined sheet pans for 7 to 15 minutes, depending on the shape of the cookie. If your oven is uneven, turn the cookie sheet front to back halfway through baking. The bottoms of the cookies should be lightly browned, while the tops should barely take on color. Let cookies sit on a cooling rack for 1 hour to set.

WHAT CAN GO WRONG? As discussed in the previous recipe, the dough needs to be properly chilled for easy rolling, and the amount of refrigerator time required may vary. It is also important to beat the butter until it is very light and fluffy for good results.

ROLLED COOKIE VARIATION

Refrigerate dough for an extra half hour (for a total of 2½ hours). On a lightly floured surface, roll dough out until it is ⅛ to ¼ inch thick, depending on the thickness desired (⅛ inch is about as thick as a quarter). Cut into shapes with a cookie cutter. Gather scraps and roll out again, cut into shapes, and repeat until all the dough is used. A ⅛-inch cookie will take 7 to 8 minutes to bake; the thicker cookie will take another minute or two.

JAM SANDWICH VARIATION

Follow directions for the Rolled Cookie Variation, rolling out the dough to a thickness of ⅛ inch. Cut dough with a round cookie cutter and place half of the circles onto parchment-lined cookie sheets. Spread a thin layer of jam (apricot and raspberry are good choices) over these circles. Using a smaller-diameter cookie cutter, cut a hole from the center of the remaining rounds of dough and place the resulting "doughnuts" on top of the jam-covered circles. Bake 10 to 12 minutes, or until done. Roll out the dough scraps to make more cookies. You can also bake the cookies first and then add the jam (see page 100 for method); in this case, bake 7 to 8 minutes.

DROP COOKIE VARIATION

Shape rounded teaspoons of dough into balls using your palms and place onto parchment-lined baking sheet about 2 inches apart. Brush with beaten egg white and sprinkle with sugar. Bake for 10 to 12 minutes, or until lightly browned.

THUMBPRINT COOKIE VARIATION

Shape rounded teaspoons of dough into balls using your palms and place onto parchment-lined baking sheet about 2 inches apart. Make an indentation in the middle of the dough with your thumb and fill with ¼ teaspoon jam. Bake for 10 to 12 minutes, or until lightly browned.

REFRIGERATOR COOKIE VARIATION

Divide the dough into 4 pieces. Take each piece and place it on a sheet of waxed paper. Mold dough into a log shape and then wrap with the waxed paper. Twist the ends to seal. Chill for 2 hours, or up to 3 days. To make cookies, unwrap and cut ¼-inch-thick cookies with a thin knife. Dip knife in water every few cookies to facilitate cutting. Bake about 14 minutes, or until lightly browned.

ALMOND VARIATION

Add ½ teaspoon almond extract along with the egg yolks. Add 1 cup toasted, slivered almonds to the dough mixture before the last 5 seconds of mixing.

CASE 22: SAND TART BAKE-OFF

How do sand tart recipes compare?

Ingredient/Technique	Classic Home Desserts	Fannie Farmer Cookbook
Flour	1 cup	2 cups
Salt	None	¼ teaspoon
Butter	1 stick	1 stick
Sugar	1 cup	1¼ cups
Egg	2 yolks	1 whole egg
Vanilla	1 teaspoon	None
Other	1 tablespoon hot water	None
Temperature	375 degrees	400 degrees

ORANGE OR LEMON VARIATION

Add ½ teaspoon orange oil (see page 36 for more information) and 2 tablespoons grated orange zest with the liquid ingredients. For lemon cookies, use ½ teaspoon lemon oil and 2 tablespoons lemon zest.

SAND TARTS

A SAND TART IS pastry dough rolled thin, brushed with egg white, maybe with a nut half pressed into its center, and definitely sprinkled with sugar and cinnamon. I wanted to create dough that was buttery, with a crisp and tender texture. It needed to be easy enough to handle and brown nicely as well. I found recipes for sand tarts in Richard Sax's *Classic Home Desserts* and in *The Fannie Farmer Cookbook*. Sax's recipe was twice as buttery and almost twice as sweet as the *Fannie Farmer* cookie. After making both of them, I found a cross between the two to be my best attempt in the areas of taste, texture, and handling. Sax calls for the use of hot water, which made little sense and, when tested, turned out to have no effect on the baked cookie.

The amount and type of egg turned out to be key. I finally settled on 1 whole egg and 1 yolk, a combination that provides rich flavor and color. This worked out well, since one needs an egg white to brush the cookies before baking. As with some of the other cookie recipes in this book, I found 400 degrees to be a bit too hot for even browning. I also have found that such a high oven temperature is asking for trouble, since many ovens are not properly calibrated. If they run hot, the cookies will be baked at more than 400 degrees, a temperature that will probably yield burned cookies. To finish off the cookies, I pressed a nut half into the dough for a simple but elegant presentation.

・・・

Sand Tarts

These are simple cookies, not unlike a butter or sugar cookie, but with a higher proportion of sugar and less butter. These should be very crisp, not rich and buttery, and they are usually baked with a pecan half pressed into the middle. I have been told that sand tarts were once thought to have a connection to the Epiphany, the church celebration commemorating the manifestation of Christ to the Magi. In that version of the cookie, three almonds are placed onto each cookie, one for each of the wise men.

MAKES ABOUT 50 TWO-INCH COOKIES

2	cups all-purpose flour
¼	teaspoon salt
12	tablespoons (1½ sticks) unsalted butter, softened but still firm
1¼	cups granulated sugar
2	large eggs (reserve 1 of the whites for the egg wash)
1	teaspoon vanilla extract
About 50	pecan halves or whole almonds (optional)
¼	cup granulated sugar mixed with 1 teaspoon cinnamon

1. Sift together the flour and salt onto a piece of waxed paper and set aside. In a large bowl, beat the butter with an electric mixer until creamy, about 1 minute, and then beat in the sugar for an additional 2 minutes, or until light. Add 1 whole egg and 1 yolk (reserve the leftover white for the egg wash) and beat for an additional 30 seconds, or until combined. Add the vanilla and then the dry ingredients and beat until combined, about 30 seconds more, or until the dough just starts to come together. (The dough should be in grape-size pieces. Do not overbeat or dough will become sticky and unmanageable.) Press the dough together with your hands to form a ball and then divide in half, shaping each piece into a 6-inch disk. Wrap in plastic or waxed paper and refrigerate until firm, about 2 hours. If dough has been refrigerated for an extended period, let sit on the counter for about 10 minutes before proceeding, so it is firm but not hard.

2. Adjust an oven rack to the middle position and heat oven to 375 degrees. Line a cookie sheet with parchment paper. Lightly beat the reserved egg white in a small bowl. Remove the dough from the refrigerator. On a lightly floured surface, roll the dough to about ³⁄₁₆ inch thick. Cut to desired shapes (2-inch rounds are common) and transfer to the prepared cookie sheet using a cookie spatula. Brush the cookies with the egg white, press a nut into the center if desired, and sprinkle with the sugar-cinnamon mixture.

3. Bake until the edges are browned, 7 to 8 minutes, turning the sheet front to back halfway through the cooking time. (Check cookies after 4 minutes.) Cool on the pan for 5 minutes and transfer to a rack to cool to room temperature.

4. Repeat steps 2 and 3 until all the cookies are baked. Store in an airtight container.

WHAT CAN GO WRONG? Incorporating the dry ingredients into the butter-sugar-egg mixture is critical. If overbeaten, the dough will collapse into a sticky mess. Dough is ready when still in grape-size clumps.

GINGERBREAD MEN

GINGERBREAD MEN USUALLY look great, have an alluring fresh-from-the-oven scent, but taste

CASE 23: SEEKING A KINDER, GENTLER GINGERBREAD MAN

Not all gingerbread men are created equal.

Ingredient/ Comments	Recipe A	Recipe B	Recipe C	Recipe D
Molasses	⅓ cup	½ cup	½ cup	¾ cup
Brown sugar	½ cup light	¾ cup dark	¾ cup	¾ cup dark
Ginger	1 tablespoon	1 tablespoon	½ teaspoon	2 tablespoons
Cinnamon	½ teaspoon	1¾ teaspoons	½ teaspoon	2 tablespoons
Cloves	½ teaspoon	¼ teaspoon	½ teaspoon	None
Nutmeg	½ teaspoon	None	½ teaspoon	None
Baking soda	¼ teaspoon	¾ teaspoon	½ teaspoon	½ teaspoon
Baking powder	½ teaspoon	1½ teaspoons	None	1 teaspoon
Salt	¼ teaspoon	¼ teaspoon	½ teaspoon	1 teaspoon
Butter	8 tablespoons	6 tablespoons	3 tablespoons	12 tablespoons
Egg	1	1	None	1
Flour	2½ cups	3 cups	2 cups	4½ cups
Comments	Good, but hard to roll out	Very hard cookie	Very hard cookie	Good texture; too many spices

awful. They are often rock hard and overspiced, as if the contents of the spice drawer had been accidentally dropped into the bowl with the flour. My question was, could one make a gingerbread man that tasted as good as it looked?

The first step was to take a look at a number of recipes and compare their ingredient lists. The most important issue was the ratio of butter to flour. Recipes B and C (see Case 23) had a very low ratio, using from 1½ to 2 tablespoons of butter per cup of flour. Both of these cookies were very hard and virtually inedible. Recipes A and D, however, used much more butter, between 2⅔ to a little over 3 tablespoons of butter per cup of flour. I found that the cookie with higher butter content (Recipe A) was hard to roll out, so I went with the cookie slightly lower in fat content (Recipe D), which had a very good texture.

Baking powder and baking soda were next on the list for review. Most recipes use too much of these ingredients. Too much leavener can cause cookies to actually become thinner during baking, since an excess of carbon dioxide is created and simply escapes from the batter. In addition, there will be a residue of baking soda left over in the cookies, which gives them an odd, soapy flavor. After some testing, I found that recipe A had it about right, so I went with ½ teaspoon baking powder and ¼ teaspoon baking soda.

Most of the recipes used about the same proportion of sugar and molasses to flour, but I did prefer dark brown sugar to light. Finally, some of the recipes had an excess of spices, which I cut back to more moderate amounts. (Recipe D called for a mouth-puckering 2 tablespoons of cinnamon!)

As for a glaze for these cookies, since many folks are concerned about raw eggs, I eliminated the usual egg white and went with a simple combination of confectioners' sugar and milk. This style of icing does take a bit longer to set up, but it works just fine. It can also be made with a bit of lemon zest, or with orange juice instead of milk, or with a bit of rum in it.

▪ ▪ ▪

Gingerbread Men

Hard, overspiced gingerbread men seem to be the norm, but I wanted kinder, gentler cookies that did not contain tongue-burning amounts of cinnamon and ground ginger, although they should have a bit of zip to them. These are gin-gerbread men that look good and are also worth eating. If you wish to glaze the cookies, see the recipe that follows.

MAKES ABOUT 75 TWO-INCH COOKIES.

3   cups all-purpose flour
½   teaspoon baking powder
¼   teaspoon baking soda
½   teaspoon salt
1   teaspoon ground ginger
½   teaspoon cinnamon
½   teaspoon ground cloves
½   teaspoon nutmeg
8   tablespoons (1 stick) unsalted butter, softened but still firm
½   cup tightly packed dark brown sugar
½   cup molasses
1   large egg

1. In a medium bowl, whisk together the first 8 ingredients (flour through nutmeg). Set aside. In a large bowl, beat the butter and sugar with an electric mixer on medium speed for 2 minutes. Scrape down the sides of the bowl. Add the molasses and beat for another 30 seconds, or until combined. Add the egg and beat for another 30 seconds, or until combined, scraping down the sides of the bowl as necessary. Add the dry ingredients and beat on low speed until just incorporated. Divide the dough in two and shape each half into an 8-inch disk. Wrap disks in plastic and chill until firm, about 2 hours. If dough has been chilled for an extended period of time, let it sit on the counter for about 10 minutes before proceeding. It should be firm but not hard.

2. Adjust an oven rack to the middle position and heat oven to 350 degrees. Line a cookie sheet with parchment paper. On a lightly floured surface, roll the dough (half at a time) to a thickness of ¼ inch. Cut to desired shapes and place on the prepared cookie sheet with a cookie spatula. Bake until the cookies are set and just beginning to brown, about 7 minutes, turning the sheet front to back halfway through the

baking time. Let cool on the baking sheet for 5 minutes and transfer to a rack to cool completely.

3. Gather the scraps of dough, reroll, and cut, until you have used all the dough. If the dough becomes too soft, refrigerate for about 15 minutes. Bake and cool as directed above.

WHAT CAN GO WRONG? As with all rolled cookies, the dough needs to be at the proper temperature. If it becomes very soft as you work with it, put it back in the refrigerator or briefly in the freezer to firm up. Also, since these cookies are dark brown, it is hard to tell when they are baked properly. Most cooks overbake them. They should still be very soft when they come out of the oven, since they will harden as they cool. Peek underneath one or two of the cookies. They should just be starting to brown. I would also be cautious about oven times, because your oven may bake differently than mine. Since these cookies take just a few minutes to bake, I suggest watching them very carefully.

GLAZE FOR GINGERBREAD MEN

These cookies can be iced (after baking and cooling) with a glaze made with 2 cups sifted confectioners' sugar and 2 to 3 tablespoons milk whisked together until smooth. Add the milk slowly to get the desired consistency. The glaze should be thick and spreadable, not too runny. If it is too thick add a few drops more milk, if too thin add more sifted confectioners' sugar. For variations, add a bit of lemon zest to the sugar or substitute 1 tablespoon of rum or orange juice for an equal amount of milk.

SABLÉS

SABLÉS ARE A TEA COOKIE, more refined than the American sugar or butter cookie. This sort of cookie is particularly good when made into a jam sandwich or when dressed up with a bit of confectioners' sugar on top. The challenge with sablés is to create a delicate, almost sandy-textured cookie, and this is determined by both the ingredients and the mixing method. I started by making recipes from a variety of baking books and found some interesting discrepancies among the ingredients. Some recipes used regular granulated sugar and others used confectioners'. I vastly preferred the confectioners' sugar variation, as the cookie was much more refined and had a better texture. I was greatly surprised to find that two of the recipes I tried used hard boiled egg yolks! These cookies were drier and more crumbly, which I did not feel was an advantage. I then tried a recipe with 1 whole egg, then tried just an egg yolk, and finally settled on 2 egg yolks for the added richness I liked in this refined French dessert cookie.

Cake flour made a cookie that did not hold up very well; all-purpose flour provides the additional strength it needs. I then tested the amount of flour by starting with a very loose dough and then adding flour in quarter-cup increments until the dough held together well without rendering the cookies dry and tough when baked. I did the same sort of testing for the sugar to arrive at a pleasantly sweet cookie without overdoing it. I particularly liked the cookie with just vanilla as a flavoring, although I did try lemon and almond variations.

I also found that the method by which the ingredients were blended was crucial. The standard method is to cream the butter and sugar, add the eggs and vanilla, and then add the flour and salt while mixing on low speed. This makes for a very blended, dull cookie. I experimented a bit and found that it was best to add the flour and salt and then mix with your hands or a rubber spatula. When the dough came together in a crumbly mixture, I wrapped it in plastic and put it into the refrigerator to firm up. This produced a more crumbly, delicate cookie, which I think is in keeping with the recipe.

Finally, I found that a lower oven setting seemed to work best. This cookie can be baked at 325 or 350 degrees successfully, but the lower setting has two advantages: it gives the baker more time to tell when the cookie is done, and it also produces crispier cookies.

• • •

Sablés (Crisp, Delicate Butter Cookies)

This is the French version of the American butter cookie. It is a bit more delicate and crumbly than our sturdy, all-purpose cookies and is particularly good when sandwiched with a layer of jam.

MAKES 25 TO 30 TWO-INCH COOKIES

1¼	cups all-purpose flour
¼	teaspoon salt
8	tablespoons (1 stick) unsalted butter, softened but still firm
½	cup confectioners' sugar
1	large egg yolk, at room temperature
½	teaspoon vanilla extract

1. Adjust a rack to the center position of the oven and heat oven to 325 degrees. Line a cookie sheet with parchment paper.

2. Sift together the flour and salt onto a piece of waxed paper. Set aside. In a medium bowl, cream the butter and sugar with an electric mixer for 2 minutes. (Start on low speed so you don't get a confectioners' facial.) Add the egg yolk and vanilla and mix to combine. Add the flour and use a spatula or your fingers to mix until all of the flour is incorporated. When the dough begins to come together, wrap in plastic and then press into a cohesive ball. The dough will be very soft. Refrigerate for 1 to 2 hours, or until the dough is slightly firm but not hard.

3. On a lightly floured surface, roll out the dough, half at a time, to a thickness of about ⅛ inch. (If dough is hard and cold, let it warm up a few minutes before rolling.) Cut into desired shapes with a cookie cutter. Lift cookies onto the prepared sheet with a spatula, placing them 1 inch apart. When the sheet is filled, place in the heated oven and bake until the edges just start to brown, about 10 minutes, checking cookies after 6 minutes and turning the pan front to back at the same time. Cool on the pan for 5 minutes and then transfer onto a rack to cool completely.

4. Gather the scraps of dough, reroll, cut, and bake as above. Continue in this way until all the dough is used. Store cooled cookies in an airtight container.

WHAT CAN GO WRONG? This cookie is typical of rolled cookies in that the dough must be firm for easy rolling. If at any point it becomes too soft, return it to the refrigerator to firm up. Be sure not to overbake the cookies. Use my oven times only as a rough guideline.

JAM SANDWICH VARIATION

Cut out rounds of dough and in half of the rounds remove the centers with a smaller cutter. Gather scraps, roll out dough again, cut into rounds, and repeat until all the dough is used. Bake as directed. When cookies have cooled completely, take all of the solid cookies and flip them over to expose the bottom (the side that was in contact with the cookie sheet). Spread that side with a thin layer of smooth jam, preferably seedless. (Apricot, raspberry, and black raspberry are good choices.) Top each jam-covered cookie with a cookie with a cutout center. Sprinkle the filled cookies with confectioners' sugar.

▼

SHORTBREAD COOKIES

ALTHOUGH MOST HOME COOKS rarely make shortbread these days, this recipe is worth mastering, since shortbread cookies marry well with almost any dessert (fresh or poached fruit,

CASE 24: HOW DO YOU PUT THE SHORT IN SHORTBREAD?

Six shortbread recipes were baked and tasted to find the best combination of flour, butter, and sugar for the perfect cookie.

Ingredient or Technique	Result
Ratio of butter to flour	1 stick butter per cup of flour is best
Ratio of sugar to flour	¼ cup sugar per cup of flour is best
Type of sugar	Granulated better than confectioners'; the cookie is less crumbly
Oven temperature	350 degrees is better than lower temperatures

custards such as crème caramel or crème brûlée, et cetera), are not difficult to make, and also store well. This classic cookie should be buttery, have a bit of crunch to it, and not be too dry or sandy. I was looking for a crunchy cookie, not a crumbly one, the sort that does not disintegrate as soon as you bite into it. A good shortbread recipe should produce a dough that is not too sticky, which will make it hard to roll out.

The ingredients are simple — flour, butter, sugar, and just a pinch of salt — but the texture and taste can vary tremendously from recipe to recipe, as I was to find out. I began by testing six recipes: a family recipe from a member of the *Cook's Illustrated* test kitchen staff, and recipes from five cookbooks, including *Myrtle Allen's Cooking at Ballymaloe House* and *Joy of Cooking*. My tests revealed that confectioners' sugar was a poor choice, as it resulted in a very crumbly, delicate cookie. I also settled on the proper ratios of butter and sugar to flour and then devised a good working recipe, which contained 2 sticks butter, 2 cups flour, ½ cup sugar, and just a pinch of salt. The basic method was simple enough. I used a food processor to work the butter into the dry ingredients (this

can also be done by hand) and then I dumped the mixture onto a work surface and smeared it with the palm of my hand until a dough formed. This took about seven or eight smears. To finish the cookies, I rolled the dough, cut shapes, and baked them.

The cookies were good, but the dough was a bit sticky and, I thought, on the edge of being too buttery, so I increased the flour from 2 cups to 2¼ cups. That solved both problems. For good measure I tried using 2½ cups of flour and thought the cookies were too dry and tough. I also tested cake flour and then a mixture of cake flour and all-purpose and liked the sturdy texture of the all-purpose better than both of the cake flour cookies. Leaving no stone unturned, I tried bleached flour and still liked the taste of the all-purpose unbleached flour best.

Since I had already tried a couple of cookies with confectioners' sugar, I did not test it any further. I did try using more and less granulated sugar in the recipe and ended with the original ½ cup. The cookies were sweet enough without being too much so. All that was left was the salt, and I settled on ¼ teaspoon (½ teaspoon was too much). To my surprise, most of the recipes I tested called for no salt at all, a major shortcoming, in my opinion. A bit of salt perks up the flavor and also adds some balance. My last ingredient test was cream of tartar, an ingredient called for in one of the recipes I tested, and it made no discernible difference.

The final frontier was baking temperature. I started testing at 300 degrees, and the cookies baked for almost twice as long (19 minutes) as the 350-degree cookies with no benefit. I then tried 325 degrees; the cookies baked for about 15 minutes, and again the extra time didn't do anything to improve them. I settled on the 350-degree temperature, which bakes them in 10 to 12 minutes and still does not cook them so quickly that it's hard to avoid overbrowning.

∎ ∎ ∎

Quick and Easy Shortbread Cookies

This recipe calls for only four ingredients, which can be mixed quickly in the bowl of a food processor. The cookies keep well and can be served with many desserts, poached or fresh fruit being a good choice. They are buttery without being over the top, and the salt, an ingredient missing from most of the cookbook recipes I tested, perks up the flavor. The butter should be malleable (the stick will bend but still be cool and not spreadable), which means that the internal temperature should be 65 to 67 degrees. If the dough becomes too soft or sticky as you are working with it, put it into the refrigerator for about 15 minutes, or until it is easy to roll out and cut again.

MAKES ABOUT 48 COOKIES

- 2¼ cups all-purpose flour
- ½ cup granulated sugar
- ¼ teaspoon salt
- ½ pound (2 sticks) unsalted butter, softened but still firm, cut into 1-inch pieces

1. Adjust a rack to center position and heat oven to 350 degrees. Line a baking sheet with parchment. In a large bowl, stir the flour, sugar, and salt to combine. Rub the butter into the flour mixture until the mixture resembles coarse meal and will stick together if squeezed into a ball. (If you have a food processor, add the dry ingredients and then the butter. Pulse to combine until the mixture takes on a slightly yellowish color and the texture changes, becoming coarser.)

2. Dump the mixture onto a work surface and smear with the palm of one hand about seven or eight times or until a dough forms. (Using a motion similar to kneading bread, press down on the mixture and push it away from you, smearing it onto the counter. Gather it together with a dough scraper, then smear again.) Stop this process as soon as the dough comes together. Gather the dough into a ball and cut in half. Dust the work surface lightly with flour. Working with half the dough at a time, roll it about ⅛ inch thick and cut into 1 x 2-inch rectangles, using as little additional flour as possible. (I find the rectangles save time and you are left with very few scraps to reroll, which keeps the dough from getting tough.) Don't worry if the dough sticks to the work surface. Transfer the cookies onto the cookie sheet with a cookie spatula, spacing them ½ inch apart. If you like, the cookies can be pricked with the tines of a fork to produce a fancier look.

3. Bake the cookies for 10 to 12 minutes, turning the cookie sheet front to back halfway through the baking time. The cookies should be very light brown at the edges and very light-colored in the center. Cool on the pan for 5 minutes and then transfer to a wire rack to cool completely.

4. Continue rolling, cutting, and baking until all the dough is used. These cookies can be stored in an airtight container for a week.

WHAT CAN GO WRONG? The trick here is having the butter at the proper temperature before you begin. When I suggest 65 to 67 degrees, I mean it! The butter should be malleable but not soft. (You should be able to bend the stick of butter like putty. It should not, however, be soft or hard.) The simplest method of checking the butter is to use an instant-read thermometer.

CHOCOLATE SHORTBREAD VARIATION

The trick to making chocolate shortbread was to find a method for producing pieces of chocolate that were the proper texture for incorporating into the dough. I wanted to avoid anything complicated, such as dipping the cookies into chocolate or piping or tempering chocolate. My first thought was to use chips, but even when chopped they were too coarse. I then tried grating the chocolate, which was rather messy. Finally, I tried shaving the chocolate from the end of a bar with a knife, and this seemed to work well (a vegetable peeler would also work). However, you can also put the chocolate into a food processor and pulse until it is ground very fine. Either method results in good chocolate flavor, an intriguing speckled appearance, and an easy but satisfying variation. In fact, most of my tasters went for the chocolate-speckled shortbread over the plain.

To make chocolate shortbread, either shave 2 ounces of semisweet or bittersweet chocolate from the end of a bar or use a food processor to finely grind the chocolate. Mix the prepared chocolate into the dough mixture after step 1 in the master recipe but before step 2. Proceed with recipe.

6

BROWNIES
AND BAR COOKIES

Bar cookies appear to have preceded brownies on the American culinary scene. A 1917 edition of Fannie Farmer's *A New Book of Cookery* includes recipes for "wafer" cookies, which are relatively thin bar cookies usually made from a shortbread crust topped with a sweet nut mixture. In the twentieth century, bars took on fancy names and recipes were offered with many variations on the basic theme. I have come across Dream Bars, Honeymoon Bars, and Lover's Morsels, to name just a few, the basic recipe harking back to the original recipe structure found in Fannie Farmer. (The Chewy Pecan Bars near the end of this chapter are a good example of this type of bar cookie.)

Brownies, however, are a more modern invention, since they are more like a cake than a cookie. Brownies were often referred to as Fudge Bars in early cookbooks. Nowadays, it seems, brownies are everywhere, and they run the gamut from dry, crumbly cakes to dense, fudgelike confections. To uncover the fundamental secrets of great brownies, I turned again to the test kitchen.

BROWNIES ON THE LIGHTER SIDE

BROWNIES ARE AS HARD TO MAKE as a good chocolate chip cookie. Some are fudgy, others cakey; some are light and dry, while others are dense and sweet; some crumble when cut, and others stick to the knife like treacle. I prefer a brownie on the lighter side — not fudgy and wet, but with good mouth-filling texture and two-fisted chocolate flavor without a cloying aftertaste.

I started with 1 stick butter, 2 ounces unsweetened chocolate, ⅔ cup cake flour, 1 cup granulated sugar, 1 teaspoon vanilla extract, 2 eggs, ¼ teaspoon salt, ½ teaspoon baking powder, and ½ cup chopped walnuts. The result was very cakelike, not at all what I had in mind. I then tried a series of tests, including refrigerating the batter for 1 hour before baking; adding 1 egg white to the batter; using bread flour instead of cake flour; using cocoa powder instead of baking chocolate; substituting light brown sugar for white sugar; and, finally, baking at 300 degrees instead of 375. None of these variations were an improvement. I did have some luck, however, when I added 1 whole egg (moister), used all-purpose flour instead of cake flour (chewier), and, most important, creamed the butter instead of melting it. This last technique produced the mouth-filling texture I was looking for.

However, the butter had to be just the right temperature — 65 to 67 degrees — for this to work properly. It needs to be firm yet warm enough to successfully incorporate air. If the butter is still in its wrapper, allow it to sit out about 2 hours in a kitchen that is 72 degrees, or until the stick is malleable — it should give when pressed — but still firm and unmelted. (To check the butter temperature, you can use an instant-read thermometer.) I also discovered that cold eggs added to creamed butter will not incorporate properly — the difference in temperature is simply too great. Leave them at room temperature for a couple of hours or immerse them in hot tap water for 2 minutes. As the eggs are added, the butter mixture should be dull, thick, and smooth, not shiny or grainy.

So the secret of the perfect brownie is all-purpose flour, 3 room-temperature eggs instead of 2, and creaming the butter. This makes terrific brownies; they have great flavor, are moist and firm but not crumbly, and have good "mouth feel" — the texture coats the tongue nicely with a very pleasant aftertaste.

▪▪▪

Moist, Light Brownies

To melt chocolate, place it in a microwave uncovered in a glass measuring cup. Heat at 50 percent power for 60 seconds and stir. Heat another 60 seconds and check. If necessary, heat for another 30 seconds. Chocolate can also be melted in a 250-degree oven, which takes about 15 minutes. The butter must be at 65 to 67 degrees for successful creaming. Leave the wrapped stick of butter at room temperature for about 2 hours, or until the butter is malleable but still firm.

MAKES 16 BROWNIES

- 8 tablespoons (1 stick) unsalted butter, at 65 to 67 degrees (pliable but not soft)
- 1 cup granulated sugar
- 3 large eggs, at room temperature
- 2 ounces unsweetened chocolate, melted and hot
- 1 teaspoon vanilla extract
- ¼ teaspoon salt
- ½ cup all-purpose flour
- 1 cup walnuts, coarsely chopped

1. Heat oven to 350 degrees. Grease an 8-inch square baking pan or line it with parchment paper (see page 106).

2. Cream the butter and sugar together in a metal bowl with a heavy-duty electric mixer for 3 minutes on high speed. (Allow 5 minutes if beating by hand or using a small hand-held electric mixer.) Scrape down the sides of the bowl every minute. Add the eggs one at a time, scraping down after every addition, beating for a total of 2 additional minutes. Add the hot melted chocolate and continue beating for 1 minute on high speed. If the mixture looks separated or grainy, heat the outside of the bowl with a kitchen towel soaked in hot tap water. Continue beating until the mixture looks smooth and dull.

3. Add the remaining ingredients and fold in gently with a rubber spatula or a wooden spoon.

4. Pour batter into baking pan and level out top. Bake 30 to 35 minutes, or until a cake tester comes out clean when inserted into center. Allow to cool in pan at least 2 hours before cutting, removing from pan, and serving.

WHAT CAN GO WRONG? It is important that the butter and eggs be at the correct temperature. If they are too cold, the mixture will appear grainy and separate when beaten. If this happens, soak a towel in hot tap water (it should be very damp but not dripping wet) and wrap it around the bowl of the electric mixer as you beat the mixture. You may have to refresh the towel with more hot water until the mixture turns dull and smooth.

LARGE PAN VARIATION

If you want to make a bigger batch of brownies, double the recipe above and bake in a 9 x 13-inch pan.

CHEWY, FUDGY BROWNIES

EVERYONE HAS THEIR OWN OPINION about the proper texture for a brownie. While I prefer a lighter brownie, many people are taken with the notion of a brownie with a rich, almost fudge-like interior and a crispy top crust. With this in mind, I set out to track down the perfect recipe.

There are two basic methods for making

THE EASY WAY TO REMOVE BAR COOKIES & BROWNIES

Line pan with two pieces of parchment paper at right angles.

Simply lift out paper when brownies are done.

REMOVING BROWNIES AND BAR COOKIES FROM THE PAN

Many cooks have trouble getting brownies and bar cookies out of baking pans. If you line the pan with two sheets of parchment paper or aluminum foil (the two pieces at right angles to each other), the entire cooled, baked bar can be removed from the pan in one piece and then easily cut with a large knife. Or you can line the bottom of a buttered pan with a square of parchment. Invert the cooled, baked brownies onto a wire rack, peel off the parchment, and invert the brownies onto a cutting surface. Either method avoids the difficulty of cutting and removing individual pieces from the pan. I prefer to use a pan that does not have rounded corners, since a perfectly straight-sided pan produces the most attractive corner pieces.

---

brownies. In one method the butter is creamed, and in the other it is simply melted. The preceding recipe, for Moist, Light Brownies, follows the first method and the result is very cakelike, typical of brownie recipes that use the creamed butter method. In my quest for a denser, fudgy brownie, I began a long series of tests — testing different types of flour (including all-purpose and bread flours), adding cocoa to the recipe, testing light brown versus white sugar, and varying the oven temperature. None of these tests proved fruitful. I was still a long away from my goal.

In desperation, I made up a batch of Chewy Fudge Brownies from *The Fannie Farmer Baking Book,* by Marion Cunningham, and, to my delight, found that they were the best so far. They were rich, moist, and fudgy, although they were not really chewy. The secret was a higher proportion of chocolate, a quarter-cup more sugar (I was using just 1 cup) to make up for the additional unsweetened chocolate, and butter melted with the chocolate, not creamed with the sugar. This last point was key — I discovered that melted butter transforms a cakelike brownie into something more akin to fudge. Another key point was that this recipe contained no baking powder; this subtraction also yielded a denser, moister product.

I was still bothered, however, by the lack of chew, and I thought that there was insufficient batter for an 8 x 8-inch baking pan. Perhaps if there were more batter, I reasoned, I could cook the outside of the brownie until it was chewier, while the inside would remain moist and fudgy. I increased the batter by 50 percent and found that my theory was correct: the top crust and sides became very crackly and chewy, while the center remained moist.

At this point, the recipe needed tweaking. Since the brownies were a bit greasy, I cut back on the butter and slightly increased the flour, using all-purpose instead of cake flour to provide more structure. I also adjusted the chocolate level downward a bit, finding that the flavor improved. Now I was almost home free, with a wonderfully moist brownie and a rich chocolate flavor. I then played with oven temperatures and found 350 degrees to be best. But I made another discovery along the way. The baking time had a major effect on the chewiness. When the brownies were baked 50 minutes, the tops were chewy but the insides were still soft. For a really chewy brownie, I simply increased the baking time by 5 to 10 minutes.

Finally, I ran across a brownie recipe in the excellent cookbook *Alice Medrich's Cookies and Brownies*. The author suggests taking the hot baking pan right from the oven and placing it in an ice water bath. This is supposed to keep the inside of the brownies very fudgy. Although I highly recommend her recipe, I found that the brownie bottoms became somewhat greasy using this method, perhaps because my recipe calls for more butter, and they lost a bit of their chew. I also like my recipe since it is a snap to make — even a five-year-old could do it — and any fussy techniques seemed to me out of place.

▪ ▪ ▪

Chewy, Fudgy Brownies

The secret to these brownies is that they use more chocolate than most recipes so that when they cool they have more chew. The butter is simply melted, not creamed with the sugar, which also results in a less cakelike texture. If you like really chewy brownies, bake them 55 to 60 minutes. The amount of sugar may seem extreme — I am no fan of supersweet desserts — but lower amounts will detract from both the chocolate flavor and the fudgy texture. I suggest you first try the recipe as is; then, if it's really too sweet for you, try reducing the sugar in 2-tablespoon increments when you make it again.

MAKES 16 BROWNIES

4	ounces unsweetened chocolate
10	tablespoons (1¼ sticks) unsalted butter
3	large eggs
2	teaspoons vanilla extract
1¾	cups granulated sugar
½	teaspoon salt
1¼	cups all-purpose flour
1	cup walnuts, in pieces (optional)

1. Heat oven to 350 degrees. Line an 8 x 8-inch baking pan with foil or parchment paper, or grease the pan with butter.

2. Melt the chocolate and butter in a microwave oven at 50 percent power for 2 minutes, or melt in a saucepan over very low heat. Whisk the eggs and vanilla together in a medium bowl. Add the melted chocolate mixture and whisk to combine (mixture will thicken considerably). Add all other ingredients and mix together with a rubber spatula or wooden spoon. The batter will be very thick and somewhat greasy-looking.

3. Scrape batter into baking pan (the batter will hang together like a bread dough) and press into place with a large rubber spatula. Bake about 50 minutes, or until a cake tester comes out clean when inserted into center. For chewier

brownies, bake an additional 5 to 10 minutes. Let cool at least 2 hours in pan before removing, cutting, and serving. (The brownies will continue cooking and become chewier as they cool.)

WHAT CAN GO WRONG? This is a very simple recipe. Note that the longer you cook them, the chewier the brownies become. When baked for 50 minutes, they will be very moist inside, almost fudgy. However, if they are baked for 55 to 60 minutes, they will be a bit drier but also chewier. I also find that these brownies are actually better the next day, since they firm up and have more chew to them.

COCONUT MACAROON BROWNIES

THE IDEA FOR THIS RECIPE came from one of my test cooks, Jeanne Maguire, who had just finished working on a recipe for coconut macaroons and decided to combine the batter with a brownie recipe. It quickly became clear that we would have to develop a hybrid brownie recipe in order to marry properly with the coconut mixture. The Moist, Light Brownies recipe was too light to hold up the macaroon batter, and the chewy version did not work very well either. After some experimentation, we ended up with something more akin to the light, cakelike variation, but we prepared them in the manner of the chewy brownie recipe, melting the butter instead of creaming it.

I then experimented with the best method for incorporating the macaroon batter. I tried swirling it into the brownie batter, but this was difficult since the coconut mixture was so thick. To solve this problem, I increased the egg whites incrementally until the mixture was light enough. Extra sugar and corn syrup helped

keep the macaroon mixture from drying out during the relatively long baking time.

■■■

Coconut Macaroon Brownies

This recipe is a combination of brownie and coconut macaroon batter, with sizable mouthfuls of macaroon scattered throughout the brownie. This recipe fits a 9 x 13-inch pan. You can halve the recipe and bake it in an 8 x 8-inch pan if you like, but then you won't have enough brownies.

MAKES 24 TO 36 BARS

For the Brownie Batter
- 4 ounces unsweetened chocolate
- ½ pound (2 sticks) unsalted butter
- 6 large eggs, at room temperature
- 2 teaspoons vanilla extract
- 2 cups granulated sugar
- 1 cup all-purpose flour
- 2 tablespoons cocoa powder
- ¼ teaspoon salt

For the Coconut Macaroon Mixture
- 6 large egg whites, at room temperature
- ⅓ cup light corn syrup
- 3 tablespoons butter, melted and slightly cooled
- 1 teaspoon vanilla extract
- ½ cup granulated sugar
- 3 cups desiccated coconut (see page 51 for more information)
- ¼ teaspoon salt

1. Adjust oven rack to the center position and heat the oven to 350 degrees. Grease a 9 x 13-inch baking pan, or line the pan with foil or parchment paper.

2. *For the brownie batter:* Melt the chocolate and butter in a double boiler or over very low heat. Stir frequently. Whisk the eggs and vanilla together in a medium bowl. Add the melted

chocolate mixture and whisk to combine (the mixture will thicken considerably). Add all other ingredients and mix together with a rubber spatula or wooden spoon. Pour the batter into the baking pan and set aside.

3. *For the coconut mixture:* Whisk the egg whites in a medium bowl until well broken up. Add the corn syrup, butter, and vanilla and whisk to combine. Stir in the sugar. Add the coconut and salt and stir or fold until well combined.

4. With a spoon or your fingers, space blobs of the coconut mixture all over the chocolate batter. Make about 3 rows of 5 each, about 15 blobs in all. Using a butter knife, make crisscross swipes through the blobs of coconut to cut them into the brownie batter. Check to see that each blob is cut into once or twice but not much more than that. The trick is to have the coconut in nice big mouthfuls and not too mixed into the chocolate.

5. Bake for about 40 minutes, or until the coconut is golden brown and the brownies are puffed and feel firm when poked with your finger in the center of the pan. Remove pan to a wire rack and cool to room temperature. Cut into pieces and serve.

WHAT CAN GO WRONG? The only trick here is to get the blobs of coconut mixture all about the same size and to use a knife to cut through each blob twice. This will leave a good mound of coconut in the center of each brownie yet mix it up enough so that the coconut is distributed throughout.

⁘

A BETTER BUTTERSCOTCH BROWNIE

BUTTERSCOTCH BROWNIES ARE CLOSE COUSINS to the more common chocolate brownie, using dark brown sugar instead of white. Yet they are also quite different, since chocolate tends to provide a denser, fudgier quality. The question was how to create an intense butterscotch flavor while achieving a pleasing texture. I went to the kitchen to conduct some tests.

There are two basic ways of proceeding with the butter: it can be creamed with the sugar or just melted. I tried both methods and wasn't entirely happy with either. I then decided to simply beat the eggs, sugar, and butter together, and I found that this produces a relatively light but still very moist texture, which I liked. Unlike chocolate brownies, which call for relatively little flour, these brownies needed a full cup of flour. I also ended up adding a small amount of baking powder to lighten the brownies, an ingredient rarely found in most regular brownie recipes.

Sugar was a big issue, because most butterscotch brownies are achingly sweet and, to my mind and palate, inedible. I tried a combination of dark brown sugar and white sugar and finally ended up with just the brown sugar, reducing the quantity from 1¼ cups to 1 cup. For butterscotch flavor, I knew that a very large amount of vanilla provides much of what we have come to expect from a butterscotch dessert, so I increased the quantity from 1 teaspoon to 1 tablespoon. I also added 1 tablespoon of molasses, which gave the taste a bit of depth. Some recipes use only 1 egg and regular brownie recipes use 3. I settled on 2.

After years of trying to cut up bar cookies in the baking pan, I have discovered that it is best to unmold the cooled brownies from the pan in one piece and then cut them into squares. To make this easier, I find that a bit of parchment paper lining is very helpful, even when using a nonstick pan. Place a cooling rack (a very light spray of vegetable oil on the rack is helpful) on top of the baking pan, invert the pan, and then remove it. Peel off the parchment paper and then invert the brownies onto a cutting surface. (Or see the illustration on page 106.)

⋯

Butterscotch Brownies

For this recipe the size of the baking pan is crucial. Only use an 8-inch square pan. Note that this recipe will produce a strong butterscotch flavor, but the brownies will be a bit more cake-like than you would expect from chocolate brownies.

MAKES 16 SQUARES

8 tablespoons (1 stick) unsalted butter, softened

1 cup packed dark brown sugar

2 large eggs

1 tablespoon vanilla extract

1 tablespoon molasses

1 cup all-purpose flour

½ teaspoon baking powder

½ teaspoon salt

¾ cup pecans, broken or coarsely chopped

1. Heat oven to 350 degrees. Butter an 8-inch square baking pan and line the bottom with parchment paper. (This is one recipe for which the size of the baking pan is important. Do not use a larger or smaller pan.)

2. Beat the butter, sugar, eggs, vanilla, and molasses in the bowl of an electric mixer on high speed for about 1 minute, or with a wooden spoon until creamy and smooth. Sift together the flour, baking powder, and salt onto waxed paper and then add to the egg mixture. Fold gently with a large rubber spatula until flour is about half incorporated. Do not overmix. Stir in nuts and continue stirring gently until flour is fully mixed in. Transfer batter to prepared pan. Spread top with spatula to make smooth and even.

3. Bake for 30 to 35 minutes, turning pan front to back halfway through. Start checking for doneness after 23 minutes. When brownies are done, the center top will be firm to the touch and spring back when pressed and the sides will start to pull away from the pan. Let cool in pan. Invert in one piece onto a lightly oiled cooling rack, remove parchment paper, and then flip back onto a cutting board. Cut into 2-inch squares and serve.

WHAT CAN GO WRONG? The easiest way to get into trouble with this recipe is to use the wrong size pan. These brownies must be baked in an 8-inch square pan. If you use a larger pan, the brownies will easily dry out and become hard rather than chewy.

⋱

CRISPY AND CREAMY LEMON BARS

LEMON BARS RANGE BETWEEN culinary nirvana and rubbery, achingly sweet confections with greasy crusts. When they are well made, the lemon curd is creamy without a hint of gluey cornstarch and just sweet enough to offset the tang of lemon, and the crust is crisp and dry to set off the moist topping. Getting there is no piece of cake.

Having tasted superb lemon bars in the test kitchens of *Cook's Illustrated* (see the May/June 1998 issue), I wasn't sure that I could make any improvements on that recipe. However, I started by fiddling with the crust and the first question, of course, was the flour. I tested unbleached all-purpose as well as cake and bleached flour and preferred the all-purpose. One trick often suggested by bakers is to add cornstarch to all-purpose flour to produce a more tender product. I tried this, in varying amounts, and preferred the tooth of the regular all-purpose flour — it was crisper and sturdier without being tough — with no additions. For sugar, confectioners' won out over granulated, which produced a crust that was too tough for this recipe. I played with the ratio of flour to butter and ended up with 1¾ cups of flour to ¾ cup unsalted butter. (These proportions were identical to the *Cook's Illustrated* recipe.) The *Cook's* recipe also suggested chilling the dough before baking, so I tested 30 and 45 minutes; the results were identical, so I stuck with the shorter chilling time.

Now I moved on to the filling. I started with a basic recipe of whole eggs, flour, sugar, lemon zest, lemon juice, salt, and milk. I found that the *Cook's* filling was just a bit too sweet for my taste (I usually prefer slightly less sweet desserts), so I reduced the sugar. I also found that a small amount of melted butter, 2 tablespoons, helped to offset the sweetness. I then slightly reduced the amount of milk to compensate for the added liquid. I tried varying the number of eggs and also adding extra yolks but to no avail; the 4 whole eggs were perfect as is. The recipe in *Cook's* also mentioned that a cornstarch-thickened lemon curd does not hold up during baking as well as one thickened with flour. I tested, and found this to be true. Cornstarch in this case also produced an odd, almost metallic flavor that I found very unappealing.

All that was left was to test the prebaking of the shell and the baking of the filling. With most recipes of this sort, I put the filling into a hot crust, and this recipe was no exception. This keeps the crust from becoming soggy. When I tested oven temperatures, I found that 350 degrees was best for prebaking the crust, but the filling worked better at 325 degrees. I also slightly increased the baking time of the crust from 20 minutes to 20 to 25 minutes. Parchment paper worked better than waxed paper for lining the pan. (This makes removing the lemon bars a snap.) As for sprinkling the bars with confectioners' sugar, as many recipes recommend, I found this unnecessary; and unless it is added just before serving, the sugar will melt.

• • •

Lemon Bars

MAKES ABOUT 24 BARS

For the Crust
Unsalted butter for greasing the pan
1¾ cups all-purpose flour
⅔ cup confectioners' sugar
¾ teaspoon salt
12 tablespoons (1½ sticks) unsalted butter, at very cool room temperature, cut into 1-inch pieces

For the Lemon Curd
4 large eggs, lightly beaten
1¼ cups granulated sugar
2 teaspoons finely grated lemon zest
3 tablespoons all-purpose flour
⅛ teaspoon salt
⅔ cup lemon juice (from 3 to 4 large lemons), strained
¼ cup whole milk
2 tablespoons unsalted butter, melted and slightly cooled

1. *For the crust:* Dot the bottom of a 9 x 13-inch baking pan with butter and line with a sheet of parchment large enough to go up and over the edges of the long sides of the pan. Dot the parchment with butter and line the pan with a second piece of parchment, large enough to go up and over the short sides of the pan.

2. Pulse the flour, sugar, and salt in a food processor fitted with a steel blade. Add the butter and process to blend 8 to 10 seconds and then pulse until the mixture is pale yellow and resembles coarse meal, about three 1-second bursts. Sprinkle the mixture into the prepared pan and press firmly with your fingers into an even layer on the bottom of the pan and about ½ inch up the sides. (The mixture will be very light and fluffy, almost like cornmeal, rather than like a pie dough. Forming the sides may

---

CASE 25: THE SECRET LIFE OF FIG BARS

Fig bars have lots of unusual ingredients in them. Here is a quick look at the hidden ingredients in a few popular recipes.

Recipe A	Recipe B	Recipe C	Recipe D
Orange zest, cocoa powder, red wine	Lemon juice, cinnamon	Citron, orange zest, cocoa powder, cinnamon, rum, Galliano	Dark rum or Marsala, cinnamon

---

appear difficult, since the mixture is so light, but it will harden during baking. Don't worry if the sides are uneven either in height or thickness. It will look much better when baked.)

3. Refrigerate for 30 minutes. While crust is chilling, heat oven to 350 degrees. Bake crust 20 to 25 minutes, until light golden brown.

4. *For the filling:* Whisk the eggs, sugar, and zest in a medium bowl. Whisk in the flour and salt and then stir in the lemon juice, milk, and butter to blend well.

5. Reduce the oven temperature to 325 degrees. Stir the filling one more time and pour into the hot crust. Bake until the filling feels firm when touched lightly, about 20 minutes. (Watch carefully, since once the filling starts to set, it will firm up quickly. Do not overbake it.) Transfer the pan to a cooling rack and cool until almost at room temperature, about 30 minutes. Pull on the long sides of the parchment paper to remove entire bar from the pan in one piece and place on a cutting board. Cut into bars about 2 inches square, wiping the knife as necessary.

WHAT CAN GO WRONG? It is likely that you will find the crust mixture to be light and fluffy and very hard to work with. (It is more like a floury coffee cake topping than a pie dough.) This will lead you to the conclusion that there is some-

thing wrong with the recipe. Just stick to it and do your best to form sides to the crust, and don't worry if it looks like a five-year-old made it. Once baked and filled, the crust will turn out just fine.

FIG BARS

FIG BARS ARE OFTEN FOUND in Italian cookbooks and consist of a crust rolled around a fig-and-nut filling. In this country, they are often made with a bottom crust placed into a baking pan and then topped with a sticky fig filling. I tried the latter method but decided that a more manageable cookie would be best (the sticky top layer makes them hard to handle), so I tried putting on a top crust. This was difficult, since rolling out and fitting the crust was no easy task. Finally, I went back to the more traditional Italian approach, which is to roll out the dough, place the filling on top, wrap the dough around the filling, cut the resulting roll into individual cookies, and then bake them.

With that decided, I now had to develop a recipe for the fig filling that truly tasted of figs and a recipe for the dough that would roll out easily, be sturdy enough to encase the filling without crumbling, and still be flavorful and tender. I consulted cookbooks by four experts: Carol Field *(The Italian Baker),* Nick Malgieri *(How to Bake),* Jim Dodge *(Baking with Jim Dodge),* and Richard Sax *(Classic Home Desserts).* The filling is made from figs, honey, and nuts, plus additional flavorings. I preferred Jim Dodge's recipe since it had the most interesting flavor. In addition to the basic ingredients, he used citron, orange zest, cocoa powder, rum, Galliano, cinnamon, and raisins. One of the other recipes had ¾ cup red wine, which was overpowering, and another version required precooking the filling, which I excluded as an option since it was too much work. The Richard Sax recipe was also good and very simple compared to Dodge's symphony of ingredients.

After devising a working master recipe, I concentrated on the dried figs. I chose Calimyrna for their availability and flavor. However, I did notice a huge difference in quality and flavor from brand to brand, so always purchase the biggest, plumpest figs you can find. These always tested the best. I liked the addition of raisins, which are used in most fig bar recipes, and settled on ½ cup. For the nuts, I went with chopped pecans. Walnuts tend to be bitter, and hazelnuts are often hard to find and have to be skinned, which is a fair amount of work. Toasting did seem to improve the flavor a lot, so I went with this extra step. As with the raisins, I ended up with ½ cup. Honey, which is used by most everyone, works nicely with the figs. The trick is to use just enough but no more. Otherwise, the filling becomes very sticky and hard to handle.

As far as spices go, these cookies definitely needed some spices to perk up the flavor, and the cinnamon was a must, although a modest amount was best, since cinnamon is so strong. I tried a bit of ground cloves but did not care for it. The cocoa powder, which at first may seem an unusual ingredient, does enhance the other flavors in the filling, making them darker and richer without being detectable itself. For the spirits, I skipped the Galliano suggested by Dodge, since it is not a common liquor cabinet staple. I tried using wine and rum, and the flavor of the rum was a better complement to the cookies. I settled on just 1 tablespoon. Finally, I tried the zest of both orange and lemon and much preferred the orange.

My only other concerns were the preparation of the filling and the amount of filling to pastry. Since these cookies are heavy in labor and ingredients, I believe the recipe should yield a decent amount. They keep nicely for up to a week in an airtight container.

For the dough, I found that both Dodge and Sax had exactly the same recipe! However, this dough seemed a bit dry and lacking in flavor. (Dodge ices his cookies, so his dough recipe is fine for that application.) Carol Field's recipe was very dense (it uses no leavening; the other recipes do) but had a rich, buttery flavor. Nick Malgieri's recipe was very good, but I thought it needed a bit of vanilla to round off the flavors.

The first discovery was that 2½ cups of flour married well with ½ cup sugar. It had great balance and the dough was very manageable. I liked the lightness of the doughs made with baking powder; I started with ½ teaspoon and then tested levels up to 2½ teaspoons. I settled on 1 teaspoon, which yielded a crust that was light but not too cakey. I also tested butter quantities and finally settled on a substantial 14 tablespoons, pushing the limit to get the maximum butter flavor and still have a workable dough. I found that 2 eggs worked well; when I tried using 1 whole egg and 2 yolks, the dough was a little more eggy-tasting and more crumbly than I wanted. As mentioned, the crust needed the vanilla taste, but I found the lemon taste to be unwelcome in this recipe.

Now I had a great recipe, but I discovered that the crust had a dull appearance, so I gave it an egg wash before baking, which dressed the cookies up a bit. These cookies are made by rolling out the dough, placing the filling on top, rolling the dough around the filling, cutting the roll into individual cookies, and then baking them. I tried baking the whole roll without cutting beforehand, but this did not work; I tried slicing the baked rolls when they were hot, warm, and even completely cooled, and they fell apart on all attempts. So they have to be cut before baking.

▪ ▪ ▪

Italian-Style Fig Bars

These bars are made in the Italian style: the dough is rolled out, topped with filling, and then rolled up into a long, thin log. Individual cookies are cut, placed on a cookie sheet, and baked.

MAKES ABOUT 48 COOKIES

For the Filling

1	pound dried Calimyrna figs, stemmed and roughly chopped
½	cup raisins
½	cup chopped, toasted pecans
½	teaspoon cinnamon
1	tablespoon cocoa powder, Dutch-process preferred
½	cup honey
1	tablespoon dark rum
	Zest from 1 orange, minced (optional)

For the Crust

2½	cups all-purpose flour
½	cup granulated sugar
1	teaspoon baking powder
½	teaspoon salt
12	tablespoons (1½ sticks) unsalted butter, at cool room temperature, cut into 1-inch pieces
2	large eggs
1	teaspoon vanilla extract

For the Egg Wash

1	large egg
1	tablespoon milk

1. Adjust an oven rack to the center position and preheat oven to 350 degrees. Line two baking sheets with parchment.

2. *For the filling:* Place all of the filling ingredients in the bowl of a food processor fitted with the metal blade and process until finely chopped but not quite pureed. The filling will be sticky. Set aside.

3. *For the crust:* Place the flour, sugar, baking powder, and salt in a large bowl and whisk to combine. Add the butter and toss to coat with the flour mixture. Using your fingertips, rub the butter into the flour mixture until the mixture resembles coarse meal. This can also be done in a food processor, but be very careful not to overprocess the dough.

4. In a small bowl, whisk together the eggs and the vanilla. Make a well in the center of the flour-butter mixture. Pour the egg mixture into the well and mix the egg into the flour mixture with a fork until the dough comes together. Gather the dough into a ball and wrap in plastic. Refrigerate for 30 minutes.

5. *To assemble the cookies:* On a lightly floured surface, roll the dough into a rectangle about 12 x 16 inches. It will be a bit less than ¼ inch thick. Cut the dough into three pieces 4 inches wide by 16 inches long. Using your hands, form the filling into long 1-inch-thick ropes down the center of each of the three strips of dough. (This step is a bit messy.)

6. Combine the egg and milk and whisk well to make the egg wash. Lightly apply a stripe of egg wash along one long edge of each strip of dough. (At this point, you will have three 4 x 16 pieces of dough. Down the center of each strip is a 1-inch-thick line of filling, and one long edge of each strip is painted with a thin coating of egg wash.) Working with one strip at a time, use your fingers to pick up the long edge of dough *without* egg wash and wrap it snugly over the filling. Now roll the partially wrapped filling toward the egg wash to fully encase the filling in dough. Carefully place the completed roll out of the way, seam side down, and proceed until all three strips have been rolled. With your fingers, flatten each roll until it is about 2 inches wide. Apply two coats of egg wash to each roll.

CASE 26: MAKING HERMITS POPULAR

Recipes for this lonely bar cookie vary tremendously in their use of sugar, eggs, and molasses.

Ingredient	Recipe A	Recipe B	Recipe C	Recipe D	Recipe E
Flour	2 cups	1⅓ cups	4 cups	2 cups	2 cups
Butter	4 tablespoons	8 tablespoons	16 tablespoons	9 tablespoons	8 tablespoons
Sugar	½ cup granulated	1 cup brown	2½ cups brown	1 cup brown	½ cup granulated
Eggs	2	1	3	1	2
Molasses	½ cup	None	⅓ cup	¼ cup	½ cup
Baking soda	1 teaspoon	¼ teaspoon	1½ teaspoons	2 teaspoons	¾ teaspoon
Baking powder	None	None	1½ teaspoons	None	¾ teaspoon
Other	None	Sour cream	Crystallized ginger	Ground ginger	None

7. With a thin, sharp knife, and using a quick motion, slice the rolls into 1-inch pieces. Place the cookies seam side down onto the prepared sheets, leaving about 1 inch between them. Bake the cookies, one sheet at a time, for about 20 minutes, turning the sheet front to back halfway through the cooking. Cool completely on a rack and store in an airtight container for up to a week.

WHAT CAN GO WRONG? Unless you are particularly skilled as a baker, you will find that your rolls of filling-encased dough will look less than perfect. It is helpful if the dough is properly chilled, since once it warms up, it can become hard to work with.

HERMIT BARS

THE PROBLEM WITH many hermit bars is that they are dry — the sort of thing that might keep well in a farmhouse pantry but would not be one's first choice as a delectable cookie. In addition, they should not, in my opinion, be too light — I like a bit of chew to these bars rather than a mouthful of cake. They should be spicy but with a flavor different from that of gingerbread, and I like a good number of raisins in the batter to give the bars some interest.

As a jumping-off point, I turned to hermit recipes in several popular cookbooks. Case 26 shows how the five cookbook recipes tested matched up. Of the five recipes, the one from Maida Heatter (recipe E in the chart) was the best, although the cookies were a bit on the cakey side. The hermits without molasses just didn't satisfy, some recipes were quite dry, and some had too much ginger and not enough flavor from other spices. So I started with Maida's recipe and went back to the kitchen.

For starters I reduced the amount of baking powder and baking soda and did not sift the flour (as called for in Maida's recipe), to see if I could make the cookies a bit denser. Now I had a denser, chewier cookie, just what I was looking for. The next test was the amount and type of sugar. When I used either light or dark brown sugar, the flavor of the molasses was diminished, so I stuck with regular white granulated sugar. The same thing happened when I tried substituting a bit of honey for some of the sugar. I finally settled on ½ cup sugar to ½ cup molasses.

For the eggs, I settled on 2. One egg made the hermits crumbly and heavy; 3 eggs made the batter spread too much during baking and the cookies were too light. For the butter, I tried 4 tablespoons and the hermits were dry; but with 12 tablespoons the dough was too soft and spread during baking, so I stuck with 8 tablespoons. For the spices, I played with a number of combinations and finally settled on allspice, mace, cloves, and cinnamon. Mace seemed a bit more aromatic than nutmeg, and ginger made the bars taste too much like gingerbread. Other flavorings, such as coffee or cocoa, just complicated the flavor and were therefore unnecessary. I like raisins in a hermit bar, so I added a full cup. I found there was no need to soak them before adding. I baked the bars with and without nuts and preferred the latter, although I list nuts as optional in my final recipe. I also found that an egg wash for glazing the cookies before baking added a nice touch and prevented the batter from spreading quite so much.

For oven temperature, all of the recipes I found suggested 375 degrees, but I found that 350 degrees was better, since the edges do not brown too much and the inside of the cookies

remains moist. Lower oven temperatures produced bars that spread too much during baking.

▪ ▪ ▪

Hermit Bars

These are the sort of cookies that keep and travel well. As for the recipe itself, I use a technique favored by biscotti bakers: I fashion the dough into logs, bake them up, and then slice them into individual cookies.

MAKES ABOUT 16 BARS

8	tablespoons (1 stick) unsalted butter, softened but still firm
½	cup granulated sugar
2	large eggs, at room temperature
½	cup molasses
2	cups all-purpose flour
½	teaspoon baking soda
½	teaspoon baking powder
½	teaspoon salt
¼	teaspoon allspice
½	teaspoon cinnamon
¼	teaspoon mace
½	teaspoon ground cloves
1	cup raisins
1	cup pecans or walnuts, coarsely chopped (optional)
1	large egg, lightly beaten

1. Heat oven to 350 degrees. Line a cookie sheet or jelly roll pan with parchment paper.

2. Beat the butter and sugar in the bowl of an electric mixer or with a wooden spoon until creamy and smooth, about 3 minutes. Add the eggs and molasses and beat until fully incorporated. (The mixture may appear grainy at first; keep beating until smooth and dull in appearance.) In a separate bowl, whisk together the next 8 ingredients (flour through ground cloves) and then gently stir into the butter-sugar mixture until just incorporated. Stir in raisins and optional nuts.

3. Using a rubber spatula, form the dough

into two logs on the prepared pan, each about 2 inches wide by 14 inches long. (When baked, the logs will spread out to 5 inches in width, so leave plenty of room between them.) Brush with the lightly beaten egg. Bake for 15 minutes, or until the tops of the logs spring back when pressed and they are lightly browned. Let cool on the pan for 15 minutes. Cut at an angle into bars about 2 inches wide. Hermits hold well in an airtight container and can also be successfully frozen.

WHAT CAN GO WRONG? You will not think that the logs of dough will spread as much as they do in the oven and may be tempted to place them too close together on the baking sheet. Each log will spread out to about 5 inches in width, so leave plenty of space between them.

● ● ●

Raspberry Rectangles

This recipe started out as an attempt to develop date squares, a common recipe from the forties and fifties in which the dough mixture used for the base is also used for a crumb topping. The filling is usually either jam or a cooked filling made from dried fruit. After reviewing a few recipes, I determined that the most common combination of ingredients was 1½ sticks butter, 1½ cups flour, 1½ cups oats, and 1½ cups granulated sugar. When I tested this recipe, I found that the bars were much too sweet, so I reduced the total sugar to 1 cup, using ½ cup of light brown sugar and ½ cup granulated. This was a marked improvement, with more flavor and a more balanced level of sweetness. I played with the nuts, preferring a pairing of sweet almonds with nutty pecans, although you can use either by itself if you like. I also added baking soda to the recipe to make the crust a bit lighter.

For the filling, I tested a variety of jams, including apricot, strawberry, and blackberry,

none of which had the bright, strong flavor of raspberry, which stands up nicely to oats and nuts. The traditional date filling was dull and unappealing by comparison. These cookies are extremely rich and buttery and will need to cool completely before cutting. I suggest letting them sit for at least 2 hours before serving.

MAKES 24 RECTANGLES

1¼	cups quick-cooking oats
1½	cups all-purpose flour
½	cup granulated sugar
½	cup packed light brown sugar
¾	teaspoon baking soda
¼	teaspoon salt
½	cup chopped pecans or almonds or a mixture
12	tablespoons (1½ sticks) unsalted butter, softened
1	cup raspberry preserves

1. Adjust oven rack to middle position and heat oven to 350 degrees. Butter a 9 x 9-inch baking pan and line with parchment (see illustration, page 106). In a large bowl, whisk together the first 7 ingredients (oats through nuts). Blend in the softened butter with a fork or with an electric mixer on slow speed for 3 to 4 minutes, or until the mixture is blended well and looks like wet sand. Place two-thirds of the mixture into the prepared pan and press onto the bottom. Spread with the preserves using a rubber spatula. Sprinkle the remaining crust mixture on top.

2. Bake for 30 minutes, turning pan front to back after 15 minutes. Completely cool before removing from pan and cutting.

WHAT CAN GO WRONG? You do want to use the correct size baking pan; otherwise the cookies will be too thin or too thick and not bake up properly. You also want to be sure to leave enough of the mixture, roughly one-third, to use as a topping. Finally, when they are baked properly, the cookies should be neither raw and moist nor hard and dry. They should be firm but still moist.

Chewy Pecan Bars

This recipe comes from Pillsbury's Fifth $100,000 Recipe and Baking Contest, which was run in 1954. A Mrs. Pope from Aberdeen, South Dakota, won a $1,000 prize for her pecan bars, which are both light and chewy, a cross between a cookie and a candy. I have faithfully reproduced the recipe below without alteration since, when tested, they needed no improvement. These cookies are similar to many recipes from the turn of the last century, which used a simple shortbread type of dough covered with a sweetened nut topping.

MAKES ABOUT 36 BARS,
EACH 1½ INCHES SQUARE

For the Crust

    1   cup all-purpose flour
    ¼   teaspoon baking powder
    4   tablespoons (½ stick) unsalted butter,
        softened but still firm
    ⅓   cup packed brown sugar
    ¼   cup pecans, finely chopped

For the Topping

    2   large eggs
    ¾   cup dark corn syrup
    ¼   cup packed brown sugar
    2   tablespoons all-purpose flour
    ½   teaspoon salt
    1   teaspoon vanilla extract
    ¾   cup pecans, chopped

1. Heat oven to 350 degrees. Grease a 9 x 9-inch pan.

2. *For the crust:* Sift together the flour and baking powder onto a sheet of waxed paper. Set aside. Using an electric mixer, beat the butter and brown sugar together for 3 minutes. Add the flour mixture and continue beating until mixture resembles coarse meal. Stir in the pecans and mix with a wooden spoon. Pat firmly into prepared pan and bake for 10 minutes. Remove from oven.

3. *For the topping:* Whisk eggs in a medium bowl until foamy. Add the next 5 ingredients (corn syrup through vanilla) and whisk until combined. Pour over baked crust. Sprinkle with chopped pecans. Bake at 350 degrees for 25 to 30 minutes. Let cool in pan and then cut into bars.

WHAT CAN GO WRONG? This is a very simple recipe. Make sure that you beat the dough until it is the texture of coarse meal. Do not overbeat it.

BLONDIES

WE HAVE ALL HAD a blondie, or congo bar — a brownie without chocolate in the batter — yet it is hard to remember eating a really good one. They are often dry and hard or gooey and too sweet. Some are bland, with very little flavor, and others are so rich that one can take only a bite. Some are high-rise and cakey, while others are so dense that they are hard to bite through. I was looking for a moist interior, some chew, and a crisp exterior, and I also knew that the bar should contain both chocolate chips and nuts. With those goals in mind, I made recipes from four cookbooks: *Best Ever Brownies* (Joan Steuer), *The Fannie Farmer Cookbook, Rosie's All-Butter Fresh Cream Sugar-Packed Baking Book* (Judy Rosenberg), and *Classic Home Desserts.*

Recipe A (see chart, Case 27) was dull, probably because of too little sugar. Recipe B was much too sweet; the dark brown sugar overpowered the other ingredients. I also missed the chocolate chips. The other two recipes were pretty good, although on the heavy and gooey side. My conclusions were that more butter

CASE 27: CONGO BONGO

Congo bars appear to be simple enough, but recipes vary tremendously in their use of eggs, sugar, and baking powder.

Ingredient/Technique	Recipe A	Recipe B	Recipe C	Recipe D
Butter	8 tablespoons	8 tablespoons	9 tablespoons	8 tablespoons
Sugar	1 cup light brown	2 cups dark brown	1¾ cups light brown	¾ cup plus 2 tablespoons light brown
Eggs	1	2	2	1
Vanilla	1 teaspoon	1 teaspoon	1¼ teaspoons	1½ teaspoons
Flour	1 cup	1½ cups	1⅓ cups	¾ cup
Baking powder/ baking soda	1 teaspoon baking powder	2 teaspoons baking powder	1½ teaspoons baking soda	½ teaspoon baking soda
Salt	¼ teaspoon	½ teaspoon	None	⅛ teaspoon
Chocolate chips	3 ounces	None	1 cup	4 ounces
Nuts	None	1 cup	½ cup	¾ cup
Pan size	8 x 8	9 x 13	9 x 13	8 x 8

would add flavor and moisture. Sugar was also important for moisture and flavor, so I went with a full 2 cups. Finally, I thought that 3 eggs rather than 1 or 2 might improve the texture as well. So my working recipe now included 12 tablespoons butter, 2 cups light brown sugar, 3 eggs, 1½ cups flour, 1 teaspoon baking powder, ½ teaspoon salt, 1 cup chocolate chips, and ¾ cup toasted, chopped pecans. The basic method included creaming the butter and the sugar, adding the eggs one at a time, adding the dry in-

gredients, and then stirring in the nuts. I baked the bars at 350 degrees for 30 minutes.

The result? They were good but still needed work. First I tested the sugar. I made the recipe using 1½ cups light brown sugar and ½ cup granulated but preferred those made with all brown sugar, since they had more flavor. I also tested cutting back the sugar to 1¾ cups. This was an improvement, as it balanced the flavors better, allowing the taste of the butter to shine through. When I tried reducing the sugar to 1½ cups, the bars were dry and tough compared to those made with 1¾ cups. Bars made with dark brown sugar tasted more like butterscotch, which I felt was heavy-handed for a simple blondie. So I left the sugar at 1¾ cups light brown.

For the eggs, I tested 4 instead of 3, and the bars were too cakey; when I used 2 eggs the bars were too dense. A teaspoon of vanilla turned out to be okay, 2 teaspoons was overpowering, and 1½ teaspoons was just right. Cake flour made the bars fall apart, since they were too crumbly. In terms of leavener, some recipes use baking soda instead of powder, but I found that the soda did not provide sufficient lift. Baking powder was clearly the way to go, and 1 teaspoon was best: more than that made the bars taller but less chewy, one of my key taste criteria, and less than a teaspoon made bars that were dense. Salt was tested and finally adjusted to ¾ teaspoon. I did not scrimp on the chocolate chips — I like the bars shot through with them — so I settled on a full cup. I also found that milk chocolate works well here, even though I am usually partial to darker chocolate. Walnuts were too bitter, so I went with pecans, which I prefer toasted and then coarsely chopped.

...

Blondies (Congo Bars)

As with all recipes that call for creaming butter, make sure that the butter is at 65 to 67 degrees, the point at which it is the consistency of clay or putty. To warm up the eggs in a hurry, place them in a small bowl of hot water for 2 minutes and then discard the water. A good technique for removing these bars from the pan is to line the pan with two pieces of parchment paper that are long enough to cover the bottom and extend an inch or so beyond the sides. The pan does not need to be greased, and to remove the bars for cutting, simply use the paper to lift them out in one piece.

MAKES ABOUT 36 BARS

- 1½ cups all-purpose flour
- 1 teaspoon baking powder
- ¾ teaspoon salt
- 12 tablespoons (1½ sticks) unsalted butter, softened but still firm
- 1¾ cups packed light brown sugar
- 3 large eggs, at room temperature
- 1½ teaspoons vanilla extract
- 1 cup chocolate chips
- ¾ cup chopped, toasted pecans

1. Adjust oven rack to the center position and heat oven to 350 degrees. Butter a 9 x 13-inch baking pan and line with parchment paper (see illustration, page 106). In a small bowl, whisk together the flour, baking powder, and salt.

2. Beat butter in the bowl of an electric mixer for 1 minute. Add sugar and beat for 3 minutes, or until the mixture becomes very light and fluffy. Add eggs one at a time, beating 20 seconds after each addition. Add the vanilla and beat to combine. The mixture should be dull and smooth. (If it looks grainy or separated, place a kitchen towel dampened with hot water around the mixing bowl with the machine on. Refresh the towel with hot water as necessary.) Add the flour mixture and beat on the lowest speed until almost combined and then add the chocolate chips and nuts. Mix on low or fold with a spatula until fully combined.

3. Turn the batter into the prepared pan and bake for 35 to 40 minutes, or until the top is shiny and cracked and feels firm to the touch. Place pan on a rack and cool completely. Cut into rectangles about 1½ x 2 inches and serve.

WHAT CAN GO WRONG? The texture of these bars will vary considerably based on baking time. If you leave them in the oven too long, they will become hard and dry.

7

CAKES

Any sort of baking can be difficult, since small changes in ingredients or pan sizes or even baking temperature can radically affect the outcome. This is particularly true of cakes, since they require just the right amount of lift during baking combined with the formation of sufficient structure to hold the height once the cake is done. This requires a balance between leavening agents, fat, flour, and eggs, and the right oven temperature.

Most cakes are quite similar. A yellow cake, the variety used as the basic building block for most recipes, is made with both egg whites and yolks. The lift is provided by baking powder and soda, and the structure is also enhanced by beating softened butter and sugar together in the process called creaming. This is also the basic method used for a chocolate cake. A white cake is similar to a yellow cake except that it has no egg yolks; this results in a finer, lighter cake, akin to one made from a boxed mix.

Some cakes use whipped egg whites for lift. These include angel food cake, sponge cake, and chiffon cake. These three cakes are quite similar, the first using all egg whites, the second

using a few yolks as well, and the third using yolks, vegetable oil or butter, and then some baking powder for lift, since the batter is heavier and fattier than that of either an angel food or sponge cake.

CAKE-BAKING BASICS

IN PREPARING THIS CHAPTER, I performed a series of tests intended to resolve common issues such as the proper rack position, the best way to grease a cake pan, how to tell when a cake is done, and so forth.

WHICH IS THE BEST RACK POSITION FOR BAKING A CAKE?

I had always assumed that the middle position was best for baking a cake. Using the bottom rack, I thought, would overcook the bottom of the cake and using the top rack would overcook the top. Since many of my dearly held theories about cooking are proved wrong when actually tested, I set out to test this theory once and for all.

CASE 28: GREASE THIS!

Which method of greasing a cake pan produces the best rise, the best color, and the best texture?

Greasing Method	Nonstick Pan	Traditional (Tinned Steel/Shiny) Pan
No grease	Domed, uneven rise	Poor rise in pan; hard to remove cake
Butter dusted with flour	Good flavor and release	Good flavor, but some sticking
Crisco dusted with flour	Best release, with even rise and firm crust	Great even, flat rise; some sticking with bottom of cake
Vegetable oil dusted with flour	Unpleasantly crunchy crust, but excellent release	Crunchy crust, but an even rise
Baker's Joy	Uneven spray; off flavors	Uneven spray; off flavors
Sprayed oil dusted with flour	Good job overall	Good job overall
Parchment paper only	Some sticking to sides of pan; otherwise worked well	Sides of cake stuck to pan
Parchment paper in a buttered and floured pan	Worked well; tender bottom; great release	Worked well; tender bottom; great release
Parchment paper in a pan greased with butter or Crisco	Worked well; must run knife around sides of pan to release	Worked well; must run knife around sides of pan to release
Butter dusted with sugar	Somewhat gritty sides and bottom	Gritty sides and bottom

I tried the top, middle, and bottom racks, as well as actually setting the cake pan directly on the oven bottom and, for a final test, setting the cake pan on a pizza stone (the stone was on an oven rack). The results were not unexpected but still fascinating.

It turned out that the middle position *is* the best position for most cakes. That is, you are less likely to run into problems. The lower rack produced a cake that was rubbery and dense, with a coarse texture. The cake baked directly on the floor of the oven was rubbery, uneven in texture, and had a burned bottom. The cake baked on the pizza stone was very rubbery and chewy. Baking on the top rack overbrowned the tops of the cake layers. For a basic yellow cake, the middle rack was the best of the lot.

However, being curious about a different style of cake, I tried a genoise — an extremely light cake, which depends on beaten egg whites for the leavening — and found that the middle rack produced uneven holes in the cake structure and a texture that was a bit dense. The unexpected winner was the upper rack, which turned out a very nice, even-textured cake, with more rise than the middle or lower racks. The top of the cake was also flat, not domed, a big plus when you are trying to make a frosted cake look professional. However, when I tried a genoise in a second, smaller oven, I found that the top did get overcooked when baked in the top third of the oven.

The conclusion? The safest rack placement is the middle, as expected, but in some ovens, and with lighter cakes, the top third of the oven may be the best place. (When baking two cake layers simultaneously, always bake them on the same rack. If you place them on different racks, they will bake unevenly.)

WHAT IS THE BEST WAY TO GREASE A CAKE PAN?

This would at first blush appear to be a rather simple issue, the method of preparing the pan having little to do with the rise or crust. It turns out, however, that the method is important and can dramatically affect not only how well the cake releases from the pan but whether it bakes up with a domed or flat top.

I decided to test both nonstick pans and regular cake pans, thinking that they might require different solutions. For both types of pan I tried the following: no greasing at all, butter dusted

with flour, Crisco dusted with flour, vegetable oil dusted with flour, Baker's Joy (a spray), sprayed oil dusted with flour, parchment paper on bottom, parchment paper in a greased pan, parchment in a greased and floured pan, and butter dusted with sugar. Case 28 summarizes the results.

The winner was lining the pan with parchment after greasing with either Crisco or butter. Dusting the pan with flour after greasing is unnecessary except for a very sticky cake. I also found that flour can leave small white splotches on the sides and bottom of a cake if the pan is not coated evenly. Crisco did have one advantage worth noting, which is that it is always just the right consistency for coating a cake pan. Butter, on the other hand, does not spread particularly well if it is too cold. However, butter has better flavor, and that's why most bakers prefer it. One added benefit of using parchment, by the way, is that it tends to make the bottom of a cake more tender. (When you peel it off, you often also peel off some of the tougher cake bottom.) The chapter "Tips, Techniques, and Shortcuts" tells you how to cut parchment rounds to fit your pans.

HOW CAN YOU TELL WHEN A CAKE IS DONE?

Many recipes suggest that a thin metal skewer is the proper tool for determining if a cake is done. Nonsense! I have found that this method is far from foolproof, and most folks do not have one of these at home anyway. But I wanted to approach this topic scientifically, so I set up an experiment using toothpicks, wooden skewers, metal skewers, an instant-read thermometer, a finger, and a fork, as well as trying to judge "doneness" using appearance or baking time alone.

None of the methods turned out to work very well on its own. I find that a combination of a wooden toothpick or skewer plus a bit of prodding with the finger (pressing the top of the cake to see if it springs back) is the most reliable

WHEN IS A CAKE DONE?

Press a fork into the center and the cake should spring back.

Or press center of cake with your fingers. Cake testers are unreliable.

combination. An instant-read thermometer is also a good indicator — at least it tells you if the cake is close to being ready. (Most cakes are done at around 200 to 204 degrees.)

HOW CAN I BAKE UP A PERFECTLY LEVEL CAKE?

Everyone who bakes cakes finds that sometimes the center of the cake bakes up higher than the circumference, which is referred to as doming, or the cake has a sunken middle. Unfortunately, this is a very complicated subject and there is no easy answer. But here is what I do know.

The problem often starts with the recipe itself. If there is too much leavener — baking powder or soda — or if there is too little flour, this can result in a fallen center. In the case of a domed cake layer, there may be too little baking powder or too many eggs. None of this matters particularly, because the home cook is unlikely to start reworking cake recipes to solve this problem. However, there are a few things that are within your control.

The most common reason for a domed or sunken cake, assuming that the recipe is well tested, is that the home cook uses the wrong pan size. A bigger size than called for often makes the cake sink in the middle, and a pan that is smaller can result in a domed center. Next, the cake pans may not have been properly greased. Angel food cake, for example, needs an ungreased tube pan so that the cake has something to hold on to as it rises. On the other hand, a yellow cake requires well-greased sides so that the cake can rise properly. (Angel food cake has little internal structure — it is little more than egg whites beaten with sugar — and therefore needs to attach itself to the side of the pan during baking. As it cools, the cake sets and can then support itself. A yellow cake, on the other hand, is made with eggs, butter, and a higher proportion of flour; this results in a sturdier structure, which can support itself during baking.)

I have also found that the correct oven temperature and placement of the cake pan in the oven can make a difference. If your oven varies by even 25 degrees, this can affect the rise of a cake. At the same time, using the wrong rack position can also have adverse consequences, especially with a delicate cake such as a genoise. I have even found that different types of cake pans can yield different results. (In my cake pan tests, there was a difference between using an aluminum and a cushioned aluminum pan, for example. See page 24.) Finally, having the ingredients (especially butter and eggs) at the proper temperature is crucial as well to generate the desired results (such as volume when beaten).

The bottom line? There is no quick fix. Have your oven calibrated properly, use the middle oven rack, use the right size cake pan made out of the right materials, grease the pan properly, make sure ingredients are at the right temperature, and follow the recipe directions carefully. All that being said, you will still have problems from time to time, since baking chemistry is

CASE 29: LET YOUR FINGERS DO THE TESTING

Which method or combination of methods is best for determining when a cake is properly baked?

Tool/Technique	Result
Toothpick or wooden skewer (insert into center of cake; cake is done when pick or skewer comes out clean)	Undercooked batter sticks well to wood; repeat tests can affect rise of cake
Fork (press top of cake to see if it springs back)	More surface area for testing; will affect rise of cake if used repeatedly
Metal skewer or cake tester (technique same as toothpick)	Can result in undercooking; batter does not stick to metal easily
Instant-read thermometer (insert into center of cake)	200 to 204 degrees was about right; does leave a largish hole in cake, however
Finger (press top of cake to see if it springs back)	Hard to judge spring; by the time cake definitely springs back it is often overcooked
Timer	Baking times are never foolproof, since all ovens bake at different rates
Appearance (cake pulls away from sides of pan)	Very hard to judge doneness from appearance alone

tricky and small variations in preparation can make a large difference in the outcome.

WHAT IS THE BEST WAY TO COOL A CAKE?

I had long wondered if it was necessary to use a cooling rack to cool a cake. What if one just left it in the pan or on a plate? Well, I tried four methods: cooling completely in the pan, or cooling briefly in the pan and then turning out onto a plate, onto a cooling rack, or onto a greased rack. The results were unambiguous. The cakes left to cool in the pan were hard to remove; some of the cake remained in the pan. The cakes cooled on a plate also had problems; some of the bottom of the cake came off when the cake was removed from the plate. The ungreased cooling rack was less than ideal, since a bit of cake stuck to the rack. The greased rack (I sprayed the rack with a vegetable oil spray) turned out best. Be sure to use only a very light film of oil. I also found that it was important to flip the cake over after a half hour to avoid the problem of grooves appearing on the cake surface.

WHAT IS THE BEST METHOD FOR REMOVING A CAKE FROM THE PAN TO A COOLING RACK?

I have always had difficulty with this step, using a combination of plates and cooling racks and getting myself into all sorts of trouble. The problems arise from the fact that this is a two-step process. First, the cake has to come out onto a flat surface. Then it needs to be flipped onto a cooling rack. If, for example, you turn the cake out onto a plate, then how do you get the upside-down cake from the plate to a rack? If it is a small, circular rack, then this is relatively easy. Just place the lightly greased rack over the bottom of the cake (be sure the *rack* is upside down at this point), then gently but se-

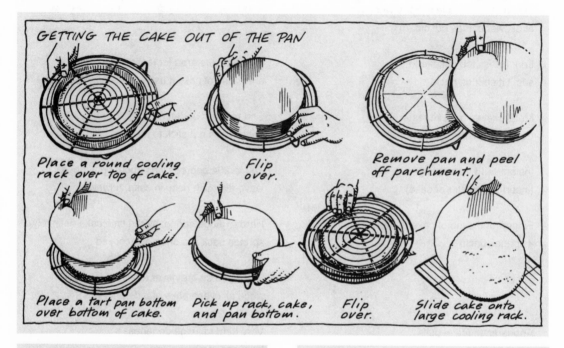

GETTING THE CAKE OUT OF THE PAN

Place a round cooling rack over top of cake.

Flip over.

Remove pan and peel off parchment.

Place a tart pan bottom over bottom of cake.

Pick up rack, cake, and pan bottom.

Flip over.

Slide cake onto large cooling rack.

FIXING DOMED CAKES is easy. Cut off dome with a serrated knife.

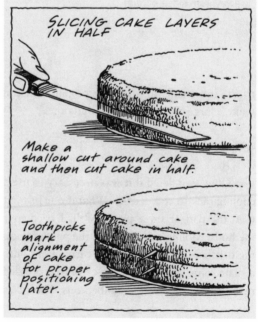

SLICING CAKE LAYERS IN HALF

Make a shallow cut around cake and then cut cake in half.

Toothpicks mark alignment of cake for proper positioning later.

curely sandwich the cake between plate and rack as you flip cake and rack right side up. (Remove the plate immediately.) If, however, you are baking a two-layer cake and are using a large cooling rack that holds two cake layers, then you have a problem.

Here is what I have found to be effective. You will either need two (preferably round) cooling racks about the size of your cake pan, or you can use removable tart pan bottoms or inverted (empty) cake pans of the same size. Very lightly spray the cooling racks (or their substitutes) with vegetable oil, or lightly grease them with oil using a paper towel (use just a whisper of oil). After allowing the cake to cool in the pan for 5 to 10 minutes, run a flat, dull knife around the sides of the pan to make sure that the cake does not stick. Place one of the cooling racks (or the bottom of a tart pan or cake pan) over the top of the cake and invert the pan and rack to transfer the cake to the rack. (Use oven mitts, since cake and pan will still be quite warm.) Remove the cake pan and peel parchment liner, if using, from cake. Now place the second cooling rack (or substitute) on the cake bottom and flip the cake over a second time. Now you have the cake right side up. To transfer it to a large cooling rack that holds both cake layers (for a two-layer cake), simply slide the cake layer onto the large rack, using a large metal spatula or pancake turner to help, if necessary.

Quick Tips for Cake Baking

Here are a few tips that should help you avoid common cake-making mistakes:

- A large rubber spatula is helpful in folding together batter ingredients. Smaller spatulas or wooden spoons require many more strokes, which are inefficient and can overwork a batter. (See illustrations and discussion of folding on pages 8–9.)

- When working with batters, use the largest bowl possible. It is difficult to mix a batter in a bowl that barely contains it.

- Never let the batter sit once it has been prepared. Make sure to grease your pans before starting a cake recipe so that the batter can be quickly put into the pans and then set into the oven. Letting the batter sit will adversely affect both the amount of the rise in the oven and the texture.

- Don't panic if the tops of your baked cake layers are not level. It is not uncommon to find a layer that is slightly sunk or domed in the middle. For a two-layer cake, use the best layer for the top. The imperfections in the bottom layer will never be seen. A bit of extra filling will disguise any depressions in the cake.

- To keep your cake plate clean while frosting a cake, first place four 2-inch-wide strips of waxed paper around the perimeter of the plate. Place the bottom cake layer on top of these strips so that about 1 inch of paper is sitting underneath the cake and the rest is sticking out. After frosting, simply pull out these strips and the plate will be perfectly clean.

- Cake flour and all-purpose flour are quite different products. The former has a relatively low gluten level, which simply means that it is made from a softer, lower-protein wheat, the actual kernels being less hard than those used for all-purpose or bread flours. This produces a finer, softer texture. If you want a bit more chew to a cake, for example, you can use all-purpose instead of cake flour. On the other hand, if you want a softer, finer product, use cake flour instead. Although different flours with different protein levels require slightly different ratios of liquid to flour, this is not a significant factor when making cakes.

- Self-rising flour already has baking powder included with the flour. Never use self-rising flour unless it is specifically called for in a recipe; otherwise you will have too much of a good thing. This will cause overproduction of carbon dioxide gas, which may result in a cake rising too much and then deflating. The amount and type of leavener (baking powder and/or baking soda) required for a particular cake depends heavily on what else is in the batter. For example, a batter that uses milk will probably require the use of baking powder, which contains an acid, to help produce the chemical reaction that provides lift. (Milk has little acid in it.) One that is based on buttermilk, which contains a great deal of lactic acid, might not need the acidic ingredient found in baking powder and therefore would use baking soda or a combination of powder and soda. Using self-rising flour when it is not called for will upset the acid-soda balance of the recipe.

ALL-PURPOSE YELLOW CAKE

THIS IS WITHOUT DOUBT the most basic and most important cake recipe in any home cook's repertoire. Unlike the basic white cake, this yellow cake uses yolks and is therefore sturdier and works with a variety of different fillings and frostings. It also lends itself to a wide variety of flavorings, which might overwhelm a delicate white cake. I started with a master recipe that I had been using for years and then performed a series of tests to see if I could improve it.

The basic recipe for any yellow cake is to cream (beat at high speed) butter and sugar and then to beat in whole eggs. A mixture of flour, salt, and baking powder is gently added along with milk to make the cake batter, which is then baked in a moderate oven. I started my testing with the flour, substituting cake flour for all-purpose. This did produce a finer-textured cake as expected, but it was still a bit tough. I then tested the quantity of cake flour, starting with 3 cups, the amount of flour called for in my original recipe. Thinking that the cake was a bit dry, I re-

duced the flour in ¼-cup increments, down to 2¼ cups, and found that 2½ cups was just right. I also tested sifting the flour, but this did not yield any discernible improvement, so I decided it wasn't worth the bother. I tried substituting vegetable oil for the butter only to find that the cake was greasy and lacking the rich, buttery flavor I associate with a good yellow cake. Even a substitution of only a few tablespoons made the cake a poor cousin to the real thing. I finally settled on 12 tablespoons butter when I discovered that more butter simply made the cake greasy and less butter produced a dry cake. I had been using 5 whole eggs in my recipe and tried both 4 and 6 without any improvement. Four whole eggs and 2 yolks as well as 4 whole eggs and 2 whites were also tried without success.

I tested various levels of baking powder and settled on 2 teaspoons: a cake made with 1 teaspoon was heavy and the cake with a full tablespoon was coarse in texture. I also tried 1½ teaspoons as well as 2½ teaspoons, but the 2-teaspoon cake was superior. For the sugar, I started with 1¼ cups and, finding that a bit low, I increased it to 1½ cups, which produced a sweeter and moister cake. More than 1½ cups sugar did not improve the cake at all. The last important test was the milk. I determined that 1 cup was the right amount when ¾ cup produced a stiff batter and dry cake and 1¼ cups made the cake, well, damp and somewhat bubbly in texture. Just for fun, I tried warming the milk before adding it to the batter and this made no difference whatsoever.

Although in many recipes, the editors of *Cook's Illustrated* have found that imitation vanilla is as good as the real thing (in a cookie, for example), I was able to tell the difference in yellow cake. (Imitation vanilla is not made from vanilla beans at all but from chemically treated wood pulp.) For the oven temperature, a moderate 350 degrees was preferred over higher or lower ovens, and rotating the cake pans halfway through baking is a must for an evenly browned and evenly risen cake. Lining the bottom of the cake pan with parchment paper is a must as well; otherwise the bottoms of the cake layers become a bit tough and unpleasant.

...

Master Recipe for All-Purpose Yellow Cake

This is the most important building-block recipe for any cake baker. This recipe can be easily modified to produce a wide variety of cakes, including spice, almond, and lemon. (See the variations below.) The trick with this recipe, which is otherwise straightforward, is to make sure that the butter is at the proper temperature before creaming, so take it out of the refrigerator about 2 hours before starting recipe. If you have an instant-read thermometer, the butter should be at 65 to 67 degrees. If you don't have a thermometer, try bending the stick of butter; it should be malleable but not soft. Cold butter will not cream properly, and the batter will appear separated when the eggs are added.

MAKES TWO 9-INCH ROUNDS

2½	cups cake flour
2	teaspoons baking powder
½	teaspoon salt
12	tablespoons (1½ sticks) unsalted butter, softened but still firm
1½	cups granulated sugar
5	large eggs, at room temperature
1	cup milk
2	teaspoons vanilla extract

1. Adjust oven rack to the middle position and heat the oven to 350 degrees. Grease two 9-inch cake pans and cover the bottom of each pan with a circle of parchment.

2. Sift together flour, baking powder, and salt onto waxed paper.

3. Beat butter in a large bowl with an electric mixer at medium speed for 30 seconds. Continue beating and gradually add the sugar. Beat until light-colored, about 3 minutes. Add eggs, one at a time, beating on high speed for 30 seconds after each addition and scraping down the bowl as necessary. After all the eggs have been added, beat for 1 additional minute. The mixture should appear thick and dull. If it appears separated or grainy and shiny, the butter and/or the eggs were too cold (to rectify, see "What Can Go Wrong?" below).

4. Add about one-third of both the flour mixture and the milk and beat on low speed or by hand until just incorporated. Add the vanilla and then the remaining flour and milk in two batches, beating between additions. Scrape down the sides of the bowl and stir by hand to finish. Be careful not to overbeat at this point.

5. Divide the batter between the prepared pans. Turn the pans back and forth on the work surface to level out the batter and then smooth the surface with a rubber spatula. Place pans in oven on the middle rack, a few inches apart, and bake for about 30 minutes, rotating the pans 180 degrees halfway through baking. Check the cakes after 22 minutes. When they are done, the tops of the cakes should be golden brown and spring back when lightly pressed in the center and a cake tester should come out clean. They should have begun to shrink back from the sides of the pan.

6. Remove the pans to a cooling rack. Let rest for 5 minutes. Run a small knife or metal spatula around the sides of the pans and invert cakes

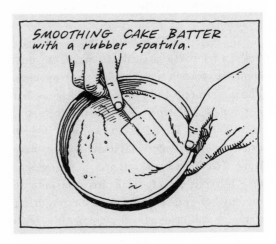

SMOOTHING CAKE BATTER with a rubber spatula.

CASE 30: THE SPICE GIRLS AND BOYS BAKE A CAKE

How spice cake recipes stack up in terms of flavorings.

Flavoring	Recipe A	Recipe B	Recipe C	Recipe D	Recipe E
Cinnamon	1½ teaspoons	2 teaspoons	1 teaspoon	2 teaspoons	1¼ teaspoons
Nutmeg	½ teaspoon		1 teaspoon	½ teaspoon	¾ teaspoon
Allspice	½ teaspoon				
Ground cloves	½ teaspoon		½ teaspoon	¼ teaspoon	
Cocoa powder	1 tablespoon				
Ground ginger				½ teaspoon	1¼ teaspoons
Cardamom		1 teaspoon			

onto lightly greased racks. Remove parchment paper. Reinvert cakes onto cooling rack. Let cool for at least 1½ hours, or until completely cooled.

FROSTING TIPS: Almost any frosting will work with this cake since it is so generic, but I prefer chocolate frostings, which have enough flavor and body to stand up to this firm-textured cake.

WHAT CAN GO WRONG? Although, as cakes go, this is a relatively easy cake to make, the most common problem is using cold butter and eggs. The butter needs to be at least 60 degrees, but not too warm either — 65 to 67 degrees is ideal. The eggs should also be warm. (Put them in a bowl of hot water for 2 minutes if they have come directly from the refrigerator.) If the butter is too cold, cut into small pieces and put into the bowl of your electric mixer. Beating it for a minute will help, as will wrapping the bowl in a kitchen towel damp with hot water. Wrapping a hot towel around the bowl while you beat is also the way to help a separated or grainy and shiny egg-butter-sugar mixture become properly thick and dull. Of course, the best solution is simply to let the butter and eggs come up to the proper temperature before starting the recipe. The other mistake, one I have made, is to let the batter sit before baking. This can lead to a tough, coarse cake. It is important to have the cake pans prepared early on, so that once the batter is ready to go, it can be poured into the pans and put right into the oven.

SPICE CAKE VARIATION

Spice cakes are simple variations on a basic yellow cake. The basic structure is the same, it is simply a matter of varying the flavorings. I started my investigations by reviewing recipes from *James Beard's American Cookery* (the spice variation on his 1-2-3-4 Cake), Richard

Sax's *Classic Home Desserts* (Rich, Soft Spice Cake), the 1997 *Joy of Cooking,* by Irma S. Rombauer et al. (Velvet Spice Cake), *The Fannie Farmer Cookbook,* by Marion Cunningham (Buttermilk Spice Cake), and Nick Malgieri's *How to Bake* (Old-Fashioned Spice Cake). I preferred my yellow cake master recipe to the base recipes used in the other books, but I did carefully review the flavoring ingredients. Case 30 shows how they stacked up.

After baking all of these cakes, I quickly determined that using a large amount of any one ingredient was a mistake. James Beard's recipe was overpowered by 1½ teaspoons of cinnamon; Nick Malgieri's spice cake almost tasted like gingerbread, with its large dose (1¼ teaspoons) of ginger; and the *Fannie Farmer* recipe also included both molasses and cayenne pepper, which were a bit too strong for what should be a delicate cake. So a moderate level of spice with a nice rounded flavor seemed best. I also discovered, after icing a few of these cakes, that strong flavors conflict with many frostings, another reason to tone down the spices.

So I cobbled together a starting mix of spices that included 1 teaspoon cinnamon, ½ teaspoon nutmeg, ½ teaspoon allspice, ½ teaspoon cloves, and 1 tablespoon cocoa. I baked up a cake and quickly discovered that the cinnamon was too strong, as were most of the other spices. I then tried a milder version, which was quite good if not frosted but was difficult to match up with any sort of frosting except whipped cream. So I tried an even milder version, cutting most of the spice quantities in half; this tasted great and also married well with a variety of frostings. I then tried this spice mixture using ½ cup of light brown sugar in place of ½ cup of the granulated sugar in the master recipe and preferred the cake with the granulated sugar because of the texture: the cake with the light brown sugar was not as soft or delicate. Finally, I tried adding small amounts of ginger and cardamom (ingredients that I had left out of the recipe until now) and decided that neither of them merited inclusion: the cardamom did not add anything of value, and the ground ginger tasted almost medicinal.

To make the spice variation, follow the Master Recipe for All-Purpose Yellow Cake (page 129), making the following changes. Sift together with the dry ingredients 2 teaspoons Dutch-process cocoa powder, ½ teaspoon cinnamon, ¼ teaspoon nutmeg, ¼ teaspoon allspice, and ⅛ teaspoon ground cloves. Reduce vanilla to 1 teaspoon. For frostings, try the Maple Meringue Frosting, a mocha buttercream, or the Dark Brown Sugar Frosting. You can also use any of the chocolate frostings. (See the next chapter for frosting recipes.)

ALMOND CAKE VARIATION

The question with the almond variation was how to introduce a natural, well-rounded almond flavor that blended nicely with the cake. Finely ground almonds added only a hint of flavor and spoiled the light, moist texture. I thought about toasting the nuts, which would have added more flavor, but counted out this approach due to the unwelcome texture. Next, I tried almond paste, which also detracted from the texture. The obvious choice was almond extract, which was good, but I was still looking for something spectacular. I decided to try an almond milk, made by blending hot milk and almonds in a blender, letting the mixture cool, and then straining it. This combination — almond extract and almond milk — gave me exactly what I was looking for: strong but balanced almond flavor.

To make this cake, follow the Master Recipe for All-Purpose Yellow Cake (page 129), but reduce the vanilla extract to 1 teaspoon. Add 1 teaspoon natural almond extract or flavor when adding the vanilla in step 4. Replace the 1 cup of milk with 1 cup of Almond Milk (below).

ALMOND MILK

I use a blender rather than a food processor, since it does a better job, but the latter will do in a pinch. Heat 1 cup milk just to the boiling point. Place ½ cup coarsely chopped almonds in a blender or food processor and pour the hot milk over the nuts. Blend until smooth. Pour into a bowl and let steep for 2 hours. Strain through a fine mesh strainer or 2 layers of cheesecloth.

LEMON CAKE VARIATION

The choices for lemon flavorings include lemon zest, lemon extract, lemon oil, and lemon juice. I knew from prior testing that natural lemon zest provides both an intensity and a range of lemon flavors that oils and extracts just cannot match. I also knew from other tests that natural lemon oils are preferred over extracts. However, I wanted to devise a recipe that was not totally dependent on oils, since they are not common pantry staples.

I started testing with the zest, testing 1, 2, and 3 teaspoons, and settled on the largest amount. However, the cake was still a bit lackluster. Adding 1 teaspoon lemon extract was the answer. It gave the boost the zest needed to produce a nice lemon layer cake. Any more extract and the cake was too lemony — lemon extract lemony. Any less extract and it was not lemony enough. That being said, use natural lemon oil if you can find it — it is vastly superior to the standard supermarket extract, which contains a great deal of alcohol. (See page 299 for the best way to zest a lemon.)

To make the lemon variation, follow Master Recipe for All-Purpose Yellow Cake (page 129), but reduce vanilla to 1 teaspoon. When adding the vanilla in step 4, add 1 tablespoon finely chopped lemon zest and 1 teaspoon natural lemon oil or, if you cannot find lemon oil, 1½ teaspoons natural lemon extract.

ORANGE CAKE VARIATION

Follow Master Recipe for All-Purpose Yellow Cake (page 129), but reduce vanilla to 1 teaspoon. When adding the vanilla in step 4, add 1 tablespoon finely chopped orange zest and 1 teaspoon natural orange oil or, if you cannot find orange oil, 1½ teaspoons natural orange extract.

▪ ▪ ▪

Buttermilk Cake

This is almost identical to the Master Recipe for All-Purpose Yellow Cake but uses buttermilk instead of regular whole milk. The texture is a little coarser but tender, and the cake has a slightly tangy flavor from the buttermilk. I have tried this cake with both 8- and 9-inch pans and find that the latter produces the best cake, with a relatively level top. I had to reduce the amount of baking powder and add some baking soda, since the buttermilk is full of lactic acid, which changes the chemistry of the batter.

MAKES TWO 9-INCH ROUNDS

2½	cups cake flour
1	teaspoon baking powder
½	teaspoon baking soda
½	teaspoon salt
12	tablespoons (1½ sticks) unsalted butter, softened but still firm
1½	cups granulated sugar
5	large eggs, at room temperature
1	cup buttermilk
2	teaspoons vanilla extract

1. Set oven rack in middle position and heat oven to 350 degrees.. Grease two 9-inch cake pans and cover the bottom of each pan with a circle of parchment.

2. Sift together flour, baking powder, baking soda, and salt onto a sheet of waxed paper. Set aside.

3. Beat butter in a large bowl with an electric mixer at medium speed for 30 seconds. Continue beating, gradually adding sugar. Beat until light and fluffy, 2 to 3 minutes. Add eggs, one at a time, beating after each addition. Scrape down sides of bowl when necessary.

4. Add about one-third of both the flour mixture and the buttermilk and beat on low

speed or by hand until just incorporated. Add the vanilla and then the remaining flour and buttermilk in two separate batches, beating between additions. Scrape down sides of bowl and stir by hand to finish.

5. Divide batter between prepared pans. Smooth surface with a rubber spatula. Place pans in oven a few inches apart and bake about 30 minutes, or until top of cake springs back when lightly pressed in the center and a wooden toothpick or skewer comes out clean. Rotate the pans 180 degrees after 15 minutes of baking, and start checking the cake after 22 minutes.

6. Remove pans to a cooling rack. Let rest for 5 minutes. Run a small metal spatula or knife around the sides of the pans and invert cakes onto lightly greased racks. Reinvert cakes onto cooling rack. Let cool for at least 1½ hours.

···

Strawberry Cake

This cake requires very ripe berries for best results. Also, the cake is a bit messy, since it tends to fall apart when sliced. However, it is a wonderful cake to serve during strawberry season.

SERVES 12

1   recipe All-Purpose Yellow Cake (page 129) or Buttermilk Cake (page 132)
1   recipe Whipped Cream Frosting (page 189)
1   quart fresh strawberries, washed, dried, and hulled
1   teaspoon granulated sugar

1. Prepare cake according to instructions and cool to room temperature on racks. Prepare frosting. Slice three-fourths of the strawberries in half lengthwise. Place in a medium bowl with sugar and toss gently to combine. Let sit for at least 20 minutes before using.

2. Place one cake round on a cake plate. Top with a thin layer of Whipped Cream Frosting. Distribute the halved strawberries evenly over

the frosting (use all of them) and then spread with another layer of frosting. Add second cake layer and frost top and sides. Decorate with remaining whole strawberries.

ALL-PURPOSE WHITE CAKE

HOMEMADE LAYER CAKES are often heavy, lacking the pillowy, melt-in-your-mouth texture of cake made from a store-bought mix. I was looking for a recipe that combined the reliability and ease of a basic yellow cake with the ethereal texture of an angel food or sponge cake. It had to be sturdy, since I intended to fill and frost it, but also so delicate that it might just rise up off the plate.

A basic yellow cake is made with whole eggs. The lift is provided by baking powder (and sometimes baking soda), and the structure is also enhanced by creaming softened butter and sugar together. A white cake, however, uses no egg yolks. The basic method is simple. Butter and sugar are creamed and then one folds in two separate mixtures: one of milk, egg whites, and vanilla extract and the other of flour, baking powder, and salt. Some recipes, however, opt to beat the egg whites and others use water instead of milk.

In my tests, I found that beating the egg whites produced a drier cake and also one not sturdy enough to use as an all-purpose layer cake. I also wanted an extremely tender crumb and therefore went with milk instead of water. I cut back on the sugar about 20 percent from more traditional recipes, slightly increased the amount of baking powder, and also reduced the ratio of butter to flour.

···

All-Purpose White Cake

I suggest that you use either the Meringue Frosting (page 189) or the Chocolate Sour

Cream Frosting (page 187) with the basic recipe or one of the variations. If you want to make a version of Sunshine Cake, a classic American dessert, make a three-layer cake (two layers of yellow cake and one of white cake) and frost it with a simple white icing, such as Meringue Frosting.

MAKES TWO 9-INCH ROUNDS

 1   cup milk
 6   large egg whites
2½   teaspoons vanilla extract
 3   cups cake flour
 4   teaspoons baking powder
 1   teaspoon salt
12   tablespoons (1½ sticks) unsalted butter, softened but still firm
1½   cups granulated sugar

1. Set oven rack in middle position and heat oven to 350 degrees. Grease two 9-inch cake pans and cover the bottom of each pan with a circle of parchment.

2. In a medium bowl, stir together the milk, egg whites, and vanilla with a fork. Sift together the flour, baking powder, and salt into a medium bowl or onto waxed paper.

3. Beat the butter in a large bowl with an electric mixer on medium speed for 30 seconds. Continue beating, gradually adding the sugar. Beat until light and fluffy, 2 to 3 minutes. Scrape down the sides of the bowl as necessary.

4. Add one-third each of the flour mixture and milk mixture and beat on low speed or by hand until just incorporated. Add the remaining flour and milk mixtures in two separate batches, beating between additions to fully incorporate. Scrape down the sides of the bowl and stir by hand to finish.

5. Divide batter between prepared pans. Smooth surface with a rubber spatula. Place pans in oven, a few inches apart, on the middle rack. After 15 minutes, rotate the pans 180 degrees. Bake a total of 25 to 30 minutes (check cake after 22 minutes), or until top of cake springs back when lightly pressed in the center and a wooden skewer comes out clean.

6. Remove pans to a cooling rack. Let rest for 5 minutes. Run a small metal spatula or knife around the sides of the pan and invert cakes, one at a time, onto a lightly greased rack. Reinvert cakes onto cooling rack. Let cool for at least 1½ hours.

FROSTING TIPS: This is a light cake and the Meringue Frosting and variations work particularly well, although since this is such a basic cake, just about any frosting can be used.

WHAT CAN GO WRONG? This is about as foolproof as a cake recipe gets. The butter does have to be creamed, so it needs to be at the proper temperature, 65 to 67 degrees. Make sure that the butter-sugar mixture is beaten until it is very light and fluffy, which could take up to 5 minutes if you are using a lower-quality electric mixer.

ALMOND VARIATION

Reduce vanilla extract to 1 teaspoon and add 2 teaspoons almond extract.

CITRUS VARIATIONS

Reduce vanilla extract to 1 teaspoon and add 1 teaspoon orange or lemon extract plus 2 tablespoons freshly grated orange or lemon zest. Add zest along with extracts.

• • •

Old-Fashioned Coconut Layer Cake

This recipe takes a bit of work but results in a three-star dessert. The cake is flavored with coconut cream and ground desiccated coconut, and the frosting contains plenty of coconut to boot. (If you cannot find coconut cream, you can make your own following the directions on page 51 or just use milk.) It is important to purchase desiccated coconut for this recipe or, at the very least, the coconut sold at natural food stores. The moist, very sweet product sold in supermarkets just won't do the trick here. It will be much too sticky for the cake. If you want to go all out, try filling this cake with Lemon Cake Filling (page 198) before frosting it. When toasting coconut, watch it closely since it burns quickly.

SERVES 12

For the Cake

1	cup lightly packed desiccated or unsweetened coconut
1	cup coconut cream OR 1 cup milk
6	large egg whites
1	teaspoon vanilla extract
3	cups cake flour
4	teaspoons baking powder
1	teaspoon salt
12	tablespoons (1½ sticks) unsalted butter, softened but still firm
1½	cups granulated sugar

For the Coconut Frosting

2½	cups lightly packed desiccated or unsweetened coconut
1	recipe Meringue Frosting (page 188)

1. *For the cake:* Grind 1 cup desiccated coconut (do not use the sweet, moist coconut sold in supermarkets) in the food processor until the texture resembles coarse sand. Set aside.

2. Set oven rack in middle position and heat oven to 350 degrees. Grease two 9-inch cake pans and cover the bottom of each pan with a circle of parchment.

3. In a medium bowl, stir together the coconut cream, egg whites, and vanilla extract with a fork. Sift together the flour, baking powder, and salt onto waxed paper.

4. Beat the butter in a large bowl with an electric mixer on medium speed for 30 seconds. Continue beating, gradually adding the sugar. Beat until light and fluffy, 2 to 3 minutes. Scrape down the sides of the bowl when necessary.

5. Add one-third of the flour mixture and one-third of the cream of coconut mixture and beat on low speed or by hand until just incorporated. Add the remaining flour and cream of coconut mixtures in two separate batches, beating between additions to fully incorporate and adding the 1 cup ground coconut with the last batch of dry ingredients. Scrape down the sides of the bowl and stir by hand to finish.

6. Divide batter between prepared pans. Smooth surface with a rubber spatula and place cake pans on the middle rack. After 15 minutes, rotate the pans 180 degrees. Bake a total of 25 to 30 minutes (check cake after 22 minutes), or until top of cake springs back when lightly pressed in the center and a wooden skewer comes out clean.

7. Remove pans to a cooling rack. Let rest for 5 minutes. Run a small metal spatula or knife around the sides of the pan and invert cakes, one at a time, onto a lightly greased rack. Reinvert cakes onto cooling rack. Let cool for at least 1½ hours.

8. *For the frosting:* Place the 2½ cups of coconut on a cookie sheet and bake at 350 degrees about 7 minutes. Watch the coconut closely, as it burns easily. Prepare Meringue Frosting and fold in only 2 cups of the toasted coconut. Place one cake layer on a cake plate, frost the top, add the second layer, and frost the top and sides. Sprinkle remaining ½ cup toasted coconut over frosted cake.

WHAT CAN GO WRONG? Make sure that you use coconut cream or milk, not cream of coconut, which is sweeter and thicker. Also, be sure to watch the coconut very carefully during browning; it burns easily.

GENOISE

GENOISE IS TO A French pastry chef what a basic yellow cake is to the American home

CASE 31: THE GREAT GENOISE BAKE-OFF

Comparing the ingredients from five famous bakers.

Cookbook	Flour	Sugar	Butter	Eggs	Other Ingredients
Joy of Cooking	1¼ cups	1 cup	⅓ cup	6	1 teaspoon vanilla
The Cake Bible	½ cup	½ cup	3 tablespoons	4	½ cup cornstarch
Baking with Julia	1 cup	½ cup	2 tablespoons	4	Vanilla and salt
How to Bake	½ cup	¾ cup	None	3 plus 3 yolks	¼ cup cornstarch
Desserts by Pierre Hermé	1⅓ cups	1 cup	4 tablespoons	6	Nothing extra

cook — an essential building-block recipe. It is lighter and more finicky than a yellow cake, since it requires beating eggs and sugar until very light, usually over simmering water, and then folding in a small amount of flour. A delicate touch is required, unlike with most American cakes, which can be blended together with an electric mixer without the threat of imminent disaster. Besides the problems inherent in making genoise, the other issues that I investigated were flavor and texture. Many genoises lack a bit in the flavor department, and some of them tend to be a little dry. I wanted a moist genoise with good flavor, the sort of cake that does not require a sugar syrup. (Many classic genoise recipes call for soaking the finished cake with a sugar syrup. If it were a nice, moist cake to start with, you wouldn't need that bloody syrup!)

The first step was my usual bake-off and tasting, which included recipes from *Joy of Cooking; The Cake Bible,* by Rose Levy Beranbaum; *Baking with Julia,* by Dorie Greenspan and Julia Child; *How to Bake;* and *Desserts by Pierre Hermé.*

I made the Pierre Hermé recipe, which was quite good, but I thought it was a bit tough and could use some salt and vanilla. The recipe from *How to Bake,* by Nick Malgieri, was on the dry side and probably could use some melted butter as suggested by the other recipes. I also discovered that I am not crazy about cornstarch, which was used by two of the recipes. The taste is a bit off and it leaves an odd sensation on the teeth. Julia Child's recipe was good, although not sweet enough — she had the lowest ratio of sugar to flour. I also noted that some bakers called for clarified butter instead of simple melted butter, a notion that deserved testing. The Hermé recipe — 1⅓ cups flour, 1 cup sugar, 6 large eggs, and 4 tablespoons melted butter — produced a very good cake, so I decided to use that as my working recipe.

First I wanted to test the notion of using clarified butter instead of melted butter. Clarified butter has been slowly melted to separate out the milk solids, which tend to burn at higher temperatures. (Clarified butter is also referred to as drawn butter and, in Indian cuisine, as ghee.) I made one cake using 4 tablespoons melted butter (cooled to room temperature) and then another one using 4 tablespoons clarified butter. I was happy to find there was no difference in the two cakes. (Disposing of unnecessary culinary tasks is one of life's great pleasures.) I then tested to arrive at the proper amount of butter, baking a cake using only 2 tablespoons of butter and another that used 6 tablespoons. The lower quantity yielded a dry cake and the higher volume of butter was good but too buttery for a genoise, which should be, at least in my opinion, relatively neutral and reserved. However, this is purely a matter of personal taste. So I stuck with the original 4 tablespoons.

Next I tested the types of flour and the use of cornstarch. I made one cake using all-purpose flour, one using equal parts all-purpose and cake flour, and one using only cake flour. The cake using entirely all-purpose flour was a bit tough. I was surprised to discover that the cake using only cake flour was structurally okay (it did not fall into itself) but was a bit too spongy. The cake made with a fifty-fifty mix was my favorite. It was more delicate than the all-purpose but not as spongy and crumbly as the cake flour cake. To further refine this marriage of all-purpose and cake flours, I made a cake using ⅓ cup cake flour and 1 cup all-purpose and then another cake using ⅓ cup all-purpose and 1 cup cake flour. The cake using mostly all-purpose was still a bit tough and the cake using mostly cake flour was still crumbly and spongy, so the fifty-fifty ratio was best. I did want to give the cornstarch one more try, so I baked a cake with ⅓ cup cornstarch, ⅓ cup all-purpose flour, and ⅔ cup cake flour. Next to the other cakes this one was my least favorite, mostly due to an off flavor. By the way, the flour in all cases was sifted onto a piece of waxed paper, which makes adding the flour to the beaten sugar-egg mixture quick and easy (plus you do not need to clean up another bowl).

The eggs were tested next. I was using 6 whole eggs and tried a long list of variations, including 5 eggs, 7 eggs, 4 whole eggs plus 4 yolks, 5 whole eggs plus 2 yolks, et cetera. You get the idea. I even tried using whole eggs plus a few whites, but to no avail. The 6 whole egg recipe was simple and not too eggy. Most of the recipes required heating the eggs and sugar over simmering water until hand hot, or about 130 degrees, while beating them. This was a step I wanted to avoid if at all possible in my search for a kinder and gentler genoise recipe. However, I was quite disappointed to discover that this step really matters. The heating produces more volume and a finer texture. If, however, you are going to fill the genoise and then frost it, you can probably get away without this step, since you are unlikely to notice the difference.

After coming this far, I thought the cake was a tiny bit too sweet. I tried making a cake using ¾ cup of sugar instead of the 1 cup I had been using so far. This seemed to reduce the volume of the egg-sugar mixture more than it should have, and the cake was not sweet enough for my taste. I made a cake with ⅞ cups sugar, and this cake was right on the money. The level of sweetness was best, and the loss of volume to the egg-sugar mixture was hardly noticeable.

Last, Pierre Hermé mixes ¼ cup of the beaten egg-sugar mixture into the melted butter before adding the butter to the batter. I found that this step helps maintain the volume of the batter. I also tested the use of salt and vanilla and found both ingredients to be necessary.

• • •

Master Recipe for Genoise

Here is the classic French building-block cake recipe. The heating of the egg-sugar mixture produces a higher cake with a finer texture and is recommended for cakes that will not be buried under an avalanche of filling and icing. You might not notice, however, if you were slapping on a load of buttercream. Make sure that your eggs are at room temperature before starting this recipe.

MAKES ONE 9-INCH ROUND

⅔ cup cake flour

⅔ cup all-purpose flour

1 teaspoon salt

⅞ cup (1 cup minus 2 tablespoons) granulated sugar

6 large eggs, at room temperature

1½ teaspoons vanilla extract

4 tablespoons unsalted butter, melted and cooled to room temperature

1. Set oven rack in the upper middle position and heat oven to 350 degrees. Grease one 9 x 2-inch round cake pan and cover the bottom with a circle of parchment. (For a two-layer cake, slice the cake in half after it has cooled — see illustrations, page 126.)

2. Sift the flours and salt onto a piece of waxed paper and set aside. Place 1 inch of water in a saucepan large enough to fit the bowl of your electric standing mixer. (If you do not have a standing mixer, just use any mixing bowl that fits over a large saucepan.) Heat the water over low heat until it is just beginning to simmer. Add the sugar and eggs to the bowl and place the bowl onto the pan of simmering water (the bowl should not touch the water). Whisk constantly by hand until the mixture is heated through to a temperature of about 130 degrees or feels hand hot. Remove the bowl from the simmering water. If you have a standing mixer, attach the bowl to the mixer and beat with the paddle attachment for 5 minutes, or until the egg-sugar mixture has tripled in volume and is shiny and a dollop dropped from the beater leaves a mark for at least 10 seconds. (Otherwise, remove the bowl from the simmering water and beat with a hand whisk or hand-held electric mixer.) Add the vanilla and mix for an additional 10 seconds. Remove the bowl from the mixer if using one.

3. Using a spoon or spatula, add about ¼ cup of the egg-sugar mixture to the melted butter and stir until well incorporated. Return this mixture to the mixing bowl. Add the flour to the egg-sugar mixture and place bowl back into mixer. Mix at the lowest speed, using the whisk attachment (or whisk gently by hand), for 10 seconds. Remove bowl from mixer and fold by hand to finish.

4. Add the batter to the prepared pan (it will almost reach the top) and place on a rack in the upper middle portion of the oven. After 15 minutes, rotate the pan 180 degrees. Bake a total of 28 to 33 minutes (check cake after 25 minutes), or until top of cake springs back when lightly pressed in the center and a wooden skewer comes out clean.

5. Remove the pan to a cooling rack. Let rest for 5 minutes. Run a small, thin metal spatula or knife around the sides of the pan and invert cake onto a lightly greased rack. Reinvert cake onto cooling rack and let cool for 1½ hours, or to room temperature.

FROSTING TIPS: The classic treatment for genoise is to soak it with a sugar syrup and not use any frosting. You can split the cake horizontally into two layers and then fill with jam or a simple lemon curd and top with powdered sugar. You can use a whipped cream frosting or buttercream. I would avoid a heavy, American-style frosting.

WHAT CAN GO WRONG? This recipe requires a fair amount of skill in folding, and the process is on the fussy side. (Well, did you expect something simple and foolproof from the French?) The key here is folding, since overworking the mixture will deflate it. I strongly recommend that you use an electric mixer on low speed to mix the batter and then finish folding by hand. (See pages 8–9 for more information.) This eliminates the biggest problem with genoise, which is that too much folding of the delicate egg-sugar mixture will deflate the batter.

LEMON VARIATION

Follow master recipe, but reduce vanilla to 1 teaspoon. When adding the vanilla in step 2, add 1 tablespoon finely chopped lemon zest and 1 teaspoon natural lemon oil or, if you cannot find lemon oil, 1½ teaspoons natural lemon extract.

ORANGE VARIATION

Follow master recipe, but reduce vanilla to 1 teaspoon. When adding the vanilla in step 2, add 1 tablespoon finely chopped orange zest and 1 teaspoon natural orange oil or, if you cannot find orange oil, 1½ teaspoons natural orange extract.

CHOCOLATE GENOISE

THERE ARE TWO WAYS to turn a basic genoise into a chocolate genoise. The most common technique is simply to substitute cocoa powder for some of the flour, whereas other recipes use melted baking chocolate instead. A quick test of these two methods proved that the cocoa method was superior; chocolate genoise made with melted chocolate did not rise sufficiently and had a wetter, denser texture. This was hardly worth the trade-off for the richer chocolate taste.

So my next series of tests involved the precise quantity of cocoa. I tested using as little as 3 tablespoons and as much as ⅔ cup cocoa with 1⅓ cups flour. The smaller amount had insufficient chocolate flavor, whereas ⅔ cup cocoa resulted in a very dry cake indeed. I finally settled on replacing ⅓ cup of the all-purpose flour with an equal amount of cocoa. The cake was good but still needed some work. Rose Levy Beranbaum, author of *The Cake Bible,* states that the true flavor of cocoa is not released unless it is first dissolved in boiling water. I tried this method and was pleased to find that she was right. (I came to the same conclusion when de-

veloping my recipe for devil's food cake.) After a few tests, I settled on mixing the ⅓ cup cocoa into a paste using 5 tablespoons of boiling water. Finally, I tested the addition of small amounts of baking powder and baking soda as suggested in one recipe and found them to be unnecessary.

▪ ▪ ▪

Chocolate Genoise

Dutch-process cocoa mixed with boiling water produces a paste that is then mixed into the batter. This creates a light, moist cake with outstanding chocolate flavor.

MAKES ONE 9-INCH ROUND

⅓ cup Dutch-process cocoa powder
5 tablespoons boiling water
⅔ cup cake flour
⅓ cup all-purpose flour
1 teaspoon salt
⅞ cup (1 cup minus 2 tablespoons) granulated sugar
6 large eggs, at room temperature
1 teaspoon vanilla extract
4 tablespoons unsalted butter, melted and cooled to room temperature

1. Set oven rack in the upper middle position and heat the oven to 350 degrees. Grease a 9 x 2-inch round cake pan and cover the bottom of the pan with a circle of parchment. Mix the cocoa and boiling water into a paste in a small bowl and set aside.

2. Sift the flours and salt onto a piece of waxed paper and set aside. Place 1 inch of water in a saucepan large enough to fit the bowl of your electric standing mixer. (If you do not have a standing mixer, just use any mixing bowl that fits over a large saucepan.) Heat the water over low heat until it is just beginning to simmer. Add the sugar and eggs to the bowl and place the bowl onto the pan of simmering water (the

bowl should not touch the water). Whisk constantly by hand until the mixture is heated through to a temperature of about 130 degrees or feels hand hot. Remove the bowl from the simmering water. If you have a standing mixer, attach the bowl to the mixer and beat with the paddle attachment for 5 minutes, or until the egg-sugar mixture has tripled in volume and is shiny and a dollop dropped from the beater leaves a mark for at least 10 seconds. (Otherwise, remove the bowl from the simmering water and beat with a hand whisk or hand-held electric mixer.) Add the vanilla and mix for an additional 10 seconds. Remove the bowl from the mixer if using one.

3. Using a spoon or spatula, add about ¼ cup of the egg-sugar mixture to the melted butter and stir until well incorporated. Stir in the cocoa paste and set aside. Add the flour to the egg-sugar mixture and fold until almost mixed, then add the butter mixture to the batter. Continue folding until the batter is fully blended.

4. Add the batter to the prepared pan (it will almost reach the top) and place on a rack in the upper middle portion of the oven. After 15 minutes, rotate the pan 180 degrees. Bake a total of 28 to 33 minutes (check cake after 25 minutes), or until top of cake springs back when lightly pressed in the center and a wooden skewer comes out clean.

5. Remove the pan to a cooling rack. Let rest for 5 minutes. Run a small, thin metal spatula or knife around the sides of the pan and invert the cake onto a lightly greased rack. Reinvert cake onto cooling rack and let cool for 1½ hours, or to room temperature.

BUTTERMILK CHOCOLATE CAKE

THIS IS SIMILAR TO a recipe I developed for *The Cook's Bible*, but I did some additional work on it. I tried adding another egg and the cake was too loose and the texture was not as

good. When I substituted oil for the butter, the cake was greasy and too moist. Sour cream in place of the buttermilk created a drier cake that was less chocolaty. It also did not rise quite as well. I then added a bit of oil to the sour cream, to solve the dry texture problem; it was moist, but the flavor was not as good as the buttermilk version. Finally, I tried sifting the cake flour, which created a wonderful cake, slightly moister than the master recipe from the *Bible*.

•••

Buttermilk Chocolate Cake

*Y*ou can bake this cake in either two 8-inch or one 9-inch round pan. (Make sure that the 9-inch pan is at least 2, and preferably 3, inches high.) By the way, if you frost a chocolate cake with orange icing, it is called Black-Eyed Susan Cake.

MAKES ONE 9-INCH OR TWO 8-INCH ROUNDS

1½	cups sifted cake flour
½	cup Dutch-processed cocoa powder
2	teaspoons instant espresso or instant coffee powder
¼	teaspoon baking powder
½	teaspoon baking soda
¼	teaspoon salt
12	tablespoons (1½ sticks) unsalted butter, softened but still firm
1¼	cups granulated sugar
2	large eggs, at room temperature
1	large egg white, at room temperature
1½	teaspoons vanilla extract
1	cup buttermilk

1. Grease the bottom of two 8-inch round baking pans or one deep (about 3 inches) 9-inch pan. Line with parchment paper. Adjust oven rack to middle position and heat oven to 350 degrees.

2. Sift the flour, cocoa, instant coffee, baking powder, baking soda, and salt onto a sheet of waxed paper and set aside.

AND TODAY'S SPECIAL DESSERT IS MINNEHAHA CAKE . . .

The Victorians were fond of playing with their food, toying with every possible combination of cake flavors, colors, and fillings to conjure up a fantastic assortment of desserts, from Black-Eyed Susan Cake (chocolate cake with orange icing) to Sunshine Cake (alternate layers of lemon-flavored yellow and white cake — four in total — finished with a meringue frosting flavored with orange zest). A Marble Layer Cake was made of yellow cake and chocolate cake batters, spooned alternately into cake pans to produce a marbled effect. Daffodil Cake was made with one layer of white cake flavored with vanilla and one layer of yellow cake flavored with orange rind. Other Victorian cakes included Jewel Cake (made with cranberries), Gold Cake (made with many egg yolks and orange rind), Snow Cake (a white cake made with egg whites and milk), Minnehaha Cake (the frosting was an Italian meringue folded together with chopped raisins and walnut meats), and Chrysanthemum Cake (a pink cake with red icing). Such a playful and prolific approach to cake baking is probably due indirectly to the Industrial Revolution, coupled with the growth of the middle class and the availability of cheap domestic help made possible by large numbers of immigrants. Freed from the burdens of housework, many middle-class women found time for the home and cooking, and cakes were popular for entertaining, often served at afternoon teas. The recipes themselves were written in shorthand, the cookbook authors having the luxury of addressing home cooks who were proficient in the art of baking.

3. Put butter in the bowl of an electric mixer and beat for 1 minute, or until light-colored. Add sugar gradually and beat on medium-high speed for 3 minutes, until mixture is very light-colored and fluffy (scrape down two or three times). Add whole eggs and egg white one at a time, beating for 20 seconds after each addition. Add the vanilla and beat for 10 seconds.

4. Add the flour mixture to the bowl in three parts alternately with the buttermilk. Beat on low speed after each addition and scrape down the sides of the bowl with a rubber spatula. Stir by hand to finish. Do not overbeat.

5. Spread the batter into pan(s) and bake a total of 25 to 30 minutes (about 10 minutes longer if using only one pan). Rotate pan(s) 180 degrees halfway through baking. Cake is done when it springs back when lightly pressed in the center and a wooden skewer comes out clean.

6. Remove pan to a cooling rack. After 15 minutes run blade of a dull knife around sides of pan and remove cake onto wire rack. Let cool fully before frosting.

FROSTING TIPS: Any chocolate frosting works well here, as does a plain buttercream.

WHAT CAN GO WRONG? This is a basic cake recipe. Just make sure that the butter and eggs are at the proper temperature before beginning. Oh, and don't try to substitute milk for the buttermilk. The recipe won't work.

MOCHA VARIATION

Substitute ½ cup strong coffee for ½ cup of the buttermilk.

HEAVENLY DEVIL'S FOOD

THE LATTER PART OF the nineteenth century, which saw the development of a lot of imaginative cakes with fancy names (see sidebar), also gave birth to one cake whose popularity hasn't waned from that period to ours, the Devil's Food Cake. Its success is a testament to its utter simplicity and to the lasting appeal of a moist chocolate cake.

The obvious question is, what is it? The short answer is that the name refers to the color of the cake, not the texture or taste. One group of food historians argues that devil's food is a black cake; others point to a reddish hue — cocoa naturally contains red pigments — as the distinguishing characteristic. For those who argue for black cakes, there is the Satan Cake, a late nineteenth-century cake that was probably synonymous with devil's food and was an obvious counterpoint to angel food. Those who favor a reddish cake would offer the "flames of hell" as the working analogy and the fact that the devil is often portrayed as a red, not a black, figure. James Beard's classic *American Cookery* offers both versions of devil's food cake: one is called Chocolate Custard or Devil's Food Cake and the other is referred to as Red Devil's Food Cake. Related to this second type of devil's food cake is the Red Velvet Cake, which is usually chocolate and contains red food coloring, the Mahogany Cake, which includes molasses, and the Oxblood Cake, which is also reddish.

One reason this cake is so difficult to define is that over time the recipe was changed and embellished to the point that different recipes had little in common. To get a better handle on this, I pulled together two dozen or so recipes from cookbooks and the Internet and baked five of them. The first thing I noticed about the recipes was that the majority called for both cocoa powder and baking soda (not baking powder), and many also suggested the addition of melted chocolate. The majority also used boiling water as the liquid of choice, although recipes early in the twentieth century preferred milk, sour milk, or buttermilk. Perhaps the most singular aspect of devil's food is the water, since milk, a standard ingredient in American layer cakes, does tend to mute the flavor of chocolate, whereas water lets it show through. (Think of milk chocolate as opposed to dark chocolate.) If one aspect of devil's food cake is an intense chocolate experience, then the use of water is key. So the four key ingredients — the ones that really stood out in our research — were chocolate, cocoa, baking soda, and water.

However, it was up to the taste test to confirm whether these simple ingredients were going to lead us to the best devil's food cake. First, all the recipes all were constructed using a basic layer cake method. Butter and sugar were creamed

and then eggs were beaten in, followed by flour, cocoa, milk or water, and other ingredients. In order to test our theory about the four key elements, we included recipes that did not use all four for comparison. My tasting quickly provided the answer to the question about whether melted chocolate was necessary. Of the five recipes tested, the one that used only cocoa was the driest and most tasteless. Clearly, a bit of chocolate was a must, and I finally settled on 4 ounces after testing smaller and larger amounts. As expected, the cake that used milk instead of water had less flavor. Baking soda was the leavener of choice in virtually every devil's food cake recipe I found, but we tested this anyway. To my great surprise, the baking powder cake produced a totally different product. It was much lighter in color but, more to the point, it was fudgy, almost like a brownie. It shared none of the delicate, velvety texture that we have come to expect of a classic devil's food. I also tested the proper amount of baking soda and settled on 2 teaspoons: a tablespoon produced the telltale "soapy" taste, which indicates an excess of soda, and 1 teaspoon didn't provide enough lift.

I continued my testing to refine the recipe and found that a mixture of cake flour and all-purpose was best. The all-purpose provided structure, but the addition of the cake flour made the cake a bit more delicate. On a lark, I made one cake by whipping the egg whites separately from the yolks, but it was much too flimsy and could not support the large amount of water, so it sank. I played with the number of eggs, trying 2, 3, and then 4 eggs, but the middle road proved best — 3 eggs was just right. White sugar was tested against brown sugar and the latter won, improving the flavor. (I noted later that many devil's food recipes call for brown sugar, whereas regular chocolate cakes tend to list white sugar.) The butter was finalized at 8 tablespoons rather than the 12 tablespoons typical of a traditional layer cake. Although milk and buttermilk had been tested against water, I did try adding sour cream to the recipe and was impressed. It deepened the flavor, added substance to the texture, and provided a richer taste experience, the chocolate flavor lingering in the mouth and coating the tongue. (Scientists are now discovering that it is not dairy fat that enhances flavor but flavor compounds carried in the fat molecules. There are more of these flavor compounds in sour cream than in milk. When the cake bakes, the compounds dissolve, carrying with them a richer taste sensation, which complements the chocolate flavor.) Finally, to determine if boiling water was necessary, I made a cake with just room temperature water and found that the cake made with boiling water had substantially better flavor. This was the same phenomenon I discovered when making the Chocolate Genoise. (It should be noted that with recipes that do not use chocolate but do call for boiling water and baking soda, I have not found a difference. One theory as to why older recipes that used baking soda often called for boiling water is that the soda would harden into clumps and hot water was necessary to dissolve and distribute the soda properly throughout the batter.)

So I had finally discovered the essence of a great devil's food cake. Unlike chocolate cake, which is usually made with milk and has a higher proportion of fat (butter), devil's food is a velvety, more intense chocolate experience. It is a particularly dark cake when made with Dutch-process cocoa, whereas a supermarket cocoa will give it a redder hue. It is a singular cake in its devotion to a pure chocolate experience, subordinating everything to this simple proposition.

▪ ▪ ▪

Devil's Food Cake

You can use either natural cocoa such as Hershey's or Dutch-process cocoa such as Droste.

IS DUTCH-PROCESS COCOA REALLY BETTER?

Dutch-process cocoa is less acidic (more alkaline) than a regular (or natural) cocoa such as Hershey's. The theory behind the process is that reducing the acidity of natural cocoa enhances sugar-amino browning reactions, which results in a darker color. Manufacturers also claim that this process results in a smoother, less bitter chocolate flavor. Natural cocoa, which is more acidic than Dutch-process cocoa, is supposed to produce a redder cake, since the red pigments in cocoa become more visible in a more acidic environment.

To determine the veracity of these claims, I conducted a head-to-head test of four unsweetened cocoas — three Dutch-process cocoas (Droste; "black cocoa," sold by the King Arthur Flour Company; and Pernigotti, a very expensive brand sold at Williams-Sonoma stores) plus regular Hershey's. The Dutch-process cocoas all produced darker cakes with more chocolate flavor than the Hershey's, bearing out my research. However, I suspect that this improved flavor may also be related to the quality of the cocoa. I noted that Droste Dutch-process cocoa was not as rich in flavor as the more expensive Pernigotti, although it was significantly better than Hershey's. The only way to adequately test the claim of Dutch-process flavor superiority would be to compare the same quality cocoa head-to-head, one being "Dutched" and one not.

As promised, the Hershey's cocoa did produce a much redder cake, but we also noticed a difference in texture. It was dry and airy without much complexity of flavor, and some tasters also detected an odd taste undertone that was described as metallic or salty. Among the Dutch-process cocoas, I also noted textural differences. The expensive Pernigotti had a very moist, soft crumb, the Droste was a bit dry with a more open crumb, and the black cocoa cake was very dense, almost spongy, although incredibly chocolaty as well. (Black cocoa is made from beans that have been roasted until they are almost burned.) So if you want a richer-tasting, darker, more velvety cake, use Dutch-process cocoa, keeping in mind that quality matters. For those who have to have a reddish color, go with regular cocoa, but the taste and texture will suffer somewhat.

The former will produce a somewhat drier, red-der, lighter cake with less chocolate flavor. The Dutch-process yields a darker color and also a more velvety, richer chocolate flavor. Keep in mind that the quality of the cocoa is key — the better the cocoa, the deeper the flavor. I like to frost this cake with a vanilla, mocha, or coffee buttercream.

MAKES THREE 8-INCH ROUNDS

1¼   cups boiling water
4   ounces unsweetened chocolate, chopped
¼   cup cocoa powder
¾   cup all-purpose flour
¾   cup cake flour
¼   teaspoon salt
1   teaspoon baking soda

WHY DO DEVIL'S FOOD CAKES USE BAKING SODA, NOT BAKING POWDER?

The conventional wisdom about baking powder is that baking powder contains roughly one-third baking soda plus acids to stimulate a chemical reaction and a stabilizer such as cornstarch. Baking soda interacts with acids (acids are found in ingredients such as buttermilk, brown sugar, chocolate, even flour) to produce carbon dioxide gas, which leavens baked goods. Since this recipe contains sour cream, which contains loads of lactic acid, one might expect that there is sufficient acid in the batter to react with the baking soda. In other words, that the acids in baking powder are not necessary for a complete chemical reaction.

My actual test kitchen experience confirms that expectation. First, I found that cakes made with natural cocoa baked up somewhat lighter in texture than the Dutch-process cakes. The reason? Natural cocoa is more acidic. This results in a more active chemical reaction (the soda has more acid to react with) and therefore a somewhat airier cake. As described earlier, the cake made with baking powder was a disaster. This conforms to my theory, which is that baking powder made the batter too acid, which produced an excess of gas at the outset of baking, causing the cake to eventually collapse.

½   pound (2 sticks) unsalted butter, softened but still firm
1½   cups packed dark brown sugar
1   teaspoon vanilla extract
3   large eggs
½   cup sour cream or plain yogurt

1. Stir boiling water, chocolate, and cocoa together and reserve. Sift together the flours, the salt, and the baking soda onto a sheet of waxed paper and set aside. Set oven rack in the middle position and heat oven to 350 degrees. Grease three 8-inch round cake pans with Crisco or butter and line the bottom of each pan with parchment paper.

2. Place butter in the bowl of an electric mixer and beat on medium high for 1 minute. Add brown sugar and vanilla and beat on high until light and fluffy, about 3 minutes. Add one egg at a time and beat on medium high for 30 seconds after the addition of each egg. Add the sour cream and beat on medium speed until combined, about 10 seconds. Scrape down bowl as necessary.

3. Stir water-chocolate mixture until smooth. Add half of the chocolate mixture and half of the flour mixture to the batter and beat on low speed for 10 seconds. Add the balance of the chocolate and flour and beat on low speed for another 10 seconds. Gently finish mixing batter by hand with a large rubber spatula.

4. Pour the batter into the prepared pans and bake at 350 degrees for 20 to 25 minutes, or until the center springs back when lightly pressed with the flat side of a fork. Rotate pan 180 degrees halfway through baking time. When cake is done, remove from oven and let cool on a rack for 10 minutes. Run a dull knife around the edges of each cake, invert cake onto a plate or wire rack, and peel off parchment paper. Invert cake onto a cooling rack and cool completely.

FROSTING TIPS: A plain buttercream is nice with this moist, light cake. You can also use a meringue frosting.

WHAT CAN GO WRONG? Be sure that the chopped chocolate has completely melted in the boiling water. You will notice that this recipe produces a thin batter. Don't worry. The cake will rise nicely and be incredibly moist. Finally, do *not* use 9-inch pans — the texture of the cake made in larger pans is inferior. Also, I have had trouble making this recipe with Scharffen Berger natural cocoa. (The cake did not rise properly.)

SKY-HIGH ANGEL FOOD

ANGEL FOOD, SPONGE, AND chiffon cakes are really quite different, although all three depend on beaten egg whites for their structure. Angel food, the purest of the three, uses no egg yolks and is nothing more than a mixture of cake flour, beaten egg whites, and flavorings. Although the ingredient list is short, if angel food cakes are not made properly, they collapse during cooling, are unbearably sticky sweet, or don't rise evenly in the pan. I wanted a foolproof recipe, one that could be whipped up quickly, a cake that had a nicely browned exterior and tender crumb and was good enough to be served on its own.

I started by testing all-purpose flour versus cake flour, the amount of flour and sugar in relation to the egg whites, the oven temperature, and also whether cream of tartar, a common ingredient in angel food recipes, is really essential. With breads, I have found that all-purpose flour is often interchangeable with bread flour; with muffins and many cakes, I have found cake flour and all-purpose to be almost identical. However, my tests showed that an angel food cake made with all-purpose flour is very coarse and unpleasant. This is one category of recipes for which cake flour is a must.

I then turned my attention to the amount of flour. I decreased the flour from my original master recipe's 1 cup to ¾ cup and discovered

that the cake collapsed during cooling. I had inadvertently made a soufflé, not a cake! There just wasn't enough flour to create a lasting structure. I then reduced the quantity of sugar, and the cake became tough and tasteless. Although an angel food cake is quite sweet, it depends heavily on the sugar content for both tenderizing and flavor. When I bumped the oven temperature from 350 to 375 degrees, I found that the outside of the cake took on a darker, more golden texture, which added a good deal of flavor. Finally, the most interesting test was the cake made without cream of tartar. It was tough and lacked structure, exhibiting a very uneven texture. (Cream of tartar, an acid, makes it more difficult for the egg white proteins to bond too tightly, which results in a better rise and a more even, more tender structure.)

The biggest issue of all was the proper quantity of egg whites. Most recipes call for 10 whites, which is what was in my original master recipe. However, when I increased the amount to 12, the cake was slightly better — a bit fluffier, a bit lighter, and a winner. I also tested 8 egg whites and found that the cake was a good deal shorter and denser, not at all what I expect from a sky-high angel food recipe.

I had also been told that water is a good addition for many cakes. Rose Levy Beranbaum, author of *The Cake Bible*, was once having trouble with a meringue cake — the texture was tough and unpleasant — and Shirley Corriher, a well-known food scientist, told her to add water to the recipe. It was a success; moister and more tender. However, when I tried adding 1 tablespoon water to my recipe, it didn't improve the cake at all; in fact, I thought that the texture was a little less substantial, a bit like cotton candy. When I tried greater amounts, the cake fell during baking and was a wet mess. The egg whites just couldn't hold that much liquid. (I have added water successfully to sponge and chiffon cakes; however, those recipes contain egg yolks.) I also tried adding a bit of lemon juice, and this did produce a whiter cake.

Traditionally, angel food cakes are baked in ungreased 10-inch tube pans. Why ungreased? As the egg whites expand in the oven, they need to "climb" up the sides of the pan, which would be impossible if it were greased. After the cake is taken from the oven, the tube pan is turned upside down, which prevents the delicate cake structure from falling in on itself during cooling (the cake hangs upside down while the protein structure is setting). Just to see what would happen, I tried greasing the pan and not turning it upside down after baking. The cake did not rise properly and did collapse on itself somewhat as well.

• • •

Angel Food Cake

Angel food cake is a bit like cotton candy; it's all air and sugar. I like to serve angel food with slightly sweetened fruit; peaches and strawberries are my favorites since they produce a lot of juices, which go well with the cake. In the winter, use frozen berries, adding just a bit of sugar to sweeten. Angel food cake can also be served with any custard or chocolate sauce, such as a basic vanilla sauce, or can be sliced and served on its own.

MAKES ONE 10-INCH TUBE CAKE

1	cup cake flour
1¼	cups granulated sugar
⅛	teaspoon salt
12	large egg whites, at room temperature
1	teaspoon cream of tartar
1	teaspoon vanilla extract
1½	teaspoons lemon juice

1. Heat oven to 375 degrees. Place the flour, ½ cup of the sugar, and the salt in a sifter. Sift onto a large piece of waxed paper and set aside.

2. Beat the egg whites in the bowl of an electric mixer at medium speed for 1 minute, or until whites begin to foam and bubble. Add cream of tartar. Turn mixer to high and beat until whites just start to form very soft peaks and have increased three or four times in volume. Slowly add remaining ¾ cup sugar and continue beating until whites just hold soft peaks. Add vanilla and lemon juice and beat until whites can just hold a 2-inch peak.

3. Placing sifter over egg whites, sift one-third of flour mixture over whites at a time. After each sifting, fold flour into egg whites using a rubber spatula. Repeat two times with balance of flour, incorporating each time into egg whites. Work quickly but smoothly — this step should take about 2 minutes in total.

4. Turn batter into an ungreased tube pan. (An ungreased pan allows the batter to cling to the sides as it rises.) Bake for 20 to 30 minutes, but check after 20. The top should be a rich gold and should spring back when touched lightly. If the top of the cake does not spring back, bake for an additional 5 to 10 minutes (check every 5 minutes).

5. Remove pan from oven and turn upside down. If pan has "feet," just set it on the counter; if not, balance on top of three or four solid mugs or glasses. After 30 minutes, run a thin knife or spatula around the outside edge of the cake, as this cake is sticky and will adhere easily to the sides. Cool completely in the pan, bottom side up.

FROSTING TIPS: Angel food cake is rarely frosted. It is simply cut and served with fresh fruit or perhaps a crème anglaise. It does take well to a citrus glaze.

WHAT CAN GO WRONG? As with many recipes in this chapter, the biggest problem is beating the egg whites and then folding in the dry ingredients. Overbeating the whites makes them dry and hard to fold. (For the proper way to beat egg whites, see the illustrations on page 9.) Overbeaten whites will also rise less during baking and tend to fall more when cooling. It is very important to know how to fold properly, so check the step-by-step illustrations on page 8.

CASE 32: HOW MUCH WATER CAN A SPONGE ABSORB?

The proportion of egg yolks to whites makes little difference, but adding water to the batter produces a great sponge cake.

Test	Results
6 egg yolks, 8 whites	Very good texture
5 egg yolks, 8 whites	Same as 6 yolks
4 egg yolks, 8 whites	Same as 6 yolks
No water added	Slightly tough and dry
¼ cup water added to batter	Moist and tender

SPONGE CAKE, AMERICAN-STYLE

A SPONGE CAKE IS quite similar to an angel food cake except that it also includes egg yolks along with the whites. The testing I had done in developing the recipe for angel food cake had already covered most of the relevant issues, including the type of flour, the amount of sugar, the baking temperature, and so on. But with regard to a sponge cake, the question still remained, what was the proper proportion of yolks to whites? I decided to base my recipe on 8 egg whites and then baked a few cakes using different numbers of yolks. Although I had tried adding water to an angel food cake with disastrous results, I also wanted to try that approach with sponge cake as well.

After trying 4, 5, and 6 egg yolks, I decided that 4 yolks was fine, since the higher quantities seemed to have no effect. The big surprise was that adding ¼ cup water made the cake significantly moister and less cottony in texture. Although I was unsuccessful adding water to an angel food cake, a sponge cake contains egg yolks. Egg yolks in turn contain lecithin, which promotes emulsification. This means that the batter can more readily absorb the additional water.

▪▪▪

American Sponge Cake

MAKES ONE 10-INCH TUBE CAKE

1	cup cake flour
4	large egg yolks, at room temperature
1½	teaspoons vanilla extract
¼	cup cold water
1¼	cups granulated sugar
8	large egg whites, at room temperature
¼	teaspoon salt
1	teaspoon cream of tartar

1. Set oven rack in lower middle position and heat oven to 375. Sift flour onto a sheet of waxed paper and set aside.

2. Place egg yolks in the bowl of an electric mixer and beat until thick and pale yellow, about 3 minutes. Add the vanilla and slowly add the water as you continue to beat. Slowly add the sugar (reserve 2 tablespoons) and beat until thick and very pale.

3. Place a 10-inch tube pan in the oven to heat. Sprinkle one-third of the flour over the beaten yolks and fold in with a rubber spatula. Repeat twice with remaining flour. Set bowl aside.

4. In a large bowl, beat egg whites for 45 seconds on high speed. Add the salt and cream of tartar. Beat until the whites just start to hold a peak. Sprinkle in the remaining 2 tablespoons sugar and continue to beat until whites can hold a 2-inch peak but are still moist.

5. Stir one-quarter of the beaten whites into the yolks to lighten, then fold in the rest gently with a rubber spatula or with your hand.

6. Pour mixture into preheated tube pan. Bake 25 to 35 minutes, or until top is golden brown and springs back when lightly pressed with a fork. If the top of the cake does not spring back, bake for an additional 5 to 10 minutes (check every 5 minutes). Let cool in pan for 1 hour. Remove from pan.

FROSTING TIPS: Like angel food, sponge cake is rarely frosted, although you can sprinkle it with confectioners' sugar or drizzle on a simple glaze.

WHAT CAN GO WRONG? As with any cake that depends on beaten egg whites for lift, you must not overbeat the whites; a light hand in folding is also important.

CITRUS VARIATION

Increase flour to 1¼ cups. Add 1 tablespoon grated lemon zest and ¼ cup orange juice to the beaten egg yolks.

FRENCH SPONGE CAKE

AN AMERICAN-STYLE SPONGE CAKE (see preceding recipe) is more or less a variation on angel food cake with the addition of egg yolks and, in the case of my recipe, ¼ cup water as well, to add moisture and tenderness. However, there is another approach to sponge cake; instead of beating the yolks and whites separately, it involves beating some of the eggs whole, much as one would with the classic French genoise. This would, I thought, produce a more tender, more delicate cake that can simply be eaten on its own with perhaps a bit of whipped cream and fresh, sweetened fruit.

Before I began my recipe testing, I wanted to understand the different types of "foam" cakes. Angel food, genoise, sponge, and chiffon are all "foam" cakes. They depend on beaten eggs to provide lift and structure. Although each of them uses an egg foam for structure, they differ in two ways: the addition of fat (butter, milk, or oil) and whether the foam is made from whole eggs, egg whites, or a combination. The leanest of the foam cakes is the angel food cake, which is made with egg whites only, using no yolks nor added fat. A genoise is made by whipping whole eggs with the addition of melted butter. A sponge cake calls for beating either whole eggs and yolks or just yolks and then folding in whipped egg whites. Traditionally, aside from the fat in the egg yolks, no fat is added. A chiffon cake, the sturdiest of the lot, is a sponge cake with a good deal of added fat, usually a half cup or so of oil or butter.

The problem with these definitions is that cookbook authors often ignore them, using the terms "foam" and "sponge" interchangeably, referring to the whole category of foam cakes as "sponge-style" cakes. The recipe for sponge cake in *Joy of Cooking,* for example, is actually a genoise recipe, since it calls for beaten whole eggs and says nothing about beaten egg whites.

I found the same situation in the sponge cake recipe that appears in *Classic American Desserts,* by Richard Sax. Despite these inconsistencies, I concluded that a classic sponge cake must call for beating at least some of the whites separately and then folding them into the whole egg or egg yolk foam; otherwise it is nothing more than a classic genoise. (To make this category of cakes even more confusing, there are variations on classic sponge cakes that add fat in the form of milk and/or butter. One very common variation is the "hot milk" sponge cake. Although technically speaking this qualifies as a chiffon cake, it seems that the determining factor is the amount of fat. The addition of just a few tablespoons of milk or butter still qualifies as a sponge cake; adding a half cup or so of fat transforms it into a chiffon cake.)

Having established the fundamental properties of foam cakes, I was ready to work with some recipes. To get things started, I tested a variety of foam cakes, and the winner was a variation on a genoise. It was delicate but springy, light but firm. But as I soon discovered, a genoise is anything but simple. This aerated mixture is dependent on the temperature of the ingredients, the ratio of eggs to flour, and even the speed with which the cake is whisked into the oven. During testing, I discovered that if the milk was added at room temperature, not hot as is suggested by most recipes, or if the eggs were a bit over- or underbeaten, the cake would not rise properly. It is a professional baker's cake, not the simple everyday cake recipe I was looking for.

My next thought was to turn to a sponge cake, which is similar to a genoise, but some or all of the egg whites are beaten separately, which delivers a more stable batter and a more foolproof recipe. I started by making a classic American sponge cake, which adds no fat in the form of butter or milk, using my own recipe (see page 147), which calls for 8 beaten egg whites folded into 4 beaten egg yolks. The cake certainly was light but lacked a bit in flavor, and

the texture, although moist and tender by sponge cake standards, could have been more delicate. (Please note, however, that my American Sponge Cake recipe is easier to make, sturdier, and more foolproof than the French Sponge Cake below.) I then tried a hot-milk sponge cake (a small amount of melted butter and hot milk are added to the whole egg foam), and this turned out much better on all counts. The added fat not only provided flavor but tenderized the crumb. This particular recipe also used fewer eggs than my sponge cake recipe.

I was now working with a master recipe that used ¾ cup cake flour, 1 teaspoon baking powder, ¾ cup sugar, and 5 eggs. I started by separating out all 5 of the whites and found that the cake was too light, with insufficient structure, resulting in a slightly sunken center. I then beat just 3 of the whites, and the resulting cake was excellent. When all-purpose flour was substituted for cake flour, the cake had more body and was a bit tougher. I then tried different ratios of the two flours, finally settling on two-thirds cake flour to one-third all-purpose. I also tested the ratio of eggs to flour and found that 5 eggs to ¾ cup flour (was best. Six eggs produced an "eggy" cake; 4 eggs resulted in a lower rise and a bit less flavor.

I thought that the baking powder might be optional, but it turned out to be essential to a properly risen cake. Although angel food and classic sponge cakes, which use no added fat, do not require chemical leavening, the addition of milk and melted butter, combined with the relatively small amount of beaten egg whites in proportion to the flour, makes baking powder essential. Two tablespoons of melted butter was just the right amount; 3 tablespoons made the cake a bit oily and the butter flavor too prominent. As for the milk, 3 tablespoons was best; larger quantities resulted in a wet and mushy texture.

A host of other tests were performed, including adding lemon juice, which is probably a holdover from angel food cakes, used to whiten the color of the cake (I noticed no benefit in either color or texture); sifting the flour more than once (many professional bakers suggest this step, but I found no improvement); and beating the whole eggs and sugar over warm water (this is a classic French technique that was both awkward and unnecessary; that being said, I found that the eggs must be at room temperature to beat up into a thick foam).

I also played with the order of the steps. Beating the whole egg foam first, and then the whites, allowed the relatively fragile foam to deteriorate, producing less rise. I found that beating the whites first was vastly better. After much experimentation, I also found it best to fold together, all at the same time, the beaten whole eggs, the whites, and the flour, and then, once the mixture was about half-mixed, to add the warm butter and milk. This eliminated the possibility that the liquid would damage the egg foam and made the temperature of the milk-butter mixture less important than it was with a genoise.

Three baking temperatures were tested: 325, 350, and 375 degrees. The middle temperature was best. I also discovered that this recipe can be made successfully in either an 8-inch or 9-inch pan, although making the entire recipe in one pan (one with high sides) is not recommended. The cake falls in the center. Determining when a sponge cake is properly cooked is a little more difficult than with a regular American layer cake. It should, however, provide some resistance and not feel as if one just touched the top of a soufflé. Another good test is color. The top of the cake should be a nice light brown, not pale golden, not dark, rich brown.

Handling the cakes once they were out of the oven was also tested. When left to cool in the baking pans, they shrank away from the sides and the edges became uneven. It is best to quickly remove them onto a cooling rack. This is tricky, however, since the cake pans are very hot. I found that the best method was to place the hot pan on a kitchen towel, cover the cake with a plate, and then use

MAKING SENSE OF EGG FOAMS

To understand how both egg white and whole egg foams work, I called a variety of scientists and discovered that foam cakes, of which the French Sponge Cake recipe is a good example, depend on the proper aeration of both whole eggs and egg whites. An egg white foam consists of egg white proteins that are partially unwound around air bubbles. (This unwinding also occurs during cooking.) These bubbles are lined with unwound protein strands that are loosely connected to one another. When the batter is heated, the bubbles increase in size and the loose, elastic strands allow this expansion without breaking their bonds. (If one overbeats egg whites, for example, the protein strands become inelastic and the mixture cannot expand.) This aeration is a good thing for leavening, but it creates a less stable, more fragile structure, since the protein has been partially denatured (unwound) through the beating process.

A whole egg foam, on the other hand, is a great deal more sensitive and unstable than an egg white foam. Unlike an egg white foam, which is based on a film or protein that traps air, a whole egg foam is created through the process of emulsification. (A good example of emulsification is the combination of oil and vinegar in a salad dressing.) Through the phospholipids found in lecithin, an ingredient in egg yolks, emulsification is made possible, in this case holding together water and air. (Water comes from the egg and the air is beaten into it by a mixer.) This produces a more fragile and complex structure than an egg white foam, since the water and the air are not naturally inclined to bond.

By folding an egg white foam into a whole egg foam, I have increased the protein content of the batter, which makes it more stable. (Egg whites are almost pure protein.) The beaten egg whites also set at a lower temperature than the whole egg foam, which means that the cake structure firms up more quickly during baking. Adding flour, a stabilizing influence, to this mixture counteracts the effects of melted butter and milk, fats that often destabilize egg foams.

the towel to protect my hands as I inverted the cake onto the plate. The cake could then be inverted onto a cooling rack.

▪▪▪

Master Recipe for French Sponge Cake

The egg whites should be beaten to soft, glossy, billowy peaks. If beaten too stiff, they will be very difficult to fold into the whole egg mixture.

MAKES TWO 8- OR 9-INCH ROUNDS

½	cup cake flour
¼	cup all-purpose flour
1	teaspoon baking powder
¼	teaspoon salt
3	tablespoons milk
2	tablespoons unsalted butter
½	teaspoon vanilla extract
5	large eggs, at room temperature
¾	cup granulated sugar

1. Adjust oven rack to lower middle position and heat oven to 350 degrees. Grease two 8- or 9-inch round cake pans and cover pan bottoms with rounds of parchment paper. (If using 8-inch pans, they must be at least 2 inches high.)

2. Whisk flours, baking powder, and salt in a medium bowl (or sift onto waxed paper); set aside. Heat milk and butter in a small saucepan over low heat until butter melts. Off heat, add vanilla; cover and keep warm.

3. Separate 3 of the eggs, placing whites in bowl of standing mixer fitted with the whisk attachment (or a large mixing bowl if using hand mixer or whisk). Reserve the 3 yolks plus remaining 2 whole eggs in another bowl. Beat the 3 whites on high speed (or whisk) until whites are foamy. Gradually adding 6 tablespoons of the sugar, continue to beat whites to soft, moist peaks. (Do not overbeat, as stiff, dry egg whites will be difficult to incorporate into the batter.) If using a standing mixer, transfer the beaten whites to a large bowl and add the yolks and

whole eggs to the bowl of the mixer (you don't need to wash the bowl).

4. Beat yolks and whole eggs with the remaining 6 tablespoons sugar at medium-high speed until eggs are very thick and a pale lemon color, about 5 minutes (or 12 minutes by hand). Return the beaten whites to the mixing bowl and then sprinkle the flour mixture over beaten eggs and whites. Mix on the lowest speed for 10 seconds. Remove bowl from mixer, make a well in one side of batter, and pour melted butter mixture into bowl. Fold mixture with a large rubber spatula until batter is evenly mixed, about 8 additional strokes.

5. Immediately pour batter into prepared baking pans; bake until cake tops are light brown and feel firm and spring back when touched, about 16 minutes for 9-inch pans and 20 minutes for 8-inch pans.

6. Place one cake pan, bottom side down, on a kitchen towel; run a knife around pan perimeter to loosen cake; cover pan with a large plate. Invert pan and plate, then remove pan from cake. Peel parchment paper from bottom of cake and invert cake onto a cooling rack. Repeat with remaining cake. Cool completely before frosting or filling.

FROSTING TIPS: Treat this cake much like a genoise, which means use only a light frosting such as a whipped cream or meringue frosting or fill it with a custard filling and sprinkle with powdered sugar. See variations below.

WHAT CAN GO WRONG? This is probably the most finicky recipe in this book. As cakes go, sponge cakes are tricky, which means that a lot can go wrong, although I have tried to make this recipe as foolproof as possible. It is crucial to beat the egg yolks, whole eggs, and sugar a long time, until the mixture is very pale and very light. This may take 5 minutes, which will seem almost forever. You will be tempted to stop beating at 3 minutes or so. If using 8-inch cake pans, be sure they are at least 2 inches high; otherwise the batter will rise above the sides of the pans. This is one cake you do not want to underbake, because it will collapse. Make sure that the middle of the cake springs back when lightly touched with your finger or a fork. If you have little baking experience, I recommend you make the American Sponge Cake (page 147), which is sturdier and simpler.

· · ·

Sponge Cake with Blackberry Jam

A simple sponge cake filled with jam and dusted with confectioners' sugar used to be called a Washington Pie after Martha Washington. Seedless black raspberry jam is best.

SERVES 12

1 recipe French Sponge Cake (page 151)
1 jar (8 ounces) blackberry jam
Confectioners' sugar for dusting

1. Make French Sponge Cake.
2. Place one cake layer on a cardboard round and set on a sheet of waxed paper (to protect your counter). Evenly spread jam over cake. Place second layer over jam, making sure layers line up properly. Dust cake with confectioners' sugar and serve.

· · ·

Sponge Cake with Rich Lemon Filling

This is another way to dress up a sponge cake for company. The cake is filled with the filling used for lemon meringue pie.

SERVES 12

1 recipe French Sponge Cake (page 151)

Rich Lemon Filling
10 tablespoons (½ cup plus 2 tablespoons) granulated sugar

3 tablespoons cornstarch
⅛ teaspoon salt
⅞ cup (1 cup minus 2 tablespoons) cold water
2 large egg yolks
⅓ cup lemon juice
2 teaspoons minced lemon zest
2 tablespoons unsalted butter

Confectioners' sugar for dusting

1. Make French Sponge Cake.
2. *For the filling:* Whisk the sugar, cornstarch, salt, and water in a 2-quart nonreactive saucepan. Bring the mixture to a simmer, whisking frequently but gently. When it starts to turn translucent and simmer, add the egg yolks one at a time, whisking gently and slowly after each addition. The filling will be very thick. Next, add the lemon juice and zest and bring the mixture back to a simmer, stirring constantly but very gently. (The filling will thin out a bit after the lemon juice is added.) Remove from heat; stir in the butter until it melts. Transfer to another container to cool to room temperature, placing a piece of waxed paper or plastic wrap directly on the surface of the filling to prevent a skin from forming. Refrigerate until the filling is firm. (Can be refrigerated overnight.) To ensure that the lemon filling does not thin out, do not whisk or vigorously stir it once it has set.
3. When ready to assemble cake, place one cake layer on a cardboard round and set on a sheet of waxed paper (to protect your counter). Carefully spoon filling over layer and spread evenly up to cake edge. Place the second cake layer on top, making sure layers line up properly. Dust with confectioners' sugar and serve.

BOSTON CREAM PIE

THE FOUNDATION FOR Boston Cream Pie was a cake referred to by James Beard as the One-Egg Cake and by Marion Cunningham in *The*

Fannie Farmer Cookbook as the Boston Favorite Cake. It is made with cake flour, sugar, butter, milk, 1 or 2 eggs, vanilla, baking powder, and salt. Using this simple building-block recipe, many different variations were created, including, according to James Beard, Washington Pie, filled with jam and topped with powdered sugar; Boston Cream Pie, filled with a pastry cream and topped with powdered sugar; Martha Washington Pie, which is either the same as Washington Pie or split into three layers, the middle one spread with jam and the bottom one with pastry cream; and Parker House Chocolate Cream Pie, which is Boston Cream Pie topped with a thin layer of chocolate butter icing. The last was invented either by a French chef, Sanzian, who was hired by Harvey Parker at his hotel's opening in October 1855 at the extraordinary annual salary of $5,000 (a good chef in Boston could be hired at that time for $8 per week), or by a German baker named Ward, who, shortly after the hotel opened, was also credited with inventing Parker House rolls. However, it is not clear whether, as Beard suggests, the term Boston Cream Pie already existed before the Parker House version. My guess is that Beard is right, since *Fannie Farmer* offers a recipe for Boston Favorite Cake and treats Boston Cream Pie as a variation. As for why it is called a pie, Jim Dodge, author of *Baking with Jim Dodge,* suggests that the cake was originally baked by early New England cooks in a pie pan. (He offers such a recipe in his book.) Why were pie pans used? My best guess is that pie pans or plates, which predated cakes in the American kitchen, were common kitchen equipment, cake pans being less widely available. No matter the origins, I found, in a blind tasting of five different cakes, that the French Sponge Cake recipe above was ideal for Boston Cream Pie. I fill it with a thick pastry cream and then drizzle on a healthy layer of chocolate glaze. As is the case with many more modern Boston Cream Pie recipes, this one allows the glaze to drip down over the sides of the cake.

▪ ▪ ▪

Boston Cream Pie

SERVES 8

1 recipe French Sponge Cake (see page 151)

For the Pastry Cream
2 cups milk
6 large egg yolks
½ cup granulated sugar
¼ teaspoon salt
¼ cup cornstarch, sifted
1 teaspoon vanilla extract
1 tablespoon rum
2 tablespoons unsalted butter (optional)

For the Rich Chocolate Glaze
1 cup heavy cream
¼ cup light corn syrup
8 ounces semisweet chocolate, chopped into small pieces
½ teaspoon vanilla extract

1. Make French Sponge Cake.
2. *For the pastry cream:* Heat milk in a small saucepan until hot but not simmering; reserve. Whisk yolks, sugar, and salt in a large saucepan until mixture is thick and lemon-colored, 3 to 4 minutes. Add cornstarch; whisk to combine. Slowly whisk in hot milk. Cook milk mixture over medium-low heat, whisking constantly and scraping pan bottom and sides as you stir, until mixture thickens to a thick pudding consistency and has lost all traces of raw starch flavor, about 10 minutes. Remove from heat; stir in vanilla, rum, and optional butter. Remove from heat, transfer to another container, place a piece of plastic wrap directly on the surface of the filling to prevent a skin from forming, and let stand at room temperature to firm up. (Can be refrigerated overnight.) To ensure that pastry cream does not thin out, do not whisk or vigorously stir it once it has set.

3. *For the glaze:* Bring cream and corn syrup to a full simmer in a medium saucepan. Remove from heat; add chocolate, cover, and let stand for 8 minutes. (If chocolate has not completely melted, return saucepan to low heat; stir constantly until melted.) Add vanilla; stir very gently until mixture is smooth. Cool until tepid, so that a spoonful drizzled back into the pan mounds slightly. (Glaze can be refrigerated to speed up cooling process; stir every few minutes to ensure even cooling and to make sure it doesn't get *too* cool.)

4. While glaze is cooling, place one cake layer on a cardboard round that has been cut to the size of the cake; place on a cooling rack set over a jelly roll pan (to catch drips). Carefully spoon pastry cream over cake and spread evenly up to cake edge. Place the second layer on top, making sure layers line up properly.

5. Pour glaze over middle of top layer and let flow down cake sides. (I prefer to let the glaze drip down haphazardly over the sides, but if you want to completely coat the sides, use a metal spatula to finish spreading the glaze.) Use a small needle to puncture air bubbles. Let sit about 1 hour or until glaze fully sets. Serve.

WHAT CAN GO WRONG? Besides the usual issues with sponge cake, you need to keep a close eye on the chocolate glaze. It must be poured over the cake when it starts to firm up, but if you wait too long, it will be too thick and not pour properly. I have also found that the glaze often takes a long time to thicken, a half hour or more, which can be frustrating. (To speed up the thickening process, pour it out of the saucepan and into a separate bowl.) I wouldn't bother trying to evenly coat the sides of the cake — it is fussy work, and in my opinion the cake looks better with the glaze simply dripping over the sides.

CHIFFON CAKE

A CHIFFON CAKE IS quite similar to an angel food or sponge cake, with one major difference. Chiffon cakes use oil and therefore less sugar is called for (in proportion to the other ingredients), producing a tender but not overly sweet cake. Both fat and sugar tenderize proteins such as those found in eggs. Since an angel food cake has little fat, a large amount of sugar is called for to make a tender cake. In a chiffon cake, less sugar is necessary, since the oil or butter does much of the tenderizing. Although an angel food cake relies exclusively on whipped egg whites for leavening, a chiffon cake contains both flour and fat, which need a chemical leavener (baking powder) to raise the structure.

My original recipe for chiffon cake called for inverting the pan while the cake cools after baking. On one occasion, when I used vegetable oil instead of butter, I watched the cake slide right out of the pan! I suspect that butter may make the cake adhere better to the sides of the pan, since it causes the sides of the cake to brown better than when oil is used. Out of curiosity, I then made a chiffon cake and did not invert the pan after baking. It turned out fine, so I suggest that you do *not* invert the pan for this recipe. The amount of fat is relatively high compared to an angel food cake, and therefore the cake is less likely to attach itself firmly to the sides of the pan.

. . .

Chiffon Cake

I often use this cake to make trifle, or it can simply be served with fresh lightly sugared fruit and whipped cream or with a thin glaze.

MAKES ONE 10-INCH TUBE CAKE

2¼ cups cake flour
1½ cups granulated sugar

2 teaspoons baking powder

¼ teaspoon salt

½ cup melted unsalted butter or corn oil
(butter is preferred)

6 large egg yolks

½ cup water

2 teaspoons vanilla extract

9 large egg whites

1 teaspoon cream of tartar

1. Adjust oven rack to middle position and heat oven to 375 degrees. Sift together the flour, 1 cup of the sugar, the baking powder, and the salt into a large bowl. Whisk to blend.

2. In a separate bowl, whisk together the butter (or oil), egg yolks, water, and vanilla. Pour the liquid ingredients into the flour mixture and beat until smooth (this can be done by hand with a whisk or wooden spoon).

3. Place the egg whites in a large bowl and, using an electric mixer, whip until frothy. Add the cream of tartar and beat until soft peaks just begin to form. Slowly add the remaining ½ cup sugar and beat until whites hold a 2-inch peak. Do not overbeat; whites should be billowy and glossy.

4. Stir one-quarter of the beaten whites into the batter to lighten. Then fold the remaining whites into the batter and pour into an ungreased 10-inch tube pan. Bake for 30 to 40 minutes, rotating pan 180 degrees after 15 minutes. Press lightly with a fork. If the top of the cake does not spring back, bake for an additional 5 to 10 minutes (check every 5 minutes).

5. Remove pan from oven and set on a wire rack to cool for at least 1 hour. Run a thin knife around the outside of the cake before removing from pan, since it is sticky and will easily adhere to the sides.

FROSTING TIPS: This cake can take any flavor glaze, including chocolate, or can simply be served with flavored whipped cream.

WHAT CAN GO WRONG? Of all the "egg white" cakes, this one is the most foolproof, since it contains egg yolks as well as butter, both of which make it sturdy. Just be sure to lighten the batter with one-quarter of the beaten whites before you fold in the rest; otherwise the mixture will be very difficult to fold together.

CITRUS VARIATION
Replace the ½ cup water with ½ cup orange juice and 1 tablespoon grated lemon zest. Reduce vanilla extract to 1 teaspoon.

UPSIDE-DOWN CAKE

UPSIDE-DOWN CAKE IS most often made with a yellow cake, and the most popular topping is pineapple. According to *The Fannie Farmer Baking Book,* this recipe was the result of a 1925 cooking contest held in an effort to promote the use of pineapple by the Dole company. Of course, many older recipes suggested using canned pineapple and maraschino cherries, whereas more modern cooks will opt for fresh fruit and skip the cherries entirely.

The basic method is simple: the butter and sugar are melted in a skillet, the fruit is added, a batter is made and then poured over the fruit, and the whole thing is baked in the skillet. I found that it was best to cook the fruit along with the butter and sugar — it gives the fruit better flavor and texture. I also played with a variety of cake types, including a basic yellow cake and a sponge cake, and ended up with a recipe that is more like a boxed cake mix. Instead of creaming the butter, I found that I preferred the texture of the cake if the butter was simply beaten with the dry ingredients and some of the buttermilk and then added to the rest of the liquid ingredients. The texture was softer and finer. I also ended up adding cornmeal to make the cake a bit more interesting. A small amount of almond extract contributed an appealing flavor note.

An iron skillet is traditional for this recipe — I didn't invent this approach — and I like the results. (You could use any relatively deep oven-proof skillet.) You can also use a cake pan, but then the topping must be made in a separate saucepan. (A 9 x 3-inch cake pan works well. You do need a very high cake pan to hold all of the batter.) The cake pan method produces a straight-sided cake, whereas the skillet will make a cake with sloping sides.

▪▪▪

Upside-Down Cake

The trick to this recipe is having the proper size skillet; an 8-inch skillet is too small and a 12-inch skillet is too large. The ideal size is 9 to 10 inches. Cast iron is traditional, but any relatively deep ovenproof skillet will do. If you do not have a skillet of the proper size, simply heat the butter-sugar mixture in a saucepan for 4 minutes, add the fruit, stir until the sugar is completely dissolved, and then pour it into a 9 x 3-inch cake pan. Pour the batter on top and bake.

SERVES 6 TO 8

For the Fruit

2   cups of fruit (peaches, plums, or pineapple) cut into ½-inch slices
1   tablespoon lemon juice
4   tablespoons unsalted butter
¾   cup packed dark brown sugar

For the Cake

⅔   cup buttermilk
4   large egg whites
3   large egg yolks
1   teaspoon vanilla extract
½   teaspoon almond extract
1½ cups all-purpose flour
¾   cup granulated sugar

1   teaspoon baking powder
¼   teaspoon baking soda
¼   cup cornmeal
½   teaspoon salt
6   tablespoons unsalted butter, at room temperature

1. Preheat oven to 350 degrees.

2. *Prepare the fruit:* Toss fruit with lemon juice and set aside. In a 9- or 10-inch cast iron skillet, melt the 4 tablespoons butter. Add the brown sugar and, stirring occasionally, heat for 4 minutes. Add the fruit and stir until the sugar is totally dissolved. Remove from heat.

3. *Make the batter:* Stir together ⅓ cup of the buttermilk, the egg whites, yolks, and extracts with a fork; set aside. In a large bowl, mix the next 6 ingredients (flour through salt) until blended. Add butter and remaining ⅓ cup buttermilk and beat on low speed or by hand until dry ingredients are moistened. Beat on medium for 1½ minutes. Scrape down sides of bowl and add half of egg-buttermilk mixture. Mix for 30 seconds. Scrape down sides of bowl, add remaining egg-buttermilk mixture, and finish beating for 30 seconds. Scrape down sides and beat 20 seconds more.

4. Pour batter over fruit in cast iron pan and smooth top. Bake about 30 minutes, or until top of cake springs back when lightly pressed in the center. Rotate pan front to back after 15 minutes and check cake after 25 minutes.

5. Remove skillet to a cooling rack. Let rest for 3 minutes. Place a serving plate over top of skillet and invert cake onto plate. If any of the fruit sticks to the pan, remove and place on top of cake.

WHAT CAN GO WRONG? The most common problem with this recipe is using the wrong pan size. Anything other than the 9- or 10-inch skillet called for in the directions will produce problems. You can use a cake pan in place of a skillet, however. See headnote. Also, getting this dessert out of a heavy skillet is no piece of cake! I find that it is best done by two people, one holding the skillet handle with both hands (with oven mitts) and the other holding the cake plate.

REGULAR MILK VARIATION

To make this cake with regular milk, simply substitute it for the buttermilk, eliminate the baking soda, and increase the baking powder to 1½ teaspoons.

WELL-ROUNDED POUND CAKE

POUND CAKE DERIVES its name from a seventeenth-century English cake that was made from 1 pound each of flour, sugar, butter, and eggs. (Another famous "ingredient" cake is the 1-2-3-4 cake, which is made from 1 cup butter, 2 cups sugar, 3 cups flour, and 4 eggs.) In fact, American layer cakes are descendants of this simple combination of ingredients. Although the old 1-pound-each formula has long gone out of fashion, modern versions of pound cake are still with us and rightly so, given the recipe's appeal and usefulness.

The bad news about pound cake is that a good one is hard to come by. I was looking for a tender, moist crumb with a good rise, a rich cake that was also light and delicate but full-flavored. Since I was not going to use baking powder for this recipe (I tested this method and did not like the texture), relying instead on the creaming of butter and sugar to lend lift to the batter, I knew that the temperature of ingredients and proper mixing methods were going to be key.

A starting recipe having been assembled, the first question was which mixing method to use. I could beat together the butter, sugar, and egg yolks, add the flour, and then whip the whites separately, folding them into the batter. This method, one used by James Beard in *American Cookery,* was okay, but the cakes were not rich and moist enough. Next, I tried the obvious method, simply beating the butter and sugar together, adding the eggs one at a time, and then folding in the flour. Having tried this method a number of times, I found that this was a chancy approach. Very often, the batter would "curdle" or separate, appearing grainy and not very thick. Flo Braker, in *The Simple Art of Perfect Baking,* published a recipe for pound cake in which she did two interesting things: she changed the proportions of ingredients and also insisted that the eggs be lightly beaten and then added little by little. She claimed that it is easier for the batter to absorb the eggs slowly, in small amounts. By increasing the sugar and the eggs, in keeping with Braker's recipe, I did get a more tender result. As for the eggs, I found that adding them in little dribbles was unnecessary as long as one beat each egg when added to the batter for a full 20 seconds on high speed.

The biggest problem, however, with pound cakes is the issue of the temperature of the butter and eggs. Cold ingredients will make a lousy cake, since they will not whip up properly to form a cohesive emulsion. On the other hand, the butter should not be at room temperature, at the point that it is very soft, almost melted. Rather, it should be soft and malleable but still have some body to it. For those who have an instant-read thermometer, simply stick it into the butter. It should read 65 to 67 degrees. If you have forgotten to leave the eggs out at room temperature, put them in a bowl of hot water for 2 minutes or so.

The last hurdle was how to deal with a batter that does curdle or separate. This can happen if the ingredients were too cold or if you did not beat in the eggs properly. The first test is to feel the outside of the mixing bowl (if you are using a metal bowl). If it is cold, an indication that the butter and/or eggs were not at the proper temperature, simply take a thick kitchen towel and soak it with very hot tap water. Being careful not to burn your hands, wring it out and then place it around the sides and bottom of the mixing bowl as the beaters are turning. You may have to repeat this a few times. Be careful not to melt the butter. If the ingredients were at the correct temperature, simply continue beating the mixture until it appears dull and thick. I have rescued many pound cake batters using this method.

* * *

Pound Cake

Do not use a glass loaf pan for this recipe. Glass is a very good conductor of heat, and since the cake bakes for over an hour, the bottom or sides can overcook. A cheap metal pan is just fine, but be sure to grease it well.

SERVES 8 TO 12

1⅔	cups cake or all-purpose flour (cake flour preferred)
½	teaspoon salt
½	pound (2 sticks) unsalted butter, softened but still firm
1½	cups granulated sugar
5	large eggs, at room temperature
1½	teaspoons vanilla extract
1	teaspoon grated lemon zest

1. Set oven rack in the center position and heat oven to 325 degrees. Grease a standard metal loaf pan, 9 x 5 x 3 inches, with Crisco or soft butter and dust with flour. Sift together the flour and salt onto a large piece of waxed paper.

2. Place the butter in a large metal mixing bowl and beat until smooth, light-colored, and creamy. This can be done by hand, about 1 minute, or in an electric mixer, about 30 seconds. Gradually add the sugar and beat until the butter turns almost white and is very fluffy, about 5 minutes by hand and 3 minutes with an electric mixer.

3. Add the whole eggs, one egg at a time,

beating for 20 seconds after each addition. The mixture should be dull and smooth after beating each egg. If the batter appears grainy or separated, the butter or eggs may have been too cold. In this case, take a thick kitchen towel and soak it with very hot tap water. Being careful not to burn your hands, wring it out and then place it around the sides and bottom of the mixing bowl as the beaters are turning. You may have to repeat this until the outside of the bowl is warm, not cold. Continue beating until the mixture appears dull and thick. Add the vanilla and lemon zest and beat 10 seconds, or until mixture is thick.

4. Add the flour in three equal parts, folding it into the mixture with a large rubber spatula after each addition, until all the flour has been incorporated and the batter is well mixed. Scrape up from the bottom of the bowl frequently.

5. Pour batter into prepared pan and bake for 1 hour and 10 minutes. Rotate pan front to back halfway through baking. The top should be split and nicely browned and a wooden cake tester or straw inserted into the center should come out clean. If not, continue baking and check every 5 minutes. When cake is done, empty it upside down onto one covered hand (use a towel or pot holder) and then place the cake right side up on a cooling rack. Cool at least 1 hour before slicing and serving.

WHAT CAN GO WRONG? Pound cake is a tricky recipe. It depends heavily on having the butter and eggs at just the right temperature. (The butter should be at 65 to 67 degrees and the eggs should be at room temperature. Immerse the eggs in hot water for 2 minutes to warm them if they are cold.) There is no chemical leavening in this recipe, which means that successfully creaming the butter is essential to a nicely risen cake. If the butter is too cold, for example, it will not beat up properly, which means it will not incorporate enough air, resulting in a dense loaf. A cold batter often appears grainy and separated, which leads to a less-than-ideal result. If this happens, follow the procedure in step 3 to heat up the mixture. Be careful not to overheat it, since butter that is too soft will not whip up properly either.

❦

FALLEN CHOCOLATE CAKE

EVERY RESTAURANT DESSERT has its life cycle. At least it seems that way to those of us who have lived through the birth and formative years of the emerging American restaurant scene. We survived the terrible twos, when cheesecake was ubiquitous; we made it through the awkward adolescence, when crème brûlée, like a body-pierced teenager, was disfigured with ingredients such as ginger and raspberries; and now we have arrived at young adulthood, featuring fallen chocolate cake, an undercooked-in-the-center mound of intense, buttery chocolate cake, which ranges from a dense, brownielike consistency to something altogether more ethereal. When cutting-edge international chef Jean-Georges Vongerichten serves several hundred of these desserts every night in his three New York restaurants, we know something is afoot.

Having tasted Jean-Georges's recipe on a number of occasions, and having also tried this dessert at other trendy eateries, such as Olives in Boston, I became intrigued with the notion of turning a restaurant showstopper into a practical recipe for home cooks. I knew that the ingredient list was short and suspected that the techniques would be relatively simple, but since restaurant recipes rarely work at home, it was clear that there would be a great deal of culinary translation ahead.

The first step, since this recipe concept encompasses a wide range of styles from half-cooked batter to a chocolate sponge cake, was to organize a tasting to decide exactly what I was looking for. I made three variations: the Warm, Soft Chocolate Cake from Vongerichten,

Fallen Chocolate Cake from Olives, created by chef-owner Todd English, and then an old favorite of mine entitled Fallen Chocolate Soufflé Cake, which was published by Richard Sax, a well-known food writer.

Sax's recipe, which is baked in a tube pan rather than in a ramekin, was quite delicious and soufflélike in texture. However, it lacked the intense whack of chocolate and the rich, buttery texture of the other two desserts. The recipe from Olives was the heaviest of the lot, very good but quite similar to an undercooked brownie. Vongerichten's cake was the tasting panel's favorite, with the most intense chocolate flavor, a relatively light texture, and a very runny center. I then wondered if I might be able to capture both the ethereal lightness of Sax's cake and the rich taste and buttery mouth feel of Vongerichten's dessert.

First I had to decide on the basic preparation method. There were two choices: I could beat the egg yolks and whites separately and then fold them together, or I could beat whole eggs and sugar to create a thick foam. The latter method proved superior, as it delivered the rich, moist texture I was looking for and at the same time made the recipe simpler. My method thus consisted of melting chocolate; beating whole eggs, sugar, and flavorings into a foam; and then folding the two together, perhaps with a little flour or ground nuts for extra body.

My next step was to determine what amount of each ingredient made the best cake. After considerable testing, I decided that ½ cup melted butter made the dessert considerably moister. Some recipes use no flour or very little (Jean-Georges Vongerichten, for instance, uses only 4 teaspoons), but I finally settled on 2 tablespoons. The amount of chocolate was key and highly variable, running from a mere 4 ounces to a high of 12 ounces in Todd English's recipe. Eight ounces provided a good jolt of chocolate without being overbearing.

The eggs, however, were perhaps the most crucial element. I tested 6 whole eggs (light and airy sponge cake texture), four whole eggs plus 4 yolks (moist and dark), and then the winner, 4 whole eggs plus 1 yolk (rich but light, moist, intense, and dark).

When baking these desserts in ramekins at 450 degrees, as called for in the Vongerichten recipe, I found that the tops were slightly burned and the center was a bit too runny. At 350 degrees, the dessert took on a more cakelike quality and was also drier. Four hundred degrees was best, yielding a light, cakelike perimeter around a moist well of intense chocolate. (When using a cake pan rather than ramekins, though, we found it best to set the oven at 375 degrees.)

At this point I had the recipe pretty well in order. To finish the translation from restaurant to home kitchen, however, I still had some work to do. The biggest obstacle was the amount of last-minute cooking. One doesn't want to run out to the kitchen during dinner, whip up an egg foam, and throw it into the oven. Having had some experience with preparing chocolate soufflés ahead of time, I tested pouring the batter into the ramekins, refrigerating them, and then baking them during dinner. This worked, the batter holding for up to 8 hours. Although the filled ramekins can be taken directly from the refrigerator to the oven with reasonably good results, the cakes rise better if allowed to sit at room temperature for 30 minutes before baking.

I also wondered if most folks have eight ramekins at home. I could find only four, the others lost to breakage and my children's craft projects. Therefore, I developed variations using both 8- and 9-inch springform pans or cake pans with removable bottoms. As an added benefit for the home cook, I discovered that in cake form this dessert can be baked up to 1 hour before serving, remaining warm right in the pan. (In a pinch, it can be held up to 2 hours in the pan, but it will become slightly more dense as it cools.)

Individual Fallen Chocolate Cakes

You can substitute 5 ounces of unsweetened baking chocolate for the semisweet if need be, but you'll also have to increase the sugar by 6 tablespoons, for a total of ⅞ cup. To melt the chocolate and butter in a microwave oven, heat chocolate alone at 50 percent power for 2 minutes; stir chocolate, add butter, and continue heating at 50 percent for another 2 minutes, stopping to stir after 1 minute. If chocolate is not yet entirely melted, heat an additional 30 seconds at 50 percent power.

SERVES 8

8 tablespoons (1 stick) unsalted butter
8 ounces semisweet chocolate, coarsely chopped
4 large eggs
1 large egg yolk
1 teaspoon vanilla extract
¼ teaspoon salt
½ cup granulated sugar
2 tablespoons all-purpose flour
   Confectioners' sugar or unsweetened cocoa powder for decoration (optional)
   Whipped cream for serving (optional)

1. Adjust oven rack to center position and heat oven to 400 degrees. Generously butter and flour (you can substitute cocoa powder) eight 6-ounce ramekins or custard/baking cups; tap out excess flour and position ramekins on shallow roasting pan, jelly roll pan, or baking sheet. Meanwhile, melt the butter and chocolate in a medium heatproof bowl set over a pan of almost simmering water, stirring once or twice, until smooth; remove from heat. (Or melt chocolate and butter in microwave oven. See instructions above.)

2. Beat whole eggs, yolk, vanilla, salt, and sugar at highest speed in bowl of a standing mixer fitted with whisk attachment until vol-

ume nearly triples, color is very light, and mixture drops from beaters in a smooth, thick stream, about 5 minutes. (Alternatively, beat for 10 minutes using a hand-held electric mixer and large mixing bowl.) Scrape egg mixture over melted chocolate and butter; sprinkle flour over egg mixture. Gently fold egg and flour into chocolate until mixture is uniformly colored. Ladle or pour batter into prepared ramekins. (At this pont they can be covered lightly with plastic wrap and refrigerated up to 8 hours. Allow to sit at room temperature for 30 minutes before baking.)

3. Bake until cakes have puffed about ½ inch above rims of ramekins, have a thin crust on top, and jiggle slightly at center when ramekins are shaken very gently, 12 to 13 minutes. Run a paring knife around inside edges of ramekins to loosen cakes and invert them onto serving plates; cool for 1 minute and lift off ramekins. Sieve a light sprinkling of confectioners' sugar or cocoa powder over cakes to decorate, if desired, and serve immediately with optional whipped cream.

WHAT CAN GO WRONG? This is not a hard recipe to put together, but baking time is key. Just a minute one way or the other is important, since the baking time is so short. Do not rely on my baking time, since your oven may be quite different. It is important to remove the cakes when the center jiggles slightly, the cakes are puffed, and they have a thin crust on top. Underbaking is better than overbaking.

SINGLE CAKE VARIATION
One large fallen chocolate cake can be prepared in either a springform pan or a cake pan with a

WHY DOES THIS CAKE TASTE SO GOOD?

One of the more interesting ideas I heard for the fantastic taste of this undercooked cake was proposed to me by Jean-Georges Vongerichten, who stated that the less one cooks chocolate, the better it tastes. I decided to check this out with Tom Lehmann, director of bakery assistance at the American Institute of Baking, who agreed with Vongerichten. Chocolate, Lehmann explained, is a very delicate substance, full of highly sensitive volatiles. During baking, some of these volatiles, which give chocolate much of its flavor, are carried away by the steam produced by the liquids in the baked product. Anyone who has been in a kitchen while a chocolate cake was baking can attest to the strong smell of chocolate produced. That aroma may be mouthwatering, but it means that some volatiles are no longer in the cake, where you want them to be. This situation is made even more acute by the fact that unwanted volatiles have already been driven off during the roasting and subsequent processing that take place in turning cocoa beans into chocolate. Additional exposure to heat, therefore, has no benefits; it simply makes the chocolate more bitter and less complex.

Another aspect of the wonderful flavor of this undercooked dessert is texture. It is my experience with many foods, including apple pie and tomato sauces, that flavor is enhanced by the presence of liquids. A juicy apple pie tastes better than a dry one, for example. In the same way, a very moist, liquid-in-the-center chocolate cake tastes better than a fully cooked one. My conjecture, which is supported by some of the food scientists I spoke with, is that liquids transport flavor to the tongue better than solids.

So are there any lessons to be learned for home cooks who bake with chocolate? First, underbaking is always better than overbaking. Dry chocolate cakes, cookies, and brownies will have much less flavor and tend to be bitter. Second, use as much fat as possible. Fat increases the retention of volatile compounds. That's why "low-fat" chocolate cookies usually don't taste much like chocolate (or they are only slightly lower in fat). Finally, as we discovered in a chocolate tasting performed in our test kitchen some months ago, expensive chocolates with subtle flavor characteristics tend to lose their flavor edge when baked, so less expensive chocolate is fine for brownies, cakes, and cookies.

removable bottom. Do not use a regular cake pan, as the cake will be impossible to remove once baked. Though the cake is best when served warm, within about 30 minutes of being unmolded, it can also be held in the pan for up to 2 hours before serving.

Follow recipe for Individual Fallen Chocolate Cakes, substituting an 8- or 9-inch springform or removable-bottom cake pan for ramekins. Decrease baking temperature to 375 degrees and bake until cake looks puffed, a thin top crust has formed, and center jiggles slightly when pan is shaken gently, 22 to 25 minutes for 9-inch pan or 27 to 30 minutes for 8-inch pan. Cool cake for 15 minutes (or up to 2 hours), run a paring knife around inside edge of pan, and remove pan sides. Sieve a light sprinkling of confectioners' sugar or unsweetened cocoa powder over cake to decorate, if desired, just before serving, and serve warm with optional whipped cream.

ORANGE CHOCOLATE VARIATION

Follow recipe for Individual Fallen Chocolate Cakes or Single Cake Variation, adding 1 tablespoon finely grated orange zest and 2 tablespoons orange liqueur (such as Grand Marnier or triple sec) to beaten egg and melted chocolate mixture before folding in the flour.

ALMOST FALLEN CHOCOLATE CAKE

HAVING SPENT COUNTLESS HOURS developing a recipe for fallen chocolate cake, I became intrigued with the notion of producing a similar recipe, one that was a bit sturdier and less gooey in the middle, something more like a cake than a pudding cake. I also wanted a recipe that could be served at room temperature, making it a bit easier to work into a busy schedule when preparing dinner for guests.

I started with the ingredient list from the In-

dividual Fallen Chocolate Cakes, which read: 8 tablespoons butter, 8 ounces semisweet chocolate, 4 whole eggs, 1 yolk, 1 teaspoon vanilla, ¼ teaspoon salt, ½ cup sugar, and 2 tablespoons flour. I began with the butter, thinking that perhaps it was a bit excessive at a full 8 tablespoons. However, 4 tablespoons yielded a spongier, drier cake, which I did not prefer, so the butter was judged to be about right. I also fiddled with the chocolate level, both up and down, and again came to the conclusion that the original quantity of 8 ounces was just fine.

The big series of tests turned out to focus on the eggs. Six whole eggs plus 2 whites produced a light and airy cake with a chiffon-cake texture. Four whole eggs plus 4 yolks made the cake very moist and dark, but I was looking for something a bit lighter in texture. Next, I tried 5 whole eggs plus 2 yolks, which was good, but a final test of 6 whole eggs, beaten until very light and thick, produced the best cake, both light and moist at the same time. Sugar tests left me with the same ½ cup I used in the original recipe.

The flour was the next test. I was starting with a meager 2 tablespoons flour, then tried 3 tablespoons, and finally ended up with ¼ cup to turn this dessert into a cake from a pudding cake. This was a simple change, but one that immediately altered the texture of the recipe. The vanilla was left at the same level, but I decided to increase the salt to give the cake a bit more flavor.

The last set of tests involved oven temperature. The recipe for fallen chocolate cake was baked at 400 degrees when using ramekins, but I had determined that the single cake version, which was baked in a springform pan, was best at 375 degrees. Since I wanted to bake this new recipe in a springform pan as well, I tested various oven temperatures and confirmed that the lower 375 degrees was best. At this temperature, the inside of the cake has time to cook fully. I liked the cake best when it cooled in the pan for only 10 to 15 minutes before slicing and serving.

···

Almost Fallen Chocolate Cake

This variation on the fallen chocolate cake earlier in this chapter is a bit more sturdy and cakelike than the original recipe. It is best when served about 15 minutes after coming from the oven, but it can be cooled completely before serving as well. Note that the cake will fall a bit in the middle during cooling, which is typical of this sort of dessert. This recipe can also be baked in a jelly roll pan, filled, and then rolled and sliced. See variation below.

SERVES 8

8 tablespoons (1 stick) unsalted butter
8 ounces semisweet chocolate, chopped
6 large eggs, at room temperature
½ cup granulated sugar
¼ cup all-purpose flour
1 teaspoon salt
1 teaspoon vanilla extract
Confectioners' sugar for dusting (optional)
Whipped cream or vanilla ice cream for
    serving (optional)

1. Adjust a rack to the center position and heat the oven to 375 degrees. Butter and flour (or dust with cocoa) an 8- or 9-inch springform pan.

2. Heat the butter and chocolate together until the chocolate is just about melted. Set aside to cool almost to room temperature. (This can be done in a microwave oven at 50 percent power for 3 to 4 minutes. Stir once every minute.) Beat the eggs and sugar in a large bowl until very light and thick — 5 minutes with a paddle attachment of a standing mixer, about 12 minutes with a hand mixer or whisk. Stir the chocolate and butter to a smooth and homogenous mixture. (If using a standing mixer, you can do this while the eggs are beating.) When the egg mixture is ready, fold about ½ cup of it into the melted chocolate. Fold the flour into the egg-sugar mixture. Add the chocolate mixture, salt, and the vanilla and fold until fully incorporated. Pour the batter into the prepared pan.

3. Bake 26 to 27 minutes for the 8-inch pan, 23 to 25 minutes for the 9-inch pan. The cake will look puffy in the center. Let cool for 10 minutes. Run a thin knife around the edge of the pan and remove pan sides.

4. Dust with confectioners' sugar and serve immediately with whipped cream or vanilla ice cream. This cake can be held and served when completely cooled, but the center will sink down a bit and the texture will not be as light.

WHAT CAN GO WRONG? You can make two mistakes here. One, if the eggs are too cold they will not whip up properly. Two, if you do not have an electric mixer or if you are not patient, you may not fully beat the eggs and sugar into a thick, voluminous foam. The foam should turn very pale yellow and be thick and quite large in volume. Be patient — this is what will provide the lift to the cake.

JELLY ROLL VARIATION

Butter a jelly roll pan or half sheet pan and line the bottom with parchment. (A jelly roll pan looks like a cookie sheet with short sides.) Butter the parchment and flour the interior of the pan. Pour the batter from the master recipe into the prepared pan and spread into a smooth layer using a rubber spatula. Bake for 10 to 12 minutes, or until the cake is set and looks dry on the surface. Let cool for 5 minutes. Run a thin knife around the edge of the pan. With the long edge of the pan facing you, grab the parchment (you may need the knife or a fork to get going on this step) and roll the cake into a log shape, leaving the parchment and cake together. Cover the roll with a damp towel and let cool completely on the pan.

After the cake is completely cooled, unroll the cake as best you can. It will not go back to a flat shape at this point. Beat 1½ cups heavy cream with ¼ cup granulated sugar and 1 tablespoon dark rum until very thick. Spread this filling in an even thin layer over the exposed surface of the cake. Roll the cake in the same manner as above, but peel the parchment away from the cake as you roll. The parchment will actually help you roll the cake, so peel it sparingly as you work. Cover the cake and refrigerate for at least 2 hours to set. Slice on an angle and serve.

CHOCOLATE SOUFFLÉ CAKE

I FIRST CAME ACROSS the notion of a soufflé cake in a book by Richard Sax, *Cooking Great Meals Every Day,* which became a staple in my dinner parties of the 1970s. In essence, it was a soufflé but with a bit of ground toasted nuts in it to give it body. It was baked in a tube pan and allowed to fall a bit after coming from the oven and was then served warm. It was not as rich or liquid in the center as the recipe for Individual Fallen Chocolate Cakes, also in this chapter. It was a cross between a soufflé and a genoise — light, subtle, and ethereal.

I went back to that recipe, not having made it for many years, and still found it quite good. But I thought it lacked depth of chocolate flavor and also needed a bit more moisture. I started my investigation by testing a variety of other recipes, some similar to fallen chocolate cake and others more like sponge cake. I started with a recipe comprised of melted semisweet chocolate, walnuts, egg yolks, sugar, and egg whites. It was good but hardly the best of its class. It was so light in both texture and flavor that it would easily qualify for the cover of *Cooking Light* magazine. I then tested adding 4 tablespoons of melted butter and was pleased with the result — the cake had a moist consistency without being greasy. The next question to be resolved was the nuts. I thought that the cake was lacking in nut flavor, using only ¼ cup, so I doubled the quantity to ½ cup toasted, ground pecans. This worked fine, the substitution of

pecans for walnuts giving the cake a somewhat sweeter, more rounded flavor as well. Now I wondered if a bit of flour might help with the texture and also produce a cake that would hold up in a regular cake pan. (The original Sax recipe was made in a tube pan, which was necessary to hold it up during baking.) This addition was also successful; the cake turned out light but a bit less springy, and it baked up nicely in a regular 8-inch cake pan. (A springform pan is a good choice here, since you do not have to invert the cake to remove it from the pan. This is helpful, because the cake will be served as is, without any frosting to hide an irregular top crust.) I then made a cake with 1 tablespoon less flour, and this was slightly wetter and not quite as good as the ¼-cup version. I also tried the cake with flour only, no nuts, and found the flavor bland.

For the eggs there were many choices. The recipe calls for beating eggs (whole or yolks) until light, then adding sugar and beating the mixture until it falls in ribbons from the beater. Just before baking, this base, to which other ingredients have subsequently been added, is folded into beaten egg whites. After testing whole eggs, yolks only, and then a combination, I found that a mix of 4 yolks and 1 whole egg was best, providing structure to the cake but also a light but moist texture. The whites were relatively easy to test: the more I used, the lighter the cake and the more it fell after baking. I tested 4, 6, and then 8 whites and settled on 6. The 4-white version wasn't enough of a "soufflé" cake, and the 8-egg white cake fell too much, looking to me like the old barn on a neighbor's farm that had fallen in on itself recently. The 6-white cake was just right, falling about an inch during cooling but maintaining enough structure so that it could be sliced into recognizable pieces.

The last important series of tests involved the proportions of sugar to eggs to flour to chocolate. I bumped the chocolate up to 5 ounces from the original 3 but also cut the sugar back to make this more of an adult dessert. I once more fiddled with the total number of eggs and left them as is, finding either a dense cake or one that was too eggy.

Finally, I added ½ teaspoon salt to balance the sugar and a teaspoon of vanilla. Baking time is a matter of personal preference: 25 to 26 minutes produced a very wet center and 30 minutes or so gave it a moist, fully cooked center. I split the difference at 28 minutes, although your baking time may vary, since all ovens are not created equal.

...

Chocolate Soufflé Cake

This is a much lighter cake than the one offered in Individual Fallen Chocolate Cakes (page 160) and is best served with some whipped cream. It can be baked in a regular cake pan, but I call for a springform pan since it is easier to remove the cake after baking. The cake will fall a bit, about an inch, as it cools, hence the word "soufflé" in the title.

SERVES 8

5	ounces semisweet or bittersweet chocolate
4	tablespoons unsalted butter
½	cup pecan halves
½	cup granulated sugar
2	large eggs, at room temperature
4	large egg yolks, at room temperature
1	teaspoon vanilla extract
¼	cup all-purpose flour
½	teaspoon salt
6	large egg whites, at room temperature

Confectioners' sugar for dusting

Whipped cream or vanilla ice cream for serving (optional)

1. Adjust a rack to lower third of oven and heat oven to 350 degrees. Butter and flour an 8-inch springform pan.

2. Melt the chocolate and butter over hot water or in a microwave (2 minutes at 50 per-cent power, stir, 1 minute, stir, and then 1 additional minute if necessary). Let cool for 10 minutes off heat. Spread pecan halves on a baking sheet and toast in oven for 5 to 7 minutes, until browned and fragrant. Let nuts cool for 10 minutes, then grind in a food processor with 1 tablespoon of the sugar.

3. Beat whole eggs and yolks until light, about 2 minutes with an electric mixer. Gradually beat in 6 tablespoons of the sugar to the ribbon stage, about 3 more minutes. Add the vanilla and mix to combine. Fold in the cooled chocolate mixture. Fold in the nuts, flour, and salt. Beat the egg whites until foamy. Add the remaining 1 tablespoon sugar and beat until they hold a 2-inch peak. Fold one-quarter of the whites into the batter to lighten, then fold in the remaining whites. Pour into prepared pan and bake for about 28 minutes. The cake will be puffy but the center will jiggle a bit.

4. Let cool for 1 hour. Run a thin knife around edge of cake and remove pan sides. Dust cake with confectioners' sugar. This cake is best served warm with whipped cream or vanilla ice cream.

WHAT CAN GO WRONG? You can make two mistakes with this recipe. First, you can beat up on the egg whites as you fold them into the batter. This will cost you height as the cake bakes, and the texture will be a bit dense. Second, the baking time is crucial, but your oven is not the same as mine, so the listed baking time is only an approximation. The cake should be puffy and the center should jiggle a bit when the cake is gently shaken. Overbaking chocolate cakes or cookies results in less chocolate flavor, so if you make a mistake, err on the side of undercooking.

CARROT CAKE

CLASSIC CARROT CAKE has many problems, the greatest of them being the signature heavy, wet texture. This is caused primarily by the carrots themselves, which contain a great deal of water. An article in the February 1998 issue of *Cook's Illustrated* by Marie Piraino and Jamie Morris solved a good deal of this problem by suggesting that grated carrots be tossed with sugar and then drained in a colander. The result was a much lighter cake, although I thought it was a bit too refined. I wanted a cake that was sturdier and richer, something closer to the original. To find a happy middle ground, I tested a variety of ingredients, including applesauce (the texture was very wet), honey (the honey flavor was too strong, and unwelcome in this cake), whole wheat flour (the soft texture of the cake was lost and the flavor was too earthy), cooked carrots (the texture suffered and the carrot flavor was weaker), and coconut (dry, flaked, unsweetened coconut did add a bit of texture and improved the flavor, but don't use the sweet supermarket variety). Taking a cue from variations on this recipe published in *Cook's*, I added a small amount of canned crushed pineapple, and I also found that toasted pecans worked well. To further boost flavor, I decided to use mostly dark brown sugar, rather than the granulated and light brown varieties, to produce a darker cake with a richer flavor. I also thought that the amount of grated carrots in the *Cook's* recipe was a bit excessive, so I reduced the quantity to 5 cups from 7. The other interesting feature of this recipe, one suggested by Piraino and Morris, is that the butter for the cake be melted and browned. This adds a lot of extra flavor, and therefore I use the same method below.

▪ ▪ ▪

Carrot Cake

*M*ost carrot cake recipes call for a combination of butter, cream cheese, confectioners' sugar, and sour cream for the frosting, often using a stick or more of butter. I find these frostings too rich, so I use only 3 tablespoons of softened butter in my cream cheese frosting.

SERVES 12

For the Cake

  5 cups coarsely grated carrots (about 6 large carrots)
  1 cup granulated sugar
2⅔ cups cake flour
  4 teaspoons baking powder
  ½ teaspoon baking soda
  2 teaspoons cinnamon
  1 teaspoon salt
  ½ pound (2 sticks) unsalted butter
1½ cups packed dark brown sugar
  5 large eggs
1½ teaspoons vanilla extract
  1 can (8 ounces) crushed pineapple packed in its own juice, drained well (about ¾ cup)
  ¾ cup toasted, chopped pecans
  ⅔ cup unsweetened, dried, flaked coconut (optional — do not use the sweet supermarket variety)

For the Cream Cheese Frosting

 16 ounces cream cheese, softened
  3 tablespoons unsalted butter, softened
  2 cups confectioners' sugar
  3 tablespoons sour cream

    Extra pecans and coconut for garnish (optional)

1. *For the cake:* Heat oven to 350 degrees and adjust rack to the center position. Grease two 9 x 2-inch round cake pans. Line the bottoms with parchment paper (this cake has a tendency to stick). Place the grated carrots in a large bowl and toss with granulated sugar. Transfer carrots to a colander and place over the bowl to drain. Whisk together cake flour, baking powder, baking soda, cinnamon, and salt in a medium bowl.

2. Melt butter in a large saucepan or skillet over medium-low heat, stirring frequently. Cook until the butter turns golden brown, about 10 minutes, and has a nutty aroma.

There should be small brown flecks on the bottom of the pan. Do not allow these flecks to turn very dark; otherwise the cake will have a bitter flavor. Pour melted butter into a large bowl and let cool for 2 minutes. Whisk in the brown sugar. Whisk in the eggs, one at a time. Add the vanilla and whisk for 10 seconds. Add the flour mixture and whisk until it is three-quarters incorporated. Using a large rubber spatula, gently fold in the carrots, drained pineapple, pecans, and optional coconut until the batter is well mixed.

3. Divide the batter evenly between the prepared pans. Smooth top surfaces with the rubber spatula. Bake until cake feels firm in the center when pressed lightly, 40 to 50 minutes. Rotate pans front to back after 20 minutes and check cakes after 30 minutes. Remove from oven and run a knife around the perimeter of each pan. Invert cakes onto a large plate and then back onto a cooling rack. Allow to cool completely before frosting. Remove cream cheese and butter from refrigerator 1 hour before preparing frosting.

4. *For the frosting:* Beat the softened cream cheese and butter with an electric mixer on low speed until homogenous, 3 to 4 minutes. Add the confectioners' sugar and sour cream and beat until well blended, up to 2 minutes longer. To frost the cake, place one layer on a cake plate, anchoring it with a small dab of frosting, and frost the top. Add the second layer, frost the top and then the sides. Garnish with extra pecans or coconut if desired.

WHAT CAN GO WRONG? The only tricky part of this recipe is browning the butter. If you cook it too much, it will have a burned, bitter flavor.

GINGERBREAD

MOST GINGERBREAD RECIPES call for ground ginger, which makes for a very dull cake indeed,

sweet, heavy, and flat-tasting. However, a few years ago I was lucky enough to order the gingerbread at the Ginger Island restaurant in Berkeley, California. The cake was made using fresh ginger. What a difference. This transformed this somewhat childish treat into an adult dessert, complex and with plenty of bite. So I started my testing by eliminating the ground ginger and substituting a full ¼ cup fresh minced ginger. This was very good but too sharp and not complex enough in taste. I cut the fresh ginger back to 3 tablespoons and added 2 tablespoons of chopped crystallized ginger, which added both depth and balance.

Most old-fashioned gingerbread recipes call for the addition of ½ cup or so of boiling water. This is a common feature of many simple one-layer cakes that depend on baking soda for lift. It is thought that the heat helps to activate the baking soda. (A similar recipe, applesauce cake, usually calls for hot applesauce and a small quantity of hot water into which the baking soda is dissolved.) However, after much testing, I found that the temperature of the milk or water made no difference. I also preferred milk (a common ingredient used instead of water), which softened the crumb, making a more tender cake.

Pan size and cooking time are very important for this recipe. You can use either a 9 x 9 or an 11 x 7 pan, the latter being preferable but harder to find. Other sizes may cause the cake to fall a bit in the center after baking. After making this cake a dozen times, I have also found it extremely important to cook the center of the cake thoroughly; if it is even slightly undercooked it will have a tendency to sink as it cools. Do not trust cake testers — they are unreliable. You need to press on the center of the cake with your finger or the flat side of a fork. It should spring back immediately.

I also tested using melted butter instead of creamed butter and found that the latter was preferable for a slightly lighter texture. It is very important that the butter be softened but still quite firm, about 65 to 67 degrees when measured with an instant-read thermometer. Also, the butter-sugar mixture should be light-colored and fluffy after beating. If it isn't, touch the side of the bowl. (It is best to use a metal bowl.) If it is very cold, then warm the outside of the bowl using a heavy kitchen towel soaked in hot water and wrung out. (The mixer should be running.) You may have to repeat this process three or four times to warm up the butter mixture sufficiently. Be careful here. You don't want to melt the butter.

I also cut back on the amount of spices. Many old-fashioned recipes go overboard, using large quantities of cinnamon, cloves, and the like. I use just ½ teaspoon each.

▪ ▪ ▪

Double-Ginger Gingerbread

This recipe uses fresh grated and chopped crystallized ginger rather than the usual ground dried ginger. I find the taste brighter and superior to that of a cake made with ground ginger, which is dull by comparison. Serve it with a bit of slightly sweetened whipped cream.

SERVES 8 TO 10

2½	cups all-purpose flour
½	teaspoon cinnamon
½	teaspoon ground cloves
½	teaspoon nutmeg
½	teaspoon allspice
½	teaspoon baking soda
½	teaspoon salt
½	pound (2 sticks) unsalted butter, softened but still firm
½	cup packed dark brown sugar
½	cup granulated sugar
2	large eggs, at room temperature
1	cup molasses
3	tablespoons peeled, minced fresh gingerroot
2	tablespoons minced crystallized ginger
½	cup milk

Sweetened whipped cream for serving (optional)

1. Set oven rack in center position and heat oven to 325 degrees. Grease an 11 x 7-inch or 9-inch square baking pan. Line the bottom with parchment or waxed paper, grease the paper, and flour the pan.

2. Sift the first 7 ingredients (flour through salt) onto a piece of waxed paper; set aside. Place the butter in a large bowl and beat for 1 minute, or until light-colored. Add the sugars gradually while beating with an electric mixer. Beat for 2 to 3 minutes or until the mixture is light and fluffy, scraping down the sides of the bowl two or three times. Add the eggs one at a time, beating for 20 seconds after each addition. Beat in the molasses. Add the dry ingredients and the fresh and crystallized ginger and beat on the lowest speed until combined. Add the milk and mix with a rubber spatula to combine.

3. Pour batter into the prepared pan and transfer it to the center of the hot oven. Bake for 55 to 60 minutes, rotating pan 180 degrees after 30 minutes. Cake is done when the top springs back quickly when lightly pressed with the flat side of a fork. Cool in the pan on a rack for 20 minutes. Cut into squares and serve plain or with a dollop of sweetened whipped cream.

WHAT CAN GO WRONG? I had a lot of trouble with this recipe. It kept falling in the middle during baking. I found that it was absolutely crucial to use the right size pan. It is also very important to beat the butter, sugar, and eggs properly. If you do not beat them enough, the cake will not have the right texture when baked.

HONEY CAKE

HONEY CAKES ARE COMMON in many cultures, including Eastern Europe. I have found a recipe for honey gingerbread in a cookbook from the turn of the last century and daintier honey tea cakes in a book from the 1940s. I decided to go down the road of a heartier cake, one that would be more welcome in a farmhouse than at high tea.

I started my testing with the flour and found that I preferred cake flour over all-purpose, the former producing a lighter, finer-textured cake. A baking powder–baking soda combination was necessary to balance the chemical reaction as the cake baked, since this recipe uses brown sugar, which is acidic. (Baking powder, you may recall, includes baking soda plus an acidic ingredient that reacts with the soda to produce carbon dioxide bubbles, which in turn produce lift. When a recipe contains an excess amount of acid, baking soda is often required in order to neutralize it.) I also increased the amount of butter in the recipe as well as the eggs, to give this a richer mouth feel. Some recipes for honey cake use quite a lot of spices, which I felt competed unfavorably with the subtle flavor of the honey itself. However, I did like the addition of strong coffee as an ingredient, and a bit of scotch didn't hurt either.

...

Honey Cake

To successfully cream the butter and the sugar, make sure that the butter is at 65 to 67 degrees. It should be firm but malleable, neither at room temperature nor cold, just out of the refrigerator.

SERVES 8 TO 10

2½ cups cake flour
½   teaspoon salt
1   teaspoon baking powder
½   teaspoon baking soda
½   pound (2 sticks) unsalted butter, softened but still firm
¼   cup packed brown sugar
¼   cup granulated sugar
3   large eggs, at room temperature
¾   cup honey
¼   cup strong brewed coffee or espresso
2   teaspoons finely chopped lemon zest
1   tablespoon scotch or bourbon (optional)
⅔   cup raisins (optional)
Confectioners' sugar for dusting (optional)

1. Adjust oven rack to the middle position and heat oven to 350 degrees. Grease and flour a 9 x 9 square baking pan or a deep 9-inch round cake or springform pan.

2. Sift together the flour, salt, baking powder, and baking soda onto a piece of waxed paper; set aside. In a large mixing bowl, beat the butter with an electric mixer for 1 minute, or until very light-colored. Add the sugars and beat for 3 minutes on high speed until the mixture is light and fluffy. Scrape down sides of bowl two or three times as you work. Add eggs one at a time, beating for 20 seconds after each addition. Continue beating until mixture is smooth. Add the honey, coffee, lemon zest, and scotch and beat to combine.

3. Add the flour mixture and beat on lowest speed to mix or combine with a large rubber spatula. Do not overmix. Stir in the optional raisins.

4. Pour batter into the prepared pan and bake for 45 to 55 minutes, or until the center of the cake springs back when pressed and a cake tester or straw inserted into the center comes out clean. Cool in the pan on a rack for at least 30 minutes. Cut into squares and serve plain or with a dusting of confectioners' sugar.

WHAT CAN GO WRONG? As with all cakes that require creaming the butter, make sure that butter is the correct temperature before starting, 65 to 67 degrees. Make sure that you use the correct pan size as well.

FRUITCAKE YOU WANT TO EAT

FRUITCAKES ARE PRIMARILY about storage. Many recipes suggest that when made with liquor-soaked fruit and wrapped in cheesecloth soaked in more booze, fruitcakes can be stored in a cool place for years. This is not a comforting thought for a modern cook but would clearly appeal to folks who lived before the advent of refrigeration.

The question then is, how does one make a fruitcake that is worth eating? My first step was to eliminate any sort of candied fruit, substituting instead dried fruits. I also discarded the notion of using any sugary coating such as fondant. The English are fond of this approach, but I find it beyond the pale of either good taste or sensible cooking.

This left me with a simple cake batter into which is folded a whole lot of liquor-soaked dried fruit. There is in fact a long tradition of this rather simple approach to fruitcakes. James Beard in *American Cookery* writes about fruitcakes that are no more than pound cakes with fruit added. In my 1917 edition of *A New Book of Cookery,* by Fannie Merritt Farmer, however, the recipe for fruitcake uses no butter and eggs, simply a mixture of raisins, whole wheat flour, white flour, sugar, molasses, coffee, baking powder, and spices. This would be a much heavier approach. I have also come across recipes calling for the addition of ale (this recipe tasted very sour to me) and many recipes based on yeast breads, which are more difficult to make and taste more like stollen or panettone than fruitcake.

So I chose to work with a simple spiced butter cake as the base for this recipe, adding nuts and real dried fruits to make it a fruitcake. This approach was easy, fresh, and produced a cake that could be eaten immediately, rather than one that needed a month of storage. I then tried three recipes for comparison: the Four Seasons'

Christmas Fruitcake from *Classic Home Desserts,* Rich Fruitcake from *La Varenne Pratique* (Anne Willan), and Dark Fruitcake from *Joy of Cooking.* The first lesson was that soaking the fruit in liquor was a good alternative to soaking the entire cake in cheesecloth-drenched liquor. The second observation was that eggs were indeed important. Recipe C (see chart), which used no eggs, was much too dry. Candied fruits were definitely out, since real dried fruit was tastier. The ratio of fruit to cake was also important — too little fruit, and the cake was dry and dull; too much, and the flavor was overwhelming and the cake too dense. So my working recipe now included 3 cups of dried fruit, 1½ cups flour, spices and salt, 16 tablespoons butter, ½ cup sugar, 3 eggs, ½ cup molasses, and a cup of toasted, chopped pecans.

So far so good, but the cake was not quite rich enough. I decided to start reworking the recipe with the fruit. I doubled the amount of fruit to roughly 6 cups, using a combination of dates, apricots, prunes, and raisins. Instead of soaking the fruit for only 1 hour in liquor, I went for an overnight soak, which did complicate the recipe but also improved the flavor substantially. Next I experimented with the cake. To deepen the flavor, I decided to add coffee, thinking that it would offer depth of flavor without sweetness. So at the same time, I increased the molasses to ¾ cup (from ½ cup) and then added ½ cup strong coffee. This was a big improvement. I then tried using brown sugar for granulated, and this was not successful. Since I had so much molasses in the recipe to start with, the regular white sugar was a better choice; the brown sugar simply muddied the flavor. With all of this extra fruit and with the addition of coffee, the cake was a bit on the wet side, so I added ½ cup flour and 1 more egg. The cake was rich and moist without being wet. Voilà! Now I had a fruitcake worth eating.

CASE 33: HOLD THAT FRUITCAKE!

What is fruitcake really made of, and why doesn't it taste better?

Ingredient	Recipe A	Recipe B	Recipe C
Fruit	1 pound dried	3⅓ cups raisins, 3⅓ cups currants, 1 cup candied orange peel, 1 cup candied citrus peel	2½ cups mixed candied fruit, 1½ cups dates, 1½ cups currants, 1½ cups golden raisins
Nuts	2 cups chopped walnuts	None	2 cups chopped walnuts
Flour	2⅔ cups	3 cups	3 cups
Spices	2½ teaspoons cinnamon, 1½ teaspoons allspice, 1½ teaspoons nutmeg, ¾ teaspoon ground coriander	½ teaspoon nutmeg, ½ teaspoon allspice	1 teaspoon cinnamon, 1 teaspoon nutmeg, ½ teaspoon mace, ½ teaspoon ground cloves
Baking powder/ baking soda	2½ teaspoons baking powder	None	1 teaspoon baking powder, ½ teaspoon baking soda
Salt	¼ teaspoon	½ teaspoon	¼ teaspoon
Butter	22 tablespoons	24 tablespoons	16 tablespoons
Sugar/molasses	1¾ cups granulated sugar, 2 tablespoons confectioners'	1¾ cups brown sugar	2 cups brown sugar, ½ cup molasses
Eggs	9	6	None
Other	Zest of 1 lemon, zest of 2 oranges, rum as needed to soak the fruit overnight	3 tablespoons brandy	¾ cup brandy, zest and juice of 1 orange and 1 lemon

···

Fruitcake Worth Eating

This recipe produces two loaves that can be eaten right away and do not have to sit. The fruit, not the cake itself, is soaked overnight in liquor, and the addition of coffee deepens the flavor. You will find that the rum-soaked fruit packs a pretty good wallop, so this is not the sort of fruitcake you should be serving to the kids. These loaves will keep for up to a month in a cool, dark place. Wrap first in cheesecloth and then in plastic wrap.

MAKES 2 LARGE LOAVES

¾ cup dark raisins
¾ cup golden raisins
1 cup dried apricots, roughly chopped
1 cup pitted prunes, roughly chopped
2 cups pitted dates, roughly chopped
1 cup rum or bourbon
2 cups all-purpose flour
½ teaspoon nutmeg
½ teaspoon allspice
½ teaspoon salt
½ pound (2 sticks) unsalted butter, softened but still firm
½ cup granulated sugar
4 large eggs
¾ cup molasses
½ cup strong coffee
1 teaspoon vanilla extract
1 cup toasted, chopped pecans

1. Soak the raisins, apricots, prunes, and dates in rum for about 8 hours or overnight.

2. Adjust a rack to the middle position and heat oven to 300 degrees. Grease and flour two 9 x 5-inch loaf pans. Alternatively, line bottoms of two loaf pans with parchment paper. Sift together the flour, spices, and salt onto a piece of waxed paper.

3. In a large bowl, beat the butter until light, about 2 minutes with an electric mixer. Add the sugar and beat an additional 2 minutes. Add the eggs, one at a time, and beat for 20 seconds after each addition. Add the molasses, coffee, and vanilla and beat about 30 seconds more, or until thoroughly combined. Add the dry ingredients and beat by hand or on the lowest speed of the mixer until combined. Add the fruit and rum and the nuts and fold with a rubber spatula until combined. Pour the batter into prepared pans and smooth tops with the spatula.

4. Bake for 65 to 75 minutes, or until the top feels firm to the touch.

CUPCAKES

MANY OF THE CAKE RECIPES in this chapter can be used to make cupcakes. After some experimenting, I discovered that the cakes that work best as cupcakes are All-Purpose Yellow Cake (page 129), Buttermilk Cake (page 132), All-Purpose White Cake (page 133), and Buttermilk Chocolate Cake (page 140). I find it easier to line the muffin pans with paper liners as opposed to greasing the entire pan. This also makes it easier to remove the cupcakes from the pan and to handle them while icing.

···

All-Purpose Yellow Cake, Buttermilk Cake, All-Purpose White Cake, and Buttermilk Chocolate Cake Cupcakes

MAKES 18 CUPCAKES
(BUTTERMILK CHOCOLATE CAKE MAKES 14)

Refer to the appropriate recipe earlier in the chapter (see page numbers above). Prepare cupcake pans with paper liners and lightly grease the top surface of the pans. You will need pans to accommodate 18 cupcakes. (Ignore the instructions for preparing the pans in step 1.) Prepare batter as instructed in steps 2 to 4. Fill the prepared pans until each cup is full up to the top of the paper liners. Bake the cupcakes in a 350-degree oven for about 20 minutes, rotating pan(s) front to back after 10 minutes. Cupcakes are done when they are golden brown, the tops spring back when lightly pressed in the center, and a cake tester comes out clean. Let the pan(s) cool for 5 minutes on a cooling rack. Remove the cupcakes from the pan(s) and allow to cool completely.

▪▪▪

Foolproof Sponge Cake Cupcakes

MAKES 16 CUPCAKES

Refer to the recipe for French Sponge Cake (page 151). Prepare cupcake pans with paper liners and lightly grease the top surface of the pans. You will need pans to accommodate 16 cupcakes. (Ignore the instructions for preparing the cake pans in step 1.) Prepare batter as instructed in steps 2 to 4. Fill the cupcake pans until the batter is up to the top of the paper liners. Bake in 350-degree oven until the tops are light brown and feel set and spring back when touched, about 16 minutes. Let the pan(s) sit for 5 minutes on a cooling rack and then remove the cupcakes. Let cool completely. These cupcakes are the smallest of the lot but are great for making Boston Cream Pie Cupcakes (recipe follows).

▪▪▪

Boston Cream Pie Cupcakes

MAKES 16 CUPCAKES

Refer to the recipe for Boston Cream Pie on page 153. Bake the French Sponge Cake as cupcakes (see directions above) and then prepare the pastry cream and chocolate glaze as stated in the recipe. When both the cupcakes and the pastry cream are cool, place the pastry cream in a pastry bag fitted with a plain tip about 3/16 inch in diameter (Ateco #8). Pierce the top of a cupcake with the pastry tip and squeeze some pastry cream into the cupcake. Continue until all of the cupcakes are filled. Each cupcake will hold about a generous tablespoon or so of cream. (There is really no way to measure how much pastry cream you are dispensing into each cupcake, but the cupcake should feel heavy compared with the unfilled cupcakes. Also, you can break one open to see how much filling you are using. There should be enough to get some cream in every bite but not so much as to make them messy.) The glaze should be cooled until it is spreadable instead of pourable. Using a small icing spatula or a butter knife, apply the glaze to the cupcakes and let sit until the glaze is set, about 1 hour. The cupcakes can also be refrigerated for several hours but should be allowed to sit at room temperature for about 20 minutes before serving.

▾▾
▾

TORTES

ACCORDING TO DESSERT MAVEN Maida Heatter, "Torte or torta is a European word meaning cake, and since many European cakes are made without flour, a torte is often defined as a cake without flour." Instead of flour, tortes usually call for ground nuts, but in many cases tortes do use a small amount of flour, either with or without the nuts. If all of this were not sufficiently confusing, many well-known tortes do not fit either of the above descriptions, and some are not even cakes. Three classic tortes that cropped up in my research were the many-layered Dobos torte; the jam-filled, chocolate ganache–covered Sacher torte; and Linzer torte, which is more of a jam-topped nut cookie than a cake. Beyond the classics, a broad range of desserts are inexplicably called tortes as well, none of which will be included in this chapter. Richard Sax, a well-known cookbook author, includes a yellow sheet cake baked with fresh fruit on top. James Beard lists his recipes for date nut tea cake and frozen lemon mousse as tortes. Rose Levy Ber-

CASE 34: BUILDING BLOCKS OF TORTES

Here is a summary of the six cakes and their principal ingredients.

Recipe	Nuts and Flour	Flavorings	Eggs
Mandel torte	1 cup almonds to ½ cup breadcrumbs	Lemon juice, cinnamon, almond extract	6
Pecan mocha torte	3½ cups pecans to 3 tablespoons flour	Coffee	6
Brottorte	1 cup almonds to 1¼ cups breadcrumbs	Lemon juice, cinnamon, sherry	6
Hazelnut torte	2 cups hazelnuts to 1 tablespoon flour	None	12 yolks, 8 whites
Small walnut torte	1¼ cups walnuts to 3 tablespoons cornstarch	Lemon juice	4
Austrian walnut torte	1½ cups walnuts to 2 tablespoons breadcrumbs	Coffee, rum	8

anbaum refers to her chocolate genoise layered with strawberry cream and banded with chocolate lattice as one, too, although this is understandable — a genoise is similar in construct to a torte, since it is made with very little flour. Chiffon cakes and sometimes angel food cakes are grouped with tortes in some cookbooks. Cakes with layers of meringue are also often referred to as tortes.

For purposes of this book, I decided to focus most of my efforts on developing a master recipe for a basic nut torte made with whole eggs, the sort of cake one could easily vary by using different nuts or flavorings. (I also thought that the Linzer torte was worth including, since it is both excellent and famous.) There are two basic methods for making classic tortes, one using whole, separated eggs and the other made with only the whites. Most common are the whole-egg tortes, in which the yolks are beaten with sugar, then folded together with ground nuts, stiffly beaten whites, and a small amount of either flour or bread-, cake, or cookie crumbs. The batter is baked in a springform pan or in individual cake pans and the torte is served in a variety of ways — as a single layer either richly glazed or simply dusted with confectioners' sugar, or split into two or more layers and then filled and frosted with buttercream, pastry cream, whipped cream, or ganache. Here is a rundown of the half-dozen recipes I tested:

• Mandel torte is an almond torte. The recipe I tried called for ground almonds and breadcrumbs, along with 6 eggs and flavorings.

The taste and texture were fine, but not exceptional, but the big problem (I soon discovered this to be true for many tortes) was that the cake sank in the middle. The cake also stuck to the sides of the cake pan, since the recipe called for buttering only the bottom of the pan.

- A pecan mocha torte worked much better than the first recipe, with the cake layers baking up nicely and springing back perfectly when pressed. The recipe called for 3½ cups of toasted pecans to only 3 tablespoons of flour, so the torte had a large crumb and chewy texture. Brushing the cake layers with cognac before filling and frosting added a welcome dimension to the dessert.

- Brottorte is unique in that it uses more breadcrumbs than ground nuts, which produces a dramatically tall, even-textured cake. (*Brot* means "bread" in German.) However, a great deal of sherry was used to soak the cake after baking, which made it my least favorite recipe.

- The hazelnut torte was odd since it used more yolks than whites. The cake was delicate, fine-textured, and tall. As it cooled, however, it seemed to shrink more than sink; it was still level, but dropped in height by about a third. Inside, this cake had an odd, beige color and coarse, porous texture that reminded me of seven-grain sandwich bread. The top had a crusty appearance similar to the pecan torte, but with the spongy texture of the almond cake. The taste was fine, but the shrinking was a serious problem.

- Small walnut torte was unique in that it called for using cornstarch instead of flour or breadcrumbs. The cake was thin, spongy, and relatively dense, almost breadlike. Not a winner.

- Austrian walnut torte used only 2 tablespoons breadcrumbs and no flour. I decided to try a test, making half of the recipe with the specified breadcrumbs and half with an equal amount of flour instead. The cake

made with flour came out twice as high as the one made with crumbs. It was fluffier and far more appealing, with a slight sponginess but no "Passover sponge cake" odor. It had a coarser crumb, but none of the "breadiness" of the previous walnut and hazelnut tortes, and a lovely golden-brown color from the coffee and visible walnuts. As it cooled, it sank slightly, but in a strangely even manner, keeping its height around the perimeter like a fallen chocolate cake. It ended up level, but with an attractive raised edge.

Now I had to cobble together a good working master recipe. I had learned many things, including that flour was better than breadcrumbs and essential for good texture, that an even number of yolks to whites was better than a higher proportion of yolks, and that coffee seemed to make a better pairing with ground nuts than lemon, another common flavoring. So I started with 8 whole eggs, ¾ cup plus 2 tablespoons sugar, 1½ cups ground nuts, 2 tablespoons flour, and 1½ tablespoons strong coffee. After making this recipe a few times, I discovered that sinking was a real problem and I was getting inconsistent results. I also found the torte a bit too sweet and cut back on the sugar by ¼ cup while adding a bit of nutmeg and vanilla to improve the flavor.

After more testing, I ended up increasing the flour to a whopping (by torte standards) ½ cup, which solved the problem of sinking. Most tortes are simply too delicate for the home cook, and I wanted a foolproof recipe. I also found that if I used only 5 whites and 6 yolks, the texture was improved as well. After doing some more research, I discovered that the food scientist Shirley Corriher suggests adding a tablespoon of water to the yolks if one is using a large amount of sugar — this helps to dissolve the sugar properly. I used rum instead of water, but I did see an improvement in the texture. I also read what cooking teacher Madeleine Kamman had to say about tortes, and her mixing method seemed to work best: a scoop of beaten whites is folded into the yolk mixture, the balance of the whites are added on top along with the flour and nuts, and then the whole mixture is folded into a final smooth batter. The real revelation came, however, after I used the folding method I have described elsewhere in this book. I used my electric mixer on low speed for 10 seconds to mix the batter, following up with a few manual strokes with a rubber spatula, and this did an excellent job of folding together the ingredients. With these refinements in place, I finally had a reliable recipe, one that did not rise as much as some torte recipes but that did not sink much at all when cooling.

⋯

Nut Torte

I use a combination of almonds and hazelnuts, but you can substitute any nuts you want, using all of one kind if you like. The nuts do not have to be toasted, but pecans and hazelnuts will benefit from this extra step, whereas almonds and walnuts won't. I suggest you fill and frost this torte with a whipped cream frosting (page 189 — the almond variation would be best) or the Maple Meringue Frosting (page 190). Take care when folding the batter together. The best method is to use an electric mixer on low speed.

MAKES TWO 8-INCH ROUNDS

Fine dry breadcrumbs for dusting pans
6   large egg yolks
½   cup plus 2 tablespoons sugar, divided
1   tablespoon rum
1   teaspoon vanilla extract
¼   teaspoon nutmeg
1½   cups nuts (almonds, pecans, walnuts, or hazelnuts), ground
5   large egg whites
¼   teaspoon cream of tartar
Pinch salt
½   cup all-purpose flour

IN A NUTSHELL

The choice of nuts in a nut torte, obviously, is just a matter of personal taste. Although my tests showed it is not absolutely necessary to toast the nuts used in a torte, I found that pecans and hazelnuts benefited from the step, while almonds and walnuts did not. Further, it was surprising to note that the volume of nuts doesn't change that much when they are ground or chopped. For example, 2½ cups (10 ounces) of very coarsely chopped almonds lost only ¼ cup in volume when ground, and 4 cups (16 ounces) coarsely chopped pecans lost only 2 tablespoons when ground.

HOMEMADE BREADCRUMBS FROM FRESH BREAD

When a recipe calls for fine breadcrumbs, most of us are brought up short. Does this mean the fine dried breadcrumbs that one purchases at the supermarket, or does it mean fresh bread chopped in a food processor? If you make your own, does the bread have to be stale?

For lining cake pans, I have found that unseasoned fine breadcrumbs purchased at the market are best. They should be extremely fine, no larger than grains of sand. (Shy away from whole wheat breadcrumbs — they are much too tough and a bit too large as well.) But if you do not have commercial breadcrumbs on hand, what do you do? I tested this and found a simple solution. Cut fresh bread into thin slices and toast it well. When it is thoroughly cool, put it through a food processor for at least a minute. You will find that the food processor is incapable of making really fine crumbs; there will be plenty of larger, somewhat soft pieces of bread in the bowl. To solve this problem, simply empty the contents of the food processor into a sieve. (You don't want to use an extra-fine strainer here because too little of the bread will pass through it. Use a medium-fine sieve.) This will remove the larger pieces, leaving you with professional-looking breadcrumbs that are fine enough to line a cake pan.

1. Set an oven rack in the middle position and heat oven to 350 degrees. Grease the bottoms of two 8-inch cake pans (don't use 9-inch pans) and line the bottoms with parchment pa-

per. *Do not grease the sides*. Butter the paper and dust with fine dry breadcrumbs.

2. In the large bowl of an electric mixer, beat the egg yolks, ½ cup of the sugar, and the rum on medium-high speed until very fluffy and at least doubled in volume, about 5 minutes. (The time will vary depending on your mixer.) The mixture should form a thick ribbon when the beaters are lifted. Add the vanilla and nutmeg and gently fold to combine. Fold in the ground nuts.

3. In another bowl with clean beaters, beat the egg whites until foamy. Add the cream of tartar and salt and continue beating, adding the remaining 2 tablespoons sugar gradually, until the mixture holds firm peaks but the whites are still glossy; do not overbeat. Stir a scoop, about one-quarter, of the egg whites into the yolk-nut mixture. Slide the rest of the whites on top of the batter and then sift the flour over the whites. Beat on the lowest speed of your mixer for 10 seconds. Remove bowl from mixer and finish combining by folding mixture gently by hand using a large rubber spatula. (Be sure to scrape the bottom of the bowl as you fold.) There should be no streaks of egg white visible. Turn batter into the two prepared pans. Smooth the top of the batter with the spatula.

4. Bake until the cake is lightly golden and springs back when gently pressed, 25 to 35 minutes. Rotate pans 180 degrees after 15 minutes and check cakes after 20 minutes. When cakes are done, remove pans from oven and invert onto a cake rack. Let cakes cool in the pans for 30 minutes. Turn cake pans right side up. Run the tip of a sharp knife around the edge of each pan to loosen cake, and remove cakes from pan and cool completely.

WHAT CAN GO WRONG? The big problem with tortes is sinking during cooling. I have added ½ cup of flour to this recipe, so this should be a minor problem, but be sure to thoroughly cook the torte; the center should really spring back when pressed with the flat side of a fork. Un-

dercooking will yield a very wet, gummy interior. Also use a light hand when folding the batter and follow my instructions carefully. A heavy hand with the batter will make a tough cake. And be absolutely sure not to grease the sides of the cake pans and to invert the pans as soon as they come out of the oven. If the sides of the pans are greased, the cakes will fall out of the pans onto the cooling rack.

THE LINZER TORTE

A LINZER TORTE IS REALLY nothing at all like the Nut Torte recipe above. It is a relatively dense tart (not a torte) made from sugar, eggs, flour, and nuts and filled with jam. It is not all that hard to make, but many recipes turn out leaden desserts, with dense, floury crusts. The other common problem is dough that is too crumbly and hard to work with, although this sort of dough often produces nice results when baked. You want three things from a Linzer torte: a relatively light crust, the strong taste of nuts, and just the right pairing of nuts and jam for perfect balance.

As usual, I started by making a half-dozen or so recipes to find out what I liked. Some recipes were much like a piecrust, cutting butter into flour and then adding sugar, nuts, and eggs, while others read more like cake or cookie recipes, creaming butter and sugar and then adding eggs, flour, and nuts. The first recipe I tried was from Maida Heatter. She cuts butter into flour in a food processor and then adds sugar, ground walnuts, eggs, and lemon. The dough was heavy, like a pie dough, and somewhat dry and crumbly from the nuts. Half the dough was pressed into a springform pan lined with parchment and baked at 400 degrees in the lower third of the oven until barely colored, about 15 minutes. Meanwhile, the rest of the dough was rolled between pieces of plastic wrap and chilled on a cookie sheet. The baked shell was sprinkled with dry breadcrumbs and then covered with raspberry jam. The chilled dough was cut into strips and then arranged in a lattice pattern over the jam. The whole thing was then baked in the top third of the oven at 350 degrees for 50 minutes, until well browned. The torte was absolutely gorgeous — it looked like it came from a European bakery. When tasted, however, the texture was relatively dense, the downfall of many Linzer tortes.

The next recipe, from James Beard, used the "cookie dough" method (creaming the butter with the sugar rather than cutting it into the flour) and called for a 2 to 1 ratio of nuts to flour, half of which were toasted hazelnuts. The dough was very soft and sticky and needed to be chilled before using. The torte was formed in much the same manner as the first recipe, but during baking the lattice spread too much, lacking the definition of the Heatter torte. It unmolded easily, even without parchment, but was hard to serve; whereas the Heatter slices could be picked up and eaten like a cookie, this torte fell apart on the plate. Worst of all, the crust itself was floury and unpleasant.

I searched for other Linzer tortes and, after discarding a half-dozen mongrel recipes, came across a Time-Life version that intrigued me. It called for hard-cooked egg yolks in the crust. I had heard of bakers using this ingredient but had never tried it. I decided anything that weird had to be worth a shot. The crust ingredients were blended in a food processor and then frozen 15 minutes. Three-quarters of the mixture was pressed into an unlined springform pan and baked in the lower third of the oven at 400 degrees for 15 minutes, until slightly colored. The sides of the crust fell in a bit, making the edges very thick, but the crust was smooth and had good color. I sprinkled 2 tablespoons ground almonds on the crust and combined 1 cup raspberry jam with ½ cup red currant jelly and poured it over the crust. For once, the remaining portion of dough held together while I formed the lattice and brushed it with egg wash. Borrowing from Maida Heatter's recipe, I sprinkled the torte with slivered almonds and baked it in the upper third of the oven at 350 degrees for almost an hour, until it was well colored. The results were spectacular. The texture was light, the torte was beautiful, and the flavor was wonderfully nutty. The torte is also easy to make, the dough being blended together entirely in the bowl of a food processor.

▪ ▪ ▪

Linzer Torte

This is nothing like the preceding Nut Torte recipe. This is a relatively dense tart, not a torte, made from flour, sugar, nuts, and flavorings. It is filled with jam and topped with a latticework. The beauty of this recipe is that even a ham-handed baker can turn out a beautiful-looking dessert, since the soft dough melts during baking and conceals any rough spots. If you are familiar with other Linzer torte recipes, you will find that this one has a more tender crust. Many Linzer tortes tend to be a bit tough and dry.

MAKES ONE 9-INCH TORTE

1½	cups all-purpose flour
½	teaspoon cinnamon
1	teaspoon grated lemon zest
2	hard-cooked egg yolks, mashed until crumbly

½ pound (2 sticks) cold unsalted butter, cut into pieces
½ cup granulated sugar
2 large egg yolks (raw), lightly beaten
1 teaspoon vanilla extract
1 cup plus 2 tablespoons coarsely chopped toasted hazelnuts
¼ cup plus 2 tablespoons coarsely chopped almonds
2 tablespoons very finely ground almonds or dry breadcrumbs
1 cup thick raspberry or red currant jam (or a mixture of the two)
1 large egg lightly beaten with 1 tablespoon cream
½ cup slivered almonds (optional)
Confectioner's sugar for dusting (optional)

1. Arrange oven racks with one in the top third position and one in the bottom third position. Heat oven to 400 degrees.

2. In a large food processor bowl, combine the flour, cinnamon, lemon zest, and hard-cooked egg yolks. Add the butter and sugar and pulse about 6 times, or until the butter is in small, pea-size pieces. Add the raw yolks, vanilla, 1 cup of the hazelnuts, and ¼ cup of the almonds to the bowl and pulse until well blended. Add the remaining nuts and process steadily until the mixture forms a ball. Wrap the dough in plastic, pat into a disk, and freeze 15 minutes, until the dough is firm but not hard.

3. Break off about one-third of the dough and roll it between sheets of plastic wrap to make an 8½-inch circle. Place on a cookie sheet and chill. Using your fingers, press the remaining dough to cover the bottom and 1 inch up the sides of a 9-inch springform pan. (Press the dough with the bottom of a drinking glass to smooth out the surface.) Bake on the bottom oven rack 15 minutes, until the dough is lightly colored. The sides may fall in a bit, which is okay.

4. Remove the pan from the oven and reduce the temperature to 350 degrees. Sprinkle the shell with the ground almonds or crumbs. Stir the jam and when it is smooth pour it over the crumbs, spreading it evenly on the crust. (Do not cover the sides with jam, even if they collapsed while baking.)

5. Take the rolled dough from the refrigerator and remove the top sheet of plastic. Cut the dough into ½-inch-wide strips. Lay 5 or 6 of the strips over the jam in parallel rows about 1½ to 2 inches apart. (Use alternating strips of dough, reserving the others to finish the latticework.) Attach the strips to the sides of the crust by pressing the ends lightly. Rotate the pan about one-quarter turn and repeat with additional strips to form a lattice. (If the strips break when transferred to the torte, repair them by loosely overlapping the broken ends.) Use any leftover dough to cover the ends of the lattice strips and form a neat edge. Note that during baking, the dough will melt a bit, smoothing out any rough spots.

6. Brush the dough with the egg-and-cream mixture and sprinkle the optional slivered almonds over the top. (The almonds add texture, but I prefer the look of the torte without them.) Bake the torte in the top third of the oven 45 to 60 minutes, until golden brown. (The sides may brown more quickly than the top.) Let cool 5 minutes before removing the sides of the pan. Cool to room temperature and dust with confectioners' sugar if desired.

WHAT CAN GO WRONG? You will have difficulty working with this dough, since it is heavy and sticky. I have also found that forming the edge is difficult; but this doesn't make much difference, since the dough melts as it bakes and looks terrific. So don't worry if this dessert looks awful as you are making it — during baking, it will transform itself into a showstopper.

▾▾
▾

CHEESECAKE

OTHERWISE REASONABLE COOKS can come to blows about what constitutes the best cheesecake. Some like it thick, rich, and dense; others prefer a lighter texture, one that has plenty of tongue-coating silkiness but is also more ethereal, dancing in the mouth before dissolving in a final burst of rich cream. I belong to the latter school, and my search for the perfect cheesecake carried me well off the culinary beaten path.

To solve the issue of texture, the most obvious test was to separate the eggs, beat the whites separately, and then fold them back into the cream cheese mixture. The basic notion was good, but the resulting cake was much too light and foamy. I finally settled on separating only 3 of the eggs, leaving the other 2 whole. This made a light but substantial cheesecake, a pleasant cross between a soufflé and a cake. I tested adding cream of tartar to the whites as they were beaten, and in fact this did stabilize the whites, producing a somewhat higher and lighter cake. A more traditional New York–style cheesecake (which is relatively dense) can be made by not separating the whites, and I have included this variation below.

The next issue was oven temperature and baking time. Over many years, I have found that lower oven temperatures work best for cheesecake. Having tested everything from 200 degrees up to 350 degrees, I find that 275 degrees is in fact the winner — low enough not to toughen the egg proteins and dry out the mixture, yet high enough not to take all day. But even with this low temperature, I did find that the top of the cake would often come out cracked and overcooked. Although I prefer to make recipes as simple as possible, it turns out that a bain marie, a hot water bath, is essential. Unfortunately, this leads to complications. A cheesecake must be cooked in a springform pan, which, if not wrapped properly with aluminum foil, will allow water to seep in. An extra-wide piece of foil is placed over the removable bottom of the pan, the pan is assembled, and then the foil is folded up around the sides. A second sheet of foil is wrapped around the bottom and sides of the pan. (See illustrations.) When the cheesecake is ready to bake, the pan is placed in a roasting pan and hot water is poured around it, enough to come halfway up its sides. The water moderates the temperatures around the pan and also provides a moister environment, one that produces a tender cheesecake.

SEALING SPRINGFORM PANS FOR WATER BATH COOKING

Place an 18-inch-wide sheet of foil over bottom of pan.

Insert bottom into pan.

Fold foil up around pan and place on second sheet of foil.

Fold up second sheet.

After much testing, I determined that it was best to let the cake sit in the turned-off oven for 2 hours after baking. I also tested a variety of baking times, from 50 minutes to 1 hour and 15 minutes. I found that a time between 60 and 70 minutes was best. (All ovens vary. Never trust baking times; always check the contents of the oven during baking.) The flavors of the cheesecake were at their peak after the cake was thoroughly chilled, which will take 3 to 4 hours in the refrigerator. Slicing a cheesecake is difficult. Use a sharp knife and run the blade under hot water between slices.

...

Light Cheesecake

The easiest way to make crumbs out of graham crackers is to place the crackers in a zip-closure bag and then crush them with a rolling pin.

SERVES 12

1	tablespoon unsalted butter, melted
2	graham crackers, crushed into fine crumbs
2	pounds cream cheese, at room temperature
1¼	cups granulated sugar
5	large eggs, at room temperature
1	teaspoon minced lemon zest
1½	teaspoons vanilla extract
½	cup heavy cream
1	cup sour cream
½	teaspoon cream of tartar

1. Adjust oven rack to the middle position and heat oven to 275 degrees. Remove bottom from a 10-inch springform pan. To prevent leakage, wrap the pan in two sheets of extra-wide aluminum foil, as shown in the illustrations at left. Brush the inside of the pan with the melted butter and then sprinkle with graham cracker crumbs, tilting the pan to coat evenly. Set springform pan in a large roasting pan and bring a large kettle of water to a boil.

2. Separate 3 of the 5 eggs. In a large bowl, beat cream cheese with an electric mixer or by hand until smooth. Gradually add sugar and beat until smooth, about 3 minutes with an electric mixer and 6 to 7 minutes by hand. Scrape bowl frequently. Add the 2 whole eggs, one at a time, and beat until just incorporated, frequently scraping down the sides of the bowl. Add the 3 egg yolks, one at a time, and beat until incorporated. Add the lemon zest, vanilla, heavy cream, and sour cream and mix on low speed until combined.

3. In a separate bowl, beat the 3 egg whites with the cream of tartar until they hold soft peaks. Fold whites into the batter with a large rubber spatula. Pour batter into prepared springform pan and then pour enough boiling water into the roasting pan to come halfway up the sides of the springform. Bake for 1 hour to 1 hour and 10 minutes, or until cheesecake is puffy and slightly browned and the center is still a bit wobbly. Turn off heat and let cheesecake sit in oven, door closed, for another 2 hours.

4. Remove springform pan from the water bath and set on a wire rack to cool to room temperature. Cover and refrigerate for 3 to 4 hours, until completely chilled. To serve, run a thin knife around the inside of the pan and remove outer ring. Run a sharp knife under hot water in between cutting individual slices.

WHAT CAN GO WRONG? Cheesecake is easy enough to make, but you could have two problems here. First, you will need an extra-wide roll of aluminum foil to make sure that the pan doesn't leak. Narrower sheets of foil will not cover the width of the pan as well as the sides. This will result in leakage during baking. The other problem is that, since this cake is baked at only 275 degrees, you may find that your baking time varies considerably. (Almost all home ovens are improperly calibrated. If your oven is actually at 240 degrees instead of 275 degrees, for instance, this will dramatically increase the baking time.) Therefore, do not rely on my suggested baking time to determine when the cake is done but use instead my description of the cake when it is properly baked.

NEW YORK–STYLE VARIATION

For a more traditional, New York–style cheesecake, do not separate the eggs; beat in the 5 whole eggs, one at a time, as described in step 2 of the master recipe. Eliminate cream of tartar and simply pour the mixture into the prepared pan after the lemon zest, vanilla, heavy cream, and sour cream have been added. The baking time will be the same, but the cake will not puff up and will not brown at all on top. It is ready when the cake is almost set, the center 2 inches or so still being slightly underbaked and wobbly. Note that this cheesecake will still be a lot lighter than a traditional and, to my palate, very dense New York cheesecake.

FROSTINGS, ICINGS, GLAZES, AND FILLINGS

For the purposes of this book, *frostings* are defined as relatively thick confections that are used to ice and/or fill a cake. An *icing* has a thinner consistency, really the same thing as a *glaze*. *Fillings* are denser, more flavorful mixtures used between layers to provide contrast in flavor. Although these definitions may be somewhat arbitrary, they do provide a simple method for organizing recipes used to frost, fill, glaze, ice, or otherwise coat a cake.

Having made a large number of recipes of this type, from both old and new cookbooks, I find that many of them are either unappealing or time-consuming. Royal icing, for example, made with egg whites and confectioners' sugar, has a truly awful taste, and a chocolate whipped cream frosting takes literally hours to make, since the cream mixture must be cooled sufficiently before whipping. Even then, it often does not whip properly, since ultrapasteurized cream is difficult to whip even under the best of circumstances. Plenty of recipes are both easy to make and delicious, so I have taken the liberty of passing over frostings, icings, and fillings that are neither.

⬩ᵛ⬩

CHOCOLATE FROSTINGS

THE FIRST CATEGORY of frostings I examined was chocolate frostings. I was not looking for a buttercream but something less fatty and with a more intense chocolate flavor. I wanted the texture of a good old-fashioned chocolate frosting, the sort of thick, smooth topping one would find on a birthday cake for a six-year-old. To get a handle on the possibilities, I made five recipes from various cookbooks. All of them began by melting chocolate with the milk or cream, cooling the mixture, adding the rest of the ingredients, and then whipping. (One recipe actually cooked the entire mixture.) The recipe I started with (recipe A on the chart) was easy enough to put together, but the frosting was too sweet for me. It was smooth and light, but the confectioners' sugar was the predominant flavor — not what I was hoping for. Recipe B was pretty good, but the mixture had to be cooked on the stove until it reached a certain temperature, which I thought was fussy; the frosting

CASE 35: FROSTINGS ON THE CAKE

How do standard recipes for chocolate frostings compare?

Ingredient	Recipe A	Recipe B	Recipe C	Recipe D	Recipe E
Chocolate	2 ounces baking	3 ounces baking	6 ounces baking	8 ounces bittersweet	8 ounces bittersweet
Butter	1 tablespoon	2 tablespoons	6 tablespoons	None	8 tablespoons
Milk	⅓ cup	1¼ cups	None	None	None
Heavy cream	None	None	1 cup	2 cups	¾ cup
Sugar	2 cups confectioners'	3 cups granulated	1½ cups confectioners'	None	None
Corn syrup	None	2 tablespoons	None	None	3 tablespoons
Vanilla	1 teaspoon	None	1 teaspoon	½ teaspoon	None
Salt	None	¼ teaspoons	None	None	None

was also somewhat too sweet. The next recipe had some of the same problems. The taste of the confectioners' sugar was too strong and the frosting too sweet.

These first three tests convinced me that any frosting that uses unsweetened baking chocolate doesn't have a very nice flavor, since I find that semisweet or bittersweet chocolates tend to be of a higher quality. The next two recipes did use bittersweet chocolate. Recipe D was the best yet but a bit rich and heavy, almost like a ganache (a classic thick chocolate frosting). Recipe E, however, was terrific, with great chocolate flavor plus butter and cream to complement and lighten the chocolate, and a light, smooth texture. The bit of corn syrup added a little more sweetness without going over the

top, and putting it together was a snap as well. Of course, I could see a few windows of opportunity for improvements. The recipe had no vanilla, which I think is a great complement to chocolate. Also, I believed the procedure could be streamlined. I didn't think the butter needed to be melted (why not just whip it into the cooled chocolate and cream mixture), the yield was skimpy, and I felt that the frosting could be a bit sweeter. My working recipe now included 8 ounces bittersweet chocolate, 8 tablespoons unsalted butter, ¾ cup heavy cream, 3 tablespoons corn syrup, and ½ teaspoon vanilla.

My first test was to incorporate room temperature butter instead of melting it with the chocolate and cream. So I started the recipe by heating the cream in a small saucepan until

FROSTING CAKES 101

Place a dab of frosting on a cardboard round that is slightly larger than cake diameter.

For a quick cake decorating stand, place cake on removable tart pan bottom on an upside-down cake pan.

Cover bottom layer with icing.

Add top layer.

Apply a skim coat of buttercream. Chill cake for one hour.

Apply frosting on top, then on sides.

To even frosting around sides, hold spatula at 45 degrees.

Move spatula across cake, pushing frosting toward center.

Simple rosettes can be piped around sides.

Use a fork to make wave patterns.

Apply nuts to outside.

Melted chocolate can be dripped on top with a fork.

A simple glaze is applied with cake on a cooling rack sitting on a jelly roll pan.

bubbling around the edges. Next, I took the pan from the heat, added the chopped chocolate and let it sit covered for 5 minutes. I then whisked the mixture until combined and transferred it to a mixing bowl. At this point I allowed the mixture to cool to room temperature. I then added the butter (cool room temperature and cut into chunks), corn syrup, and vanilla and beat the mixture with an electric mixer. While I loved the fresher taste of the butter this way, I thought the frosting was too bitter and therefore added 1 more tablespoon corn syrup, but the frosting was still not sweet enough. I finally decided that confectioners' sugar was the answer, so I started adding confectioners' sugar in 1-tablespoon increments. Using Callebaut chocolate, I found I needed 6 tablespoons confectioners' sugar to adjust the sweetness. (If you use a sweeter brand of chocolate, you may get away with a bit less.)

Though this was a great frosting recipe, I felt that a little more testing was in order. I played with the amount of chocolate and found 6 ounces was too little and 10 ounces produced a bitter taste. I tried reducing the butter to 6 tablespoons, but the result wasn't as smooth in taste or texture. When made with 10 tablespoons butter, the frosting began to taste like a buttercream, so I settled on 8 tablespoons. I tried using less than ¾ cup cream and it became too difficult to incorporate the chocolate, but with more than ¾ cup there were a number of problems — the mixture was too thin, it took longer to cool to the correct spreadable consistency, and the taste was not improved. I stuck with ¾ cup.

Next I wanted to test different brands of chocolate to see how this might affect the quantity of sugar. First I tested Ghirardelli, which, I discovered, needed only 4 tablespoons confectioners' sugar, instead of the 6 tablespoons I was using with Callebaut, my chocolate of choice. When I tested Valhrona, however, I found that a full ½ cup confectioners' sugar was required. As a result, I have written the recipe

so that you may vary the amount of sweetness as you go along. You will add ¼ cup confectioners' sugar to start with, taste the frosting, and then add more as necessary. One final comment: the recipe depends heavily on the quality of the chocolate. If you don't like the taste of it out of the wrapper, you won't like the frosting either.

■■■

Old-Fashioned Chocolate Frosting

This is the sort of frosting that was probably used in a Norman Rockwell painting. It is thick, smooth, and with a deep chocolate flavor nicely balanced with the taste of butter and cream. Use the best chocolate you can find (I suggest Callebaut, which is my favorite baking chocolate). Do not use cheap supermarket brands. Note that this recipe calls for a variable amount of confectioners' sugar, since different brands of chocolate display different levels of sweetness. The frosting keeps well in an airtight container for up to 2 days (after 2 days, the fresh, buttery taste is a bit compromised); just rewhip it before icing the cake. To rewhip, allow it to sit out on the counter until it reaches a cool room temperature, about 20 minutes, and then beat with an electric mixer until it achieves a spreadable consistency. Be sure to keep the frosted cake in a cool place, but be aware that a refrigerated chocolate cake needs to come up to room temperature before serving. If you serve it cold, you will find the frosting dense and the cake itself dry. Use this frosting with a basic yellow or white cake.

MAKES ABOUT 4 CUPS, ENOUGH TO FROST AN 8- OR 9-INCH TWO-LAYER CAKE

¾ cup heavy cream

8 ounces bittersweet or semisweet chocolate, coarsely chopped

¼ cup light or dark corn syrup

8 tablespoons (1 stick) unsalted butter at cool room temperature, cut into 1-inch chunks

½ teaspoon vanilla extract
¼ to ½ cup confectioners' sugar

1. Place the cream in a small saucepan over low heat until it is just simmering and small bubbles are forming around the edges of the pan. Remove from heat; add the chocolate, cover, and let sit for 5 minutes. Remove cover and whisk mixture until homogeneous, shiny, and smooth. Transfer to a mixing bowl and allow to cool to room temperature.

2. To the bowl add the corn syrup, butter, and vanilla and beat with an electric mixer until well combined, about 1 minute. Add ¼ cup confectioners' sugar and beat on low to combine. Increase the speed to high and continue mixing for about 5 minutes more, or until the mixture has lightened in color and texture and thickened to a spreadable consistency. Taste for sweetness. At this point you may add the remaining confectioners' sugar in 1-tablespoon increments until desired sweetness is reached. If the icing will not whip to a light, spreadable consistency, refrigerate for 15 minutes and try again. Repeat this last step until the frosting whips.

WHAT CAN GO WRONG? The temperature of the mixture before whipping is important, since it will not whip properly if too warm. A brief spell in the refrigerator may be necessary to cool it off sufficiently for proper whipping. The butter also needs to be firm but malleable, about 65 degrees or so on an instant-read thermometer.

MILK CHOCOLATE VARIATION
This frosting is even lighter than the master. However, it must be made with a delicious milk chocolate; otherwise don't bother. This variation does not need the additions of either vanilla or confectioners' sugar. I like this frosting on basic yellow cake. Follow the master recipe, using a top-notch milk chocolate and omitting the vanilla and confectioners' sugar. This recipe makes about 3 ½ cups frosting.

CHOCOLATE SOUR CREAM FROSTING

THE BEAUTY OF SOUR CREAM frostings lies not only in the tang of the major ingredient; they are also easy and quick to make. There is no cream to cool and then whip, and the sour cream also gives the frosting a wonderful creamy texture. The basic procedure is simple enough. Chocolate is melted and then whisked into sour cream with the addition of a sweetener and perhaps a few other flavorings. As the chocolate cools, it hardens, providing enough structure to make a thick frosting.

The big question was which type of sweetener worked best. I tried confectioners' sugar, corn syrup, and sugar. The confectioners' sugar produced a sugary taste, as if the sugar were a thin mask over the underlying tartness of the sour cream. Granulated sugar was better but still didn't marry well with the sour cream. I also found that the frosting became quite stiff when cooled. Finally, I tested corn syrup, and this proved to be the solution. It not only made the best-tasting frosting, it also made the frosting shinier and more spreadable. It can and should be added to taste depending on the chocolate. While ¼ cup corn syrup was fine for a frosting made with grocery store chocolate, I needed a full ½ cup when using bittersweet Callebaut. Add the syrup bit by bit until the desired sweetness is achieved.

▪▪▪

Chocolate Sour Cream Frosting
This is a great recipe, since the taste of chocolate and sour cream is a good marriage and the recipe is easy and quick to make. Use the best semisweet or bittersweet chocolate you can find. The instant coffee is unnecessary with a really good brand of chocolate, but it is helpful if you are using an inexpensive supermarket

chocolate. Use this frosting with a basic yellow or white cake.

MAKES ABOUT 4 CUPS

> 12 ounces semisweet or bittersweet chocolate
> 1 teaspoon instant espresso or instant coffee powder (optional)
> 1⅔ cups sour cream
> ¼ to ½ cup light or dark corn syrup
> ½ teaspoon vanilla extract

1. Chop the chocolate into small pieces with a large knife (or in the bowl of a food processor). Combine the chocolate and optional instant espresso in the top of a double boiler or in a heatproof bowl set over simmering water. Let sit for 5 minutes, or until the chocolate has melted. Remove from heat and let cool until tepid. (The chocolate can also be melted in a microwave oven at 50 percent power. Heat for 2 minutes, stir, heat for 1 minute, stir, and then heat for 1 additional minute if necessary.)

2. Place sour cream, ¼ cup corn syrup, and vanilla in a medium bowl and stir to combine. Add the tepid chocolate and stir until the mixture is uniform. Taste for sweetness. If needed, add corn syrup in 1-tablespoon increments until desired sweetness is achieved. Let cool in the refrigerator (this should take no more than 30 minutes) until frosting is of spreadable consistency. If the frosting becomes too cold and stiff, simply leave at room temperature until it is easy to spread.

WHAT CAN GO WRONG? This is a very easy frosting to make. Just keep a close eye on the frosting as it cools so you catch it at the right consistency, which is thick but still spreadable. It will get pretty hard if left too long in the refrigerator.

WHIPPED CREAM FROSTINGS

WHIPPING SWEETENED AND FLAVORED heavy cream and using it as a frosting is nothing new. Whipped heavy cream tends to break down over time, however, and so I experimented with the notion of adding a stabilizer to give it more substance. Chocolate performs this task well, since when it cools it adds structure to the whipped cream. (The bad news is that the chocolate-cream mixture needs to cool before whipping, which can take hours.) But I still needed to find the right ingredient for frostings flavored with something other than chocolate. I finally tried gelatin, which turned out to be the solution. It gives the whipped cream body and helps to retard its breakdown.

The problem with these frostings is first and foremost the heavy cream itself. I find that most ultrapasteurized American supermarket creams have little flavor and therefore, in a frosting, one is tasting the sugar and the flavoring, not the cream itself. If possible, try to purchase organic pasteurized cream (not ultrapasteurized, which is heated to a higher temperature) that is produced locally.

I also spent months working on chocolate and mocha variations to the master recipe and found that since the cream needs to be heated with the chocolate and then cooled, this meant that the recipe had to be started hours ahead of time for proper chilling. I also found that the cream mixture was hard to whip properly with the addition of chocolate. Finally, if you want a good chocolate frosting, forget about using a flavored whipped cream. Go for the real thing and use either of the two chocolate frostings printed earlier in this chapter.

···

Master Recipe for Whipped Cream Frosting

Note that this recipe uses gelatin to stabilize the whipped cream. I suggest that you use this frosting on cakes that are to be eaten the same day, since even with the addition of gelatin, this sort of topping will not hold well for 24 hours. This frosting is best with lighter cakes, such as genoise or sponge cakes.

MAKES ABOUT 3¾ CUPS

1	teaspoon unflavored gelatin
2	tablespoons water
2	cups heavy cream
⅓	cup granulated sugar
½	teaspoon vanilla extract

1. Chill bowl and beaters of an electric mixer in the freezer for at least 10 minutes.

2. Sprinkle gelatin over 2 tablespoons water in a small saucepan. Let dissolve for 4 minutes. Over very low heat, melt gelatin mixture, about 3 minutes.

3. Place heavy cream, sugar, melted gelatin, and vanilla in the chilled bowl. Beat on low speed for 30 seconds, until gelatin is thoroughly mixed into cream. Increase speed to high and beat until stiff, being careful not to overbeat (the cream will become grainy or curdled-looking).

WHAT CAN GO WRONG? There is no trick to whipping cream, but I find that ultrapasteurized cream does take more effort than simple pasteurized cream. Therefore, it is best to throw the bowl and beaters into the freezer for 10 or 15 minutes before beginning.

LEMON, ORANGE, OR ALMOND VARIATION

Substitute lemon, orange, or almond extract for the vanilla. If you can find lemon oil or orange oil (oils have a purer, stronger flavor than extracts), use this instead of the extract.

LIQUOR VARIATION

Add 1 tablespoon of any liquor such as dark rum, bourbon, brandy, or Cointreau along with the heavy cream.

···

Meringue Frosting

This is a classic recipe for an "Italian" meringue. A hot sugar syrup is poured over beaten egg whites, which are then whipped a bit longer to incorporate the syrup. This sets the whites, giving them lots of body. An instant-read thermometer is helpful to determine when the sugar syrup is properly cooked, although the traditional "soft ball" test will do in a pinch. (A bit of the hot sugar syrup is dropped into a glass of cold water. If it sets up into a soft, gummy ball, it is done.) I have found, however, that the exact temperature of the sugar syrup is not absolutely crucial. The frosting always turns glossy and stiff, even if you are off a few degrees. This frosting works with most any cake but is especially good with devil's food cake, basic white cake, genoise, and sponge cake.

MAKES ENOUGH TO FROST A TWO-LAYER CAKE

1¼	cups granulated sugar
⅓	cup water
3	large egg whites
1	teaspoon vanilla extract
¼	teaspoon cream of tartar
⅛	teaspoon salt

1. Combine sugar and water in a small saucepan. Bring to a boil, swirling pan occasionally to wash down sides of pan. Boil until sugar mixture reaches 238 degrees on a candy thermometer, or until a drop of the syrup makes a soft, gummy ball when dropped into a small bowl of cold water. This will take about 7 minutes. (The time will vary a lot depending on your pan and the heat output of your burner.) Remove from heat and let cool for 5 minutes.

2. Beat egg whites in a medium bowl with an

electric mixer or by hand with a large whisk for 45 seconds. Add the vanilla, cream of tartar, and salt. Increase speed to high and beat until stiff but still glossy. Whites should still be moist, not dry and cottony. (This can be done without an electric mixer but will take a few minutes of intense beating with a large whisk.)

3. With the mixer on medium high, add the sugar syrup to the egg whites in a thin, steady stream. Continue beating until the frosting can hold a 2-inch peak and is very shiny. Cool to room temperature.

WHAT CAN GO WRONG? This is a reasonably foolproof recipe, since the hot syrup makes it difficult to overbeat the whites. However, getting the sugar syrup to the right temperature takes a little practice, because the type and size of the saucepan and the heat output of your burner will make all the difference in how long it takes. This is one recipe for which an instant-read thermometer is really helpful. Also note that the sugar syrup will come up to 230 degrees rather quickly but then gain in temperature more slowly. This frosting does not last well overnight, so it is best served within a few hours of being made.

▪▪▪

Maple Meringue Frosting

This frosting uses the same principle as the meringue frosting above: a hot sugar syrup is poured onto the whites as they are beaten. Since maple sugar (a granulated product) is sometimes hard to find, you can substitute a syrup made with 1 cup granulated white sugar and ¼ cup water; after beating the cooled syrup into the whites, add ¼ cup dark maple syrup. In old cookbooks, this sort of frosting was often referred to as a foam. This is one of the best recipes in this book and is terrific with the All-Purpose Yellow Cake (page 129) or the Spice Cake Variation (page 130).

MAKES ENOUGH TO FROST A TWO-LAYER CAKE

1¼   cups maple sugar (or see substitution above)
  3   large egg whites
  ¼   teaspoon cream of tartar
  ⅛   teaspoon salt

1. Place maple sugar in a small saucepan (no water is needed). Bring to a boil over medium-high heat, swirling pan occasionally to wash down sides. Boil until sugar syrup reaches 238 degrees on a candy thermometer, or until a drop of the syrup makes a soft, gummy ball when dropped into a small bowl of cold water. This will take about 7 minutes. Remove from heat and let cool for 5 minutes.

2. Beat egg whites in a medium bowl with an electric mixer or by hand with a large whisk for 45 seconds. Add the cream of tartar and salt. Increase speed to high and beat until stiff but still glossy. Whites should still be moist, not dry and cottony. (This can be done without an electric mixer but will take a few minutes of intense beating with a large whisk.)

3. With the mixer on medium high, add the sugar syrup to the egg whites in a thin, steady stream. Continue beating until the frosting is very stiff and shiny. Cool to room temperature.

BROWN SUGAR FROSTING

ONE OF THE MORE UNUSUAL frosting recipes I came across in my research was something called brown sugar frosting, and it was made with butter, eggs, water, salt, and brown sugar. The mixture was cooked briefly, cooled, and then whipped. I thought this was an interesting approach and also might make a good all-purpose frosting, so I went into the kitchen to test the recipe.

The results were disappointing, to say the least. The frosting was much too sweet, had a strong egg flavor, and never reached the right consistency for spreading on a cake. I almost gave up at this point but plunged on with a few variations. First, since the frosting was too thin, I eliminated the water; this made the butter and sugar too difficult to combine and produced a slightly flat taste. Next I substituted cream for the water, which did help. I changed the egg yolks to whole eggs, which eliminated the eggy flavor, but the frosting was still too sweet and too grainy. I then tried dark brown sugar versus the light brown called for in the recipe and liked the results. The frosting was mellower, with better flavor and a smoother consistency. A bit suspicious of this result, since the difference between light and dark brown sugars is only a bit of molasses, I made two more frostings, one with light and one with dark brown sugar, and the comparison held up.

Still, the frosting was a bit intense and also a bit heavy. To lighten it, I added 4 tablespoons room temperature unsalted butter to the cooled frosting before whipping. This really took it over the top for me. The addition of fresh butter at this stage rounded the flavor, and the texture was light, smooth, and very spreadable. Finally, I made a batch and added vanilla, but this addition masked the brown sugar taste.

My only other issue was volume. The recipe produced a skimpy 2 cups of frosting, whereas 4 cups is required for most layer cakes. I simply doubled the ingredients except the salt.

▪ ▪ ▪

Dark Brown Sugar Frosting

This is an unusual frosting recipe, but it works very well with the spice cake on page 130. The eggs need to be lightly beaten; otherwise the whites will start to cook when added to the hot sugar mixture. This is a fairly thick frosting and therefore goes best with a sturdier cake, such as a basic yellow cake.

MAKES ABOUT 4 CUPS

2   cups lightly packed dark brown sugar
8   tablespoons (1 stick) unsalted butter
¼   cup heavy cream
½   teaspoon salt
2   large eggs, lightly beaten

To Finish the Frosting
8   tablespoons (1 stick) unsalted butter, at cool room temperature, cut into pieces

1. Place the sugar, 8 tablespoons butter, cream, and salt in a small saucepan over medium-low heat, stirring occasionally. Cook until the butter is melted and the mixture begins to simmer. (The time will vary, depending on your pan and your cooktop.) Remove from heat.

2. Add the eggs and stir to combine. Return the pan to the heat and simmer while stirring for 2 to 6 minutes, or until the mixture is quite thick and foamy. Cool completely.

3. Place the cooled frosting mixture in a medium mixing bowl or the bowl of an electric mixer. Add the room temperature butter and beat until the butter is completely blended and the frosting has lightened in color and texture and is very smooth, 1 to 2 minutes. (Scrape the bottom and sides of the bowl as you work.) Use immediately or refrigerate for up to 3 days. If refrigerated, the frosting will need to come to room temperature and then be rewhipped before using.

WHAT CAN GO WRONG? If the brown sugar mixture sits too long, a few hours say, before the butter is added, it can get very thick and hard to blend with the butter. It is best to whip in the butter as soon as the mixture cools.

CASE 36: THE GERMANS FROST A CAKE

What is German chocolate frosting made out of, anyway?

Ingredient	Recipe A	Recipe B	Recipe C
Milk	1 cup evaporated	1 cup evaporated	1 cup evaporated
Sugar	½ cup white plus ½ cup brown	1 cup white	1 cup white
Eggs	6 yolks	3 yolks	2 yolks
Butter	4 tablespoons	8 tablespoons	8 tablespoons
Vanilla	¾ teaspoon	None	None
Coconut	1 cup shredded	1⅓ cups shredded	1⅓ cups shredded
Nuts	1⅓ cups walnuts	1⅓ cups pecans	1 cup pecans
Miscellaneous	1 tablespoon cornstarch, ⅛ teaspoon salt		

GERMAN CHOCOLATE CAKE FROSTING

EVERYONE IS FAMILIAR WITH this frosting. It is the thick, buttery frosting containing coconut and pecans which is served with German chocolate cake. The problem with these frostings is that they are often much too sweet and the balance between coconut, nuts, butter, and sugar is not right. The coconut should add a fluffy component, not be dense and heavy, and the taste of butter and toasted nuts should each come through clearly, not muddled together in a wet, sticky goo.

I started by making three recipes from different cookbooks. Using these recipes as a guide, I fashioned a working recipe that included 1 cup evaporated milk, 1 cup sugar, 3 egg yolks, 8 tablespoons butter, ½ teaspoon vanilla, 1 cup sweetened shredded coconut, and 1 cup chopped pecans. All of the recipes heated the milk, sugar, eggs, and butter until simmering and then allowed the mixture to cook for a couple of minutes. After removing it from the heat, the vanilla, coconut, and nuts were added. The frosting was cooled until spreadable and then used to assemble the cake or refrigerated until needed.

For my first test, I made two versions of this recipe, one using evaporated milk and one using heavy cream. I favored the rich, buttery flavor of the heavy cream version, but I thought both were too sweet and the balance between the coconut (the chewy stuff) and the sugar-cream mixture (the gooey stuff) was off. I definitely wanted more chew and less goo, so I took the sugar down to ¾ cup and increased the coconut to 1½ cups and made two more versions of the recipe, again using heavy cream and evaporated milk. Although I still preferred the heavy cream versions, I wondered how they would hold up in the refrigerator. Unfortunately, the heavy cream frostings became dull and grainy after just a few hours, the buttery taste having disappeared into the ether! The evaporated milk versions held up much better, although I was not particularly fond of the flavor.

Still not completely satisfied with the evaporated milk, I tried milk and half-and-half. They were no improvement, producing a loose frosting that did not hold up as well as the evaporated milk. I then tried sweetened condensed milk in place of the evaporated milk, eliminated the sugar, and discovered a winner. The frosting held up as well as the evaporated milk version, remaining smooth, shiny, and spreadable even after a rest in the refrigerator, and the flavor was much improved. Still, I missed the buttery flavor of the heavy cream variation, so I increased the butter from 8 to 10 and then 12 tablespoons and settled on the last amount. This produced a frosting that held well in the refrigerator and also had a nice buttery taste.

I then went on to test the other ingredients. The cornstarch, which was used in the first cookbook recipe tested, was deemed unnecessary. For the yolks, I tried 2 yolks and found the topping wasn't rich enough. I discovered that 4 yolks made the topping slightly eggy tasting. I then tried 2 whole eggs and the topping was wetter but not richer, so I stuck to the yolks, settling on 3. I increased the vanilla to 1 teaspoon and liked the slight boost of flavor. Since I wanted more chew and less goo to this frosting, I increased the coconut to 2 lightly packed cups. I also tested unsweetened coconut, but the frosting was too dry and not sweet enough. I toasted the chopped pecans to enrich the nut flavor.

However, I was still stuck with a relatively heavy, waxy topping, so I decided to test whipping the butter with the cooked base, and this worked much better than simply melting the butter. Finally, a light frosting that was not sticky and gooey, the texture of wax!

▪ ▪ ▪

German Chocolate Cake Frosting

Use sweetened coconut, not unsweetened, to give the frosting the right level of sweetness and moisture. This frosting is usually served with a sturdy chocolate cake.

MAKES ABOUT 5 CUPS

1   can (12 ounces) sweetened condensed
    milk
3   large egg yolks
1   teaspoon vanilla extract
12 tablespoons (1½ sticks) unsalted butter,
    cool but pliable
2   cups lightly packed sweetened shredded
    coconut
1   cup pecans, toasted and chopped

1. Place the milk and yolks in a small saucepan and stir to combine. Cook over low heat, stirring frequently, until the mixture thickens and leaves a thick coating on the back of a spoon. This will take about 5 minutes. (Time will vary a lot depending on your saucepan, heat level, and type of stove.) Do not boil. If any lumps form, immediately remove the pan from the heat and whisk until smooth. Remove from heat, add the vanilla, and stir to combine. Transfer to a medium mixing bowl and cool to room temperature.

2. Beat with an electric mixer on high for about 3 minutes, or until mixture is light-colored and thickened. Add the butter, 1 or 2 tablespoons at a time, and beat until light and all the butter is completely incorporated. (At this point, the mixture can be held in the refrigerator, tightly covered, for 48 hours and then beaten again before using.) Add the coconut and pecans and beat on low to incorporate.

CASE 37: MY LITTLE BUTTERCREAMS

There is more than one way to make a buttercream.

Ingredients/Method	Results
3 cups granulated sugar, 1 cup water, 1 pound butter, and 7 yolks; make sugar syrup and whip into beaten yolks	Much too sweet, but the texture was good
1 cup granulated sugar, ½ cup water, ½ pound butter, and 4 yolks; same method as above	Good flavor and texture and not as sweet as the recipe above; a bit dense, however
1½ cups granulated sugar, ½ cup water, 1 pound butter, 6 yolks, and 2 whole eggs; same method as above	A very good buttercream, but rich
1¼ cups confectioners' sugar, ¼ pound butter, and ⅞ cup heavy cream; mix ingredients in a food processor for 5 minutes and then beat with an electric mixer for 20 minutes	Okay, but not really a buttercream, and it takes forever to make

WHAT CAN GO WRONG? If the milk mixture gets too hot, it can curdle the egg yolks. Stir frequently and watch the mixture closely.

BUTTERCREAM

To MY SURPRISE, buttercream can be made in many different ways. The most common method is to make a sugar syrup by heating water and sugar to 238 degrees and then whisking this into beaten egg yolks. When the mixture cools, the butter is beaten into it. However, Nick Malgieri, a well-known baker, simply beats egg whites (no yolks are used) and then adds sugar and butter. Julia Child uses a mix of yolks and whole eggs. Another recipe suggests using a food processor to mix confectioners' sugar, butter, and cream for 5 minutes and then whipping the mixture for 20 minutes with an electric mixer. In addition, the amount of sugar varies tremendously, from as much as 3 cups to as little as 1 cup per pound of butter.

After testing all of these approaches, I came to a few conclusions. First, I wanted to avoid making a sugar syrup, a step that requires both extra time and a bit of experience or, at the very least, a good instant-read or candy thermometer. Second, the long cooling time for the beaten yolks bothered me. I wanted a quicker recipe. Finally, I did not want a dense, extremely rich buttercream (of course, all buttercreams are inherently rich), nor did I want a light, fluffy version that would not hold up well over time. That probably meant using whole eggs instead of just yolks or just whites.

I started with the classic approach — using a sugar syrup — and devised a recipe that included 1 cup sugar, ½ cup water, 4 egg yolks, and 12 ounces of softened but cool unsalted butter. Of the classic buttercream preparations I had tasted, I thought that this was the best, but I wondered if I could lighten the mixture and also streamline the process. So I jettisoned the sugar syrup and used whole eggs instead of yolks. The recipe now included 3 whole eggs, 1 cup sugar, and 1 pound butter. As for the method, I placed the eggs and sugar in the bowl of my standing electric mixer and set the bowl over a pan of simmering water. I whisked the mixture frequently until the temperature reached 160 degrees, hot enough to make the eggs safe from bacteria. I then removed the bowl from the heat, attached it to the standing mixer, and beat for about 5 minutes on medium high. At this point, the butter was beaten in, 2 tablespoons at a time. This made a relatively light buttercream and simplified the process as well. I did think, after tasting it, that it was a bit too buttery, so I added 1 more egg and the result was excellent, a smooth, rich texture and a very simple list of ingredients that is easy to multiply for larger quantities.

...

Master Recipe for Not-So-Classic Buttercream

I can't claim that this is a "light" recipe, given the ingredient list, but it does have a lighter texture than classic buttercreams. It also avoids the problem of making a sugar syrup, and the mixture cools down fairly quickly, in about 5 minutes, rather than the usual 20 minutes for most buttercream recipes. Buttercreams can be used with just about any cake, but I particularly like to pair them with sturdier cakes such as chocolate cakes.

MAKES ABOUT 4 CUPS

4   large eggs
1   cup granulated sugar
1   pound unsalted butter, at cool room temperature
⅛   teaspoon salt

1. Place the eggs and sugar in the bowl of your standing electric mixer. Place this bowl over a pan of simmering water to form a double boiler. Whisk frequently but gently, allowing the egg-sugar mixture to warm to 160 degrees. (Use an instant-read or candy thermometer to check the temperature.) Remove from heat and attach bowl to mixer.

2. Beat on medium high until the mixture is very light-colored, very airy, and completely cooled, about 5 minutes. With the mixer on medium speed, add the butter a couple of tablespoons at a time. To finish, add the salt and beat the buttercream on high speed for 1 minute. Use immediately or refrigerate in an airtight container for up to 5 days (after which the fresh butter taste is compromised). If refrigerated, let the buttercream come up to a cool room temperature and rewhip before using.

WHAT CAN GO WRONG? This recipe is best made with a good standing mixer, because it requires a great deal of whipping. The only part that is at all tricky is bringing the egg-sugar mixture up to 160 degrees over simmering water. For this you will need an instant-read or candy thermometer.

CHOCOLATE VARIATION

Make buttercream according to recipe and then add 6 ounces melted and cooled (room temperature) bittersweet or semisweet chocolate, beating mixture until fully incorporated.

WHITE CHOCOLATE VARIATION

Make buttercream according to recipe and then add 6 ounces melted and cooled (room temperature) white chocolate, beating mixture until fully incorporated.

RUM/LIQUOR VARIATION

Make buttercream according to recipe and then add 3 tablespoons rum or liquor, beating mixture until fully incorporated. Try Tia Maria, Kahlúa, and other flavored liquors.

LEMON VARIATION

Make buttercream according to recipe and then add 1 cup Lemon Cake Filling (see page 198), beating mixture until fully incorporated.

RASPBERRY VARIATION

Puree a pint of raspberries in the bowl of a food processor along with ⅓ cup granulated sugar. Taste, and add more sugar if necessary. Strain. Make buttercream according to recipe and then add ¾ cup raspberry puree, beating mixture until fully incorporated.

COFFEE VARIATION

To make the coffee flavoring, dissolve 3 tablespoons instant espresso powder in 3 tablespoons warm water. Make buttercream according to recipe and then add coffee flavoring, beating mixture until fully incorporated.

MOCHA VARIATION

To make the mocha flavoring, mix 4 ounces melted and cooled (room temperature) bittersweet or semisweet chocolate with 1 tablespoon instant espresso powder dissolved in 1 tablespoon warm water. Make buttercream according to recipe and then add mocha flavoring, beating mixture until fully incorporated.

⋮

ICINGS AND GLAZES

Frostings ARE THICK, whereas icings and glazes are relatively thin. They can be as simple as melting chocolate with a bit of butter (Chocolate Veneer, below) or slightly more complicated and thicker, approaching the notion of a frosting (Creamy Chocolate Glaze, page 197). Many glazes, especially those made with copious amounts of confectioners' sugar, look better than they taste, so they should be used sparingly.

•••

Royal Icing

This is a very basic recipe — egg whites are beaten with a large amount of confectioners' sugar. Unfortunately, it tastes bloody awful, due, I assume, to the cornstarch content of the confectioners' sugar. On the bright side, it is easy to make and the consistency is good for piping decorations. But since it is hardly edible, I do not recommend it. (If you have not been deterred by my description, whip 2 egg whites for 30 seconds in the bowl of an electric mixer. Add 3 cups sifted confectioners' sugar and beat until the mixture holds a soft peak. It is best to sift the sugar to avoid lumps, which will clog the nozzle of a pastry bag. This recipe makes about 1½ cups, for decorating only. Never use it as an icing, since it will ruin the cake or cookie with its daunting flavor.)

•••

Chocolate Veneer

The idea of pouring a bit of liquid chocolate over an already frosted cake is not new, but it is simple and effective. Melt 2 ounces of bittersweet or semisweet chocolate with 2 teaspoons of butter in a microwave for 2 minutes on 50 percent power. Stir. If still not melted, heat another minute at 50 percent. When the mixture is cool but still liquid, drizzle over a frosted cake.

•••

Confectioners' Sugar Glaze

This is nothing more than confectioners' sugar with a hint of milk added. If one adds just a bit more liquid to achieve a pourable consistency, it can be used as a glaze for coffee cakes, pound cakes, sticky buns, cookies, and so on. Of course, you do not have to use milk. To flavor this icing, you can use lemon juice, orange juice, wine, rum, liqueurs, and more. See variations below. I should point out that this glaze has the same problem as royal icing. It has a raw flavor due to the confectioners' sugar, so it should be used sparingly.

MAKES ABOUT 1¼ CUPS

3	cups confectioners' sugar, sifted
2 to 4	tablespoons milk

Place the sugar in a medium bowl. Add 2 tablespoons of milk and mix with a whisk or electric mixer until all of the sugar is moistened. Continue adding milk until the icing is smooth and spreadable. For an icing of drizzling consistency, continue adding liquid a teaspoon at a time until the desired consistency is reached. Remember, if you are to drizzle this onto something warm, use just enough milk to make a fairly thick icing, since it will become thinner when it hits a warm surface (drizzle a bit to test the consistency). Use immediately.

LEMON OR ORANGE VARIATION

For this variation, simply substitute lemon juice or orange juice for the milk. A tablespoon of grated zest helps to boost the flavor as well.

LIQUOR VARIATION

Substitute an equal amount of liquor for the milk. (I have found that ½ teaspoon grated orange zest works nicely with a rum variation.)

•••

Creamy Chocolate Glaze

This is a simple glaze to be poured over the cake when it has been placed on a wire rack. It's easier to use than a frosting and provides an elegant, glossy look. Determining when the glaze is ready to be poured over the cake is the only crucial step. To test this, drizzle a spoonful of the glaze back into the pan. When the glaze is ready, it should mound up a little as it touches the glaze in the pan. It's like drizzling honey into honey, although the glaze won't be quite that thick.

MAKES ABOUT 1½ CUPS

8	ounces semisweet chocolate
1	cup heavy cream
¼	cup light corn syrup
½	teaspoon vanilla extract

1. Chop the chocolate into small pieces using a large knife. (You can also chop it in a heavy-duty food processor.)

2. Combine cream and corn syrup in a saucepan. Bring to a simmer. Add chocolate and cook over low heat, stirring constantly. Remove from heat and let stand for 8 minutes. (If chocolate is not completely melted, place mixture back over low heat and stir constantly until melted.)

3. Add vanilla and stir very gently until mixture is smooth.

4. Allow glaze to cool until tepid. Drizzle a spoonful of glaze back into the pan. If it mounds a little, the glaze is ready for pouring over the cake. (You can refrigerate the glaze to speed up the cooling process, but check it every few minutes, stirring the mixture gently. Otherwise it may set up too quickly.)

5. Place cake to be frosted on a wire rack set on a roasting or jelly roll pan to catch the drippings. Pour contents of saucepan over middle of cake. Use a metal spatula if necessary to completely cover cake. Use a small needle to punc-

ture air bubbles in the glaze. Let sit about 1 hour, or until glaze fully sets.

WHAT CAN GO WRONG? Waiting for the glaze to reach the proper consistency before pouring requires a bit of patience. It should mound up as it is drizzled from a spoon back into the bowl. If the mixture is too thin when poured, the glaze will run off the top of the cake and not coat it properly. If too thick, it will not spread out to cover the cake but simply mound up like a frosting.

FILLINGS

One can certainly fill a cake with icing or frosting, but for a special occasion, it is nice to have a different flavor and texture between cake layers. Cake fillings are pretty much a lost art, but cookbooks a century ago offered dozens of fillings such as fig filling, sour cream prune filling, custard filling, rhubarb filling, et cetera.

Lemon Cake Filling

This is similar to the filling I use with lemon meringue pie. The lemon flavor is clear and the filling is not overly sweet.

MAKES ABOUT 2 CUPS

10	tablespoons (½ cup plus 2 tablespoons) granulated sugar
3	tablespoons cornstarch
⅛	teaspoon salt
⅞	cup (1 cup minus 2 tablespoons) cold water
2	large egg yolks
⅓	cup lemon juice
2	teaspoons grated lemon zest
2	tablespoons unsalted butter

1. Whisk the sugar, cornstarch, salt, and water in a 2-quart nonreactive saucepan. Bring mixture to a simmer over medium heat, whisking frequently but gently. When it starts to turn translucent and simmer, add the egg yolks one at a time, whisking gently and slowly after each addition. The filling will be very thick. Next, add the lemon juice and zest and bring the mixture back to a simmer, stirring constantly but very gently. (The filling will thin out a bit after the addition of the lemon juice.)

2. Remove from heat and stir in the butter until it melts. Transfer to another container to cool to room temperature, placing a piece of plastic wrap directly on the surface of the filling to prevent a skin from forming. Refrigerate until the filling is firm. (Can be refrigerated overnight.) To ensure that the filling does not thin out, do not whisk or vigorously stir it once it has set.

WHAT CAN GO WRONG? Cornstarch is a delicate thickener, much more so than flour, although it is also more powerful. Once the filling starts to thicken, stir gently. A heavy hand at this point can damage the structure of the filling, leading to a thinner consistency.

Custard Filling (Pastry Cream)

Pastry cream, which is really just a soft custard, makes an excellent filling for cakes or profiteroles and can be flavored in many different ways. See pages 344–45 for the master recipe and variations.

Fudge Filling

This is a ganache, a simple combination of melted chocolate and cream plus a few other ingredients. The Creamy Chocolate Glaze, earlier in this chapter, is also a ganache, but it is slightly thinner in consistency. This recipe will turn out a thicker product when chilled, which is great for use as a filling. It can, however, also be used as a glaze. Obviously, the success of this recipe depends entirely on the quality of the chocolate being used.

MAKES ABOUT 1¼ CUPS

- ½ cup heavy cream
- 2 tablespoons unsalted butter
- 2 tablespoons light corn syrup
- 8 ounces semisweet or bittersweet chocolate, chopped into ½-inch chunks or smaller
- 2 tablespoons liquor (optional; see variation below)

Bring the cream, butter, and corn syrup to a strong simmer in a small or medium saucepan over low heat. Remove from heat and add the chocolate. Cover and let sit for 5 minutes. Un- cover and add the optional liquor and stir or whisk until smooth. Use immediately for a glaze, or refrigerate until spreadable for a filling.

WHAT CAN GO WRONG? This simple recipe is really a thin glaze, so if you want to make a fill- ing out of it, it needs to cool properly first. This will take some time (as it rests in the refrigera- tor), and you will need to watch it carefully to catch it at the point it is thick but not too thick to spread.

Liquor Variation

Add 2 tablespoons cognac, dark rum, Grand Marnier, framboise, kirsch, Frangelico, amaretto, Kahlúa, Tia Maria, or port.

9

∵

BRIOCHE

AND FRITTERS

The two principal recipes in this chapter, a brioche tart and fruit fritters, are both unusual choices for dessert for American bakers, since most of us have no experience with either dish. Brioche, an extremely buttery French yeast bread, is rolled out and formed into a tart shape, filled with fruit or a custard filling, and then baked until light and puffy. In my testing, I found that most recipes turned out a very dry bread, which is remedied in the recipe on page 203. This is a good recipe to master, since brioche can be used for many nondessert applications as well, especially as a breakfast bread.

Fruit fritters are another dish that usually causes problems. The recipes I tested inevitably turned out a soggy coating. The quest was to find a technique for developing a crispy fritter with a fruit filling that was not overcooked. Once that problem was solved, I had a batter that took just a couple of minutes to prepare, other than the time for heating the oil.

The Brioche Tart is an excellent choice for a holiday dessert, since the recipe is both singular and spectacular. The Crispy Fruit Fritters are a great last-minute recipe that can be made quickly with common pantry staples plus 2 or 3 apples or bananas.

∵

BRIOCHE

THIS IS NO BREAD BOOK, but the French do know a thing or two about making desserts using their classic yeast bread brioche. Its distinguishing characteristic — what sets it apart from any other bread — is the huge amount of butter incorporated into the dough, making it soft and incomparably sumptuous. It is a puffy, pillowy bread, soft and moist at its best, the perfect partner for a simple sauce or ripe fruit. Having made quite a few brioche recipes over the years, however, I have found that they are often on the dry side and sometimes not quite as tender as I would like. So my first step in developing a master brioche dough recipe was to review a number of recipes and perform a few side-by-side tests.

The first thing I learned from the tests was that milk is crucial for a tender dough: the two

CASE 38: WHO PUT THE BUTTER IN BRIOCHE?

Seven brioche recipes were tested and compared to find the best way to make a rich, buttery brioche.

Ingredient	Recipe A	Recipe B	Recipe C	Recipe D	Recipe E	Recipe F	Recipe G
Yeast	2¼ teaspoons	2½ teaspoons	2½ teaspoons	5 teaspoons	2½ teaspoons	2½ teaspoons	1½ teaspoons
Flour	3½ cups	3½ cups	4½ cups	5½ cups	2¾ cups	2¼ cups	1½ cups
Sugar	⅓ cup	⅓ cup	¼ cup	½ cup	3 tablespoons	3 tablespoons	3 tablespoons
Salt	1 teaspoon	1½ teaspoons	2 teaspoons	1½ teaspoons	1 teaspoon	½ teaspoon	½ teaspoon
Eggs	5	4	6	4 yolks, 1 white	3	2	3
Butter	12 tablespoons	12 tablespoons	16 tablespoons	11 tablespoons	12 tablespoons	6 tablespoons	8 tablespoons
Milk	⅓ cup	⅓ cup	None	1 cup	⅓ cup	½ cup	None
Water	None	3 tablespoons	½ cup	None	None	None	2½ tablespoons

recipes that used water instead of milk were significantly tougher. Second, one recipe used an initial sponge (a mixture of flour, water, and a small amount of yeast is allowed to sit for hours in order to develop flavor), and although the brioche was quite good, other recipes without this extra step were equally delicious. Finally, the higher levels of butter and eggs delivered the richness I expected in a brioche. A second-rate brioche is dry and tough, and eggs and butter are important ingredients for adding moisture and tenderness.

The next step was to cobble together a work-

ing recipe based on the two test winners. I was now using ⅓ cup milk, 1 package (2½ teaspoons) active dry yeast, 3½ cups flour, ⅓ cup sugar, 1 teaspoon salt, 5 large eggs, and 12 tablespoons butter. The process was time-consuming but relatively easy. First I heated the milk until warm (about 100 degrees) and then sprinkled on the yeast. (There is no need to proof yeast these days as long as the expiration date has not been reached, but this step does kick-start the yeast, which saves a little time later on.) Next I put the flour, sugar, and salt into the bowl of an electric mixer fitted with a dough hook and added the milk-yeast mixture and the eggs. The ingredients were mixed on low until they came together into a rough dough and then beaten on medium speed for about 10 minutes. I added the butter, cut into large chunks, with the mixer on low and beat until the dough was smooth and very soft, about 5 minutes. The dough was formed into a ball, placed in a buttered bowl, and let rise until about 1½ times the original size. I then gently punched down the dough and placed it into the refrigerator for at least 4 hours, or until it was puffed but quite firm. (Further testing proved that an overnight rest in the refrigerator worked very well.) Now it was shaped, allowed to proof (i.e., rise) for about 45 minutes, and then baked off.

My first test was the flour. I tried using bread flour, but the resulting brioche was too tough. I then added some acid (lemon juice) to the dough — a common baker's trick to tenderize dough — but the unbleached all-purpose flour version was still better. Cake flour produced a crumbly, tight bread, and bleached all-purpose flour produced a brioche that was lacking in flavor. Next I tried using 1 cup bread flour to 2½ cups all-purpose, and the brioche was still tough. Finally, I combined 1 cup cake flour with 2½ cups all-purpose, and the texture of that brioche was not quite as open and light as the brioche using only all-purpose. Many brioches later, I came back to the original recipe, settling on 3½ cups unbleached all-purpose flour.

The next ingredient I tested was the yeast. I wanted to try making brioche using rapid-rise yeast in order to speed up the proofing time. This turned out to be a dead end, since the dough has to sit a long time in the refrigerator anyway to firm up the butter. In addition, I found the brioche made with rapid-rise yeast to be lacking in flavor. This is one dough that does need to rise slowly to develop flavor. I then tested to determine the proper yeast level, using regular active dry yeast. Two teaspoons was not quite enough and 3 teaspoons made the dough too active — so 2½ teaspoons was just right.

Eggs were next on the list. Brioche made with 5 eggs was very good, but 6 eggs produced a wet popover, not a brioche. Four whole eggs and 2 yolks was not substantially different than the simpler 5 whole eggs, so I left it at that. The sugar level was fine, but I did increase the salt to 1½ teaspoons. Finally I worked with the butter. Although most brioche recipes use 1½ sticks (12 tablespoons) butter per 3½ cups flour, I found the resulting bread to be on the dry side. I increased the butter to a full 2 sticks and was pleased with the results. The brioche browned nicely, it was moist and rich, and the taste was also improved. I then tried 2½ sticks, but the dough was impossible to handle, becoming so soft and floppy that I could not work with it.

Reviewing the recipe, I was hoping to find a way to make it simpler. The dough was to be proofed for a couple of hours and then chilled for at least 4 hours, shaped and allowed to rise again for 45 minutes, and then baked. Was there a simpler method? I tried to eliminate the first rise entirely, simply putting the dough into the refrigerator as soon as it was kneaded, but this did not save very much time. I was successful, however, when I tried shaping the dough and then letting it sit in the refrigerator overnight. After a brief rise the dough can then be baked off first thing in the morning. This works well for a breakfast loaf but is of no benefit for cooks using this recipe for a tart base. So in the end, the method stood as is. It is time-consuming but worth the wait for a special dessert.

One final note. This bread dough really cannot be kneaded by hand. You will need a strong electric mixer with a dough hook. I finally settled on a two-step method. The dough is kneaded for 10 minutes, then the cool butter is added and the dough is kneaded for an additional 5 minutes. Make sure that the butter is no warmer than 65 to 67 degrees, since the dough will become oily instead of soft and smooth.

...

Moist, Buttery Brioche Dough

To make this recipe, you will need a sturdy standing mixer with a dough hook. Although this recipe is simple enough to make, it will take all day, since the dough must sit in the refrigerator in order for the butter to firm up. If you start in the morning, you can have the dough ready to go by dinnertime. It is very important that the butter be cool but pliable. Warm, room temperature butter will produce an oily, droopy dough. This recipe makes enough dough for two 10-inch tarts. I always make a full recipe, since it takes no more effort and the extra can be baked off for breakfast (see Brioche Loaf, below).

MAKES ENOUGH DOUGH FOR TWO 10-INCH TARTS

⅓	cup whole milk
2½	teaspoons active dry yeast (1 envelope)
3½	cups all-purpose flour
⅓	cup granulated sugar
1½	teaspoons salt
5	large eggs
½	pound (2 sticks) unsalted butter, softened but still cool

1. Heat the milk in a small saucepan over low heat to 110 degrees but no hotter. Remove pan from heat, sprinkle the yeast over the milk, and let sit for 10 minutes. During that time the yeast will foam across the top of the milk. Meanwhile, combine the flour, sugar, and salt in the bowl of an electric mixer fitted with the dough hook.

2. Add the milk-yeast mixture to the flour mixture along with the 5 eggs. Mix on low until the ingredients come together to form a rough dough. Increase the speed to medium and mix (knead) for 10 minutes. After the first few minutes the sides of the bowl should be fairly clean and the bulk of the dough should be wrapped onto the hook, whacking the side of the bowl as it spins around. After 10 minutes the dough will look smooth but be quite stiff.

3. With the mixer on very low, add the butter in chunks (a couple of tablespoons each). The dough will now look very scrappy as it tries to incorporate the butter. Once it comes together again, increase mixer speed to medium and mix for at least 5 additional minutes, or until the dough is smooth, wet, and droopy. The dough will slap against the side of the bowl as it is being kneaded. Form the dough into a ball with your hands and place in a large buttered bowl. Cover bowl with plastic wrap and let dough sit at room temperature for about 2 hours, or until it increases in volume by 50 percent.

4. Very gently press down on the dough to deflate. Cover bowl with plastic wrap and refrigerate dough for 4 to 12 hours, or until it is quite stiff and slightly puffy. It is now ready to shape, proof, and bake. (See recipes below for instructions on using the dough.)

WHAT CAN GO WRONG? The proofing time may vary quite a bit, depending on the temperature in your kitchen. Also be sure to use very cool butter that is firm but pliable, about 65 to 67 degrees. Room temperature butter will ruin the dough. Finally, this is one recipe for which a high-quality standing mixer is a must. Don't try it with a cheap machine that doesn't have much horsepower.

BRIOCHE LOAF

If you make a whole brioche recipe and use only half of it for a tart, here is an easy way to use up the other half.

MAKES 1 LOAF

½ recipe Moist, Buttery Brioche Dough

1. Butter a standard loaf pan. After the full recipe of dough has risen the first time (step 3), punch it down and cut it in half, reserving one half for the tart. On a very lightly floured surface, gently press the other half of dough into a rectangle, about the length of the loaf pan. Roll up the dough from the long side nearest you

and pinch together the seam. Place dough in pan, seam side down. Press dough into pan so that it touches all four sides. Cover pan with plastic wrap and place in refrigerator overnight, or for at least 4 hours.

2. Remove pan from refrigerator, loosen plastic wrap, and place pan in a warm spot in the kitchen. Let dough rise for about an hour, or until it has doubled in size. (The time will vary; this may take as much as 2 hours if dough is in a cool place.)

3. Meanwhile, adjust oven rack to middle position and heat oven to 375 degrees. Place loaf pan in oven and bake about 30 minutes (turn halfway through baking), or until the top of the loaf is dark brown and the internal temperature measures about 185 degrees with an instant-read thermometer. Due to the high butter content, brioche loaves will turn very dark as they bake.

▪▪▪

Master Recipe for Brioche Tart

This recipe is nothing new, but it does make a spectacular dessert. You can fill the tart with fruit or with a custard sauce. The trick is shaping the tart itself. The dough is rolled out, edged, allowed to rise for about half an hour, and then baked. After much testing, I uncovered a few secrets.

First, it is best to roll out this dough to a diameter of 14 inches. This will take some work but is worth it. You want a wide circle so that you have plenty of dough to form the edges. If the edges are not high enough, a custard sauce, for example, will leak out. Second, brush the perimeter of the dough with a simple egg wash before forming the edges. This ensures that the dough will stick to itself as you fold it over and will not come apart. Finally, I found it best to contain the dough with the outer ring of a 10-inch springform pan. This helps the tart to keep its shape as it bakes.

MAKES ONE 10-INCH TART

½ recipe Moist, Buttery Brioche Dough (page 203)
1 lightly beaten egg
1 recipe filling (see variations below)

1. Place the chilled brioche dough on a lightly floured surface and roll into a circle 14 inches in diameter. Transfer to a cookie sheet. Brush the outer 2 inches with the beaten egg (refrigerate leftover egg wash for step 2) and then fold this 2-inch border back toward the middle to form an edge. (I work counterclockwise around the circle of dough, slightly overlapping the previous fold.) Now fold the edge in half, so that the border is approximately 1 inch in width. Place the unlocked outer ring from a 10-inch springform pan around the circle of dough and then lock in place. Press the edges of the tart back against the metal ring in order to give them more height. Cover loosely with plastic and let sit in a warm place 30 to 45 minutes, or until the dough looks swollen.

2. Set oven rack in middle position and heat oven to 350 degrees. Press down the center of the dough with your fingers to flatten. (Do not touch the edging.) Brush the edge with remaining beaten egg. Add the filling and bake for 20 to 25 minutes, or until edges are very brown. Let cool for 30 minutes before serving.

CUSTARD VARIATION

This custard filling is simply poured into the tart before it is baked.

1 cup heavy cream
1 tablespoon sour cream (optional)
1 large egg
¼ cup granulated sugar
1 tablespoon cornstarch
½ teaspoon vanilla extract
Small pinch (about ¹⁄₁₆ teaspoon) salt

Whisk all of the ingredients together in a medium bowl. Pour into the tart just before baking. Bake 20 to 25 minutes, or until the custard is just set and still wiggles when shaken. Let cool for 30 minutes before serving.

WHAT CAN GO WRONG? A lot. The dough can rise up and push the custard out of the center and onto the bottom of your oven! That is why it is crucial to use the springform pan ring for this recipe, to form a high edge, and to press down the center of the tart before adding the filling.

CARAMELIZED APPLE VARIATION

This is a simple, year-round variation. I simply cook a few apples in butter, sugar, lemon juice, and brandy until they turn nicely brown and the juices caramelize. I prefer to use a juicy apple here, such as Macoun, Cortland, Winesap, Rhode Island Greening, and so on. Stay away from Granny Smith and Golden Delicious, since they will exude few juices, and also McIntosh, which will cook down to applesauce.

3 large apples
1 tablespoon lemon juice
3 tablespoons butter
3 tablespoons granulated sugar
1 tablespoon brandy or cognac

Peel, core, and slice apples into 12 slices each and toss with lemon juice. Heat butter in a sauté pan and when melted add apple slices. Sprinkle with sugar and brandy and sauté until soft and nicely browned, about 10 minutes on medium high. Place filling in brioche tart and bake as directed in master recipe. This variation can be served as is, with whipped cream, or with the white wine zabaglione below.

FRUIT WITH WHITE WINE ZABAGLIONE VARIATION

This recipe does have to be made at the last minute, but the warm sauce with the fresh fruit and warm brioche is divine. Note that the tart shell itself is baked without a filling (bake it 20 to 25 minutes). The fresh berries are added just before serving.

5 large egg yolks
5 tablespoons granulated sugar
5 tablespoons white wine or champagne
2 cups ripe berries, washed

Whisk the egg yolks in the top of a double boiler over low heat. Add the sugar and whisk to combine. Add the wine and whisk to combine. Whisking constantly, cook the mixture until thick and foamy and the consistency of homemade mayonnaise, about 10 minutes. If the zabaglione starts to curdle, remove from heat and whisk vigorously. Fill the baked, warm brioche tart with the fresh fruit and serve with the warm zabaglione sauce.

FRUIT FRITTERS

A FRUIT FRITTER IS merely fruit coated with a simple batter and fried. The problem? Well, every recipe that I tried stayed crispy for only 30 seconds or so. I also found that the fruit inside almost always became very mushy and unappealing after frying in the hot oil. So the goal was to develop a stay-crisp fritter with lively, perfectly cooked fruit.

There are three approaches to fritters. Batters can be made with whipped egg whites, with beer or wine, or with egg yolks, similar to a French choux paste. When tested, the first two batters were very foamy and light, but after they were fried they immediately became soggy and horrible. The choux paste approach, with egg yolks, produced fritters that were shiny and puffy, much like chicken fingers from third-rate Chinese restaurants. The use of milk in the batter resulted in a coating that became soggy.

I went back to the drawing board and decided to start with a simple batter made from equal parts flour and water. This produced a tough, cardboard casing. Next I tried using a bit of salt and sugar and working butter into the flour to make the coating more flavorful and tender. This did improve the flavor, but the texture was still tough. I finally hit upon the solution when I added baking powder. This gave the fritters a light, crispy texture, which remained even after they had been on a rack for several minutes. The addition of lemon juice brightened the flavor a bit. I substituted ½ cup milk for the same amount of water and once again found that the fritters turned out soft rather than crispy.

Finally, the oil temperature turned out to be critical. All of the recipes I found suggested 350 degrees as the ideal temperature, but the fritters always turned out soggy. I then tried much higher temperatures and settled on 390 degrees. The fritters were perfect — the outside was crisp and the fruit inside was cooked but not soggy.

▪ ▪ ▪

Crispy Fruit Fritters

Unlike the other recipes I tested, these fritters stay crispy for a few minutes after frying. Be sure to use very hot oil, about 390 degrees; otherwise the fritters will quickly turn soggy. For the ideal fritter, the oil should be hot enough so that the fritters cook in just 1 minute. It is best to serve these fritters as soon as they are cool enough to eat, about 5 minutes after frying.

SERVES 8

1   quart canola oil
1   cup all-purpose flour
1   tablespoon granulated sugar
1   teaspoon baking powder
½   teaspoon salt
1   tablespoon unsalted butter, at room
    temperature
1   cup water
1   teaspoon lemon juice
5   cups bananas, apples, or pineapples cut
    into ½-inch slices
Confectioners' sugar or granulated sugar for
    dusting (optional)

1. Heat the oil in a large heavy pot (cast iron preferred) over medium heat for about 7 minutes, or until it reaches 390 degrees on a candy thermometer. (If you do not have a candy thermometer, you can experiment with one fritter at a time until the fritter cooks to a dark golden brown in 60 seconds.) Have a cooling rack set into a jelly roll pan near the pot of oil.

2. Place the flour, sugar, baking powder, and salt in a medium bowl and stir to combine. Add the butter and rub it into the flour mixture until it is fully combined and no traces of butter remain. Combine the water and lemon juice and add to the flour mixture. Whisk to a smooth batter.

3. Place 2 to 3 pieces of fruit at a time into the batter. Turn with a fork to be sure all sides are coated and then, using the fork, add them one at a time to the hot oil. They should immediately bubble wildly and start to brown. After 30 seconds or so, turn them over. If they will not turn (sometimes an air pocket prevents them from turning over), use a spoon to carefully baste the top of the fritters to ensure even browning. Cook each fritter until it is dark golden brown and then remove with a slotted spoon onto the cooling rack. Let cool for about 5 minutes before serving. Repeat with the remaining fruit. Sprinkle with confectioners' sugar or roll in granulated sugar if desired.

WHAT CAN GO WRONG? The batter itself is a snap to make, so the only potential problem is the temperature of the oil. It needs to be very hot, about 390 degrees, for the fritters to cook properly and turn out crispy. I suggest placing a frying or candy thermometer in the oil, attached to the side of the pot, so that you can monitor the temperature as you cook. You will probably have to adjust the heat level as you fry.

10

P I E S

Anyone who has ever made a pie knows the problem. In a word, it's the crust. It can be tough, short, dry, wet, crackly, and bubbly. It can shrink so much that there is hardly any room for filling. It can be hard to roll out, the dough so dry that it is impossible to keep together on the work surface. It can be so sticky that no matter how much flour you put on the dough, it still ends up sticking to the rolling pin.

The problem with cookbook writers and food experts is that they sometimes know too much. They instinctively know when the butter has been cut into the flour enough. They know if a dough has the right amount of moisture just by rubbing it between their fingers. Then, forgetting that most home cooks are not armed with all of this experience, they go off on long diatribes about the benefits of pastry flour over all-purpose. They also give you a dozen different recipes including pâte brisée, pâte sucrée, flaky crust, extra-flaky crust, sour cream crust, cream cheese crust, you name it. What most of us really need is a foolproof recipe, a method of preparing pie pastry dough that is simple and reliable.

IN SEARCH OF FOOLPROOF PIECRUST

To THIS END, I set out on a very long journey, making as many pie dough recipes as I could get my hands on. I made several recipes from Rose Levy Beranbaum's *Pie and Pastry Bible* and then sampled recipes from Carole Walter's *Great Pies and Tarts* as well as from *James Beard's American Cookery.*

In *The Pie and Pastry Bible,* Rose Beranbaum uses a unique method for many of her doughs, which is to freeze the flour and some or all of the butter (which has been cut into small pieces). She then uses a food processor to combine them, adding water and vinegar (for tenderizing the pastry) during the processing. The dough is placed into a 1-gallon plastic bag, kneaded briefly, and then shaped into a disk and refrigerated. In her Deluxe Flaky Pie Crust, the butter is frozen but left in larger pieces, which can be problematic, since if the butter is not worked into the dough sufficiently, the dough will be tough and crackly. I then made her Pâte Brisée, a classic French pastry that is similar to an American pie pastry except that it includes an egg. She makes this dough by hand, without a food processor, and this turned out to be the flakiest crust of them all. I thought that this dough would be good for prebaked pie shells or for tarts, for which shrinking is often a problem. I then made the Pâte Sucrée, another French classic, which uses flour, butter, ¼ cup sugar, an egg yolk, and a bit of heavy cream. The result was a very short, sweet, cookielike crust that was delicious. The downside was that the very soft, fragile dough was hard to roll out. I would not suggest this dough for a beginner. Finally, I tested the Cream Cheese Pie Crust, which is similar to the basic flaky crust but includes cream cheese. It made a very smooth dough that was easy to roll out. When baked, it was flaky and tender, but I could taste the vinegar in this dough.

I then moved on to *Great Pies and Tarts*, by Carole Walter, and tried her Flaky Pie Pastry I, in which she uses half butter and half vegetable shortening (Crisco). The proportion of fat to flour (for 1¼ cups flour, the amount used for a one-crust pie, she uses 4 tablespoons butter and 4 tablespoons Cricso) was about right, although perhaps a bit on the lean side, especially for beginners. She suggests making the pastry by hand using a pastry blender. It is a good, straightforward recipe, with the caveat that many home cooks may not have or are not adept at using a pastry blender. However, the pastry turned out well and was light and flaky. James Beard, in *American Cookery*, uses either all vegetable shortening or a combination of butter and vegetable shortening (½ cup shortening to ⅓ cup butter for 2 cups of flour). I made the dough by hand as instructed and it worked well, although the amount of fat was excessive. I would opt for a slightly lower percentage of fat to flour.

After all of this testing, I came to a few general conclusions. First, more emphasis should be placed on how easy a pie dough is to roll out and fit into a pie pan than on how flaky it is.

Many doughs are very hard to work with because they are crumbly or too sticky. Next, the recipe ingredients ought to consist of simple pantry items. I have little patience for recipes that call for special flours—or for ingredients that don't measurably affect the final result, such as baking powder or vinegar. Third, the process of making the dough ought to be as simple as possible, without jumping through hoops. I don't want to have to go through ten steps to make a simple pie pastry. (Do we really need to freeze the flour?) Finally, the cook should have the option of making the dough by hand or using a food processor.

Then I looked at specific variables in terms of ingredients and technique, performed many tests, and came to the following conclusions:

- Butter Versus Vegetable Shortening (Crisco): Butter adds flavor and vegetable shortening makes a piecrust flaky. I tested this head-to-head and found it to be true. One reason that vegetable shortening is relatively foolproof is that it is stable and will not change texture under different conditions. If butter gets too warm, it will melt, which is disastrous, since the dough will turn soft and sticky. Vegetable shortening always maintains the same texture, even on a hot day. An experienced baker can make an all-butter crust, but most of us are advised to use at least some Crisco in our crust to ensure success. Although I personally prefer more butter than Crisco, I thought that equal proportions of the two types of shortening might be best for a foolproof recipe. It may lack a bit of flavor, but an easy-to-make, workable dough was more important.
- Refrigerating Versus Freezing: I have found over the years that refrigerated butter turns soft rather quickly when it is cut into pieces to be used in pie pastry. For this reason, I felt that Rose Beranbaum's freezer method was a very good idea, although I ended up reducing the freezing time to 15 minutes, which was fine.

- Pastry Flour Versus All-Purpose Flour: The notion of special flours (pastry flour, bleached all-purpose) for pie doughs makes little sense to me. There is not a great difference in the final product and, since most people have only all-purpose at home, I see no point in using anything else. (I tested Beranbaum's Basic Flaky Pie Crust with all-purpose flour instead of the pastry flour called for in the recipe. It was slightly less tender than the pastry flour variation but still very good; the difference would not be noticeable unless the crusts were sampled side by side.) I have also tested bleached flour versus unbleached and prefer the latter for flavor; bleached flour does produce a light, delicate pie pastry, albeit with a metallic aftertaste.

- The Question of Vinegar: Many cooks claim that the acid in vinegar helps to prevent the gluten in the flour from toughening. I tested this head-to-head and found that the pastry was slightly lighter, although the improvement was marginal. The ratio of fat to flour and one's skill in cutting the fat into the flour are much more important than adding vinegar. The big drawback with vinegar is that it leads to rapid browning of the pie pastry, which is a serious problem. This means that the edges of the crust need to be covered, which is extra work. I say forget the vinegar and make life simple.

- What About Baking Powder? This is another ingredient often thrown into pie pastry doughs. I made two pies, one with baking powder and one without, and found that it makes little difference.

- Is Sugar Necessary? Yes. Without any sugar, I find, pie pastry is dull-tasting. Sugar brings out flavors and makes the pastry more lively.

- When Should the Water Be Added? It was very clear to me after the testing that liquid should *never* be added to pie dough while it is in a food processor. You never know how much you will need, which can easily lead to overprocessing. Use a food processor for cut-

ting in the shortening, but remove the dough to a bowl before adding the liquid.

- How Much Water Should Be Added? *The single biggest mistake home cooks make is to not add enough water to the dough.* Cookbook authors who warn about excessive water are doing a great disservice. Their fear is that a wet dough will be tougher. Although I have found only small variations in tenderness based on water content, the more important issue is whether one can roll out the dough in the first place. Besides, a wet dough can be fixed easily by adding a bit more flour. A dry dough is a disaster; it cannot be rolled out. (This is the major complaint I had with many of Beranbaum's recipes.) So add sufficient water to allow you to easily press the dough into a ball. Even if the dough is a bit sticky, that's okay. Simply sprinkle a bit of flour on it before shaping it into a disk. Oh, and consider the amount of water called for in a recipe as only a rough guide, since the actual amount you need will almost always vary due to the condition of the flour, how well you cut the butter or Crisco into the flour, and a number of other factors.

- Eggs and Egg Yolks: A basic American pie dough really does not need an egg, which produces a somewhat sturdier dough. However, I did test this sort of dough for a tart shell that requires prebaking, since one needs a dough that is unlikely to shrink very much. (See next chapter.)

- What About Lard? Most older American pie pastry recipes call for lard. When I tried using today's supermarket lard, I found that the crust tasted like bacon; it was harsh and unpleasant. Knowing, however, that lard 100 years ago was quite a different product, I called a friend of mine who is a farmer in Connecticut. He gave me a large quantity of leaf lard, which is what bakers used to use. (Leaf lard is the fat around the kidneys in a pig. Today's lard is an inferior product and comes from all over the animal.) I tried a pie pastry with it and loved it. It does have a

CASE 39: PIES IN THE SKY

Perfecting a foolproof recipe for American pie dough.

The Test	Rolling Dough	Texture When Baked
Butter not frozen	Okay	Good; a little heavy
Pulse Crisco before frozen butter	Okay	Good
Pulse frozen butter before Crisco	Okay	Good; a little heavy
Pulse frozen butter and Crisco together	Okay	Very good, very flaky
Reduce Crisco to 4 tablespoons	Okay	Not quite as flaky
Use softened butter	Hard to roll out	Too short and soft
Use 6 tablespoons Crisco and 4 tablespoons butter; pulse Crisco first for 5 seconds	Dough falls apart	Short and light, much like a cookie crust
Add ½ teaspoon vinegar	Okay	Crust browns too fast
Add 2 tablespoons sour cream	Falls apart a bit	Heavier than basic recipe
Use milk instead of water	Very crumbly	Very short crust
Use leaf lard	Okay	Good flaky crust; slight bacon flavor
Use ¼ cup cream cheese	Easy to roll out	Not flaky but soft
Pulse 12 times instead of usual 8	Okay	Short crust

slight savory flavor with just a hint of bacon, but the pastry was light and flaky. I would use leaf lard with any sort of savory pie, such as chicken pot pie, and I might also use it for something sturdy such as apple pie. But if you can't get good leaf lard, as most people cannot, forget it.

FOOLPROOF AMERICAN PIE DOUGH

ALL OF THIS DETECTIVE WORK led to a simple recipe. Using 1¼ cups of flour as the basic

PREPARING BUTTER FOR PIE DOUGH: Quarter the butter lengthwise and then cut across the stick into small pieces.

spoons ice water. This is a heavy ratio of fat to flour, but it makes the recipe relatively foolproof. I also wanted a master recipe that used a food processor, since making a pie pastry by hand takes some experience. I now performed a series of tests to settle on a final recipe. The tests and my observations are summarized in Case 39.

So now I had it. The butter is cut into small pieces and then frozen for 15 minutes. The Crisco and frozen butter are added to the flour, salt, and sugar at the same time and then pulsed 8 times. This step is crucial, and a keen eye is helpful here. Since everyone has a different idea about how long a "pulse" is, one really needs to keep an eye on the dough mixture. It is not done if the mixture appears powdery and white. On the other hand, if overprocessed, the dough will become wet and sticky. The perfect dough will start to look mealy and take on a slightly yellowish cast from the butter. Yet there should be

amount for a one-crust pie, I used ½ teaspoon salt, 2 tablespoons sugar, 5 tablespoons chilled Crisco or other vegetable shortening, 5 tablespoons chilled unsalted butter, and 4 to 5 table-

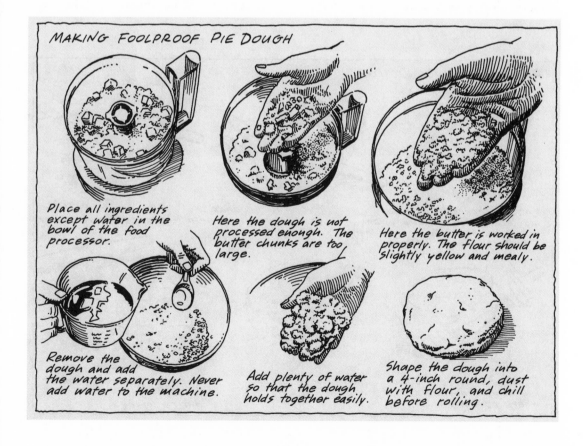

MAKING FOOLPROOF PIE DOUGH

Place all ingredients except water in the bowl of the food processor.

Here the dough is not processed enough. The butter chunks are too large.

Here the butter is worked in properly. The flour should be slightly yellow and mealy.

Remove the dough and add the water separately. Never add water to the machine.

Add plenty of water so that the dough holds together easily.

Shape the dough into a 4-inch round, dust with flour, and chill before rolling.

small pieces of butter still in the mixture. These are usually referred to as "pea-size" pieces, but I find that the texture of the flour mixture is more important than the size of the butter pieces. When it starts to get a bit heavier and more yellow, losing its light, floury texture, then it is done. Another good tip is that the dough should almost appear pebbly — not clumpy, and not light and powdery.

I then take the pastry dough out of the food processor, place it in a bowl, and slowly add the water. I have found that the best method for incorporating the water is to use a large rubber spatula. You want to keep your hot little hands off the dough; otherwise it will start to get soft, resulting in a very short, cookielike crust. It is also good to not rush this step, since it takes a while for the water to be distributed evenly throughout the dough. Always start with half the water called for in the recipe and then add water as you go. Also be aware that the amount of water will vary somewhat, depending on the

condition of the flour and the humidity of the kitchen. Never follow a pie pastry recipe blindly in this regard. Use just enough water so that the dough will come together in a ball. Don't short-change yourself, however. A dry dough will be very difficult if not impossible to roll out.

Finally, I find that a light dusting of flour is helpful. I put the ball of dough onto a lightly floured surface and shape it into a disk. I flour the top very lightly and then place it in a plastic bag and let it sit in the refrigerator for about an hour. If the dough has been left overnight in the refrigerator, it will need to warm up a bit before you roll it out. Otherwise it will be difficult to work. As for rolling out the dough, here are some tips:

- I prefer a thin, tapered rolling pin for rolling out circles of dough. It gives you a better feel for the dough and makes it easier not to overwork it.
- The basic method for rolling a circle of dough is to roll a quarter circle of the dough

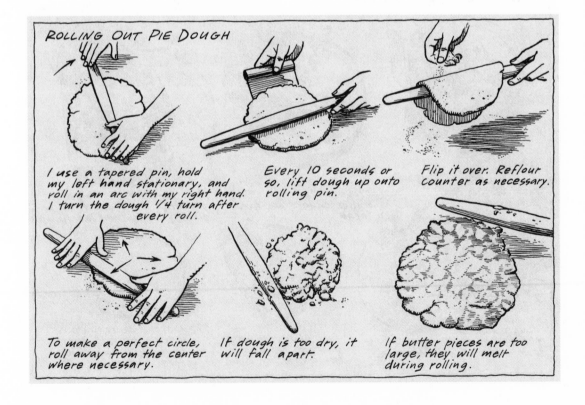

ROLLING OUT PIE DOUGH

I use a tapered pin, hold my left hand stationary, and roll in an arc with my right hand. I turn the dough 1/4 turn after every roll.

Every 10 seconds or so, lift dough up onto rolling pin.

Flip it over. Reflour counter as necessary.

To make a perfect circle, roll away from the center where necessary.

If dough is too dry, it will fall apart.

If butter pieces are too large, they will melt during rolling.

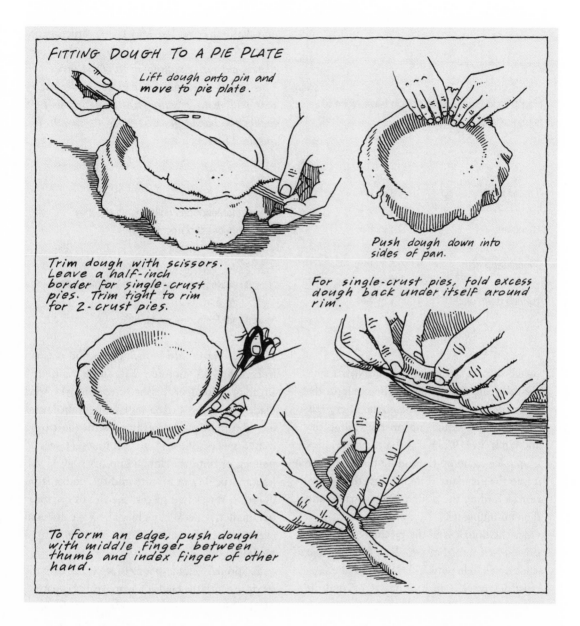

FITTING DOUGH TO A PIE PLATE

Lift dough onto pin and move to pie plate.

Push dough down into sides of pan.

Trim dough with scissors. Leave a half-inch border for single-crust pies. Trim tight to rim for 2-crust pies.

For single-crust pies, fold excess dough back under itself around rim.

To form an edge, push dough with middle finger between thumb and index finger of other hand.

toward you, with your left hand stationary on the pin and the right hand rolling the pin toward you.

- After every roll, move the dough a quarter turn counterclockwise. This will prevent the dough from sticking to the work surface. This also means that the basic rolling motion is always exactly the same, which makes it easy to control.
- After every few rolls, the dough will need to be picked up onto the rolling pin and turned over; this will also allow you to reflour the work surface if need be. Use a bench knife, also called a pastry scraper, and flip the dough up onto the pin. The dough will be draped over the pin. It can then be unrolled easily, the former top side now being the bottom.
- Use the dough scraper to even out the edges of the round of dough as you work.
- When the circle of dough is about 7 or 8 inches wide, it is becoming too thin to rotate without lifting it off the work surface. I now

CASE 40: DOES SIZE MATTER?

How big does rolled-out dough have to be to fit into different pie plates?

Pie Plate Diameter	Dough Diameter
9 inches	13 inches
10 inches	14 inches
9-inch deep dish	14 inches
10-inch deep dish	15 inches

switch over to another method. Now I simply roll from the middle of the circle to the outer edges to even up the circle. Every few rolls, pick the dough up on the rolling pin and flip it over. When it is the right size, pick it up once again on the rolling pin and place it into the pie plate. (I find this method superior to folding the dough into quarters and then unfolding it.)

- Once the dough is in the pie plate, push the sides down into the pan. This is important since it will help reduce shrinkage. For a one-crust pie, leave ½ inch of pastry beyond the rim of the pan. For a two-crust pie, cut it even with the edge of the pie pan. I find that scissors work best for this.

•••

Master Recipe for Foolproof Food Processor Pie Dough

A combination of butter and lard (or in this case Crisco) is nothing new. I have found recipes that are 100 years old which suggest using this pairing. Having tested this extensively, I know that butter provides a great deal of flavor and the Crisco yields a flaky pastry. Freezing the butter for 15 minutes stops it from being completely cut into the flour in the food processor. This leaves small pieces of butter in the pastry that will melt, creating steam, which in turn makes the baked piecrust flaky. Be sure to use unsalted butter.

MAKES PASTRY FOR A SINGLE-CRUST
8- OR 9-INCH PIE

5	tablespoons cold unsalted butter
1¼	cups all-purpose flour
½	teaspoon salt
2	tablespoons granulated sugar
5	tablespoons cold all-vegetable shortening (e.g., Crisco)
4 to 5	tablespoons ice water

1. Cut butter into ¾-inch pieces and place in freezer for 15 minutes. Mix flour, salt, and sugar in a food processor fitted with the steel blade. Place the Crisco in 1-tablespoon lumps into the food processor along with the frozen butter pieces. Pulse 8 to 12 times (1-second pulses), or until the dough appears slightly yellow and pebbly in texture and the butter is reduced to very small pieces, the size of tiny peas or smaller. Check dough after 5 pulses and every pulse thereafter. Turn mixture into a medium bowl.

2. Sprinkle 3 tablespoons of ice water over the mixture. With the blade of a large rubber spatula, use a folding motion to mix, then press down on dough with the broad side of the spatula until the dough sticks together, adding up to 2 tablespoons more water if dough will not come together. Work slowly, mixing the dough to evenly distribute the water. This should take about 1 minute. The dough should be very wet and sticky at this point. *It is better to add too much water than too little.* Shape dough into a ball with your hands, turn onto a lightly floured surface, and flatten into a 4-inch-wide disk. Dust very lightly with flour, wrap in plastic, and refrigerate for at least 30 minutes before rolling.

THE GREAT CRISCO VS. BUTTER DEBATE

Crisco (vegetable shortening) is hydrogenated vegetable oil — hydrogen atoms are pumped into vegetable oils — which is a solid, stable product even at room temperature. This process creates a relatively unhealthy saturated fat, but the good news is that it works wonders with pie dough. (As for the health issues, Americans consume very little vegetable shortening through home cooking, so I doubt this is much of an issue. However, it is used extensively in convenience foods, which is where the lion's share of our consumption occurs.) The reason I like to use both Crisco and butter is that the Crisco does a good job of coating the flour, which makes the dough flaky and tender, while the butter adds flavor. Unlike butter, Crisco will hold its shape even in hot conditions, which makes the dough almost foolproof, immune to overworking. Butter, of course, has lots of flavor, while an all-Crisco crust will be disappointing in terms of taste. Experienced bakers use only butter, but I find that most home cooks (myself included) are better off using a 50-50 combination of Crisco and butter.

WHAT CAN GO WRONG? The first mistake many people make is not cutting the butter and Crisco into the flour enough. Make sure that the flour is coated properly. It should turn slightly yellow and mealy-looking. (It is always better to over-process the fat than underprocess it. The former will lead to a shorter, more crumbly dough. The latter leads to a very tough dough.) Second, don't listen to cooking experts who tell you to add "just enough water until the dough holds together." That's nonsense. Add all of the water you need to get the dough to hold together firmly. In fact, the dough should actually be quite wet and sticky, and then you can dust it with flour. It will be very soft, almost like a kneaded yeast dough. Dry dough is impossible to roll out. That being said, take your time stirring the water into the dough. It takes a while for the water to be dispersed evenly throughout

the mixture. Finally, *never* add the water to the food processor; this is a surefire way to ruin your dough, since the food processor is so powerful that it can turn dough into mush in a mere second or two. The machine will do less damage to a dry flour mixture than a wet one. Move the dough mixture to a separate bowl, *then* add the water.

▪▪▪

Master Recipe for Foolproof Handmade Pie Dough

Grating frozen butter and Crisco with a box grater works very well and isn't that much more work than using a food processor. The freezing makes it less likely that you will overwork the dough as you cut the fat into the flour.

MAKES PASTRY FOR A SINGLE-CRUST
8- OR 9-INCH PIE

5	tablespoons cold unsalted butter
5	tablespoons cold all-vegetable shortening (e.g., Crisco)
1¼	cups all-purpose flour
½	teaspoon salt
2	tablespoons granulated sugar
4 to 5	tablespoons ice water

1. Freeze the butter and vegetable shortening (Crisco) for 30 minutes. Combine flour, salt, and sugar in a large mixing bowl. Grate butter and shortening into the bowl. Toss flour and fat mixture about 8 to 10 times, until all the butter and shortening are coated with flour and distributed evenly throughout the flour. Break up any clumps with your fingers as you toss the mixture. The flour should no longer appear light and powdery but take on a mealy texture, slightly heavier and a bit more yellow in color. Do not overwork or the butter will melt and the dough will become unworkable when rolled out.

2. Sprinkle 3 tablespoons of ice water over the mixture. With the blade of a rubber spatula, use a folding motion to mix, then press down

on dough with the broad side of the spatula until the dough sticks together, adding up to 2 tablespoons more water if dough will not come together. Work slowly, mixing the dough to evenly distribute the water. This should take about 1 minute. The dough should be very wet and sticky at this point. *It is better to add too much water than too little.* Shape dough into a ball with your hands, turn onto a lightly floured surface, and flatten into a 4-inch-wide disk. Dust very lightly with flour, wrap in plastic, and refrigerate for at least 30 minutes before rolling.

For the following variations, see either of the master recipes above for instructions. Note that for the hand method both the butter and vegetable shortening (Crisco) will have to be frozen for 30 minutes; for the food processor method the butter must be frozen for 15 minutes.

SINGLE-CRUST 10-INCH REGULAR AND 9-INCH DEEP-DISH VARIATION

These ingredient amounts are for oversized single-crust pies. Refer to either of the master recipes above for instructions.

- 6 tablespoons cold unsalted butter
- 6 tablespoons cold all-vegetable shortening (e.g., Crisco)
- 1½ cups all-purpose flour
- ½ teaspoon salt
- 2 tablespoons granulated sugar
- About 5 tablespoons ice water

DOUBLE-CRUST 8- OR 9-INCH VARIATION

The dough should be divided into two balls, one slightly larger than the other. The larger one is used for the bottom crust, the smaller for the top. Refer to either of the master recipes above for instructions.

- 9 tablespoons cold unsalted butter
- 9 tablespoons cold all-vegetable shortening (e.g., Crisco)
- 2¼ cups all-purpose flour
- ¾ teaspoon salt
- 2 tablespoons granulated sugar
- About ½ cup ice water

DOUBLE-CRUST 10-INCH REGULAR OR 9-INCH DEEP-DISH VARIATION

The dough should be divided into two balls, one slightly larger than the other. The larger one is used for the bottom crust, the smaller for the top. With these larger quantities, make sure that the butter and vegetable shortening (Crisco) are sufficiently processed into the flour. Otherwise, the crust will be very tough and will shrink if prebaked. Refer to either of the master recipes above for instructions.

- 10 tablespoons cold unsalted butter
- 10 tablespoons cold all-vegetable shortening (e.g., Crisco)
- 2½ cups all-purpose flour
- ¾ teaspoon salt
- 2 tablespoons granulated sugar
- 8 to 10 tablespoons ice water

HOW TO PREBAKE A PIE SHELL

THE SINGLE MOST DIFFICULT culinary task for the home cook is prebaking a pie shell. It is a ubiquitous recipe directive that instills fear and loathing into even the most practiced pie maker. The crust shrinks, it cracks, and one ends up with a disfigured miniature shell that can hold only half the filling. I suspected that there had to be a better way.

The first question was what sort of recipe to use for the pie dough itself. My master recipe for pie dough has a bit too much fat in it for prebaking. This causes the dough to shrink as it bakes, leaving the edges melted and lacking in definition. I tested this extensively and finally settled on 5 tablespoons Crisco and 3 tablespoons butter rather than the 5 tablespoons of

PREBAKING A PIE SHELL

Press extra-wide foil into corners of frozen pie shell.

Fill with pie weights.

You can use ceramic weights or dried beans.

If done properly, a prebaked pie shell will not shrink very much.

each called for in my original recipe. Less fat results in a nice-looking prebaked shell, but too little fat, as is the case with many published recipes, creates a shell that is tough. I also found that a slightly higher proportion of Crisco resulted in a shell that was more immune to shrinking.

The next question was the process of prebaking itself once the dough is made. The first important step is to allow the dough to rest, wrapped in plastic wrap, for at least a few hours and preferably overnight. This allows the gluten to rest and the dough to hydrate (the water to distribute) evenly. I then roll out the dough, fit it to the pie plate, and flute the edge. At this point, one has many options. Before baking, the dough should be briefly refrigerated or even put into the freezer for a short stay. After much testing in the *Cook's Illustrated* test kitchen, it was decided that a 40-minute rest in

the refrigerator and then 20 minutes in the freezer provided the best results. This dramatically reduced shrinkage. I then tested the notion of pricking the dough with a fork (this is supposed to cut down on the dough's bubbling as it bakes; this process is referred to as docking), which I found was completely unnecessary. However, a sheet of aluminum foil and pie weights (dried beans or rice will also work) were useful in keeping the pie shell in place. (I find that pressing the foil snugly against the bottom and sides of the shell is a good idea as well.) I bake the shell at a constant 375 degrees for about 21 minutes, or until the dough sets up and loses its wet, soft texture. (I tested other oven temperatures, but 375 was best.) I then remove the foil and weights and continue baking the shell. How long one continues the baking process depends on how the shell will be used. If the filling requires no baking at all, continue baking the shell until it is well browned, 15 to 20 more minutes. For fillings that will require 20 minutes or less baking, leave the shell in the oven another 7 minutes. For fillings that require more than 20 minutes of baking, leave the shell in the oven only another 4 minutes.

•••

Master Recipe for Prebaked Pie Shell

I provide two methods here. The first and by far the easiest and most reliable method uses a food processor. The second is a variation made by hand (see next page). Make sure that your dough is not too dry or it will be impossible to roll out. If you need to add a bit more water to form a cohesive ball of dough, don't be afraid to use it. This recipe is enough for one single-crust pie shell. Note that I use less butter and shortening for this recipe than I do, say, for the Foolproof Food Processor Pie Dough on page 214. This is because a somewhat lower ratio of fat is preferable for a prebaked pie shell in order to maintain the distinct shape of the edging. With higher ratios, the edging tends to melt. If you do not wish to wait an hour for the dough to rest before rolling it out, place it in the freezer for 20 minutes. (The refrigerator method is, however, preferable.)

MAKES ONE 8- OR 9-INCH PREBAKED SHELL

3	tablespoons cold unsalted butter
1¼	cups all-purpose flour
½	teaspoon salt
1	tablespoon granulated sugar
5	tablespoons cold all-vegetable shortening (e.g., Crisco)
4 to 5	tablespoons ice water

1. Cut butter into ¾-inch pieces and place in freezer for 15 minutes. Mix flour, salt, and sugar in a food processor fitted with the steel blade. Place the Crisco in 1-tablespoon lumps into the food processor along with the frozen butter pieces. Pulse about 8 times (1-second pulses), or until the dough appears slightly yellow and pebbly in texture and the butter is reduced to very small pieces, the size of tiny peas or smaller. Check dough after 5 pulses and every pulse thereafter. Turn mixture into a medium bowl.

2. Sprinkle 3 tablespoons of ice water over the mixture. With the blade of a large rubber spatula, use a folding motion to mix, then press down on dough with the broad side of the spatula until the dough sticks together, adding up to 2 tablespoons more water if dough will not come together. Work slowly, mixing the dough to evenly distribute the water. This should take about 1 minute. The dough should be very wet and sticky at this point. *It is better to add too much water than too little.* Shape dough into a ball with your hands, turn onto a lightly floured surface, and flatten into a 4-inch-wide disk. Dust very lightly with flour, wrap in plastic, and refrigerate for at least 30 minutes before rolling.

3. If dough has spent more than 1 hour in the refrigerator, let warm up a few minutes on the counter before proceeding. Roll out dough and place into an 8- or 9-inch pie pan (see illustrations, page 212). Push dough gently down the sides of the pan. Trim dough around edge of pan, leaving a ½-inch border. Fold excess dough underneath the edge of the dough and shape edge using fingers (see illustrations, page 213) or press with the tines of a fork. Place in refrigerator for at least 40 minutes. Place in freezer for 20 minutes. Heat oven to 375 degrees.

4. Remove pie shell from freezer and fit a double thickness of heavy-duty aluminum foil (the extra-wide rolls are best; if the foil is too narrow, use two sheets) over shell, fitting foil carefully into bottom of pie shell and pressing against the sides. Add pie weights or dried beans, enough to generously cover bottom of pie plate. Pile up the weights around the sides of the shell to help hold them in place.

5. Bake on lower rack for about 21 minutes, or until sides of pie shell are set. (They should

not be moist and should be firm.) Remove foil and weights and bake another 15 to 20 minutes if the filling requires no baking, 7 minutes if filling requires 20 minutes or less of baking time, and 4 minutes if the filling needs more than 20 minutes of oven time. Remove from oven and cool on a rack.

WHAT CAN GO WRONG? Prebaking a piecrust is the number one problem for most home cooks. If you follow my directions closely, you should be fine, but do not be tempted to skip the refrigeration or freezing of the shell; these are crucial steps to avoid shrinkage during baking. It is also helpful when fitting the dough to the pie plate or tart pan to gently push the sides of the dough down toward the bottom before trimming. This helps to avoid shrinkage, a major problem when it comes time to add the filling. Finally, be absolutely sure to cut the butter and vegetable shortening thoroughly into the flour. You do not want big pea-size pieces of butter for prebaked shells. These large pieces will melt in the oven and can cause bubbling and shrinking.

HAND VARIATION

If you do not have a food processor, the dough can also be made by hand. A simple box grater works well for cutting up the butter and shortening. Since the butter and Crisco are grated, be careful not to work them too much into the flour mixture. They will quickly turn warm and the dough will become soft, sticky, and impossible to work with.

    5   tablespoons cold all-vegetable shortening
        (e.g., Crisco)
    3   tablespoons cold unsalted butter
    1¼ cups all-purpose flour
    ½   teaspoon salt
    1   tablespoon granulated sugar
4 to 5 tablespoons ice water

1. Freeze the vegetable shortening (Crisco) and butter for 30 minutes. Mix flour, salt, and sugar in a large bowl with a whisk for 30 seconds. Grate the butter and shortening into the bowl containing the flour mixture. Use your fingers to gently toss the grated butter and shortening with the flour. The flour mixture should turn slightly yellow and take on a coarse, cornmeal-like texture. Do not overmix at this point or the butter will melt and the dough will become sticky and hard to handle.

2. Sprinkle 1 tablespoon ice water onto the mixture and gently toss with your fingers to mix. Add an additional tablespoon and toss and then a third. Check the mixture by taking a handful and squeezing. If the dough holds together, it is done. (It is better to use too much water than not enough.) If not, add another tablespoon of water, toss, and then squeeze a handful to check. Gather the dough into a ball, turn onto a lightly floured surface, and flatten into a 4-inch disk. Dust very lightly with flour, wrap in plastic, and refrigerate for at least 30 minutes before rolling.

3. Follow the master recipe above, starting with step 3.

▪ ▪ ▪

Graham Cracker Crust

The bottom of a drinking glass is effective for pressing the crumbs into the pie plate. Note that when this crust comes out of the oven after prebaking, it will appear a bit dry and loose. However, it will set nicely as it cools. This crust is best for creamy pies, such as Chiffon Pie or Lemon Meringue Pie.

MAKES ONE 8- OR 9-INCH PIECRUST

    11 graham crackers, processed to fine crumbs
        (1¼ cups)
    3   tablespoons packed brown sugar
    5   tablespoons butter

1. Heat oven to 350 degrees. Process graham crackers to fine crumbs in the bowl of a food processor. Add sugar and process a few seconds

to mix. Melt butter. Add butter and process until well blended. (To do this by hand, place crackers in a sturdy plastic bag and pound with a heavy saucepan. Place in a bowl and stir in the sugar and then the melted butter. Stir until well mixed.)

2. Press mixture into bottom and sides of an 8- or 9-inch pie plate.

3. Chill in refrigerator for 20 minutes. Bake in preheated oven for about 15 minutes. Remove from oven just before crust starts to brown. Allow to cool before filling.

WHAT CAN GO WRONG? The crust will seem very loose before baking, but it will harden as it cools. The most difficult part is pressing the crumbs into the pie plate evenly. I find that the flat bottom of a drinking glass is helpful, but even so the crust will vary in thickness, especially around the edges of the bottom. I wouldn't worry too much about this, it is hardly noticeable once the pie is filled and served.

THE SECRETS OF FRUIT PIES

THE PROBLEM WITH fruit pies is the thickener. How does one get both a fresh fruit taste and a slice of pie that doesn't ooze onto the serving plate like melted cheese off the end of a slice of pizza? To get the answer, I set up a few kitchen experiments to see what would work best.

I baked 3 cups blueberries with 1 teaspoon lemon juice, ½ cup sugar, and then 2 tablespoons of one of various thickeners: tapioca, cornstarch, arrowroot, and all-purpose flour. I also baked one batch with 4 tablespoons of flour. The flour and cornstarch tests both yielded dull fruit, lacking in bright flavor and noticeably less acid. As a result, the mixture tasted sweeter and heavier. Both the arrowroot and the tapioca were clear winners, the tapioca showing a bit more thickening power. The flour

test with 4 tablespoons was very gummy and almost inedible.

Next, I contacted Shirley Corriher, the *Cook's Illustrated* consulting food scientist, and also the folks at Kraft Foods to explain the test results. I found that there are two basic types of starchy molecules used for thickening: amylose starch and amylopectin. Cornstarch and flour both contain amylose, which forms a long chainlike bar that bonds with itself and other ingredients. A fruit pie thickened with cornstarch, for example, will be very thick and gluey the next day due to the superior bonding properties of amylose. This is the same chemical action that is responsible for the hard, clumpy texture of day-old rice. The downside of amylose is that the mixture will be cloudy (the bonding of the amylose is responsible for this as well), and I personally find that the resulting texture is a bit gluey, especially for a fruit pie (this was confirmed by the test results). Flour, by the way, does have a lot of amylose in it, but it also has a number of other things. As a result, flour is a less pure form of starch and you need nearly twice as much of it by volume to end up with the same thickening properties as, say, cornstarch. This amount of flour will also adversely affect your fruit pie — you can taste it.

The second type of starch is amylopectin, which has branches that inhibit bonding with itself and other ingredients. This more delicate bonding agent may not be as strong a thickener as cornstarch, but it provides a crystal-clear pie and one with a more delicate texture. Arrowroot and tapioca fall into this category. Keep in mind, however, that all thickeners contain both types of molecules; some have a higher percentage of one over the other (cornstarch, for example, has 28 percent amylose, and tapioca has about 17 percent). Amylopectin is also preferred by commercial bakers because it freezes well. Pies made with cornstarch or flour (amylose) will lose water from the bonded structure when frozen and thawed.

In the course of choosing a thickener, I had

to consider that both sugar and acidity may adversely affect the thickening process. It is true that sugar robs the thickener of water, necessary to the thickening process. (Sugar is also absorbed into the cells of the fruit and helps it keep its shape during baking.) A thickener can absorb up to 100 times its weight in water, but sugar will compete for the water, bonding water around its molecules. In a fruit pie, however, the proportion of sugar is low enough that there is sufficient free water for the thickening agent to do its work. In addition, acidity is said to have an adverse effect because it reduces the molecular weight of the starch, thus inhibiting thickening. In a lemon meringue pie, for example, this is a problem, so the lemon juice is usually added after thickening occurs. However, in a fruit pie with only 2 teaspoons of juice per 6 cups of fruit, the home cook need not worry.

When developing recipes for berry pies, I decided to choose Minute Tapioca as the thickening agent. Based on the initial testing, flour and cornstarch rob the fruit of its bright, fresh flavor, and Minute Tapioca performed much better in a subsequent head-to-head test with arrowroot. (I baked two blueberry pies using 6 cups of fruit and 4 tablespoons of thickener — one pie with Minute Tapioca and the other with arrowroot — and the tapioca pie turned out considerably thicker.) Minute Tapioca is also cheaper than arrowroot (an 8-ounce box costs about $2.49, whereas a 1.87-ounce jar of McCormick's arrowroot costs $3.89). During additional testing, I found that the amount of Minute Tapioca should be varied depending on the juiciness of the berries. If you like a more juicy pie, you might try 3 tablespoons of Minute Tapioca with 6 cups of fresh blueberries. If you like a really firm pie with no juices, increase the quantity to 5 tablespoons. When the test kitchen staff at Kraft were queried about their tapioca-heavy back-of-the-box recipe (they suggest about 1 tablespoon of Minute Tapioca per cup of fruit), they explained that they like to operate with a large

margin of safety — that is, they suggest using a larger amount of tapioca to be absolutely sure that the pie firms up properly. (They also, I would guess, like to sell more tapioca!) I like some juice and therefore opt for the lower quantity recommended in the master recipe.

When I made a lattice-top pie, I ran into trouble. At the time, I was testing pearl tapioca (these are the large, fish-eye rounds that become translucent when cooked), and I found that the tapioca on top of the fruit baked into hard bits that made me feel like I was eating Tic-Tacs. (I encountered a similar problem with Minute Tapioca.) For an open or lattice pie, therefore, I suggest mixing the Minute Tapioca with three-quarters of the fruit, filling the pie, and then adding the balance of the fruit on top. By the way, if you find only pearl tapioca in your pantry, just place the tapioca in a spice grinder, blender, or food processor and grind away. Now you have "instant" Minute Tapioca. The other solution, suggested by one manufacturer, is to allow pearl tapioca to soak in water before using. However, upon testing, I found that the thickening powers were greatly diminished because the thickener had already sucked in about as much water as it could handle before baking. However, high heat does increase the ability of a thickener to absorb water, so it did thicken somewhat, albeit at a greatly reduced rate. As a result, I don't recommend presoaking.

I also found that it is important to let fruit pies sit and cool, as this allows the juices to thicken. A fresh fruit pie will not completely set until it comes to room temperature (allow at least 1 hour).

▪ ▪ ▪

Master Recipe for Fruit Pie

This master recipes requires a bit of common sense. Both the sugar and the tapioca are variable in this recipe, depending on the sweetness and juiciness of the fruit. Tart blueberries, for example, can take a full cup of sugar. Very sweet berries, however, can do with ¾ cup or even a bit less. The tapioca will also depend on the fruit and the cook's preference for juiciness in the sliced pie. If you want perfect individual pieces, with no juice running out onto the pie plate, go with the 4 to 5 tablespoons. Less juicy fruit will firm up nicely with only 3 to 4 table-spoons.

MAKES ONE 8- OR 9-INCH DOUBLE-CRUST PIE

1	recipe Foolproof Food Processor Pie Dough or Foolproof Handmade Pie Dough, Double-Crust 8- or 9-Inch Variation (page 216)
8	cups fruit, prepared (peeled, cored, sliced)
1	teaspoon grated orange or lemon zest
2	teaspoons lemon juice
¾ to 1	cup granulated sugar
3 to 5	tablespoons Minute Tapioca

1. Make the pie dough and refrigerate for at least 30 minutes (let warm up for 10 minutes at room temperature if refrigerated for more than an hour).

2. Toss the fruit with the other ingredients and let sit for 15 minutes. (If you are making a lattice-top pie, toss the fruit with all ingredients except the tapioca. Set aside one-quarter of the fruit mixture and toss the balance with the tapioca. When filling the pie shell, add the larger amount of fruit first and then top with the quarter without tapioca.)

3. Heat oven to 400 degrees. Roll out half of the chilled pastry dough so that it fits an 8- or 9-inch pie dish with a ½-inch overlap. Push dough down into edges of plate and then cut with scissors so it is even with the rim of the pie plate. Add fruit mixture. Place in freezer while working with top crust. Roll out remaining dough,

WHERE DO THICKENERS COME FROM?

Arrowroot comes from arrowroot roots (*Maranta arundinacea*), tapioca comes from the root of the cassava plant (also called the tapioca plant or manioc), cornstarch is made from corn, rice starch from rice, sago starch from the pith of palm trees, and wheat starch from wheat.

The tapioca plant is grown in much of the world and is harvested when its roots are 6 to 12 inches long. The root itself can be boiled and eaten. It is a substitute in many countries for rice or potatoes. When the starch is removed from the plant, it is separated from the plant and cellulose material. The starch molecules are contained in granules. These granules are, in their natural state, insoluble and only begin to absorb water with the introduction of energy in the form of heat. An unrefined starch will absorb water to the granule-bursting point, letting the starch molecules escape from the granules. This results in a less pleasant, slimier texture to the cooked product. That is one reason manufacturers further process starches, such as Minute Tapioca, to avoid bursting granules, preserving a creamier, more pleasant texture during thickening. The processing also makes starches less likely to have their thickening properties impaired by acids such as lemon

juice. For example, you may have noticed bags of tapioca starch in Chinese groceries. This is a very inexpensive starch refined for thickening, but it is apt to hydrate more quickly, resulting in starch granules that burst more readily than will a further processed starch.

Raw materials used in manufacturing commercial starches are inexpensive, ranging from 2 cents per pound for cornstarch to 8 cents per pound for tapioca. Cornstarch is relatively inexpensive because it is a domestic product and because manufacturers sell off the processing by-products, including corn oil and animal food, whereas tapioca is imported from Thailand and incurs extra shipping costs.

Pearl tapioca is made from tapioca starch, which is heated into pearls. To create Minute Tapioca, the starch is partially gelatinized and then pressed into pellets to improve its thickening powers. For example, a processed starch, as compared with a raw starch, is less likely to lose its viscosity when in the presence of an acid such as lemon juice. The starch granules are also less likely to burst, which detracts from the texture and mouth feel of the thickened food.

place over pie, and trim, leaving ½-inch of over-lap. Fold edge of top crust under bottom crust and crimp with your fingers or the tines of a fork. Cut three small slits in top of crust for air vents. If pie dough is very soft, place in freezer for 10 minutes before baking.

4. Set pie on a baking sheet, place in oven, turning oven down to 350 degrees. Bake for 1 hour. Check after 35 minutes and rotate if pie is not browning evenly. Juices should bubble before removing pie from oven.

5. Let pie sit and cool to room temperature before serving so that juices thicken (allow at least 1 hour).

WHAT CAN GO WRONG? The problem with fruit pies is judging the amount of sugar and thickener to use. The condition of the fruit is key. For example, some blueberries are sweet, some tart; some are very juicy and others are mealy. This requires a bit of experience, but just keep in mind that both the quantities of sugar and Minute Tapioca are variable and will have to be adjusted each time you make this recipe.

STRAWBERRY-RHUBARB VARIATION

Use 3 cups hulled and sliced strawberries and 3 cups rhubarb cut into 1-inch pieces. Use 1 tablespoon orange zest (instead of 1 teaspoon of lemon). Add ¼ teaspoon vanilla extract to the fruit mixture.

PEACH VARIATION

Add ½ cup brown sugar, reduce white sugar to ¼ cup, and add 1 tablespoon crystallized ginger diced into small pieces, ¼ teaspoon nutmeg, ¼ teaspoon allspice, and ¼ teaspoon salt to the peach mixture.

BLUEBERRY VARIATION

Omit the orange or lemon zest. Add ¼ teaspoon allspice and a pinch of nutmeg to blueberry mixture. Use ¾ cup sugar if blueberries are sweet. I do not recommend frozen blueberries — in a

taste test against fresh, they were deemed virtually inedible.

CHERRY VARIATION

Use 4 cups of pitted, canned sour cherries packed in water (drain the cherries). If cherries have been canned in a syrup, drain and rinse with water, then drain again. Toss fruit with 1 cup sugar, ⅛ teaspoon allspice, ⅛ teaspoon cinnamon, ⅛ teaspoon almond extract, 1 tablespoon brandy, 2 teaspoons lemon juice, and 4 tablespoons Minute Tapioca (use 3 tablespoons tapioca if cherries were packed in syrup). Omit the orange or lemon zest.

FRUIT PIE FOR IDIOTS

MOST OF US ARE, excuse the expression, idiots when it comes to making a fruit pie. The bottom crust has to be rolled out and transferred to a pie dish, and then the filling must be added and a top crust rolled out and properly fitted over the pie, with the edges neatly crimped. What one usually ends up with is not a Martha Stewart centerpiece but something out of the Addams family: cruelly shaped and tortured-looking. Not only that, I have often found myself wishing that pies had a higher proportion of crust to fruit — a really crispy crust and plenty of it. I set out to remedy these problems.

In Europe, there is a tradition of simply rolling out dough, topping it with fruit, folding up the sides, and then baking. These doughs are often referred to as galette doughs and tend to be very soft, often made with cream cheese. I started my testing by trying five different galette doughs from various cookbooks, all of which used cream cheese as a key ingredient. For 1 cup of flour, these recipes used anywhere ¼ to ½ cup cream cheese plus 6 to 8 tablespoons butter. The doughs came together with very little water added and were smooth and easy to roll out. I soon discovered a few problems, however. The first was that many of these doughs are relatively soft, even when baked. I find this to be a disappointing partner for baked fruit. As with a pie, I wanted some crispness and flake to the crust to marry with the fruit. The more fat-laden recipes were so rich that I found them hard to digest. After a few more tests, I decided to go back to my basic pie dough recipe. This turned out to be a winner. It's simple, it's flaky, it's crisp, and it marries well with the fruit. If it works well with a two-crust pie, why not use it for this simple one-crust dessert as well?

For the fruit, 2 cups turned out to be about right. All of the other recipes I came across called for the same ingredients: 2 tablespoons flour, 1 tablespoon white sugar, and 1 tablespoon brown sugar. I found this combination too heavy on the flour and too light on the sugar. In fact, I found that most fruit needs no flour at all. If the fruit is cooked long enough, the juices mix with the sugar and form a thick syrup when cooled. The flour simply dulls the flavor of the fruit. I also found that white sugar is better than brown sugar, since it doesn't interfere with the flavor of the fruit.

So I went back into the kitchen and tried my basic pastry dough recipe, used 2 cups fruit mixed with 3 to 4 tablespoons sugar, and baked at 400 degrees for about 45 minutes, or until the fruit was bubbling and the crust was nicely browned. I let the pie cool for an hour for the juices to set. The end result is intensely flavored filling (the fruit has cooked down with the sugar) married to a crispy, toothsome crust and, best of all, even an idiot like me can make it!

• • •

Fruit Pie for Idiots

This "pie" is much easier to make than a traditional two-crust pie. One layer of dough is simply rolled out; it doesn't have to be fitted into a pie dish and there is no fussing with the

edging. *There is also a better ratio of crust to filling (this recipe uses 2 cups of fruit instead of the 6 to 8 cups for a standard fruit pie), which makes it an easy and superior method for cooking up fruit. Note that the amount of sugar will depend on the fruit. Use 3 tablespoons with very ripe, sweet fruit and 4 tablespoons if the fruit is tart or less than perfectly ripe.*

SERVES 6 TO 8

1 recipe Foolproof Food Processor Pie Dough (page 214) or Foolproof Handmade Pie Dough (page 215)
2 cups ripe summer fruit (berries, peaches, plums)
3 to 4 tablespoons granulated sugar

1. Prepare pie pastry according to recipe directions and chill for 30 minutes in refrigerator.

2. Heat oven to 400 degrees. Prepare the fruit. Berries just need to be washed and dried with paper towels. Stone fruits such as peaches or plums can be skinned or not, pitted, and then sliced thinly. (To skin, place in rapidly boiling water for 25 seconds, immerse in ice water for at least 1 minute, and then remove skin with a small paring knife.)

3. Roll out the dough into a large round on a sheet of parchment paper. (The dough should be about the thickness of a quarter and 12 inches or so in diameter.) Or, roll it out on any lightly floured work surface and then transfer to a baking sheet. Toss the fruit with the sugar and place in the middle of the dough, leaving a 2½-inch border all around. Drape the border up over the fruit in overlapping folds. Note that the fruit in the center will remain uncovered.

4. Bake in preheated oven for about 45 minutes, or until the fruit is bubbling and the crust is very brown. Let cool for at least an hour before serving. Slice into 6 pieces for hungry adults.

WHAT CAN GO WRONG? This is an easy-to-assemble pie but has the same problem as do all fruit desserts — the amount of sugar has to vary depending on the condition of the fruit.

AN APPLE PIE FOR ALL SEASONS

LIKE MOST COOKBOOK AUTHORS, I started my search for the best apple pie recipe with a taste test of apples. I tried seventeen varieties and picked out my favorites, including Winesap,

WAS THERE A GRANNY SMITH?

Yes, there was a Granny Smith. She lived in Australia in the nineteenth century, and the tart green apple that is available in every supermarket these days bears her name. Another famous apple, the Red Delicious, was discovered on an Iowa farm in 1874, when a farmer repeatedly cut down a young apple tree only to have it reemerge the next season. Finally, figuring that anything that struggled against death so persistently might have a good reason to live, he tended the tree, grew the fruit, and entered it in competition at a state fair, where it won first prize. Later, a powerful nursery family from Missouri, the Stark brothers, bought the Hawkeye (its original name) and turned it into the ubiquitous, mediocre apple that it is today. After World War II, the Red Delicious became the staple of many growers out in Washington State, its classic shape and deep cherry color becoming emblematic of the ideal American apple. But we all know what it tastes like. It is, to borrow a phrase, a "gorgeous fraud" — the skin is thick and bitter, and the fruit is soft, sweet, and lacking in the tartness that most apple growers and cooks find synonymous with a good eating apple. It has made many a grower a fortune, since it ships and stores well, and consumers still buy it, regardless of its shortcomings.

The tale of the Red Delicious is one of serendipity — a tree grows from a chance seedling, barely escapes with its life, and then goes on to become the bestselling apple in history. But the tale of America's apple industry is less romantic. In the nineteenth century, apples were grown and consumed locally, with literally thousands of varieties on the market. Some apples were as small as cherries, some as large as grapefruit; some were pale white in appearance and others almost black; some even looked like potatoes and others like a sheep's nose (the Yellow Sheepnose). The Watermelon apple had bright red fruit, the Court Pendu Plat had rough, scabby skin (it would never sell today) but a unique pecanlike sweetness. Other apples had lyrical names: Maiden Blush, Rainbow, Newtown Pippin, Wolf River, Fallawater, Red Winter Pearmain, Summer Banana, and Esopus Spitzenberg. It was an industry that reflected the spirit of nineteenth-century America — a diversity of tastes and regions served by hardworking entrepreneurs who grafted and planted, fought scab and mildew, and battled the apple moth and plum curculio, insects that had to be laboriously shaken from trees rather than killed easily through spraying.

Over the past fifty years, all that has changed. An industry spokesperson once told me, "There are only three kinds of apples in America today: red, yellow, and green." He meant that supermarket buyers know that consumers purchase on looks alone, the classic case of beauty only being skin deep. They prefer dark green Granny Smith apples to light ones, yet the paler, somewhat yellow-skinned specimens are actually riper and sweeter. A collection of nineteenth-century apples would be a study in diversity; modern supermarket apples are almost indistinguishable except for color: they all have the same shape, size, and smooth, glossy skin. Although not all "heirloom" apples are worth saving — many were bitter, had tough skin, or didn't store well — the apple business today is one of DNA engineering, no longer subject to the serendipity of a chance seed beating the odds to become a Golden Delicious or a McIntosh.

Macoun, Northern Spy (it was originally called Northern Pie since it was so good in pies), Rhode Island Greening, and Cortland. The problem, however, was that I could not get most of these apples out of season and they were also not available nationwide. So I quickly restricted my search to year-round, nationally distributed supermarket apples. Of those apple varieties that are ubiquitous, I tested the top nine sellers and determined that Red Delicious, the number one American apple, made terrible pies but that Granny Smith and McIntosh both had excellent qualities. The former was tart with good texture, and the latter had excellent flavor. But each of them also had drawbacks: a pie made with just Grannies was too sour and a bit dull in flavor and the McIntosh pie was too soft, more like applesauce than apple pie. A pie made with both varieties, however, was outstanding. The Grannies held up well during cooking, while the Macs added flavor and their mushy texture was actually welcome. It provided a nice base for the harder Grannies and soaked up some of the juice. Finally, I had a good year-round combination.

I also took a close look at the other filling ingredients. I had always used butter in my pies, up to 6 tablespoons in a deep-dish pie. Over the years I had cut this back to a more modest 2 tablespoons, but when pies were taste-tested with and without butter, the leaner pies won hands down. Butter simply dulls the fresh taste of apples. Lemon juice, however, is absolutely crucial to a good pie. By properly balancing sweet with tart, a good apple pie tastes like a crisp October morning rather than a muggy August afternoon. In the end, I settled on 1½ tablespoons of juice with 1 teaspoon of zest. (However, one cannot take an overly sweet apple and balance it successfully with lemon juice. The citric acids in lemon juice have different flavor characteristics than the malic acids found in apples. It would be like substituting vinegar for lemon juice. It is equally difficult to balance the flavor of an overly tart apple using sugar, since white granulated sugar is entirely different from the fructose found in an apple.)

Spices were another matter. In order to give the apples the upper hand, we used only small amounts, ¼ teaspoon or less, of cinnamon, nutmeg, and allspice, the last adding unexpected balance to the lemon juice. Vanilla was voted down by my tasters as a meddlesome addition. The choice of sugar was clear-cut. Plain white sugar didn't overpower the fruit, whereas light or dark brown sugar obscured flavors.

Even a cursory review of apple pie recipes reveals a wide range of preferences for thickeners, flour, tapioca, and cornstarch being the most common. I did try flour and tapioca and found them unnecessary, the Macs reducing nicely, creating their own thickener. (The one exception to this rule is if you are using extremely juicy apples in the height of the season. Then I find that 2 tablespoons of flour is necessary. However, as the apples sit in storage, they tend to become drier and therefore no thickener is needed most of the year.) In addition, a bit of tart, thin juice gives an apple pie a breath of the orchard, whereas a thick, syrupy texture is dull by comparison.

Many cookbooks claim that letting sliced apples sit in a bowl with the sugar, lemon juice, and spices, a process known as macerating, is a key step in developing flavors and juice. I found, however, that this simply caused the apples to dry out, making them rubbery and unpleasant. In addition, the apples themselves lose flavor, having exuded their fruitiness into the juice. So macerating, a frequent step in apple pie making, was clearly out.

I ran across the same texture issue once again when investigating the thickness of the apple slices. At first I thought that I could control texture by varying the thickness of slices. When tested, this was found not to be the case. A ½-inch slice cooked no more slowly than a ¼-inch slice. It turned out that baking time was the more crucial issue. I had been baking pies for 20 minutes at 425 degrees and then 25 minutes at

375 and found that the apples were under-cooked, often turning rubbery. When I increased baking time to 55 minutes (25 minutes at 425 and 30 minutes at 375), the juices bubbled, the crust turned a rich brown, and the apple slices were cooked through.

Many home cooks are concerned about pies in which the top crust sets up quickly, leaving an air space between it and the apples, which reduce in volume as they cook down. (To solve the problem, some bakers precook the apples, which, by the way, was a common method of making apple pies in the eighteenth century. The stewed and strained apples were poured into a crust, or paste as they called it, and then baked with the usual spices, although rose water was sometimes suggested as an ingredient as well. I have tested this method and find that the resulting pie loses the fresh, tart flavor of the apples.) With my crust recipe, however, this is not an issue. There is sufficient shortening cut into the flour that the crust sinks down onto the apples as they cook. I did notice, however, that this high ratio of shortening does produce a very flaky crust, one that is not easily cut into perfect slices. In addition, there is still a fair amount of juice, which I find essential for good flavor, and the filling may spread slightly once the pie is cut into individual slices.

I also wondered if I could solve the problem of the soggy bottom crust. Partial prebaking of the crust is the obvious solution, but one that is not practical for a two-crust pie and, in my opinion, not worth the effort. I tried coating the bottom of the crust with egg whites and, in a separate test, sprinkling a layer of breadcrumbs on the crust, but neither helped. I tested four different types of pie plates — glass, ceramic, metal with holes, and metal without holes — and it didn't make much difference, although glass is cheap, cleans up easily, and does a slightly better job of browning the crust. I did find that overall cooking time was a factor, the longer, 55-minute baking period being substantially better. With longer baking times in a glass pie plate, I did have some success. The outside of the crust was crisp while the inside was still moist, and none of my tasters found this particularly objectionable.

I then looked into what sort of wash might be applied to the top of the pie to give it color. Whole eggs, with or without milk, turned the pie an unpleasant yellow. Egg yolks only yielded dark yellow splotches, and when paired with cream created a shiny top surface reminiscent of store-bought apple pies sold at third-rate diners. I did like, however, a simple mixture of egg whites and sugar. The pies had a pretty, frosted appearance, maintaining a natural, lighter color. To finish up the testing, I tried baking a pie with no air vents, and it turned out just fine. My pastry recipe is so flaky that steam found its own way through small cracks in the top crust. Vents are attractive, however, and probably make sense with tougher doughs that use less shortening.

Finally, I wanted to find out if a pie could be assembled, frozen, and then baked later. I tried this, baking the pie after 1 day, after 2 weeks, and then after a month. The overnight freezing was pretty good, the 2-week method yielded flavor that was a bit muted and apples that were slightly on the spongy side, and the full month of freezing was a disaster. The apples were puffy, without much flavor, and the crust was oily and dense. If you wish to freeze a pie for up to 2 weeks, put it in the freezer for 2 to 3 hours, then cover it with a double layer of plastic wrap and return it to the freezer. To bake it, remove the pie from the freezer, brush it with the egg wash, sprinkle with sugar, and place directly into a preheated oven. After baking it for the usual 55 minutes, reduce the oven to 325 degrees, cover the pie with foil so as not to overcook the crust, and bake for an additional 20 to 25 minutes.

⋅⋅⋅

All-Season Apple Pie

*P*lease note that this filling is loose, not thick and firm, which means that the individual slices will not be picture perfect. However, through extensive testing I have found that a somewhat juicier pie has dramatically better flavor.

SERVES 6 TO 8

1   recipe Foolproof Food Processor Pie Dough or Foolproof Handmade Pie Dough, Double-Crust 8- or 9-inch Variation (page 216)

For the Filling

4   Granny Smith and 4 McIntosh apples (about 8 cups sliced)
1½ tablespoons lemon juice
1   teaspoon grated lemon zest
¼   teaspoon salt
¾   cup granulated sugar
¼   teaspoon nutmeg, freshly ground preferred
¼   teaspoon cinnamon
⅛   teaspoon allspice
2   tablespoons all-purpose flour (use only with very juicy apples)

1   egg white, lightly beaten
1   tablespoon granulated sugar for topping

1. Make the pie dough and refrigerate for at least 30 minutes.

2. Remove both balls of dough from refrigerator. The dough is ready to be rolled when it is still cool to the touch but you can push your finger halfway down through the center. If the dough has been chilled for more than 1 hour, it may have to sit on the counter for 10 to 20 minutes to soften. Heat oven to 425 degrees.

3. Roll out larger piece of dough on a lightly floured surface into a 12-inch circle, about ⅛ inch thick, the thickness of a quarter. Transfer and fit dough into a 9-inch glass pie pan, leaving dough that overhangs the lip in place without trimming. Refrigerate until ready to use.

4. Roll out smaller piece of dough on a lightly floured surface into an 11-inch circle. Transfer to a baking sheet and refrigerate until ready to use.

5. *Prepare filling:* Peel apples, quarter, and remove core. Slice each quarter lengthwise into thirds, about ½ inch thick. Toss with lemon juice, lemon zest, salt, sugar, and spices. Only use the flour for very juicy apples.

6. Remove pie dough from refrigerator. Turn fruit mixture, including any juices, into pie shell. Lay the top pastry over top. Trim top and bottom edges to ½ inch beyond pan lip. Tuck this rim of dough underneath itself so that folded edge is flush with pan lip. Flute dough in your own fashion, or press with fork tines to seal. Cut four slits at right angles on dough top to allow steam to escape. (Pie can be prepared to this point and frozen for up to 2 weeks; see instructions above for storing and baking.) Brush egg white on top of crust and sprinkle 1 tablespoon of sugar evenly over the top.

7. Place pie on bottom rack of oven. Bake until crust is lightly golden, 25 minutes. Reduce oven temperature to 375 degrees and continue to bake until juices bubble and crust is deep golden brown, 30 to 35 minutes more. The bottom crust should be golden and the juices from the pie bubbling.

8. Transfer pie to a wire rack. Let cool to almost room temperature, about 4 hours. Pie is best eaten after it has completely cooled, even the next day.

WHAT CAN GO WRONG? If you do not properly cut the butter and vegetable shortening into the flour, the dough will be tough and will not melt down onto the apples as they bake. This creates a large air space between the top crust and cooked fruit, a situation that some home cooks find objectionable. The bigger problem is the apples. In season, apples are relatively juicy, but after months of storage they tend to become drier. Therefore, you might want to add some flour (2 tablespoons) if the pie is made in October with very juicy apples, whereas an apple pie baked in April may require no thickener. It is also true that no two Granny Smith apples (or any other variety) are the same. One might be ripe and juicy and another might be tart, hard, and dry. As a result, every apple pie you make will be slightly different. Although I suggest using a mixture of McIntosh and Grannies, since they are almost always available, do not be afraid to use local apples in season. I find it is always best to mix varieties (as one would with cider). Try three or four different kinds in a pie and see what happens. Do not be afraid to experiment. Look for one apple that is very sweet, one that is very tart, one that holds its shape well during baking, et cetera.

CRYSTALLIZED GINGER APPLE PIE

Add 3 tablespoons chopped crystallized ginger to apple mixture.

DRIED RAISIN, CHERRY, OR CRANBERRY APPLE PIE

Combine 1 cup dried fruit (chopped coarse if large) with the lemon juice and 1 tablespoon applejack, brandy, or cognac. Let sit for 30 minutes. Toss with apple mixture.

FRESH CRANBERRY APPLE PIE

Add 1 cup fresh or frozen cranberries to apples, and increase sugar to 1 cup from ¾ cup.

* * *

Apple Pie for Idiots I

The idea for this recipe comes from Jacques Pépin, who included a similar one in Jacques Pépin's Table. *I use a pastry dough with more butter and also prefer a tarter apple than Golden Delicious, which he uses, but the results are similar. This recipe is incredibly quick and easy and is used in my household as the quintessential last-minute dessert when I have nothing in the house but a few apples and pantry staples. The concept is simple. Place peeled, cored, and halved apples on pie dough, roll up the sides, sprinkle with a little sugar, and bake.*

Be sure to chill the pastry dough for at least 30 minutes before rolling, since a relatively thin dough is required. If you do not have apricot jam, try using applesauce instead.

SERVES 4

For the Pastry Dough

- 3 tablespoons unsalted butter
- ¾ cup all-purpose flour
- ¼ teaspoon salt
- 1 tablespoon granulated sugar
- 2 tablespoons all-vegetable shortening (Crisco)
- About 2 tablespoons very cold water

For the Filling

- 2 large tart apples (Granny Smith, Empire, Braeburn, etc.), peeled, cut in half, and cored
- Juice of 1 lemon
- 2 tablespoons apricot jam or applesauce
- 1 tablespoon granulated sugar
- ¼ teaspoon nutmeg

1. *For the pastry dough:* Cut butter into ¾-inch pieces and place in freezer for 15 minutes. Mix flour, salt, and sugar in a food processor fitted with the steel blade. Place the Crisco in two 1-tablespoon lumps into the food processor along with the frozen butter pieces. Pulse a few times (1-second pulses), or until the dough appears slightly yellow, pebbly in texture, and the butter is reduced to very small pieces, the size of tiny peas or smaller. Check dough after 3 pulses and every pulse thereafter. Turn mixture into a medium bowl.

2. Sprinkle 2 tablespoons cold water over the mixture. With blade of a large rubber spatula, use a folding motion to mix, then press down on dough with the broad side of the spatula until dough sticks together, adding more water if dough will not come together. Work slowly, mixing the dough to evenly distribute the water. This should take about 1 minute. Shape dough into a ball with your hands, turn onto a lightly floured surface, then flatten into a 4-inch wide disk. Dust

very lightly with flour, wrap in plastic, and refrigerate for at least 30 minutes before rolling.

3. Heat oven to 425 degrees. Remove dough from refrigerator and roll out on a well-floured surface to a 10-inch-diameter circle. (To make rolling easier, you can sandwich the dough between two layers of plastic wrap.) Place rolled dough in the refrigerator on a baking sheet.

4. *For the filling:* Toss apples with lemon juice and then hollow them out slightly with a 1-teaspoon metal measuring spoon or a small melon baller. Chop the scooped-out bits. Place ½ tablespoon of jam into the cavity of each halved apple and place apples, cut side down, in the center of the rolled-out dough. Sprinkle the chopped apple around the halves.

5. Fold the edge of the dough up over the apples to create a border and to hold in the juices while baking. Mix together the sugar and nutmeg and sprinkle over the pie. Bake about 20 minutes, reduce heat to 375 degrees, and bake another 25 to 35 minutes, or until apples are thoroughly cooked and the crust is nicely browned.

WHAT CAN GO WRONG? This is one recipe in which the apple variety and condition matters a lot, since the apples are simply cut in half, not sliced. A dull, mealy apple, such as a poor Golden Delicious, will make a less than exceptional dessert.

• • •

Apple Pie for Idiots II

This pie is similar to the recipe above except that instead of using halved and cored apples, I use apples prepared as they would be for a regular apple pie: peeled, cored, and sliced. Be sure to use a baking pan with sides so that any juices that may leak out do not end up on the floor of your oven. In terms of selecting the apples, it is crucial that you use juicy apples for this recipe. Dry Granny Smiths are no good, since they will not exude enough juices to mix with the sugar. On the other hand, McIntosh apples have excellent flavor but will cook down and become

mushy, something I do not find objectionable in this recipe. You might also use Golden Delicious since they are a common variety, but I find them a bit lacking in acidity. The best way to choose an apple, since the condition of the apple is at least as important as the variety, is to simply taste one first, hoping to find an apple that is tart, firm, and juicy.

SERVES 6 TO 8

1 recipe Foolproof Food Processor Pie Dough (page 214) or Foolproof Handmade Pie Dough (page 215)
3 firm, tart, juicy apples
1 tablespoon lemon juice
5 tablespoons granulated sugar
   Generous pinch cinnamon (optional)
   Generous pinch nutmeg (optional)
   Vanilla ice cream for serving

1. Roll out pastry to an 11-inch circle and place on a jelly roll pan lined with parchment paper. Fold the edge of the pastry over about ¾ inch all the way around. Now fold the pastry over a second time to create a thick rim of crust. (The center of the pie should be about 9 inches in diameter.) Use your fingers to pinch the edging together to make it higher. Complete the edging by fluting it with your fingers. (Hold the thumb and forefinger of one hand about ½ inch apart on the outside of the edge and then push dough between them with the index finger of your other hand.) Chill in refrigerator for 30 minutes.

2. Adjust oven rack to middle position and heat oven to 400 degrees. When the crust is almost chilled, peel, core, and slice the apples into twelfths. (Quarter them and then cut each quarter lengthwise into thirds.) In a medium bowl, toss them with the lemon juice, 4 tablespoons of the sugar, and the optional cinnamon and nutmeg. Remove chilled crust from the refrigerator and sprinkle with the remaining 1 tablespoon sugar. Next, place the prepared apples in the center of the crust. Spread them as evenly as possible over the surface of the tart.

3. Bake in the heated oven for 15 minutes and then lower the oven to 350 degrees. Bake for an additional 30 minutes, or until the crust is browned and the apples are soft. Cool for at least 10 minutes. Serve with vanilla ice cream.

WHAT CAN GO WRONG? Just make sure that you cook the apples enough. Undercooked apples are tough and unpleasant to eat.

CHIFFON PIE

CHIFFON PIES ARE MADE with a simple stovetop custard, thickened with cornstarch and then gelatin, which is folded into whipped cream and then poured into a prebaked pie shell. Some recipes don't set up properly; you can't get a nice clean slice. Others are too tough — the cream mixture loses that light, silky quality and becomes heavy on the palate. I was searching for a moist, rich pie with plenty of flavor but still delicate, and with a texture that was firm yet pleasant.

I started with a basic recipe that used 2 whole eggs, 2 egg yolks, 2 cups milk, 1¾ cups heavy cream, ¾ cup sugar, 2 tablespoons cornstarch, one packet of unflavored gelatin, plus salt, a bit of butter, and flavorings. My first test was to determine whether the cream should be whipped until stiff or just until firm. I discovered that a stiff whipped cream is very hard to fold into a rapidly thickening custard base, so I whipped the cream until firm *but not stiff*. This method worked fine.

I then wondered if the amount of cornstarch was right. I made a pie with 3 tablespoons and it was slightly thicker, although the master recipe was also fine. I like a cream pie that sets up but is still a little wobbly and very moist, so I stayed with the lesser amount. I tried making the custard with all milk instead of 2 cups milk and 1 cup heavy cream and the result was unappealing: not as creamy and definitely lacking

in substance. When I tried using 4 egg yolks instead of 2 whole eggs and 2 yolks, however, the pie was silky smooth, with just the texture I was looking for.

I also found that using an ice water bath for the custard once it comes off the stove dramatically shortens preparation time (place the custard in a metal bowl set in a larger bowl containing cold water and ice cubes). The vanilla and butter are whisked in and then the gelatin is dissolved in ⅓ cup milk, which is then stirred in as well. Now it takes just 10 minutes for the gelatin to kick in, thickening the custard (if you don't use a water bath, this step will take a good half hour). Be sure to stir the custard frequently as it sets; otherwise you may find it has thickened too much for folding.

- - -

Master Recipe for Chiffon Pie

There are two secrets to a really good chiffon pie. First, use all egg yolks instead of a combination of whole eggs and yolks. This produces a silky, rich texture. Second, don't whip the cream until it is stiff. A firm but still moist whipped cream will fold more easily into the setting custard base. This recipe has endless variations.

SERVES 6 TO 8

1 recipe Prebaked Pie Shell (page 218)

For the Filling

4 large egg yolks
2 tablespoons cornstarch
¾ cup granulated sugar
¼ teaspoon salt
1 tablespoon dark rum or cognac
2 cups milk
1¾ cups heavy cream
2 teaspoons vanilla extract
1 tablespoon unsalted butter
1 packet (¼ ounce) unflavored gelatin
½ teaspoon freshly grated nutmeg
2 tablespoons superfine sugar

1. Follow instructions for Prebaked Pie Shell, baking for about 35 minutes, or until a rich nut-brown.

2. Whisk together the first 5 filling ingredients in a medium bowl. Heat 1⅔ cups of the milk (reserving ⅓ cup for gelatin) and 1 cup of the cream (reserving ¾ cup) in a large saucepan until bubbling around the edges. Whisk into egg mixture slowly. Place custard back into saucepan and heat, stirring constantly, until mixture thickens, 3 or 4 minutes. Do not let mixture boil (if mixture starts to steam heavily, remove from heat and whisk rapidly to cool down). Strain into a metal bowl to remove lumps and whisk in vanilla and butter. In a small saucepan, sprinkle the gelatin over remaining ⅓ cup milk and when softened, place over very low heat until dissolved. Stir into warm custard.

3. Place bowl of custard in a larger bowl half filled with cold water and ice cubes. Stir custard mixture every minute until it starts to set (about 10 minutes). Meanwhile, in a separate bowl, whip remaining ¾ cup heavy cream until it starts to thicken. Add nutmeg and sugar and continue beating until firm *but not stiff*. Stir one-third of the remaining whipped cream into the custard. Fold custard and remaining whipped cream together. Pour into fully prebaked shell and chill for 2 hours before serving.

WHAT CAN GO WRONG? The custard needs to be watched very carefully as it starts to thicken. If you are not careful, it can set up too much, to the point that it is impossible to fold with the whipped cream. On the other hand, if it is too loose, it will not fold properly either. The custard should be the texture of a loose pudding. Also keep in mind that the time it takes to thicken will vary considerably, depending on the type of bowl you use as well as the quantity of water and ice cubes. I say 10 minutes in the recipe, but it could easily be a lot longer.

CHOCOLATE VARIATION

Melt 8 ounces semisweet chocolate in a small saucepan in a 250-degree oven (about 15 minutes) or use a microwave oven (50 percent power for 3 to 4 minutes; stir after 2 minutes). Stir chocolate into custard just before straining.

COCONUT VARIATION

Add 1 cup grated dried coconut to the whipped cream just before folding into the custard. Top with ⅓ cup toasted dried coconut (toast coconut in a 375-degree oven for about 8 minutes — check frequently to avoid burning).

CUSTARD PIE

CUSTARD PIES HAVE many shortcomings, as I discovered after baking up a half dozen of them from various cookbooks. Among the problems are a tough, overbaked outer ring of custard (the perimeter overbakes by the time the center is set), soggy, milk-soaked piecrust, an eggy taste that is less than delightful in a dessert, and long cooking times that are anything but precise. I set out to create a custard pie with a crisp crust, a tender yet flavorful filling, and a relatively fool-proof cooking method. The first question was which type of liquid is best. I tried, in order of rising cholesterol count, skim milk, whole milk, half-and-half, light cream, and heavy cream. The skim milk version had a hollow taste and a thin texture; the custard made with whole milk had good flavor but did not set up that well; the half-and-half version was good; the one made with light cream was a bit fatty; and the heavy cream was much too much of a good thing. I played a bit more with proportions and settled on 2 cups of whole milk to 1 cup heavy cream. (Half-and-half runs about 10 percent butterfat, whole milk around 4 percent, and heavy cream is between 36 percent and 40 percent. So a mixture of 2 parts milk to 1 part heavy cream is about 15 percent butterfat, richer than half-and-half but less heavy than light cream, which is about 30 percent butterfat.)

Before I pursued this recipe any further, however, I had to deal with the issue of the crust. With all custard-based pies such as pumpkin, the *Cook's* test kitchen prebakes the crust, adds a hot filling, and then finishes the baking in the oven. I was certain this would work well for a simple custard pie, since the crust would already be light brown and crispy and the oven time would be dramatically reduced. I tried this method with a simple combination of milk, eggs, sugar, and vanilla, but found the cooking time for the filling to be much too long, well over a half hour. This produced a soggy bottom crust, since the pie dough could not be prebaked to the point where it was browned and crispy, since it would overcook during the long oven time. Because I wanted to prebake the crust as much as possible, I had to get the filled pie in and out of the oven fast. So the question was, how could I speed up the thickening process?

I naturally turned to the issue of the thickener itself. After some reflection, I thought that a combination of cornstarch and eggs might be best. The reason for this pairing lies in understanding the science of thickeners. When cornstarch is added to an egg custard mixture, the viscosity is greater (the mixture is thicker). This causes heat to be transmitted throughout the custard more evenly, which solves the problem of the overcooked perimeter. At the same time, eggs also add flavor and provide emulsification, which ensures a longer-lasting custard mixture that is less likely to "weep" in the refrigerator the next day. Finally, it is a well-known fact among bakers that cornstarch helps prevent eggs from curdling. One theory is that swelling starch granules make it more difficult for egg proteins to bond, the immediate cause of curdling. Therefore, I thought, a good balance between cornstarch and eggs should produce the best and most foolproof custard pie.

So I started a new round of tests, using corn-starch along with the eggs. (I later discovered that custard pies that use eggs and cornstarch are common in the South, where they are referred to simply as custard pies or sometimes silk pies.) The standard custard pie recipe uses 4 whole eggs and 3 cups of liquid (milk and heavy cream). I started my tests by decreasing the eggs to 3 and adding 2 tablespoons cornstarch. The pie had difficulty setting up properly, so I went back to 4 eggs, which worked fine. The pie was evenly cooked throughout, including the edges, and had a delicate, light texture, an improvement, I thought, on a standard eggs-only custard pie. I also tried both 3 and 4 tablespoons cornstarch, but with 4 eggs in the mix, the extra cornstarch was not necessary. For the eggs, I tried using 4 and then 3 egg yolks (no whites) and found both versions to be a bit too rich, with a strong egg yolk flavor. I then tried 3 whole eggs and 1 yolk, which was not quite as good as the 4 whole egg approach.

Now the issue was finding the best way to assemble the filling. Most custard recipes suggest that one simply add the cold filling ingredients to the unbaked shell. I knew from experience that prebaking the crust and heating the filling would produce a much crispier crust, but the question was how to heat the filling. I could simply heat the milk-cream mixture and add it to the eggs, cornstarch, sugar, and flavorings, or I could heat the entire filling. Over months of testing, I found that simply heating the milk and cream was both easier and more foolproof. When I heated the entire mixture, including the cornstarch, the pie often did not thicken properly, resulting in a very finicky recipe. Much to my surprise, the easier method did not result in longer oven time: both methods required 15 to 20 minutes in the oven.

To finish off the testing, I fiddled with the sugar and settled on ⅔ cup — this was enough to add flavor but less than the ¾ cup or more called for in most recipes. A pinch of salt made a big difference, rounding out flavors and adding depth as well. (Sugar, by the way, tends to slow the thickening process and salt enhances it.) I liked the addition of nutmeg, but only ⅛ teaspoon. I also found it best to mix the cornstarch with ¼ cup of the milk-cream mixture (in order to dissolve it) and then to add this back to the milk and cream when it had been brought to a simmer. I also played with variations for coconut, butterscotch, and nutmeg pies. These variations follow the master recipe.

...

Master Recipe for Custard Pie

The objective here is to get a good crispy crust and to yield a light, tender custard that is not too eggy or overcooked. Most custard pies take so long to set up in the center of the pie that the edges become overcooked. However, adding cornstarch to the custard mixture and preheating the filling before baking mean the center of the pie sets up in about 15 minutes, quick enough so that the edges do not overcook and become tough.

SERVES 6 TO 8

1   recipe Prebaked Pie Shell (page 218)

For the Filling
2   cups whole milk
1   cup heavy cream
2   tablespoons cornstarch
4   large eggs
⅔   cup granulated sugar
1½ teaspoons vanilla extract
⅛   teaspoon nutmeg
⅛   teaspoon salt

1. Follow instructions for Prebaked Pie Shell and bake shell for about 10 minutes after removing the foil, until lightly browned but not dark, rotating pan front to back halfway through baking.
2. After the foil has been removed, pour the milk and heavy cream into a heavy saucepan.

Remove ¼ cup of the mixture to a small bowl. Add the cornstarch to the bowl and stir thoroughly with a fork until completely dissolved; reserve. Heat the milk and cream in the saucepan over very low heat while the pie shell is browning.

3. When pie shell is ready, remove it from the oven. Bring the milk-cream mixture to a simmer and stir in the cornstarch mixture. Place the eggs, sugar, vanilla, nutmeg, and salt in a medium bowl and whisk until combined. (Do not do this ahead of time.) Now gently whisk in the hot milk-cream mixture, pouring slowly.

4. Place pie shell back in oven and carefully pour in filling. Bake for 15 to 20 minutes, or until custard is set around the outside but still wobbles a bit in the center 2 inches. (I find that it takes closer to 20 minutes.) Cool for 2 hours before serving.

WHAT CAN GO WRONG? This is a straightforward recipe, but be very attentive to the custard filling after 15 minutes of baking. Once it starts to set, it will firm up quickly and needs to be checked every minute. You will find it almost impossible to make yourself remove this pie from the oven before the filling is completely set, but you must! The center 2 inches or so should still be very wiggly, although the perimeter will have set and puffed up. Have faith in the recipe and remove the pie at this point. It will continue cooking and setting after it comes out of the oven. If you overcook the custard filling, it will become tough, weep, and remind you of the reason you don't like custard pies!

Butterscotch Variation

Butterscotch is a tricky flavor, since most of us think of commercial butterscotch puddings or candy from our childhood. This taste memory is based on a flavor that is hard to replicate at home, because the flavor we remember was engineered using artificial ingredients. However, when working on a recipe for butterscotch pudding, I discovered that the secret is to use lots of vanilla, dark brown sugar, and a hint of alcohol.

Use ⅔ cup dark brown sugar instead of white granulated. Increase vanilla to 3 tablespoons. Add 1 teaspoon bourbon or scotch. Eliminate nutmeg.

LEMON OR ORANGE VARIATION

Add ¼ cup lemon or orange juice plus 1 tablespoon grated zest to the mixture. Eliminate nutmeg.

NUTMEG VARIATION

Increase nutmeg to 1 teaspoon.

▪ ▪ ▪

Coconut Custard Pie

*M*any cooks are confused about the difference between cream of coconut and coconut cream. The former is sweetened and thick, the sort of mixture used in summer drinks. (It is often sold under the Coco López name.) Coconut cream is not sweetened and is made with the meat of the coconut plus either water or milk. (One common brand is Thai Kitchen Pure Coconut Milk. Although it is referred to as milk, it is actually a coconut cream.) If you cannot find coconut cream, use cream of coconut but reduce the sugar in the recipe to ½ cup. For the very best coconut custard pie, do not use the sweetened flaked coconut sold in supermarkets. Use unsweetened coconut or desiccated coconut, sold at natural food stores. (If you use supermarket coconut, reduce the sugar to ½ cup. If you use both cream of coconut and sweetened supermarket coconut, reduce the sugar to ¼ cup.)

SERVES 6 TO 8

1 recipe Prebaked Pie Shell (page 218)

For the Filling

1½ cups whole milk
1 cup heavy cream
½ cup coconut cream (see headnote)
2 tablespoons cornstarch

WHAT ABOUT A SLIPPED CUSTARD PIE?

Fannie Farmer offers a recipe for a slipped custard pie which calls for prebaking a piecrust and then baking the filling separately in an identical buttered pie dish. The cooled filling is then gently coaxed out of its pie plate and into the waiting crust. Our test kitchen tried it and found that first, one needs to use a smaller pie plate for the filling than for the crust; otherwise the filling is too big. Second, once the custard starts to slip, look out! It's almost impossible to make a nice-looking, perfectly fitting custard filling.

Marion Cunningham, who undertook the first major revision of *The Fannie Farmer Cookbook* back in the 1970s, noted that I had trouble with this recipe, so she hopped on a plane to give me a personal demonstration. The first try was not a success, since the filling was still hot out of the oven, which caused the custard to fall apart as it was transferred to the prebaked shell. However, for the second attempt, we allowed the custard to cool completely before slipping it into the pie shell, and this worked just fine. Although I think that experience counts with this approach, it is one method of solving the soggy crust problem common to custard-style pies.

4 large eggs
⅔ cup granulated sugar
½ teaspoon vanilla extract
⅛ teaspoon salt
¾ cup unsweetened dried coconut (see headnote), toasted or untoasted

1. Follow instructions for Prebaked Pie Shell and bake shell for about 10 minutes after removing the foil, until well browned but not dark, rotating pan front to back halfway through baking.

2. After the foil has been removed, pour the milk, heavy cream, and coconut cream into a heavy saucepan. Remove ¼ cup of the mixture to a small bowl. Add the cornstarch to the bowl and stir thoroughly with a fork until completely dissolved; reserve. Heat the milk and cream in

the saucepan over very low heat while the pie shell is browning.

3. When pie shell is ready, remove it from the oven. Bring the milk-cream mixture to a simmer and stir in the cornstarch mixture. Place the eggs, sugar, vanilla, and salt in a medium bowl and whisk until combined. (Do not do this ahead of time.) Now gently whisk in the hot milk-cream mixture, pouring slowly. Stir in the coconut.

4. Place pie shell back in oven and carefully pour in filling. Bake for 15 to 20 minutes, or until it is set around the outside but still wobbles a bit in the middle 2 inches. (I find that it takes closer to 20 minutes.) Cool for 2 hours before serving.

WHAT CAN GO WRONG? Be sure not to substitute cream of coconut for coconut cream without adjusting the sugar level. See recipe headnote and page 51 for more information.

▪ ▪ ▪

Master Recipe for Diner Cream Pie

This recipe is what most Americans would refer to as a cream pie. It is thicker than a regular custard pie, since it uses cornstarch, and has a whipped cream topping. This is diner food similar to the great, thick slabs of pie that one finds in the refrigerator cases behind the counter. I tested different numbers of egg yolks and found that 8 yolks was best, producing a somewhat smoother filling than 7 yolks. It is very important to let the custard cook sufficiently in the saucepan, so that it thickens up properly, about the consistency of mayonnaise. Otherwise, it will never properly set up. Yes, the heavy cream is necessary. After all, this is a cream pie! Versions with a higher proportion of milk just didn't have the right texture. I also tried using evaporated milk, a traditional ingredient in this sort of recipe, which helped the pie to set up nicely, but I preferred the fresh milk version.

SERVES 8 TO 10

1   recipe Graham Cracker Crust (page 219) or Prebaked Pie Shell (page 218)

For the Filling
  ½   cup plus 2 tablespoons granulated sugar
  ⅛   teaspoon salt
  3   tablespoons cornstarch
  8   large egg yolks
2½   teaspoons vanilla extract
1½   cups whole milk
  2   cups heavy cream
  2   tablespoons unsalted butter, at room temperature
  1   teaspoon brandy or rum

1. Prepare and bake either piecrust according to directions. If using a prebaked piecrust instead of the Graham Cracker Crust, bake shell for 15 to 20 minutes after removing the foil, until well browned, turning pan front to back halfway through baking.

2. In a medium saucepan, whisk together ½ cup of the sugar, the salt, and the cornstarch. Add the yolks and 2 teaspoons of the vanilla, then slowly pour in the milk and 1 cup of the heavy cream, whisking constantly. Cook over medium heat, stirring frequently with a straight-edge wooden spoon, until mixture starts to steam, then stir constantly, scraping the bottom of the pan as you stir. When mixture thickens to the consistency of mayonnaise, remove from heat and whisk in butter and brandy. Place custard in a bowl, lay plastic wrap directly on the surface, and refrigerate until cold. Place a metal mixing bowl and beaters from an electric mixer (or a metal bowl and a whisk) in the refrigerator or freezer while custard is cooling.

3. When custard is cold, combine remaining 1 cup heavy cream, remaining 2 tablespoons sugar, and remaining ½ teaspoon vanilla in the chilled bowl and beat on medium speed for 60 seconds. Increase speed to high and whip until peaks are firm and smooth. (If beating

by hand, just whisk until peaks are firm and smooth.)

4. Place chilled custard into pie shell and top with whipped cream.

WHAT CAN GO WRONG? Any cornstarch-thickened custard is tricky. You want to be very gentle with the mixture once it starts to thicken; otherwise you can destroy its thickening power. I have also noticed over the years that the time a custard takes to thicken will vary considerably depending on the amount of heat used and the type of saucepan. Therefore, my cooking times may be quite different from yours.

Coconut Cream Pie Variation

Reduce vanilla extract in custard to 1 teaspoon. Heat oven to 350 degrees. Place 2 cups shredded sweetened coconut in a single layer on a large baking pan. Toast 5 to 7 minutes, stirring frequently to promote even cooking. Remove when golden brown. Add 1½ cups toasted coconut to the filling in the saucepan once the milk has been whisked in. Sprinkle the remaining ½ cup coconut over the top of the whipped cream, once the pie is assembled.

Chocolate Cream Pie Variation

The problem with chocolate cream pie is that the excessive amount of dairy in this recipe dulls the deep flavors of the chocolate, resulting in a very mild chocolate taste. However, I still don't find too many slices left over when I serve it.

Reduce vanilla extract in custard to 1 teaspoon. Melt 4 ounces semisweet chocolate in a microwave at 50 percent power for 2 minutes; stir and heat another 1 to 2 minutes until melted (or melt in a double boiler or in a heavy bowl placed over a saucepan of simmering water). Add to the custard mixture along with the butter. Stir until combined.

Banana-Rum Cream Pie Variation

Substitute 2 tablespoons dark rum for the brandy. Slice 2 large ripe bananas into ³⁄₁₆-inch slices. Place half the filling in the pie shell, cover with bananas, and cover with remaining filling. Top pie with whipped cream.

Lemon Meringue Pie

LEMON MERINGUE PIE ought to be a brilliant pairing of tart, lemony filling and luxurious, smooth topping cradled in a buttery, crisp crust rather than what most of us have come to expect from the local diner — a thin, rather tasteless filling topped with an airy, weeping foam served in a gummy, undercooked shell. Determining how to make the perfect lemon meringue pie was a serious challenge.

The first issue was the filling. Most fillings are made from cornstarch, water or milk, sugar, egg yolks, salt, butter, and lemon zest and juice. Starting with a basic combination, I found the filling to be uninspired — starchy, dull, too sweet, and lacking in bright, lemony flavor. Reducing the sugar was a big help. I used less than two-thirds of the quantity called for in most recipes. I also reduced the amount of both cornstarch and water. The filling was now smoother and richer and much less gummy. Using milk for some or all of the water, I found, simply muted the lemon flavor of the filling while dulling the color to a pale yellow; so milk was out. I was using 3 egg yolks and found that increasing the quantity to 5 yolks made the filling richer and smoother. Six yolks was too much of a good thing.

The foamy topping of a typical lemon meringue pie has always bothered me; it is too airy to pair successfully with the filling. My first thought was that an Italian meringue (made by whipping egg whites with a hot sugar syrup) would be a good choice, since it is smooth and satiny rather than airy and in-substantial. I started with a meringue made with 3 egg whites, 6 tablespoons sugar, 2 table-spoons water, ¼ teaspoon cream of tartar, and ½ teaspoon vanilla. One tablespoon of cornstarch mixed with ⅓ cup water, cooked into a paste, was used to stabilize the topping. (The use of cornstarch to prevent a meringue topping from weeping was reported in *Cook's Illustrated* in an article by Pam Anderson.) The topping was a bit too stiff and not plentiful enough, so I added another egg white, with ex-cellent results.

Finally, I overcame the problem of a pasty, undercooked crust by prebaking it, adding the hot filling to the warm shell. I also found that since the meringue needs to be browned, a mod-erate oven temperature is best. A hot oven will make the top of the meringue bead.

■ ■ ■

Lemon Meringue Pie

SERVES 6 TO 8

1 recipe for Prebaked Pie Shell (page 218)

For the Filling

1 cup plus 3 tablespoons granulated sugar
5 tablespoons cornstarch
¼ teaspoon salt
1¾ cups cold water
5 egg yolks
⅔ cup lemon juice
1 tablespoon grated lemon zest
2 tablespoons unsalted butter

For the Meringue Topping

2 teaspoons cornstarch
¼ cup water
4 large egg whites, at room temperature
¼ teaspoon cream of tartar
6 tablespoons granulated sugar
½ teaspoon vanilla extract

1. Follow instructions for Prebaked Pie Shell and bake shell for about 15 minutes after re-moving the foil, until well browned but not dark, turning pan front to back halfway through baking. When it is done, remove it from the oven, leave the oven door open for 1 minute, and reduce the temperature to 325 de-grees. Adjust oven rack to the middle position.

2. *For the filling:* Combine the first 4 ingredi-ents (sugar through cold water) in a 2-quart nonreactive saucepan. Bring mixture to a sim-mer, stirring frequently. When it starts to turn translucent and simmer, add the egg yolks one at a time, whisking after each addition. If at any time the mixture starts to lump, remove it from the heat and whisk gently. Next, add the lemon juice and zest and bring the mixture to a sim-mer, whisking constantly but gently. The filling will be very thick. Remove from heat, stir in the butter until it melts, and cover to keep warm.

3. *For the meringue topping:* Place the corn-starch and 2 tablespoons of the water into a small saucepan and, over low heat, stir con-stantly. The mixture should turn into a translu-cent paste. Remove from heat.

4. In a large bowl of an electric mixer, beat the egg whites until frothy. Add the cream of tartar and beat until soft peaks form.

5. In a small saucepan, combine the sugar with the remaining 2 tablespoons water. Bring to a boil and cook until the mixture reaches 238 de-grees (a digital instant-read thermometer is help-ful here), or when a small amount dropped into a glass of cold water forms a soft, gummy ball.

6. Start beating the whites again with the mixer. Add the hot sugar syrup in a thin stream. Add the cornstarch paste and vanilla. Beat until the meringue forms 2-inch peaks and is stiff but still smooth and moist.

7. Place pie filling back on the stove and re-heat over low heat until hot. Immediately pour into the warm pie shell. Working quickly, dis-tribute the meringue over the top of the pie with a rubber spatula, being careful to attach the topping to the crust all the way around the

edge. (This will prevent shrinking.) Use a spoon or fork to create small peaks on the surface of the meringue. Bake until the meringue is golden brown, about 15 minutes. Cool pie on a wire rack to room temperature before serving. Serve at room temperature or chilled.

WHAT CAN GO WRONG? This is a relatively complex dessert, and there are a number of key issues. First, since this pie has a meringue topping, it is best done on a cool, dry day. Hot, humid weather almost always causes meringues to weep. Second, be gentle with the cornstarch-thickened filling. Once it starts to thicken, use a light hand stirring; otherwise you can impair its thickening power. Finally, an instant-read thermometer is extremely helpful in determining when the sugar syrup is ready. Note that the sugar syrup will quickly reach 230 degrees or so, but the last few degrees takes some time, which will vary depending on the saucepan used and the amount of heat.

PECAN PIE

Everyone in America, it seems, has their favorite recipe for pecan pie. Yet I rarely come across a piece of pecan pie that I truly love. How many times have you tucked into a piece only to find that the filling seems curdled, or hard around the edges, or too sweet, or grainy? Some pecan pies border on being treacly confections, not at all my ideal, with a tough top layer of pecans that have to be cut through with a steak knife. I want a creamy pecan pie, not too sweet, with a smooth, rich texture, a slice of pie that I can cut through delicately with a dessert fork.

The first step was to cut back on the tooth-aching sweetness of the typical pecan pie. By using more corn syrup than sugar, the former having about half the sweetening power of the latter, I managed to reduce the sweetness while keeping a nice texture. My recipe now uses only

½ cup dark brown sugar, less than half the amount called for in many other recipes. I also found that ½ cup cream dramatically changes the filling from a jellylike consistency to a creamier texture, just what I was looking for. Many pecan pies use a great deal of butter, which produces an extremely oily product. I tried a number of variations and settled on 2 tablespoons as the proper amount, just enough to add flavor.

Finally, I discovered that it was best to toast the pecans first in a 375-degree oven for about 7 minutes. I then chopped them coarsely, which solves the problem of cutting through the top of a slice.

■ ■ ■

Pecan Pie

This version is the quick and easy method. For a superior pecan pie, I prebake the crust and also preheat the filling (see Crisp-Crust Variation, below). For a more elegant presentation, bake your pecan pie in a tart pan.

SERVES 8

1 recipe Foolproof Food Processor Pie Dough (page 214) or Foolproof Handmade Pie Dough (page 215)

For the Filling
1½ cups pecan halves
3 large eggs
1 cup dark corn syrup
½ cup packed dark brown sugar
½ teaspoon vanilla extract
1 tablespoon bourbon or dark rum
½ cup heavy cream
¼ teaspoon salt
2 tablespoons unsalted butter, melted

1. Spread out the pecans on a baking sheet and toast in a 375-degree oven, about 7 minutes. Check frequently to avoid burning. Chop coarsely. Heat oven to 425 degrees.

2. In a large bowl, beat the eggs with a whisk

until blended. Whisk in the corn syrup, brown sugar, vanilla, bourbon, heavy cream, salt, and melted butter.

3. Roll out the pastry dough and fit into a 9-inch pie pan. Trim, leaving a ½-inch overlap. Fold the excess dough back under the crust and crimp with a fork or fingers.

4. Fold pecans into filling, pour filling into pie shell, and bake for 10 minutes. Reduce heat to 375 degrees and bake for another 20 minutes or so, or until a knife blade inserted in the center comes out clean. (The center of the pie should still be a bit wobbly.) Be careful not to overbake, as filling will become tough and hard. Cool to room temperature before serving.

WHAT CAN GO WRONG? Don't overcook this pie. The perimeter will become tough and chewy if you do. Take the pie out of the oven when the center is still a bit wobbly and you will have a more tender, creamier result.

CRISP-CRUST VARIATION

Although this is more difficult, it is best to pre-bake the crust and also heat the filling. This shortens the oven time and results in a crispy crust. Follow the directions for Master Recipe for Prebaked Pie Shell on page 218, baking the crust about 7 minutes after the foil has been removed. Prepare filling and heat in a medium saucepan until hot but not bubbling. Pour into hot, prebaked crust and bake 12 to 14 minutes in a 425-degree oven.

⬩⬩⬩

PUMPKIN PIE

PUMPKIN (OR SQUASH OR sweet potato) pie is nothing more than a custard pie made with pumpkin puree instead of milk and flavored with traditional spices. As I learned through test-baking, pumpkin pies are often dry and overcooked. A good pumpkin pie is moist and light, tender and not too eggy, solid but just cooked, with a tender texture and a clear, but not overpowering, note of spice. The first issue, then, was whether to use fresh pumpkin rather than the canned variety. I have found this not to be worth the trouble; the canned, nonspiced variety works just fine. It was then a question of how many eggs to use, and 3 seemed just right: with only 2 eggs, the pie did not set up properly, and 4 eggs produced a heavier, eggy texture. I voted for heavy cream for a silky, rich texture and flavor, and was a bit conservative with the spices, although pumpkin or similar fillings can stand a heavier hand than most other foods. I tried using lower oven temperatures, but it turned out that more heat worked just fine and also reduced the baking time. The most important discovery, however, is that it is best to heat the filling and then pour it into a hot, just pre-baked pie shell. This yields a crispy, nonsoggy crust. Finally, be sure to remove the pie from the oven before the center is fully cooked. It will finish cooking and setting outside the oven.

●●●

Pumpkin Pie

If the crust starts to overcook during baking, cover with aluminum foil, leaving the filling still exposed. If you like a smooth pie, pumpkin puree is best. If you prefer a bit more texture, use the squash or sweet potato filling (see variation below). Note that it is important to add the hot filling to a hot pie shell to produce a crisp crust.

SERVES 6 TO 8

1   recipe Prebaked Pie Shell (page 218)

For the Filling
2   cups canned pumpkin
¾   cup packed brown sugar
3   tablespoons molasses
½   teaspoon salt
¼   teaspoon nutmeg

¼   teaspoon ground ginger
½   teaspoon cinnamon
⅛   teaspoon ground cloves
1⅓ cups heavy cream
3   tablespoons bourbon
3   large eggs

Sweetened whipped cream or vanilla ice cream
    for serving

1. Follow instructions for Prebaked Pie Shell and bake shell for 4 minutes after removing the foil.

2. Increase oven temperature to 425 degrees. Whisk together all filling ingredients except the eggs in a medium saucepan. Place over low heat and cook, stirring occasionally, until bubbling. Remove saucepan from heat and whisk in eggs one at a time. Pour filling into still-hot prebaked pie shell and place on a baking sheet in the oven. Bake for 10 minutes and then lower heat to 350 degrees. Turn pie around so that filling bakes evenly. If the crust starts to become too brown, cover it with strips of aluminum foil. (Or, you can purchase metal piecrust covers in specialty cookware stores.) Bake 10 to 15 minutes longer, but start checking the pie after 8 minutes and every minute thereafter. A custard pie will set up quickly. Check by jiggling pie slightly. The mixture will puff up slightly but it should still shimmy and shake a bit when jiggled. This is the time to remove the pie from the oven. (Unlike the case with many custard pies, the filling of this one will not set from the edge in, leaving a wobbly center. Most of the filling will be slightly loose when you take it from the oven.) Note that the sweet potato and squash versions of the pie will set up a bit more quickly. Check these versions after 7 minutes instead of 10. Remove from oven and let cool on a rack for at least 1 hour before serving. Serve with sweetened whipped cream or vanilla ice cream.

WHAT CAN GO WRONG? As with the pecan pie, overbaking is the biggest problem. It will firm up a great deal after having been removed from the oven. (An overcooked pumpkin pie has a cracked top and is dry-tasting.) It takes fortitude to remove this pie from the oven when the filling still appears loose, but take heart. This is the secret to a moist, tender pumpkin pie.

SWEET POTATO OR BUTTERNUT SQUASH VARIATION
If using sweet potatoes, wrap them in aluminum foil and bake for 30 minutes in a 400-degree oven. When cool, remove the skin and mash. To prepare butternut squash, cut the squash in half lengthwise and remove the seeds. Lightly oil a baking sheet and place squash, cut side down, onto sheet. Roast in a 375-degree oven for 1 hour, or until the squash is very soft. Scoop out the flesh and mash. (I tried other varieties of winter squash with less success. Their texture was too wet or too slippery, or they did not have sufficient flavor.) Use 2 cups of either prepared vegetable in place of the canned pumpkin in the master recipe above.

SWEET POTATO PIE

THERE ARE TWO KINDS of southern cooking: lady food and down-home food. Sweet Potato Pie belongs to the latter category, since sweet potatoes were cheap, available, and the original recipes for this dessert were short on eggs, milk, and white sugar. Instead, country cooks relied more heavily on the natural sweetness and texture of the sweet potatoes themselves, combined with sorghum syrup or molasses instead of scarce white sugar. This resulted not in a custard-type pie as we know it today (see Pumpkin Pie recipe, above, for the more common version of this dessert), but in a toothier slice of pie, something more akin to a delicate version of mashed sweet potatoes. Since sweet potatoes were grown in abundance in the South and then stored in root cellars throughout the winter and spring, sweet potato pie was, unlike the seasonal pumpkin pie, an everyday dessert, not baked only at Thanksgiving or Christmas. But all that is history. The question I had to answer was how to create a distinctive sweet potato pie, a recipe that honored the texture and flavor of sweet potatoes while being sufficiently recognizable as a dessert pie. Neither a custardy pumpkin-style pie nor mashed potatoes in a crust would do.

Despite my keen interest in the history of this recipe, I realized that sweet potato pie had been adapted and modified so many times through the years that a wide range of recipes would have to be tested to get a handle on the possibilities. Very often the most authentic recipe is hardly the best. A review of more than thirty recipes led me to five distinctive approaches, from mashed sweet potatoes with a modicum of milk and eggs, to Louisiana chef Paul Prudhomme's Sweet Potato Pecan Pie, which was soaked in a sweet pecan pie syrup, to more custardy pumpkin pie styles. Some recipes separated the eggs and whipped the whites, some used evaporated milk, others used a combination of white and sweet potatoes, and most of them used a profusion of spices. To my surprise, all of them had abandoned molasses or sorghum for either white or brown sugar.

Although the classic pumpkin pie style was good, my tasters were drawn to more authentic recipes, especially one published in *Dori Sanders' Country Cooking,* which had more potato-like texture and better sweet potato flavor. The downside of these recipes, however, was that nobody was excited by the notion of eating mashed potatoes in a pie shell. I had to make this recipe work as a dessert, not as a savory side dish to a turkey dinner. This would require some fiddling with the amount of milk, eggs, and sugar, as well as with the method of preparing the potatoes. Second, I felt that all of these recipes had been modernized — for example, they all used white sugar — and I wondered if a bit of detective work might bring this recipe back to its roots, to a dessert that had more character than the white-tablecloth pie it has become.

The first step was to determine the best method of preparing the sweet potatoes. One group of tasters was keen on slicing cooked sweet potatoes and then layering them in the pie shell. This method was quickly discarded, since it bore little resemblance to a dessert. I also gave up on using an electric mixer to beat the cooked potatoes; this resulted in a very smooth, custard pie texture. I found that simply mashing the potatoes worked well, leaving the mixture with a few small lumps. This also made the recipe simpler, since the mashed sweet potatoes did not have to be passed through a sieve as called for in some of the more refined, "lady" recipes. Finally, I tested the microwave for precooking the sweet potatoes. It took just 10 minutes, without having to first boil water or preheat an oven. The only minor drawback was that different-size potatoes did cook at slightly different rates, but larger potatoes can simply be zapped for an extra minute or two. So the microwave was the answer.

Next, I discarded the notion of using a bit of white potato in the recipe (a technique often used by traditional southern cooks to lighten the texture), since it made it both more complicated and a bit grainy as well. Separating the eggs and whipping the whites, another common procedure, produced an anemic, fluffy dessert without enough moisture or flavor. Sweetened condensed milk did not improve the flavor, and I preferred regular milk over half-and-half. I added 2 yolks to 3 whole eggs for a moister texture; melted butter was preferred over margarine; orange zest and lemon juice were tried and discarded since they detracted from the delicate flavor of the sweet potato itself; and a bit of bourbon was added to pick up the flavor. A major problem with modern sweet potato pies is that they call for the usual array of pumpkin pie spices, which overwhelm the taste of the sweet potato. The solution was to use only a modest amount of nutmeg. White sugar worked just fine, but since older recipes often call for molasses (I also discovered recipes that use sorghum syrup, cane syrup, dark corn syrup, or even maple syrup), I decided to test this and settled on 1 tablespoon molasses, replacing 2 tablespoons of white sugar. This modest addition adds flavor without overpowering the pie with the distinctive malt taste of molasses. (Even 2 tablespoons molasses was too much.)

Even after all of these changes, I felt that the pie was still a bit dull. Based on the notion of pecan pie flavorings, which were used in Paul Prudhomme's recipe, I made a few pies to see if I could create two layers: one of sweet potato filling and one similar to the sweet filling in a pecan pie to jazz things up. It turned out that it was difficult to create two separate layers without a lot of extra work, so I simply sprinkled the bottom of the crust with brown sugar before adding the filling, which worked well. I also tested adding toasted pecans, a common sweet potato

pie ingredient, to the bottom layer, but they came out soft and leathery rather than crisp.

As usual with most of my one-crust pies, I prebake the crust so that it remains crisp even with a wet filling. The baking temperature was tested and a moderate 350 degrees was best. Be sure to bake this pie just until the edges start to set. It will continue cooking out of the oven.

▪ ▪ ▪

The Best Sweet Potato Pie

Sweet potatoes cook quickly in the microwave but can also be pricked with a fork and baked uncovered in a 400-degree oven until tender, 40 to 50 minutes. Some tasters preferred a stronger bourbon flavor than others in the filling, so I give a range below. If you like molasses, use the optional tablespoon; a few tasters felt it deepened the sweet potato flavor. Whipped cream is a perfect foil for the rich, thick filling.

SERVES 6 TO 8

SORGHUM SYRUP, CANE SYRUP, AND MOLASSES

In my research for this recipe, I came across southerners who swear by sorghum syrup, cane syrup, and molasses as key baking ingredients, and not just for sweet potato pie. (Many older sweet potato pie recipes call for these sweeteners.) After a few phone calls, I discovered that sorghum is a cereal grass that looks a great deal like corn, with broad leaves and tall, pithy stalks. It is grown primarily for animal feed in the United States, but a few southern growers still press the stalks, extract the juice, and then boil it down into a thick syrup that can be used much like molasses or maple syrup — poured on top of biscuits, used in baking, or drizzled over cornmeal mush or other cereal. It is a lighter color than molasses (which ranges from very dark brown to black) and has a buttery, more refined flavor. Cane syrup, another southern specialty, is simply sugar cane juice boiled down to make a syrup. It is almost identical to light molasses in flavor, with a distinctive malted mineral taste. Molasses, like

cane syrup, is also made from sugar cane, but it is the syrup left over after some or all of the sugar crystals are extracted from the boiled cane juice. The first boiling of the juice produces light molasses; the second boiling produces dark molasses; and the third boiling produces blackstrap molasses, which is very dark and somewhat bitter. (If all of the sugars are extracted from molasses, it is used as animal feed rather than for human consumption.) In a tasting, I found that cane syrup was somewhat sweeter than molasses, perhaps because the sugar crystals had not been extracted. Cane and sorghum syrups (also called sorghum molasses) are, at least in the North, available only by mail order. To place an order, contact the Lee Brothers at 843-720-8890 or hook up to their Web site at **www.boiledpeanuts.com.** You can also purchase cane syrup and molasses from Steen's Syrup, which has been in business for eighty-five years. Their Web site is **www.steensyrup.com.**

▪ ▪ ▪ ▪ ▪ ▪ ▪ ▪ ▪ ▪ ▪

THE TRULY SOUTHERN POTATO

Virtually all of the yams sold in American supermarkets are in fact sweet potatoes. Real yams are thick, tropical-vine tubers that can grow up to 7 feet long, depending on the species. Although many southern growers refer to their crops as yams, they are in fact sweet potatoes — edible roots that are part of the morning glory family. There are two basic types of sweet potatoes grown in the United States: those with light-colored flesh and thin skins, and darker-skinned varieties that are often erro-neously labeled yams. We used the latter type for our recipe since it was more readily available. The term "yam" may come from a Caribbean term, *nyami*, which means "good to eat." If you would like to purchase high-quality sweet potatoes from a southern grower, contact Wayne Garber of Garber Farms at 318-824-6328. I taste-tested his sweet potatoes (he stole a few last May from his father's secret stash, since his inventory was de-pleted) and found them superior to those available in lo-cal Boston markets. He sells sweet potato gift boxes during the holiday season.

▪ ▪ ▪ ▪ ▪ ▪ ▪ ▪ ▪ ▪ ▪

1 recipe Prebaked Pie Shell (page 218)

For the Sweet Potato Filling

2	pounds sweet potatoes (about 4 medium)
2	tablespoons unsalted butter, softened
3	large eggs plus 2 yolks
1	cup granulated sugar
½	teaspoon nutmeg
¼	teaspoon salt
2 to 3	tablespoons bourbon
1	tablespoon molasses (optional)
1	teaspoon vanilla extract
⅔	cup whole milk
¼	cup packed dark brown sugar

1. Follow instructions for Prebaked Pie Shell and bake shell for 4 minutes after removing the foil. Remove from oven; reduce oven tempera-ture to 350 degrees.

2. Meanwhile, prick sweet potatoes several times with fork and place on double layer of pa-per towels in microwave, making sure they do not touch. Cook at full power for 5 minutes; turn potatoes and continue to cook at full power until tender but not mushy, about 5 minutes longer. Cool 10 minutes. Halve each potato crosswise. Fold doubled layer paper towels into quarters and use to hold one potato half in one hand; insert small spoon between skin and flesh and scoop flesh into a medium bowl; discard skin. Repeat with remaining sweet potatoes; you should have about 2 cups. While potatoes are still hot, add butter and gently mash with large wooden spoon or fork but *not* a potato masher or food processor; small lumps of potato should remain. It is *crucial* not to overwork the pota-toes. If you do, they will become glutinous and the filling will be tough and unappealing.

3. Whisk together eggs, yolks, sugar, nutmeg, and salt in a medium bowl; stir in bourbon, mo-lasses (if using), and vanilla, then whisk in milk. Gradually add egg mixture to sweet potatoes, whisking gently to combine.

4. Heat partially baked pie shell in oven un-til warm, about 5 minutes. Sprinkle bottom of pie shell evenly with brown sugar. Pour sweet potato mixture into pie shell over brown sugar layer. Bake until filling is set around edges but center jiggles slightly when shaken, about 45 minutes. Transfer pie to wire rack; cool to room temperature, about 2 hours, and serve.

WHAT CAN GO WRONG? Do not overcook the potatoes and, most important of all, mash them very lightly. If you overwork the sweet potatoes, they will become starchy and glutinous, produc-ing a tough, barely palatable filling. Different types of sweet potatoes (although they are often called yams in supermarkets) will impart differ-ent colors and flavors to this dessert. Some are a rich orange color, while others are merely yel-low. The recipe will work with any type, but the flavor will be different with each variety.

11

TARTS

One might ask whether an American home cook really needs to know how to make a tart. After all, we are steeped in the English tradition of pies, and tarts seem the province of a French pastry chef. In addition, most French tart doughs, made with eggs and sugar, are notoriously sticky and hard to work with. However, if an easy-to-roll-out tart dough is available, tarts make a lot of sense. Unlike an American pie shell, which demands a rather substantial filling (pie plates are relatively deep compared to tart pans), the tart can handle a wider range of more interesting fillings — rich chocolate, for instance, or a thin layer of sweet almond filling (frangipane tart). Finally, the crust is a bigger player in a tart than in a pie, and I find the pairing of a delicious, well-browned tart pastry with a thin layer of intensely flavored filling to be not only an entirely different experience than the American pie but a bit more elegant.

The recipes in this chapter have been developed for a 9-inch tart pan with removable bottom. (The removable bottom makes it possible to remove the tart easily from the pan.) I have tested both the dark-colored and shiny metal

pans and prefer the latter. You will also find that tart pans come in different depths. The deeper ones might be fine for a quiche, but for a delicate dessert tart, the pan should be just 1 inch in depth. (Deeper pans are 1¼ to 1½ inches deep.) You will also want to use a tart pan with vertical sides. Some models come with sides that flare outward, which can cause problems during prebaking of the crust.

Here are a few tips I have learned after spending many months testing the recipes for this chapter:

• The recipe I have developed for the tart dough is relatively easy to work with, but getting dough into a tart pan is never easy. You will inevitably have to patch the dough with your hands, because pieces will break off as you work. The edges of the tart pans are sharp and often cut through the dough as you lay it into the pan. Do not be afraid to take bits and pieces of dough and patch your shell. A small amount of water brushed onto the area to be patched will help the patch to adhere properly. You can then dust with just

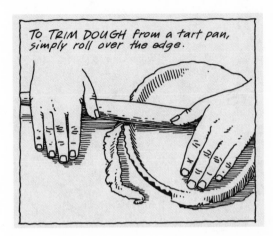

To TRIM DOUGH from a tart pan, simply roll over the edge.

a light sprinkle of flour to get rid of any excess moisture. It may look like something done by a ham-handed surgeon, but when baked it will look great.

- Press the sides of the dough down into the pan as you fit the dough. This will help reduce shrinkage as the tart shell bakes.
- On a very hot day, rolling out the tart dough will be difficult. The dough will soften quickly. I suggest that you not attempt these recipes in very hot weather. If the dough does start to become too soft as you work with it, put it back into the refrigerator to cool down before trying again.
- Always keep a can of vegetable shortening (Crisco) in the refrigerator if you are apt to make pies and tarts. The shortening must be cold for best results. If it is at room temperature, scoop it into tablespoon-size pieces, wrap in plastic, and freeze for 10 minutes before using.
- Prebaking a tart shell is necessary for most of these recipes. This means that the dough has been fitted into the tart pan, refrigerated and then frozen, fitted with aluminum foil and pie weights, and then placed into a 375-degree oven for 20 minutes. Always refrigerate the tart shell for 40 minutes and then freeze for 20 minutes before baking. This will reduce or eliminate shrinkage. Never just throw the tart shell into the oven after

rolling it out and fitting it to the pan. The dough will shrink and you will blame the recipe!

- Most experts caution you against using too much water when making tart or pie dough. I disagree. It is much better to have a slightly wet dough than a dry one. The latter simply cannot be rolled out. In addition, a slightly wet dough can be corrected by adding flour as you work with it. However, to avoid adding an excess of water, work the dough slowly with a large rubber spatula after the butter and vegetable shortening have been cut in. It takes time for the moisture to hydrate evenly throughout the dough, and haste at this point will cause you to add too much water.
- Always rotate tarts in the oven every 10 minutes or so as they bake. Ovens never bake evenly, and I am a great believer in cooking the tart dough until it is very dark. This brings out the flavor of the dough and also makes it look more attractive. The frequent turns will ensure that no side of the tart is overcooked.
- Although I like well-baked tart shells, I do not like overbaked fillings. Don't forget that most fillings (especially custard-style fillings) will continue to cook after being removed from the oven. Generally speaking, the center of the tart (when using eggs and milk or cream) should still jiggle a bit and not be completely set when it is time to remove the tart from the oven.

PASTRY DOUGH FOR TARTS

AN APPLE PIE, or any two-crust pie for that matter, is much easier to deal with than a single-crust pie or tart that requires prebaking. This process often results in shrinkage, the sides of the crust reducing in height to the point that the shell cannot hold the proper amount of filling.

CASE 41: THE MYSTERIES OF TART PASTRY

I tested five recipes for a sweet tart dough. Each recipe contained 1¼ cups flour, ½ teaspoon salt, and the ingredients listed below in the chart.

	Sugar	Butter	Crisco	Egg	Comments
Test 1	¼ cup	4 tablespoons, frozen	4 tablespoons	1	Easy to roll out; tender
Test 2	½ cup	4 tablespoons, frozen	4 tablespoons	1	Impossible to roll out; tougher than the first test
Test 3	¼ cup	8 tablespoons, frozen	None	1	Disastrous; major shrinking during prebaking; tough
Test 4	¼ cup	8 tablespoons, frozen	None	None	Same as test 3
Test 5	¼ cup	8 tablespoons, soft	None	1	Easy to roll out; didn't shrink; a bit tough in texture

This problem is exacerbated in a tart shell, which has relatively low edges, and even a small amount of shrinkage will both look unprofessional and leave one with little room for filling indeed. (A rustic look is fine for pies, but tarts, with their perfectly scalloped edges, demand a more precise appearance.)

In the pie chapter, I provide a recipe for prebaked pie shells that uses less total shortening than a regular two-crust pie dough and a slightly higher proportion of Crisco to butter. However, after some testing, I decided that a sturdier dough was called for when making tarts, since shrinkage is such a crucial issue. Just to see how different doughs reacted, I tested thirteen different pie pastry recipes from well-known cookbooks to see how they stood up to prebaking. The results were clear. Whether a recipe was made by hand or food processor made no difference. The oil-based recipe shrank the least but was relatively inedible due to its texture and complete lack of flavor. The cream cheese crust shrank the most, but those based on vegetable shortening maintained their shape well when prebaked. Crusts made exclusively with butter become very hard to work with during hot weather and were more likely to shrink or bubble in a hot oven. All in all, crusts with a combination of butter and vegetable shortening seemed to be the best bets: they had good flavor and only shrank a small amount.

Additional testing, however, led me to the conclusion that a French pastry dough such as a pâte sucrée or pâte brisée also has something to offer. These are doughs with more sugar than an American pie dough, and they also include egg instead of simply using water. The egg makes the dough more substantial and less prone to shrinkage. However, I have found that many French tart doughs have two drawbacks:

CASE 42: WHAT IF I HAVE THE WRONG SIZE TART PAN?

Here are the relative surface areas of different size tart pans. Note that a 1-inch difference in diameter makes a substantial difference in volume. I have used a 9-inch pan as the standard. If your pan is smaller or larger than this, decrease or increase the ingredients for the filling by the amount shown in the chart. Note that the recipe for tart pastry that follows makes enough for an 8- or 9-inch pan. For larger size pans, the recipe would have to be increased.

Pan Diameter	Surface Area Relative to a 9-Inch Pan
8 inches	20 percent less than a 9-inch pan
9 inches	The standard size
10 inches	25 percent greater than a 9-inch pan
11 inches	50 percent greater than a 9-inch pan

they are hard to roll out, since they are so sticky, and they are also a bit heavy for my taste. So I decided to begin with my own well-tested pie dough recipe — the one I use for pre-baking — and then modify it by adding more sugar, experimenting with the addition of egg, and perhaps taking a fresh look at whether I could make an all-butter crust, as the French do, or whether the vegetable shortening was in fact necessary. Case 41 shows the results from my first five tests. For them I determined that ¼ cup sugar was about right, the ½-cup recipe producing a tougher dough that was hard to roll out. It also seemed that the Crisco-plus-butter dough did better than the all-butter versions. This, I surmised, was because butter contains a lot of water and Crisco doesn't. The water turns to steam during baking, which leads to shrinking. I also suspected, however, that freezing the butter for 15 minutes — a technique I use for regular American pie pastry — was a problem with a tart dough. This came to light with tests 3 and 4, which used only butter. When baked, the dough shrank a great deal and became un-

even. This was because the frozen butter did not properly coat the flour during mixing. However, the soft-butter dough (test 5) was also not perfect; it was a bit tough when baked.

So I decided to try cold butter instead, without freezing and without bringing it to room temperature. I also wanted to test whether an egg yolk, instead of a whole egg, would be better and wanted a final matchup between the all-butter and Crisco-butter versions to make sure I was right. (The French would probably shoot any cook who uses Crisco in a classic pâte sucrée recipe!) After a further round of tests, the results were unambiguous. The two all-butter doughs (one with yolk and one with a whole egg) shrank more than the Crisco-butter version. The latter did not shrink at all, maintaining its shape perfectly in the shell. In addition, the flavor of the crust did not suffer terribly, being almost as good as the all-butter version. Also, the yolk fared better than the whole egg, producing a somewhat more tender crust. It turned out that cold butter was indeed better than either frozen or room temperature butter, since all three tests were better than the first batch. So, after two weeks' baking and twenty-one tests, I finally had the perfect tart dough, one that was easy to make and roll out and that did not shrink during baking. The final recipe used 1¼ cups of flour, ½ teaspoon salt, ¼ cup sugar, 4 tablespoons each cold butter and cold Crisco, 1 egg yolk, and up to 2 tablespoons cold water. Both a handmade version and a food processor version of the recipe are provided below.

▪ ▪ ▪

Master Recipe for Food Processor Tart Pastry

This is an unorthodox recipe for what the French call a pâte sucrée. I use a combination of Crisco and butter, which I found, after extensive testing, produced a dough that did not shrink at all during baking. It also helps to make a dough that is easy to roll out and fit into the tart pan. Some recipes for this dough call for cream instead of water, which I did not test, figuring that most folks do not have heavy cream on hand. I wanted this recipe to be easy to make from ingredients found in all kitchens.

MAKES ONE 8- OR 9-INCH TART SHELL

1¼	cups all-purpose flour
½	teaspoon salt
¼	cup granulated sugar
4	tablespoons chilled all-vegetable shortening (e.g., Crisco)
4	tablespoons chilled unsalted butter, cut into ¼-inch pieces (see page 211)
1	large egg yolk
1 to 2	tablespoons cold water

1. Mix flour, salt, and sugar in a food processor fitted with the steel blade. Place the vegetable shortening (Crisco) in 1-tablespoon lumps into the food processor along with the butter pieces. Pulse 8 times (1-second pulses) and then run food processor continuously for 12 to 15 seconds, or until the mixture changes texture, be-coming thicker. It will also mound up around the side of the workbowl and then start to slide back down, acting much like cornmeal. There should be no visible lumps of butter — the mixture should be totally processed and very fine. Turn mixture into a medium bowl.

2. Whisk the egg yolk with 1 tablespoon of the water and sprinkle over the mixture. With the blade of a large rubber spatula, use a folding motion to mix, working for up to 1 minute, to distribute the egg-water mixture evenly throughout the dough. The dough will probably need a bit more water, up to 1 tablespoon. Note that it is better to use too much water here than too little. To test the dough, use your hands to press the dough together into a ball. If it holds together easily, it is done. If it doesn't, add a bit more water. Place the dough onto a floured work surface and then lightly sprinkle flour over the top. Turn the dough over a few times, lightly shaping it into a 4-inch-wide disk. Wrap in plastic and refrigerate for at least 2 hours before rolling.

WHAT CAN GO WRONG? This recipe requires that one more thoroughly cut the shortening into the flour than for an American pie dough. Do not leave pea-size pieces of butter in the dough. Process the mixture until it is very fine. Also, make sure you use enough water so that the dough comes together easily. A dry dough will be impossible to roll out.

▪ ▪ ▪

Master Recipe for Handmade Tart Pastry

A tart dough needs to be sturdier than the standard two-crust American pie dough. This is because most tarts require prebaking, and even a small amount of shrinkage results in both an unattractive tart and one with very low sides that cannot hold a sufficient amount of filling. The secret? There is more than one. The use of both Crisco and butter, a lower proportion of fat to flour than with American pie pastry, more sugar, and the addition of an egg yolk. All of these changes make a sturdy dough that can still be rolled out easily, and which is flavorful and reasonably tender.

When making tart pastry by hand, be sure to cut the cold butter and shortening into small bits, so they can be worked relatively quickly into the dry ingredients. (You can cut the butter into small pieces by cutting the stick lengthwise into quarters and then crosswise into ¼-inch pieces; see illustration on page 211.)

MAKES ONE 8- OR 9-INCH TART SHELL

1¼	cups all-purpose flour
½	teaspoon salt
¼	cup granulated sugar
4	tablespoons chilled unsalted butter, cut into small pieces
4	tablespoons chilled all-vegetable shortening (e.g., Crisco), cut into small pieces
1	large egg yolk
1 to 2	tablespoons cold water

1. Combine flour, salt, and sugar in a medium mixing bowl. Add the cold butter and shortening pieces and toss flour and fat mixture about 8 to 10 times until all the butter and shortening are coated with flour and mixed evenly throughout the flour. Break up any clumps with your fingers as you toss the mixture. The flour should no longer appear light and powdery but take on a mealy texture, slightly heavier and a bit more yellow in color. There should be no pieces of butter or shortening still visible; it should all be evenly incorporated with the flour. However, do not overwork or the butter will melt and the dough will become unworkable when rolled out.

2. Whisk the egg yolk with 1 tablespoon of the water and sprinkle over the mixture. With the blade of a large rubber spatula, use a folding motion to mix, working for up to 1 minute, to distribute the egg-water mixture evenly throughout the dough. The dough will probably need a

bit more water, up to 1 tablespoon. Note that it is better to use too much water here than too little. To test the dough, use your hands to press the dough together into a ball. If it holds together easily, it is done. If it doesn't, add a bit more water. Place the dough onto a floured work surface and then lightly sprinkle flour over the top. Turn the dough over a few times, lightly shaping it into a 4-inch-wide disk. Wrap in plastic and refrigerate for at least 2 hours before rolling.

WHAT CAN GO WRONG? This is a tricky recipe since the butter and Crisco need to be fully worked into the flour, yet too much handling produces a sticky, unworkable dough. I highly recommend the food processor version, which is relatively foolproof. However, if you must do this by hand, don't attempt this recipe in a hot kitchen and work quickly when tossing the flour and fat so that the butter does not have time to melt.

■ ■ ■

Master Recipe for Prebaked Tart Shell

This is a foolproof technique for prebaking a tart shell. Note that it requires both refrigeration and freezing before baking; both techniques are necessary to produce superior results. Once the aluminum foil has been taken off the shell (after 21 minutes), you then have to decide how much longer to bake the pastry. If the filling is to be placed into the shell without any further baking, bake an additional 12 minutes, or until the crust is well browned. For fillings that will undergo long baking (20 minutes or more), remove foil from the shell and bake an additional 4 minutes. For fillings that are to be baked less than 20 minutes, bake an additional 7 minutes after foil is removed.

MAKES ONE 8- OR 9-INCH TART SHELL

1 recipe Handmade Tart Pastry or Food
  Processor Tart Pastry (page 249)
Flour for sprinkling dough and work surface
8- or 9-inch tart pan with a removable bottom
Pie weights or dried beans
Aluminum foil

1. Take the tart dough out of the refrigerator and let sit about 20 minutes before rolling. When the dough is no longer hard but still very firm, place on a floured surface and hit the dough with a rolling pin four or five times, moving from one side of the dough to the other. Turn the dough 180 degrees and repeat. Do this until the dough is about 6 inches in diameter.

2. Pick up the dough, reflour the work surface, and turn the dough over. Flour the top of the dough lightly. Roll out the dough until it is 2 inches greater in diameter than the diameter of the tart pan. (See illustrations, page 212). Pick up the dough on the rolling pin a few times as you work, reflouring the work surface and turning the dough over. If you don't do this, the dough will stick to the work surface, making it very difficult to pick up and move to the tart pan.

3. When dough is rolled out, drape it over rolling pin to transfer to tart pan, then unroll dough over pan. Immediately push the sides of the dough down into the pan. Once dough has been fit snugly into pan, roll over edges of the pan with the rolling pin to remove excess dough. Patch any holes in the bottom or sides of the shell. If any of the sides are very thin, reinforce them with scrap dough. (Very thin sides have a tendency to shrink when baked.) Place finished shell in the refrigerator for 40 minutes. Heat oven to 375 degrees. Place shell in the freezer for 20 minutes; remove from freezer.

4. Fit a sheet of aluminum foil over the frozen tart shell and press it down into the bottom of the shell and into the edges. Make sure that the edges are completely covered with foil. Add the pie weights (metal or ceramic weights are best, since they conduct heat well). Place in the preheated oven on a cookie sheet on the lowest rack.

5. Bake for 10 minutes and turn pan around in oven. Bake an additional 11 minutes and then remove foil and weights. If the filling requires no baking, bake shell an additional 12 to 15 minutes, or until the crust is well browned. For fillings that are to be baked less than 20 minutes, bake shell an additional 7 minutes after foil is removed. For fillings that require longer baking times (20 minutes or more), remove foil and bake an additional 4 minutes.

WHAT CAN GO WRONG? If you have added enough water to the dough to start with, then the dough should roll out fairly easily, but keep in mind that this dough is relatively sticky, since it uses an egg yolk and ¼ cup sugar. It will be very hard to work with in a hot kitchen. If you have trouble rolling it out, I suggest that you place the dough between sheets of waxed paper, plastic wrap, or parchment paper and then roll it. It is likely that the dough will crack or fall apart a bit when it is placed into the tart pan. I find that the sharp top edge of the pan often cuts into the dough as I lay it in place. Don't panic. Just press it all together with your fingers. Finally, be sure to press the dough down into the corners of the pan before trimming it. This helps reduce shrinkage during baking.

▾
▾

LEMON TART

MOST LEMON TARTS are made with lemon curd, which consists of egg yolk with sugar, lemon juice, butter, and lemon zest. The curd is usually heated and then poured into a partially baked pie shell, which is then put back into the oven to finish. I find this approach a bit rich for my taste, preferring instead something lighter and more refreshing. So I set out looking for a different sort of lemon tart, the sort of dessert that would end a meal with a light, smooth burst of lemon without an eggy aftertaste.

My first thought was to add cream to the mixture in an effort to dilute the texture and flavor of the eggs. This was a good start. But I also thought that the ratio of eggs to lemon juice needed fixing. Most lemon curd recipes use 8 eggs, mostly yolks, to ½ cup lemon juice. I decided that a lower ratio of eggs to juice would be better, but I wasn't sure how to proceed. Remembering a lemon tart I had at Fredy Girardet's restaurant in Crissier, Switzerland, many years ago, I looked up the recipe in his cookbook. He uses 3 whole eggs and 1 yolk to the juice of 3 lemons and 1 orange. I fiddled with this recipe a bit and liked it a lot — the orange juice cut the bitterness of the lemon juice and added an extra dimension of flavor — but I finally decided to slightly adjust the lemon juice down to ½ cup (a large lemon will yield ¼ cup of juice, so I was using 2 lemons instead of the original 3) and add a bit of zest to boost flavor. I started with a full tablespoon of zest and then worked down to 2 teaspoons, which was less bitter. I also added 2 teaspoons of orange zest, which complemented the lemon flavor nicely.

Many cooks like a nice deep filling for a lemon tart, but I prefer a thinner filling because it makes for a better marriage with the crust. This is an intense filling, and a small amount goes a long way.

● ● ●

Lemon Tart

In order to achieve a crisp crust, the shell is partially prebaked and then the cold filling is poured into the hot crust and the tart is placed back in the oven to finish. Note that the tart will start to set up very quickly toward the end of cooking. Watch it carefully as it begins to set, checking it every minute. Remove from the oven when the middle 2 inches are still wobbly. It will continue cooking on the counter. This recipe is best made in an 8-inch tart pan, although it can also be baked in a 9-inch pan. The cooking time will be significantly shorter. One last trick. When mixing the filling ingredients, do so gently so that there is minimum froth. Otherwise, the top of the baked tart will appear foamy.

SERVES 6 TO 8

1   recipe Prebaked Tart Shell (page 250)

For the Filling
⅓   cup orange juice
½   cup lemon juice
2   teaspoons grated lemon zest
2   teaspoons grated orange zest
3   large eggs plus 1 egg yolk
⅔   cup heavy cream
¾   cup granulated sugar

1. Follow instructions for Prebaked Tart Shell and bake shell for about 4 minutes after removing the foil, until light brown.

2. Just before the tart shell is ready, lightly whisk together the ingredients for the filling. With the hot tart shell on a cookie sheet on the bottom rack of the oven, pour in the filling. (You can pull out the cookie sheet a bit to make this easier. Push the cookie sheet back into the oven before adding the last half cup so the filling does not spill.) Bake at 375 degrees until the perimeter sets but the center 2 inches are still loose, about 20 to 25 minutes. Turn tart after 12 minutes of baking. Watch tart very closely toward end of baking, as it will set up quickly.

WHAT CAN GO WRONG? The only tricky part is keeping an eye on the tart as it bakes. Once it starts to set, it will go quickly. Even 1 minute can make a difference, so once the perimeter of the custard starts to firm up, watch it like a hawk. Also, remember to take the tart out of the oven before the center 2 inches is set. The tart will continue to bake after it is removed from the oven.

TRUFFLE TART

UNLIKE THE BAKED chocolate tart on page 254, this is an unbaked tart: chocolate and butter are melted on the stovetop, cream is added, and then the mixture is simply poured into a freshly prebaked tart shell. It doesn't get much easier than this.

However, as with all recipes, things can go wrong. I found that this tart can produce a very bitter chocolate flavor. Eggs made a good addition, but since the tart is not baked, I could not use them for safety reasons. So I had to find just the right mix of ingredients to produce a rich, moist chocolate mixture without using eggs.

The first test was the chocolate itself. I tested semisweet, milk, and unsweetened chocolates. The semisweet variety was quite good — the flavor was excellent — but I found that the milk chocolate had a more buttery flavor and better texture. The unsweetened chocolate was problematic, because adding sugar to the chocolate was difficult and the texture was adversely affected. The solution was to use a mixture of semisweet and milk chocolates for a dark, glossy dessert with a creamy, buttery taste and texture.

The next issue was the dairy element. I had to add milk or cream to improve the texture and to mellow the taste of the chocolate. Half-and-half and light cream were both too thin to stand up to the chocolate, but heavy cream worked just fine. The addition of 1 egg was good, but as I stated at the outset, I felt that using raw eggs was off limits. I did try adding salt but found that it overpowered the chocolate and cream. I also found that butter was a must in this recipe. It moderates the bitterness of the chocolate and makes the tart just a bit less thick, which is good.

Additional flavorings were tried, and I found much to my dismay that any sort of liquor made the chocolate sweat and easily overpow-

ered the tart. The one success was the use of mint flavoring, which seemed to work well with the chocolate although, since extracts are alcohol based, I did notice that the chocolate sweated. As a result, I decided to keep this recipe simple, using just chocolate, cream, and butter.

• • •

Quick and Easy Truffle Tart

The chocolates and butter are melted in a saucepan, the heavy cream is added, and then this mixture is simply poured into a freshly prebaked tart shell. It is a rich, elegant-looking dessert with a thin layer of chocolate married to a crisp, buttery crust.

SERVES 6 TO 8

1 fully prebaked 9-inch tart shell, cooled (page 250)

For the Filling
3 ounces semisweet or bittersweet chocolate, chopped
3 ounces milk chocolate, chopped
2¾ tablespoons unsalted butter
½ cup heavy cream

1. Prepare tart shell as directed in master recipe, baking until well browned, about 35 minutes. Allow to cool completely.

2. Melt the chocolates and the butter over low heat in a small, heavy saucepan (or use a double boiler) until just melted. Remove from heat, add heavy cream, and stir until smooth. If necessary, place back on low heat and stir until the mixture is smooth. (The cold heavy cream can thicken the chocolate, making it difficult to incorporate.)

3. Pour mixture into the cooled tart shell and cool until set. Keep in a cool place until ready to serve.

WHAT CAN GO WRONG? Almost nothing can go wrong here, since the filling is simply poured into the prebaked shell. You may have to place the filling back on the stove if the mixture is not smooth after adding the heavy cream.

RICH CHOCOLATE TART

THE PRECEDING RECIPE provides a thin, intense layer of chocolate, almost more of a cookie than a tart. I was also looking to develop a chocolate tart recipe that had a thicker filling and was a bit lighter, but that also delivered an intense chocolate experience.

I noted, as I was developing the recipe for the truffle tart, that the addition of eggs improved the texture, making it silkier and lighter, but I could not use them since the tart was not baked. Since this recipe is baked, I fiddled with different quantities and finally settled on 2 whole eggs. Larger amounts drowned out the taste of the chocolate and produced a somewhat rubbery texture. (I was using 6 ounces of chocolate; lesser amounts produced a light-colored confection without enough chocolate punch.)

Next, I sorted out the type of chocolate, testing milk chocolate, semisweet chocolate, bittersweet chocolate, and cocoa powder. The milk chocolate was good, and it might work well as an alternative, but I preferred the taste of bittersweet and semisweet chocolates. Cocoa powder, however, was a disaster, since it turned out a very dry tart indeed, with a bitter, lingering aftertaste.

For flour, I tested ¼ cup, ½ cup, and a full cup and ended up with ½ cup. Too much flour makes the filling dry and rubbery and overpowers the chocolate flavor. Butter was also an important ingredient, and I settled on 8 tablespoons. For flavorings, brandy and vanilla were winners. I did not like the taste of mint in this recipe.

Baking time was the most important issue. Many recipes suggest baking this sort of tart for 20 to 25 minutes. I found that slightly underbaking the tart was best, pulling it from the oven after about 12 minutes, when the center was still quite wet. This preserves the intense flavor of the chocolate and also makes for a moist, tongue-coating texture. At 20 minutes of baking time, the tart is relatively tough and lacking in chocolate flavor.

• • •

Rich Chocolate Tart

The secret to this tart is underbaking rather than overbaking. This keeps the tart moist, with an intense, rich chocolate flavor. This recipe is for a 9-inch tart shell.

SERVES 6 TO 8

1   recipe Prebaked Tart Shell (page 250)

For the Filling
6   ounces semisweet chocolate, chopped
8   tablespoons (1 stick) unsalted butter, cut into pieces
½   cup all-purpose flour
½   cup granulated sugar
3   large eggs
1   teaspoon vanilla extract

1. Follow instructions for Prebaked Tart Shell and bake shell for about 7 minutes after removing the foil.

2. After prebaking the shell, increase oven temperature to 400 degrees. Melt chocolate and butter over very low heat in a heavy saucepan or use a double boiler.

3. Whisk together the flour, sugar, eggs, and vanilla in a medium bowl. When the chocolate and butter have melted (stir occasionally as they melt) and are smooth, pour into the egg mixture and stir until smooth. Let cool for 1 minute.

4. Pour filling into the prebaked shell, place in oven, and bake for 12 to 14 minutes, or until the perimeter is set but the center is still wet. Do not overbake this tart. Cool for at least 30 minutes and then serve.

WHAT CAN GO WRONG? Overbaking this tart results in a tough, brownielike dessert with a reduced chocolate flavor. Slightly underbaking will yield a moist, rich interior with lots of flavor.

Fruit Custard Tart

This is a simple summer dessert. Fresh, ripe fruit is placed in a prebaked tart shell, a bit of custard mixture is poured over it, and the tart is then baked about 20 minutes. The trick is to have just the right balance between custard, fruit, and tart shell and, of course, to use the right fruit. Too much fruit, too much custard, or a hole in the bottom of your tart shell can all lead to a less than spectacular dessert.

My first inquiries focused on the custard itself. I tested using no eggs, 2 eggs, 3 eggs, and then 4 yolks. I was surprised that the custard with no eggs was actually rather good and that the whole egg versions were disappointing; I could taste the egg whites, and the texture was grainy. The 4-yolk version was excellent, although I eventually cut that to 2 yolks since I ended up using less custard than I had originally planned.

I then tested sugar. Three tablespoons of white sugar was tested against half that amount and against no sugar at all, and the winner was the middle road, a modest 1½ tablespoons. When tested, brown sugar gave the custard an unpleasant dirty brown color, and honey was a very strong flavor that overpowered the dessert.

The next question was what to do about the dairy component. After a number of tests (Case 43 shows the results), light cream was declared the winner, providing just enough fat for good custard flavor without overpowering the fruit.

The next issue was settling on the proper type of fruit. I tried blueberries, sour cherries, peaches, grapes, plums, and apples. The winners were the blueberries, peaches, and apples.

CASE 43: THE DAIRY MAID BECOMES A TART

Which type of milk product is best for a simple fruit custard tart?

Test	Comments
¾ cup heavy cream	Too sweet; too rich
½ cup light cream	Good fruit flavor; a classic
¼ cup heavy cream	A bit eggy; too thick
½ cup half-and-half	Hollow finish; too thin
½ cup sour cream	Sour cream taste too strong
½ cup milk	Too thin; not enough flavor

The cherries were overpowered by the custard, the grapes were surprisingly good — it would be worth trying this with different varieties, such as champagne grapes — and the plums were a bit tart, although this would also vary depending on the variety and their ripeness.

Finally, I fiddled with the custard recipe a bit more. A little brandy added depth of flavor; flour was unnecessary and cloying; more fruit overpowered the custard. Baking the crust and the fruit before adding the custard mixture turned out to be a good idea, producing a flakier crust and a smoother custard, almost like a pudding.

•••

Master Recipe for Fruit Custard Tart

I find that when using berries, the fruit should sit in the tart shell in one layer. It makes for a prettier presentation, rather than having some berries sitting on top of others. This recipe is for a 9-inch tart shell.

SERVES 6 TO 8

1   recipe Prebaked Tart Shell (page 250)

For the Filling
2   cups prepared fruit (apples, peaches, berries, plums, etc.)
2   large egg yolks
½   cup light cream (or a mix of milk and heavy cream)
½   teaspoon brandy, rum, or bourbon
½   teaspoon vanilla extract
1½ tablespoons granulated sugar

1. Follow instructions for Prebaked Tart Shell, baking the shell about 20 minutes, or until the sides of the tart set up and can stand on their own. Remove the foil and bake an additional 7 to 8 minutes, until very light brown.

2. While crust is baking, prepare fruit if you have not already done so. For stone fruits, pit, peel if necessary, and slice thinly. For apples, core, peel, and slice thinly. For berries, wash and dry. You may need somewhat less than 2 cups berries, since you want only one layer of fruit in the tart shell. When tart shell is light brown, remove it from oven, place fruit in shell, and return to oven for 8 minutes.

3. Lightly whisk together the yolks, cream, brandy, and vanilla, then whisk in the sugar. Try not to incorporate too much air into the mixture, which will result in bubbles on the surface of the finished tart. After fruit has baked for 8 minutes, pull out the oven rack and pour custard mixture over fruit. Bake until the custard is set around the perimeter (about 15 minutes) but still wobbly in the very center. It is best to turn the tart shell around in the oven halfway through baking to ensure even cooking.

4. Remove tart from oven and allow to cool thoroughly before serving.

WHAT CAN GO WRONG? Make sure that the fruit is not wet when you put it in the tart shell, and take the tart out of the oven before the custard is totally set. Also, use ripe fruit. Tasteless, semiripe fruit is not worth the trouble.

▾▾▾

JUST-FRUIT TARTS

I HAD AN AWAKENING about fruit tarts one summer at the home of Julia Child. She often has potluck get-togethers, and Jim Dodge, a well-known chef and author of *The American Baker,* brought a simple apricot tart that changed my view about fruit desserts. It was nothing more than a tart shell filled with perfectly ripe, halved apricots sprinkled with a bit of sugar. It was simple, beautiful, and the fruit itself was the star.

Of course, simplicity is often more difficult to achieve than something more elaborate, as I was about to find out. The problem with simple fruit tarts is the fruit. In any given batch some specimens are ripe and juicy and others are relatively hard and dry. For example, one Granny Smith apple may be full of juice and another may exude almost no juices at all, to say nothing about the differences between various types of apples. In addition, peaches are juicier than apples, which are, in turn, quite different from plums. The nature and condition of the fruit will affect cooking time, and the juices are important, since they mix with the sugar and flour to form a thickened liquid. Blueberries, for example, exude very few juices, and therefore sugar will simply sit on top of them throughout the baking period.

Since I was performing these tests in August

at the height of the peach season, that was my first test, and I was lucky the first time out. I used 3 large, very ripe peaches, removed the skin, and then sliced them very thinly. I arranged them in a fan pattern on an unbaked tart crust, sprinkled them with 2 tablespoons of sugar, and then placed the tart in a 400-degree oven. At first, the tart shell filled up with juices, but as time went on, some of the juice evaporated. The result was excellent, but there was still a bit too much juice for my taste. So I decided to put the tart through a series of tests.

The first was to determine what sort of thickener I would need and how to apply it. I tried flour, cornstarch, tapioca, cake crumbs, and cookie crumbs, and flour emerged as the thickener of choice. The next issue was how to use the thickener. I tried tossing the fruit with it, but it seemed better to simply coat the bottom of the tart with the flour before adding the fruit. (Some fruit does not exude a lot of juice; as a result, the flour never really comes off the fruit during cooking, making the fruit taste a bit dry.) I found that 1 tablespoon was plenty, even with juicier fruits such as peaches.

The next issue was sugar. I tested both white and brown sugar and found that white sugar seemed to melt easier and didn't disturb the natural taste of the fruit. I tried ⅓ cup sugar, which was too much, then only 2 tablespoons, which I thought was a bit too little. It seemed that ¼ cup was about right, although really sweet fruit might do fine with only 3 tablespoons. A tip from a local chef resulted in sprinkling on 2 tablespoons of the sugar at the outset and then adding the balance after 20 minutes of baking. It made only a small difference, but the fruit seemed to have a nicer finish when baked. I also tried adding butter, but this left a greasy aftertaste that I found unappealing.

The biggest issue was which fruit worked best for this recipe. My first choice was ripe peaches. The tart was drop-dead gorgeous after baking, and the flavor was sublime. Apples are dicey, since you really want juicy apples that

CASE 44: THE TART THICKENS

Which sort of thickener works best with a simple fruit tart?

Type of Thickener	Results
Cornstarch	Good, but odd aftertaste
Tapioca	Grainy texture like Tic-Tacs
Cake crumbs	Appearance lumpy; flour better
Cookie crumbs	Spongy texture; stale flavor
Flour	Worked nicely
No thickener	Okay for less juicy fruits

bake up nicely. Some apples, dry Granny Smiths in particular, end up like dried apples with no juices. In terms of year-round supermarket apples, I would vote for McIntosh or Golden Delicious, both of which will cook down nicely and have some juice, although they will get very soft and lose their shape. Berries are not recommended, since they do not release many juices. I tried blueberries, which I had to cook for an hour, and the sugar never dissolved. I also did not care much for cherries, for the same reason. Plums were pretty good, but use juicy varieties. Apricots are terrific, but full-flavored ripe specimens are virtually impossible to find. Grapes were too sweet. So peaches, apples, and plums were best.

Finally, I found that a long cooking time

really makes this recipe. The crust gets very dark, the excess juices have time to evaporate, and the flour, sugar, and remaining juices combine in the bottom of the tart to make a nice syrup. The fruit also cooks down nicely, concentrating its natural flavors. Fifty minutes to 1 hour seems about right to me. Just be sure that you don't burn the edges of the tart. I discovered that refrigerating and freezing the tart shell before baking slows down the cooking process and also makes it less likely that the tart dough will shrink during baking.

• • •

Master Recipe for Just-Fruit Tarts

This is about as simple as it gets. Thinly sliced fruit is placed into an unbaked tart shell with some flour and sugar and then baked for almost an hour. I suggest trying this with peaches first, since they have the most flavor and make the most beautiful tart. I like to peel peaches before baking them, but to simplify this recipe, you can skip this step. I use 4 tablespoons of sugar for most fruit unless it is extremely sweet to begin with. Note that in the early stages of cooking, especially when using peaches, the tart will fill with liquid. As the baking continues, these juices will mingle with the flour and sugar, reducing down to a thick syrup on the bottom of the tart.

SERVES 6 TO 8

1   unbaked 9-inch tart shell (see recipe for
    Prebaked Tart Shell, page 250,
    through step 3)
3   large, ripe peaches (or apples or an
    equivalent amount of plums)
1   tablespoon all-purpose flour
3 to 4   tablespoons granulated sugar

1. Prepare the tart pastry, roll it out, and fit it to a 9-inch tart pan. Refrigerate the unbaked shell for 40 minutes, then freeze it for an additional 20 minutes.

2. Heat oven to 400 degrees. If you wish to peel the peaches before slicing them (this is optional), bring a medium saucepan of water to a boil. Half fill a medium bowl with ice and water and set near the saucepan. Immerse each peach in boiling water for 30 seconds, remove it to the ice water for at least 1 minute, and then peel. The skin should now come off easily. (If you are using apples, peel, core, and quarter. Plums should be pitted.)

3. Spread the tablespoon of flour over the bottom of the tart shell. Thinly slice (this is important) the fruit and place the slices on the bottom of the shell. (You can arrange them in a fancy fan pattern if you like — or just throw them in as evenly as possible.) Sprinkle fruit with 2 tablespoons of the sugar. Place tart in the preheated oven.

4. After 20 minutes, rotate tart 180 degrees and sprinkle with remaining 1 to 2 tablespoons sugar. Bake for a total of 50 minutes to 1 hour, turning the tart every 10 minutes to ensure even cooking. Remove from oven before the edges of the tart burn. The juices should cook down, forming a thick syrup at the bottom of the tart shell. Cool to room temperature and serve.

WHAT CAN GO WRONG? This is an easy recipe, but you can run into trouble if you use dry apples. Bite into one of the apples as a test. If it isn't juicy, don't make this recipe. You need juicy fruit to combine with the sugar and flour to make a rich syrup.

NUT TARTS

WHEN I SET OUT to develop a recipe for a nut tart, I wasn't exactly sure what they were. In fact, there are many different approaches to this dessert, but the one I like best is more or less the equivalent of a pecan pie. That is, the filling is made from eggs, corn syrup, sugar, butter, nuts, and flavorings. I had always thought that pecan pie was too much of a good thing, so using a thin layer of filling in a crisp tart shell seemed to promise a more grown-up, more appealing dessert. But getting the texture exactly right, firm but not overcooked, required a lot of testing and just the right combination of ingredients and cooking time.

After a fair amount of research, I started off with a working recipe that contained pecan halves, eggs, white sugar, light corn syrup, melted butter, vanilla, and salt. (I had tested the use of flour and decided that it was unnecessary for thickening and simply confused the flavors.) The result had a soggy crust, the filling did not hold up well when the tart was cut into slices, and the crust seemed to separate from the filling. It needed a lot of work.

The first series of tests was aimed at determining which type of liquid sweetener to use. Case 45 shows how the various sweeteners stacked up. After all of the testing, I finally settled on light corn syrup as the simplest and best solution. However, I also liked mixing maple syrup with light corn syrup, so if you have maple syrup on hand, simply use equal parts maple and light corn syrups.

In terms of sugar, I knew that I wanted to use either light or dark brown sugar to provide depth of flavor. It turned out that light brown sugar did not have enough punch, whereas dark brown sugar, which has twice the molasses content of light brown sugar, was richer in both appearance and flavor. (Light and dark brown sugars are white sugar to which molasses has been added: 3.5 percent for light brown and 6.5 percent for dark brown.) I tested 2 tablespoons, 4 tablespoons, and then 6 tablespoons of dark brown sugar and settled on the ¼-cup measurement. In addition to achieving the proper level of sweetness, the amount of sugar also affects the thickness of the custard. Anything less than ¼ cup produced a somewhat liquid custard.

Butter was also tested, because I not only wanted a more luxurious custard but also needed something to cut the sweetness. I found that a

CASE 45: SWEET TARTS

Which type of liquid sweetener, or combination, is best when making a nut tart?

Sweetener	Results
Honey	Custard not thick enough; too sweet
Maple syrup	Flavor nice, but custard a bit thin
Dark or light corn syrup	Both work well
Maple syrup plus light corn syrup	Maple flavor is subtle; nice custard and good color
Molasses	Dark, smoky flavor; overpowering; sugar crystals
Molasses plus light corn syrup	Texture a bit grainy

mere 2 tablespoons was just fine. Larger amounts of butter yielded a greasy filling and a soggy bottom crust. Eggs were necessary for setting the filling, and I tried 1, 2, and 3 eggs. One egg produced a filling without enough body — it was just a loose syrup — and 2 eggs also did not provide enough thickening. At 3 eggs, however, I produced a firm custard that was light, not rubbery, and the flavor seemed well balanced. I tried adding brandy and rum and found they were either distracting or contributed nothing of value.

I then moved up to a testing of different nuts. Pecans were very good, producing an effect much like a pecan pie. However, they were better in coarsely chopped pieces than in halves;

this also made it easier to cut the tart for serving. Walnuts were fine; cashews were too sweet with the filling; macadamia nuts were also relatively sweet; and almond slices became rubbery during cooking. So pecans were my first choice, followed by walnuts; and, having tested different amounts, I finally settled on 1 cup. I was also interested in how to prepare them. Should they be toasted or ground before baking? The good news was that untoasted nuts were almost as good as the toasted version, although, since the oven is already preheating, it isn't too much trouble to toast them for a few minutes, and toasting does bring out their flavor. I did not like the texture of the ground nut variation. I also wondered if I should place the nuts in the tart shell and then pour the filling over them or simply mix them in with the custard. It turned out that it didn't matter.

For most tarts, I prebake the crust, but in this case I wanted the crust to absorb a bit of the filling to make it less greasy. I finally hit on a good compromise, which was to bake the crust for 6 minutes before adding the filling. This gave me a crispy bottom crust and also improved the filling. I also tried cooking the filling on top of the stove first and then adding it to the crust. (I use this method for many single-crust pies in order to speed up baking time and improve the crispiness of the crust.) However, since this tart has such a thin layer of filling, I found that cooking the filling made no difference and simply complicated the recipe.

When I make a traditional pecan pie, I find that heavy cream in the filling cuts the sweetness and makes for a more palatable dessert. This makes a lot of sense with a thick slice of pie, but for a thin tart a more concentrated, caramelized filling works best.

・・・

Nut Tart

This is more or less a pecan pie filling baked in a thin layer in a tart shell. Since there is much less filling than with a regular slice of pie, I have opted to make the filling a bit more intense and slightly sweeter than I would prefer for a pie. In fact, I prefer this recipe to regular pecan pie, since the proportion of crust to filling is higher, which cuts the sweetness and provides a better balance of textures. In a pinch, you don't have to toast the nuts, and if you have maple syrup on hand, try ¼ cup maple syrup combined with ¼ cup light corn syrup.

SERVES 6 TO 8

1	unbaked 9-inch tart shell (see recipe for Prebaked Tart Shell, page 250, through step 3)
1	cup pecans or walnuts, coarsely chopped
3	large eggs
¼	cup packed dark brown sugar
½	cup light corn syrup OR ¼ cup maple syrup plus ¼ cup light corn syrup
2	tablespoons unsalted butter, melted
½	teaspoon vanilla extract
¼	teaspoon salt

1. Prepare the tart pastry, roll it out, and fit it to a 9-inch tart pan. Refrigerate unbaked shell for at least 2 hours.

2. Heat oven to 375 degrees. Toast nuts about 5 minutes in oven until golden. (This step is not crucial.) Place the tart shell in the oven for 6 minutes.

3. Meanwhile, whisk together the eggs, sugar, syrup, butter, vanilla, and salt and then stir in the nuts. Pour filling into the hot shell.

4. Bake until the custard edges are firm but the center still quivers when jiggled, about 15 minutes or so. Do not overbake. Cool for 2 hours before serving to allow filling to set properly.

WHAT CAN GO WRONG? This is a simple recipe, but overbaking will make the filling tough. Make sure that you remove the tart from the oven before the center sets. It is also important to give this tart plenty of time to set before slicing. Allow at least 2 hours.

Fresh Fruit Tarts with Pastry Cream

THIS IS A CLASSIC French invention and is a good way to serve perfectly fresh fruit without having to bake it. The pastry cream, a custard filling, acts as a foil for the fruit, which would be a bit naked sitting in a prebaked tart shell by itself. The process is straightforward enough: the shell is baked, the pastry cream is made on top of the stove and poured into the crust, and then fresh fruit is arranged over it. The only issue of significance is how to make a pastry cream that has enough body to produce clean, upstanding slices. I went into the kitchen to find out.

Since I had already perfected a recipe for pastry cream (see page 344), I was left with the issue of how to make it a bit sturdier. One can simply use pastry cream as is, but I find that it makes for messy slices, and this is the sort of dessert that calls for a nice appearance, unlike more family-style desserts such as fruit cobbler or a fruit buckle. The obvious solution was to use gelatin. I started with a full ¼-ounce packet (2 teaspoons) of gelatin dissolved in 3 tablespoons cold water to thicken 1¼ cups pastry cream. This produced neat slices, although I did feel that there was a slight bitter aftertaste from the gelatin. However, lesser amounts of gelatin did not always produce perfect slices, so I decided to stick with the full 2 teaspoons.

That settled, I tried a few techniques for jazzing up the tart. The French are keen on using glazes, so I tried the classic — apricot — and it worked fine. Purchase apricot jelly, heat it up in a saucepan, and then let it bubble for 2 minutes. If you can only find apricot preserves, be sure to strain them first, since you need a thin glaze to apply to the fruit. I tried brushing the inside of the baked crust with both dark and white chocolate and found these variations too fussy. They take more work and don't improve the finished product. I also tried brushing the inside of the crust with egg white; this improved the crunchiness of the crust only marginally, so I decided it wasn't worth the effort. (The white is supposed to protect the baked crust from the moisture in the pastry cream.) I also, in a fit of culinary insanity, tried adding a thin layer of cake to the shell before adding the pastry cream. Not only did this put the recipe over the top in terms of preparation, but it simply distracted from the simple but pleasant confluence of pastry cream, crust, and fruit.

▪ ▪ ▪

Master Recipe for Fresh Fruit Tart with Pastry Cream

This is the classic summer dessert you have probably seen in French restaurants. It has been abused by many modern chefs who, finding nothing better to do with certain exotic fruits, cover the pastry cream with slices of kiwifruit. Whoever invented this variation ought to be brought to justice. Please, stick with ripe berries and be done with it. There is nothing pedestrian about perfectly ripe summer blueberries or handpicked blackberries. Leave the kiwi in the fruit basket. If you like, you do not have to use the glaze, but it adds a nice extra flavor and makes the fruit look more attractive.

SERVES 6 TO 8

1   recipe Pastry Cream (page 344)
1   fully prebaked 9-inch tart shell, cooled (page 250)
¾   cup apricot jelly or strained apricot preserves
1½   teaspoons unflavored gelatin (about one ¼-ounce packet)
3   tablespoons cold water
2   cups ripe, flavorful blueberries, hulled strawberries, blackberries, or raspberries, washed and dried

1. Prepare Pastry Cream and refrigerate as directed in the master recipe.

2. Prepare tart shell as directed in the master recipe, baking until well browned, 30 to 35 minutes. Allow to cool completely.

3. Make a glaze by placing the apricot jelly or strained preserves in a small saucepan and heating until bubbling. Simmer for 2 minutes and then set aside in a warm spot. If glaze hardens, reheat until melted. Do not overcook the glaze or it will become thick and hard to spread over the fruit.

4. Brush the inside of the prebaked tart shell with a thin layer of glaze. Remove pastry cream from the refrigerator. Sprinkle the gelatin over the 3 tablespoons water in a small saucepan and let sit for 1 minute. Heat mixture until the gelatin melts. Combine with the pastry cream and immediately pour into the shell. Let filling cool for a few minutes and then place fruit on top.

5. Brush the warm glaze over the top of the fruit in a thin layer. Cool and serve.

WHAT CAN GO WRONG? This recipe is a bit fussy but not hard. The only part I have had trouble with is brushing the fruit with glaze. If you overcook the glaze, it will become thick and hard to spread.

⋎

FRANGIPANE TART

ALTHOUGH THIS IS in essence an almond tart, it is quite different from the Nut Tart recipe earlier in this chapter. Instead of being a cousin to a pecan pie, a frangipane tart is made without corn syrup or brown sugar, being a more sophisticated dessert in which the taste of the almonds has to shine through. I found few similarities among the frangipane tart recipes in other cookbooks, so I had to start pretty much from scratch.

I knew that I was going to use eggs, white sugar, almonds, butter, and vanilla and that I might also have to use some flour as well. The trick was going to be to balance the flavor of the almonds with the other ingredients and to achieve a texture that was not gritty, too greasy, or too sweet. The first question was how to deal with the almonds. Grinding them in a food processor was better than in a blender, which tended to make them sticky. I then tested toasting them and found that this added a great deal of flavor. I also tested varying amounts of nuts and finally settled on a modest ¼ cup; larger amounts were too much of a good thing.

For butter, I finally settled on 2 tablespoons after testing larger amounts, which made the filling greasy and overpowered the taste of the almonds. I also found that the recipe needed the addition of flour. Initially, I had settled on ½ cup, but I soon changed my mind when I tested the eggs. I tried 1 egg, 2 eggs, and 2 yolks, and then tried separating 2 eggs, beating the whites. This last turned out to solve many of the problems of a dense, greasy custard filling. It also meant that I needed hardly any flour, and I finally settled on 1 tablespoon. I then moved on to test the amount of sugar and found that ⅓ cup was about right; ¼ cup was not sweet enough and ½ cup was too much like an overly sweet, commercial marzipan. It was also grainy.

I tested both almond extract and an almond-flavored liqueur. Both worked well, but the liqueur was slightly better. Imitation almond extract, the choice for most supermarket shoppers, is mostly alcohol, which can yield a slightly off flavor. However, since I use only ¼ teaspoon of extract, this is a minor point. I also tried rum, which was recommended by one recipe I consulted, but it competed with the almond flavor and was therefore rejected.

Baking time is crucial here. If you overbake the tart, the filling will deflate to a very thin layer upon cooling. (Your guests will never know, however, and it will still taste great.)

...

Frangipane Tart

This is an almond tart and is more delicate than the Nut Tart recipe on page 260. The thin layer of marzipan-flavored filling works well with the nicely browned crust. The trick to this recipe is separating the eggs and whipping the whites. This recipe is for a 9-inch tart shell.

SERVES 6 TO 8

1   recipe Prebaked Tart Shell (page 250)
¼   cup almonds
2   tablespoons unsalted butter, softened but still firm
⅓   cup granulated sugar
2   large eggs, separated
1   teaspoon vanilla extract
2   teaspoons almond liqueur (¼ teaspoon almond extract will do in a pinch)
1   tablespoon all-purpose flour

1. Follow instructions for Prebaked Tart Shell, baking the shell an additional 7 minutes after the foil is removed.

2. Heat oven to 400 degrees. Grind almonds in a food processor until very fine. Place on a baking sheet and toast in oven for 3 to 4 minutes, or until golden brown. Watch carefully, as they can burn quickly. Cool for 10 minutes.

3. Cream the butter and sugar with an electric mixer for 2 minutes, or until light and fluffy. Add the egg yolks (reserve whites for later), ground almonds, flavorings, and flour. Mix until smooth.

4. Whip the egg whites until soft peaks form. Take one-quarter of the whites and stir into the nut mixture. Fold in the rest of the whites until just combined.

5. Pour filling into the prebaked shell and bake for about 15 minutes, or until the top is a very light brown. Do not overbake. Cool before serving.

WHAT CAN GO WRONG? Make sure that you remove the tart from the oven just when the top has a very light brown color. If you overcook this filling, it will deflate a lot during cooling, which will not ruin the dessert but will result in a very thin layer of custard.

12

FRUIT DESSERTS

Most of us are very confused by the difference between crisps, crunches, crumbles, and betties. Simply put, there are lots of old-fashioned desserts consisting of fruit baked with bread, cake crumbs, flour and butter, oats, crackers, and the like. In the days when home cooks were frugal, this was an easy way to use up stale leftovers while providing a bit of variety in terms of texture and flavor. All of these American home desserts are most likely based on older European recipes. One such European dish is called a Veiled Maiden or Country Lass with a Veil and is pretty much a betty, or a crunch, made with fruit and browned breadcrumbs. It may also include a bit of jam. The earliest version of this recipe I have found comes from Denmark.

A *crisp* is fruit baked with a topping made from butter, sugar, and flour. However, many variations qualify as crisps, including those made with ingredients such as nuts, cake or cracker crumbs, or cornflakes. A *crunch,* although it is often confused with a crisp by many authors, is, according to *Joy of Cooking,* fruit sandwiched between two layers of buttered breadcrumbs. A *betty,* however, is fruit baked with buttered breadcrumbs, not necessarily sandwiched in two layers, which makes it pretty close to a crunch. (I have seen recipes for betties that do call for a top and bottom layer of breadcrumbs.) A *crumble,* for which there seems to be some consensus, is a crisp that uses oats along with the flour. All of these definitions aside, common usage suggests that crisps have a top layer of streusel, crumbles are crisps using oats, and crunches and betties are fruit layered with breadcrumbs. A *cobbler* is fruit baked with a biscuit topping, although pie pastry dough can also be used.

There are many faces to these desserts, but the essence of most truly great fruit desserts is the perfect marriage between the clear, sparkling flavor of fresh fruit and a rich, indulgent crust. Cobblers or crisps that try to wed heavily sweetened fruit with rich, sugary crusts do the fruit and the dish a great disservice. Fruit desserts are also about simplicity — picking fruit fresh from the orchard and topping it with whatever is on hand, be that sweetened breadcrumbs, baking powder biscuits, or a quick pie dough. There is no need for elaboration. When poaching fruit, I take the same approach, using a very light, not-too-sweet poaching syrup that is refreshing rather than heavy and dull.

After years of making fruit desserts, I have developed a method that works for many recipes. I bake the fruit uncovered for a bit and then add the topping. This ensures that the fruit is properly cooked and that the topping is not overbaked. For some recipes — a cobbler with a cookie dough crust, for example — I have even tried baking the topping separately and then adding it just before serving. This produces a very crisp crust, which partners nicely with the bubbly, soft fruit.

It goes without saying (although I will say it again anyway) that a good cobbler or buckle is only as good as the fruit. I find that blueberries and peaches are ideal for these recipes. Note that the sugar levels are only approximate, since that will depend on the quality and ripeness of the fruit. I tend not to use much thickener for these desserts, since I like plenty of juice with my topping. Fruit pies need to slice neatly, but a cobbler should be a big dish of bubbling juices and soft fruit.

FRUIT COBBLER

ALTHOUGH IT IS DIFFICULT to improve on the heady perfume of a sun-drenched, ripe peach, its juices bursting out of the skin on the first bite, a well-made fruit cobbler is the next best thing. The marriage of summer fruit and simple cobbler dough is classic; the tender puffs of dough sitting atop pools of sweet juices is a taste memory that only grows stronger in winter. But just the right proportions are important here, without tarting up this simple American dish.

First, the fruit has to be ripe. You can make a decent cobbler from second-rate fruit but never a great one. I have also tested a variety of op-

tional ingredients, including ginger, lemon rind, and vanilla, and find that simple fruit and sugar work best with just a touch of lemon juice. Thickening is another matter. You do need some thickener; otherwise the fruit mixture will be too loose and thin. I find that just 1 tablespoon of Minute Tapioca works best, having also tested flour, cornstarch, and arrowroot. Flour and cornstarch are too gluey, masking the taste of the fruit. Arrowroot works well but is too expensive. By the way, use a full 10 cups of fruit, not the meager 6 called for in some recipes. It takes little extra time, fits a standard 2-quart baking dish, and you are unlikely to have leftovers.

Cobblers are usually topped with a simple biscuit dough, which puffs up light and tender, the perfect foil for the syrupy juices. However, the problem with biscuit dough is that it is often too much of a good thing, the fluffy biscuits overpowering the fruit. I was looking for a richer topping, one that was less like bread and more like dessert. Starting with my own recipe from *The Yellow Farmhouse Cookbook,* I increased the amount of shortening substantially, to 6 tablespoons butter and 4 tablespoons Crisco. To make the dough even richer and more tender, I also added an egg yolk to the milk. Finally, I increased the sugar to ¼ cup. Now I had a rich cobbler topping that really felt like dessert.

The secret to this recipe, however, is how the dough is handled. Instead of baking the topping on the fruit for the entire cooking time, I start off with just the fruit in a 375-degree oven and then add the topping after 15 minutes, increasing the oven temperature to 425 degrees. This allows the fruit extra time to cook, concentrating the juices while not overbaking the dough. It is also best to cut the dough into shapes before topping the fruit, since the dough is too soft to handle in large pieces.

▪▪▪

Master Recipe for Fruit Cobbler

If you only have an 8-inch square pan, use 6 cups of fruit; a 9 x 11-inch pan can take a full 10 cups. If the fruit is not particularly juicy, you can eliminate the Minute Tapioca altogether.

SERVES 8

For the Fruit Mixture

   10   cups prepared fruit (see headnote)
        Juice of half a lemon
   ½   teaspoon minced lemon zest (optional)
   ½ to ¾ cup granulated sugar
    1   tablespoon Minute Tapioca

For the Cobbler Dough

    2   cups all-purpose flour
   ½   teaspoon salt
    1   tablespoon baking powder
    5   tablespoons granulated sugar
    6   tablespoons unsalted butter, cut into small pieces, chilled
    4   tablespoons vegetable shortening (e.g., Crisco), chilled
   ¾   cup milk
    1   large egg yolk

Heavy cream or vanilla ice cream for serving

1. Preheat oven to 375 degrees.

2. *For the fruit mixture:* Prepare fruit (wash, peel, hull, core, etc.) and cut into bite-size pieces if necessary. Make sure that fruit is well drained. Toss fruit with lemon juice, optional zest, sugar, and tapioca. Pour fruit into a 2-quart baking dish.

3. *For the cobbler dough:* In the bowl of a food processor, combine the flour, salt, baking powder, and 4 tablespoons of the sugar and pulse for 2 seconds to mix. Then add the cold butter pieces and the vegetable shortening (in 1-tablespoon lumps) and process in 1-second bursts until flour is slightly yellow in color and the texture of coarse meal. This will take 10 to

12 bursts. (This can also be done by hand in a large bowl. Whisk together the dry ingredients and then cut in butter and shortening with a pastry blender or two knives.)

4. Whisk together the milk and egg yolk. Transfer flour mixture to a large bowl and gradually add two-thirds of the milk mixture, mixing with a rubber spatula. If necessary, add more of the milk mixture so that the dough holds together easily in a ball. (If you need additional milk, go ahead and add it.) Now lightly press dough together into a rough ball. The dough will be extremely soft.

5. Place dish with fruit mixture into oven. Bake for 10 minutes and then toss fruit with a large spoon. Meanwhile, roll out dough to a size smaller than the baking dish. Cut into rounds, squares, or triangles. When fruit has cooked for a total of 15 minutes, remove from oven. Increase oven temperature to 425 degrees. Top fruit with dough shapes. Sprinkle dough with the remaining 1 tablespoon sugar.

6. Return dish to oven and bake for an additional 20 minutes, or until dough is browned and fruit is bubbly and tender. Allow to cool for 30 minutes before serving with heavy cream or vanilla ice cream.

WHAT CAN GO WRONG? The juiciness of this dessert depends largely on the quality and type of fruit as well as the baking time. Some fruits will deliver a lot of juices and others will give off very little juice. I have indicated that you should add 1 tablespoon of Minute Tapioca for thickening, but you can leave this out if the fruit is on the dry side. Unlike a pie, which needs to be cut into neat slices, a cobbler is more casual and can be very juicy; the liquids mix nicely with the biscuit topping.

BLUEBERRY VARIATION

Use 10 cups blueberries, adding ¼ teaspoon allspice to fruit mixture. Since blueberries range from very sweet to quite tart, the amount of sugar required will vary from a mere ½ cup for very sweet berries to a full cup for tarter fruit.

STRAWBERRY-RHUBARB VARIATION

Use 5 cups rhubarb and 5 cups strawberries. Substitute 1 teaspoon orange zest for the lemon zest. Add ¼ teaspoon vanilla extract to the fruit mixture and use 1 to 1¼ cups sugar.

BLUEBERRY-PEACH VARIATION

Use 5 cups of blueberries and 5 cups of peaches. Add ¼ teaspoon allspice, ¼ teaspoon freshly grated nutmeg, and ½ teaspoon lemon juice to fruit mixture.

PEACH-RASPBERRY VARIATION

Use 6 cups peaches and 4 cups raspberries. Add ¼ teaspoon freshly grated nutmeg, ¼ teaspoon allspice, and ¼ teaspoon salt to fruit mixture. Increase tapioca to 3 tablespoons — raspberries give off a lot of juice during baking.

GINGER-PEACH VARIATION

Use 10 cups peaches. Replace sugar with ½ cup packed brown sugar and ¼ cup granulated sugar. Add 1 tablespoon crystallized ginger diced into small pieces and ¼ teaspoon freshly grated nutmeg to the fruit.

▪ ▪ ▪

Cookie Crust Cobbler

This variation on a simple fruit cobbler uses a cookie crust in place of a biscuit dough as a topping. I use a version of a sugar cookie dough and simply top the partially baked fruit with this. It provides a thicker, sweeter topping than pie dough and is less overpowering than a biscuit topping. I use a modest ⅓ cup sugar to 10 cups fruit in this recipe. If you like sweet desserts or are using fruit that is on the tart side, you could increase the sugar to ½ cup. Since neither the fruit nor the topping is excessively

sweet, this is a good dessert to serve with vanilla ice cream.

SERVES 8 TO 10

For the Cookie Dough Topping
- 1¾ cups all-purpose flour
- ¼ teaspoon salt
- ¼ teaspoon baking powder
- ¼ teaspoon nutmeg
- 10 tablespoons unsalted butter, at 65 degrees (firm, not soft)
- ⅓ cup plus 1 tablespoon granulated sugar
- 1 large egg
- 1 teaspoon vanilla extract

For the Fruit Mixture
- 10 cups prepared summer fruit (peaches, plums, berries, etc.)
- Juice of half a lemon
- 1 teaspoon minced lemon zest (optional)
- 1 tablespoon minced crystallized ginger (optional)
- ⅓ cup granulated sugar, approximately

Heavy cream or vanilla ice cream for serving

1. *For the topping:* Whisk together the flour, salt, baking powder, and nutmeg in a medium bowl. In a large bowl, using an electric mixer, cream the butter and ⅓ cup sugar for 2 minutes at medium speed. Scrape down the sides of the bowl. Add the egg and vanilla and beat until combined, about 30 seconds. Add the flour mixture and beat until combined, about 30 seconds more, or until the dough just starts to come together. Press the dough together with your hands to form a ball, dust with flour, and then wrap in plastic and refrigerate until firm, about 2 hours.

2. Preheat oven to 375 degrees.

3. *For the fruit mixture:* Prepare fruit (wash, peel, hull, core, etc.) and cut into bite-size pieces if necessary. Make sure that fruit is well drained. Toss fruit with lemon juice, optional

zest, optional ginger, and sugar. Pour fruit into a 9 x 13-inch baking dish.

4. Place dish with fruit mixture in oven. Bake for 30 minutes, tossing fruit two or three times as it bakes to mix evenly with juices. Meanwhile, roll out dough on a piece of waxed paper or parchment to the dimensions of the baking dish. (The dough should be slightly smaller to fit easily into the dish.) Place dough back in the refrigerator until fruit has baked 30 minutes. Remove baking dish from oven, flip the dough over the fruit, and peel off the paper, Sprinkle dough with remaining 1 tablespoon sugar and return dish to oven. Bake for another 20 minutes, or until the dough has puffed, become firm, and turned light brown. Note that the juices may bubble up over part of the dough as it bakes. Allow cobbler to cool for at least 30 minutes before serving with heavy cream or vanilla ice cream.

WHAT CAN GO WRONG? The cookie dough topping will be relatively soft, since it bakes on top of the fruit. This, in effect, steams the dough. If you want a really crisp cookie topping, see the variation below, which calls for baking the dough separately and adding it just before serving.

CRISP COOKIE VARIATION

If you bake the topping apart from the fruit, the cookie dough will turn out crisp rather than soft. Follow the recipe above through step 3. Then bake the fruit for 40 minutes uncovered, tossing every 10 minutes or so with a large spoon. Meanwhile, place the dough on a sheet of parchment paper and roll out to a size just slightly smaller than your baking dish. Place parchment paper on a cookie sheet and refrigerate dough until needed. When fruit is done, bake the cookie dough for 15 to 20 minutes, or until edges turn brown and the top turns a light brown. Let cool on a rack. Place on top of fruit just prior to serving.

• • •

Apple Pandowdy

This is nothing more than fruit baked in a shallow dish, topped with a layer of pie dough. Halfway through baking, the fruit is typically removed from the oven and the crust is cut and pushed down into the fruit, a process referred to, according to Richard Sax in Classic Home Desserts, *as "dowdying." (I have also seen recipes that simply call for inverting the dessert after it is baked, the crust being served on the bottom and not broken up and mixed with the filling.) Having tested this, however, I saw no point in mixing the crust and fruit halfway through cooking. This simply made the crust soggy. Instead, I prefer to mix crust and fruit after baking, right before serving. Note that the pear variation below does require a thickener and less sugar, since pears are both more watery than apples and sweeter.*

SERVES 6 TO 8

1	recipe Foolproof Food Processor Pie Dough (page 214)
8	cups prepared apples
1½	tablespoons lemon juice
1	teaspoon grated lemon zest
¼	teaspoon salt
¾	cup plus 1 tablespoon granulated sugar
¼	teaspoon nutmeg, freshly grated preferred
¼	teaspoon cinnamon
⅛	teaspoon allspice
1	large egg white, lightly beaten

Heavy cream or ice cream for serving

1. Prepare the pie pastry and chill, wrapped in plastic wrap, for at least 1 hour. Set oven rack at the bottom position and heat the oven to 425 degrees.

2. Peel, core, halve, and slice the apples about ½-inch thick, tossing with lemon juice in a large bowl as you work. Add the lemon zest, salt, ¾ cup sugar, and spices and toss with your hands to combine.

3. Turn fruit mixture, including any juices, into a large (at least 9-inch) pie pan or shallow baking dish (a 9 x 12 or 7 x 13 pan is fine). Roll out the chilled pie pastry and place over the top of the fruit, trimming the sides to fit the baking dish. Don't worry about any tears or holes, since the crust will be cut into small pieces after baking. Cut three parallel slits in top of dough to allow steam to escape. Brush egg white (in a pinch, you can use water) on top of crust and sprinkle remaining 1 tablespoon sugar evenly over the top.

4. Place baking dish in oven. Bake for 15 minutes at 425 degrees and then lower oven temperature to 375 degrees and bake for another 25 minutes, or until top crust is well browned, the apples are cooked through, and the juices are bubbling. Remove from oven and place on a wire rack. Cool for 20 minutes to allow juices to thicken a bit.

5. Using the thin front edge of a metal pancake turner, cut the pie pastry into 1-inch squares; use a spatula to press the pastry down into the filling. Serve warm with heavy cream or ice cream.

WHAT CAN GO WRONG? This dessert depends entirely on the quality and condition of the apples. Keep in mind that some apples are very juicy while others will be very dry; some are too sweet, some are very acidic; and so on. This means that you will have to taste the apples before using them to adjust the sugar level. I also find that very dry apples, such as unripe Granny Smiths, make lousy baked desserts.

Pear Pandowdy Variation

Substitute pears for apples. Since pears are juicier than apples, add 4 teaspoons Minute Tapioca along with the lemon zest, salt, sugar, and spices and reduce the ¾ cup sugar to ⅔ cup.

Fruit Grunt

A GRUNT IS SIMILAR TO a cobbler except that the mixture is cooked on top of the stove in a covered Dutch oven so that the dumplings steam rather than bake. Although the dumplings are not particularly attractive on top, since they are steamed, they are soft and fluffy and absorb some of the sweet fruit juices.

In an effort to find the best recipe for grunt, I started with the fruit. I like to use at least 8 cups of fruit for these sorts of desserts, and I prefer a light hand with the sweetener. I tried everything from ½ cup to a full cup of sugar and found that the best range was between ½ and ¾ cup. Sweet peaches, for example, need less sugar, whereas tart blueberries require a bigger dose. There are many different points of view about thickening, but I am partial to a fair amount of juice, so I use only 1 tablespoon of Minute Tapioca, which is my thickener of choice for cooked fruit. In any case, the dumplings soak up a good deal of the juices, so minimal thickening is in order.

The dumpling dough was a bit tricky and unlike a biscuit dough, which is made from cold butter cut into flour. I found that melted butter worked best here, for a soft, fine texture and good flavor. I also played with the amount of liquid and found that about 1 cup of buttermilk was good with 2 cups of flour. I didn't want the dough overly sticky, which would make it hard to shape into dumplings. During cooking, it is helpful to place a sheet of aluminum foil under the lid of the Dutch oven to keep in the steam.

• • •

Master Recipe for Fruit Grunt

This dish is best served after sitting for 15 or 20 minutes. A grunt should be warm, not hot, to let the full flavors of the fruit shine through. I prefer to make this recipe with either blueber-

ries or peaches. I find that frozen blueberries are very sweet and need only ½ cup sugar.

SERVES 8

For the Fruit Mixture

  8 cups washed and well-drained fruit
  Juice of half a lemon
  ¼ teaspoon allspice (optional)
  ¼ teaspoon nutmeg
½ to ¾ cup granulated sugar, depending on the sweetness of the fruit
  1 tablespoon Minute Tapioca

For the Dumpling Dough

  2 cups all-purpose flour
  ¼ teaspoon salt
  1½ teaspoons baking powder
  ½ teaspoon baking soda
  2 tablespoons granulated sugar
  4 tablespoons unsalted butter, melted
¾ to 1 cup buttermilk, approximately

  Heavy cream for serving

1. *For the fruit mixture:* Toss fruit with lemon juice, allspice, nutmeg, sugar, and tapioca in a cast iron Dutch oven.

2. *For the dumplings:* Whisk together the flour, salt, baking powder, baking soda, and 1 tablespoon of the sugar in a mixing bowl. With a rubber spatula, stir in the melted butter and then add as much of the buttermilk as needed to produce a wet biscuit dough.

3. Cover the Dutch oven and bring the berries to a simmer over medium-high heat. Lower the heat to maintain a steady simmer, uncover, and spoon small (golf ball–size) dumplings over the fruit. Sprinkle with the remaining 1 tablespoon sugar.

4. Cover the Dutch oven with aluminum foil and then replace the lid. Continue simmering for about 15 minutes, or until the dumplings are cooked through.

5. Let stand uncovered for 15 to 20 minutes to cool. Spoon individual servings into bowls and serve with heavy cream.

WHAT CAN GO WRONG? The cooking time will vary a lot depending on your pot, your stovetop, and the fruit. Just make sure that you thoroughly cook the dumplings.

FRUIT BUCKLE

ONE OF THE BEST summer fruit desserts and one of the kitchen's best-kept secrets is the buckle. Usually made with berries (blueberries are the most common choice), buckles are simple and rustic. Fresh berries are folded into a yellow cake batter, topped with sugar, spices, and nuts, and then baked in an 8-inch square pan. But even the simplest recipes offer plenty of techniques that demand testing.

First, most yellow cake batters, the foundation for a buckle, are made by creaming the butter, sugar, and egg yolks together. Starting with a basic yellow cake recipe, I added an extra egg white to fluff up the batter, making it airier and more delicate. This is an old-fashioned technique used to make tender white cakes, such as a classic birthday cake. I also tested how many eggs are optimal and settled on 3 large eggs to 10 tablespoons of butter and 1 cup of flour, a fairly high proportion. I dramatically cut down on the sugar level, to a meager ½ cup; I want to taste the sweet fruit, plus I use a sweet topping as well. I also added a bit of lemon zest, which goes well with the fruit. Some recipes suggest tossing the berries with a small amount of flour so that they are more easily incorporated into the batter. I found this unnecessary; in fact, it actually complicated the process, since the flour became gooey and held the fruit together in clumps. The butter needs to be creamed (beaten at high speed in an electric mixer or by hand), so it must be at just the right temperature, about 65 to 67 degrees. (The butter should be malleable but still firm.) If it is colder, the batter will not come together properly, resulting in a denser, less risen cake. The topping itself is a simple combination of nuts, brown sugar, spices, and softened butter. Toasting the nuts adds a great deal of extra flavor.

...

Master Recipe for Fruit Buckle

This is really a simple cake with fruit added and a crumb topping. In a taste test of five cobblers, a betty, a crisp, and a blueberry buckle, the buckle won a surprising first place from the tasters. The combination of cake, topping, and fruit makes this recipe a winner. Blueberries are the fruit of choice.

SERVES 8

3   cups washed and well-drained fruit
    (blueberries, raspberries, blackberries, or
    cut-up peaches)

For the Cake Batter
1   cup plus 2 tablespoons all-purpose flour
1½ teaspoons baking powder
¼   teaspoon salt
10 tablespoons unsalted butter, softened but
    still firm
½   cup granulated sugar
1   teaspoon vanilla extract
3   large eggs
1   large egg white
½   teaspoon minced lemon zest

For the Topping
½   cup all-purpose flour
¼   cup lightly packed light brown sugar
1   tablespoon granulated sugar
¼   cup pecans or walnuts, toasted
¼   teaspoon cinnamon
¼   teaspoon freshly grated nutmeg
½   teaspoon minced orange zest
4   tablespoons unsalted butter, slightly
    softened, cut into small pieces

Heavy or whipped cream or ice cream for
    serving (optional)

1. Heat oven to 375 degrees. Prepare fruit (wash, peel, hull, core, etc.) and cut into bite-size pieces if necessary. Make sure that fruit is well drained. Butter an 8-inch square baking dish.

2. *Prepare the batter:* Whisk together the flour, baking powder, and salt in a small bowl. In a separate bowl, whip the butter, sugar, and vanilla on high speed in an electric mixer until light, about 4 minutes. Beat in the eggs, one at a time, and the egg white until incorporated, scraping the sides of the bowl with a spatula between additions. Add lemon zest. Gently mix flour mixture into the batter and fold in fruit. Place into prepared pan and spread evenly.

3. *For the topping:* Place all the ingredients except the butter in a medium bowl and mix with an electric mixer until thoroughly combined, about 30 seconds. Add the butter and mix until topping is crumbly, about 3 minutes. Scatter over the cake batter.

4. Bake 45 to 55 minutes, or until cake is set in the middle and a tester comes out clean. Cool on a wire rack. Serve warm, in large bowls, with heavy cream (whipped or liquid) or ice cream.

WHAT CAN GO WRONG? For best results, it is important to drain the fruit well before folding it into the batter.

FRUIT CRISPS

THERE IS NOTHING CRISP about a crisp. This simple baked dessert, typically made from sweetened apples topped with a combination of sugar, butter, and flour, inevitably comes out of the oven with a soggy top crust. A few recipes go so far as to refer to this classic dish as a crunch, a term that has no relation to the flat, dull, overly sweetened crumble that serves as a streusel. The task, therefore, was quite simple. I wanted to put the crunch back in the crisp.

To make sure that others shared my opinion, I asked the *Cook's* test kitchen to bake a crisp from the new *Joy of Cooking,* by Irma S. Rombauer et al., and then a second recipe from *A Feast of Fruits,* by Elizabeth Riely. The former produced a very light, sandy-colored topping that was not at all crisp, and the topping from the Riely book was almost runny in texture. Both used a combination of sugar, flour, and butter, and neither was satisfactory. Additional testing revealed that this combination of ingredients, regardless of proportions, would not produce a crispy topping.

My first thought was to use oats. In *The Cook's Bible,* my master fruit crisp recipe called for an oat-and-flour topping and, after much testing for that book, I concluded that a 1-to-1 ratio of flour to oats was best, although other recipes called for a wide range of ratios, from a 2-to-1 ratio of oats to flour to a 3-to-1 ratio of flour to oats. Although I preferred my recipe, I was nonetheless disappointed with the topping, because it was more chewy than crisp, a bit like soggy cardboard. In fact, I wondered if I wouldn't prefer baking the apples without any topping at all.

Still in search of a crunchy topping, I moved on to test a variety of other ingredients, including cornflakes, cookie crumbs made from vanilla wafers, graham crackers, and Grape-Nuts. The cornflakes were crispy but made for an odd combination with the baked apple mixture; cookie crumbs were also crispy but too sweet; graham crackers were relatively crispy, but the flavor was unwelcome on the fruit; and Grape-Nuts created the effect of chewing on tiny pebbles. I excluded cake crumbs because very few home cooks have extra slices of cake sitting around the house. I also left out breadcrumbs, since they are used on the baked fruit dessert usually referred to as a betty or crumble, not a crisp. Having seemingly run out of options, I reviewed my crisp recipe from *The Cook's Bible* and found a variation using nuts instead of oatmeal. This turned out to be a win-

ner. The nuts produced a crispy streusel and added a pleasant complementary flavor to the underlying fruit. I preferred pecans and almonds to walnuts, the latter having a slightly bitter aftertaste.

The next question was one of technique. It turned out that how one cuts the butter into the flour is crucial. This is one task ideally suited to the food processor, although a hand method can produce good results (see Hand Variation, page 274). For the food processor method the butter, a key ingredient, must be very cold, taken straight from the refrigerator. I found it best to use three 4-second pulses to combine the flour and butter and then five to six 1-second pulses once the nuts were added. With a pie pastry, one wants the flour to resemble a coarse meal. With a crisp, the topping should be more thoroughly processed, until it has the consistency of wet sand. The flour must be thoroughly coated with butter; otherwise the streusel will be floury and not at all crisp. However, over-processing will cause the mixture to clump together. If the butter is melted, by the way — we tried this method — the topping turns to mud.

The next issue was the sugar. Some recipes use all granulated sugar, some all brown sugar, and others use a mixture. The all-granulated version had little flavor, the all–dark brown sugar version was too strong, and the all–light brown sugar seemed a bit soggy. I found that half granulated and half light brown was best. It was crisp but also had a nice flavor. The ratio of sugar to flour was also crucial. Too much sugar and the topping was hard and too sweet. Too little, and the topping was bland and floury-tasting and did not hold together. The best ratio turned out to be ½ cup sugar to ⅓ cup flour. I also wanted to test whether the nuts should be toasted first and found that toasting was unnecessary — they toasted during the baking time. I also discovered that ¾ cup nuts was the proper amount.

How to sweeten and thicken the fruit was also problematic. Many recipes don't call for sweetening the fruit at all, simply placing a layer of very sweet streusel on top and then baking. The problem with this is that the fruit itself is lackluster. This is especially true if tart apples are used. (It is much like what happens if you try boiling pasta in unsalted water, expecting the sauce to carry the flavor: you simply end up with dull, unsalted pasta.) On the other hand, I found that it is best to keep the fruit mixture on the tart side to provide a nice contrast with the sweeter topping. So for 8 cups of apples, ⅓ cup of sugar was deemed optimal; with 6 cups, use ¼ cup of sugar. With ripe peaches, which are sweeter, you can easily reduce the sugar to ¼ cup when using 8 cups of fruit. Although this recipe cries out for a juicy filling (the juices carrying a great deal of flavor), I decided to try using a thickener. Based on a prior series of tests with baked fruit desserts, I chose Minute Tapioca as the thickener to try, since it absorbs liquid nicely without adding a gummy texture or a starchy aftertaste. Two tablespoons was too much; there were almost no juices left in the pan after baking. One tablespoon was better, but no thickener at all was best, the juices resulting in a much brighter-tasting dessert.

In terms of flavorings, I opted for a fairly high concentration of lemon juice (the juice of half a lemon) plus ½ teaspoon lemon zest. This is consistent with the recipe for apple pie on page 228. A very small amount, ¼ teaspoon each, of cinnamon and nutmeg was a nice addition. Other recipes we found had a heavy hand with the spices (one recipe used a whopping 1½ teaspoons of cinnamon), which dulls the fresh, tart flavor of the apples. A little freshly grated gingerroot can be added for a variation. For the apples themselves, I am fond of the McIntosh–Granny Smith combination I devised for my apple pie recipe, since both varieties are available year round. The Macs have good flavor and the Grannies keep their shape. Of course, a good firm, tart seasonal apple is also recommended. A blind tasting determined that Macoun, Royal Gala, Empire, Winesap, Rhode Island Green-

ing, Cortland, and Northern Spy were all excellent choices.

I have worked up two quantities for this recipe: one using 6 cups of apples and then a double recipe for bigger pans. The basic recipe can be baked in either a deep-dish 9-inch pie plate or an 8 x 8 x 2 baking dish. Use a 9 x 13-inch dish for the double recipe. Baking temperatures were also tested, starting at 325 degrees and running up to 425 degrees in 25-degree increments. At 325 and 350 degrees, the filling was overcooked by the time the topping browned and crisped properly, although the lower temperature never actually browned the streusel satisfactorily. At the two higher temperatures, the fruit never cooked all the way through before the topping started to burn. The 375-degree oven was just right, delivering cooked fruit and a nicely browned topping. In a final refinement, I found that raising the oven temperature to 400 degrees for the last 10 minutes of baking produced a slightly crispier streusel. Be sure to cook the apples thoroughly. The Macs should cook down into a sauce and the Granny Smiths should be soft but still hold their shape. Undercooking yields leathery fruit and too much excess liquid.

...

Master Recipe for Fruit Crisp with Nut Topping

A crisp is a casual cobbler. A simple streusel is tossed over a dish of fruit and baked. The problem with most crisps is that the topping often becomes sticky and soft and the oats, an ingredient used in many crisps, are tough and taste like cardboard. This recipe is best made with apples or peaches. I tested plums and nectarines and found them to be unsatisfactory. You can, however, add blueberries to the peaches, or raspberries to the apples. If you have a food processor, use it for the topping; otherwise see the Hand Variation below.

SERVES 6 TO 8

For the Fruit Mixture

- 6 cups prepared apples (peeled, cored, and cut into 1-inch dice)

    OR

- 6 cups prepared peaches (peeled, halved, stone removed, and cut into ½-inch wedges, then cut in half crosswise)

- Juice of ½ lemon
- ¼ cup granulated sugar
- ½ teaspoon minced lemon zest
- ½ teaspoon grated fresh gingerroot (optional)

For the Topping

- ⅓ cup all-purpose flour
- ¼ cup packed light brown sugar
- ¼ cup granulated sugar
- ¼ teaspoon cinnamon
- ¼ teaspoon freshly grated nutmeg
- ¼ teaspoon salt
- 5 tablespoons cold unsalted butter
- ¾ cup chopped pecans, walnuts, or almonds, or a combination

Heavy cream or vanilla ice cream for serving

1. Heat oven to 375 degrees. Toss prepared fruit with lemon juice, sugar, lemon zest, and optional ginger in a large bowl. Set aside.

2. In the bowl of a food processor, pulse together flour, brown sugar, sugar, cinnamon, nutmeg, and salt. Cut cold butter into ½-inch pieces. Add to dry ingredients and pulse 3 times for 4 seconds each. The mixture will first appear like dry sand, with large lumps of butter, then like coarse cornmeal. Add nuts, then pulse again, 5 to 6 times, 1 second each. At this time, the topping should look like slightly clumpy wet sand. Be sure not to overmix, or mixture will become too wet and homogenous.

3. Place fruit in a deep-dish 9-inch pie plate or a square 8 x 8 x 2-inch baking dish. Sprinkle topping over fruit and bake 30 minutes. Increase oven temperature to 400 degrees and

bake for an additional 10 minutes. (Fruit mixture should be bubbling, and topping should be a deep golden brown.) Let cool for 15 minutes. Serve with heavy cream or vanilla ice cream.

WHAT CAN GO WRONG? The key part of this recipe is processing the topping until it looks like wet sand.

DOUBLE RECIPE VARIATION

Double all of the ingredients and use a 9 x 18-inch baking dish.

HAND VARIATION

Note that for this version the butter that goes in the topping should be cool but slightly softened, not cold. (You can measure the temperature of the butter with an instant-read thermometer. The ideal temperature is 65 to 67 degrees.) Follow step 1 of the master recipe. Next, in a medium bowl, combine the first 6 ingredients of the topping recipe (flour through salt) and toss with your hands to combine. Rub cut-up butter into the dry ingredients until the mixture looks crumbly and well mixed. The flour must be thoroughly coated with the butter. Add the nuts and toss with your hands to incorporate. *Be sure not to overmix,* or else the topping will become a sticky mass. (If this happens, place the topping in the refrigerator until it becomes firm and then break it into crumbs.) Proceed with step 3 of the master recipe.

BISCUIT-STYLE SHORTCAKE

AFTER REVIEWING A DOZEN shortcake recipes, I realized that they were nothing more than biscuits with fruit. The issue, then, was how to make the perfect shortcake biscuit. For starters, I tested buttermilk versus regular milk and found, as I have with pancakes and waffles, that the former makes a substantially lighter, fuller biscuit because of buttermilk's high lactic acid content, which reacts at room temperature with baking soda, creating lots of carbon dioxide and hence imparting lift to the dough. I also found through testing that it was best to let the cut biscuits rest for 10 minutes before baking — this increases the rise.

Some recipes call for an egg or egg yolk to be added to the dough. I tested the egg yolk version and found that this gives the biscuits more tooth, which helps them stand up to the fruit. Most recipes also add some sugar. Three tablespoons of sugar picked up the flavor nicely. Some cookbooks suggest that the biscuits be topped with a sugar-nut mixture before baking (an almond topping is the most common variation), and although this is not a pure shortcake, it is an easy alternative. There are also endless fruit variations, one of which follows the master recipe.

I also tested which type of shortening to use and settled on 5 tablespoons of butter and 2 tablespoons Crisco to 2 cups flour. The butter provides the flavor and the Crisco improves the texture.

▪▪▪

Master Recipe for Old-Fashioned Biscuit Shortcake

This is a simple recipe for a quick summer dessert. The food processor makes short work of the biscuit dough.

SERVES 6

For the Fruit
4	cups fresh berries (strawberries, blueberries, blackberries, or raspberries)
¼ to ½	cup granulated sugar
½	teaspoon minced lemon zest (optional)

For the Biscuits
2	cups all-purpose flour
½	teaspoon salt
2	teaspoons baking powder
½	teaspoon baking soda
3	tablespoons granulated sugar
5	tablespoons cold unsalted butter
2	tablespoons cold vegetable shortening (e.g., Crisco)
1	large egg yolk
¾	cup buttermilk, approximately
½	teaspoon vanilla extract

For the Whipped Cream
1½	cups heavy cream
2	tablespoons granulated sugar
1	teaspoon vanilla extract

1. *For the fruit:* Mix berries, sugar, and optional lemon zest and let stand at room temperature for 45 minutes. Chill. Place the bowl of an electric mixer or any metal bowl in the freezer or refrigerator along with a whisk or beaters from an electric mixer.

2. *For the biscuits:* Heat oven to 425 degrees. Combine the flour, salt, baking powder, baking soda, and sugar in the bowl of a food processor. Process for 2 seconds to mix. Add the butter, cut into 1-tablespoon bits, and pulse 7 times for 1 second each. Add shortening in 1-tablespoon lumps and pulse another 6 times, or until mixture looks like coarse meal (the flour should take on a slightly yellowish hue from the butter). Turn mixture into a large bowl.

3. Whisk the egg yolk into the buttermilk with a fork along with the vanilla. Gradually add to the flour-butter mixture, folding together with a rubber spatula. When mixture starts to hold together, press the dough with the side of the spatula to form a rough ball. Note that you may use a little more or less than the ¾ cup buttermilk called for in this recipe.

4. Turn dough onto a floured surface and roll out very gently to a thickness of ½ inch. Use a biscuit cutter (I use a 2½-inch cutter to yield 6 servings of 2 biscuits per person) to cut, and then place on an ungreased cookie sheet 1½ inches apart and bake in the preheated oven for about 10 minutes, turning sheet front to back after 5 minutes in oven. Remove from oven.

5. *For the whipped cream:* Whip cream with

the sugar and vanilla, using chilled bowl and beaters.

6. Serve the fruit with 2 biscuits per person and whipped cream. Traditionally, the biscuits are cut in half for serving, but I prefer them whole, as they do not get as soggy from the fruit syrup.

WHAT CAN GO WRONG? As with all biscuit recipes, use a very light hand when working with the dough, rolling it out as gently as possible.

HAND VARIATION

Freeze the butter and Crisco for 30 minutes. After heating the oven in step 2, whisk together the flour, salt, baking powder, baking soda, and sugar in a medium bowl. Then grate the cold butter and shortening onto the flour mixture. Using your fingertips, work the butter and shortening into the flour mixture until the flour is slightly yellow in color and the texture of coarse meal. This will take 2 to 3 minutes. Proceed with step 3.

ALMOND VARIATION

Add ½ teaspoon almond extract to the dough along with the vanilla. Moisten tops of cut biscuit dough with milk and sprinkle with ½ cup sliced almonds. Top with a sprinkling of sugar and bake as directed.

BLUEBERRY-PEACH VARIATION

Use 2 cups each of blueberries and peeled, sliced peaches. Assemble fruit mixture and let sit for 1 hour before proceeding with recipe.

...

Master Recipe for Fruit Pudding

There are all sorts of puddinglike desserts that are mixed with fruit. A clafouti, which I don't much care for, is one example; the texture is fleshy, like a very starchy, tough custard. Although the outside edges of this pudding are much like a clafouti, the inside should be soft and custardy. You can use this recipe with most any fruit, although traditionally it is most often paired with apples. (I have also tested it with blueberries and peaches, and I find sweet, ripe peaches work best.) The fruit does end up on top of the pudding, which is just fine for a simple country dessert. By the way, this recipe should be served within an hour of baking. The texture of the custard is vastly better when it is warm, not at room temperature.

SERVES 6 TO 8

3	cups prepared fruit, peaches preferred (peeled, pitted, and cut into bite-size pieces)
1	tablespoon lemon juice
2	teaspoons grated lemon zest
⅔	cup all-purpose flour
¼	teaspoon salt
¼	teaspoon nutmeg
½	cup granulated sugar
1	cup milk
½	cup heavy cream
4	large eggs
2	teaspoons vanilla extract

1. Heat oven to 350 degrees. Butter a shallow casserole or oval baking dish (the sides should be low and the pan should be wide — an 8 x 12-inch pan is about the right size). Toss the fruit with the lemon juice and zest and pour into the baking dish.

2. Whisk together the flour, salt, nutmeg, and sugar. In a separate bowl, whisk together the milk, heavy cream, eggs, and vanilla. Add the flour to the milk mixture and stir very gently with a whisk just until smooth. Do not overbeat. Pour over fruit.

3. Bake 30 to 40 minutes, or until custard sets. The center 2 inches should still be wet and custardy. It will finish baking out of the oven. Remove from oven and serve warm, not hot, but no longer than 1 hour after baking.

WHAT CAN GO WRONG? Knowing when to take a custard out of the oven is always tricky. Make sure that you remove it before it completely sets up — the center 2 inches should still wiggle when the dish is shaken.

APPLE VARIATION

Soak ⅓ cup raisins in ⅓ cup bourbon for 1 hour and then drain. Use apples for the fruit, peeling, coring, and cutting them into bite-size pieces. Toss raisins along with apples.

FRUIT GRATINS

A FRUIT GRATIN is simple. Fresh fruit of any kind is placed in a broilerproof dish and then a bit of sweetened, dairy-based topping is added — pastry cream, sour cream, goat cheese, vanilla yogurt, crème fraîche, et cetera. The dish is then quickly broiled (no more than 5 minutes) and served immediately. It's simple, it's fresh, and it's not too sweet, the perfect way to turn simple summer fruit into a fancy dessert.

There are really only a few possibilities for the toppings: prepared sauces such as zabaglione or pastry cream; simple dairy products such as sour cream, yogurts, and crème fraîche; cheeses such as mascarpone, cream cheese, and goat cheese; and finally, simple combinations of sugar and an acid (lime or lemon juice) or sugar and alcohol (brandy). Even so, this amounted to fifteen different toppings that had to be tested, and I tried them on seven different types of fruit: mixed berries, bananas, mango, apples, rhubarb, grapefruit, and stone fruits. This worked out to be about 100 combinations, the mother of all kitchen tests.

The recipe was the same for most of the toppings (except those with sugar): 2 cups fruit, ¼ cup topping, and 4 teaspoons dark brown sugar. Not surprisingly, the results were all over the place, since certain toppings did better with some fruits than others. For example, zabaglione looked awful on rhubarb, since the topping disappeared into the fruit, yet it was wonderful with berries and bananas. Sour cream worked nicely with the rhubarb but was a poor choice as a topping for bananas.

The chart "It Takes Two to Mango" (page 278) shows the most successful combinations, but I felt this still left an unwieldy number of possibilities, so I went back into the kitchen in an effort to create a few toppings that worked for most fruits. The most likely candidate was the combination of sugar, butter, and lime juice, since it worked so well with a wide variety of fruits. The recipe I settled on is provided below.

My next thought was to try a combination of cheeses. There are times when you want more than just sugar, butter, and lime juice, and I thought that cheese mixed with a bit of sugar and cream or milk seemed like a good possibility. I concocted four variations: a goat cheese mix, a cream cheese mix, a Neufchâtel cheese mix, and a combination of goat and cream cheeses. I played with the ingredients and finally decided on a mix of cheese, half-and-half, vanilla, white sugar, and brown sugar. The winner was the combination of goat and cream cheeses, although the Neufchâtel mix was also good. However, since Neufchâtel is not a cheese available to everyone, I decided to stick with the simpler goat cheese–cream cheese combination. The recipe for this gratin is also given below.

...

Master Recipe for Mix-and-Match Fruit Gratin

Look at the chart on the next page in order to determine which fruits go best with which toppings. This recipe will only be as good as the fruit, which should be ripe and free of blemishes that will show up readily in the final dish. The recipe is easily increased or decreased. I have designed it for only 2 cups fruit since this dish must be served quickly after broiling — it will not keep.

SERVES 2 TO 4

2   cups prepared fruit
¼   cup topping of choice (zabaglione, pastry cream, sour cream, vanilla yogurt, mascarpone, goat cheese, or Neufchâtel cheese)
4   teaspoons dark brown sugar

1. Preheat broiler, placing a rack about 4 inches from heat source. Wash fruit, dry, and then cut into bite-size pieces. Place in individual heatproof bowls or gratin dishes or in one larger baking dish. Top with the topping of choice and then sprinkle with the dark brown sugar.

2. Place dishes under broiler and cook for 4 to 5 minutes. The time will vary depending on your oven. Watch carefully and remove from heat as soon as the topping melts and browns. Serve immediately.

WHAT CAN GO WRONG? Using a broiler is always tricky, since they often do not brown evenly and you need to place the fruit at just the right distance from the heat source (the surface of the fruit should be 2 inches from the heat). Watch the topping very carefully, as it can burn easily.

▪ ▪ ▪

Fruit Gratin with Sugar, Butter, and Lime Juice

I tested lemon juice and preferred the flavor of lime juice. This gratin needs only 2 to 3 minutes of broiling. This recipe works with berries, bananas, mangoes, stone fruits (such as peaches or plums), and grapefruit.

SERVES 2 TO 4

2   cups prepared ripe fruit (berries, bananas, mangoes, stone fruits, or grapefruit)
2   teaspoons unsalted butter
2   tablespoons packed dark brown sugar
4   teaspoons lime juice

CASE 46: IT TAKES TWO TO MANGO

More than 100 combinations of topping and fruit were tested to determine the best pairings for fruit gratin. Here are the preferred combinations.

Topping	Fruit
Zabaglione	Berries, banana
Pastry cream	Berries, stone fruits
Sour cream	Rhubarb, grapefruit
Vanilla yogurt	Mango, stone fruits
Mascarpone	Rhubarb
Goat cheese	Rhubarb
Neufchâtel cheese	Berries
Sugar, butter, lime juice	Berries, banana, mango, stone fruits, grapefruit
Sugar and brandy	Grapefruit

1. Preheat broiler, placing a rack about 4 inches from heat source. Wash, dry, and then cut fruit into bite-size pieces. Place in individual heatproof bowls or gratin dishes or in one larger baking dish. Dot with butter and sprinkle with sugar and lime juice.

2. Place dishes under broiler and cook for 2 to 3 minutes. The time will vary depending on your oven. Watch carefully and remove as soon as the topping melts and browns. Serve immediately.

WHAT CAN GO WRONG? Using a broiler is always tricky, since they often do not brown evenly and you need to place the fruit at just the right distance away from the heat source (the surface of the fruit should be 2 inches from the heat). Watch the topping very carefully, as it can burn easily.

• • •

Fruit Gratin with Sweet Cheese Topping

This is an unusual recipe, since it uses a combination of both goat cheese and cream cheese. It also contains a bit of half-and-half to lighten the mixture, vanilla, and dark brown sugar. Use this recipe rather than the one above if you want a more luxurious fruit gratin. If you use rhubarb, increase the granulated sugar to 1 tablespoon.

SERVES 4

2   cups prepared ripe fruit (use any fruit except grapefruit)
2   tablespoons fresh goat cheese (do not buy aged goat cheese), at room temperature
2   tablespoons cream cheese, at room temperature
2   tablespoons half-and-half
½   teaspoon vanilla extract
1   teaspoon granulated sugar
1   tablespoon packed dark brown sugar

1. Preheat broiler, placing a rack about 4 inches from heat source. Wash, peel, and cut fruit into bite-size pieces; place in a broilerproof gratin dish. Combine the cheeses, half-and-half, vanilla, and white sugar with a fork in a small bowl. Spoon over fruit and then sprinkle with brown sugar.

2. Broil for 5 to 6 minutes, or until the cheese starts to brown. The cooking time may vary a great deal, so watch the dish carefully. Serve immediately.

WHAT CAN GO WRONG? Using a broiler is always tricky, since they often do not brown

evenly and you need to place the fruit at just the right distance from the heat source (the surface of the fruit should be 2 inches from the heat). Watch the topping very carefully, as it can burn easily.

• • •

Fruit Gratin with Breadcrumb Topping

Another approach to a fruit gratin is to use breadcrumbs processed with butter and sugar as the topping. The benefit of this method is texture. The browned crumbs provide a nice contrast to the soft fruit. This recipe can also be made with frozen fruit (see variation below), an idea I picked up from Jacques Pépin's excellent dessert book, Sweet Simplicity.

SERVES 6 TO 8

4   cups prepared ripe fruit (raspberries, blackberries, peaches, nectarines, plums, or apricots)
1   tablespoon lemon juice
6 to 7   tablespoons granulated sugar
3   medium-thick slices white bakery or European-style bread
3   tablespoons cold unsalted butter
¼   teaspoon salt
Sour cream, whipped cream, or vanilla ice cream for serving (optional)

1. Adjust oven rack to center position and heat oven to 400 degrees. Prepare fruit (wash, peel, hull, core, etc.) and cut into bite-size pieces if necessary. Toss fruit with lemon juice and 2 to 3 tablespoons of the sugar. Place in an 8-inch square baking pan or in a 9-inch pie pan.

2. Tear bread into large pieces and pulse with butter, salt, and remaining 4 tablespoons sugar in the bowl of a food processor to produce breadcrumbs. The butter should be in pieces no larger than lentils. Sprinkle crumbs on top of fruit.

3. Bake for 15 to 20 minutes, or until the fruit is juicy and the topping is well browned.

Cool for 5 minutes and then serve with sour cream, whipped cream, or vanilla ice cream.

WHAT CAN GO WRONG? The type of bread will affect the quality of this dish. I do not recommend a tough bread or a sourdough. This recipe is best made with a sweet or buttery bread such as challah or brioche. However, any well-made sandwich bread is fine, as long as you avoid extra-light supermarket sandwich breads.

Frozen Fruit Variation

You can use frozen fruit for this recipe. Use one 12-ounce package of frozen raspberries or strawberries (raspberries are best), top with the breadcrumb topping, and bake at 400 degrees for about 20 minutes. Serve with sour cream.

How to Poach Fruit

A COMMON SHORTCOMING in poached fruit recipes is the poaching liquid — it is simply too sweet. A heavy poaching syrup often calls for 1½ cups sugar to 2 cups liquid, a good formula for doing in your wealthy, diabetic grandmother but otherwise a culinary disaster. The lightest syrup I found uses ½ cup sugar to 2 cups liquid. After much testing, I discovered that ½ cup sugar per 3 cups liquid suited me about right for most recipes. Heavy syrups are dull and not refreshing.

In addition to the level of sugar, I tested a variety of flavoring ingredients, including peppercorns, bay leaves, mint, rosemary, and thyme. For a more complex flavor, I tried toasted cardamom seeds, and, of course, liqueurs are an obvious variation — use ¼ cup per 3 cups liquid. The fruit itself should be firm and just ripe. Overly ripe fruit will become too soft and unappealing in a hot poaching syrup. Unripe fruit will have little flavor and still be hard after poaching (you can simmer unripe fruit in a poaching syrup to soften texture, but the flavor will be bland).

HOW TO SKIN A PEACH

Peaches are usually served skinless, yet they are hard to peel. The secret to quick peeling is to immerse them in boiling water for exactly 30 seconds (I tested shorter times, which did not work as well) and then place them immediately into ice-cold water to stop the cooking. The peel should now come off readily. However, peaches that are not quite ripe may still be a bit difficult to peel. Try boiling them for 45 seconds, although underripe peaches will never be as easy to peel as succulent, ripe specimens.

To test poaching times, I used just-ripe peaches and poached them in four separate batches: one batch was placed into the simmering liquid and immediately removed from the heat; one was simmered for 3 minutes; one for 6 minutes; and the last batch was simmered for a full 10 minutes. The results were immediately clear. The first batch, the one that was immediately removed from the heat, was the winner since it had the firmest texture. However, it also became apparent that there were only small differences among the batches. That is, the fruit poaches and softens considerably even when sitting in a hot liquid off the heat.

I also tested orange slices and found that they should not be simmered at all. In fact, the syrup should be cooled first and then poured over the slices. Otherwise, the oranges will lose their bright flavor and the texture will suffer.

Master Recipe for Poached Fruit

This recipe yields a very light syrup. If you prefer a sweeter, thicker syrup, use ¾ cup sugar. If you have fresh herbs available, don't be afraid to throw a few sprigs of rosemary, thyme, or mint into the poaching syrup. Rosemary is particularly good with pears (see variation).

SERVES 6

For the Basic Poaching Syrup

2	cups water
1	cup white wine
½	cup granulated sugar
1	bay leaf
3-inch strip orange zest	
½	stick cinnamon
2-inch piece vanilla bean sliced in half lengthwise OR ¼ teaspoon vanilla extract	

For the Fruit

1	quart (about 3 pounds) berries, peaches, or apricots, or a mixture

1. Combine ingredients for poaching syrup in a large saucepan (large enough to also hold the fruit), bring to a boil, and simmer for 5 minutes.

2. Prepare the fruit (berries should be washed, peaches should be peeled, pitted, and quartered; apricots should be halved and pitted, not peeled). Add fruit to the syrup, remove from heat, and cover. Let sit until syrup reaches room temperature.

3. Place fruit with syrup in refrigerator. Serve chilled.

WHAT CAN GO WRONG? The real key to this recipe is the fruit itself, not the cooking technique. You will need full-flavored, ripe fruit that is firm, not soft.

POACHED PEAR VARIATION

Peel, core, and halve 3 pounds pears. Follow master recipe but omit cinnamon and add 20 crushed black peppercorns and ¼ cup sweet dessert wine to poaching syrup.

POACHED PLUM VARIATION

Cut 3 pounds plums in half and remove pits. Use red wine instead of white wine in poaching syrup. Omit cinnamon and add ⅛ teaspoon allspice.

▪▪▪

Poached Oranges

To peel an orange for this recipe, use a large, very sharp chef's knife. Slice off the top and bottom of the orange and place the orange on its now flat bottom. Cut off the peel in vertical strips, following the contour of the fruit, being sure to remove all of the white pith. At this point, you can either cut the orange into rounds or segment the orange, the latter technique yielding pieces without pithy membranes. However, rounds are more attractive for serving.

SERVES 4

4	large seedless oranges
¾	cup water
¼	cup white wine
¼	cup granulated sugar
1	teaspoon aniseed

1. Juice one of the oranges and put ½ cup of the juice in a heavy saucepan. Peel the remaining oranges and slice into thin rounds.

2. Add the water, wine, and sugar to the saucepan with the orange juice and bring to a boil. Add aniseed and simmer gently for 2 minutes. Let liquid cool for 1 hour. Pour room temperature liquid over sliced oranges.

3. Refrigerate for at least 1 hour. Serve.

WHAT CAN GO WRONG? Almost nothing can go wrong here. Just be sure to use seedless oranges. Oranges with thick, bitter membranes will also detract from this recipe.

▪▪▪

Peaches with Ginger

This recipe requires perfectly ripe peaches, as they are not really poached; the flavoring syrup is cooled before it is added to the fruit. If your peaches are underripe, I suggest pouring the hot syrup over them and then chilling. Crystallized ginger is found in the spice section of supermar-

kets. This dessert can be served with ice cream, a dense cake, or cookies such as biscotti or shortbread. To peel the peaches, place them in boiling water for 30 seconds and then immerse them in ice water to stop the cooking. The skins will now peel off easily if the peaches are ripe.

SERVES 4

1	lime
½	cup granulated sugar
1	cup water
1	cup white wine
¼	cup crystallized ginger
4	ripe peaches

1. Juice the lime. Combine the sugar, water, wine, and ginger in a saucepan. Bring to a boil, reduce to a simmer, cover, and cook for 7 minutes. Remove from heat and add 1 tablespoon of the lime juice. Chill in refrigerator for 1 hour.

2. Peel, pit, and slice the peaches. Toss fruit with remaining lime juice and reserve in a non-reactive bowl.

3. Pour syrup over peaches and toss. Refrigerate for 1 hour.

4. Serve slightly chilled but not cold from the refrigerator.

WHAT CAN GO WRONG? The success of this recipe depends on the fruit itself, not the cooking technique. You will need full-flavored, ripe peaches that are firm, not soft.

▪▪▪

Pears Poached in Sherry with Ginger

Instead of a sweet dessert wine or sherry, you can use a drier, slightly sweet wine such as a Sancerre or Tokay. That being said, any decent white wine will do in a pinch. The ripeness of the pears is crucial to this recipe. Pears that are too hard will have no flavor. Pears that are too soft will be mushy. A good ripe pear will give

just a smidge when pressed at the stem end, but is still firm.

SERVES 4

1	cup water
¼	cup honey
6	slices (¼-inch thick) peeled fresh ginger
2-inch piece cinnamon stick	
12	whole cloves
4	ripe but firm pears
2	tablespoons lemon juice
½	cup sweet dessert wine or sherry

1. Bring the first 5 ingredients to a simmer.

2. While the poaching liquid is heating, peel, quarter, core, and stem the pears and place in a bowl and toss with lemon juice.

3. Add the pears and the wine to the liquid mixture and bring back to a simmer. Immediately remove from heat and let cool. Serve pears with plenty of poaching syrup.

WHAT CAN GO WRONG? The key to this recipe is the fruit itself, not the cooking technique. You will need full-flavored, ripe pears that are firm, not soft. Many pears in the supermarket are hard and tasteless. To ripen pears, leave in a closed paper bag. This usually takes 2 to 3 days.

▪▪▪

Apple Compote with Prunes and Apricots

You can make a variety of substitutions here, using pears instead of apples, using a combination of both, or using different dried fruits, such as figs or peaches. For a cleaner flavor, use water instead of apple cider and add ½ cup sugar to the mixture. Beware of organic Turkish apricots. I have purchased them at a local health food store and find that they are very dark with very little fruit flavor. I prefer dried apricots that have a bright orange color. (However, in baking, the Turkish apricots are preferred, since heat brings out their flavor.) The most important part of this recipe is cooking the apples to the point that they are cooked through yet still hold their shape. Since all apple varieties are a bit different, you will have to adjust the cooking times accordingly.

SERVES 4

2 cups apple cider
1 cup white wine
¼ cup granulated sugar
1 bay leaf
4 whole cloves
3-inch strip orange zest
½ stick cinnamon
¼ teaspoon salt
½ cup dried apricots (if whole, cut in half)
½ cup pitted prunes
4 tart, firm medium-size apples
1 tablespoon lemon juice
¼ teaspoon vanilla extract
Plain yogurt for serving (optional)

1. Combine the first 8 ingredients (apple cider through salt) in a wide saucepan and bring to a simmer. Add the apricots and prunes to the simmering liquid, cover, and cook for about 15 minutes. Meanwhile, peel, core, and then cut the apples into twelfths (quarter them and then cut each quarter into thirds), tossing them with lemon juice in a medium bowl as you work. Add the apples to the saucepan and continue cooking until tender, 5 to 7 minutes. (The time will vary a great deal depending on the type, size, and freshness of the apples.)

2. Pour fruit mixture into a large strainer set over a bowl. Pour the juices, along with the cinnamon stick, orange zest, and bay leaf, back into the saucepan and place the fruit in the bowl. Over medium-high heat, boil the apple cider mixture until you have 1½ cups of liquid, about 3 minutes. Let cool for 10 minutes off the heat, discard the zest, bay leaf, and cinnamon,

add the vanilla, and then pour over the fruit. Cool to room temperature for serving. Serve with plain yogurt, if you like.

WHAT CAN GO WRONG? All apples are different and therefore they will all cook differently. You want them to be thoroughly cooked but not so much so that they turn into applesauce.

■ ■ ■

Baked Peaches with Bourbon and Brown Sugar

In earlier times, peaches were often baked or broiled and then served with game or as simple desserts, sometimes with a flavored custard sauce. As is often the case, too much sugar (and sometimes bourbon) was used in older recipes, detracting from the fresh flavors of the fruit. Here is a simple, lower-sugar recipe. Note that the juices from the peaches combine with the other ingredients in the dish to make a simple sauce.

SERVES 6

¼ cup packed light brown sugar
Pinch nutmeg
3 peaches, peeled, halved, and pitted
1 tablespoon butter
1 tablespoon bourbon
Vanilla ice cream for serving

Heat oven to 400 degrees. Butter a 2-quart baking dish and evenly coat bottom and sides with the brown sugar, sprinkling a pinch of nutmeg on top. Place peaches in the dish, cut side down. Cut butter into small pieces and scatter around the peaches. Add bourbon. Cover with aluminum foil and bake for 15 minutes. Remove from oven, remove foil, and check to see if the butter and sugar are forming a sauce at the bottom of the dish. Stir, if necessary, to combine. Cover and continue baking for 10 minutes, or until peaches are just soft. This will vary based on the size and ripeness of the peaches. Remove from oven and cool for 5 minutes. Invert each peach half into a bowl and top with a scoop of vanilla ice cream. Spoon sauce over top and serve.

WHAT CAN GO WRONG? The size and ripeness of the peaches will affect both the baking time and the quality of this dessert.

• • •

Stewed Rhubarb

This is simple to make and a good way of using up a large rhubarb patch. I found that using all honey instead of sugar overpowered the taste of the rhubarb, but a bit of honey makes the dish more interesting.

MAKES ABOUT 4 CUPS

1 pound rhubarb, leaves removed, cleaned and cut into 1-inch pieces (about 3½ cups)
½ to ¾ cup granulated sugar
2 tablespoons honey
1 teaspoon minced lemon zest
2 tablespoons lemon juice
¼ cup water

Combine ingredients in a medium saucepan. Bring to a boil, cover, and simmer for 6 minutes. Uncover and simmer an additional 6 to 7 minutes, or until thick. Stir gently, only once or twice, to preserve the texture of the rhubarb.

WHAT CAN GO WRONG? Overstirring will break down the rhubarb, turning it into a soup. Stir gently and infrequently.

• • •

Rhubarb Fool

In a traditional fool, the fruit and whipped cream were often not folded together but added to the goblets in separate layers. Make sure that the stewed rhubarb is cooled when you make this recipe.

MAKES 4 LARGE SERVINGS

1 cup heavy cream
2 tablespoons granulated sugar
½ teaspoon vanilla extract
1 recipe Stewed Rhubarb (above), chilled, or at least cooled to room temperature

Put a metal mixing bowl and beaters or whisk in refrigerator or freezer for 30 minutes or more. When you are ready to whip the cream, place cream, sugar, and vanilla in chilled bowl and beat with an electric mixer on medium speed for 1 minute. (Cream can also be beaten by hand with a whisk.) Increase to high speed and beat into stiff peaks. Fold rhubarb into whipped cream. Spoon the mixture into large goblets or wineglasses and chill before serving. (The whipped cream and rhubarb can also be served in alternating layers.)

WHAT CAN GO WRONG? The only trick is stewing the rhubarb, which is easy enough.

13

SOUFFLÉS

Julia Child once told me that she had to make twenty separate soufflés trying to get the right texture and flavor when developing a recipe for a raspberry soufflé. At the time, that sounded excessive, even compulsive, but I now realize that she was right; soufflés are temperamental, and each type of soufflé requires a different approach. However, this often overlooked dessert, a relic from the days of haute cuisine, is worth every minute of attention. At its best, a soufflé has a crusty exterior packed with flavor, a dramatic rise above the rim, an airy but substantial outer layer, and a rich, loose center that is not completely set. A great soufflé must also convey a true mouthful of flavor, bursting with the bright, clear taste of the main ingredient. From the start, I knew it was going to take a lot of detective work to find the secrets of this delicate thoroughbred of a dessert.

Soufflés are a combination of a base and whipped egg whites; the base provides the substance and flavor, and the whites provide the lift. For the purposes of my investigation, I divided soufflés into four different categories, depending on what sort of base they use:

chocolate, fruit puree, cream cheese, or thickened dairy bases such as béchamel (flour, butter, milk), bouillie (flour, milk), and pastry cream (flour, milk, sugar, eggs). Each type of soufflé seemed to be a bit different and might, I thought, require a slightly different approach. However, all soufflés require a thorough knowledge of egg whites, how to beat them, and how they work.

THE SECRETS OF EGG WHITES REVEALED

THE FIRST QUESTION I wanted to answer was whether the temperature of the egg whites made any difference in the baked soufflé. I discovered that cold egg whites actually produced more volume when whipped, although when they are baked, the difference between cold and warm egg whites diminishes. (The soufflé made with cold whites rose ¼ inch higher than the one made with warm whites.) On the other hand, room temperature whites produced a more even

CASE 47: GOING THE EGGSTRA MILE

Can soufflés be made with powdered or pasteurized egg whites?

Type of Egg White	Volume When Beaten	Soufflé Rise	Cooking Time	Comments
Fresh	1 cup	½ inch	16 minutes	Even rise
Powdered	½ cup	Sank, then coned in middle	17 minutes	Horrible flavor; whites deflated easily when folded into base
Pasteurized	1½ cups	¼ inch	20 minutes	Center never cooked, while sides became brown and crunchy
Fresh with water added	1½ cups	Sank	17 minutes	Watery

rise and a more stable soufflé, so cold versus warm whites was pretty much a toss-up.

I then wondered about the eggs themselves. What would happen if I whipped powdered egg whites, pasteurized whites, or egg whites to which a bit of water has been added, as suggested in some recipes? Case 47 shows the results of my tests.

Once again I discovered that the volume of the beaten whites is not a good indication of the volume of the finished soufflé. In fact, the egg whites beaten with water produced 1½ cups of volume raw, but when they were baked, the soufflé sank. The whites need to be stable and sturdy enough to lift the base during cooking. An insubstantial structure will simply collapse on itself. (I have found, however, in other tests, that water can be successfully added if the final foam has a lot of fat in it, as with chiffon cakes. When tested with lighter angel food cakes, this method was a disaster, but the egg yolks and vegetable oil in chiffon cakes provide plenty of structure for the added water.)

THE BEST WAY TO WHIP EGG WHITES

MANY COOKS, especially those trained in France, argue that there is no substitute for a copper bowl to whip egg whites. I had tested this premise a number of times over the years and found no difference in volume of the beaten whites. However, I had never tried actually baking with the whites, so to test the mystique of the copper bowl, I decided to see if it would produce a superior soufflé.

I began my tests by hand beating whites to the soft peak stage in both a stainless steel and a copper bowl. As I expected, the two bowls produced the same volume of whites. (Each produced ¾ cup when starting with 2 egg whites.) However, I was surprised to find that the finished soufflés were quite different. The copper bowl whites turned out a soufflé with a ½-inch rise (as opposed to only a ¼-inch rise for the stainless steel bowl), the flavor was bright, not eggy and dense, and the crust had a beautiful brown color. The stainless steel bowl, on the other hand, turned out a soufflé that rose unevenly, had inconsistent air bubbles, and collapsed easily. I hated to admit it, but the French do actually know something about soufflés. Those copper bowls really do work. I then repeated this test using a standing mixer and found similar results. Although in this test both soufflés rose the same amount, the copper bowl soufflé had a nicer-looking rise, with great

THE SCIENCE OF EGG WHITES

Egg whites are about 88 percent liquid (water) and about 11 percent protein. (The remaining 1 percent consists of minerals and carbohydrates.) So egg white foams are basically made up of gas bubbles separated from each other by very thin liquid-protein films. When you agitate or beat egg whites, the tightly wound protein molecules relax and begin to unfold and stretch. With continued beating, the stretched proteins begin to overlap, creating a long, elastic surface. This is known as the "soft peak" phase — the air bubbles are relatively large and the foam is unstable because the proteins have not sufficiently unwound and bonded to create a rigid enough structure for holding the air pockets. If one continues beating, the proteins further bond and envelop the air bubbles, trapping and separating them. Consequently you get smaller air bubbles but an increased quantity of them, held in a three-dimensional network of united protein molecules. The key is to establish a fine, even foam that is still moist and elastic enough not to break. Without the addition of sugar (see below for explanation), the margin between beating to maximum volume and overbeating is slim. If you overbeat or heat foams too quickly or too slowly, the proteins will overcoagulate. They become too rigid and rupture, squeezing out the liquid held within their mesh. Technically called syneresis, this process is the one home cooks call weeping or curdling.

When an egg white foam goes into an oven, the heat will further coagulate (unite) the proteins around the air cells, creating a structure to stabilize the foam. Egg white coagulation takes place between 144 and 149 degrees Fahrenheit. (Yolks coagulate between 149 and 158 degrees, whole eggs between 144 and 158.) Part of this range in temperature is due to the fact that egg whites contain a variety of protein types that coagulate at different temperatures. This is not discussed much in books (because it is a bit technical), but it is key to the slow and steady stabilization of egg white foams in an oven. It could be likened to the building of a house: the proteins that coagulate first create a foundation, others the framing, and so on. The proteins that are slower to coagulate are key to foam expansion because they maintain elasticity while the structure is beginning to stabilize.

I also discovered that a pinch of cream of tartar added to egg whites makes a big difference in the final volume and texture of a soufflé. Cream of tartar is an acid, and it is particularly good at denaturing (unwinding) the strands of protein in the egg whites. It enhances their bonding properties while at the same time making them slower to coagulate — the proteins remain more elastic, which results in a more stable, more structured soufflé. Until the protein strands unwind, it is more difficult for them to join together (when the strands are coiled like a snake, many of the molecules are hidden and not available for bonding). In our tests, we discovered a substantial increase in the volume of the baked soufflé with the use of cream of tartar. In addition, the texture was lighter and less cakey.

I was also curious about why sugar beaten with egg whites made for a better result. It turns out that, like acid, sugar also delays foam formation. It separates protein molecules, slowing the bonding process. Thus it helps to prevent overbeating. It also stabilizes the foam, particularly in the oven, because it attracts water and thus delays water evaporation, giving the protein structure time to set up. So whether you are using a sugar syrup or plain sugar, the risk of overbeating decreases as the amount of sugar increases, because it impedes the bonding of proteins.

CASE 48: BETTER WHIPPING THROUGH CHEMICALS

How do vinegar, cream of tartar, and salt affect the beating of egg whites?

Technique	Volume of Beaten Whites	Soufflé Rise	Comments
Copper bowl, cream of tartar, salt	1¼ cups	¾ inch	Salty; cakelike texture
Copper bowl, vinegar cleaning, cream of tartar	1¼ cups	1½ inches	Great flavor, even rise, even bubbles
Stainless steel bowl, cream of tartar	1½ cups	1 inch	Rise a bit uneven, but nice texture

color, great crust, and even bubbles. The conclusion? Well, either bowl will do nicely, but copper is best if you can afford it.

To understand the science behind these results, I consulted a few food scientists, who told me that the copper ions combine with conalbumin, an egg white protein, to slow the coagulation process. The result is an increased stability of the foam, increased moisture retention, and an increase in the temperature at which coagulation occurs. As I found in my tests, it does not increase the volume of the foam when beating, but it stabilizes it so well that the foam can better tolerate expansion in the oven. Thus the finished product will have greater volume.

I then set out to perform a series of tests with a variety of additives. For example, should the bowls first be cleaned with a bit of white vinegar? What about adding cream of tartar or salt? These were ideas I'd read of or heard about over the years. I tried each of these items out with copper and stainless steel bowls, whipping 2 egg whites by machine to the soft peak stage. As the Case 48 test summary shows, the best method was to clean a copper bowl with white vinegar, wipe it out, add the room temperature

whites, and beat them with a bit of cream of tartar. However, beating whites in a stainless steel bowl with cream of tartar was a very good second choice.

The last set of tests involved the use of sugar. The first issue was whether the whites should be beaten with or without sugar. I tested this and found that when beaten with even just a small amount of sugar, the whites became more stable, which makes them more foolproof and more resilient to a heavy hand during folding. The question then became, which is better, granulated or confectioners' sugar? I also wanted to know whether the sugar should be added at the beginning or only during the whipping process. (Again, the tests involved beating 2 whites until they held a 2-inch peak.)

As the chart "Sweet Success" shows, the obvious lesson from these tests is never to add granulated sugar at the outset of whipping the whites. The foam becomes overdeveloped, and therefore the soufflé is less stable and too sweet. For the best rise, I recommend using granulated sugar but adding it during whipping. Confectioners' sugar produces a good volume of beaten egg whites, although they rise less when baked.

CASE 49: SWEET SUCCESS

A face-off between granulated and confectioners' sugar delivers surprising results.

Technique	Volume of Beaten Whites	Soufflé Rise	Comments
Granulated, added at outset	1½ cups	¾ inch	Uneven rise; too sweet
Granulated, added during whipping	1 cup	1 inch	Even rise; better flavor
Confectioners', added at outset	1¼ cups	¾ inch	Nice foam; stable soufflé
Confectioners', added during whipping	1 cup	½ inch	Good foam; stable soufflé

SOUFFLÉ RULES

Now that I had done my homework on egg whites, I wanted to investigate other factors might be consistent for all types of soufflés. The first issue was the correct proportion of egg whites to egg yolks. Soufflé recipes vary a lot in this regard. I've seen cookbooks calling for 4 yolks and 4 whites, while others tell you to use 8 whites with 4 yolks. It turns out that there is no right answer for all soufflés. Fruit soufflés, chocolate soufflés, cream cheese soufflés, and savory soufflés all must be treated differently.

The next variable was oven temperature. All types of soufflés work well at the standard 375 degrees, but I found through testing that a slightly higher oven temperature produced a more dramatic rise. I finally settled on 385 degrees, since I found that 400 degrees was living a bit too dangerously — sometimes the top of the soufflé would turn very dark and almost burn. I then tested the notion of using a water bath (the baking dish was placed in a roasting pan half-filled with hot water) in the hope that this might moderate the heat around the dish and make a more delicate soufflé. In all cases, the outside of the soufflé turned out wet and gelatin-like, although the flavor was fine. This was a disaster.

Finally, I tested a few other variables. I found that a 1½-quart soufflé dish works best. A 2-quart dish is too large; you don't get that nice high rise and creamy, moist center. (Make sure to use a soufflé dish, with perfectly straight sides.) When folding together the base and the beaten egg whites, use a large, flexible rubber spatula or, in a pinch, your hands, which are actually well suited to the task. After the baking dish is filled, run a table knife or your finger around the mixture, about 1 inch in from the perimeter. This will give the risen soufflé a nice flat top. Be sure to bake soufflés on the middle rack of your oven. I found that the bottom of the soufflé burned on the lowest rack. The soufflé will rise into the top of the stove or the heating elements if it is baked on the top rack. Finally, and most important of all, never overcook a soufflé. It should be very wet in the middle and firm around the outside, almost like a pudding cake. The center should not be liquid but still quite loose and very moist. I find that once you can smell a soufflé baking in the oven, it is about ready to come out.

❖

BASIC DESSERT SOUFFLÉS

THERE ARE A number of possible ways to prepare the soufflé base, which is the thick, flavored mixture into which the beaten egg whites are folded. In a Grand Marnier soufflé, the base is usually a béchamel, a thick French sauce made from butter, flour, and milk. However, pastry cream is often used as a base, as is a bouillie, a simple flour-milk paste, similar to a béchamel but without butter. The test kitchen at *Cook's Illustrated* prepared a blind tasting using each of these three methods. Although we expectd the béchamel version to win, the bouillie soufflé had the creamiest, richest texture. However, it did taste a bit like scrambled eggs. To solve this problem, we stirred 2 tablespoons of butter into the bouillie, which eliminated the eggy aftertaste.

Our tastings also confirmed that most recipes produce foamy rather than creamy soufflés, and the solution to this problem was to increase the amount of flour used in the base. Although a standard bouillie or béchamel calls for 3 tablespoons of flour to 1 cup of milk, we experienced the best results using 5 tablespoons of flour. We also wondered if milk was the right choice as opposed to heavy cream or half-and-half. When this was tested, however, the tasters preferred milk; the flavor was livelier than either of the other versions and also superior to half milk and half heavy cream.

Next, I tested the proportion of egg whites to yolks. Five of each turned out to be best (see Case 50), so my working recipe for a basic dessert soufflé called for 5 egg whites plus 5 yolks, the yolks whisked into a base made from 1 cup milk, 5 tablespoons flour, and 2 tablespoons butter. This variety of soufflé base is excellent for citrus flavors and for liquor-flavored soufflés such as Grand Marnier.

CASE 50: HOLD THOSE WHITES!

What is the best proportion of whites to yolks for a rich, creamy soufflé?

Test	Comments
5 whites to 5 yolks	Rich, luxurious texture
5 whites to 4 yolks	Very good
6 whites to 4 yolks	Good, but on the light, foamy side
7 whites to 4 yolks	Good, but airy
8 whites to 4 yolks	Too airy and foamy

•••

Grand Marnier Soufflé

To prepare this recipe in individual ramekins, bake for 16 to 18 minutes. When tested on the bottom oven rack, this soufflé was a disaster. The bottom was ruined and the outside was burned. It is best to bake a soufflé on the middle rack (the upper position is often too close to either the top of the oven or the electric coils in an electric oven). If you are pressed for time when serving this to company, you can prepare the soufflé dish, make the base, whisk in the flavorings, put the egg whites in the mixing bowl, and preheat the oven (steps 1 and 2 of the recipe) all well ahead of time. Then, half an hour before serving, whip the whites, fold them

into the base, fill the soufflé dish, and bake. Al-
though the soufflé will not rise quite as well us-
ing this method (a freshly made base produces a
better soufflé), your guests won't know the dif-
ference, and you will be spared a lot of last-
minute work.

SERVES 6

Softened unsalted butter for coating soufflé
   dish
¾   cup granulated sugar
5   tablespoons all-purpose flour
⅛   teaspoon salt
1   cup whole milk
2   tablespoons unsalted butter
1   tablespoon grated orange zest
3   tablespoons Grand Marnier
5   large egg yolks
¼   teaspoon cream of tartar
5   large egg whites

1. Heat the oven to 385 degrees. Generously
butter the inside of a 1½-quart soufflé dish
and add ¼ cup of the sugar. Shake and turn
dish to distribute sugar evenly and knock out
excess.

2. Put flour, salt, and ¼ cup of the sugar in a
small, heavy saucepan and whisk to combine.
Add milk slowly, whisking until smooth, about
10 seconds. Place pan over high heat, add the 2
tablespoons butter, and bring to a boil, whisking
constantly, until mixture has thickened and pulls
away from the sides of the pan, 2½ to 3 minutes.
Remove from heat and turn contents into a large
bowl. Whisk in orange zest and Grand Marnier.
Whisk in yolks one at a time, whisking 10 seconds after each addition.

3. Combine cream of tartar with remaining ¼
cup sugar. In a mixing bowl, beat egg whites for
30 seconds on medium speed. Turn mixer to high
and slowly add the sugar mixture. Beat until
whites hold a 2-inch peak.

4. Add one-quarter of the beaten whites to the
base and whisk together. Add the remaining
whites and fold mixture as gently as possible,
using a rubber spatula.

5. Turn mixture into prepared soufflé dish
and run your index finger or a table knife
around the perimeter of the soufflé, an inch in
from the sides. (This helps the soufflé to rise
properly.) Bake in the middle of the oven 20 to
25 minutes, checking soufflé after 20 minutes.
The top should be brown but the soufflé should
still wiggle a bit when gently shaken and, when
cut into, the center should be wet and a bit
loose. Serve immediately.

WHAT CAN GO WRONG? Obviously, this recipe
is about beating egg whites and folding them
properly into the base. Adding cream of tartar
and some sugar to the whites makes the beaten
whites considerably more stable and less apt to
be damaged by a heavy hand while folding.
However, you can still deflate the whites if your
folding technique leaves something to be desired. (See page 8 for step-by-step instructions.)
Perhaps the most difficult part of making a
soufflé is knowing when it is done. It should still
be slightly liquid in the very center, so it should
have a bit of jiggle to it when you take it from
the oven.

SHAVED CHOCOLATE VARIATION
Mix 2 teaspoons of sifted cocoa powder with
the ¼ cup sugar in step 1 before adding to the
buttered soufflé dish. In step 4, add ⅓ cup
(about ½ ounce) grated bittersweet chocolate to
the base after the beaten whites have been
added. (The easiest way to grate chocolate is to
use a rotary cheese grater.)

ESPRESSO VARIATION
Follow instructions for master recipe, substituting Kahlúa for Grand Marnier and adding ⅓
cup finely ground espresso-roasted coffee beans
to the base after the beaten whites have been
added (step 4).

...

Lemon Soufflé

The lemon oil is optional, but it does add a bit of extra zip to the taste of this soufflé. I do not like lemon extract very much, so unless you have the oil on hand, just forget about this ingredient. I find that small lemons turn out about 3 tablespoons juice but a large one at room temperature can produce a full ¼ cup.

SERVES 6

Softened unsalted butter for coating soufflé
    dish
¾ cup granulated sugar
5 tablespoons all-purpose flour
⅛ teaspoon salt
1 cup whole milk
2 tablespoons unsalted butter
1 tablespoon grated lemon zest
¼ cup lemon juice
¼ teaspoon lemon oil (optional)
5 large egg yolks
¼ teaspoon cream of tartar
5 large egg whites

1. Heat the oven to 385 degrees. Generously butter the inside of a 1½-quart soufflé dish and add ¼ cup of the sugar. Shake and turn dish to distribute sugar evenly and knock out excess.

2. Put flour, salt, and ¼ cup of the sugar in a small, heavy saucepan and whisk to combine. Add milk slowly, whisking until smooth, about 10 seconds. Place pan over high heat, add the 2 tablespoons butter, and bring to a boil, whisking constantly, until mixture has thickened and pulls away from the sides of the pan, 2½ to 3 minutes. Remove from heat and turn contents into a large bowl. Whisk in zest, lemon juice, and optional lemon oil. Whisk in yolks one at a time, whisking 10 seconds after each addition.

3. Combine cream of tartar with remaining ¼ cup sugar. In a mixing bowl, beat egg whites for 30 seconds on medium speed. Turn mixer to

high and slowly add the sugar mixture. Beat until whites hold a 2-inch peak.

4. Add one-quarter of the beaten whites to the base and whisk together. Fold in the remaining whites as gently as possible, using a rubber spatula.

5. Turn mixture into the prepared soufflé dish and run your index finger or a table knife around the perimeter of the soufflé, an inch in from the sides. (This helps the soufflé to rise properly.) Bake in the middle of the oven 20 to 25 minutes, checking soufflé after 20 minutes. The top should be brown but the soufflé should still wiggle a bit when gently shaken and, when cut into, the center should be wet and a bit loose. Serve immediately.

...

Butterscotch Soufflé

This variation was the brainchild of the Cook's *test kitchen. I didn't think that the butterscotch flavor would come through but it did, and with flying colors. The secret is brown sugar, butter, and lots of vanilla extract.*

SERVES 6

4 tablespoons unsalted butter, softened
¾ cup packed dark brown sugar
5 tablespoons all-purpose flour
⅛ teaspoon salt
1 cup whole milk
1 tablespoon vanilla extract
5 large egg yolks
¼ teaspoon cream of tartar
¼ cup granulated sugar
5 large egg whites

1. Heat the oven to 385 degrees. Using 1 tablespoon of the butter, grease the inside of a 1½-quart soufflé dish and add ¼ cup of the brown sugar. Shake and turn dish to distribute sugar evenly and knock out excess.

2. Combine flour and salt in a small bowl and gradually whisk in the 1 cup milk until no lumps remain, about 10 seconds. Set aside.

3. In a small, heavy saucepan, heat remaining 3 tablespoons butter over medium heat until foaming. Add remaining ½ cup brown sugar and cook until bubbling and fragrant, about 30 seconds. Add flour-milk mixture and whisk constantly until mixture has thickened and pulls away from the sides of the pan, 2½ to 3 minutes. Remove from heat, turn contents into a large bowl, and whisk in vanilla. Whisk in yolks one at a time, whisking about 10 seconds after each addition.

4. Combine cream of tartar with the granulated sugar. In a mixing bowl, beat egg whites for 30 seconds on medium speed. Turn mixer to high and slowly add the sugar mixture. Beat until whites hold a 2-inch peak.

5. Add one-quarter of the beaten whites to the base and whisk together. Add the remaining whites and fold mixture as gently as possible, using a rubber spatula.

6. Turn mixture into the prepared soufflé dish and run your index finger or a table knife around the perimeter of the soufflé, an inch in from the sides. (This helps the soufflé to rise properly.) Bake in the middle of the oven 20 to 25 minutes, checking soufflé after 20 minutes. The top should be brown but the soufflé should still wiggle a bit when gently shaken and, when cut into, the center should be wet and a bit loose. Serve immediately.

Fruit Soufflés

I HAVE MADE MANY fruit soufflés in my time, using pureed raspberries or canned peaches or dried apricots simmered in a sugar syrup. None of them has been half as good as a simple chocolate or béchamel-base soufflé. Fruit puree simply does not have enough fat in it to balance the light,

foamy nature of beaten egg whites. As I described in *The Cook's Bible,* one can make a béchamel-base soufflé and then add a fruit puree to it, but I still find this sort of dessert unsatisfactory, since the fruit flavor is too mild. There are plenty of better choices, so why bother with second best?

Chocolate Soufflés

IN A CHOCOLATE SOUFFLÉ, the chocolate high notes should be clear and strong. A balancing act between egg whites, chocolate, yolks, and butter is the essence of a great chocolate soufflé. But the problem with most chocolate soufflés is that they are made with a generous amount of milk, which mutes the chocolate. The milk is part of the soufflé base. To understand this problem, let's review some soufflé basics.

A primary consideration when trying to create such a soufflé is what to use as the base, the mixture that gives substance and flavor to the soufflé. After much testing, I had decided that a butter-enhanced bouillie was better than either pastry cream or a classic béchamel. But after a week of refining a recipe, I held a tasting and it was noted that the chocolate was muted by the milk used in the bouillie. Now I had to start all over again. Stephen Schmidt, a frequent contributor to *Cook's Illustrated,* had made an interesting discovery while preparing a chocolate truffle cake during a cooking class. He forgot to add the flour and came up with a dessert that was soufflélike in texture but with a more intense chocolate flavor than most soufflés.

Starting with this idea, and a suggestion from the *Cook's Illustrated* test kitchen to try an egg yolk–sugar base, I removed the flour from the recipe, separated the eggs (whipping the whites separately), more than doubled the amount of chocolate, used 6 whole eggs, and reduced the amount of butter. This approach resulted in a base of egg yolks beaten with sugar until thick. This gave the soufflé plenty of volume but eliminated the milk, the ingredient that was holding back the chocolate. The result was fantastic — the most intense chocolate dessert I had ever tasted.

My chocolate soufflé now had the intense flavor I had been looking for, but I still wasn't completely happy with the texture, because the outer layer was a bit cakey. After several more experiments, though, I discovered that adding 2 egg whites resolved the problem, giving the soufflé more lift and a better texture.

I also tested the theory that a chilled soufflé dish improves the rise, and discovered that it did cause chocolate soufflés to rise higher but made little difference with nonchocolate soufflés. During the course of all this testing, I also found that there are three ways to know when a chocolate soufflé is done: when you can smell the chocolate, when it stops rising, and when only the very center of the top jiggles when the dish is gently shaken. Of course, these are all imprecise methods. If you are not sure if your soufflé is done, take two large spoons, pull open the top of the soufflé, and peek inside. If the center is still soupy, simply put the dish back in the oven! Contrary to what you might expect, this in no way harms this type of soufflé.

When I moved on to test flavorings, my first test was whether an orange liqueur, such as Grand Marnier, or a chocolate liqueur, such as a crème de cacao, would be better. The Grand Marnier was fine as a variation on the theme, but it overpowered the chocolate. I vastly preferred the crème de cacao, which provided an intense flavor boost. I then tested the chocolate component of the recipe, comparing soufflés made with semisweet chocolate, bittersweet chocolate, and cocoa powder. The semisweet version tasted a bit washed-out to me, and the cocoa powder soufflé was a disaster, with a bitter, shallow chocolate flavor, almost like a sinfully rich cup of dark coffee. The cocoa also produced a very dry and dense soufflé. On the other hand, the soufflé made with bittersweet chocolate was impressive,

a great mix of cake and pudding, almost like eating a premium bar of chocolate.

Just for fun, I also tried substituting ground nuts (I tried almonds) for the flour; the soufflé was chewy and macaroon-like and collapsed almost immediately. It also had a strange mushroom shape on top. When I tried making the recipe with chocolate chunks instead of melted chocolate, I found a layer of chocolate on the bottom of the dish, none of it having remained suspended in the batter.

•••

Chocolate Soufflé

Rather than one large soufflé, you can make individual ones. To do so, completely fill eight 8-ounce ramekins with the chocolate mixture, making sure to clean each rim with a wet paper towel, and reduce baking time to 16 to 18 minutes. If you are microwave oriented, melt the chocolate and butter at 50 percent power for 3 minutes. You can use semisweet chocolate, but I found that bittersweet produced a deeper flavor.

SERVES 6 TO 8

	Softened butter and granulated sugar for coating soufflé dish
8	ounces semisweet or bittersweet chocolate, coarsely chopped
4	tablespoons unsalted butter, cut into 1-inch chunks
⅛	teaspoon salt
½	teaspoon vanilla extract
1	tablespoon crème de cacao
1	teaspoon grated orange zest
6	large egg yolks
6	tablespoons granulated sugar
8	large egg whites
¼	teaspoon cream of tartar

1. Adjust oven rack to lower middle position and heat oven to 385 degrees. Butter inside of 2-quart soufflé dish with softened butter, then coat inside of dish evenly with a tablespoon or

so of sugar, gently shaking out excess sugar. Refrigerate until ready to use.

2. Melt chocolate and the 4 tablespoons butter in a medium bowl set over a pan of simmering water, or heat in a microwave oven for 2 minutes at 50 percent power, stir, heat another minute at 50 percent, stir, and then heat an additional minute if necessary. Off heat, stir in salt, vanilla, crème de cacao, and orange zest; set aside.

3. In a medium bowl, beat yolks and 4 tablespoons of the sugar with an electric mixer set on medium speed until thick and pale yellow, about 3 minutes. Fold into chocolate mixture. Clean beaters.

4. Put the egg whites in a large metal mixing bowl. Whip on medium-high speed for 30 seconds, add the cream of tartar, and then add the remaining 2 tablespoons sugar gradually, beating until the whites hold a 2-inch peak. They should still be soft and glossy.

5. Vigorously stir one-quarter of the whipped whites into the chocolate mixture. Gently fold remaining whites into mixture until just incorporated. Spoon mixture into prepared dish; bake until exterior is set but interior is still a bit loose and creamy, about 25 minutes. (Soufflé is done when fragrant and fully risen. Use two large spoons to pull open the top and peek inside. If center is not yet done, place soufflé back in oven.) Serve immediately.

WHAT CAN GO WRONG? This recipe is all about beating. It is important to fully beat the yolk-sugar mixture and to properly whip the whites until they hold a 2-inch peak but are not dry and stiff. The benefit of using chocolate in a soufflé is that it provides a lot of structure, so much so that one can use two spoons to peek inside the soufflé and then put it back in the oven if it is not yet done!

Mocha Variation

Dissolve 1 tablespoon of instant coffee powder in 1 tablespoon hot water and add to the chocolate mixture along with the vanilla.

Grand Marnier Variation

Substitute Grand Marnier for the crème de cacao and eliminate the grated orange zest.

The Make-Ahead Chocolate Soufflé

FOR YEARS, I had heard rumors about chefs who had devised secret recipes for chocolate soufflés that were prepared ahead of time, then refrigerated or frozen, and baked at the last minute. I wanted to develop just such a recipe to take the last-minute worry out of soufflés for busy cooks.

For the first test, I tried simply refrigerating and freezing the soufflé batter in individual ramekins. (I had discovered through earlier testing that individual soufflés hold up much better in the refrigerator or freezer than a full recipe held in a soufflé dish.) When I baked them, the refrigerated soufflés were a disaster (they hardly rose at all and were very wet inside), but the frozen versions worked fairly well. However, they were cakelike, without the loose center I was seeking.

For the second test, I heated the sugar with 2 tablespoons of water just to the boiling stage and added it to the yolks while beating. Although this produced more volume, the final soufflé was only slightly better than in the first test. Finally, I also added 2 tablespoons of confectioners' sugar to the whites. This version was a great success, producing a soufflé that was light and airy, with an excellent rise and a nice wet center. The actual texture of the whites changed as they were beaten, becoming stable enough so they held up better during freezing. I did find that these soufflés ended up with a domed top, but increasing the oven temperature to 400 degrees solved this problem. I had my make-ahead soufflé at last!

···

Make-Ahead Chocolate Soufflé

This technique only works for individual chocolate soufflés, which can be made and frozen up to 2 days before baking.

SERVES 8

Softened butter and granulated sugar for
    coating ramekins
8 ounces bittersweet chocolate, coarsely
    chopped
4 tablespoons unsalted butter, cut into 1-inch
    chunks
⅛ teaspoon salt
½ teaspoon vanilla extract
1 tablespoon crème de cacao
⅓ cup plus 3 tablespoons sugar
6 large egg yolks
1 teaspoon grated orange zest
8 large egg whites
¼ teaspoon cream of tartar

1. Butter eight 1-cup ramekins with the softened butter, then coat inside of them evenly with sugar, shaking gently to remove excess sugar. Refrigerate until ready to use.

2. Melt chocolate and 4 tablespoons butter in a medium bowl set over a pan of simmering water, or heat in a microwave oven for 2 minutes at 50 percent power, stir, heat another minute at 50 percent, stir, and then heat an additional minute if necessary. Off heat, stir in salt, vanilla, and crème de cacao; set aside.

3. Make a sugar syrup by bringing ⅓ cup of the sugar mixed with 2 tablespoons water to a boil in a small saucepan. In a medium bowl, beat yolks with an electric mixer set on medium speed, drizzling in the sugar syrup. Beat until the yolks are thick and pale yellow, about 3 minutes. Fold into chocolate mixture along with the orange zest. Clean beaters.

4. Put the egg whites in a large metal mixing bowl. Whip on medium-high speed for 30 seconds, add the cream of tartar, and then add the remaining 3 tablespoons sugar gradually, beating until the whites hold a 2-inch peak. They should still be soft and glossy.

5. Vigorously stir one-quarter of the whipped whites into the chocolate mixture. Gently fold remaining whites into mixture until just incorporated. Fill each ramekin almost to rim, wiping excess filling from rim with a wet paper towel. Cover with plastic wrap and freeze until firm, at least 3 hours and up to 2 days.

6. Adjust oven rack to middle position and heat oven to 400 degrees. When oven is preheated, remove soufflés from freezer, uncover, and bake until fully risen, 16 to 18 minutes. Do not overbake.

WHAT CAN GO WRONG? Make sure that the soufflés go into the oven directly from the freezer. Do not thaw first — they will not rise properly.

THE CREAM CHEESE SOUFFLÉ

I HAVE TRIED A VARIETY of "alternative" bases for soufflés, including applesauce, pureed bananas, apricot baby food (it seemed like a good idea at the time) — just about everything — but the one nontraditional ingredient that shines above all the others is cream cheese. It has enough substance to work much like a béchamel, providing some fat and flavor to the beaten egg whites. It makes a wonderful sauce if you cook the soufflé properly, leaving the center loose and undercooked.

I beat the egg yolks with sugar to start and found that 3 yolks was the right amount with 5 egg whites. I also discovered that I preferred confectioners' sugar to granulated in this recipe. I added the cream cheese to the yolks and sugar and whipped the mixture until it was light and fluffy. It is very important to use room temperature cream cheese or it will be difficult to beat properly. I then experimented with other ingredients and found that ½ cup heavy cream was helpful in lightening the cream cheese mixture. I also liked a tablespoon of melted butter for flavor along with a teaspoon of vanilla.

Finally, I played around with additional flavorings and remembered a recipe from *Cook's Magazine* from the 1980s which called for ground cardamom. I tried it here and loved it. It adds an unusual but complementary flavor to the cream cheese. Some cooks serve this substantial type of soufflé with a fruit sauce. This is an excellent pairing, but the soufflé is perfectly fine on its own with a good cup of coffee or espresso.

···

Cream Cheese Soufflé

This is one of the few recipes for which ground cardamom is a key ingredient. It lends an exotic perfume to an otherwise straightforward dish. Note that cream cheese soufflés have a rather smooth, tough-looking top, unlike the more extravagant visuals offered by classic soufflés. Inside, however, the soufflé is rich and exciting. It is very important to leave the center of this soufflé runny; the still-liquid cream cheese makes its own sauce.

SERVES 6 TO 8

Butter and granulated sugar for coating
    soufflé dish or ramekins
3   large egg yolks, at room temperature
½   cup confectioners' sugar
8   ounces cream cheese, at room
    temperature
1   tablespoon all-purpose flour
½   cup heavy cream
1   tablespoon melted butter
1   teaspoon vanilla extract
¼   teaspoon ground cardamom
Pinch of salt
5   large egg whites, preferably at room
    temperature
¼   teaspoon cream of tartar
1   tablespoon granulated sugar

1. Adjust oven rack to lower middle position and heat oven to 385 degrees. Butter the inside of a 1½-quart soufflé dish or 6 to 8 individual ramekins, then add a tablespoon or so of granulated sugar to coat evenly.

2. Beat the yolks and confectioners' sugar together with an electric mixer until light yellow and fluffy, 2 to 3 minutes. Add cream cheese in 1-ounce lumps and continue beating until light and fluffy, another 2 minutes. Add flour, heavy cream, melted butter, vanilla, cardamom, and salt. Mix until just combined.

3. Put the egg whites in a large metal mixing bowl. Whip on medium-high speed for 30 seconds, add the cream of tartar, and then add the 1 tablespoon sugar gradually, beating until the whites hold a 2-inch peak. They should still be soft and glossy.

4. Stir one-quarter of the whipped whites into the cream cheese mixture. Gently fold remaining whites into mixture with a large rubber spatula. Spoon the soufflé mixture into the prepared dish(es) and bake for about 18 minutes for individual ramekins and 20 to 25 minutes for a soufflé dish. The center should still be very moist and a bit loose. (To check for doneness, remove from oven and use two large spoons to pull open the top. If center is not sufficiently cooked, place back in oven.)

5. Serve as is or with a fruit sauce.

WHAT CAN GO WRONG? The cream cheese mixture is relatively heavy, and folding in the whites requires some skill. Stirring one-quarter of the beaten whites into the base mixture to lighten it before folding in the rest makes this easier.

THE PERFECT CHILLED LEMON SOUFFLÉ

THERE ARE RECIPES that arrive at the kitchen door one day with no letter of introduction and then go on to quietly claim a room in the house of American culinary history. Chilled lemon soufflé — a soufflé that doesn't go near the oven — is such a recipe. Based on a classic Bavarian cream, it is most often a mixture of a custard base, gelatin, whipped cream, beaten egg whites, sugar, and lemon flavorings. But like any good mongrel American classic, chilled lemon soufflé covers a wide range of recipes, from baked pudding cakes, which are then cooled and served at room temperature, to minimalist combinations of lemon juice, sugar, and beaten whites.

Despite its various guises, how should it taste? For me — and I have happily eaten lots of them — a chilled lemon soufflé is an unusual marriage of cream and foam, of sweet and sour, of high lemony notes and lingering rich custard. It starts at the tip of the tongue with the sharp tingle of lemon zest and then slides slowly down the throat, filling the mouth with cream and pudding and a soft, long finish. At least, that's what it is supposed to do. The question is, how can a home cook make this delicate balance of ingredients and technique turn out just right? I set out to test as many recipes as possible.

I quickly discovered that there are five basic approaches to this dessert. The most elaborate begins with a custard base that is then combined with gelatin, whipped cream, and beaten egg whites. Many recipes, however, leave out the custard, using only beaten egg yolks and sugar as the base, while some classic French versions of this dish also leave out the egg whites. Other recipes omit the egg yolks altogether, using just sugar, lemon juice, whipped cream, and beaten egg whites. If the whipped cream is eliminated in a further act of reductionism, you have what is known as a lemon snow pudding. I also looked up recipes for lemon mousse and found that mousse is usually made without gelatin, the key ingredient in chilled lemon soufflé.

I began my testing with the simplest approach, just beaten egg whites, gelatin, sugar, and lemon juice. The result was a foamy con-

fection, much like being served a mound of beaten egg whites. This dessert needed some fat for texture and flavor. I then thought I would try a recipe with whipped cream as well. This was quite good, rated number one by some of my tasters. It had lots of lemon punch but a somewhat airy, foamy texture which, I thought, still needed a bit more fat. Next, I added beaten egg yolks to the mixture, perhaps the most common approach to chilled lemon soufflé, but the texture of this version of the dessert was tough. I tried a second variation on this theme and was still unsatisfied with the texture. I then left out the egg whites and produced a dense, rubbery lemon dome, the sort of dessert that might hold up nicely in Death Valley in July. Finally, I started with a custard base made with sugar, egg yolks, milk, lemon juice, and gelatin and then added this to the whipped cream and beaten whites. This was highly rated, but the lemon flavor was a bit muted.

Reviewing my testing results, I decided that a compromise might be reached between the two test winners. The dessert made with lemon juice, whipped cream, and beaten egg whites was light and lemony but too foamy; the custard-base dessert had a better finish and mouth feel but was lacking the bright, clear flavor of lemon. I worked up a new master recipe that called for softening a package of gelatin in ½ cup lemon juice. (I tried 2 packages of gelatin and ended up with a rubbery orb.) Next, a cup of milk was heated with sugar while I beat 2 egg yolks with an extra 2 tablespoons of sugar. The milk and the beaten yolks were combined on top of the stove and heated until the mixture began to steam. Finally, the cooled custard was folded into whipped cream (I used ¾ cup heavy cream), and 6 beaten egg whites were folded into the result. This was the best variation to date, but it still needed a few refinements.

First, I cut back the whites to 5 from 6 to give the dessert a bit less air and more substance. Next, I added ¼ teaspoon cornstarch to the custard mixture to prevent the yolks from curdling too easily. (For more information on this technique, see "Really Good Custard Pie" in the May/June 1999 issue of *Cook's Illustrated*.) I then wondered if either lemon oil or lemon extract might be better than zest, so I made a side-by-side comparison. I settled on the zest, since it produced a more complex range of flavors. I also discovered that to maintain a more consistent texture it was better to whisk a small part of the beaten egg whites into the custard base before folding the mixture together.

Many recipes call for using individual ramekins, but most home cooks do not have these on hand. I thought that a soufflé dish was best (after all, this is a chilled lemon *soufflé*), and to make it look even more like its baked cousin, I added a simple collar of aluminum foil and increased the recipe to the point that it would rise above the rim of the dish, much like a real soufflé. I was also curious about how well this dessert would hold up in the refrigerator. After 1 day, it was still good but slightly foamy, losing the creamy, tender undercurrent that is its hallmark when well made. After 2 and 3 days, it quickly deteriorated. This is a dessert that is best served the day it is made.

▪ ▪ ▪

Chilled Lemon Soufflé

To make this lemon soufflé "soufflé" over the rim of the dish, use a 1-quart soufflé dish and make a foil collar for it by tearing off a piece of foil 3 inches longer than the circumference of the dish. Now fold the foil in half lengthwise and then in half again so that the "collar" is just a few inches high. Wrap it around the soufflé dish so that the foil extends about 2 inches higher than the rim, and tape together the overlapping ends. Also tape the foil to the outside of the dish. Carefully remove the collar before serving. For those less concerned about appearance, the soufflé can be served from any 1½-quart serving bowl. For best texture, serve the soufflé after 1½ hours of chilling. It may be chilled for up to 6 hours; though the texture will stiffen slightly because of the gelatin, it will taste just as good. Be sure to zest the lemon(s) before juicing them.

SERVES 4 TO 6

- ½ cup lemon juice
- 2 teaspoons unflavored gelatin (one ¼-ounce packet)
- 1 cup whole milk
- ¾ cup granulated sugar
- 2 large egg yolks, at room temperature
- ¼ teaspoon cornstarch
- 2½ teaspoons grated lemon zest

THE RIGHT WAY TO ZEST

Once I decided that fresh lemon zest was a better choice for flavoring my chilled lemon soufflé than oils or extracts, I wanted to test the best method for removing it from the fruit. First, we should define the term "zest": the zest is the outer peel of the lemon, without any of the white pith. (A zester is a handheld instrument with sharp-edged small holes in the blade that remove the peel in thin strips.)

Cooks from the *Cook's Illustrated* test kitchen tried five tools: a flat, moderately coarse grater (holes about ⅛ inch); a flat, very fine grater; the finest side of a box grater; a zester (the zest was then minced with a knife); and a vegetable peeler (the zest was then minced). After making a chilled lemon soufflé using each method, we declared the coarsely grated zest the winner. The fine grater produced a light, flaky, dry zest. The box grater version was frustrating, since so much of the zest was lost in the grater. The zester produced a dry, flaky product, and it required a fair amount of pressure to pull the zester across the outside of the lemon, making it awkward to use. Finally, we found the vegetable peeler to be difficult to control — it was easy to take too much of the bitter white peel — and the resulting zest was short on lemon flavor. The conclusion? Coarsely grated zest contains more flavor than the finely grated variety.

5   large egg whites, at room temperature

¾   cup heavy cream

1. If you are using a 1-quart soufflé dish, attach an aluminum foil collar to the dish as instructed above. Set dish aside. Place lemon juice in a small nonreactive bowl; sprinkle gelatin onto surface of juice. Set aside.

2. Heat milk and ½ cup of the sugar in a medium saucepan over medium-low heat, stirring occasionally, until milk is steaming and sugar is dissolved, about 5 minutes. Meanwhile, whisk together yolks, 2 tablespoons of the sugar, and cornstarch in a medium bowl until pale yellow and thickened. Whisking constantly, gradually add hot milk to yolks. Return milk and egg mixture to saucepan and cook, stirring constantly, over medium-low heat until foam has dissipated to a thin layer and mixture thickens to the consistency of heavy cream and registers 185 degrees on an instant-read thermometer, about 4 minutes. Strain into a clean bowl; stir in lemon juice mixture and zest. Set bowl of custard in a large bowl of ice water; stir occasionally to cool.

3. While custard mixture is chilling, in bowl of standing mixer fitted with whisk attachment (or in large mixing bowl if using hand mixer), beat egg whites on medium speed until foamy, about 1 minute. Increase speed to medium high; gradually add remaining 2 tablespoons sugar and continue to beat until whites are glossy and hold a soft peak when beater is lifted, about 2 minutes longer. Do not overbeat. Remove bowl containing custard mixture from ice water bath; gently whisk in about one-third of egg whites, then fold in remaining whites with a large rubber spatula until almost no white streaks remain.

4. In same mixer bowl (washing not necessary), with mixer fitted with whisk attachment, beat heavy cream on medium-high speed until soft peaks form when beater is lifted, 2 to 3 minutes. Fold cream into egg white mixture until no white streaks remain. Pour into prepared soufflé dish or 1½-quart bowl. Chill until set but not stiff, about 1½ hours (can be refrigerated up to 6 hours); remove foil collar, if using, and serve.

WHAT CAN GO WRONG? This recipe has many parts to it, making it a bit complicated. The only tricky step is making the custard (step 2). Many cooks may wait for the mixture to become very thick (like a pudding), whereas it really should be more like heavy cream. An instant-read thermometer is very helpful in this situation. The custard is done when the temperature reads 185 degrees.

White Chocolate Variation

The white chocolate in this variation subdues the lemony kick. The difference is subtle, but the sweeter, richer flavor and texture were popular among tasters.

Follow recipe for Chilled Lemon Soufflé, adding 2 ounces finely chopped white chocolate to warm custard before adding lemon juice mixture and zest. Stir until chocolate is melted and fully incorporated.

14

PUDDINGS

F ew home cooks still make puddings, due to the popularity of store-bought box pudding mixes or the feeling that puddings are a bit old-fashioned. (Of course, the English still serve plenty of puddings for dessert, some of them quite elegant, such as pears baked in a custard with ground black pepper.) For purposes of this chapter, I have included the basic vanilla and chocolate puddings but also rice puddings, mousse, jellies, Bavarian creams, bread pudding, Indian pudding, pudding cake, steamed pudding, and trifle. Most of these recipes are relatively easy and, when well made, are a whole lot better than a whole lot of the more fashionable offerings in pricey restaurants.

All of the recipes in this chapter depend on some sort of thickener or thickening process. Some puddings, such as chocolate, are thickened with cornstarch. Others use eggs, tapioca, rice, or flour. Some, such as an apple charlotte, are simply cooked down to a thick paste using no starch thickener whatsoever. Therefore it is important to know a bit about how thickeners work to truly understand what separates a good pudding from a great one.

THICKENERS AND HOW THEY WORK

MOST THICKENERS are starches. Starch is a component of many common foods such as potatoes, rice, corn, and wheat. Rice is approximately 80 percent starch, wheat 70 percent, and potatoes run around 20 percent. The first choice of thickener for most American pudding recipes such as vanilla or chocolate is cornstarch. It is preferred over flour since it is a purer form of starch and brings no additional flavors with it. Flour, since it is only 70 percent starch, can mask the pure flavor of a pudding, rendering it a bit doughy in taste. In addition, about one-third more flour than cornstarch has to be used to achieve the same thickening power, which adds to the flavor problem. But exactly how does cornstarch, or any other starch, really work?

Think of starch granules starting out as de-flated beach balls. As they come into contact with heat and water, they start to swell, absorbing water molecules. This begins the thickening process and is referred to by scientists as "gelatinization." As more heat is provided, chains of molecules start to leach out of the starch granules into the surrounding liquid. This forms a network of linked starch molecules that help to trap water molecules between them, forming a mesh, which results in thickening. When a pudding is overcooked, the starch granules break apart, releasing water molecules back into the mixture. In the case of a cornstarch-thickened pudding, vigorous stirring once it is up to temperature can also break down the fragile mesh formed during thickening, resulting in a thinner product.

It is also helpful to know that the addition of sugar to a cornstarch pudding will result in a somewhat thicker product but one with weaker bonds. Salt improves the thickening power of the cornstarch, whereas acidic ingredients, such as lemon juice, inhibit thickening, weakening the bonds. Cornstarch, besides being a powerful thickener, is also known as one that is not particularly tender. Potato starch or arrowroot excel in this regard. However, tenderness is not much of an issue in a pudding recipe, since a fairly thick, sturdy dessert is what most people expect.

Although cornstarch is the most common thickener for puddings, there are other choices. Tapioca pudding is made from a modified starch, a process that improves the cooking qualities of the starch. Rice contains a great deal of starch, and when it is cooked long enough, as in a rice pudding, sufficient starch will leach out to thicken the surrounding milk or cream. (To a lesser extent, the same is true of potatoes. If they are sliced and baked in a liquid, the liquid will thicken during cooking.) Finally, eggs are used as thickeners as well (think of bread pudding), but eggs are more finicky than starches since they are easier to overcook. That's why many pudding recipes use both cornstarch and eggs, the former making it a lot less likely that the eggs will curdle.

The last thickener of note is gelatin, which is used in puddings such as Bavarian creams. Gelatin is made from the skin and bones of animals, not from plants. Gelatin thickens as it cools and, in many recipes, the cook must watch carefully, since whipped cream or beaten egg whites are usually folded into the thickening gelatin mixture just at the point that it is thick but not set. Some pudding recipes use a combination of eggs, cornstarch, and gelatin, but in my testing I have found that this simply complicates the recipe rather than making it better.

VANILLA PUDDING

At first, producing a recipe for vanilla pudding sounded simple, but as with most seemingly basic recipes, the process turned out to be more complicated than I had thought. Since vanilla pudding has so few ingredients, balance is critical to achieving a texture that is both firm yet soft and full of flavor. Bland, rubbery vanilla pudding is actually quite easy to achieve; a more sublime dessert took some investigation.

Having reviewed recipes from the obvious sources, such as *Joy of Cooking,* by Irma Rombauer et al., *James Beard's American Cookery,* and Marion Cunningham's *Fannie Farmer Cookbook,* I soon realized that there are three basic variables: the type of thickener, the type of liquid, and the use of eggs. The basic recipe for vanilla pudding goes like this. Cornstarch, sugar, and a bit of milk are mixed together (this is often referred to as a slurry), and then the rest of the milk is added. The mixture is placed over low heat until it thickens, at which point vanilla extract is stirred in. The pudding is then left to cool. Eggs and butter are optional ingredients. To get a better sense of the possibilities, I performed a series of tests.

The testing revealed a number of clues to the perfect vanilla pudding. The first is that flour makes a lousy thickener, since it gives the pud-

CASE 51: PLAIN VANILLA

Which combination of thickener, milk product, and eggs makes the best vanilla pudding?

Thickener	Milk Product	Eggs	Comments
Flour	Milk	Yolks	Texture like congealed gravy; flavor too eggy
Cornstarch	Milk	None	Bland texture and flavor
Cornstarch	Half-and-half	None	Rich, creamy, not too sweet
Cornstarch	Milk	Whole eggs	Bland and too soft

ding more of a thick gravy consistency than a light, clean pudding texture. On the other hand, cornstarch worked well, delivering a creamy, smooth texture, although I did run into trouble overheating the cornstarch, which in one test led to a broken pudding. Second, half-and-half turned out to be a better choice than the usual ingredient, milk. In additional testing, I also discovered that the proper ratio of vanilla to sugar is important, as is the total amount of each ingredient. I have found that sugar is crucial in bringing out the taste of vanilla, and this is a dessert that desperately needs just the right amount of vanilla taste to make it worth the preparation time. Eggs and butter did not seem to help much in this recipe. I suspect this is because vanilla pudding is such a simple dish that additional flavors easily throw the dessert off balance.

▪▪▪

Vanilla Pudding

This is a simple recipe, but the balance of cornstarch, half-and-half, vanilla, and sugar is crucial. This is not my favorite recipe in this book, since it is much less flavorful than a more assertive chocolate or butterscotch pudding. If you want a plain vanilla puddinglike dessert with a more delicate, more sophisticated texture, try the Panna Cotta on page 340.

SERVES 4

⅓ cup granulated sugar
2½ tablespoons cornstarch
⅛ teaspoon salt
2 cups half-and-half
1½ teaspoons vanilla extract

Combine sugar, cornstarch, and salt in a heavy saucepan. Whisk in about ⅓ cup half-and-half until smooth, then whisk in the rest of the half-and-half. Cook over medium heat, stirring constantly but very gently, until thickened, about 5 minutes (time will vary). Reduce heat to low and continue stirring gently and slowly until mixture comes to a simmer. Cook 1 minute more, not stirring, and remove from heat. Stir in vanilla, and pour into 4 serving dishes. (Do not stir pudding again.)

WHAT CAN GO WRONG? If you stir the pudding once it has thickened, it will turn out loose and thin. This is the major drawback of using cornstarch, which unlike flour is more sensitive to a heavy hand when stirring.

⋎

CHOCOLATE PUDDING

CHOCOLATE PUDDING IS a classic case of fancy cooks taking a simple, no-nonsense American recipe and turning it into something unnecessarily complicated. This disgraceful lack of proportion and common sense abounds in recipes calling for puddings baked in water baths or those that taste more like a mousse or ganache than a simple pudding. Although many of these are perfectly good desserts, they are not simple American puddings, which to my mind should be easy to make and thickened with cornstarch.

Let's review some of the possibilities. The first decision was whether to bake the pudding or stir it on top of the stove. The first recipe I tested called for baking the custard in a water bath for 45 minutes. The flavor wasn't at all bad, but the pudding had an unappetizing gray color and a strange, crackly top crust. The texture was a bit pasty and was noticeably grainy from the seeds of the vanilla bean. Not only was this a complicated recipe, but it garnered low marks in the tasting. Next, I made a second batch, following a different baked pudding recipe, and found that the pudding took forever to set in the oven and never formed the "lighter spot the size of a quarter on top" as indicated in the instructions. The flavor and sweetness levels were quite good, however, and the appearance was darker and more appetizing than the first recipe. Once again, however, the texture was a serious problem, approaching the consistency of refried beans. So I discarded baking as a method and moved on to the stirred, stovetop method.

The first stovetop recipe was pretty good, just milk, cocoa, and bittersweet chocolate, all thickened with cornstarch only, no egg yolks. It was a bit pedestrian but simple in concept and pleasantly familiar to a cook who grew up in the fifties and sixties. The second recipe, a pudding from *Cook's Illustrated*, was quite good but light in color and with a fluffy, mousselike consistency, not thick enough to pass my spoon test. (When a spoonful of pudding is taken from the bowl, the hole should remain intact.) It was also a bit too rich for my ideal, less of a simple weeknight pudding than something one would serve at a dinner party. A third recipe was similar to the first but made with cream and a higher proportion of chocolate. It had an amazing, velvety mouth feel but was a bit too rich and never completely set up, reminding me of a pourable chocolate icing rather than a pudding. Finally, I made a recipe called Old-Fashioned Chocolate Pudding with Maple. It was a basic cornstarch pudding but included butter and liqueur and used only cocoa, no chopped chocolate. It was quite good—humble and satisfying, just the right sort of approach to this simple dessert.

I went on to perform a few additional tests. Using only milk, I found, made a pudding that was just a bit too thin for my taste, so I used half-and-half (or two thirds milk and one third heavy cream). I also found that I preferred a pudding that was not "candy bar sweet" and therefore cut back a bit on the sugar level. Whisking the pudding as it cooks tends to reduce the thickening power of the cornstarch, so once the mixture was properly combined, I used a wooden spoon instead. I also tested using Dutch-process cocoa versus regular cocoa and found that the former had a more intense chocolate flavor. The standard cocoa, by comparison, was a bit bland and one-dimensional.

I also wondered about using additional fat. Many pudding recipes also use egg yolks, so I added two of them toward the end of cooking. The texture was silkier, but the chocolate flavor was diminished. Next, I tried adding 2 tablespoons butter and had the same difficulty — the pudding was lighter in color and lacking in rich chocolate flavor. This is one recipe where it pays to keep it simple, since added fat merely masks the pure, sharp flavor of chocolate.

••••

Chocolate Pudding

This is not a fancy restaurant pudding but the sort of dessert that would serve nicely for a weeknight dinner. Use Dutch-process cocoa if you can find it (Droste is one widely available brand), for a richer chocolate flavor. Note that the pudding will appear relatively thin after cooking and will only become thick during chilling.

SERVES 4

2 tablespoons Dutch-process cocoa powder
⅛ teaspoon salt
¼ cup granulated sugar
2 tablespoons cornstarch
1 teaspoon vanilla extract
½ ounce bittersweet chocolate, finely chopped or grated
2 cups half-and-half OR 1⅓ cups whole milk plus ⅔ cup heavy cream

1. Sift the cocoa, salt, sugar, and cornstarch onto a piece of waxed paper. Place the vanilla and chopped chocolate into a small bowl; set aside.

2. Pour sifted ingredients into a medium saucepan set over low heat. Whisk in half-and-half. Increase heat to medium and whisk for 2 minutes. Stir constantly, but gently, with a wooden spoon for an additional 3 to 5 minutes, or until mixture starts to bubble and thicken. At this point, the mixture will still be loose, much thinner than a set pudding.

3. Add the chopped chocolate and vanilla and cook for 1 additional minute, stirring very gently but constantly. Make sure that all of the chocolate has melted. If it has not, take pan off heat and continue to stir. Pudding should reach 180 degrees on an instant-read thermometer. Pour into individual ramekins or into a bowl.

Chill for at least 2 hours before serving. Pudding will thicken as it cools.

WHAT CAN GO WRONG? The most common problem with puddings is that they do not set up properly. This is caused by too much vigorous stirring or by not bringing the pudding up to 180 degrees. Once cornstarch begins to set, the starch granules enlarge, absorbing liquid. Too much stirring can break these granules, which causes the pudding to thin out. You also need the pudding to reach 180 degrees, not only the temperature at which the starch granules become large and saturated with liquid but also the point at which starch molecules leak out into the surrounding liquid, creating a network that traps additional water.

CINNAMON VARIATION

Add ¼ teaspoon ground cinnamon to the cocoa mixture before sifting.

CARDAMOM VARIATION

Add ¼ teaspoon ground cardamom to the cocoa mixture before sifting.

BUTTERSCOTCH PUDDING

BECAUSE I GREW UP in the fifties and sixties, my frame of reference for butterscotch pudding has either been the kind served in elementary school, which was probably delivered to the kitchen in 50-gallon vats, or the boxed puddings that my sister and I would make at home, a bit of sweet alchemy with a predictable if not joyous outcome. So it was perfectly natural that I started my detective work by making a Royal Cook 'n' Serve Butterscotch Pudding. It tasted like . . . well, like butterscotch. But it was an artificial flavor and not particularly desirable.

I then tried three recipes, two from magazines and one by Richard Sax, one of my favorite cookbook authors, but none of them quite filled the bill. The first called for gelatin, egg yolks, and cornstarch — three different thickeners — and was about as complicated as could be, since it used four different bowls. The texture was good, but the flavor was just okay. The next recipe used a caramel syrup for flavoring, which I thought would be better than simply using brown sugar; it did provide a wonderful caramel taste, but its flavor reminded me more of a crème caramel than butterscotch pudding. In any case, I wanted to avoid making a sugar syrup if possible, since it requires an extra step and the pot has to be cleaned, a messy job. The last recipe called for an excess of egg yolks — four of them — along with a good deal of cornstarch and milk, no cream. Both times I tried it, the mixture curdled.

Now the question I had to answer was, what does butterscotch really taste like? Is it caramel? Is it that strong artificial butterscotch flavor we all know from our childhood? I concluded that butterscotch is a combination of three things: cream, brown sugar, and vanilla. Butterscotch has to be rich and smooth (the cream), have a slight molasses edge to it (the brown sugar), and also have a strong punch of vanilla.

With that in mind, I went back to the first recipe, which was a bit too complex yet had the most promise. I started by switching from milk to half-and-half, which increased the depth of flavor. Next, I used dark brown instead of light brown sugar, which also made for a deeper butterscotch experience. I eliminated the gelatin, figuring that three thickeners were a bit much. I also streamlined the preparation method, modeling it after a simple chocolate pudding recipe. The dry ingredients are sifted and then whisked together with the half-and-half over low heat. (In the original recipe, the cornstarch was first whisked in a separate bowl with a small amount of milk. This step was unnecessary.) When the mixture starts to thicken, after about 5 minutes, it is poured into a bowl with 2 whisked egg yolks and the vanilla. The mixture is put back onto the stove and heated for 1 minute over medium-low heat and then poured into ramekins.

Now I really had a solid butterscotch taste, yet something was missing. I decided that just a touch of liquor would make the difference, opting for just a teaspoon of bourbon rather than the 1 to 2 tablespoons I found in other recipes, an amount that overpowers the flavor and leaves an unpleasant, raw flavor. (If you can find a butterscotch schnapps, a rare commodity in most liquor stores, go ahead. Hiram Walker makes one.) This gives the pudding the extra kick of flavor that most people expect, having grown up on the taste of commercial butterscotch products.

Finally, I played with proportions, trying 3 tablespoons of cornstarch and ending up with a glutinous blob; varying the amount of sugar and deciding that butterscotch pudding needs a full ⅔ cup to intensify the flavor (chocolate pudding does fine with just ½ cup); and working with the amount of butter and vanilla extract. In most puddings, butter is an unnecessary ingredient, but the extra fat is welcome here since it deepens the butterscotch flavor. The same was true of the 2 tablespoons of vanilla. The taste of butterscotch is entirely dependent on a major burst of vanilla flavor.

...

Butterscotch Pudding

MAKES 4 SERVINGS

2   tablespoons cornstarch

⅛   teaspoon salt

⅔   cup packed dark brown sugar

2   large egg yolks

2   tablespoons vanilla extract

1   teaspoon bourbon or scotch OR
    2 teaspoons butterscotch schnapps
    (Hiram Walker ButterNip)

2   cups half-and-half OR 1⅓ cups whole milk
    plus ⅔ cup heavy cream

3   tablespoons unsalted butter, cut into pieces

1. Sift the cornstarch, salt, and dark brown sugar onto a piece of waxed paper. Whisk together the egg yolks, vanilla, and bourbon in a medium bowl; set aside.

2. Pour sifted dry ingredients into a medium saucepan set over low heat. Whisk in half-and-half. Increase heat to medium and whisk for 2 minutes. Add butter and stir constantly with a wooden spoon, not a whisk, until the mixture starts to bubble and thicken, about 3 additional minutes.

3. Whisk hot mixture into the egg yolk mixture. Pour back into saucepan and heat over medium-low heat, stirring constantly, for 1 minute. Pour into individual ramekins or into a bowl. Chill for at least 2 hours before serving.

WHAT CAN GO WRONG? The problem many of us have with this sort of recipe is that the cooking time varies a great deal from household to household. It will depend on the type of saucepan you are using, your stovetop, and how much heat you are using. So if your mixture has not started to "bubble and thicken" after 3 minutes, that's okay. Stay the course and stir gently with a wooden spoon (not a whisk) until the mixture thickens.

TAPIOCA PUDDING

THE PROBLEM WITH MOST old-fashioned recipes for tapioca pudding is that they use pearl tapioca. Made from the tapioca plant, which is grown throughout much of the world, pearl tapioca is tapioca starch that has been heated into pearls. (The starch granules are separated from the plant and cellulose material. These granules contain starch molecules, which absorb water only when heated. Processed starches such as Minute Tapioca are superior to unrefined starches, since the resulting granules are less likely to burst as they absorb water. Burst molecules result in an unpleasant "slimy" texture. Refined starches also are better thickeners because acids, such as lemon juice, are less likely to impair their ability to absorb water.) These large orbs, however, are difficult to cook with since they require extensive soaking (an hour and a half) and cooking (30 minutes). In addition, the resulting tapioca is a bit coarse, containing the large "fish-eye" pieces familiar to any adult over the age of forty. I made three different recipes from a variety of older cookbooks; none was satisfactory and all were rather complicated.

Still searching for a simple, more refined dessert, I looked on the back of the Minute Tapioca box. The recipe there was much quicker to make, and the smaller bits of tapioca made a smoother pudding. (Minute Tapioca is also made from tapioca starch, but it is partially gelatinized and then pressed into tiny pellets. It requires no soaking, which speeds up preparation. Minute Tapioca is also excellent for thickening baked fruit desserts such as pies, cobblers, and crisps.) However, as is the case with many packaged food products, the manufacturers call for too much of their own product to stimulate consumption. As a result, the pudding was overly gelatinous. I reduced the tapioca from 3 tablespoons to 2, and the resulting pudding still set but was more tender. The basic recipe calls for milk only — no cream — and I thought it was a bit thin in both flavor and mouth feel. Therefore, I substituted 1 cup cream for 1 cup milk. I also slightly increased the amount of sugar and worked up a few simple variations. If, however, you like a less creamy dessert, go ahead and use all milk.

I also discovered that many of the old-fashioned recipes were really a tapioca cream, with the pudding folded into whipped heavy cream. I tried this variation and found that the resulting dessert was not an improvement over the basic pudding.

Tapioca Pudding

SERVES 4 TO 6

1 large egg
⅓ cup plus 1 tablespoon sugar
2 tablespoons Minute Tapioca (do *not* use
   pearl tapioca)
1¾ cups whole milk
1 cup heavy cream
1 teaspoon vanilla extract

Whisk the egg in a 2-quart saucepan until well beaten. Whisk in the remaining ingredients except the vanilla and let stand 5 minutes. Over medium heat and stirring constantly, cook the mixture until it reaches a full boil. The mixture will still be thin. Remove from heat and stir in vanilla. Cool 20 minutes, stir, and then spoon into individual serving dishes or glasses. Chill before serving.

WHAT CAN GO WRONG? Not much can go wrong. The Minute Tapioca is a very effective thickener and is able to withstand a heavy hand while stirring. Even your kids can make this recipe.

ORANGE AND ALMOND VARIATION
There is an established tradition of adding fruits or other flavorings to tapioca pudding, the most common additions being almonds, raisins, citron, currant jelly, and sherry. This is a simpler approach, pairing only orange and almond. To make it, add 1 teaspoon minced or grated orange zest and 2 tablespoons finely chopped almonds to the master recipe when adding the vanilla.

ROSE WATER, PISTACHIO, AND CARDAMOM VARIATION
Add ½ teaspoon rose water, ¼ teaspoon ground cardamom, and 2 tablespoons finely chopped pistachios to the master recipe when adding the vanilla.

CHOCOLATE MOUSSE

BACK IN THE 1970s, chocolate mousse was ubiquitous, the equivalent of today's flourless chocolate cake. At any given restaurant on any given night, one might experience a frothy foam of whipped egg whites and cream or a dense, mouth-puckering sea of fudge without a hint of the ethereal promise of this common but exceptional dessert. The ingredient list is short and the technique simple, so I set out to explore why there could be such alarming variation.

The essence of chocolate mousse consists of four elements: semisweet chocolate, egg yolks, whipped egg whites, and heavy cream. The chocolate is melted, the egg yolks are whisked in, and then both the whites and the heavy cream are whipped and folded in. Some recipes add butter, others a bit of strong coffee or liquor for flavoring, and some even use gelatin for setting the mousse. The trick is balance. Too much chocolate and the texture becomes dense and the flavor dull. Too little and the flavor fades quickly on the tongue.

Most recipes start with 4 eggs, and so did I. After some experimentation, I decided on 8 ounces of semisweet chocolate. Some recipes use 4 and others 6; if I am going to make a chocolate mousse, I want the full chocolate experience. However, the texture suffered a bit (as the melted chocolate cools it hardens, and this affects texture), so I also had to increase the amount of heavy cream, from the standard ½ cup to ¾ cup. This maintained serious chocolate flavor but also perked up the texture.

I did find that a bit of butter added silkiness to the mousse, and I settled on 4 tablespoons, which is melted along with the chocolate. I am not enthusiastic about overly sweet desserts and therefore added only 2 tablespoons of sugar, since I was using sweetened chocolate to begin with. In my opinion, more sugar flattens the taste profile of the chocolate; in this recipe one can taste deeper, earthier chocolate tones. Finally, I tested beating the egg yolks separately with some sugar, rather than whisking them into the melted chocolate. This was time-consuming and simply added more volume to the final mixture, which reduced the chocolate flavor. I also found that it was best to let the mousse sit a few hours in the refrigerator before serving, allowing time for the flavors to blend. Most chocolate mousse lovers serve it with additional whipped cream, a pleasant counterpoint to this rich chocolate experience.

▪▪▪

Chocolate Mousse

This recipe adds both butter and whipped cream to the mousse. Many older recipes were simply made with egg yolks, chocolate, and whipped egg whites. The key to this recipe is balance; the chocolate, egg whites, and heavy cream need to be used in just the right proportion for maximum chocolate flavor with a light, tongue-coating texture.

SERVES 8 TO 10

8	ounces semisweet chocolate
4	tablespoons unsalted butter
⅛	teaspoon salt
1	teaspoon vanilla extract
4	large eggs, separated
½	teaspoon cream of tartar
2	tablespoons granulated sugar
¾	cup heavy cream

Whipped cream for serving

1. Melt chocolate with the butter in a microwave oven. Use 50 percent power for 2 minutes, stir, and then go another 1 to 2 minutes until done. Or, melt in a double boiler or heavy saucepan over low heat. Stir in salt and vanilla

and then whisk in yolks, one at a time. Cool mixture for 5 minutes.

2. Beat egg whites with cream of tartar until soft peaks just begin to form. Add sugar and beat until whites are firm but still glossy and smooth. Whisk one-quarter of the beaten whites into the chocolate mixture. Fold in remaining whites with a large rubber spatula.

3. Whip the heavy cream until firm and fold into chocolate mixture. Spoon into individual serving dishes or glasses or into a large bowl. Cover and refrigerate for at least 2 hours. Serve with additional whipped cream.

WHAT CAN GO WRONG? The only part of this recipe that requires some skill is folding the egg whites into the melted chocolate. The chocolate mixture is very thick, and even after whisking some of the whites into the chocolate first, you will need to take care not to overwork the delicate whites.

Mocha Variation

Mix 1 tablespoon instant coffee powder with 2 tablespoons hot water. Stir into the cooled chocolate mixture along with the salt and vanilla.

Rum Variation

Add 2 tablespoons rum, bourbon, or brandy to the cooled chocolate mixture along with the salt and vanilla.

Cinnamon Variation

Add ½ teaspoon cinnamon to the heavy cream just before whipping.

Dessert Jellies

Jellies were quite popular during Victorian times, and recipes were still offered in early editions of Fannie Farmer's cookbook. Perhaps the advent of Jell-O has diminished their culinary reputation, but a sweet jelly, when properly made, is delicate and refreshing, the perfect dessert when something light is called for. The trick is to use just the right amount of gelatin. I tested a variety of gelatin amounts, finally settling on 2 envelopes (4 teaspoons): more gelatin caused the jelly to be tough and unpleasant-tasting, and when I made this recipe with 1½ packets, it never fully set up. Be aware that this recipe does need to sit overnight in the refrigerator to firm up.

...

Tawny Port Dessert Jelly

You cannot make this recipe on the day you are going to serve it; it needs to firm up in the refrigerator overnight. A small amount of flavored whipped cream is a nice accompaniment.

SERVES 4

- 4 teaspoons unflavored gelatin (about two ¼-ounce packets)
- 1 cup cold water
- 2 cups boiling water
- 1 cup granulated sugar
- 1 cup sweet wine, sherry, or port
- 1 tablespoon brandy
- Juice of 1 lemon

In an 8-cup glass measuring cup, sprinkle the gelatin over the 1 cup cold water. Let sit for 5 minutes. Add the boiling water and sugar and stir to dissolve. Add the wine, brandy, and lemon juice and stir. Pour into individual molds or ramekins or into one large bowl or mold. Chill overnight. To unmold, briefly dip molds into hot water, dry the outside of the mold, and invert onto a serving plate.

WHAT CAN GO WRONG? You must let this jelly sit overnight in the refrigerator for it to firm up properly. You cannot make this recipe in the morning and then serve it for dinner. Also note that the amount of gelatin by weight and vol-

ume in small Knox gelatin packets is not consistent. I noted this difference when preparing this recipe and passed my observations along to the *Cook's Illustrated* test kitchen, which weighed more than 25 packets. Some of the packets had a discrepancy of over 20 percent in weight, so I suggest that you use the 4-teaspoon measurement rather than the "2 packets" quantity for the sake of accuracy.

STOVETOP RICE PUDDING

ONE CAN BAKE RICE PUDDING or simply make it on the stovetop, the latter method being almost identical to making risotto. The former method tends to produce a drier, firmer pudding, whereas the latter method makes a creamy, loose dessert, which I prefer. The stovetop method is simple: Rice is cooked with water in a large saucepan until most of the water is absorbed. Milk and sugar are then added and the mixture continues to cook until it thickens and turns very creamy and rich. At the end of cooking, flavorings are added, either traditional spices such as cinnamon or Indian-inspired ingredients such as rose water or cardamom.

I started by doing some homework on different types of rices. There are three basic types in terms of length: short, medium, and long. Short rice, the type served in Chinese restaurants, is sticky and ideal for use with chopsticks, with sushi, in puddings, in paella, or cooked as risotto (arborio rice, an Italian short-grain variety, is used for risotto). The longer varieties are more popular in Western cultures, as they are less starchy and therefore fluffier when cooked. Medium-length rice is more similar to short-grain than long-grain in terms of cooking properties and may be used as a substitute, but short- and long-grain rices are never interchangeable. There is very little difference in nutritional value among the different grain lengths. Long-grain rice kernels are three to five

WHY IS SHORT-GRAIN RICE STICKY?

Rice is mostly starch, and all starches, including wheat starch, tapioca, arrowroot, and cornstarch, contain both amylose and amylopectin. The ratio between these two elements is the primary determinant of stickiness in rice and is also the key factor in thickening power. Amylose, which produces a less sticky rice, occurs in a higher percentage in long-grain rice than short-grain. Conversely, amylopectin is more dominant in the short-grain varieties. Amylopectin increases the water absorption capacity of starch; short-grain rice can absorb almost three times more water than long-grain and is therefore stickier. Stickiness is also a function of other characteristics, including protein — a higher-protein rice generally produces a firmer, less sticky grain. Protein content is affected by the strain of rice and also by where it is grown.

times longer than they are wide; a kernel of short-grain rice is less than twice as long as its width.

I tested the three basic lengths of rice and preferred, as I thought I would, the short-grain rice, although a medium-grain rice will also work relatively well. The reason for my preference is that short rice has more thickening power, turning the milk into a creamy, thick sauce. I also played with the amount and ratio of water to milk and ended up with much more liquid to rice than one would expect from a standard savory rice recipe, the reason being that I wanted to create a sauce, not a bowl of sticky rice. I kept the amount of sugar relatively modest and experimented with flavorings, preferring a bit of orange zest and nuts to the usual cinnamon-and-nutmeg combination. (I have included a variation for this standard approach as well.) The cooking time will vary a lot depending on your stovetop and your saucepan, so occasional stirring is not a bad idea, especially for those who do not have heavy-bottomed cookware, to prevent scorching.

Master Recipe for Stovetop Rice Pudding

Rice is full of starch. That's why rice pudding doesn't need eggs or other thickeners. Just cook short-grain white rice in water and then with milk on top of the stove until it thickens (short-grain rice is starchier than long-grain rice). This is a relatively loose pudding compared with a thick baked rice pudding, but it is creamier and more delicate. For a thicker pudding, let it sit covered on top of the stove after cooking for up to 2 hours.

SERVES 6

½ cup short-grain white rice
2½ cups water
2 cups milk
½ teaspoon vanilla extract
7 tablespoons granulated sugar
2 teaspoons minced orange zest
¼ cup almonds, finely chopped

Combine the rice and water in a large saucepan and bring to a boil. Reduce heat to a simmer and cook for 40 minutes, or until most of the water has been absorbed. Add the milk, vanilla, and sugar, bring back to a boil, reduce heat to a simmer, and cook until mixture is the consistency of a thick porridge, about 1 hour, 10 minutes. Add the orange zest and almonds, stir to combine, and serve hot, warm, or at room temperature.

WHAT CAN GO WRONG? The longer this pudding sits after cooking, the thicker it gets. If you want a looser dessert, serve it immediately. Just don't be surprised if it thickens in the pot while you eat your main course.

ROSE WATER, PISTACHIO, AND CARDAMOM VARIATION

Follow recipe above but substitute 1 teaspoon of rose water for the orange zest, use pistachios instead of almonds, and add ½ teaspoon ground cardamom.

Cinnamon and Nutmeg Variation

Follow recipe above but substitute 1 teaspoon cinnamon for the orange zest, eliminate the almonds, and add ¼ teaspoon freshly grated nutmeg.

▼

Bread Pudding

BREAD PUDDING IS a bit like baked beans; both have origins deep in the culinary past and, over time, so many styles have emerged that the "real thing" may be difficult to uncover, even if a modern cook might find it worth the effort. Yet, as is true with all cooking, recipes are not entirely subjective. Recipes do have beginnings; they are usually born out of necessity or a chance mixture of readily available ingredients; and, especially with such a sturdy recipe as this, they show, as a nineteenth-century Vermonter might say, "good proofs of usefulness." Bread pudding is no exception.

This dessert is found in virtually all European home cooking, often referred to as *brotpudding*, and is simply a mixture of bread, milk and/or cream, sugar, eggs, and flavorings. So what's to discover? Well, the styles vary tremendously, from a baked custard with slices of French bread on top (as with the famous Coach House Bread and Butter Pudding, one of James Beard's favorite recipes) to a rich, treacly pudding with sauce, really more of a rich pudding cake. I tried them all, from recipes snagged from the Internet to buttermilk bread puddings to recipes from *Joy of Cooking*, *The New Basics Cookbook* (Julee Rosso and Sheila Lukins), *The Wooden Spoon Dessert Book* (Marilyn M. Moore), and many others. For months I ordered bread pudding for dessert whenever it was on the menu, a herculean task not appreciated a bit by my wife who, getting back into shape after the arrival of

our fourth child, was in no mood to be tortured at close quarters by a dinner partner who could shamelessly down a thousand calories in mere seconds. I consumed every conceivable sort of bread pudding, from those in which the bread seemed to have melted into the custard, to dry slices of bread that were slightly moistened, sweetened, and baked, to puddings shot through with a surfeit of ingredients from raisins to pecans, orange zest, coconut, and, in one unfortunate instance, pineapple chunks.

This massive intake of calories yielded some valuable clues. I wanted contrast between the crust and the filling in both texture and flavor, as many recipes were dull little desserts, all pudding and no chew. The choice of bread was going to be crucial, as some loaves simply melted into the custard, whereas tough, rustic breads seemed too muscular to succumb to the soft embrace of milk, cream, and eggs. I was not favorably inclined toward bread puddings that were nothing more than egg custards topped with bread. The consistency of the "pudding" was important, my tastes tending to land halfway between a custard and a sauce. The balance between bread and filling was also going to be critical. Some recipes were dry from too much bread; others used so little that it disappeared during baking. I wanted a modest amount of sugar, not something that would indulge the indefatigable sweet tooth of my hyperactive three-year-old son. Finally, I decided to dispense with a sauce, since the pudding would be plenty rich without it and it added extra work in a recipe that calls out for simplicity.

Near the end of my trials, and at the point at which my wife had mastered the stony watchfulness of a predator, apparently ready to lunge with total abandon at my last tender spoonful of silky custard, we dined at the Deer's Head Inn in the Adirondacks. There I had a bread pudding epiphany. Atop this excellent, plain dessert were crispy pieces of bread, a deep golden brown and with great chew. Underneath, instead of the usual layer of thin custard, was an interesting not-too-sweet pudding/custard, some of the bread having been soaked and dissolved into the filling. This was a humble bread pudding that spoke heavily of bread, with a crusty top and a thick, creamy bottom layer.

Back in the test kitchen, I started building my ideal recipe. First, I tackled the bread. I tried rustic Italian, a fine-textured French pullman loaf, Pepperidge Farm raisin bread, Pepperidge Farm country white, supermarket Italian bread, challah, brioche, and potato bread. The winner was the French loaf (this was not a baguette but more of a dense sandwich loaf), the fine dense texture holding up well during cooking. Other, more tender loaves such as challah and brioche were too soft and spongy. Additional testing discovered that any substantial white bread is fine, but avoid tough rustic loaves with heavy crusts and excessive chew. This sort of loaf will not soften sufficiently during soaking and baking. At the other extreme, do not buy a packaged supermarket bread, although Pepperidge Farm country white was the best of the lot. Purchase, if you can, a bakery loaf, a firm white sandwich bread baked in a local oven.

I also discovered that there was no point removing the crusts other than for appearance; that using stale or dried bread did not make a difference; and that cubes were preferred over sliced bread, since they were easier to measure (8 cups is a more precise measurement than 8 slices) and also to work with, large slices tending to curl at the corners when baked. Finally, I tested buttering the bread and found that this added an excessive amount of fat and was unnecessary. However, I did discover that the key to a crisp, crunchy top layer was to separate 2 cups of the cubed bread, placing it on top of the pudding just before baking. Brushing these cubes with melted butter added a rich color to the dessert.

The next issue was the custard. As stated above, I wanted a richer, silkier feel to the filling, not simply a thin egg custard. This, then, required using cream along with milk, and it turned out, after many tests, that half milk and half cream was about right. For eggs, another factor that af-

fects the texture of the custard, I finally settled on 4 whole eggs plus 1 yolk for a rich pudding, many recipes using as few as 2 or 3 eggs. The amount of sugar was a matter of some dispute in the tasting, some tasters preferring a full cup whereas I preferred a more modest amount, slightly more than ¾ cup suiting me just fine. A low oven temperature, 325 degrees, was best and, although a water bath seemed to provide a slightly improved texture, I opted not to include it in the final recipe, since it was more work. In terms of flavorings, modest amounts of nutmeg and cinnamon were fine, but all other additions were unwelcome, other than bourbon, which made a nice counterpoint to the creamy custard, cutting through the richness of the cream and eggs. In order to provide more contrast between the topping and filling, I also decided to sprinkle the cinnamon on top of the pudding, along with 2 tablespoons of sugar, just before it was placed in the oven. This gave the bread topping a separate flavor from the nutmeg-laced custard.

I also tried an unusual experiment. Before baking, I placed 2 cups of the custard-bread mixture into a food processor and pureed it, then mixed it back in with the other ingredients. This resulted in a sauce rather than a custard, which some tasters liked and others didn't. If you are looking for real comfort food — "baby food," in one taster's estimation — this technique works nicely. For the majority, and I include myself in this category, the master recipe is fine as is.

Determining just when to remove the pudding from the oven turned out to be a bit of a trick. Overcooking results in a separated, weepy custard, and undercooking makes for a very loose sauce. After two score or more of tests, we determined that the bread pudding should "wobble like a Jell-O mold." (Remember that it will continue to cook once removed from the oven.) Another helpful visual clue is not to cook the pudding to the point at which it inflates and rises up high in the pan. It is done when this process begins, when the edges of the pudding are just starting their upward climb.

···

Classic Bread Pudding

*M*ost *bread puddings are an egg custard on top of which float pieces of bread. This recipe, however, makes a creamier custard/pudding with a crisp top layer of buttered and sugared bread. It is better to undercook this dessert than overcook it, since overcooked custard is tough and weepy. If you are looking for real comfort food, a bread pudding with a loose sauce underneath a crisp top layer, remove 2 cups of the mixture after soaking (approximately 1 cup of bread and 1 cup of liquid) to a food processor or blender and process until smooth, about 10 seconds. Return it to the rest of the mixture and stir to combine before adding to the baking dish.*

SERVES 8 OR MORE

4	large eggs plus 1 egg yolk
¾	cup plus 2 tablespoons granulated sugar
2½	cups whole milk
2½	cups heavy cream
1	tablespoon vanilla extract
3	tablespoons bourbon
¼	teaspoon salt
¾	teaspoon freshly grated nutmeg
8	cups firm white bakery (not supermarket) bread, cut into 1½-inch squares from slices that are approximately ⅜ inch thick
1½	tablespoons unsalted butter, melted
½	teaspoon cinnamon

1. Adjust rack to center of oven. Preheat oven to 325 degrees. Butter a 9 x 13-inch baking dish.

2. Whisk eggs and ¾ cup of the sugar together in a large bowl until well blended. Whisk in next 6 ingredients (milk through nutmeg). Add 6 cups of the bread pieces to the custard mixture, thoroughly mixing to coat. Allow to sit for 20 minutes.

3. Transfer this mixture to prepared baking dish. Top evenly with remaining 2 cups of bread pieces, pushing down gently so they are par-tially submerged. Brush top of exposed bread cubes with the melted butter and sprinkle with the remaining 2 tablespoons sugar and the cinnamon. Place in oven and bake for 40 to 45 minutes, or until bread pudding is a deep golden brown and holds together but the center is still wobbly when shaken, a bit like a Jell-O mold. Remove the pudding from the oven before it puffs up. Do not overcook. Let stand for at least 30 minutes before serving.

WHAT CAN GO WRONG? This is actually a tricky dish to get just right. It is important to push down the bread cubes placed on top of the pudding so that they soak up some of the custard. The cooking time is also a bit hard to judge. When overcooked, this dish is not worth eating. Therefore, be sure to take it out of the oven when the center is still a bit wobbly. The baking time will vary a lot depending on the type of baking dish you use and your oven, so only use the stated times as a rough guide. Also, be sure not to substitute a different size baking pan. A different size will dramatically change the baking time and also the outcome.

RAISIN BREAD PUDDING VARIATION
Some folks just can't stand raisins in puddings, and therefore I offer this only as a variation. Soak ½ cup raisins in ¼ cup rum and let stand while the bread is soaking in the custard. (I prefer to use the Pavich Family Farms brand of raisins found in health food stores or Dole raisins; they are plumper and moister than Sunkist.) Drain raisins and add to the bread mixture just before pouring into the prepared baking dish.

INDIAN PUDDING

I NDIAN PUDDING IS a version of hasty pudding, which was simply cornmeal mush either cooked as a porridge and served hot for breakfast or allowed to cool (like polenta) and then sautéed or fried. To make Indian pudding, molasses and spices were added and milk or cream was used instead of water. The term Indian, according to Richard Sax in *Classic Home Desserts*, simply referred to the use of cornmeal ("Indian meal"), not to a recipe patterned after a Native American tradition. The American settlers were less than interested in the local cooking.

The problem with this recipe — one that is unavoidable — is that it takes long, slow cooking. I did find recipes that called for a 350-degree oven and a baking time of only 1 hour; other, more traditional preparations suggested a 275-degree oven and 3 hours of baking. Testing proved that the latter was preferable. I also discovered that frequent stirring with a whisk was crucial to a creamy result. Simply letting the pudding bake unattended produces a tougher, less desirable texture. Almost all recipes call for eggs, but I found that omitting them yields a more delicate pudding. Instead of using all milk, I use a combination of milk and cream. The cornmeal has to be whisked into hot milk and then cooked and whisked into the pudding mixture until smooth. This is crucial to removing lumps. I also limit the spices to ginger and nutmeg; cinnamon only muddies the flavors.

•••

Slow-Cooked Indian Pudding

This pudding takes some time to make, but it is delicate and creamy and worth the effort. Stirring the pudding during baking is crucial for a smooth texture. Do not overcook this pudding — it should be just set in the middle, so that it turns out creamy.

SERVES 6 TO 8

1	quart milk
¼	cup granulated sugar
¼	cup lightly packed dark brown sugar
¼	cup molasses
1	teaspoon salt

3	tablespoons unsalted butter, at room temperature
1	teaspoon ground ginger
½	teaspoon nutmeg
½	cup yellow cornmeal
1	cup heavy cream

Vanilla ice cream or additional heavy cream for serving

1. Heat oven to 275 degrees. Whisk together 2 cups of the milk with the next 7 ingredients (granulated sugar through nutmeg) and reserve. Butter a 2- to 3-quart casserole or soufflé dish.

2. Heat the remaining 2 cups milk in a medium saucepan over medium heat and slowly whisk in cornmeal. When mixture is smooth, whisk in the reserved pudding mixture and, whisking constantly, bring mixture to a boil over medium-high heat. Turn heat to low and simmer for 5 minutes, stirring frequently, until the mixture is quite thick (like a thick pea soup) and leaves a thick coating on the back of a spoon.

3. Pour into the prepared casserole, pour heavy cream over the mixture, cover, and bake for 3 to 3½ hours, whisking or stirring every half hour for the first 2½ hours. The pudding is done when it is just set in the middle and still soft. Let cool for 20 to 30 minutes and serve with vanilla ice cream or additional cream.

WHAT CAN GO WRONG? It is important to bake this pudding covered. If baked uncovered, it will not firm up properly and take forever to bake.

LEMON PUDDING CAKE

RECIPES FOR PUDDING CAKES are hard to come by. They rarely show up in modern cookbooks, as they are considered too lowbrow by most of today's food writers. Made with cake flour, milk, a few eggs, sugar, and flavorings, they are simple desserts that bake into two layers, the top layer being a light cake and the bottom being a pudding. The challenge is to produce just the right balance of cake to pudding. This is no simple task, since this recipe can easily become cakey, the bottom layer turning thick and firm, or wind up as a pudding with hardly a whisper of cake about it. Looking over a variety of recipes, I first considered whether to whip the egg whites separately. Some pudding cakes have a top layer of cake and a sweet sauce, rather than a pudding, underneath. I preferred a lighter texture to the cake and therefore went with beaten egg whites. In terms of the ratio of flour to liquid, some cookbooks call for 1 cup flour to 1½ cups milk or other liquid, whereas others use a full cup of milk to a mere ¼ cup flour. After a good deal of testing, I found that a minimal amount of flour was best. I tried 3, 4, and then 5 tablespoons flour and found that 4 tablespoons was ideal: less flour produced too much pudding and 5 tablespoons produced too much cake. I did add a bit of cream of tartar to the egg whites, which lightened up the texture of the cake. A quarter cup of lemon juice was fine; larger quantities dramatically increased the pucker factor. Most recipes call for eggs, and I discovered that 3 was the right number, producing a nice thick pudding without being either too runny or too eggy. Finally, a small bit of salt and vanilla, ingredients often not included in this recipe, helped to punch up flavors.

⋯

Lemon Pudding Cake

Since it is related to a soufflé, especially the top cake layer, this pudding cake is best served immediately. It will tend to sag a bit if left on the counter. Although I did reduce the amount of sugar, and the addition of the lemon juice cuts down on sweetness, this is the sort of dessert that kids will love and is not well suited to a sophisticated dinner party. This is weeknight fare or perhaps good for midweek suppers. (For a more elegant, restaurant version of this sort of recipe, see Souffléed Lemon Custard on page 375.)

SERVES 8

¾ cup plus 2 tablespoons granulated sugar
¼ cup cake flour
¼ teaspoon salt
3 large eggs, separated, at room temperature
1 cup milk
1 tablespoon finely chopped lemon zest
¼ cup freshly squeezed lemon juice
½ teaspoon vanilla extract
½ teaspoon cream of tartar

1. Adjust rack to center position and heat oven to 325 degrees. Grease and flour an 8-inch square baking pan.

2. In a medium bowl, combine ¾ cup of the sugar, flour, and salt. In a small bowl, beat the egg yolks, milk, lemon zest, lemon juice, and vanilla. Pour the egg mixture over the flour mixture and blend well with a rubber spatula.

3. Beat the egg whites until they foam and bubble. Add the cream of tartar and beat until they hold soft peaks. Add the 2 remaining tablespoons sugar and beat until the whites hold a 2-inch peak. Fold the egg whites into the yolk mixture with a rubber spatula.

4. Pour the batter into the buttered baking pan. Bake 35 minutes, or until the surface of the cake is lightly browned and springs back when lightly pressed. Serve immediately.

WHAT CAN GO WRONG? This dessert does not take well to sitting around after baking. The cake portion on top will deflate, ruining the appearance. Eat it as soon as it comes out of the oven.

STEAMED CHOCOLATE PUDDING

THIS IS PERHAPS an odd choice for a modern dessert cookbook, since so few of us make steamed puddings these days. Granted, the steaming does take some time, and a pudding mold is helpful in yielding an evenly cooked confection, but steamed puddings are delicious and worth making for the holidays. However, there are lots of approaches to this dessert and also a fair number of problems to solve.

I decided at the outset that I was looking for a light chocolate pudding, something that was rich but not heavy and wet. Of course, there were some obvious ingredients — eggs, sugar, chocolate, milk or cream, bread of some sort, flavorings, and butter — but the proportions and techniques were going to be important to achieve the desired texture. My first thought was to beat the eggs with the sugar to make the pudding lighter. Then I tried whipping just the yolks with the sugar, beating the whites separately and folding them in at the end. This worked even better, producing a very light dessert indeed. I played with the number of eggs — 4 seemed about right — and also adjusted the butter and sugar levels. Fresh breadcrumbs are traditional for this sort of dessert and worked well. I preferred a good country white bread or challah. I liked the bread to be almost spongy in texture. I also found that smaller cubes of bread were better than the huge chunks called for in many recipes, since they yield a finer, more even texture.

For the chocolate, I settled on 8 ounces semisweet, since I could get a better quality semisweet chocolate than unsweetened. I finished off the testing with some instant espresso, vanilla, and bourbon or rum for flavoring.

It turned out that getting the ingredients just right was only part of the battle with this recipe; also key was how to steam it. The first thing I

noticed in my testing was that a lidded pudding mold really is vastly preferable to simply using a foil-covered bowl. Very often, I found, the pudding at the bottom of a bowl (which will be the top of the pudding when unmolded) was not quite cooked. Steamed pudding molds have a hollow tube in the center, which makes for quicker and more even cooking. The molds really are a better choice than bowls for a perfectly cooked steamed pudding.

The molds themselves come in two sizes. This recipe fills an 8-cup mold; halve the recipe for the 5-cup model. To determine when the pudding is cooked, you should stick a knife deep into the pudding (it should come out clean), but you should also press the top with your fingers. It should be firm and springy. This may sound obvious, but you should check that the pudding mold will easily fit into the pot or steamer. Be sure that it can be removed easily, because a scorching hot metal mold is quite tricky to work with if there is little clearance in the pot. By the way, you don't have to use a steamer. Any large covered pot will do. Simply set the mold on a trivet or cooling rack placed in the bottom of the pan.

Steamed Chocolate Pudding

After many tests, I have come to the conclusion that the only way to make this recipe properly is to use a lidded pudding mold rather than a foil-covered bowl. A pudding mold has a hollow tube in the center, which speeds up the cooking time and also allows the pudding to cook more evenly than if it were simply steamed in a bowl. Be sure to check the pudding after two-thirds of the cooking time stated below. These puddings are easier to unmold and serve if they are cooled for a full hour after cooking. This recipe is for an 8-cup mold; halve it if you are using a 5-cup mold.

SERVES 8

8 ounces semisweet chocolate

2 tablespoons instant espresso powder

6 cups fresh coarse breadcrumbs

8 tablespoons (1 stick) unsalted butter, melted

2½ cups milk

1 cup heavy cream

4 large eggs, separated

1¼ cups granulated sugar

2 tablespoons bourbon, brandy, or rum

2 teaspoons vanilla extract

½ teaspoon salt

Whipped cream or ice cream for serving

1. Set a rack or trivet in the bottom of a wide, deep pot. (A large Dutch oven works well — make sure that the pudding mold fits easily into the pot.) Add water to come up even with the bottom of the rack. Bring water to a simmer while preparing the ingredients.

2. Butter an 8-cup pudding mold. Melt chocolate with instant espresso in the top of a double boiler or in a microwave. (If using a microwave, heat chocolate for 2 minutes uncovered on 50 percent power, stir, heat again for 1 additional minute, stir, and then heat again for another 30 seconds to 1 minute to finish.) In a large bowl, toss breadcrumbs with melted butter. Add milk and cream and set aside. In another bowl, whip the egg yolks for 2 minutes with a hand mixer or with a whisk. Add 1 cup of the sugar and beat an additional 2 minutes on high speed or whisk vigorously. Add the liquor, vanilla, and salt. Gently stir in the melted chocolate and then fold into the breadcrumbs.

3. Whip egg whites until billowy. Add the remaining ¼ cup sugar and beat until they hold a 2-inch peak. Fold into pudding mixture.

4. Pour pudding into prepared mold, cover mold with waxed paper, and then snap lid in place. Make sure that water in steamer is up to a simmer, place mold on rack, and cover pot. Steam pudding for about 2¼ hours, or until a knife inserted into the center comes out clean and the top is firm and springy to the touch. If using a half recipe in a smaller pudding mold, check at 40 minutes, and when using the larger mold and a full recipe, check after 1½ hours. Remove from pot and let cool on a rack for 1 hour before removing lid, unmolding, and serving. Cut into wedges and serve warm with whipped cream or ice cream.

WHAT CAN GO WRONG? You may be tempted to use a bowl instead of a pudding mold for this recipe but don't! The pudding at the bottom of the bowl will not set properly. You really need a mold with a tube in the center to make sure that the mixture cooks evenly and thoroughly.

BAVARIAN CREAM

THE FIRST QUESTION I had to answer with respect to this dessert was "What is it?" I had made a Bavarian cream before but had noted that there were plenty of variations on the theme. In general, however, one can define this dessert as an almost-set stirred custard of gelatin, sugar, milk, whole eggs, and vanilla into which is folded whipped cream. It is chilled, unmolded, and then usually served with fruit. Flavor variations are numerous, including lemon and orange.

After some more research, I decided to test three distinctly different recipes to get a better handle on which way I wanted to proceed. I started with a recipe from James Beard which called for separated eggs, with the yolks forming the custard and the whites (optionally) folded in at the end, after the cream. Cooking teacher and author Madeleine Kamman states that "true Bavarian cream has no egg whites [although] some add them to improve texture." So I decided to conduct a test, using egg whites with half of the recipe and none with the rest. The texture of the pudding without egg whites was excellent — firm, creamy, with an appealing matte finish. It didn't have the glossy sheen or gelatin-like wiggle I expected from an un-molded dessert. But it lacked flavor — it wasn't sweet enough, and only hinted of vanilla. The pudding with egg whites had the texture of a mousse — it was too light and fluffy. The flavor was even milder than the original, diluted as it was with egg whites, and it didn't unmold as well. The only benefit to this version was that it held up better over time in the refrigerator. While the rest of the puddings became too dense after several days, this one kept its ultra-light texture.

A second test recipe was from the Internet and was similar to Beard's recipe except that it also used cornstarch and vanilla ice cream was added at the end. The result was unappealing to say the least, producing a dense, pasty texture. Moving on, I tried an unusual recipe from *Bon Appétit* from 1984, which was made in a blender. Gelatin is softened in a blender and then boiling water, flavorings, sugars, eggs, salt, and whipping cream are added and everything is blended on high speed for 2 or 3 minutes. Crushed ice is added at the end and then the mixture is poured into a mold. This pudding had the smooth, glossy finish of the Bavarian creams pictured in old cookbooks, but it was relatively dense and thick, not as light as those with either whipped cream or cream with beaten egg whites folded in. This was clearly a wiggly, somewhat spongy "gelatin" dessert and was, without a doubt, the easiest recipe to make so far. Since it was so easy and also delicious, I decided to refine the recipe. The recipe called for lemon juice and zest, but I wanted a simpler master recipe and therefore simply used water and increased the vanilla to 2 teaspoons. I fiddled with the amount of blending that was required and found that if the mixture was underprocessed, the cream would not set up properly and was difficult to ummold. There-fore, I made yet another version and this time was careful not to overprocess the gelatin-water mixture but did process the mixture for a full 3 minutes once the cream was added. The results were quite good, producing a firm but not tough Bavarian cream that was easy to unmold and held its shape nicely. (For a more compli-cated but in many ways superior variation on this dessert, try the Chilled Lemon Soufflé on page 299).

Master Blender Recipe for Bavarian Cream

This is not a traditional recipe for Bavarian cream in that whipped cream is not folded into the mixture at the end. Instead, heavy cream is simply processed in a blender along with the other ingredients. The recipe takes only 10 min-utes to prepare, and the results are very good if not as rich and light as a more traditional recipe for this dessert. For a more classic preparation, see the recipe for Chilled Lemon Soufflé on page 299. Note that if you use a metal mold, it is best not to let the dessert sit in it overnight, since the metal can discolor it. (Unmold it once it is set, after 4 hours or so.) Also be aware that this recipe uses uncooked eggs, which always entails some health risk.

SERVES 6 TO 8

¼ cup cold water
4 teaspoons unflavored gelatin (two ¼-ounce packets)
½ cup boiling water
1 cup granulated sugar
1 cup heavy cream
3 large eggs
¼ teaspoon salt
2 teaspoons vanilla extract
1 cup crushed ice
Fresh berries for serving

Put cold water in a blender and then sprinkle with gelatin. Let stand until softened, about 5 minutes. Add boiling water; blend just until gelatin is dissolved. Add sugar, cream, eggs, and salt; blend at high speed 3 minutes. Add vanilla and ice, and blend until ice has melted. Pour into a 4-cup metal ring mold and chill until set, about 4 hours. Unmold onto serving platter and surround with fresh berries.

WHAT CAN GO WRONG? Not much. The only potential problem is unmolding. If you have problems, dampen a kitchen towel with hot water and place over the bottom of the mold for a few seconds to loosen.

LEMON OR ORANGE VARIATION

Substitute 1 teaspoon lemon or orange oil (or use extract instead) for the vanilla.

▾▾▾

THE TROUBLE WITH TRIFLE

MY QUIBBLE WITH most trifle recipes is that they have tarted up a rather simple dessert, one that is not that different from Italian tiramisù, which has suffered the same indignities. Trifle is — or should be — nothing more than leftover bread or cake with some custard, whipped cream, and jam. However, some older American recipes call for a much more elaborate dessert, one that might include finely broken biscuits, sweet yeast bread (a "rusk"), or spice cake, soaked with wine, covered with boiled custard, topped with a syllabub (made in the old days from whipped egg whites, white wine, grated lemon zest, and cream), and then garnished with jelly and flowers. Even back then, it had become a showstopper.

For a modern kitchen, I find that chiffon cake brushed with a bit of amaretto makes an excellent base, and then I add a good deal of custard (most trifles are wanting in this regard) folded into whipped cream. I do not use jam, which makes it too sweet, or the small almond cookies that are frequently included but that are, in my opinion, a complication and detract from the dessert. Instead, I use fresh berries, or I simply sift a bit of cocoa, which adds both color and a nice contrast in flavor, onto each layer and then on top of the dessert.

▪▪▪

Trifle

This recipe takes an investment in time, although it can be prepared early in the day and refrigerated. In fact, the cocoa version of this dessert, below, tastes better the next day, as the custard has time to work its magic on the cake; and since it has no fresh fruit, there is no bleeding of colors, which can make this dish look a bit shopworn if it sits too long.

SERVES 8 TO 10

1	recipe Chiffon Cake (page 154), cut into 2 layers and then cut into ¾-inch slices
4	recipes Pastry Cream (page 344)
1	cup heavy cream, very cold
¼	cup granulated sugar
⅓	cup amaretto or Grand Marnier or other liqueur
4	cups fresh, ripe berries such as raspberries, blueberries, or strawberries, washed and thoroughly dried

1. Bake the chiffon cake, cool, and slice. Make a quadruple recipe of the pastry cream and press a piece of waxed paper onto the surface of the custard to prevent a skin from forming. Refrigerate until cold. You can make the pastry cream a day ahead of time. Just before using, stir gently until smooth.

2. Place a large bowl and a whisk or the beaters from an electric mixer in the refrigerator or freezer and chill for at least 30 minutes. Remove from refrigerator, add the cream and sugar to the bowl, and beat on low speed (if using an electric mixer), gradually increasing the speed over the next minute until the mixer is on high. Beat until the cream is thick and can easily hold a 2-inch peak. Fold the chilled pastry cream into the whipped cream.

3. To assemble the trifle, select a clear glass

bowl with tall, straight sides. (It can also be made in any large bowl if you do not care about presentation.) The bowl should hold about 16 cups. Arrange cake slices in a fallen domino pattern around the perimeter of the bottom of the bowl. (The slices may have to be trimmed to fit properly in the bowl.) Fill in the center with additional slices. (You should have used about a third of the cake slices at this point.) Brush cake slices with one-third of the amaretto. Scatter one-third of the fruit over the cake. Spread a third of the pastry cream mixture over the fruit.

4. Repeat the sequence of layers twice, using up all (or most) of the cake and all of the amaretto, fruit, and pastry cream.

5. Place trifle in refrigerator for at least 2 hours (or it can be made a day ahead) before serving.

WHAT CAN GO WRONG? This trifle recipe is really a combination of other recipes in this book. However, during assembly, don't forget to fold the pastry cream into the whipped cream. (I have forgotten this step twice.) It is also best to use a glass trifle bowl, which has a flat bottom and straight sides and holds about 16 cups. The only other potential problem is slicing the cake properly and overlapping the pieces in the bowl. The objective is to produce nice even layers of cake. Don't worry if you do not use all of the cake — you may find that 25 percent or so of the cake is left over after the trifle is asssembled.

COCOA VARIATION

This recipe is easily made into an American version of tiramisù. Simply eliminate the fruit and replace it with ½ cup cocoa powder. Sprinkle one-third of the cocoa over each layer of pastry cream. This variation holds better for a longer period in the refrigerator than a fruit-based trifle. The fruit softens after a time, and the colors tend to bleed into the cake and pastry cream.

15

CUSTARDS

Unlike puddings, which are generally thickened with cornstarch or flour, custards combine milk, eggs, sugar, and flavorings. As a result, they are often more problematic, since eggs are easily overcooked, resulting in tough custards or even curdling. I have found that understanding a bit about the science of eggs is helpful in avoiding cooking problems.

As eggs are heated, individual protein molecules begin to unfold, stretch out, and become more likely to bond with one another. (Think of a bird's nest of dried pasta. As it cooks, the individual strands of pasta unwind and stretch out.) As the strands of protein bond, water molecules become trapped between them. Now the custard starts to thicken. The problem with egg custards, however, is that overcooking (i. e., overheating) readily results in more frenzied, tighter bonding, which forces the water molecules out of this fragile framework, resulting in weeping. In order to avoid overcooking, most custard recipes call for relatively low oven temperatures or the use of a water bath. Both methods, by slowing down the cooking process, increase the window of time between a properly

cooked custard and an overcooked one. This provides the home cook with more time to remove the custard from the oven. In a high-heat situation, this safety margin is smaller, leading to more overcooked custards if the cook is not attentive. In addition, low oven temperatures and water baths mitigate the problem of overcooking part of a custard mixture (the perimeter as opposed to the center), since lower heat cooks more evenly.

To avoid overcooking custards, remember that they will continue to cook and set up once out of the oven. Therefore, they should be removed from the heat when the center 2 inches or so is still not quite set. Waiting until the entire custard is firm will result in an overcooked dessert. When making a stovetop custard such as crème anglaise, I find it best to add a small amount of cornstarch to the mixture, since this helps to avoid curdling. This trick of adding cornstarch to custards is a good one, a technique often used by professional bakers. I have also found that cooking times for individual ramekins (when making crème caramel or crème brûlée) can vary tremendously depending on their position in the roasting pan that holds the water bath. Keep that in mind and be prepared to remove individual pots of custard as they firm up, knowing that the variance in cooking times is often 50 percent or more. Finally, cooking times, especially on the stovetop, can vary because saucepans and stoves vary greatly. In my kitchen, a crème anglaise may take 7 minutes; in yours it might take 15! Use the cooking times in this chapter as a rough guide only. Use your eyes, nose, and experience instead of the timer.

After many hours of making custards, I have a few tips to offer:

- Do not let the eggs and sugar sit together too long unmixed. As soon as you add them to the bowl, whisk them together. If you don't, the texture of the eggs will start to change.
- Overwhisking a hot milk or cream mixture with eggs and sugar is another problem. This incorporates too much air, which results in foamy custard, not a welcome outcome. A custard should be firm and perfectly solid.
- A water bath really is necessary to modify

the heat around custard cups to prevent overcooking. This is standard operating procedure for many classic custard recipes and an important step. For this technique, the baking dish or ramekins are placed in a roasting pan that has a thin kitchen towel or paper towels lining its bottom. (The towel prevents slipping.) The custard ingredients are poured into the dish(es) and then the pan is filled partway with very hot water. If the baking dish or one of the custard cups touches up against the side of the pan, or if a water bath is not used, the heat will become too intense and the custard can curdle or cook unevenly.

- Determining when custard is done takes a careful eye. When the custard is jiggled, the perimeter should be set but the center inch or so should still shake and wiggle a bit. The custard will continue cooking once it is out of the oven. I have tried inserting a knife into the center of the custard (a clean knife indicates that the custard is done), but this method is unpredictable, and most cooks have a very hard time telling when the knife is "clean."
- Ramekins and custard cups are pretty much the same thing. Both are small ovenproof dishes used to prepare individual servings. Some models are taller and narrower, with curved sides, while others are shallower and have perfectly straight sides. I find the latter easier to work with since, when unmolded, the custard is less likely to lose its shape. (A taller, narrower ramekin produces a custard that will spread easily if not baked to the perfect consistency.) They also come in different sizes. The standard 6-ounce cup actually holds just less than 6 ounces (¾ cup) when filled. The larger cups, with a capacity of 1¼ cups (10 ounces), are typically used for a serving of about 9 ounces. I find that larger ramekins seem to work a bit better than smaller sizes. Since the larger cups are not normally filled all the way, the high sides

WHAT IS THE DIFFERENCE BETWEEN CRÈME CARAMEL AND CRÈME BRÛLÉE?

Actually, they are almost the same thing. A crème caramel is a simple egg custard cooked in ramekins that have been lined with a caramel syrup. Once cooked and cooled, the custard is unmolded, the syrup cascading over the custard and pooling onto the plate. A crème brûlée (brûlée means "broiled") is made from a similar custard mixture. The custard is baked first, then a caramel syrup is poured on top. To finish, the ramekins are run under a broiler, transforming the syrup into a thin, brittle layer. The custard used for crème brûlée tends to have a heavy, thick consistency, containing both heavy and light cream. Crème caramel calls for either all milk or a mixture of milk and cream. But that difference aside, they are very similar in construct.

CASE 52: WOULD YOU LIKE CREAM WITH THAT?

Investigating how different liquids affect the taste and texture of crème caramel.

Liquid	Texture	Taste	Comments
Condensed milk	Heavy, like an overripe banana	Sweet, cloying	Too rich, too sweet
Whole milk plus coffee	Rubbery, jiggles	Slightly bitter	Good variation
Light cream	Solid, no jiggle; fatty aftertaste	Sweet and buttery	Too thick and heavy
Whole milk plus light cream	Creamy; good balance	Flavor lingers; no heavy aftertaste	Firm and delicate; great flavor
Whole milk	Delicate; very custardy	Not too sweet; quick finish in the mouth	Too fragile; doesn't linger in the mouth
Flavored nondairy creamer	Firm; doesn't melt in the mouth	Artificial taste; too sweet	Forget about it

provide some protection for the top and keep it from browning too quickly.

CRÈME CARAMEL

CRÈME CARAMEL IS, on the face of it, a simple dessert; but it is full of secrets and complexity. A knowledge of egg cookery and the science of sugar syrups is helpful, since balance and attention to detail are key. The custard itself must be silky, not cloying, sweet but not saccharine, and the caramel sauce must be cooked just right to provide depth of flavor without being burned. Although simple enough in construct, this recipe requires precision and careful execution.

For a kitchen detective, the issues were intriguing and numerous. The first issue was the liquid. I tested condensed milk, milk and coffee, light cream, milk and light cream, milk, and a flavored nondairy creamer. (Case 52 summarizes my testing notes.) I finally settled on a mix of milk and light cream, because it produced a well-balanced custard that is not as rich as crème brûlée, a dessert that coats the tongue. Crème caramel should have a cleaner finish, not slippery like an American custard, but with enough substance to visit in the mouth for a few seconds before moving on.

The next issue was the sweetener. Sugar was the obvious choice, but I also tried honey, which gave the crème caramel a beautiful color, although it slumped a bit when unmolded. However, the flavor was flowery, the honey coming through strongly, which I felt was inappropriate for this relatively sophisticated dessert. All in all, honey makes this a more rustic, country dish, one that is not in keeping with the spirit of crème caramel.

Next, I played with the issue of whole eggs versus yolks. Using all yolks, I found that the custard was buttery and melted like liquid gold in the mouth. It was silky smooth and rich. However, the downside was the prominent egg flavor and the yellow color. I then tried whole eggs, which produced a very stiff custard lacking body. Once it hit the mouth it was off and running, heading straight down the throat without a wisp of taste memory. The solution was to use both whole eggs and yolks together.

One of the great surprises of this series of tests was the use of salt. When baked without salt, the structure was weakened, although the flavor was not substantially different. The custard did not stand up under its own weight and slumped when unmolded. I also tested covering the custard cups with aluminum foil during baking, since I noticed that the tops tended to brown when baked uncovered. This turned out to be an important test — both taste and texture were improved markedly. The custard was extremely smooth and the tops of the custards in the ramekins were pale, without any skin formation.

Finally, I played around with the caramel sauce itself. To make a caramelized sugar syrup, one melts sugar either with or without water, and I found that the addition of water made this method almost foolproof. (I used 1 part water to 2 parts sugar. Some recipes use 1 part water to 3 parts sugar, which I found to be a bit risky. The syrup darkens very quickly, since the water boils off so fast. To make the syrup, one begins by cooking the sugar-water mixture in a covered saucepan for 2 minutes at a rousing boil. Once the cover is removed, the next trick is to know when to take the syrup off the heat. Three minutes after the pot is uncovered, the sugar syrup will start to froth and bubble. Watch the pot carefully. When the syrup starts to take on

the color of Budweiser, swirl the pot constantly, taking it off the heat and putting it back on. The syrup will darken quickly at this point and will continue to cook even when removed from the burner. In terms of color, the syrup is ready when it reaches a rich honey color, rather than the color of Budweiser. You want flavor but not an overpowering bitter aftertaste. Note that for even cooking you should swirl the sugar syrup in the pot, not stir it.

The other issue with a sugar syrup is hardening. In some of my tests, when the custards were unmolded, the caramel syrup was hard at the bottom of the ramekin rather than being liquid. I realized that this is why recipes usually suggest swirling the caramel syrup around the inside of the ramekin before pouring in the custard. This way, there is only a thin layer of syrup between the custard and the container, which means that the syrup is less likely to harden. A thick layer of caramel syrup on the bottom of the ramekin, however, is more likely to remain hard. Since swirling can be difficult — you have to work very quickly before the syrup hardens — I wondered if there was some other way to solve this problem. I noted in an article in *Cook's Illustrated* that we had suggested using both corn syrup and lemon juice in order to avoid crystallization when making the sugar syrup. We also discovered that the caramel syrup did not have to be swirled in the ramekins. I wondered if perhaps the corn syrup and lemon juice not only had an effect on the crystallization but also kept the caramel syrup liquid. So I performed a test. I added 2 tablespoons of corn syrup to my next batch of caramel syrup (hoping that the lemon juice was unnecessary) and found that the problem was solved! The corn syrup kept most of the caramel from hardening after baking.

I also came across many other tips that I found useful. They are:

- The best tool for removing custard cups from a hot water bath is jar grippers sold with canning supplies. They are designed

WHY DOES CORN SYRUP KEEP THE CARAMEL FROM HARDENING?

To make corn syrup, cornstarch is treated with acid or enzymes that break down the long chains of glucose molecules. This creates a syrup consisting of short glucose chains suspended amidst a tangle of longer chains of glucose. In crème caramel, this tangle of longer chains makes it difficult for other molecules to move about and interact. Specifically, it prevents sucrose molecules (in table sugar) from forming crystals. Instead, they remain suspended, which means that the sugar syrup does not become granular or harden. Corn syrup is also used in cookie recipes. Since it is attracted to water, it suspends moisture, which keeps the cookies fresh longer.

much like tongs, but the "grabbing" end is encased in rubber and they are wide. This provides a sure grip for a slippery, hot ramekin. If you do not own a pair, try sliding a pancake turner under the ramekin and then steady the top with an oven mitt.

- Do not try to unmold crème caramel until it is completely cooled to room temperature. A few vigorous shakes should free the custards. However, if you are having trouble, place the ramekins in a roasting pan and then add a half inch or so of hot water. Dip each ramekin up and down a few times before unmolding. Note that even with the use of corn syrup some of the caramel syrup will remain hard and stick to the bottom of the ramekin.
- If you have to refrigerate this dessert, bring it to room temperature before unmolding and serving. On some occasions, I found that the caramel sauce was a bit hard when cold. Allow at least a half hour at room temperature.
- The best way to clean the saucepan used to make the sugar syrup is to fill it halfway with water, cover, and place on high heat. Boil for about 5 minutes, or until all of the caramel has dissolved.

Crème Caramel

I tried two flavor variations, one with cinnamon and nutmeg and the other with citrus. The spices were nice, adding a bit of depth and complexity to the dish. The citrus (I used lime zest and juice) created problems for the texture. The custard never set up properly. However, I found that a bit of lemon or orange oil works fine (see Citrus Variation, below).

ENOUGH FOR EIGHT 6-OUNCE RAMEKINS

For the Caramel
- ½ cup water
- 1 cup granulated sugar
- 2 tablespoons light corn syrup

For the Custard
- 1½ cups whole milk
- 1½ cups light cream
- 3 large eggs
- 3 large egg yolks
- ⅓ cup granulated sugar
- ⅛ teaspoon salt
- 1 teaspoon vanilla extract

1. Heat oven to 350 degrees. Place a thin kitchen towel or paper towels evenly over the bottom of a roasting pan large enough to accommodate the ramekins. Place eight 6-ounce flat-bottomed ramekins (or six 9-ounce ramekins) on the towel (to prevent slipping), making sure that they do not touch the sides of the pan.

2. *For the caramel:* Place water, sugar, and corn syrup in a heavy saucepan over medium heat. Do not stir but swirl the pan frequently until the sugar dissolves. Increase heat to high and bring syrup to a boil. Cover and cook for 2 minutes. Uncover pan and continue to cook, still at high heat. After about 3 minutes, the syrup will froth and bubble. When the syrup begins to take on color, start swirling the pan constantly, removing it from the heat for a few seconds at a time so the syrup does not darken

too quickly. Remove pan from heat when the syrup is a rich honey color. Be careful. Once the syrup starts to darken it will change color rapidly. It will also continue to darken off the heat. Pour 1 to 2 tablespoons caramel into one ramekin at a time, swirling to coat the bottom evenly.

3. *For the custard:* Heat the milk and cream in a heavy saucepan. In a medium bowl, gently whisk the eggs, yolks, sugar, and salt until just combined. Try not to incorporate air as you work. When the milk mixture starts to steam, pour about ½ cup of it into the eggs and whisk gently to combine. Slowly add the rest of the hot milk, stirring gently with the whisk. Add the vanilla. Strain custard into a large measuring cup or pitcher, then pour into prepared ramekins.

4. Cover each ramekin with aluminum foil, pricking the foil to allow steam to escape. Pour very hot tap water around the ramekins until the water reaches two-thirds of the way up their sides. Carefully place the roasting pan in the heated oven and bake custards for 40 to 60 minutes. Cooking time will depend on the size and shape of your ramekins. Check the custards individually and remove each from the oven as it is done. When ready, the center of the custard should still wobble slightly when shaken but a knife should come out clean when inserted into the custard. (Do not stick the knife all the way in. It will pierce the bottom of the custard, which makes it unattractive when served.)

5. When custards are done, remove from the water bath, uncover, and cool completely at room temperature before unmolding. (The best way to remove hot ramekins is to lift them out with jar grippers sold with canning supplies. Or slide a pancake turner under the ramekin and steady it with an oven mitt.) If holding for a long time before serving, you may refrigerate the custards, but bring back to room temperature before unmolding and serving to loosen the caramel. To unmold, run a thin knife around the edge of the custard. Place a shallow bowl or deep-edged serving plate on top of the ramekin and flip them both over together. If the custard does not come out of the mold (it should), dip the ramekin in warm water and try again.

WHAT CAN GO WRONG? The two steps that can be tricky are removing the sugar syrup from the heat before it turns too dark and unmolding the custard. For the first problem, keep in mind that once the syrup starts to take on color, it will darken very quickly. Take the pan on and off the heat and swirl the contents frequently once you see some color. Also keep in mind that the syrup will continue to darken once it is off the heat but still in the hot pan. As for unmolding, be sure to use a sharp knife around the edges of the custard. It is important to keep the knife up against the side of the ramekin; otherwise it will cut into the custard, marring the presentation. The custard may need a few sharp downward shakes to unmold. If this doesn't work, dip the bottom of the ramekin in hot water for a few seconds, towel it off, and then repeat the process. Note that no matter what you do, some of the caramel syrup will remain in the ramekin after unmolding.

CINNAMON-NUTMEG VARIATION

Add ½ teaspoon cinnamon and ¼ teaspoon nutmeg to the custard along with the vanilla.

CITRUS VARIATION

Substitute ½ teaspoon lemon or orange oil (or extract) for the vanilla.

CRÈME BRÛLÉE

CRÈME BRÛLÉE IS A particularly velvety custard, much richer than a simpler crème caramel or an American baked custard. The difference lies mostly in the type of milk product used. Crème caramel uses milk and light cream,

CASE 53: RICE MILK CRÈME BRÛLÉE?

Which liquid provides the best texture and flavor?

Liquid	Texture	Taste	Comments
Light cream	Tight, dense	Good; a little eggy	Good overall; texture a bit thin
Heavy cream	Too thick	Rich	Too heavy
Half-and-half	Not creamy	Good flavor	Not thick enough
Skim milk	Light, silky	Light on flavor	Flavor weak
Whole milk	More like custard than crème brûlée	Flavors are good	Too thin
Rice milk	Didn't set up	Did not even taste it	Forget it

whereas a crème brûlée is often made exclusively with heavy cream. But the problem most cooks have in making crème brûlée is the topping. Traditionally, sugar was sprinkled on top and then the ramekin was run under a broiler or browned with a hot salamander (an old-fashioned metal disk attached to a handle; it was heated and then used to brown foods). Modern chefs often use a small handheld butane torch, but this seemed completely out of the question for most home cooks. So I set out to perfect not only the taste and texture of the custard itself, but to find a way around the last, most difficult step.

The first set of tests involved the type of liquid. I tested light cream, heavy cream, half-and-half, skim milk, whole milk, and rice milk. (Rice milk is a product much like soy milk, but made from rice. I decided to try it since many health-food enthusiasts like to substitute these sorts of products for milk or cream.) Case 53 summarizes the test findings. As a result, I finally settled on a combination of light cream,

which on its own was a bit light for crème brûlée, and heavy cream, which I found too heavy when used by itself. Now the custard was rich and silky and had very good flavor.

The next big issue was the eggs. Most recipes I looked at called for egg yolks only, using none of the whites. A 3-yolk crème brûlée had a very loose consistency, much like crème anglaise. A 4-yolk custard was firmer but still without sufficient body, and custards made with more yolks were firm and creamy but had an overpowering egg yolk flavor, to the point that all other flavors were lost. I then went on to perform a simple test of whole eggs, yolks only, and whole eggs plus yolks and discovered that whole eggs won hands down. The yolks-only version was too "yolky"-tasting; the yolks plus whole eggs version was better, but I still detected too much yolk flavor. The whole eggs produced a wonderful custard that was creamy, melted in the mouth, and had a subtle egg taste. I settled on 3 whole eggs as the perfect quantity.

As for the sugar, I tried 2 tablespoons, ¼ cup, ½ cup, and honey. The quarter cup came out a winner, enough to boost flavor overall without making the custard too sweet for the sugar crust. The honey, as I have found in other custard tests, had two problems: the custard did not set up properly and the honey flavor was overpowering. I also wondered whether salt made a difference or not. It turned out that salt produces a somewhat firmer custard and helps to round out the flavor. Scientists agree that salt assists in the thickening process, whereas sugar and acidic ingredients can weaken the bonds.

Now that I had a good custard, I was still left with the problem of the topping. I tried white sugar, brown sugar, and then a mixture, testing them using the broiler method, assuming that most home cooks are not going to have a blowtorch handy. The sugar topping was spotty at best, very often grainy or even burned in spots, and in some cases, the custard separated and was marred by large fissures. I also found that my broiler was very uneven in terms of cooking time: one custard might be done long before another. I then turned to the restaurant technique of using a small culinary blowtorch. This was even worse. I managed to ignite the brown sugar topping, which turned the sugar into a hard, black mass. After the effort it took to get to this point, I had no interest in any method that was so unpredictable.

I then wondered what would happen if I made a caramel syrup on top of the stove, as I did for crème caramel, and then poured it on top of the baked crème brûlée. In fact, this worked well. I made the syrup and then poured a thin layer over the baked custard, swirling to coat the top evenly. It set up quickly and produced a smooth, glassy crust that crackled nicely when cut into with a spoon. Here at last was a foolproof method and one that produced a gorgeous-looking dessert to boot. Now crème brûlée can be made at home, reliably and easily.

...

Foolproof Crème Brûlée

This recipe avoids the problem of caramelizing the top under a broiler or with a blowtorch, the first method being unreliable at best, often resulting in separated custard and burned spots, and the second being beyond the pale for the home cook. A caramel syrup is made on top of the stove and then simply poured on top of the cooked custard. The syrup hardens into a smooth and glassy surface that crackles when cut into with a spoon.

SERVES 6

For the Custard
- 1 cup heavy cream
- 1 cup light cream
- 3 large eggs
- ¼ cup granulated sugar
- Pinch salt
- 1 teaspoon vanilla extract

For the Caramel Topping
- ¼ cup water
- ½ cup granulated sugar

1. Heat oven to 300 degrees. Place a thin kitchen towel evenly over the bottom of a roasting pan large enough to accommodate the ramekins. Place six 6-ounce ramekins on top of the towel, making sure that they do not touch the sides of the pan. Bring a kettle full of water to a boil.

2. *For the custard:* Heat the heavy and light creams in a saucepan until the mixture simmers. Meanwhile, gently whisk the eggs, sugar, salt, and vanilla in a medium bowl. Slowly add about a cup of the hot cream mixture to the egg mixture, whisking gently until combined. Now add the rest of the cream mixture, stirring gently with a spoon to mix. Strain mixture through a fine strainer into a large measuring cup or pitcher, then pour evenly into the 6 ramekins. Pour hot water into the roasting pan until it

comes two-thirds of the way up the sides of the ramekins.

3. Bake for approximately 40 to 70 minutes (it may take longer in some ovens), or until the custards are set but still quiver in the center when gently shaken. Remove from the water bath and let cool completely. (Note that if you use a larger, shallower ramekin — 9-ounce size, for example — the custard will cook more quickly, in as little as 30 minutes.)

4. *For the caramel syrup:* Place water and sugar in a heavy saucepan over medium heat. Do not stir but swirl the pan frequently until the sugar dissolves. Increase heat to high and bring syrup to a boil. Cover and cook for 2 minutes, still on high. Uncover pan and cook until syrup begins to take on color. After about 3 minutes, the syrup will froth and bubble. After about 8 minutes, it will start to darken quickly. Swirl pan constantly at this point, placing pan on and off the heat as you work so the syrup does not darken too quickly. Remove pan from heat when the syrup is light mahogany in color. Be careful. Once the syrup starts to darken, it will change color rapidly. It will also continue to darken off the heat. Pour a *thin layer* of the hot syrup into one ramekin at a time, swirling each cup to completely cover the custard. It is best to add the syrup all at once to each custard cup for an even top layer. The syrup hardens very quickly, so if you add it in batches, the top surface will be uneven in both thickness and color.

WHAT CAN GO WRONG? Aside from making the sugar syrup, the only potential problem is pouring either too much or too little syrup onto the custard. If you use too little, it will not cover the top completely, and if you then add a bit more, the topping will come out uneven in thickness and color. If you pour too much on, the top crust will be a bit too thick for easily breaking into with a spoon. Also, the size of the ramekin can dramatically affect the cooking time. If you have only 9-ounce cups, the custard may cook

in as little as 30 minutes. In addition, within a given batch, some cups may cook much faster than others if the amount of custard is not exactly the same for every cup. I would start checking the custards at 25 minutes of baking time and keep a close eye on them until they are set.

CRÈME ANGLAISE

CRÈME ANGLAISE IS a sauce, not a custard per se, but is quite similar in construct to a crème caramel. (They both use 2 egg yolks per cup of liquid.) It is cooked briefly on top of the stove rather than baked in the oven, and then it is allowed to cool, reaching a consistency much like heavy cream rather than a pudding. It is used as a dessert sauce and is often served with rich one-layer chocolate cakes, poached pears, or many baked fruit desserts as well. Of course, it is also used as the base for floating islands — cooked, sweetened egg whites that float on a pool of crème anglaise (see recipe, page 335).

I have always found crème anglaise to be a bit of a mystery. It does not thicken very much, changing from the consistency of milk to cream, so knowing when it is done is difficult. One must constantly be on the watch for overcooking the eggs, which results in curdling. I wanted to create a recipe for crème anglaise that was unlikely to curdle and that had clear, specific directions indicating exactly when it was properly cooked.

Starting with a simple recipe (milk, egg yolks, and sugar), I once again tried the traditional method of bringing the milk to a simmer in a saucepan while whisking the sugar and yolks in another saucepan until they were thick and light-colored. I slowly whisked the hot milk into the yolk mixture and then put the saucepan onto medium-low heat. I stirred with a wooden spoon for 5 minutes, then 10 minutes, and then

CASE 54: PLEASE PASS THE MILK

What type of liquid is best for crème anglaise?

Liquid	Taste	Texture	Comments
Light cream	Rich flavor	Thick like a milkshake	Too thick
Half-and-half	Liquid ice cream	Thick and velvety	A bit thick but has great flavor
Whole milk	Vanilla comes through	Smooth and not too thick	Best choice
Nondairy creamer	Too sweet; artificial	Rubbery; very thick	Too thick and awful flavor
Rice milk	Awful	Thin; watery	Tastes like fake vanilla pudding
Skim milk	Pretty good	A bit thin	Works pretty well as a lower-fat version

a whopping 15 minutes and the mixture still hadn't reached the point at which it coated the back of the spoon, whatever that meant.

Determined to make this a more scientific and predictable process, I started another batch, this time adding ½ teaspoon cornstarch to the egg mixture. I have found that cornstarch "protects" egg yolks during cooking, making them less likely to overcook. I also thought that the cornstarch would aid in the thickening process, speeding it up or at least making it more noticeable. My second idea was to measure the temperature of the custard as it was heated. I reasoned that this would provide a more precise measurement of when the sauce was done.

It turned out that I was right on both counts. The cornstarch did in fact make the thickening more obvious. At 6 to 7 minutes, the custard changed over from milky to creamy. The custard on the back of the wooden spoon was no longer watery-looking; rather, it was more opaque and thicker. I noted the temperature as I cooked, using an instant-read thermometer, and found that the crème anglaise was done when it reached about 178 degrees.

Most recipes give the impression that crème anglaise is not ready until it "thickens," and therefore many home cooks cook it too long. Remember, this is a dessert sauce, not a pudding; it should never get thick in the traditional sense of the word. It simply becomes creamier, more opaque on the spoon, and seems a bit denser and heavier when stirred.

Having developed a reasonably foolproof method, I then went back to test the ingredients and their proportions. The first, and most obvious, series of tests concerned the type of liquid. The results were not unexpected. Milk was my first choice, since a crème anglaise should be a relatively thin, not thick, sauce. The nondairy creamer was awful, as was rice milk. The surprise of the taste test was the skim milk, which actually worked rather well. Feel free to use it if you are inclined toward low-fat cooking. As for me, I'll stick with the whole milk.

I then moved on to test eggs. I tried 2 whole eggs versus 4 yolks versus 6 yolks versus 8 yolks. The whites in the whole eggs were a problem. The sauce turned out more like a vanilla-flavored pudding, and some of the whites actually overcooked, turning solid. I also found that the whites coagulate too quickly, increasing the chances that the crème anglaise will overcook before one pulls it off the heat. This was a failure on all counts. The 4-yolk version was excellent. This is the standard number of yolks found in most cookbooks. I also tried 6 and 8 yolks, and both made the custard too "yolky."

I was surprised to discover that the amount of sugar affected the texture as well as the flavor. When I used a paltry 2 tablespoons, the sauce was thin and watery. The quarter cup of sugar was the right amount, the sauce being smooth and not too sweet. A half cup of sugar made for a cloying, heavy aftertaste. I also tried maple syrup, which to my surprise worked nicely, although the sauce was a bit thin. I would use this variation for a dessert cooked with nuts such as walnuts or pecans. It might also be nice with poached pears.

In an effort to make this a quicker process, I also tried a cold-start crème anglaise, neither heating the milk beforehand nor beating the yolks with the sugar. (The ingredients were simply mixed together in a saucepan and then heated.) The result was disappointing — a thin custard that tasted like overcooked eggs. The flavors of the vanilla, the milk, the sugar, and the eggs were not properly balanced.

During the course of the tests, I discovered a few other cooking tips:

- Use a wooden spoon for stirring after the yolks and sugar are whisked together. This reduces the amount of air incorporated into the mixture.
- The heat level is going to be different for every stove and saucepan. Low on my stovetop with my All-Clad Master Chef 2-quart saucepan may not translate for your kitchen. In fact, the heat should be slightly higher than low but nowhere near medium. The temperature will, of course, affect the cooking time, which I have left at 5 to 8 minutes in the directions. (You can use a higher heat setting initially, until the mixture gets to about 160 degrees. This saves a lot of cooking time.)
- Although the mixture may steam as soon as it is put onto the stove, this is not a sign that it is ready. However, if, after 5 to 8 minutes of cooking, it does start to emit a puff of steam, this is a rough indication that the custard is almost done. An instant-read thermometer will provide a foolproof gauge: the crème anglaise is done when it reaches 178 degrees.
- Many recipes suggest using a water bath to cool down the mixture after cooking. This is utter nonsense. I pour the hot mixture through a strainer and into a 4-cup Pyrex measuring cup. I then stir for 1 minute to help it cool. I then just let it sit at room temperature. After just 1 minute of stirring, the temperature dropped from 178 degrees to 150 degrees! So much for needing an ice bath. After 5 minutes, the temperature had dropped to 136 degrees.
- Crème anglaise does not keep well. It tends to thin out and lose its delicate flavor. I would hold it at room temperature and use it within 2 hours. If you must refrigerate it, do so for no more than 3 or 4 hours and make sure that it comes up to room temperature before serving for full flavor.

···

Cheater's Crème Anglaise

Why is this for cheaters? Well, I add a bit of cornstarch, which makes this recipe a snap. It is much easier to tell when the mixture has thickened, and the egg yolks are less likely to curdle. A crème anglaise is best used quickly, not left overnight in the refrigerator, where the texture and flavor suffer. For low-fat cooking, skim milk does work surprisingly well here. If you are using only a small amount of crème anglaise to splash on a dessert, you can also use half-and-half for a superrich, velvety texture and flavor. This sauce can be served with any of the one-layer chocolate cakes in the book, with stewed rhubarb, or with poached pears.

MAKES 2½ CUPS

- 2 cups whole milk
- 4 large egg yolks
- ¼ cup granulated sugar
- ½ teaspoon cornstarch
- ½ teaspoon vanilla extract

1. Heat milk to a simmer in a small saucepan.

2. Meanwhile, whisk the yolks, sugar, and cornstarch together in a heavy-bottomed 1- or 2-quart saucepan until thick and light, about 3 minutes. Whisk ½ cup of the hot milk into the eggs. Now slowly pour in the rest of the hot milk, stirring with a wooden spoon to combine. Place onto medium-low heat (closer to low than medium).

3. Stir the mixture constantly and use an instant-read thermometer to check the temperature of the custard. It is done when it reaches 178 degrees. This will take 5 to 8 minutes, but may take longer depending on the heat source and your pan. The consistency of the sauce will change from that of milk to light cream and the sauce on the back of the wooden spoon will look creamy rather than thin and watery. You will also note that the mixture seems to become a bit thicker as you stir. Just about the time it is done, you may also notice a puff of steam coming from the saucepan. However, the mixture will still be relatively thin, nothing like a pudding or heavy sauce.

4. Pour custard through a strainer into a small bowl or 4-cup Pyrex measuring cup. Stir for 1 minute to cool. Stir in the vanilla. Let sit at room temperature for up to 2 hours before serving. (This sauce is best not refrigerated but can be chilled for 2 to 3 hours. Serve at room temperature for best flavor.)

WHAT CAN GO WRONG? The big problem with this recipe is cooking time. Saucepans and stoves vary greatly, and therefore your crème anglaise may take a lot more or less time than mine did. The addition of cornstarch makes it easier to determine when the custard sauce has thickened, another common problem with this recipe. By far the best method of solving this problem is to use an instant-read thermometer, which should register 178 degrees when the sauce is done. Keep in mind that this is supposed to be a relatively thin sauce, so do not expect it to thicken up like a pudding. It will get a bit thicker and heavier as it cools but will remain fairly thin, a bit like heavy cream.

Maple Syrup Variation

Substitute maple syrup for sugar. Serve with desserts containing pecans or walnuts or perhaps with a poached pear.

Floating Islands

ANY REASONABLE HOME COOK would immediately stop at the mention of this consummate restaurant dessert and shout, "You've got to be kidding. Nobody in their right mind would bother to make this at home!" True enough, since most traditional recipes call for poaching small scoops of beaten egg whites in hot milk, a

CASE 55: BAKED, POACHED, OR BROILED?

Looking for the best method for cooking meringue.

Method	Taste and Texture	Ease of Preparation
Baking	Light, "carved" texture; not as wet and creamy as other methods; flavor good but not as good as poached	Simple; just throw egg whites into a casserole and bake at 250 degrees
Poaching	Outside of meringue is wet; has nice flavor	Have to cook in batches; not easy to determine when they are done
Broiling	Nicely browned exterior; flavor not as good as poached meringue	Easier than poaching but still tricky; easy to over- or undercook

process that is fussy, time-consuming, and not for the novice cook. But since I am quite fond of this dish — the combined texture of meringue "islands" floating on a pool of simple crème anglaise is divine — I wondered if a bit of sleuthing would uncover an easier, more practical method of preparation.

So I set out to perform three separate tests with the meringues. I baked the beaten egg whites, I poached them, and I also tried broiling them. First, a bit about each method. Each of these techniques starts out the same: egg whites are whipped with salt, cream of tartar (to act as a stabilizer), sugar, and vanilla. For the baked method, the mixture is placed into a buttered and powdered (with sugar) casserole and then baked at low temperature. For the poached method, dollops of egg whites are poached in simmering milk; it takes about 2 minutes for each batch, and many batches are required since the saucepan can only handle so many at one time. Finally, broiling entails placing the dollops of egg whites in simmering milk in a casserole dish and then running them under the broiler. My test results are shown in the chart "Baked, Poached, or Broiled?"

Although I found the baked meringue to be a bit on the dry side, the other two methods produced meringues that were quite wet on the outside and looked unprofessional. The baked meringue had a pleasant brown accent around the top and edges and was easy to carve into pieces, making for an exceptional presentation on the plate. Now, I subscribe to the theory that well-prepared food always looks good on the plate, but this is one dessert for which a bit of elegant presentation is not misplaced. Of course, baking the egg whites makes this recipe a snap. I simply would not prepare it if I had to broil or poach them. There is one other benefit to baking, which is that the meringue cooks slowly, giving you plenty of time to tell when it is done. With poaching or broiling, timing is crucial — even a few seconds can make a big difference.

The next issue was one of sugar content. How much sugar was necessary with the egg whites, not only for flavor, but for structure as well? I tested three different levels of sugar with

CASE 56: SWEET DREAMS

How much sugar is the right amount for floating islands?

Sugar	Baking	Poaching	Broiling
1½ cups	Limp, heavy foam; too sweet and too brown	Wet outer skin; too sweet	Very brown skin; too sweet
½ cup	Light foam; only moderate browning	Puffs nicely; only a thin outer skin	Nicely browned, but a bit too sugary
None	Not tested	Tripled in size and then fell; tastes like milk foam	Looks like cooked marsh-mallows; dollops deflated; salty

12 egg whites and with each of the cooking methods (baking, poaching, and broiling): 1½ cups, ½ cup, and no sugar. The results were fascinating. As my testing notes document — see Case 56, "Sweet Dreams" — the ½-cup version turned out the best meringue.

I was also keen on discovering the truth about stabilizers. Cream of tartar is often added to egg whites as they are whipped. (Cream of tartar, which is acidic, makes it more difficult for the egg white proteins to bond too tightly. As a result, the proteins remain more elastic; they are slower to coagulate yet stable enough to maintain structure. Consequently, the air cells come up against less resistance when they expand under heat, resulting in more volume.) I tested this by preparing the recipe with and without the cream of tartar and found no difference in the finished product; therefore I do not include it in the final recipe. Since this result was at odds with my testing for the soufflé chapter, I wondered why. After more research, I discovered that sugar also acts as a stabilizer. Thus, because there is a fair amount of sugar in the meringue, the cream of tartar is simply un-

necessary in this particular recipe. This, however, would not be the case where there is little or no sugar beaten with the egg whites.

So now I had what I set out to discover, a recipe for floating islands that was eminently easy. A simple custard sauce is made and set aside to cool. Egg whites are beaten with a bit of salt and sugar, turned out into a prepared casserole dish, and baked at a low 250 degrees. The meringue is then cut into pieces and served on top of the crème anglaise. This is a simple dessert which can be made ahead, perfect for entertaining.

▪▪▪

Easy, Make-Ahead Floating Islands

The secret of this recipe is baking the meringue, which takes this preparation out of the realm of the restaurant and squarely into a home kitchen. Baking also gives the home cook plenty of time to check if the meringue is done. Other methods, such as poaching or broiling, call for precise timing, which can easily result in under- or overcooked meringue. To make this dessert extra special, you can make a caramel sauce and drizzle it over individual portions just before serving (see recipe below).

SERVES 6

1 recipe Cheater's Crème Anglaise (page 333)

Butter and confectioners' sugar for preparing baking dish

For the Meringue

12 large egg whites, at room temperature

⅛ teaspoon salt

Scant ½ cup granulated sugar

1 teaspoon vanilla extract

Optional Caramel Sauce for drizzling (recipe below)

1. Prepare the crème anglaise, cool to room temperature, and cover with plastic wrap. If not using within 2 hours, refrigerate for up to 3 hours. Bring to room temperature before assembling desserts.

2. Heat oven to 250 degrees. Butter a deep 9 x 13 baking dish and then coat with a light dusting of confectioners' sugar.

3. Place egg whites in the bowl of an electric mixer. Beat at slow speed until they begin to foam. Add salt and turn mixer to medium high. Beat until mixture is light and shiny and the whites just start to hold a peak. Gradually add sugar and whip until incorporated. The whites should be moist and glossy but should be able to hold a stiff 2-inch peak. Add the vanilla and mix on medium for a few seconds until incorporated. Place in prepared casserole dish, smooth the top, and put into oven.

4. Bake for 35 to 40 minutes, or until the meringue is cooked through and firm to the touch. (The top will be a bit sticky, but a knife inserted into the middle of the meringue should come out clean. The top and edges will also brown slightly.) Cool to room temperature and

turn casserole upside down to unmold. (The meringue will shrink as it cools.)

5. Cut meringue into 2-inch chunks. Place crème anglaise on dessert plates (use shallow bowls) and top with meringue. Just before serving, prepare Optional Caramel Sauce and drizzle over each portion.

WHAT CAN GO WRONG? This is a fairly simple recipe, but you can overcook the egg whites, which will result in tough, dry meringue. It is better to undercook the whites slightly than overcook them. Remember that the top of the meringue will still be slightly sticky when the whites are done.

OPTIONAL CARAMEL SAUCE

Place ¼ cup water and ½ cup sugar in a heavy saucepan over medium heat. Do not stir but swirl the pan frequently until the sugar dissolves. Increase heat to high and bring syrup to a boil. Cover and cook for 2 minutes. Uncover pan and cook until syrup begins to take on color. After about 3 minutes, the syrup will froth and bubble. After about 8 minutes, it will start to darken quickly. Swirl pan constantly at this point, placing pan on and off the heat as you work so the syrup does not darken too quickly. Remove pan from heat when the syrup is a rich honey in color. Be careful. Once the syrup starts to darken, it will change color rapidly. It will also continue to darken off the heat. Thinly drizzle sauce over individual servings.

CHOCOLATE POTS DE CRÈME

WHAT ARE POTS DE CRÈME exactly? Well, they are custards much like a crème caramel or crème brûlée but without a caramel syrup. In fact, they have all the problems of custard, including the need for slow cooking to avoid a tough, curdled texture, and the need to find the proper balance of milk versus cream and eggs

CASE 57: POTS DE CRÈME

Determining which liquid makes the best pots de crème.

Liquid	Texture and Taste	Comments
Whole milk	Nice custard; more like a pudding than a pot de crème; good chocolate flavor	Good lower-fat option, but not in the tradition of a rich dessert
Heavy cream	Velvet texture; a bit too rich; buttery; nice dark color	Too rich for my taste; almost sinful
Light cream	Light and airy; much like a mousse	Body lacking something; not a bad choice overall
Skim milk	Waxy mouth feel; watery; hollow taste	Serve this to the low-fat police and let them suffer!
Rice milk	Loose custard; malted milk flavor; awful	Even a macrobiotic devotee could not love this insipid dessert
Half whole milk, half heavy cream	Intense chocolate taste; nice texture	The winner

versus egg yolks in order to produce a rich dessert that is not too eggy. On top of these obvious concerns is the issue of the chocolate. What type is best? What about using cocoa powder or chocolate syrup? How does one avoid a grainy texture when using chocolate? Chocolate pots de crème are a delicate balancing act between chocolate and dairy, sweet and bitter, eggs and milk. When done properly, they yield a clean, bright chocolate flavor that is rich but not dense and a creamy, smooth texture, neither thin nor puddinglike.

I started off with a test of liquids, trying whole milk, skim milk, rice milk, half whole milk and half heavy cream, heavy cream, and light cream.

Once again, as a result of my tests, I ended up with half whole milk and half heavy cream. This combination seems to work well for most custards, although in some cases I use light cream instead of heavy cream. Milk on its own simply lacks sufficient texture and mouth feel; heavy cream by itself is too much of a good thing.

I then went on to investigate the use of eggs. I tried whole eggs versus egg yolks only versus whole eggs mixed with additional egg whites. The whole eggs won out; the texture was smooth and creamy, allowing the chocolate to shine through, with no egg aftertaste. When using 4 yolks, I found the custard to be firm but not creamy and also a bit too rich. Six yolks was better, but not quite as good as the whole eggs.

Since the extra fat didn't improve the custard, I opted out of this version. When I used whole eggs with additional whites, the custard became foamy, light in color, and without enough chocolate flavor. Chocolate needs fat to convey its rich flavor, and this version was anemic.

I played with the amount of sugar, trying amounts between 2 tablespoons and ½ cup and found the lesser amount preferable. The chocolate shone through nicely, the mouth feel was good, and the custard lingered on the palate as it slid down the throat. This also gives the pots de crème a more sophisticated touch than a pudding, which is more of a sweet blunt instrument. Honey had many virtues, including a nice creamy texture to the custard, but it overpowered the chocolate. I might reconsider this sweetener if trying other flavors of pots de crème.

The key to great chocolate pots de crème is, of course, the chocolate. I started with semisweet chocolate alone, but the flavor was a bit weak. I then tried just cocoa powder, which yielded a less creamy, almost grainy, custard. The flavor was good, but texture was inferior. Chocolate syrup (don't ask me why I tried this) resulted in something close to canned pudding; it was too sweet and very commercial in flavor and texture. A mocha version (with coffee and chocolate) was a bit too liquid, slightly grainy, and had a bitter edge to it. To make this version work, one would need to use all heavy cream (no milk) and 6 egg yolks instead of 4 whole eggs. It needed more fat to balance out the thin, acidic coffee. Finally, I tried half cocoa powder and half melted chocolate, and this was a winner. It had a nice creamy texture, and the cocoa powder provided depth of flavor.

I ended my testing by trying three flavor alternatives: caramel, vanilla, and black raspberry. For the caramel variation, I simply added a caramel syrup to the mixture and ended up with something close to crème caramel. I decided that crème caramel was better, so I discarded this variation. Next, I tried a vanilla pot de crème; it was buttery, but I vastly preferred the chocolate version. Finally, I tried a black raspberry custard, and it came out much like fruit yogurt. In addition, the custard was grainy and not at all smooth. For my money, the chocolate is the best flavor for pots de crème.

▪ ▪ ▪

Chocolate Pots de Crème

This is a very simple recipe and makes a heavenly, rich, but intensely chocolate dessert. The use of both cocoa powder and melted chocolate kicks up the chocolate flavor, and the combination of milk and heavy cream lends a nice smooth texture and has enough fat to help the chocolate surround the palate. Other flavor variations are good, but chocolate is the standout.

SERVES 6

2	ounces semisweet or bittersweet chocolate
1	cup heavy cream
1	cup whole milk
4	large eggs
2	tablespoons granulated sugar
⅛	teaspoon salt
¼	cup Dutch-process cocoa powder
1	teaspoon vanilla extract

Heavy cream or sweetened whipped cream
   for serving

1. Heat oven to 350 degrees. Place a thin kitchen towel or paper towels evenly over the bottom of a roasting pan large enough to accommodate the ramekins. Place six 6-ounce ramekins on the towel, making sure they do not touch each other or the sides of the pan. Place chocolate in a Pyrex measuring cup or bowl and place in a microwave oven. Heat for 2 minutes on 50 percent power. Stir. Heat for 1 minute at 50 percent and stir again. Heat for up to 1 additional minute, or until chocolate is melted. (Or, chop chocolate and place in a double boiler to melt.)

2. Place cream and milk in a heavy-bottomed saucepan and bring to a simmer.

3. Meanwhile, combine the eggs, sugar, salt, cocoa powder, and melted chocolate in a mixing bowl and whisk just until blended. Do not overbeat, incorporating air.

4. When milk and cream are simmering, add ½ cup of the hot liquid to the egg mixture and whisk slowly to combine. Add the rest of the hot milk in a steady stream, mixing with a wooden spoon, not a whisk. Strain the mixture into a large measuring cup or pitcher, then pour into the ramekins. If using custard pots, put on the covers. If not, cover each ramekin with aluminum foil, pricking the foil to allow steam to escape. Pour very hot tap water into the roasting pan until it reaches two-thirds of the way up the sides of the ramekins.

5. Bake until center of custard quivers gently when shaken, 35 to 40 minutes. (Check the ramekins individually and remove each from the oven as it is done.) Remove custard cups from water bath, uncover, and allow to cool. When the custard has reached room temperature, place in the refrigerator to chill. Serve cold with a drizzle of heavy cream or with sweetened whipped cream.

WHAT CAN GO WRONG? I find that the cooking time varies tremendously from one ramekin to the next in the same batch, depending on where it is located in the roasting pan. In fact, some custard cups may take up to 20 minutes' more cooking than others. Start checking for doneness after 25 minutes, and take the ramekins out of the oven as they are done. Don't take them out all at the same time.

❦

Panna Cotta

This is perhaps one of the most misused terms in cooking. I have seen traditional custards (thickened with eggs) called panna cotta on restaurant menus when, as far as I can tell, a panna cotta (the name means "cooked cream") is nothing more than a sweetened, flavored milk-and-cream mixture that is thickened with gelatin. There are no eggs and no baking. This makes it one of the simplest recipes in this book.

The problem in making panna cottas is getting just the right amount of gelatin so that they set up properly without being rubbery. I tried varying amounts of gelatin, from 2½ to 5 teaspoons per 4 cups of dairy and finally settled on 2¾ teaspoons. This is just enough gelatin to produce a cohesive panna cotta that can be unmolded, although it is easier to simply serve this dessert in a wineglass, which requires no unmolding. Higher amounts of gelatin quickly turn a soft, luscious dessert into something rubbery and unpleasant. I tried using confectioners' sugar instead of granulated and did not like the taste, so I stuck with the latter. Some recipes suggest using a flavored oil (such as almond oil) to grease the ramekins, but I found that butter was superior for release and the oil did not add much in the way of flavor. I played with the relative proportion of milk to cream and found that a 1-to-1 ratio was a bit thin, whereas a 3-to-1 ratio of cream to milk was about right.

Another problem is flavor. Today's ultrapasteurized cream doesn't have much flavor, so older recipes, which depended on the cream itself to make the dessert delicious, have to be revised. First, you need to use enough sugar to punch the flavor. Second, I found that for simple variations, the use of orange or lemon oil is recommended. Just a bit of lemon or orange peel steeped in the milk-cream mixture (as suggested by many recipes) doesn't really do it. Unlike extracts, which contain a great deal of alcohol and off flavors, oils are strong and clean-tasting. They are easier to use and vastly better than using rind as a flavoring. I tested the use of rose water or orange flower water instead of extracts or oils and discovered that the flavors were too subtle to stand up to the cream. Another trick for flavoring is to use a caramel sauce in the ramekins, as one does for crème caramel. This makes a great counterpoint to the rich custard and balances the flavors nicely. (See the variation on page 341). Finally, I tried steeping the milk and cream with toasted almonds, but the flavor was too mild to show up against the cream.

■ ■ ■

Master Recipe for Panna Cotta

This dessert's success begins with the quality of the cream. Regular pasteurized cream usually tastes better than the ultrapasteurized variety. I strongly suggest using orange or lemon oil for this dessert (see Citrus Variation, below) — the vanilla version will be a bit plain unless served with some sort of sauce (the Caramel Sauce Variation, next page, is especially good) or fresh fruit. Note that the amount of gelatin listed here will produce a relatively soft panna cotta, which tastes better than those made with more gelatin but may be a bit tricky to unmold. If you want to serve this recipe on a plate rather than in a wineglass and want the panna cotta to retain its shape, increase the gelatin to 3 teaspoons, although it will be slightly less appealing when eaten. If you use the higher amount of gelatin, you can also unmold the panna cotta after only 3 or 4 hours of chilling.

SERVES 8

2¾ to 3	teaspoons unflavored gelatin (see note above)
1	cup whole milk
3	cups heavy cream
½	cup granulated sugar
2	teaspoons vanilla extract
⅛	teaspoon salt
	Fresh berries or fruit sauce for serving

1. In a small bowl, sprinkle the gelatin over ¼ cup of the milk. Let stand until softened, about 5 minutes. Butter eight 6-ounce ramekins and set aside on a tray. (You may also serve this dessert in goblets or wineglasses; these should not be buttered, since they will not be unmolded.)

2. Place the rest of the milk, the cream, and the sugar in a 2-quart saucepan over medium heat. Bring just to a boil and remove from heat. Add about ½ cup of the hot liquid to the gelatin mixture and whisk to dissolve, then pour the gelatin mixture back into the hot milk and cream. Add the vanilla and salt and then whisk mixture again to combine.

3. Strain the mixture through a fine-mesh sieve into a large measuring cup or pitcher. Divide among the prepared ramekins and cover with plastic wrap. Refrigerate until set, at least 5 hours. (The ramekins can also sit overnight.)

4. To unmold, run a knife around the edge of each custard, and shake or tap the ramekins to loosen completely. Invert onto chilled dessert plates. Serve with fresh fruit (berries or segmented oranges) or a simple fruit sauce. This dessert can also be served without unmolding if chilled, for example, in wineglasses.

WHAT CAN GO WRONG? The panna cotta does need to be chilled a long time to set up properly. It is best to make this recipe in the morning (or even a day ahead) if serving it for dinner. If you are short of time, or to produce a sturdier panna cotta that will unmold easily, use 3 teaspoons of gelatin. Shallower, straight-sided ramekins are best, since the narrower, taller custard cups produce a panna cotta that is more prone to losing its shape when unmolded. To avoid this problem entirely, simply serve the panna cotta without unmolding, as you would a pudding.

BUTTERMILK VARIATION

For a slightly tangier flavor, substitute ½ cup buttermilk for ½ cup of the heavy cream in the master recipe.

CITRUS VARIATION

Substitute 1 teaspoon orange oil or lemon oil for the vanilla extract.

ALMOND VARIATION

Substitute 1 teaspoon almond extract for the vanilla extract.

CARDAMOM-ORANGE VARIATION

Substitute 1 teaspoon orange oil for the vanilla in the master recipe and also add ¼ teaspoon ground cardamom to the strained mixture.

CARAMEL SAUCE VARIATION

Prepare the panna cotta according to the master recipe (use 3 teaspoons gelatin for easier unmolding) to the point that it is ready to pour into the ramekins. Combine ¾ cup granulated sugar and ¼ cup water in a heavy-bottomed saucepan over medium-high heat. Cook to a light caramel color, which will take 5 to 10 minutes. (Once the syrup starts to take on color, remove it from the heat and swirl the contents of the pan. Place it back on the heat for a few seconds at a time and then remove and swirl. Continue until you have a light brown caramel sauce.) Remove from heat and add 2 tablespoons water, stirring quickly. Pour about 1 tablespoon caramel into each ramekin, tilting quickly to cover the bottom. Add the warm panna cotta mixture on top and chill until set, at least 4 hours. Unmold onto chilled plates and serve.

AMERICAN BAKED CUSTARD

AT FIRST, an American baked custard seemed a simple dish. Some milk, eggs, and sugar are baked until set. But producing a tender, silky custard, I found, requires just the right proportion of ingredients, the proper oven temperature, and the appropriate cooking method. For starters, I had to test using all milk versus a combination of milk and half-and-half or cream. Many custards later, I discovered that 2 cups of milk to 1 cup of heavy cream was

best; half-and-half just didn't produce the rich, velvety texture I was looking for, and the all-milk version was too slippery and lean. A combination of 3 whole eggs plus 2 yolks did the trick; fewer yolks can't produce a really smooth custard.

As with most egg cookery, low heat was best. I used a 325-degree oven and a water bath, which promoted even, gentle cooking. Without the water bath, the edges of the custard tend to overcook before the inside is done.

Finally, it bears repeating that a good custard must be taken out of the oven before it is fully cooked. The center should be wobbly and barely set. It will continue to cook and set up after it is removed from the oven. Overcooking will result in a tough custard, especially around the perimeter. The reason? When cooked, egg proteins form a mesh that holds in water much like a sponge. When overcooked, that mesh tightens, becomes tougher, and expels much of the water, resulting in a dry, tough dessert.

■ ■ ■

American Baked Custard

This dessert is best served chilled during summer months, spooned into extra-large bowls with perhaps an extra dusting of freshly grated nutmeg. Resist the temptation to dress it up with puréed fruit sauces, sugar syrups, or fresh fruit. This is an honest, simple dessert that shouldn't be tarted up. Be sure to remove the baking dish from the oven before the center is perfectly set. It should still be wobbly.

SERVES 6 TO 8

- 2 cups whole milk
- 1 cup heavy cream
- 2 large egg yolks
- 3 large eggs
- ½ cup granulated sugar
- ⅛ teaspoon salt
- 1 teaspoon vanilla extract
- Freshly grated nutmeg

1. Heat oven to 325 degrees. Butter a 1½- to 2-quart baking dish or 8 custard cups. Place a thin kitchen towel or paper towels evenly over the bottom of a roasting pan and set the baking dish or cups on the towel, making sure they do not touch each other or the sides of the pan. Bring a kettle of water to a boil.

2. Heat the milk and heavy cream in a heavy-bottomed saucepan until bubbly around the edges.

3. Whisk together the yolks and eggs in a medium bowl. Stir in the sugar, salt, and vanilla and then slowly whisk in the hot milk mixture. Pour through a fine sieve into a large glass measuring cup or pitcher.

4. Pour the custard mixture into the prepared dish or cups, top with a dusting of freshly ground nutmeg, and then place the roasting pan in the oven. Pour the hot water into the pan to a depth of 1 inch.

5. Bake 15 to 20 minutes for the cups and 40 to 50 minutes for a baking dish. The center of the custard should still be wobbly and barely set. Remove from the water bath and let stand at room temperature until cooled. May be served warm or refrigerated. Dust with additional freshly grated nutmeg if desired.

WHAT CAN GO WRONG? The biggest problem with this recipe is overcooking. Be sure to remove the custard from the oven when the center is still wobbly and not quite set. It will continue to cook after having been removed from the oven.

PASTRY CREAM

PASTRY CREAM IS no more than a very thick custard sauce with the addition of flour or cornstarch or both as an added thickener. It is used to fill pastries such as éclairs or profiteroles and is often used as a filling for cakes such as Boston Cream Pie. It is usually flavored with vanilla extract, but you can also use a liquor such as rum or bourbon or substitute lemon or orange oil or extract as a flavoring.

For all of its versatility as a building-block recipe, pastry cream can be a problem. It often does not thicken properly or can curdle because of overheating. It can be too thick and gummy, with a strong egg yolk or flour flavor. My objective was to make this a simple recipe, one unlikely to be problematic for the home cook. I was particularly interested in developing a cream that thickened properly, as I have made plenty of pastry creams that never quite set up the way they should have.

WHAT IS THE DIFFERENCE BETWEEN FLOUR AND CORNSTARCH FOR THICKENING?

As many home bakers have noted, cornstarch is a more powerful thickener than flour. One reason is that flour contains many ingredients other than starch, whereas cornstarch is relatively pure. Cornstarch consists of two starch molecules — amylose and amylopectin. When heated in water, the granules begin to absorb water and swell, becoming increasingly viscous. Ultimately the starch reaches the point of gelatinization (between 144 and 158 degrees Fahrenheit). At this point the starch granules start to leak amylose, which diffuses into the solution to form a network, trapping additional liquids.

Although cornstarch produces a clearer solution than flour and has about twice the thickening capacity, it is more delicate than flour, which contains other binding elements, including proteins and lipids. There are three ways in which a cornstarch-thickened liquid can break down: through excessive heat, with the addition of acid or enzymes (lemon juice, for example), and when the mixture is beaten too vigorously once gelatinization has occurred. These handicaps make flour the thickener of choice for this recipe: it is dependable, resilient, and much less likely to break down if subjected to a heavy hand during whisking.

CASE 58: PASTRY CREAM

Which components make the best pastry cream?

Ingredient	Texture	Taste	Comments
Skim milk	Thin	Hollow flavor	Lightweight; needs more taste and texture
Whole milk	Not firm enough	Good flavor; tastes strongly of vanilla	Good, but needs more body
Light cream	Okay	Heavy, fatty taste	Too buttery
Heavy cream	Thick; creamy	Like ice cream	Too rich, but good texture
Half-and-half	Good firm texture	Full flavor; nice	First choice
1 yolk	Not thick enough	Nice flavor; like good ice cream	Very nice flavor, but thin
1 whole egg plus 1 yolk	Rubbery	Raw egg flavor	Leave the egg whites out!
4 yolks	Thick; custardy	Eggy	Too much egg flavor
3 yolks	Thick enough	Custardy	Perfect!
Cornstarch	Thin; watery	Smooth flavor	Thin texture
Cornstarch plus flour	Full mouth feel	Good balance	Works well
Flour	Thick and full	Good flavor when cooked enough	Works as well as the combination above

The first test, as usual with custards, was which type of milk product to use, whether to use whole eggs or just yolks, and which type of thickener was best. The results (see Case 58, "Pastry Cream") were clear. Half-and-half was the liquid of choice (milk made a thin pastry cream; heavy cream was too fatty), 3 egg yolks provided just the right amount of flavor and thickening power, and flour worked nicely and was simpler than a cornstarch-flour combination (cornstarch produces a thinner pastry cream). Egg white in the cream was a disaster, making it rubbery.

I then fiddled with the amount of sugar and discovered that ¼ cup was the right amount. When I tried ½ cup, the pastry cream was so sweet it had an almost painful finish in the mouth. Maple sugar, to my surprise, worked nicely as well, giving the pastry cream a caramel color and a maple cream flavor. Although not appropriate for most applications, this makes a nice variation. I also found that just a pinch of salt is crucial to balance and bring forth the flavors.

I still had a few problems to work out. The first is that the eggs, flour, sugar, and salt need to be whisked until light and fluffy. If this is not done, the final pastry cream will be thin. I found that it is best to accomplish this by hand, right in the saucepan in which the pastry cream will be cooked. Next, I wanted to avoid overcooking the mixture. It's not possible to specify a cooking time and temperature that will work for everyone because stoves and saucepans vary so widely. What is low heat to you might be medium heat to me or vice versa. By whisking constantly, however, this problem is somewhat mitigated. Also, a good visual clue is to watch for steam. Once a pastry cream, or any custard, starts to give off steam, it is getting hot and should be taken off the burner and whisked for 10 to 15 seconds before being put back on again. Finally, flour does have flavor, since it is not a pure starch. Additional cooking once the pastry cream has thickened eliminates the "raw flour" taste.

...

Pastry Cream

This recipe makes a thick, flavorful pastry cream with a deep yellow color and is relatively foolproof. It uses sufficient egg yolks and flour to ensure a thick result (many recipes turn out thin and watery if not prepared just right). Just remember to whisk constantly and watch the custard for steaming.

MAKES ABOUT 1½ CUPS

- 1   cup half-and-half
- 3   large egg yolks
- ¼   cup granulated sugar
- 1½ tablespoons all-purpose flour
- Pinch salt
- 1   teaspoon vanilla extract

1. Heat half-and-half in a small saucepan until it just begins to simmer.

2. Meanwhile, whisk the egg yolks, sugar, flour, and salt in a medium heavy-bottomed saucepan for 1 minute, until light and fluffy. Add about ½ cup of the hot half-and-half to the egg mixture, whisking constantly but gently. When mixed, slowly pour in the remaining half-and-half, whisking slowly to incorporate.

3. Place pan over low heat and, whisking gently but constantly, heat until mixture thickens, 4 to 7 minutes. (Time will vary depending on the stovetop and the saucepan.) Continue whisking gently for an additional 3 minutes, or until mixture loses its floury taste.

4. Strain custard into a small bowl. Add vanilla and stir gently to incorporate. Smooth top with a rubber spatula and place waxed paper directly on the surface of the pastry cream. Refrigerate until needed.

WHAT CAN GO WRONG? The cooking time can vary tremendously, depending on what sort of saucepan and stovetop you are using. Although low heat is called for, if you use too little heat, for fear of curdling the eggs, it may take a very long time for the custard to thicken. Be sure to use a heavy saucepan to avoid hot spots, which can easily overcook part of the custard mixture.

CHOCOLATE VARIATION

Stir 2 ounces of melted semisweet chocolate into the mixture after it has been strained.

COFFEE VARIATION

Dissolve 2 teaspoons instant coffee or espresso powder in 1 tablespoon boiling water. Let cool and then stir into strained custard.

MOCHA VARIATION

Stir 1 ounce melted semisweet chocolate into the coffee variation.

BUTTERSCOTCH VARIATION

Use dark brown sugar instead of white sugar, increase vanilla to 1 tablespoon, and stir 1 teaspoon bourbon and 1 tablespoon soft butter into the strained, warm custard.

PINEAPPLE VARIATION

Replace vanilla with 1 teaspoon lemon juice and add ½ cup well-drained crushed pineapple to the cooked and strained filling.

LEMON VARIATION

Replace vanilla with ½ teaspoon lemon oil (or ¾ teaspoon extract) and add 1 teaspoon grated lemon zest to the cooked and strained filling.

ORANGE VARIATION

Replace vanilla with ½ teaspoon orange oil (or ¾ teaspoon extract) and add 1 teaspoon grated orange zest to the cooked and strained filling.

ZABAGLIONE

ZABAGLIONE CONSISTS OF egg yolks, sugar, and Marsala wine, whisked over simmering water until the mixture lightens and forms soft peaks. It can be eaten as is or used as a sauce for other desserts. Even with but three ingredients, this simple dessert can be tricky, since balance of flavors is crucial. A slight misstep in any direction yields a foam that is not worth eating.

The first test was whether to use whole eggs or just egg yolks. Whole eggs were a disaster, since they curdled easily. I then investigated the ratio of yolks to sugar to wine and discovered that 2½ tablespoons sugar and 4 tablespoons Marsala were best with 4 egg yolks. Other combinations produced a variety of unwelcome outcomes, including a strong eggy flavor, a harsh liquor flavor, and a dessert that was too sweet. Salt was deemed not necessary. I also tested honey instead of sugar and I liked it very much, the zabaglione becoming a little less foamy and richer. Although sugar is the best all-round choice, I would use honey if serving the zabaglione with a sour or strongly flavored dessert, since the assertive taste of honey would marry well with bolder flavors. In addition to using Marsala, I also tested Chambord (raspberry) liqueur, pear juice, orange juice, and white wine. The Chambord and the pear juice were winners, but the orange juice version was too foamy (it tasted like the famous Orange Julius from New York) and lackluster in flavor, and the white wine version tasted yeasty and bitter.

In terms of technique, I also wondered if all of the ingredients should be cooked together or whether the yolks and sugar should be cooked first, adding the Marsala later. It turned out that cooking the ingredients together was best, since this produced a more cohesive foam and the Marsala flavor was less overwhelming. I also tried adding cornstarch to the mixture (in an effort to make the foam more stable), but the flavor was starchy, flat, and bitter, with a grainy texture.

When assembling this simple dessert, make sure that the egg yolks and sugar do not sit for any length of time before whisking and cooking. The yolks will change chemically, resulting in many flecks of hard yolk. Temperature control is also important. The bowl should not touch the simmering water underneath and, unfortunately, the mixture must be whisked constantly. I found that the best method for controlling the heat level was to remove the bowl briefly from the saucepan rather than adjusting the flame.

This provides instant temperature reduction and helps to avoid curdling. The foam is ready when it holds soft peaks and the whisk leaves a trail through the bottom of the bowl. If you like, you can strain zabaglione before serving, but I don't bother. (This will remove any clumps or hard pieces of yolk.) Be aware that zabaglione will not hold for more than 5 or 10 minutes, so it must be served immediately.

▪ ▪ ▪

Zabaglione

You can substitute Chambord (a raspberry liqueur) or pear juice (the liquid from canned pears) for the Marsala. Honey can also be used instead of sugar; this variation has a sweeter, more assertive flavor and goes particularly well with a sour dessert. Zabaglione does not hold well and must be served immediately.

SERVES 2 AS A DESSERT OR 4 IF USED AS A SAUCE

- 4   large egg yolks
- 2½ tablespoons granulated sugar
- ¼   cup Marsala wine (or Chambord liqueur or pear juice from canned pears)

1. Bring 1 inch of water to a simmer in a saucepan wide enough to accommodate your metal or Pyrex mixing bowl. Whisk egg yolks and sugar in the bowl until they are very light, about 2 minutes. Whisk in the Marsala.

2. Place bowl on top of saucepan with simmering water. The bowl must not touch the water. Whisk constantly for 5 to 7 minutes, or until the mixture forms soft peaks and the whisk leaves a trail through the mix. If you see clumps or pieces of hard-cooked yolk in the mixture, strain before serving. Serve immediately in goblets or use as sauce with another dessert.

WHAT CAN GO WRONG? To avoid flecks of yolk in your zabaglione, do not combine the eggs and sugar until you are ready to start cooking. Remember to whisk the mixture constantly once it is over (but not touching) the simmering water, and remove the bowl from over the heat occasionally to avoid overheating.

16

FROZEN DESSERTS

Making frozen desserts at home seems to be a lost art, so lost that the new revision of *Joy of Cooking* did not even include a chapter on this topic. Part of the problem is the ice cream machine. The models that require prechilling the canister in the freezer compartment of your refrigerator often do not work well, since the temperature of your freezer must be very cold — 0 degrees Fahrenheit — for them to work properly. The $200 White Mountain ice cream freezer, the one I prefer, is heavy and bulky, not suited for apartment dwellers. The $400 Simac machine is also wonderful but suffers from the same problems as the White Mountain, plus it is almost prohibitively expensive.

That being said, most of the recipes in this book are relatively easy to make, and the difference between homemade ice cream and store-bought is substantial. You can also easily vary the flavorings in the following recipes, which gives you a wide range of possibilities. Finally, since few home cooks prepare frozen desserts anymore, they have the added advantage of luxuriousness, an unexpected and welcome end to a meal.

Most cooks ask what the difference is between ice cream, gelato, granita, Italian ice, sherbet, sorbet, and frozen yogurt. *Ice cream* and *gelato* are almost the same thing — basically just flavored, frozen egg custards — except gelato has more intense flavors and a lower sugar level. (Many cookbook authors use the term "gelato" broadly, even applying it to recipes that are more sorbet than ice cream. I think of it as ice cream for adults.) Gelatos are most often made with assertive flavors such as hazelnut, coffee, chocolate, or combinations. A *granita* is a combination of water, sugar, and lemon juice, fruit puree, or coffee that is frozen into coarse chunks. An *Italian ice* is pretty much the same thing except that it is processed in an ice cream maker, which produces a finer, softer texture. A *sorbet* should be creamier and smoother than a granita, and this is usually achieved by using a higher proportion of sugar to water, lots of fruit puree, and a bit of alcohol as well to soften the texture. A *sherbet* is often confused with a sorbet. In my experience, however, a sherbet is sorbet made with dairy products, usually milk, although light cream, heavy cream, sour cream, and buttermilk are all possibilities. *Frozen yogurt* is what the name implies: yogurt combined with sugar and flavorings and frozen.

Many frozen desserts are exceedingly simple to make. A strawberry granita is nothing more than a frozen puree of strawberries, sugar, water, and lemon juice. An ice cream is a bit more complicated, since it requires heating a custard on the stovetop first. Here are a few tips I have found useful when preparing frozen desserts:

- It is important to purchase the right type of ice cream machine. There are two things to look for. First, I have found that models with an electric motor for churning are superior. They produce a smoother result. (Hand-cranked machines only mix the contents intermittently, since nobody will stand there for 20 minutes cranking.) I also suggest taking a close look at the size of the bowl or canister. Most models hold 1 quart, but I prefer the larger 1½- to 2-quart models. (If you are going to make ice cream, make a lot of it.) My favorite model is the White Mountain ice cream machine with the electric motor. (There is also a hand-cranked model.) It makes 2 quarts, and although it requires ice and rock salt, both are readily available. The benefit of this machine is that it does not require any prechilling in a home freezer, it can produce a full 2 quarts, and it does an excellent job of freezing, since the ice and freezing water keep the canister very cold. It is not really practical for an apartment dweller since the wooden tub that holds the motor and canister is quite large. The $400 Simac machine also performs well, although is very heavy, very large, and very expensive. It has a built-in freezer unit, which means no ice, no rock salt, and no need to make room in your freezer.
- If you are using a machine with a liner that requires freezing, make sure that your freezer is cold enough. If it does not reach 0 degrees,

you will have trouble. (One common problem making many home freezers too warm is overcrowding, which causes poor air circulation.) I have had only modest luck with these machines. A good trick when using one of them is to chill the custard mixture (or other base) to 40 degrees in the refrigerator, then place it in the freezer for a few minutes until it reaches 38 degrees, and only then put it in the prechilled liner. This will help a great deal.

- When making ice cream or gelato, it is very helpful to have an instant-read thermometer. This will tell you exactly when the custard base is properly cooked.
- Frozen desserts require freezer time after churning to get them to the right texture. They are usually too soft when they come right out of the machine.
- If the frozen ice cream has been left for a long time in the freezer, it is often best to soften it a bit in the refrigerator before serving. Try some first and, if it is too hard, simply place it in the refrigerator for 10 minutes or so.
- Homemade ice cream is best eaten within a day or two of being made. The flavors are fresher and the texture is better.

ICE CREAM

THE PERFECT ICE CREAM is creamy but not too rich, neither icy nor so cream- and egg-laden that it coats the mouth with a heavy film. A great ice cream is the ultimate balancing act between fat and flavor, producing a clean, fresh flavor with enough substance to slide slowly down the back of the throat. I started my investigation by trying all egg yolks versus a combination of whole eggs and yolks. I found that I preferred 1 whole egg plus 2 yolks to just 4 yolks. I also tried different amounts of sugar and determined that ⅔ cup was optimum. This is a slightly lower amount than used in most recipes, but it allows the flavor of the cream and vanilla to shine through. I also used a higher proportion of heavy cream to milk (2 cups cream to 1 cup milk), which made the ice cream richer. Try to avoid ultrapasteurized heavy cream, since it has little flavor. If you can find organic heavy cream (it will probably be pasteurized), this has the sweetest, most complex flavor. Of course, if you can find real unpasteurized heavy cream from a local dairy, then you can experience the real thing, rich, sweet, and full of complex flavor.

...

Master Recipe for Ice Cream

MAKES ABOUT 1 QUART

4-inch piece of vanilla bean
   OR 1½ teaspoons vanilla extract
1   cup whole milk
⅔   cup granulated sugar
2   cups heavy cream
1   large egg plus 2 egg yolks

1. Split the vanilla bean in half lengthwise, scraping both sides with a paring knife. Reserve both the pod and the scrapings. Combine milk, ⅓ cup of the sugar, the heavy cream, and the reserved vanilla pod and scrapings in a heavy saucepan over medium-high heat. (If using vanilla extract, do *not* add it now.) Bring mixture to 175 degrees on an instant-read thermometer, stirring occasionally.

2. Meanwhile, combine the whole egg and egg yolks with the remaining ⅓ cup sugar in a medium bowl and beat with an electric mixer or whisk by hand until pale yellow and thick, about 2 minutes with a mixer or 4 minutes by hand.

3. Remove ½ cup of the hot milk mixture from the saucepan and add slowly to the beaten egg yolks while whisking vigorously. Whisk this mixture back into the saucepan. Over low heat, cook mixture until it reaches 180 degrees, stirring constantly (about 5 minutes). The custard should be the thickness of heavy cream but should not boil or bubble. If the mixture starts to give off a fair amount of steam, take it off the heat for a few moments and stir vigorously. This is a sign that the custard is about to boil.

4. Pour custard through a fine-mesh strainer into a nonreactive bowl. Remove vanilla pod (if using) from strainer and add to mixture. If using vanilla extract, stir it into the custard now. Place bowl into a large bowl filled halfway with ice water to cool. When mixture reaches room temperature, cover bowl with plastic wrap and refrigerate. It is best to refrigerate the custard overnight or for at least 6 hours. (The temperature is less critical if you are using an expensive electric ice cream machine or the old-fashioned models such as White Mountain that depend on ice and rock salt for cooling. However, newer machines with removable liners that are chilled in the freezer cannot successfully make ice cream with a warm custard base.)

5. When mixture is chilled, remove and discard vanilla pod (if using), stir, and place into ice cream machine. Follow manufacturer's directions. When done, transfer ice cream to an airtight container. Freeze until firm, 1 to 2 hours. (The ice cream will still be soft after churning in the machine.)

WHAT CAN GO WRONG? The biggest problem is the use of ice cream machines with removable liners that must be frozen in your freezer. The freezer temperature must be 0 degrees Fahrenheit to make this work efficiently. (One of my freezers was 11 degrees and the machine never worked. Other neighbors tested their freezers and most were in the 5- to 7-degree range.) That's why I recommend the White Mountain system, since it avoids this problem completely. The other common problem is that home cooks are often not patient enough to properly cool the custard base before churning. Try chilling it to 40 degrees in the refrigerator and then putting it in the freezer to chill to 38 degrees before you put it in your ice cream machine.

CHOCOLATE CHIP VARIATION

Add 3 ounces chopped semisweet chocolate (or chocolate chips) 1 minute before churning is completed.

OREO COOKIE VARIATION

Add 1 cup coarsely crumbled Oreo cookies 1 minute before churning is completed.

CHOCOLATE VARIATION

Increase sugar to 1 cup, adding ¾ cup to the milk mixture and the balance to the eggs. Beat ⅓ cup unsweetened cocoa powder into the whipped egg mixture (step 2).

COFFEE VARIATION

Stir 3 tablespoons of instant coffee or espresso powder into the milk mixture before heating.

▪▪▪

Burnt Sugar Ice Cream

Although this sounds like an odd recipe, it is one of the best in the book. It is a simple variation on the master recipe.

MAKES ABOUT 1 QUART

4-inch piece of vanilla bean
   OR 1½ teaspoons vanilla extract
1 cup whole milk
1 cup granulated sugar
2 cups heavy cream
1 large egg plus 2 egg yolks

1. Split the vanilla bean in half lengthwise, scraping both sides with a paring knife. Reserve both the pod and the scrapings. Combine milk, ¼ cup of the sugar, the heavy cream, and the reserved vanilla pod and scrapings in a heavy saucepan over medium-high heat. (If using vanilla extract, do *not* add it now.) Bring mixture to 175 degrees on an instant-read thermometer, stirring occasionally.

2. Meanwhile, combine the whole egg and egg yolks with ¼ cup of the sugar in a medium bowl and beat with an electric mixer or whisk by hand until pale yellow and thick, about 2 minutes with a mixer or 4 minutes by hand.

3. Remove ½ cup of the hot milk mixture from the saucepan and add slowly to the beaten egg yolks while whisking vigorously. Whisk this mixture back into the saucepan. Over low heat, cook mixture until it reaches 180 degrees, stirring constantly (about 5 minutes). The custard should be the thickness of heavy cream but should not boil or bubble. If the mixture starts to give off a fair amount of steam, take it off the heat for a few moments and stir vigorously. This is a sign that the custard is about to boil.

4. Combine the remaining ½ cup sugar with ¼ cup water in a heavy saucepan over medium heat. Do not stir but swirl the pan frequently until the sugar dissolves. Increase heat to high and bring syrup to a boil. Cover and cook for 2 minutes. Uncover pan and continue to cook until the syrup begins to take on color. Swirl pan constantly at this point, moving pan on and off heat as you work so syrup doesn't darken too quickly. Remove from heat when syrup is dark and mahogany-colored. Pour into the custard mixture and stir to combine.

5. Pour custard through a fine-mesh strainer into a nonreactive bowl. Remove vanilla pod (if using) from strainer and add to mixture. If using vanilla extract, stir it into the custard now. Place bowl into a large bowl filled halfway with ice water to cool. When mixture reaches room temperature, cover bowl with plastic wrap and refrigerate. It is best to refrigerate the custard overnight or for at least 6 hours. (The temperature is less critical if you are using an expensive electric ice cream machine or the old-fashioned models such as White Mountain that depend on

ice and rock salt for cooling. However, newer machines with removable liners that are chilled in the freezer cannot successfully make ice cream with a warm custard base.)

6. When mixture is chilled, remove and discard vanilla pod (if using), stir, and place into ice cream machine. Follow manufacturer's directions. When done, transfer ice cream to an airtight container. Freeze until firm, 1 to 2 hours. (The ice cream will still be soft after churning in the machine.)

WHAT CAN GO WRONG? Aside from the usual problems associated with freezer temperature and insufficiently cooled custard (see master recipe above), the only tricky part is making the caramel sauce. Remember that once the sugar syrup starts to take on color, it will darken quickly, so swirl the syrup in the pan, removing the pan from the heat for a few seconds at a time as you work. You also do not want a really light syrup here — this is *burnt* sugar ice cream — so go for a rich, deep mahogany instead of a honey-colored syrup.

FRESH BERRY ICE CREAM

THE PROBLEM WITH fruit ice cream is that the flavor of the fruit usually gets lost. The pieces are frozen and icy and they are easily overwhelmed by the sugar, dairy, and eggs. The question I set out to answer was, how do you taste the fruit and not just the ice cream?

I started by testing my Master Recipe for Ice Cream (page 349) as a base for fresh fruit ice cream and the rich texture and flavor simply overwhelmed the delicate fruit. I therefore reduced the fat level to produce a fresher, livelier flavor, using less heavy cream and more milk. I also tried to reduce the number of eggs, but I found that when made with only 2 whole eggs, the ice cream became very icy and airy and had little flavor. I determined, after much experimentation,

that 4 yolks were best, especially when paired with milk and only ¼ cup heavy cream. Although this sort of ice cream is a bit icier than the smoother master recipe, I find it more refreshing and in keeping with the notion of fruit ice cream.

The biggest problem, however, was the fruit. Simply adding fresh strawberries to ice cream resulted in chunks of frozen, icy fruit with little flavor. At *Cook's Illustrated*, we tried briefly cooking the fruit, which did add a lot of flavor and also reduced the moisture content. However, in my opinion, the fruit lost some of its fresh taste. In further testing, I discovered that mixing the fruit with sugar and lemon juice and then letting the mixture sit overnight did the trick. The berries became infused with the sugar syrup, which made them turn less icy when chilled with the ice cream. In addition, 1 tablespoon of liqueur helped to reduce iciness further. Although most of my testing was done with strawberries, raspberries and blackberries also work nicely. Pureeing half the fruit and adding it to the ice cream base boosted the fruit flavor a great deal. The rest of the fruit was then added near the end of the freezing process.

Fresh Berry Ice Cream

MAKES ABOUT 1 QUART

1 pint strawberries (washed, hulled, cut into quarters lengthwise, and sliced into ¼-inch slices, about 3 cups) OR 1 pint whole blackberries or raspberries (washed)
½ teaspoon lemon juice
1 cup granulated sugar
1 tablespoon Grand Marnier or other liqueur
2 cups minus 2 tablespoons whole milk
¼ cup heavy cream
4 large egg yolks
1 teaspoon vanilla extract

1. In a medium bowl, combine the prepared fruit, lemon juice, and ⅓ cup of the sugar. Let

stand, stirring occasionally, until the sugar is dissolved and a syrupy liquid forms in the bowl. Add the liqueur and refrigerate for several hours or overnight, until the berries have absorbed the liquid and are soft and cold.

2. Position a fine sieve over a medium bowl that has been set in an ice water bath. Set aside. Heat milk, cream, and ⅓ cup of the sugar in a medium-size heavy saucepan over medium-high heat until steam appears, 5 to 6 minutes. Turn off heat.

3. Meanwhile, whisk the egg yolks with the remaining ⅓ cup sugar in a medium bowl until just combined. Do not overmix, which creates excess foam. Stir half of the warmed milk into the beaten yolks until just blended. Return this mixture to the saucepan containing the rest of the milk. Over medium-low heat, stir mixture constantly until it reaches 180 degrees on an instant-read thermometer. Steam should appear, the foam should subside, and the mixture should just begin to thicken. Do not let the mixture boil or the egg yolks will curdle. Remove from heat and immediately strain custard into the chilled bowl set in the water bath. Stir in the vanilla. Cool custard mixture to room temperature and then cover and refrigerate at least 4 hours or overnight. (The temperature is less critical if you are using an expensive electric ice cream machine or the old-fashioned models such as White Mountain that depend on ice and rock salt for cooling. However, newer machines with removable liners that are chilled in the freezer cannot successfully make ice cream with a warm custard base.)

4. Meanwhile, strain the liquid from the chilled berries. Puree half the berries in a blender or food processor. Add the puree to the chilled custard and pour into an ice cream freezer. Follow manufacturer's directions. When the ice cream is the consistency of soft-serve ice cream, 25 to 30 minutes, add the remaining berries and allow to mix 2 minutes longer. Transfer ice cream to an airtight container. Freeze until firm, 1 to 2 hours.

WHAT CAN GO WRONG? This recipe has the same potential problems as the Master Recipe for Ice Cream (page 349). Be sure to use ripe, flavorful fruit.

GELATO

IN THE HUNT FOR the perfect gelato, I started off with a simple question. What is it? Unfortunately, the recipes I reviewed indicated that gelato was something between a sorbet and a particularly rich ice cream. No two recipes were alike. Some, including a strawberry gelato from Marcella Hazan, used no eggs whatsoever; others used milk and eggs; and still others used cream and eggs. In the end, I decided that gelato is nothing more than the Italian word for ice cream, with one twist — the flavors are intense, much more so than with American ice cream, which is mildly flavored by comparison.

The major issue to be resolved was how to make the custard base. I started with a simple recipe that called for cream and sugar, no eggs at all. I found this gelato to be too icy, as I did a second recipe, which used just milk and sugar. These tasted more like a sherbet to me than a rich gelato. Deciding that eggs were an important component, I then tried a recipe from the Time-Life cookbook series which used 2 cups each of heavy cream and light cream mixed with 8 egg yolks and only 6 tablespoons of sugar (about half as much as other recipes). I found this recipe to be a bit fatty, with an unpleasant waxy aftertaste. I also noted that the recipe suggested adding the heavy cream just before freezing, without any cooking. In my opinion, this contributed to the problem. The good news is that I liked the lower sugar level, a clear departure from American-style ice cream. However, I needed to cut the richness and bump up the flavor.

My next test was to make a gelato using all milk and no cream whatsoever. This was an improvement, but I finally settled on a 1-to-1 ratio

CASE 59: YOU SAY GELATO

What sort of custard base makes the best gelato?

Custard Ingredients	Cooked or Uncooked	Result
Cream only, no eggs	Uncooked custard	Icy, not custardy
Milk only, no eggs	Uncooked custard	Icy and watery when warmed for serving
Milk only, 6 yolks	Cooked custard	Gluey texture
Heavy cream, light cream, 8 yolks	Cooked custard	Waxy aftertaste
2 parts milk, 1 part heavy cream, 4 yolks	Cooked custard	Thin texture
1 part milk, 1 part heavy cream, 4 yolks	Cooked custard	Perfect texture and flavor

of milk to heavy cream as preferable. I then reduced the egg yolks to just 1 yolk per cup of liquid (down from 2 yolks in the Time-Life recipe), which helped to lighten the texture and improve the aftertaste. I also ditched the notion of adding unheated cream to the custard just before freezing — heating all of the cream with the milk solved the problem of the filmy coat-your-tongue texture.

I wanted to make a coffee gelato, so next I turned to the coffee flavor. To give this gelato a strong coffee jolt, I used ¼ cup espresso beans and a tablespoon of instant espresso powder. Testing revealed that it was best to lightly crush the coffee beans and then steep them in the scalded milk mixture. For a truly intense experience, I added some of the crushed beans to the custard before freezing. I also ended up adding

a strip of lemon zest and a bit of vanilla extract as well. Now I had both the perfect texture and a strong coffee flavor, true to the notion of an authentic Italian gelato.

▪▪▪

Coffee Gelato

Gelato is an intensely flavored ice cream that has a lower percentage of sugar than traditional American recipes. If using the standard ice cream maker with a removable bowl, make absolutely sure that the custard mixture reaches 38 degrees before putting it in the machine. This will require a short stay in the freezer after a long chilling period in the refrigerator to cool down the cooked custard base. To crush the coffee beans, place them in a plastic storage bag

*on a cutting board and whack them gently with
the bottom of a saucepan.*

SERVES 6

1½ cups whole milk
1½ cups heavy cream
2-inch strip lemon zest
 ¼ cup espresso-roasted coffee beans, lightly
    crushed
 1 tablespoon instant espresso powder
 4 large egg yolks
 6 tablespoons granulated sugar
 ½ teaspoon vanilla extract

1. Combine the milk, cream, lemon zest,
crushed espresso beans, and espresso powder in
a large saucepan over medium heat. Bring just
to a simmer, being careful not to let the mixture
boil. Remove from heat and allow the coffee
beans to steep for 20 to 30 minutes. Meanwhile, in a heavy bowl beat the egg yolks and
sugar together with a whisk (or use an electric
mixer) until the mixture is pale, thick, and falls
in ribbons when the whisk is lifted, about 2 to 3
minutes.

2. Return the milk to the stove and heat to
175 degrees on an instant-read thermometer.
(This is below a simmer. A small amount of
steam should start rising from the surface.) Reduce the heat to very low. Add about ½ cup of
the hot milk to the yolks in a thin stream, stirring constantly until well blended. Transfer the
yolk mixture to the saucepan and raise the heat
to medium. (The mixture will cool down a bit
due to the addition of the yolk mixture.) Cook
the custard, stirring constantly, but do not allow it to boil or it will curdle. Heat until custard
reaches 180 degrees. Reduce heat if custard
threatens to boil. Remove from heat and strain
into a bowl, allowing some of the coffee bean
particles to fall into the custard if you wish. Stir
in the vanilla.

3. Cool to room temperature, cover, and chill
until the mixture reaches 38 to 40 degrees,
preferably overnight. This may require a short

spell in the freezer, 10 to 15 minutes, to get the
mixture down to 38 degrees. (This step is unnecessary if you are using an expensive electric
machine, such as Simac, which has a built-in
freezer unit.) Churn in an ice cream maker, following manufacturer's directions. Transfer to
an airtight container and freeze until firm.

WHAT CAN GO WRONG? As with all ice cream,
make sure that the custard mixture reaches 38
degrees before putting it in the ice cream maker.

▪▪▪

Hazelnut Gelato

*N*ow *that I had a master recipe, I wanted to
test it using hazelnuts, a classic Italian gelato
flavor that is both distinctive and delicious. I replaced the coffee beans with double-toasted,
skinned, ground hazelnuts, and replaced the
vanilla with Frangelico, a hazelnut liqueur. As
with the coffee beans, I did not strain the milk
before combining it with the egg yolks in the
saucepan, but I soon discovered that I should
have. Much of the thickened custard clung to
the ground nuts, reducing the volume of churn-
able custard considerably, and a significant
amount of the more finely ground hazelnuts
slipped through the strainer, giving the gelato a
slightly grainy, muddy texture. This problem
was easily rectified by coarsely chopping the
hazelnuts instead of grinding them.*

SERVES 6

 2 cups hazelnuts
1½ cups whole milk
1½ cups heavy cream
2-inch strip lemon zest
 4 large egg yolks
 6 tablespoons granulated sugar
 2 tablespoons hazelnut liqueur (e.g.,
    Frangelico)

1. Toast the hazelnuts on a baking sheet in a
375-degree oven for 7 to 10 minutes, until they

are fragrant and starting to brown, and then rub them in a kitchen towel to remove the skins. Coarsely chop. (Finely chopped nuts will muddy the texture of the gelato.) Place back in oven and toast again until browned, another 4 to 5 minutes.

2. Combine the milk, cream, lemon zest, and chopped nuts in a large saucepan over medium heat. Bring just to a simmer, being careful not to let the mixture boil. Remove from heat and allow the nuts to steep for 20 to 30 minutes. Strain to remove nuts. Meanwhile, in a heavy bowl beat the egg yolks and sugar together with a whisk (or use an electric mixer) until the mixture is pale, thick, and falls in ribbons when the whisk is lifted, 2 to 3 minutes.

3. Return the milk to the stove and heat to 175 degrees on an instant-read thermometer. (This is below a simmer. A small amount of steam should start rising from the surface.) Reduce the heat to very low. Add about ½ cup of the hot milk to the yolks in a thin stream, stirring constantly until well blended. Transfer the yolk mixture to the saucepan and raise the heat to medium. (The mixture will cool down a bit due to the addition of the yolk mixture.) Cook the custard, stirring constantly, but do not allow it to boil or it will curdle. Heat until custard reaches 180 degrees. Reduce heat if custard threatens to boil. Remove from heat and strain into a bowl. Stir in the liqueur.

4. Cool to room temperature, cover, and chill until the mixture reaches 38 to 40 degrees, preferably overnight. This may require a short spell in the freezer, 10 to 15 minutes, to get the mixture down to 38 degrees. (This step is unnecessary if you are using an expensive electric machine, such as Simac, which has a built-in freezer unit.) Churn in an ice cream maker, following manufacturer's directions. Transfer to an airtight container and freeze until firm.

WHAT CAN GO WRONG? Be sure to coarsely chop the hazelnuts; finely chopped nuts produce a slightly grainy, muddy texture. And, of course, make sure the custard mixture is sufficiently chilled before putting it in the ice cream maker.

GRANITA

A GRANITA IS a frozen mixture of sugar, water, and a liquid flavoring (such as lemon juice, fruit puree, coffee, or even wine). It is a relatively coarse frozen dessert because, instead of being churned in an ice cream machine, it is simply placed in the freezer compartment of the refrigerator in a shallow pan and then stirred and scraped every 20 minutes or so until it achieves the proper consistency, which can take 2 to 3 hours. (An Italian ice is, as far as I can tell, the same thing as a granita except that is has been churned in an ice cream freezer, not simply frozen into a coarse ice.) Although simple in concept, granitas turn out to be relatively complicated and involve a bit of mathematics in order to achieve the perfect balance of sweet and tart (in the case of fruit granitas) and a texture that is icy and on the grainy side of smooth (*granita* means "grained" or "grainy").

I decided to start with a basic lemon granita. The first major issue to be decided was sugar content. Recipes I checked ranged from 15 percent sugar concentration by weight up to 25 percent. Further reading turned up research by Harold McGee, the well-known food scientist and author of *On Food and Cooking*, who states that granitas should have a 15 to 20 percent concentration, although he notes that anything less than 25 percent severely reduces the "scoopability" of the dessert. Since I favored a slightly softer dessert, I tried the higher percentage, 20 percent, which produced a grainy but not flaky texture. The added benefit of this higher proportion of sugar is that the granita can be held overnight and, after a bit of thawing and additional stirring and scraping, can be served the next day. (This cannot be done with

Testing the relative ratios of lemon juice, water, and sugar in granitas.

Lemon Juice	Sugar	Water	Comments
1 cup	½ cup	1¼ cups	Tart, coarse, grainy
1 cup	1 cup	1¼ cups	Too sweet, too tart, too soft
1 cup	1 cup	1 cup	Too sweet, too tart; needs more water
½ cup	½ cup	1½ cups	Great balance of sweet and tart; not too grainy and not too soft

most traditional granitas.) It does lose a bit of its freshness in flavor and snap in the texture, but it is still quite good.

The next issue was the ratio of lemon juice to water. Lemon granitas are often too bitter, which means that the sugar level has to be upped, which makes them both bitter and sweet at the same time. After testing, I found the correct balance, the point at which the acidity of the lemon was held in check. In fact, I ended up using only ½ cup each of lemon juice and sugar to 1½ cups of water. This was surprising, since other recipes use half as much water. However, it made the granita light and refreshing, rather than a heavy, sweet slush with a bitter undercurrent.

Another issue was the use of a food processor. In a *Cook's Illustrated* article it was determined that one could freeze the granita, throw it into a food processor, and then serve it. This did work well, but I did not object to the old-fashioned method of checking the freezer every half hour or so. I found that the window was fairly broad for stirring and scraping, from 15 to 30 minutes, so it didn't matter if one was pre-

cise in one's timing. In addition, I am usually in the kitchen for at least 2 hours when cooking for company, the sort of occasion where I would indeed make a granita. However, you can follow the master recipe below, freeze the mixture, and then simply break it up in the food processor when you are ready to serve.

I also wanted to test the issue of whether it was necessary to boil the sugar and water together to dissolve the sugar. Most older recipes suggest that this is an important step. However, I discovered that I could not tell the difference if I simply stirred the sugar into the lemon juice and water without cooking. So why use an extra pan?

In addition to lemon, I tested other granita flavorings and preferred lime, strawberry, and pineapple, since they are strong and distinctive.

■ ■ ■

Master Recipe for Granita

A lemon granita is probably the best approach for this simple, grainy, refreshing dessert. You could substitute a dry white wine for some of the water, but if you use a sweet wine, such as a dessert wine, you would have to cut back on the sugar level to compensate. Champagne works well.

SERVES 3 TO 4

½ cup lemon juice (2 to 3 lemons)
½ cup granulated sugar
1½ cups water

In a large glass measuring cup or pitcher, combine all ingredients and stir well to dissolve the sugar. (This will take up to 2 minutes.) Pour the mixture into a shallow pan or dish and freeze, stirring once after 45 minutes and every 20 minutes or so thereafter. Scrape bottom and sides of pan too, to help mixture freeze evenly. When done, the mixture will be frozen but slightly mushy, about 2 to 3 hours total.

WHAT CAN GO WRONG? If you do not stir the granita as it freezes, scraping sides and bottom of pan, it will not have the proper texture. You can, however, simply freeze it and then use a food processor to churn it into pieces. This avoids the stirring.

∎∎∎

Strawberry Granita

*M*ake sure that you are using strawberries that taste as good as they look. Flavorless berries produce a lousy granita.

SERVES 3 TO 4

1½ cups hulled, washed, and halved
     strawberries
7 tablespoons granulated sugar
2 tablespoons lemon juice
¾ cup water

Puree the strawberries in a food processor, which should yield about 1 cup of puree. In a large glass measuring cup or pitcher, combine all ingredients, including the strawberry puree,

and stir well to dissolve the sugar. (This will take up to 2 minutes.) Pour the mixture into a shallow pan or dish and freeze, stirring once after 45 minutes and every 20 minutes or so thereafter. Scrape bottom and sides of pan too, to help mixture freeze evenly. When done, the mixture will be frozen but slightly mushy, about 2 to 3 hours total.

∎∎∎

Lemon Italian Ice

A granita and an Italian ice are pretty much the same thing, except that the ice has been churned in an ice cream freezer, whereas the granita has been frozen into coarser chunks. This ice must be served immediately, since it will turn hard if stored in the freezer.

SERVES 4

½ cup fresh lemon juice
½ cup granulated sugar
1¼ cups water
1 tablespoon vodka
2 teaspoons grated lemon zest

Combine all ingredients in a large glass measuring cup or pitcher. Stir until the sugar has completely dissolved. Chill until the mixture reaches 40 degrees, then transfer to the freezer until the temperature drops to 38 degrees, about 10 minutes more. (This step is unnecessary if you are using an expensive electric machine, such as Simac, which has a built-in freezer unit.) Transfer to an ice cream machine and churn following manufacturer's directions. Serve immediately, directly from the ice cream machine.

WHAT CAN GO WRONG? If using a liner-style ice cream machine, check your freezer temperature before starting — it must go down to 0 degrees — and I would also make sure to get the mixture down to 38 degrees before transferring to the ice cream maker. This will require time in the refrigerator, as well as a short stay in the freezer.

⁂

FRUIT SORBETS

A GRANITA IS A dessert ice with a coarse, granular texture, whereas a sorbet should be softer to the palate. Not only should a sorbet have a creamy texture when it comes from the ice cream freezer, it should also retain this desirable texture after having been frozen for some time. I have found that many recipes are great at the just-frozen point but lose their appeal and become more like a coarse granita after a brief stay in the freezer.

The problem in making fruit sorbets is how to achieve this texture. The ingredients are simple enough: fruit juice and/or pulp, sugar, water, and citrus juice (usually lemon). The first major variable is the amount of sugar. Harold McGee has done a great deal of research into frozen ices and determined that recipes with 15 to 20 percent sugar, which he refers to as "medium-sweet ices," are best served as soon as they are made, since they will harden in the freezer. If, however, one makes a sorbet with 30 percent or more sugar, then the dessert is still somewhat soft after freezing. The problem with just adding more sugar is that the sorbet is unpleasantly sweet. I wanted to solve the problem of texture using other methods.

The first thought I had was that fruit pulp contains pectin which, according to McGee, "interferes with water crystallization, forcing the crystals apart and lubricating them." I tested this idea with strawberries and found that, indeed, the sorbet had a softer texture than one made simply with juice, such as a lemon ice. I also found that the pectin in the strawberries reduced the puddling that often occurs during the brief thawing period that is used to soften up sorbet before serving.

So far, so good. But I was still unhappy with the recipe, seeking out a creamier texture and a bit more flavor. I thought that a touch of alcohol would help with texture, since it raises the freezing temperature, so I tried adding 1 tablespoon of vodka, which worked well, intensifying the flavors. However, I still felt that the strawberry flavor was a bit weak. I read that Madeleine Kamman, a well-known cooking teacher and author, raves about using fruit preserves in her sorbet recipes. The reason? Preserves have a lot of pectin in them, they are packed with flavor since the fruit has been concentrated through cooking, and they also contain a high percentage of sugar. I then made the strawberry sorbet recipe again, substituting 3 tablespoons of strained, good-quality strawberry preserves for ¼ cup of the sugar. The result was excellent — creamy texture straight from the freezer and vibrant strawberry flavor, without the sugary aftertaste. At the height of a fruit's season, I imagine the preserves would have less impact on flavor; but in early May, when most of us are using big, beautiful, tasteless California strawberries, preserves are essential. I suggest adding preserves of the same fruit, or a complementary one, to high-pectin sorbets, to boost the flavor and improve the texture.

So now I had perfected sorbet using fruit puree, sugar, vodka, lemon juice, and fruit preserves. It was smooth, creamy, intense, and retained its soft texture even when frozen. This recipe could be used for strawberries, pineapple, mango, papaya, plums, peaches, or any other fruit that has usable pulp. (The higher the pectin content of the fruit, the better. Less ripe fruit has more pectin, although less flavor, than riper specimens.)

But using pulp and preserves was not going to work for citrus fruits such as lemon, lime, or orange. Achieving a creamy texture, even with a lemon sorbet, wasn't the problem; the real issue was making a creamy citrus sorbet that wasn't too sweet. I started with a recipe from *Cook's Illustrated* — a lemon sorbet — that produced

CASE 61: A SOFTER SORBET

Vodka, fruit preserves, egg whites, sugar levels, and lemon curd are tested for their effect on the texture of fruit sorbets.

Ingredient	Comments
Sugar	Higher sugar levels make smoother sorbets but leave unpleasant aftertaste
Fruit puree	Produces better texture and flavor
Fruit preserves	Intensifies flavors and adds pectin for smoother texture
Alcohol	Increases freezing point for a softer sorbet; doubling quantity did not seem to help
Foamed egg whites	Produced an airy, unpleasant texture

a lovely rind-flecked, pale yellow dessert that was creamy right from the freezer, with good acidity — but oh, so sweet. Without the benefit of lemon jam, I reviewed the other texture enhancers suggested by various sources: gelatin, corn syrup, alcohol, and egg whites. I rejected gelatin as being too difficult, since I was not making a sugar syrup or heating any part of the mix, and several sources noted that it produces a gummy texture. Corn syrup seemed like an inferior substitute for honey or jam, and the *Cook's* article noted that it masks fruit flavor. I considered strained orange marmalade, but I didn't want to alter the lemon flavor. I knew alcohol had potential, and egg whites were an interesting option that came up in several sources.

As with the strawberry sorbet, the addition of vodka did help with both the texture and flavor. Adding foamed egg whites, as some cookbooks suggest, just before churning was not successful. The sorbet never set, presumably be-

cause the egg whites raised the temperature of the sorbet mixture above 40 degrees. I repeated the effort, chilling the mix to 35 degrees before adding the egg white, and the mixture set. Rather than being creamy, however, the texture was snowy, and the sorbet was very pale in color and lacking in flavor.

I was reluctantly coming to the conclusion that sugar truly was the key to creamy citrus sorbets, but I still had one more idea. I added 2 tablespoons of lemon curd to the mixture before freezing. While I knew it wouldn't add pectin in the same way preserves would, I hoped that its thickened, custardy texture would enrich the sorbet. The result was disappointing: snowy, pale, and lacking in flavor.

At this point, I conceded to the sugar theory. I returned to the *Cook's Illustrated* recipe, performing one last test. I reduced the sugar by 2 tablespoons and increased the vodka by 1 tablespoon. Neither the flavor nor the texture improved by this change, so for citrus sorbets, the *Cook's Illustrated* recipe is as good as it gets.

•••

Master Recipe for Sorbet with Fruit Puree

This recipe works with any fruit that can be made into a usable puree, such as strawberries, pineapple, apricot, peaches, plums, et cetera. Note that fruit with little flavor will produce a dull sorbet. If you do not have a preserve that matches the fruit, use a complementary flavor. Cherry or plum works well with strawberry, apricot can be used with peaches, and so on. Note that you will need to use more than 2 cups of fruit to produce 2 cups of puree. Many cooks suggest that the fruit puree and preserves be strained, but I find this to be an annoying and unnecessary extra step. If you make this recipe with strawberries, which I recommend, you will need about 13 ounces of fruit.

SERVES 4

2	cups fruit puree (2 to 3 cups fruit processed with ½ cup water)
¾	cup granulated sugar
1½	tablespoons lemon juice
1	tablespoon vodka
3	tablespoons high-quality strawberry preserves

Combine all ingredients in a large glass measuring cup or pitcher. Stir until the sugar has completely dissolved. Chill until the mixture reaches 40 degrees, then transfer to the freezer until the temperature drops to 38 degrees, about 10 minutes more. (This step is unnecessary if you are using an expensive electric machine, such as Simac, which has a built-in freezer unit.) Transfer to an ice cream machine and churn following manufacturer's directions. Scoop into a plastic container, seal well, and transfer to the freezer for several hours. If sor-

bet is hard to scoop, let sit at room temperature for several minutes to soften.

WHAT CAN GO WRONG? The keys to success are to use great fruit and chill the mixture to 38 degrees before churning.

•••

Master Recipe for Citrus Sorbet

This recipe is designed for lemon, lime, or orange ice, although it is most often made with lemon. It is sweeter than the prior recipe, since the extra sugar is necessary to keep the sorbet creamy and soft.

SERVES 4

½	cup fresh citrus juice, preferably lemon
1½	cups water
1¼	cups granulated sugar
1	tablespoon vodka
2	teaspoons grated zest (lemon, lime, or orange)

Combine all ingredients in a large glass measuring cup or pitcher. Stir until the sugar has completely dissolved. Chill until the mixture reaches 40 degrees, then transfer to the freezer until the temperature drops to 38 degrees, about 10 minutes more. (This step is unnecessary if you are using an expensive electric machine, such as Simac, which has a built-in freezer unit.) Transfer to an ice cream machine and churn following manufacturer's directions. Scoop into a plastic container, seal well, and transfer to the freezer for several hours before serving. If sorbet is hard to scoop, let sit at room temperature for several minutes to soften.

WHAT CAN GO WRONG? This recipe is as easy as it gets. Just heed my advice elsewhere in this chapter about ice cream machines with removable liners. Your freezer needs to be at 0 degrees for them to work properly. It is worth using a freezer thermometer to make sure yours is cold enough before attempting any frozen dessert.

SHERBET

THE FIRST PROBLEM WITH sherbet is trying to define it. My definition is simple — sherbet is sorbet with dairy products (usually milk, although light cream, heavy cream, sour cream, and buttermilk are all possibilities). Now, Julia Child would disagree with me, saying that "sorbet and sherbet are one and the same. . . . Sorbet is contemporary cuisine chic-speak," while other cooks such as Shirley Corriher would concur with my simple definition. The only other common additive that cooks often associate with sherbet is egg whites. I have tested the use of egg whites with sorbets and found them to be useless, producing a light, not very flavorful ice. However, I did come across a recipe in *James Beard's American Cookery* that called for stiffly beaten egg whites that are folded into a partially frozen base. Since I had only tested foamed egg whites added to the base before freezing, I decided to give this recipe a try. The result was disappointing: crumbly and grainy straight from the machine; hard, icy, and not very flavorful after freezing. I then tried a variation on this recipe, one suggested by a fellow cookbook author, which was to add ½ cup whole milk. This was also disappointing, resulting in snowy, fine flakes, which more than doubled in volume after churning. It was icy and very bland; the milk diluted the flavor and did nothing to improve the texture.

The next step, in order to concentrate flavors and improve the texture, was to replace 1 cup of the water in the sorbet recipe with an equal amount of milk rather than to simply add milk. This worked well, producing a creamier, more intense sherbet. I still wanted a more intense flavor, so I did more research and uncovered a tip from Julia Child, who suggested processing lemon or lime zest with half the sugar in a food processor, a technique that boosted the flavor significantly as a result of the release of the citrus oils.

I was left with only one question, which was why did the milk not curdle when added to the lemon juice? According to one source, the sugar buffers the cream so that it does not curdle. Rather, it thickens when the lemon juice is added. A scientist at the University of Massachusetts thought that the amount of lemon juice was insufficient to cause significant curdling, and that any curdling that might take place would end up being dispersed in the network of ice crystals. He went on to say that this small amount of curdling would actually assist in the gelling process, giving the sherbet a creamier texture.

▪ ▪ ▪

Master Recipe for Citrus Sherbet

Sherbet is a sorbet with the addition of milk. This recipe can be made with either lemon or lime juice and zest. This sherbet has a bright citrus flavor, not too rich or sweet, and a creamy texture (scoopable directly from the freezer), with just a hint of iciness that lightens the texture. You don't have to process the sugar and zest together, but the sugar will dissolve faster if you do. Instead, the zest can be grated directly into the sugar–lemon juice mixture. Be sure to use fresh *lemon or lime juice, as bottled juice will give the sherbet a harsh, unpleasant flavor.*

SERVES 4

½   cup fresh lemon or lime juice
½   cup water
2   tablespoons vodka
1   cup granulated sugar
Zest from 1 large lemon or lime, removed
    with a vegetable peeler in strips
1   cup very cold whole milk

1. In a large glass measuring cup or pitcher, combine the lemon juice, water, and vodka. Process the sugar and zest in a processor, using on/off turns, until the zest is finely chopped. Add to the lemon juice mixture and stir until the sugar is completely dissolved and the mixture is syrupy.

2. Chill until the mixture reaches 40 degrees, then transfer to the freezer if necessary to bring the temperature down to 38 degrees, about 10 minutes more. (This step is unnecessary if you are using an expensive electric machine, such as Simac, which has a built-in freezer unit.) Add the milk and stir well to combine. Transfer the mixture to an ice cream machine and churn following manufacturer's directions. Scoop into a plastic container, seal well, and transfer to the freezer for several hours.

WHAT CAN GO WRONG? If using a liner-style ice cream machine, check your freezer temperature before starting — it must go down to 0 degrees — and I would also make sure to get the sherbet mixture down to 38 degrees before transferring to the ice cream maker. This will require time in the refrigerator, as well as a short stay in the freezer.

▾

SHERBETS WITH FRUIT PUREES

WHEN I STARTED to develop a recipe for sherbet using fruit puree, I went back to the Master Recipe for Sorbet with Fruit Puree (page 360) as a template. In order to turn this recipe into a successful sherbet, I discovered, an increase in the amount of alcohol and lemon juice was necessary, as well as the elimination of the water and the addition, of course, of milk, the signature ingredient in a sherbet. (The sorbet recipe calls for ½ cup water instead of milk.) This concentrated the flavors nicely. I did find, however, since sherbets are less intense than sorbets, that the quality of the fruit was crucial. In addition,

I found that it was useful to taste the mixture before freezing to adjust the amount of lemon juice, sugar or honey, alcohol, and preserves. I had made a mango sorbet that was a bit dull — the mangoes were not totally ripe — and determined that it needed more assistance from the other ingredients, unlike a strawberry sherbet that was made with just-picked, luscious fruit.

The variations for this recipe include cantaloupe, strawberry, and mango. I found that each fruit required slightly different proportions of ingredients (see variations below). A small amount of honey makes a nice addition to sherbet, giving it a deeper, smoother flavor. Although most sherbets are best served the day they are made, this recipe produced a dessert that could be frozen and then served days later. The sherbet will be a bit icier but still relatively smooth.

•••

Master Recipe for Sherbet with Pureed Fruit

It is a good idea to taste the mixture before chilling it, adjusting the sugar, honey or preserves, lemon juice, and alcohol if necessary. Underripe or dull fruit makes a lousy sherbet, so don't bother. Feel free to try just about any sort of alcohol you like, including a flavored brandy. Note that many of the ingredients are listed in ranges. Specific quantities are listed in the variations that follow the master recipe.

SERVES 4 TO 6

2	cups pureed fruit
¾	cup granulated sugar
2 to 3	tablespoons lemon or lime juice
2	tablespoons vodka or light rum
1 to 3	tablespoons good-quality preserves or honey
1 to 1¼ cups very cold whole milk	

1. Combine the fruit puree with the sugar, lemon juice, vodka, and 1 tablespoon of pre-

serves in the bowl of a food processor and process until the sugar is dissolved and the mixture is syrupy. Taste the mixture, adjusting the sweetness to taste by blending in lemon juice or preserves as needed. If using berries and/or preserves, you may wish to strain to remove the seeds and any pieces of unblended fruit. However, I find this unnecessary, since chunks of fruit or preserves simply add to the texture.

2. Chill until the mixture reaches 40 degrees, then transfer to the freezer if necessary to bring the temperature down to 38 degrees, about 10 minutes more. (This step is unnecessary if you are using an expensive electric machine, such as Simac, which has a built-in freezer unit.) Add the milk and stir well to combine. Transfer the mixture to an ice cream machine and churn following manufacturer's directions. Serve immediately, or scoop into a plastic container, seal well, and transfer to the freezer for 2 hours to firm. (Most home ice cream machines cannot get the mixture cold enough to serve immediately. A short stay in the freezer is usually advisable to firm up the texture.)

WHAT CAN GO WRONG? If using a liner-style ice cream machine, check your freezer temperature before starting — it must go down to 0 degrees — and I would also make sure to get the sherbet mixture down to 38 degrees before transferring to the ice cream maker. This will require a short stay in the freezer, as well as time in the refrigerator.

CANTALOUPE VARIATION

Use 4 cups of cubed melon, which will yield about 2 cups puree. Add 3 tablespoons lime juice, 2 tablespoons vodka, 1 to 2 tablespoons honey, and 1 cup milk.

MANGO VARIATION

Use 3 cups cubed mango to yield 2 cups puree. Add 3 tablespoons lemon or lime juice, 2 tablespoons light rum, 1¼ cups milk. Honey may not be necessary.

STRAWBERRY VARIATION

Use 4 cups whole berries to yield about 2 cups puree. Add 2 tablespoons lemon juice, 2 tablespoons vodka or light rum, 3 tablespoons strawberry preserves, and 1¼ cups milk.

FROZEN YOGURT

THE FIRST QUESTION I had to ask about frozen yogurt was "Why?" Ice cream is clearly superior from most perspectives, so why bother at all? This is no health cookbook, so I would not include a low-fat recipe simply as a matter of saving calories. However, I finally decided that the tangy, slightly sour taste of yogurt is simply different from ice cream and, for many people, is desirable. Perhaps the best answer to "Why?" is that frozen yogurt is so easy to make. A few ingredients are mixed together and then frozen. There is no stirring, no custard, no pots and pans to clean, and no long chilling period. Nothing could be easier.

My objective, then, was to determine how to make frozen yogurt with the smooth, creamy texture of ice cream but the distinctively tangy flavor of yogurt. As with other dairy-based frozen desserts, the base flavor for the master recipe would be vanilla. Out of idle curiosity, I began my testing by trying to freeze vanilla yogurt straight from the container, to see how it would freeze. The 3.5 percent fat Colombo French Vanilla was somewhat icy, and definitely not sweet enough on its own. Yoplait Custard Style Vanilla Yogurt was not sweet enough either, but had a better texture, thanks to its added cornstarch and gelatin, which were somewhat noticeable in the finished product. I also tried low-fat yogurts; these provided more flavor but were too icy. In any case, vanilla-flavored yogurt has potential as a recipe base, but neither brand made an acceptable dessert on its own. Now I had to start work on a frozen

CASE 62: MIXING IT UP WITH YOGURTS

Which style of yogurt makes the best frozen yogurt?

Yogurt	Other Ingredients	Comments
2 cups nonfat plain	½ cup honey, ½ cup milk, vanilla	Icy; honey overpowering
1 cup nonfat plain	½ cup sugar, vanilla	Creamier than first test, but still icy; flavor improved
1 cup whole plain	½ cup sugar, scraped vanilla bean	Creamy and good texture; vanilla flavor too strong
½ cup whole plain plus ½ cup nonfat vanilla	6 tablespoons sugar	Vanilla flavor weak; texture okay
1 cup whole plain	½ cup superfine sugar, vanilla, 1 tablespoon corn syrup	Good texture, but a little too sweet
1 cup low-fat vanilla	None	Not sweet enough for a dessert
1 cup whole plain	¼ cup sugar, vanilla, 1 tablespoon corn syrup	Excellent texture and flavor
1 cup nonfat plain	Same as above	More tang, but texture suffers; needs whole yogurt
1 cup low-fat vanilla	Same as above	Too sweet; cloying
1 cup whole plain	¼ cup sugar, vanilla, corn syrup, strawberries	Very good, but better when left at room temperature before serving
1 cup whole plain	¼ cup sugar, vanilla, 1 tablespoon corn syrup	This was left to sit before freezing; improved flavor
1 cup custard-style, low-fat vanilla	None	Not sweet enough for a dessert

yogurt recipe using unflavored store-bought yo-gurts to which I would add my own flavorings.

I considered four factors: the fat content of the yogurt, the type and amount of sweetener, the source of the vanilla flavoring, and other added ingredients. Since most store-bought frozen yogurts are fat-free, I began with nonfat yogurt; but I quickly realized that whole-milk yogurt offered far better texture. For sweetener, granulated sugar was best. Honey left a pro-nounced aftertaste, and while superfine sugar dissolved more quickly into the yogurt base, it wasn't necessary, since the regular sugar dis-solved completely after a short time. I liked the flavor of purchased vanilla yogurt better than my own extract or bean versions, but I did not want to rely on it for my master recipe, since it is hard to find vanilla-flavored full-fat yogurt in the supermarket. The only additional ingredi-ents I opted for were corn syrup, which im-proved the texture of the finished product, and strawberries, which I tested at the end to see if the master recipe would stand up to a variation.

Now that I had the components figured out, the issue was proportion. I was working with a recipe using 2 cups of unflavored yogurt that was combined with sugar, vanilla, and corn syrup in a glass measuring cup, stirred well, and then left to sit for 5 minutes to completely dis-solve the sugar. I then poured the mixture into an ice cream machine, churned for 20 minutes, and then froze the yogurt in a plastic container for 2 hours. My first alteration was to reduce the amount of sugar to ¼ cup to cut the sweet-ness and then increase the corn syrup to 1 ta-blespoon, which slightly improved the texture, making it a bit smoother and less icy. The result was very creamy, not overly sweet, and just a little tangy.

I then wondered if using vanilla-flavored yo-gurt would be an improvement. Since flavored whole-milk yogurts are hard to find, I used Colombo low-fat vanilla and the result was overly sweet, with an overpowering vanilla fla-vor. To see if the master recipe would stand up

to variation, I tried it with strawberries: I blended strawberries and sugar in a processor until fairly smooth, then added the strawberry mixture to the yogurt, corn syrup, and vanilla, churned 25 minutes, and froze 2 hours. The re-sult was pale pink, with red flecks and good strawberry flavor. The texture was very light but a little icy. The only odd thing was that even though the strawberries were very sweet and ripe, the yogurt tasted less sweet than the vanilla version. The following day, I left the frozen yogurt at room temperature for 1 hour, checking the texture at 15-minute increments. After an hour, the texture was rich, smooth, and creamy, not icy at all. As the strawberry bits melted, they brightened the flavor of the yogurt substantially.

Additional testing revealed that allowing the strawberry yogurt to sit in the refrigerator for a while before freezing heightened flavors. (I came across this discovery by accident since my freezer bowl was not cold enough and the yo-gurt had to be held in the refrigerator for a few hours.)

▪ ▪ ▪

Master Recipe for Frozen Yogurt

The beauty of this recipe is its simplicity. Only four ingredients are mixed together and then churned in an ice cream freezer. I recommend using whole yogurt; the low-fat varieties tend to get icy.

SERVES 4

2 cups whole-milk plain yogurt (use low-fat yogurt only as a last resort)
½ cup granulated sugar
1 teaspoon vanilla extract
2 tablespoons corn syrup

In a large glass measuring cup or pitcher, combine the yogurt, sugar, vanilla, and corn syrup. Stir well to combine. Let the mixture stand for 5 minutes until the sugar is completely dissolved. Pour into an electric ice cream machine and churn following manufacturer's directions. When the yogurt is frozen but still soft (20 to 30 minutes), transfer it to an airtight plastic container and freeze until firm, about 2 hours.

WHAT CAN GO WRONG? Not much. Just make sure that your freezer is cold enough for ice cream machines with a removable liner. (The freezer should be at 0 degrees, not 5 to 10 degrees, for success.)

STRAWBERRY VARIATION

In a food processor, blend 4 cups of strawberries and 1 tablespoon rum with the sugar until smooth. Combine with the remaining ingredients and let stand 30 minutes before proceeding as above. Let the yogurt stand at room temperature for 1 hour (or several hours in the refrigerator) before serving.

17

RESTAURANT DESSERTS
AT HOME

Once in a while, I come across restaurant desserts that have the look and taste of a classic and also appear to be worth translating to the home kitchen. This chapter is devoted to those desserts, the sort one might make for a special occasion.

The process of translating restaurant recipes to the home requires a bit of explanation. I began by making the recipe exactly as it was given to me by the restaurant, adjusting for the number of servings. However, whenever a recipe utilized a basic dessert recipe that had been tested elsewhere in this book, I then tested it a second time, reverting to my version but modifying it by adding components or flavorings as called for by the restaurant version.

This process led me to a simple observation. Restaurant desserts are packed with cream, eggs, and colossal amounts of sugar, the sort of desserts one would never seriously consider for home consumption. When we go out to dine, we are happily ignorant of the recipe details, and a celebratory mood often overtakes our normal instinct for self-regulation. Offering these recipes in print for home use, however, requires that they

undergo a good deal of slimming down, especially in cases where I think that the slightly less sweet or less fatty versions are actually better. A chocolate banana bread pudding is served with both an intensely sweet caramel sauce and a chocolate sauce at Fog City Diner in San Francisco, but this excess seems out of place for home dining. In fact, I prefer this excellent pudding as is, without the sauces. Nevertheless, I leave the reader with the option of going overboard, providing variations or additional complementary recipes whenever possible.

You will note that this chapter does not have a wide range of offerings. In fact, a high percentage of the recipes that follow are flavored with either lemon or chocolate. For better or worse, these are the desserts that are found most often on restaurant menus, and therefore this selection is representative. I want to thank all of the pastry chefs who were so kind as to let me play with their recipes at home, not improving them, but simply adapting them to the more limited resources of us home cooks. I also want to thank Jean-Georges Vongerichten, who was kind enough to help me develop the recipe for fallen chocolate cake, another restaurant favorite, on page 160.

WARM CHOCOLATE BROWNIE CUSTARD WITH MARSALA CREAM SAUCE

(adapted from Tra Vigne, Napa Valley, California)

TRA VIGNE SERVES SUBLIME California cuisine, which means incredibly fresh ingredients served with a complete lack of fear of the culinary unknown. The centerpiece of this dessert, the brownie custard, is common enough these days in restaurants, but the original recipe also called for a Marsala butterscotch sauce flavored with bay leaves and freshly ground black pepper. I made the recipe and served it to my family, who loved the custard but found the butterscotch sauce a bit over the top. However, the flavorings were interesting, so I adapted the recipe to a simple heavy cream reduction, which complements the brownie custard and is considerably less sweet. Of course, this recipe can be baked and then served with either whipped cream or a splash of heavy cream.

I found the brownie custard recipe to be simple enough as received from the pastry chef, and so testing was limited. I tried both semisweet and unsweetened chocolate and preferred the latter. Most of us are stuck with a limited selection of unsweetened baking chocolates — Baker's being the most common — but Baker's worked out fine when tested. A better-quality chocolate would of course make for a richer flavor. I tried both large and small ramekins for this recipe and stuck with the smaller 6-ounce size — this is a rich dessert, and a small serving is more than satisfying.

You don't want to underbake this dessert, because it will not hold its shape when unmolded. Also, if baked correctly, the top (which becomes the bottom when unmolded) will form a nice crust, which adds texture to the dessert.

Warm Chocolate Brownie Custard with Marsala Cream Sauce

*T*he sauce is rather simple to make and dresses up what would be a pretty straightforward dessert. For simpler occasions, the brownie custard can be served with a splash of heavy cream or with whipped cream.

SERVES 6

1 cup heavy cream
4 tablespoons (½ stick) unsalted butter
3 ounces unsweetened chocolate, finely chopped
¾ cup granulated sugar
3 tablespoons cornstarch
¼ teaspoon cinnamon
¼ teaspoon salt
2 large eggs

Optional Garnishes
Marsala Cream Sauce (see below)
Fresh raspberries
Unsweetened whipped cream

1. Heat oven to 350 degrees. Lightly butter six 6-ounce custard cups. In a small heavy-bottomed saucepan over medium heat, bring the cream and butter to a boil. Remove from heat and stir in the chocolate until completely melted and smooth, up to 15 minutes.

2. Sift the sugar, cornstarch, cinnamon, and salt onto waxed paper. In a large bowl, whisk the eggs together and then whisk in the dry ingredients until the mixture is very smooth and thick, about 20 seconds. Gradually whisk the chocolate mixture into the eggs, beating constantly. Strain into a large measuring cup or pitcher and divide the custard between the buttered custard cups, filling each half to two-thirds full.

3. Bake until the custards are just set, 25 to 30 minutes. Let stand 5 minutes, and loosen sides with a butter knife if necessary.

4. To serve, puddle a few spoonfuls of warm Marsala Cream Sauce onto each dessert plate. Unmold a custard onto the center of each plate and garnish with a few fresh raspberries or unsweetened whipped cream.

WHAT CAN GO WRONG? As with any custard, the trick is knowing when the custard is done. The center should be not quite set, as it will firm up during cooling. You may find that not all of the individual custards will cook at the same rate, some being ready before others.

Marsala Cream Sauce

The original sauce was a Marsala butterscotch sauce, but it was deemed too sweet, even by my nine-year-old. This cream-based sauce goes nicely with the brownie custard and is quite easy to make.

MAKES ABOUT 2 CUPS

½   cup Marsala wine
2   cups heavy cream
½   cup packed dark brown sugar
2   tablespoons unsalted butter
3   bay leaves

In a medium saucepan, reduce (boil) the Marsala to ¼ cup. Add the remaining ingredients, bring to a boil, and simmer for 5 minutes, or until you have about 2 cups of sauce. Watch mixture carefully and stir frequently. The cream can boil over easily. Remove bay leaves and serve chilled.

BANANA CHOCOLATE BREAD PUDDING

(adapted from Fog City Diner, San Francisco)

THIS IS A CLASSIC Fog City Diner recipe — deeply satisfying to the point of being overwhelming. The restaurant is the brainchild of

Cindy Pawlcyn, who also founded a number of other highly successful San Francisco area eateries including Tra Vigne and Mustard's. Fog City is an eclectic American diner, and this recipe is a good example of Cindy's exuberant, full-flavored offerings. Unlike Tra Vigne, which targets a more sophisticated palate, Fog City hits you right between the eyes with big, bold flavors.

At its core this recipe is actually quite simple. It is a chocolate banana bread pudding served on a pool of caramel sauce, drizzled with orange-flavored chocolate sauce, and garnished with seasoned pecans and whipped cream. Take away the sauces and the nuts and you have a quick and easy dessert.

The original called for using real vanilla beans for flavor, but this required heating and then cooling the cream, which made the recipe fussy and time-consuming. I skipped the bean and went for vanilla extract. Real vanilla beans are only worthwhile in recipes in which vanilla is the predominant flavor, and this recipe is over the top with the flavors of banana, chocolate, and caramel. For the bread, the original called for brioche, but I substituted challah, which is more readily available. If you can find neither, use a firm-textured white bread — a rustic white bread works well, but avoid sourdough. The recipe also called for baking the pudding with a buttered piece of parchment paper on top and covered with aluminum foil. At first I thought that this step would be unnecessary, but after many tests, I preferred this approach, since the pudding turned out creamier and more tender. With these simple modifications, the recipe now took just a few minutes to throw together and pop into the oven. The combination of bread, pudding, melted chocolate, and banana is outstanding and not overly sweet.

As for the sauces, you can skip them entirely, although they are easy to make. If you are only going to prepare one of them, I would opt for the caramel sauce, since the pudding already contains chocolate. The original recipe calls for serving the pudding on a pool of caramel sauce. I tried this and found the result to be a bit too sweet. Instead, I would drizzle the pudding lightly with caramel sauce for just a hint of sweetness. I decided to skip the nuts entirely. This is fine for a restaurant, but sugaring and frying pecans in peanut oil is a bit too involved for a home cook.

...

Banana Chocolate Bread Pudding

This is a simple dessert to make — one of the easiest in this book — and the balance of banana, chocolate, custard, and bread flavors is outstanding. The parchment paper cover really does make for a better, more delicate texture, even though it is an extra step.

SERVES 8 TO 10

6	cups 1-inch bread cubes (challah or rustic white bread, crusts removed)
4	ounces semisweet chocolate, chopped
7	large egg yolks
¾	cup granulated sugar
2	cups heavy cream
2	teaspoons vanilla extract
2	cups whole milk
2	ripe bananas

Caramel and/or Chocolate Sauce for drizzling (optional; see below)

1. Heat oven to 325 degrees. Place about 4 cups of the bread into the bottom of a casserole that is approximately 8 x 11 inches with 4-inch-high sides. Sprinkle the chocolate on top of the bread and then cover with the remaining bread.

2. Whisk the egg yolks with the sugar for 1 minute and then whisk in the cream, vanilla extract, and milk. Place the peeled bananas into the bowl of a food processor and pulse to mash. Add 1 cup of the cream mixture and process 15 to 20 seconds, or until completely smooth. Scrape down the sides of the processor bowl if necessary.

3. Whisk the pureed bananas back into the cream mixture and then pour over the bread and chocolate in the baking dish. Press bread down with a rubber spatula to soak. Let stand for 10 minutes to allow bread to soak up liquids, submerging bread three or four times more.

4. Place a piece of buttered parchment paper directly on top of the pudding and then cover casserole with aluminum foil. Place in oven and bake for about 40 minutes. Remove paper and foil and bake another 40 to 45 minutes, or until the top is nicely browned and the pudding puffs up a bit. The pudding will jiggle at the very center but otherwise be firm, not loose.

5. Let stand out of the oven for 20 minutes before serving. This bread pudding can be served as is or drizzled with a small amount of either or both of the sauces below. Too much sauce will overpower the pudding.

WHAT CAN GO WRONG? The problem here is one of over- or undercooking. If baked too long, the pudding will become dry and grainy; if undercooked, however, it will be very loose, almost like a milk shake. The pudding should be set — though it will still jiggle a bit in the center — and should puff up a bit around the sides.

OPTIONAL CARAMEL SAUCE

Combine 3 tablespoons unsalted butter, ½ cup packed light brown sugar, ½ cup packed dark brown sugar, and ⅔ cup light corn syrup in a saucepan. Bring to a rolling boil, stirring to melt the sugar. (Sauce will darken as it cooks.) Stir in ⅔ cup heavy cream, return to the boil, then remove from heat. Cool until sauce is thickened and just slightly warm, which will take 15 to 20 minutes. Makes about 2 cups

OPTIONAL CHOCOLATE SAUCE

Combine 6 ounces semisweet chocolate, cut in chunks; 6 tablespoons unsalted butter; 1½ tablespoons brandy; 2 teaspoons triple sec; and ½ cup light corn syrup in a saucepan over low heat. When the chocolate softens, remove from heat and whisk the ingredients together. When the mixture is smooth, stir in ½ cup heavy cream. Makes about 1½ cups.

PANNA COTTA WITH STRAWBERRIES TOSSED WITH BALSAMIC VINEGAR

(adapted from Tra Vigne, Napa Valley, California)

A TRADITIONAL PANNA COTTA IS usually a Bavarian cream without the whipped cream, but the original recipe for this dish was more like a pot de crème — creamy, rich, and puddinglike. Using all heavy cream and a very high proportion of egg yolks to liquid, I found the baked custard difficult to unmold from the ramekins, since the texture was so creamy. In order to lighten this dessert somewhat, I adapted my recipe for crème caramel (without the sugar syrup), which uses a lower proportion of eggs to liquid, uses whole eggs and yolks, and calls for an even mix of milk and light cream. The custard is served with strawberries tossed in vinegar. The original recipe called for a mango vinegar, but I switched it to balsamic, which is more readily available and tastes just fine.

▪ ▪ ▪

Panna Cotta with Strawberries Tossed with Balsamic Vinegar

The use of cinnamon and ginger in the custard is unusual but fantastic — it takes a simple recipe and makes it special. You can also serve this custard right in the ramekins without the strawberries for a simple dessert.

SERVES 4

For the Custard

1½ cups whole milk
1½ cups light cream or half-and-half
1   cup granulated sugar
⅛   teaspoon salt
1   teaspoon vanilla extract
¾   teaspoon cinnamon
½   teaspoon ground ginger
3   large eggs
3   large egg yolks

For the Strawberries

1   pint strawberries, washed, hulled, and sliced
1   teaspoon balsamic vinegar
Coarsely ground black pepper

1. Heat the oven to 325 degrees. Put a kettle of water on to boil. Lightly butter six 6-ounce custard cups and place them on a kitchen towel in a roasting pan, making sure they do not touch each other or the sides of the pan.

2. In a small saucepan, stir the milk, cream, sugar, and salt together over medium heat until the sugar is dissolved and the mixture reaches 140 degrees on an instant-read thermometer. (It should be very hot but not yet at a simmer.) Whisk in the vanilla, cinnamon, and ginger, and remove from heat.

3. Beat the whole eggs and yolks to blend in a large bowl. Gradually add the hot cream mixture, whisking constantly. Strain into a large glass measuring cup or pitcher. (Some of the cinnamon will be left behind in the strainer — this is okay.) Pour the custard mixture into the prepared custard cups, then pour boiling water into the roasting pan until it comes two-thirds of the way up the sides of the ramekins. Bake until the custards are set, 40 to 50 minutes. They should be barely set in the center, but do not underbake, since they have to be unmolded when cold. Remove from water bath to cool to room temperature, then chill until cold.

4. To serve, slip a butter knife around the edge of each custard to loosen, then invert onto individual plates. Surround each serving with sliced strawberries that have been tossed at the last minute with balsamic vinegar and a dash of coarsely ground pepper.

WHAT CAN GO WRONG? Here, you do want to make sure that the custard is completely set before taking it from the oven; otherwise it will be hard to unmold. It is crucial to butter the ramekins, since the custard will be impossible to unmold if you don't.

CHOCOLATE CRÈME BRÛLÉE

(adapted from Pinot Bistro, Los Angeles)

THIS IS A PRETTY STRAIGHTFORWARD chocolate crème brûlée recipe, but it needed some streamlining in order to make it accessible to the home cook. (The original recipe called for 85 egg yolks and 2 gallons of cream!) When I developed a recipe for crème brûlée (see page 329), I found that melting the sugar topping was very difficult at home — broilers heat unevenly, resulting in cracked, overcooked custard and burned sugar. So I opted for topping the custards with a caramel syrup. For this recipe, I found that the custard was fine without the topping, served warm, neither hot nor at room temperature. If, however, you are adventurous, you can try the brûlée method at home, although I had very mixed results with this in my kitchen.

I played with light cream versus heavy cream and stayed with the latter. I substituted vanilla extract for vanilla beans and melted the chocolate directly into the hot cream mixture to help simplify the recipe. I find that turbinado sugar, which is often called raw sugar or sold under the label Sugar in the Raw, works best as a topping for the broiling. Don't use brown sugar, which is hard to sprinkle evenly.

• • •

Chocolate Crème Brûlée

SERVES 6

½ cup whole milk
1½ cups heavy cream
½ cup granulated sugar
4 ounces semisweet or bittersweet chocolate, finely chopped
4 large egg yolks
1 teaspoon vanilla extract
6 teaspoons turbinado sugar (optional)

1. Heat oven to 325 degrees. Place six 6-ounce ramekins on a kitchen towel in a roasting pan just large enough to hold them without touching each other. Boil a pot or kettle of water.

2. In a medium saucepan, bring the milk, cream, and ¼ cup of the granulated sugar to a boil. Remove from heat and whisk in the chopped chocolate until melted. Combine the egg yolks, remaining ¼ cup granulated sugar, and vanilla in a 4-cup glass measuring cup or pitcher. Slowly whisk about half the warm chocolate mixture into the egg yolks, stirring constantly. Whisk the egg mixture into the remaining warm chocolate mixture in the saucepan. Pour the custard back into the measuring cup through a fine-mesh strainer, then pour mixture evenly into the 6 ramekins. Pour hot water into the roasting pan until it comes two-thirds of the way up the sides of the ramekins.

3. Bake until custards are set but still quiver in the center when gently shaken, about 45 minutes. The cooking time will vary depending on the size of your roasting pan and your oven. Remove from the water bath and let cool. Serve warm or at room temperature.

4. If you want to make this a showpiece restaurant dessert, you can try the brûlée method. At serving time, evenly sprinkle the surface of each custard with 1 teaspoon of turbinado sugar and broil. Note that broilers do not heat evenly and you must watch this step very carefully; some custards cook much more quickly than others. I also found that it is best not to place the ramekins too close to the broiler; otherwise, the sugar will burn quickly.

WHAT CAN GO WRONG? Deciding when to remove custards from the oven is always tricky.

Keep in mind that they will continue cooking outside the oven, so they should still be not quite set in the center. The broiling step just before serving is very difficult, since broilers do not cook evenly. You will need to watch this extremely carefully, removing some of the custard cups before others. This is a terrible time to take a phone call! You can also ruin the custard during this step, reducing it to a liquid if the ramekins heat up too much in the process. If the custard does get overheated, let it cool in the refrigerator to regain its texture. (To avoid these problems, you could try my "mock" brûlée method — see next recipe, step 5.)

the bottom of the ramekin, since the lemon curd was already there. Instead, I reverted to my "mock" crème brûlée approach, which is to pour a thin layer of caramel sauce on top of the baked custard. This worked very well. Now I had a layer of lemon curd on the bottom, a thick layer of custard, and a very thin layer of crackly caramel on top.

For the custard itself, I went back to my master recipe for crème caramel (page 326), which was slightly different from the Aqua recipe. Although the original custard called for vanilla flavoring, I decided to use an orange liqueur, as I thought it would work better with the lemon curd.

LEMON CURD CRÈME BRÛLÉE

(adapted from Aqua, San Francisco)

So MANY OF THE FANCY restaurant recipes these days are crèmes brûlées, and this is one of the more interesting variations. The original recipe is quite complicated and is served at Aqua in San Francisco as Lemon Curd Crème Caramel. It is a crème caramel that is assembled in layers with baked phyllo dough and topped with quenelles of whipped cream and a plum compote. The dessert is simply beyond the time or skills of most of us home cooks. However, the notion of combining a lemon curd with a custard was interesting, so I set out to develop a recipe that worked at home.

The first step was to eliminate the phyllo and compote. That left a lemon curd and a custard. I also wanted to serve this dessert in the ramekins rather than unmolding, which can be tricky, so I thought that I would begin by making a lemon curd and placing it in the bottom of the ramekins. This worked, but only after I discovered that the curd needs to chill thoroughly before adding the hot custard mixture, otherwise it starts floating to the top.

Next, I decided not to use a caramel sauce in

Lemon Curd Crème Brûlée

To make this recipe a bit simpler, forget about the caramel coating; the recipe is fine without it. However, for a special occasion, the extra layer of crackling caramel does add a special touch.

SERVES 6 TO 8

For the Lemon Curd

  2 large egg yolks
  2 large eggs
  6 tablespoons granulated sugar
  Zest of 2 lemons, finely chopped
  ½ cup lemon juice
  ¼ cup crème fraîche OR ¼ cup whipping cream
    mixed with 1 tablespoon buttermilk
  8 tablespoons (1 stick) unsalted butter, cut
    into 1-tablespoon pieces

For the Custard

  1½ cups whole milk
  1½ cups light cream or half-and-half
  3 large eggs
  3 large egg yolks
  ⅓ cup granulated sugar
  ⅛ teaspoon salt
  1 teaspoon orange-flavored liqueur

For the Caramel Topping

½ cup granulated sugar

¼ cup water

1. *For the lemon curd:* In a medium saucepan, whisk together the yolks, eggs, sugar, zest, and lemon juice. Heat over very low heat, stirring constantly, until the mixture is thick enough to mound in the pan. (It should be the texture of pudding.) Remove from heat and add all the crème fraîche and then the butter, one-third at a time. Stir after each addition, then continue stirring to melt the butter. Strain through a fine sieve into a bowl, cover tightly, and chill at least 6 hours or overnight.

2. *For the custard:* Heat the milk and cream in a heavy saucepan. In a large bowl, gently whisk together the eggs, yolks, sugar, and salt until just combined. Try not to incorporate air as you work. When the milk mixture starts to steam, pour about ½ cup of it into the eggs and whisk gently to combine. Slowly add the rest of the hot milk, stirring gently with the whisk. Add the liqueur. Strain into a large measuring cup or pitcher. Refrigerate until cold.

3. Heat oven to 350 degrees. Place a thin kitchen towel or paper towels evenly over the bottom of a roasting pan large enough to accommodate the ramekins. Place eight 6-ounce flat-bottomed ramekins (or six 9-ounce ramekins) on top, making sure that they do not touch each other or the sides of the pan.

4. Spread a heaping tablespoon of lemon curd in the bottom of each ramekin. Pour the chilled custard over the lemon curd, filling each ramekin three-quarters full. Pour hot tap water into the roasting pan until it comes two-thirds of the way up the sides of the ramekins. Cover pan loosely with a sheet of aluminum foil and bake until the custards are set but still quiver in the center when gently shaken, 40 to 50 minutes. Remove from the water bath and let cool to room temperature.

5. *For the caramel syrup:* Place water and sugar in a heavy saucepan over medium heat.

Do not stir, but swirl the pan frequently until the sugar dissolves. Increase heat to high and bring syrup to a boil. Cover and cook for 2 minutes. Uncover pan and cook until syrup begins to take on color. (After about 3 minutes, the syrup will froth and bubble. After about 8 minutes, it will start to darken quickly.) Swirl pan constantly, taking pan on and off the heat as you work so the syrup does not darken too quickly. Remove pan from heat when the syrup is light mahogany in color. Be careful. Once the syrup starts to darken, it will change color rapidly. It will also continue to darken off the heat. Pour a *thin layer* of syrup into one ramekin at a time, swirling each cup to completely cover the custard. It is best to add the syrup all at once to each custard cup for an even top layer. The syrup hardens very quickly. If you add it in batches, the top surface will be uneven in both thickness and color.

WHAT CAN GO WRONG? Make sure that the lemon curd is well chilled before adding the custard mixture; otherwise it tends to float to the top of the custard cup. The sugar syrup is optional, but if you do make it, keep in mind that once the syrup starts to darken, it will turn color very quickly. I take the saucepan off the heat as soon as I see the color change, swirl the contents a few times, and then put it back on the stovetop. I continue this process of removing the pan and swirling the sugar syrup until I get the color I want. It is easy to overcook the syrup, which can become almost black and very bitter.

SOUFFLÉED LEMON CUSTARD
(adapted from Hamersley's Bistro, Boston)

HAMERSLEY'S IS BOTH my neighborhood restaurant and, in my opinion, the best all-round restaurant in Boston. This is one of their signature desserts, and although it takes some work, it is sublime and can be made well ahead of time. It reminds me a bit of a pudding cake, but it is richer, smoother, and more sophisticated. When I tested the original recipe, I liked the balance between the lemon juice and sugar, but I thought that there was too much of both. I reduced the sugar to a little less than 1¼ cups from 1½ cups and the lemon juice to ¾ cup from 1 cup and liked the results. It still had plenty of sweetness, but it wasn't overpowering.

This recipe is best made in a 10-inch cake pan. I tried a springform pan, but unless you line it properly with aluminum foil (see page 180), it will leak, since it must sit in a water bath. If you use a different size pan, it will dramatically affect the cooking time, and the custard may end up undercooked in the center if the pan is smaller.

· · ·

Souffléed Lemon Custard

This dessert will not rise very much, and the top will be fairly sturdy, much like a light cake, when it is ready to come out of the oven. The top should, however, be well browned. This recipe can be served at room temperature, so it can be made well ahead of time.

SERVES 8

8 tablespoons (1 stick) unsalted butter, softened but still firm
1¼ cups granulated sugar
6 large egg yolks, at room temperature
¾ cup lemon juice (3 to 4 lemons' worth)
⅔ cup all-purpose flour, sifted
1 tablespoon finely chopped lemon zest
⅛ teaspoon salt
2 cups whole milk
1 cup heavy cream
6 large egg whites, at room temperature
¼ teaspoon cream of tartar

1. Heat oven to 350 degrees. Bring kettle of water to a boil. Make sure that you have a 10-inch cake pan and a roasting pan large enough to accommodate it.

2. Beat the butter and all but 1 tablespoon of the sugar until fluffy, about 3 to 4 minutes in an electric mixer. Add the 6 egg yolks, one at a time, beating 20 seconds after each addition.

3. Mix in the lemon juice, flour, zest, and salt on low speed for 10 seconds. Scrape the bowl and mix another 5 seconds. Fold ingredients together by hand with a large rubber spatula to finish. Gently whisk in the milk and cream until smooth.

4. Beat the egg whites with the cream of tartar for 30 seconds and then gradually add the remaining 1 tablespoon sugar. Beat until the whites hold soft 2-inch peaks. Fold whites into the custard mixture. Pour into a 10-inch cake pan that has been set into a roasting pan. Pour the hot water around the cake pan until it comes halfway up the sides. Place roasting pan in oven and bake about 50 minutes, or until custard is just set in the middle. Turn pan halfway through cooking and check custard for doneness at 40 minutes.

5. Remove pan from water bath to cool and serve at room temperature. (Use a large serving spoon to ladle out individual portions.)

WHAT CAN GO WRONG? The biggest problem with this recipe is getting the right size cake pan. You really do need a 10-inch pan, and a springform pan will probably leak unless properly lined with foil. Smaller cake pans will not hold the batter.

ALMOND CAKE WITH RED WINE–POACHED PEARS

(adapted from the Gotham Bar and Grill, New York)

THE RECIPE AS SERVED at the Gotham Bar and Grill combines poached pears, a granita made with the poaching liquid, and almond cake. I was interested in the notion of making a frozen ice out of the same liquid used to poach the pears but thought that it would be a bit too much work for the home cook, so I dropped this part of the recipe. However, out of curiosity I did test throwing the liquid into an ice cream freezer; it worked well enough, but I found that the flavor of vanilla ice cream was a better partner with the pears and cake than the sorbet, which tasted just like the pears. Since you can use store-bought ice cream, this also greatly simplifies the recipe.

I tested the restaurant's recipe for the almond cake and found it a bit greasy, so I cut back on the butter. The recipe also called for almond flour — an ingredient that no home cook has in his or her pantry — so I substituted toasted ground almonds instead, plus a small amount of almond extract. Generally speaking, I am not a fan of almond extract, but the nuts alone were insufficient to lend enough almond taste. I played with a variety of pan sizes so that I would end up with squares of cake that would nicely match the poached pear halves. I ended up with a 9 x 13-inch pan, which is a common size, and which yielded six large pieces.

* * *

Almond Cake with Red Wine–Poached Pears

This is not a particularly difficult recipe but is quite elegant. The reduced poaching liquid is outstanding with the pear and cake, and don't forget some high-quality store-bought vanilla ice cream.

SERVES 6

For the Poached Pears

3	ripe Bartlett pears
1	cinnamon stick
½	vanilla bean
½	tablespoon grated lemon zest
½	tablespoon grated orange zest
1½	cups orange juice
3½	cups cabernet sauvignon
¾	cup granulated sugar

For the Almond Cake

10	tablespoons (1¼ sticks) unsalted butter, at room temperature
½	cup granulated sugar
⅔	cup blanched almonds, toasted and finely ground
2	large eggs
½	teaspoon almond extract
1	cup all-purpose flour
½	teaspoon baking powder
½	teaspoon baking soda
½	teaspoon salt
½	teaspoon cinnamon
⅔	cup sour cream
2	tablespoons slivered almonds
	Vanilla ice cream for serving

1. *For the poached pears:* Peel the pears and then halve them end-to-end. Remove the core from each half using a melon baller or a 1-teaspoon measuring spoon. Place the pears in a small saucepan and add the remaining ingredients. Partially cover the pan, bring to a simmer, and poach the pears gently for 1 hour. Cool the pears in the poaching liquid overnight. Be sure to reserve poaching liquid.

2. *For the almond cake:* Heat oven to 350 degrees. Lightly grease a 9 x 13-inch pan and line the bottom with parchment paper. Cream the butter and sugar until fluffy. Add the ground almonds. Add the eggs, one at a time, and the almond extract, beating well after each addition. Combine the dry ingredients and add to the batter, mixing well. Fold in the sour cream and pour the batter into the prepared pan, smoothing the surface with a spatula. Sprinkle slivered almonds over top of batter. Bake until the cake is golden brown and starts to pull away from the sides of the pan, about 30 minutes. Cool in the pan 5 minutes, then invert onto a rack to cool completely.

3. To serve, remove pears from saucepan, bring poaching liquid to a boil, and reduce by half. Cut the cake evenly into 6 rectangles and arrange them right side up on dessert plates. Arrange the pear halves cut side up on top of cake. Drizzle with reduced poaching liquid (I don't strain it, but you can if you like) and top with a scoop of vanilla ice cream.

WHAT CAN GO WRONG? There is nothing hard about this recipe. The cake does involve creaming the butter, which means that the butter should be at 65 to 67 degrees for best results. (The butter should feel like putty, malleable but still firm.) Be sure to reduce the poaching liquid to use as a sauce. It really makes the dessert.

LEMON CURD CHEESECAKE

(adapted from Aqua, San Francisco)

THE IDEA FOR THIS RECIPE comes from Aqua in San Francisco, which serves individual lemon curd cheesecakes. I tested their recipe and liked it a lot but felt that it was too much work for the home cook — it is easier to make a whole cheesecake, top it with lemon curd, chill it, and then serve individual slices. So I adapted my Light Cheesecake recipe (page 181) and paired it with Aqua's lemon curd recipe to end up with the recipe below.

• • •

Lemon Curd Cheesecake

SERVES 12

For the Cheesecake
- 1 tablespoon unsalted butter, melted
- 2 whole graham crackers, crushed into fine crumbs
- 1½ pounds cream cheese, at room temperature

- 1 cup granulated sugar
- 4 large eggs
- 1 teaspoon minced lemon zest
- 1¼ teaspoons vanilla extract
- ⅓ cup heavy cream
- ¾ cup sour cream

For the Lemon Curd
- 2 large egg yolks
- 2 large eggs
- 6 tablespoons granulated sugar
- Zest of 2 lemons, finely chopped
- ½ cup lemon juice
- ¼ cup crème fraîche OR ¼ cup whipping cream mixed with 1 tablespoon buttermilk
- 8 tablespoons (1 stick) unsalted butter, cut into 1-tablespoon pieces

1. *For the cheesecake:* Adjust oven rack to the middle position and heat oven to 275 degrees. Remove bottom from a 10-inch springform pan. To prevent leakage, wrap the pan in two sheets of extra-wide aluminum foil, as shown in the illustrations on page 180. Brush the inside of the pan with the melted butter and then sprinkle with graham cracker crumbs, tilting the pan to coat evenly. Dump out excess crumbs. Set springform pan in a large roasting pan and bring a large kettle of water to a boil.

2. In a large bowl, beat cream cheese with an electric mixer or by hand until smooth. Gradually add sugar and beat until smooth, about 3 minutes with an electric mixer and 6 to 7 minutes by hand, scraping bowl once or twice. Add the 4 eggs, one at a time, and beat until just incorporated, frequently scraping down the sides of the bowl. Add the remaining cheesecake ingredients and beat on medium speed for 10 seconds to incorporate.

3. Pour batter into prepared springform pan and then pour enough boiling water into the roasting pan to come halfway up the sides of the springform. Bake for 1 hour to 1 hour and 10 minutes, or until cheesecake is set but the

center is still a bit wobbly. (Unlike the recipe on page 181, the cake will not puff up.) Turn off heat and let cheesecake sit in oven, door closed, for another 2 hours. Remove from oven and remove cheesecake from water bath.

4. *For the lemon curd:* Start preparing the lemon curd 1 hour before cheesecake is ready. In a medium saucepan, whisk together the yolks, eggs, sugar, zest, and lemon juice. Heat over low heat, stirring constantly, until the mixture is thick enough to mound in the pan. (It should be the texture of a loose pudding. This should take 8 to 10 minutes, although time will vary. To speed things up, start at medium low until the mixture reaches 150 degrees on an instant-read thermometer and then reduce the heat to low.) Remove from heat and add all the crème fraîche and then the butter, one-third at a time. Stir after each addition, then continue stirring to melt the butter. Strain through a fine sieve into a bowl. Let cool to room temperature and then gently spread on top of cooled cheesecake.

5. Cover and refrigerate for 3 to 4 hours, until completely chilled. To serve, run a thin knife around the inside of the springform pan and remove outer ring. Run knife under hot water before cutting individual slices.

WHAT CAN GO WRONG? It is important to use the right size springform pan, since a smaller pan will not allow enough room for the lemon curd topping. Also, be sure to follow the directions closely for lining the pan with aluminum foil. If this is done improperly, the pan will leak and the cake will become watery. You will need an extra-wide roll of foil to do this successfully. The lemon curd can take a long time to thicken, depending on the type of pan you use and your stovetop. I use medium-low heat to start and an instant-read thermometer to monitor the temperature of the mixture. Once the curd is up to 150 degrees, I reduce the heat to low. The mixture will thicken at around 158 degrees. Note that a small bit of egg white may cook (turn white) while the curd is heating. This is okay. It will be removed when the mixture is strained.

ROASTED APPLE BREAD PUDDING

(adapted from the Claremont Café, Boston)

IN THE EARLY 1990s, the Claremont Café was the first upscale eatery to locate on the less popular and less developed end of Columbus Avenue in Boston's South End. Today, the entire South End has become a mecca for diners from all over Boston, yet the Claremont Café still manages to keep its small-scale neighborhood character. My wife and I recently ordered their apple bread pudding and found it to be both a bit unusual and the best we had ever had. The secret, as I learned from pastry chef Dianne Devlin, is roasting the apples with sugar and cinnamon first and then adding them to the pudding mixture. This produces a rich, caramelized apple flavor missing from puddings that do not require precooking.

• • •

Roasted Apple Bread Pudding

If you want to double this recipe, I suggest using a 9 x 13 pan.

SERVES 6

4	large apples, peeled, cored, and cut into ⅜-inch slices (about 5 cups)
¾	cup granulated sugar
¾	teaspoon cinnamon
½	loaf high-quality white bread, such as brioche, pullman loaf, or challah
1¼	cups milk
1¼	cups heavy cream
2	large eggs
5	large egg yolks
⅛	teaspoon nutmeg
⅛	teaspoon salt

1½ teaspoons vanilla extract

Whipped cream for serving (optional)

1. Heat oven to 375 degrees. Toss prepared apples with ½ cup of the sugar and the cinnamon. Place on a well-buttered jelly roll pan and roast in oven for 10 to 15 minutes, or until apple slices are soft. Cool for 15 minutes.

2. Remove and discard bread crusts and cut bread into 1-inch cubes. (You should have about 5 cups.) Place in an 8-inch square baking pan. Bring a kettle of water to a boil.

3. Place milk and cream in a saucepan and bring to a simmer. When mixture is hot, but not before, combine eggs, yolks, and remaining ¼ cup sugar in a mixing bowl and whisk with the nutmeg, salt, and vanilla. Slowly whisk in hot milk mixture. Pour custard over bread, turning bread to make sure that it is thoroughly soaked. Top with roasted apples and drizzle with any caramelized pan juices.

4. Cover baking pan with aluminum foil, place in a large roasting pan, and add hot water until it comes halfway up sides of baking pan. Bake for 45 minutes to 1 hour, until the perimeter of the pudding is set but the center is still a bit loose and wet. Serve warm as is or with whipped cream.

INDEX

(Page numbers in *italic* refer to illustrations.)